Big Five Assessment

Big Five Assessment

Edited by

Boele de Raad
University of Groningen, The Netherlands

Marco Perugini
University of Essex, United Kingdom

 Hogrefe & Huber Publishers
Seattle • Toronto • Bern • Göttingen

Library of Congress Cataloging-in-Publication Data

is now available via the Library of Congress Marc Database under the
LC Catalog Card Number 200210211

Canadian Cataloging in Publication Data

Main entry under title:

Big five assessment

Includes bibliographical references.
ISBN 0-88937-242-X

1. Personality assessment. I. Raad, Boele de, 1945–, II. Perugini, Marco

BF698.4.B53 2002   155.2'83   C2002-900938-3

USA: P.O. Box 2487, Kirkland, WA 98083-2487
                        Phone (425) 820-1500, Fax (425) 823-8324
CANADA: 12 Bruce Park Avenue, Toronto, Ontario M4P 2S3
                        Phone (416) 482-6339
SWITZERLAND: Länggass-Strasse 76, CH-3000 Bern 9
                        Phone (031) 300-4500, Fax (031) 300-4590
GERMANY   Rohnsweg 25, D-37085 Göttingen
                        Phone (0551) 49609-0, Fax (0551) 49609-88

Printed and bound in Germany

ISBN 0-88937-242-X

Contents

List of contributors

Ashton, Michael C. Dept. of Psychology, Brock Univ., St. Catharines, Ontario, L2S 3A1, Canada, e-mail: mashton@cogito.psyc.brocku.ca

Barbaranelli, Claudio Dept. of Psychology, Univ. of Rome "La Sapienza", Via dei Marsi 78, 00185 Rome, Italy, e-mail: claudio.barbaranelli@uniroma1.it

Barrett, Paul Mariner7 Ltd, 640 Great South Road, Private Bag 92-106, Manakau, Auckland, New Zealand, e-mail: paul.barrett@mariner7.com

Bassett, Jonathan F. Dept. of Psychology, Georgia State Univ., University Plaza, Atlanta, GA 30303-3083, USA, e-mail: gs07jfb@panther.gsu.edu

Caprara, Gian Vittorio Dept. of Psychology, Univ. of Rome "La Sapienza", Via dei Marsi 78, 00185 Rome, Italy, e-mail: caprara@uniroma1.it

Costa, Paul T., Jr. National Institute on Aging, Gerontology Research Center, 5600 Nathan Shock Drive, Baltimore, MD 21224-6825, USA, e-mail: paulc@lpc.grc.nia.nih.gov

De Fruyt, Filip Dept. of Psychology, Ghent Univ., H. Dunantlaan 2, B-9000 Ghent, Belgium, e-mail: filip.defruyt@rug.ac.be

De Raad, Boele Dept. of Psychology, Univ. of Groningen, Grote Kruisstraat 2/1, 9712 TS Groningen, e-mail: b.de.raad@ppsw.rug.nl

Di Blas, Lisa Dept. of Psychology, Univ. of Trieste, Via S. Anastasio 12, 34134 Trieste, Italy, e-mail: diblali@univ.trieste.it

Eber, Herbert W. Psychological Resources Inc., 74 Fourteenth Street, NW, Atlanta, GA 30309, USA, e-mail: herb.eber@psychologicalresources.com

FormyDuval Hill, Deborah Section of Neuropsychology, Wake Forest Univ., School of Medicine, Medical Center Boulevard, Winston-Salem, NC 27157-1043, USA, e-mail: dfhill@wfubmc.edu

Goldberg, Lewis R. Oregon Research Institute, 1715 Franklin Boulevard, Eugene, OR 97403-1983, USA, e-mail: lewg@ori.org

Harkness, Allan R. Dept. of Psychology, The Univ. of Tulsa, 600 South College Avenue, Tulsa, Oklahoma 74104-3189, USA, e-mail: allan-harkness@utulsa.edu

Hendriks, A.A. Jolijn Dept. of Medical Psychology, Academic Medical Center/Univ. of Amsterdam, PO Box 22660, 1100 DD Amsterdam, The Netherlands, e-mail: jolijn.hendriks@planet.nl

Hofer, Scott M. Dept. of Human Development and Family Studies, The Pennsylvania State Univ., 110 Henderson South Bldg., University Park, PA 16802, USA, e-mail: smh21@psu.edu

Hofstee, Willem K.B. Dept. of Psychology, Univ. of Groningen, Grote Kruisstraat 2/1, 9712 TS Groningen, The Netherlands, e-mail: w.k.b.hofstee@ppsw.rug.nl

Hogan, Joyce Hogan Assessment Systems, 2622 E. 21st St., Tulsa, OK 74114, USA.

Hogan, Robert Hogan Assessment Systems, 2622 E. 21st St., Tulsa, OK 74114, USA, e-mail: robert@hoganassessments.com

Jackson, Douglas N. Dept. of Psychology, The Univ. of Western Ontario, London, Ontario N6A 5C2, Canada, e-mail: dnj@sigmaassessmentsystems.com

Jónsson, Friðrik H. Dept. of Psychology, Univ. of Iceland, 101 Reykjavík, Iceland, e-mail: fhj@rhi.hi.is

Kashiwagi, Shigeo Job Placement Center, Josai International Univ., 1 Gumiyou Togane Chiba 283-8555, Japan, e-mail: skashi@jiu.ac.jp

Kihm, Jenifer A. IntelliMark, 2300 Cottondale Lane, Suite 250, Little Rock, AR 72202-2054, e-mail: jkihm@intellimark-it.com

McCrae, Robert R. National Institute on Aging, Gerontology Research Center, 5600 Nathan Shock Drive, Baltimore, MD 21224-6825, USA, e-mail: jeffm@mvx.grc.nia.nih.gov

McNulty, John L. Dept. of Psychology, The Univ. of Tulsa, 600 South College Avenue, Tulsa, Oklahoma 74104-3189, e-mail:john-mcnulty@utulsa.edu

Mervielde, Ivan Dept. of Psychology, Ghent Univ., H. Dunantlaan 2, B-9000 Ghent, Belgium, e-mail: ivan.mervielde@rug.ac.be

Paunonen, Sampo V. Dept. of Psychology, Univ. of Western Ontario, London, Ontario, N6A 5C2, Canada, e-mail: paunonen@uwo.ca

Perugini, Marco Dept. of Psychology, Univ. of Essex, Wivenhoe Park, Colchester CO4 3SQ, United Kingdom, e-mail: mperug@essex.ac.uk

Robie, Chet College of Business Administration, Niagara University, NY 14109, USA, e-mail: crobie@niagara.edu

Saucier, Gerard Dept. of Psychology, Univ. of Oregon, Eugene, OR 97403-1227, USA, e-mail: gsaucier@oregon.uoregon.edu

Schmit, Mark J. EPredix, Inc., 601 2nd Avenue South, Minneapolis, MN 55402, USA, e-mail: schmit_mark@hotmail.com

Tremblay, Paul F. Centre for Addiction and Mental Health, 100 Collip circle, Suite 200, London, Ontario, N6G 4X8, Canada, e-mail: ptrembla@uwo.ca

Trobst, Krista K. Dept. of Psychology, York Univ., 4700 Keele Street, Toronto, Ontario, Canada M3J 1P3, e-mail: trobst@yorku.ca

Trull, Timothy J. Dept. of Psychological Sciences, 106C McAlester Hall, Univ. of Missouri-Columbia, Columbia, MO 65211, USA, e-mail:trullt@missouri.edu

Tsaousis, Ioannis Dept. of Preschool Education, Univ. of the Aegean, Karpathou 98-100 Str., 185 39 Piraeus, Greece, e-mail: tsaousis@matrix.kapatel.gr

Widiger, Thomas A. Dept. of Psychology, 115 Kastle Hall, Univ. of Kentucky, Lexington, KY 40506-0044, USA, e-mail: widiger@pop.uky.edu

Wiggins, Jerry S. Dept. of Psychology, York Univ., 4700 Keele Street, Toronto, Ontario, Canada M3J 1P3, e-mail: jerwiggins@aol.com

Williams, John E. Dept. of Psychology, Georgia State Univ., University Plaza, Atlanta, GA 30303-3083, USA, e-mail: psyjew@panther.gsu.edu

Zuckerman, Marvin Dept. of Psychology, Univ. of Delaware, Newark, DE 19716-2577, USA, e-mail: zuckerma@udel.edu

Preface

This Big Five Assessment volume bridges a gap in the personality literature and represents a unique opportunity for students, researchers, and practitioners to find just about everything concerning the evaluation of the Big Five within the cover of a single book. The volume aims to present a comprehensive account of the various instruments that are constructed to assess the Big Five factors, often named (I) Extraversion, (II) Agreeableness, (III) Conscientiousness, (IV) Emotional Stability or Neuroticism, and (V) Intellect, Intellectual Autonomy, or Openness to Experience. Both well-known and frequently used and less well-known or less frequently used inventories, questionnaires, and trait adjective lists are described. During the last decade or so, the field of personality assessment has rapidly changed its orientation towards a full and extensive account of the constructs and sub-constructs that are captured by the Big Five model. One of the persistent issues in the literature on the Big Five factors is given in the great many forms each of the factors can take, even where the names of the factors are the same. Extraversion, for example, may sometimes take a more expressive connotation, and at other times a more energetic or even aggressive connotation. Factors from different studies may allow for two, three, four, five, or more facets. The formats of the original items may be abstract and adjectival or more behavioral. All of these issues come about most explicitly in the development of assessment instruments. This volume not just offers a view on the different instruments, their uses, and their applications, but also on the struggles researchers may go through in striving at operationalizing their conceptualizations of the Big Five constructs.

This book has been preceded by a few others that had the Big Five model as a main theme, such as Costa and Widiger's (1994) volume dedicated to personality disorders, Halverson, Kohnstamm, and Martin's (1994) volume dedicated to developmental aspects of the five-factorial model, Wiggins' (1996) volume on theoretical aspects of the Five-Factor Model, and De Raad's (2000) monograph on the psycholexical approach to personality. The latter book had a restricted focus on largely historical, procedural, and theoretical considerations that gave rise to the present day formulation of the Big Five model. That book was originally intended to have an assessment chapter with quite an extensive scope, but that plan soon outgrew its original frame. That chapter was dropped, which action was immediately superseded by a much more pretentious plan, namely to review all Big Five assessment instruments in a separate handbook. That plan is now virtually realized. This Big Five Assessment book contains 20 chapters with descriptions of at least 18 different instruments that can be used to assess the Big Five factors in a variety of contexts – organizational, clinical, developmental, research. The mere conjoining of instruments that are competitors in the commercial world is an interesting fact in itself, which does not mean that the contributors perform a concert in close harmony. On the contrary, opposing views on various issues are spelled out in different chapters, which fact witnesses the liveliness of the field: it signals an approach at work and it testifies that there are still unresolved aspects.

This book is the product of many individuals. Thanks are due to the contributors who made this book to a real handbook of Big Five assessment. We would like to acknowledge those who served as manuscript reviewers, in particular Alois Angleitner, Filip De Fruyt, Jolijn Hendriks, Wim Hofstee, Karen Van Oudenhoven-Van der Zee, and Fons Van de Vijver. Special thanks should go to Hanny Baan who processed the text to the present form from the first to the last page.

Boele De Raad
Marco Perugini

References

Costa, P.T., Jr., & Widiger, T.A. (Eds.) (1994). *Personality disorders and the Five-Factor Model of personality*. Washington, DC: American Psychological Association.

De Raad, B. (2000). *The Big Five personality factors: The psycholexical approach to personality*. Göttingen: Hogrefe & Huber Publishers.

Halverson, C.F., Jr., Kohnstamm, G.A., & Martin, R.P. (Eds.) (1994). *The developing structure of temperament and personality from infancy to adulthood*. Hillsdale, New Jersey: Lawrence Erlbaum.

Wiggins, J.S. (Ed.) (1996). *The Five-Factor Model of personality: Theoretical perspectives*. New York: The Guilford Press.

Chapter 1

Big Five factor assessment: Introduction

Boele De Raad
Marco Perugini

Introduction

The Big Five model of personality traits derives its strength from two lines of re-search, the psycholexical and the questionnaire tradition (John & Srivastava, 1999; McCrae & John, 1992). While the names Big Five model and Five Factor Model are often used interchangeably, they respectively originate in those two traditions. The two traditions have produced similar five-factor structures that mark a point of no return for personality psychology. Extensive reviews of history and theory with respect to the Big Five can be found in De Raad (2000) and Wiggins (1996).

The Big Five factors have been endorsed with a distinctive status, derived from the extensive, omnibus-character of the underlying *psycholexical* approach, and based on two characteristics, namely its *exhaustiveness* in capturing the semantics of personality and its recourse to *ordinary language*. Though both these characteristics may be improved upon, in comparison to other approaches to personality, the psy-cholexical approach outranks regarding semantic coverage, and it has optimized the level of communication on personality traits by faring merely on readily intelligible units of description.

Of the Big Five factors, Extraversion and Neuroticism had been identified as the "Big Two" by Wiggins (1968) within the *questionnaire approach* because these two dimensions had shown up in most personality questionnaires. Costa and McCrae (1976, 1985) added a third dimension, Openness to Experience, with which they touched a large audience, but with their addition of Agreeableness and Conscien-tiousness the questionnaire approach "cashed in", so to speak, more fully the fruits of the psycholexical approach. Since, the questionnaire approach has been tuned to-wards the coverage of especially those five dimensions. Several studies (e.g., An-gleitner & Ostendorf, 1994) have been supportive of a Big Five factor structure among scales from different instruments (see, e.g., John & Srivastava (1999) for a

Big Five Assessment, edited by B. De Raad & M. Perugini. © 2002, Hogrefe & Huber Publishers.

portrayal of the convergence between the Big Five and other structural models). With the emphasis on full coverage of the trait domain, and thus on a representation of the lexicon of trait-descriptive items, also the questionnaire approach essentially turned lexical.

The Big Five model has served as a basis for the development of assessment instruments of various kinds. In paragraphs to follow, different assessment forms   based on the Big Five model are briefly described, including Big Five trait-markers, Big Five inventories, and some instruments that have been shaped after the Big Five framework. Different examples of each of those forms can be found in the various chapters of this book. These brief descriptions are preceded by a discussion of the different uses of the Big Five model, and by a description of the Big Five constructs and their relevance.

Uses of the Big Five model

With reference to the ordinary language character of the psycholexical approach and of the Big Five model, one interesting use of the model is that it may serve as a standard medium of communication, in terms of which other psychological-technical concepts can be expressed. For example, Strelau's Strength of Excitation (SE; Strelau, Angleitner, Bantelmann & Ruch, 1990) correlates substantially with Big Five factors Extraversion and Emotional Stability, and Eysenck's Psychoticism (P; Eysenck, 1992) factor correlates substantially (negatively) with Big Five Agreeableness and Conscientiousness. Because of those relationships, the Big Five factors give insight in the semantics of Strength of Excitation and Psychoticism.

Apart from this, and especially because of its distinctive status, the Big Five model can function, and has done so, as a *template*, suggesting a general function of the model as a reference-framework, underlying various uses. The model can thus serve as a reference system for other systems, suggesting that with the Big Five factors one can find a peg for almost every hole.

While the Big Five approach may boast this distinctive status, the Big Five factors form also a model of personality-traits next to other models. In that capacity, it contains a well-founded set of basic concepts with which traits of persons can be described at an abstract level. At that abstract level, the model has a certain range of coverage by which it can compete with other models. In addition, the model can serve as a basis for the development of assessment instruments. Also in this respect the psycholexical approach provides for a good starting-point to compete with other systems of assessment. The circumplex representation, especially in its Abridged Big Five Circumplex (AB5C) format (De Raad, Hendriks, & Hofstee, 1992; Hofstee, De Raad, & Goldberg, 1992), with its systematic and detailed stratification of the semantic domain, gives the psycholexical approach the extra dimension that sustains its competitive status. Moreover, because alternative methods to arrive at domain-covering assessment-instruments are restricted by theory or problem-orientation, the psycholexical approach justifiably claims its exceptional position, which position, obviously, ultimately can be maintained only on the basis of empirical results.

In addition to developing assessment instruments, some other uses of the Big Five model and of the AB5C-system are distinguished. These are the use of the AB5C-system and of the Big Five model to classify various kinds of personality descriptors, the use of the AB5C-system to clarify discrepancies in interpretation of Big Five factors (e.g., Johnson & Ostendorf, 1993), and the role of the Big Five model in theory-building. These various uses of the Big Five not only sustain the template function of the model, but also illustrate its relevance.

The different uses and functions of the Big Five model provided here do not exhaust the possible roles the model may fulfil; they are given to showcase the potential of the model in many different directions. The Big Five model is used in many different types of investigations, running from the judgments of faces (Henss, 1995), to the comparison of polar workers with a normative population (Steel, Suedfeld, Peri, & Palinkas, 1997), to the construct validation of the concept of 'argumentativeness' (Blickle, 1997).

The Big Five as a classification-system

We give two examples that showcase the Big Five framework as organizer of semantic material collected for the purpose of describing individual differences. In both cases, the semantic material had not been collected from the Big Five viewpoint. Yet, it turned out that a description of the semantics of individual differences in those studies did not need important categories beyond the confines of the Big Five.

Assuming that the AB5C-framework provides a fair and full map of the semantics of personality traits, De Raad and Doddema-Winsemius (1999) used that system to accommodate a list of 323 *instincts*. That list, being a reduction of a larger list of 985 instinct-references, had been put together according to a psycholexical pattern in which hundreds of books, articles, and newspapers were carefully examined for instinct-expressions, many of which turned out to be descriptors of individual differences in personality (Bernard, 1924). 238 instinct-terms could be classified, leaving a set of 85 terms that could not be placed mainly because the instinct-terms were too ambiguous in meaning, or too specific. The majority of instinct-terms could thus be classified into the five categories corresponding to the Big Five. The results thus support the power of the inclusive character of the semantics of the Big Five framework.

Kohnstamm, Halverson, Mervielde, and Havill (1998) used the Big Five categories to classify *free descriptions* of children provided by parents (cf. Havill, Allen, Halverson, & Kohnstamm, 1994; Kohnstamm, Slotboom, & Elphick, 1993). Kohnstamm *et al.* (1998) summarized studies performed in seven different countries, each study revolving around the question put to parents: "Can you tell me what you think is characteristic of your child". Each study produced a host of words and phrases to be considered as representing the cultural lexicon of personality. In order to classify the many thousands of descriptors, 14 categories were used, five of which formed by the Big Five labels. The vast majority of expressions were accommodated by the Big Five, which provides an overwhelming support for the inclusive power of the Big Five categories. The other categories that were considered necessary for classification caught less than 20 per cent of the expressions on average.

Role of Big Five in theory building

A theory is a set of conventions that enable to represent empirical facts in an organizing and integrating scheme. With such a simplified and abstract form, also the Big Five scheme forms a theory that allows the incorporation of empirical findings. Its utility is in its descriptive scope. The inclusive potential of the Big Five system has been demonstrated in the preceding paragraphs. The structural features of the Big Five system, with horizontal and vertical aspects, and with the periodicity or circumplexity of the AB5C representation, provide ample opportunity for the clarification and scrutiny of the interrelationships of the many trait concepts that belong to the personality trait domain.

A very instructive example in this respect is the study by Digman (1997), who analyzed factor correlations from 14 studies. In all of these studies five primary factors had been produced, identified as the Big Five. The 14 sets of correlations between those Big Five factors were factored to produce higher-order factors. In all of the 14 studies two factors were typically evident, initially labeled *alpha* and *beta*. Factor alpha was indicated by Big Five factors Agreeableness, Emotional Stability, and Conscientiousness, and factor beta was indicated by Extraversion and Intellect or Openness to Experience.

Apart from the hierarchical organization of the trait constructs, there is the possibility, as suggested by Digman (1997), that these two higher-order factors link the Big Five to various theoretical systems of personality. Factor alpha might be a social desirability factor; alternatively the factor may represent the socialization process or represent what personality development is about. Factor beta may be conceived of as a personal growth factor, reflecting the actualization of self, being open to experience, and using one's intellect.

A different approach towards assessing relationships among Big Five factors is followed by Hofstee (2001). Because the large majority of social desirable traits form a positive manifold, and their undesirable opposites form a negative manifold, it makes sense, parallel to conceptualizations of intelligence, to speak of a general personality factor, called the *p*-factor. Hofstee proposes this single personality factor as the top trait in a sophisticated hierarchy, the meaning of which might be social desirability, or more probably, a construct that may stand midway between competence and coping.

Also at the more specific level of this hierarchical model progress is made. Peabody and Goldberg (1989) suggested that each of the Big Five factors might have its own realm of application; for example, Conscientiousness was suggested to have particular relevance in the realm of work and tasks. Such information is important for the Big Five in order to arrive at a full bearing in everyday and professional contexts. Ten Berge and De Raad (2001, in press) report about a first situational specification of traits from the Big Five domain. They not only developed a taxonomy of situations that is particularly relevant for trait psychology; they also found clear indications that the so-called temperament factors, Extraversion, Emotional Stability, and also factor V, Intellectual Autonomy, give rise to more situational differentiation than the so-called character-factors, Agreeableness and Conscientiousness (Ten Berge & De Raad, in press).

The Big Five as organizer in fields of experience and research

The Big Five factors have become acknowledged or re-acknowledged as relevant and valid dimensions of personality in various fields of research. Barrick and Mount (1991), for example, who investigated the role of the Big Five factors relative to job performance, judged the availability of an orderly classification scheme like the Big Five as essential for the communication and accumulation of empirical findings, in any field of science. Their meta-analysis of the relation of the Big Five to job performance criteria for five occupational groups showed Conscientiousness to be a valid predictor for all groups, and Extraversion and Openness to Experience to play a more restricted role.

Another example is Smith and Williams (1992) who expected the Big Five model to facilitate progress in the study of how personality influences health. They reviewed literature concerning the question whether personality is causally related to physical illness, and actually investigated whether traits from the Big Five have been specifically involved. Smith and Williams (1992) concluded that a more coherent conceptual and empirical foundation for the study of personality and health would likely occur from efforts to apply the five-factor model.

De Raad and Schouwenburg (1996) reviewed the literature on personality in learning and education. They exploited the Big Five model as a reference system for the evaluation of the comprehensiveness of the literature reviewed, and in particular they organized the literature on personality, learning and education using the periodic system of the Big Five factors and facets (AB5C) as an accommodative framework.

Many more examples of exploitation of the Big Five framework can be mentioned, such as in *behavior genetics* where the Big Five factors have been taken to classify behavior genetic findings with respect to adult personality (e.g., Bouchard, 1993). In *psychotherapy* the Big Five model can be utilized to facilitate psychotherapy treatment (e.g., Miller, 1991). Van Dam (1996) shows that the Big Five model provides for a useful framework to understand the ways selectors perceive the personalities of job applicants.

Finally, Buss (1991) embraced the Big Five factors as the most important dimensions of the 'social landscape' to which humans had to adapt: they are considered to be the dimensions along which people act upon differences in others, which is, from an evolutionary perspective, crucial for solving problems of survival and reproduction (cf. Buss, 1996).

The Big Five constructs

The Big Five constructs, Extraversion, Agreeableness, Conscientiousness, Emotional Stability, and Intellect/Autonomy, made a long journey, covering about a whole century, towards a strong performance in the psychological arena during the last decade of the twentieth century. A count of the references made to each of the presently identified Big Five constructs in abstracts during this century provides an interesting picture of the appreciation of the pertinent constructs. Of the total number of 17,262 references found in the relevant abstracts, made available on CD-rom, accredits Extraversion (and Introversion) and Neuroticism (and Emotional Stability) as absolute winners with totals of about 8,500 and 6,200, respectively. This picture sustains the historical "Big Two" of temperament (Wiggins, 1968). The historical third, Intellect, with about 1,500 references, may refer to both traits and abilities. Agreeableness and Conscientiousness started playing a role of importance only since the last one or two decades. The counts for those constructs are around 500.

Extraversion and Introversion

Guilford and Braly (1930) already remarked that "No single pair of traits of personality has been quite so widely discussed and studied as that of extroversion and introversion" (p. 96). Their main understanding at the onset of their appearance was Jungian. Though there are references in the literature to these traits before Jung, their main understanding at the onset of their appearance was Jungian. To Jung (1917) Extraversion is the outward turning of psychic energy toward the external world, while Introversion refers to the inward flow of psychic energy towards the depths of the psyche. Extraversion is denoted by habitual outgoingness, venturing forth with careless confidence into the unknown, and being particularly interested in people and events in the external world. Introversion is reflected by a keen interest in one's own psyche, and often preferring to be alone.

Extraversion is a dimension in almost all personality inventories of a multidimensional nature, which fact sustains its relevance and its substantive character. Moreover, many studies have provided behavioral correlates of this construct (e.g., Watson & Clark, 1997), such as the number of leadership roles assumed, and frequency of partying, and also nonverbal decoding skills in social interaction, but only when this is a secondary task (Lieberman & Rosenthal, 2001). Mak and Tran (2001) provided evidence of the relevance of Extraversion for intercultural social self-efficacy. Extraversion has also been found to predict employees' absenteeism (Judge, Martocchio & Thoresen, 1997), the use of networking as a job-search method among unemployed (Wanberg, Kanfer, & Banas, 2000), and the objective sales volume and managerial ratings of salesperson performance (Vinchur, Schippmann, Switzer, & Roth, 1998). Extraversion has been found to be positively related to level of salary and promotions (Seibert & Kraimer, 2001). Extraversion is also very relevant in contexts of learning and education (De Raad & Schouwenburg, 1996), and the construct appeared to be related to various health-related behaviors (Scheier & Carver, 1987). For example, it predicts subjective well-being (DeNeve & Cooper, 1998), at midlife (Siegler & Brummett, 2000) as well as for centenarians (Adkins, Martin, & Poon, 1996); and it is negatively associated with avoidance coping in dealing with cardiac catheterisation (Bosworth, Feaganes, Vitaliano, Mark, & Siegler, 2001).

Agreeableness

Agreeableness is the personality dimension with the briefest history. This may come as a surprise, since longtime constructs as Love and Hate, Solidarity, Conflict, Cooperation, Kindness are part and parcel of this dimension. While those different constructs may have been pivotal to the organization of social life throughout the history of mankind, as a personality dimension it essentially popped up with the rise of the Big Five. Graziano and colleagues have described the details of the history of this construct (e.g., Graziano & Eisenberg, 1997). The Agreeableness dimension is probably the most concerned with interpersonal relationships. Wiggins (1991) theorizes about Agreeableness as being dominated by 'communion', which is the condition of being part of a larger spiritual or social community (cf. Hogan, 1983).

In the interpersonal domain there are several correlates of Agreeableness, including more elevated ratings of peer performance on group exercises (Bernardin, Cooke, & Villanova, 2000), interpersonal skills in teams (Neuman & Wright, 1999), and several aspects of social relationships between university students (Asendorpf & Wilpers, 1998). Agreeable persons select tactics that minimize disruption during conflict episodes, and they continue to talk more with their conflict partners after a conflict (Jensen-Campbell & Graziano, 2001). McCullough, Bellah, Kilpatrick, and Johnson (2001) found that Agreeableness was negatively related to vengefulness. In health psychological research, Agreeableness plays also a documented role. For instance, coronary heart disease is more likely to develop in competitive and hostile people than in those who are more easygoing and patient (cf. Dembroski & Costa, 1987; Graziano & Eisenberg, 1997). Moreover, agreeable people are less likely to engage in risky health behaviours and are more optimistic about their future health risks (Vollrath, Knoch, & Cassano, 1999). While Tett, Jackson and Rothstein (1991) conclude that personality measures in general have a place in the personnel selection research (cf. Barrick & Mount, 1991), several studies support the specific role of Agreeableness, for instance, as a predictor of training proficiency (e.g., Salgado, 1997).

Conscientiousness

Conscientiousness has been drawn upon as a resource in situations where achievement is an important value, that is, in contexts of work, learning and education. The construct represents the drive to accomplish something, and it contains the characteristics necessary in such a pursuit: being organized, systematic, efficient, practical, and steady (cf. Goldberg, 1992).

There is an impressive list of studies emphasizing the importance of conscientiousness and related facets in learning and education. Successful boys at grammar school received higher ratings in persistence than unsuccessful boys (e.g. Astington, 1960). Smith (1967) found 'strength of character' to be an important nonintellective correlate of academic success. Wiggins, Blackburn, and Hackman (1969) found conscientiousness among the best predictors of graduate success. Conscientiousness plays a prominent role in the HSPQ (Cattell, Cattell, & Johns, 1984) as predictor of school grades (e.g. Schuerger & Kuna, 1987). Recently, Wolfe and Johnson (1995) have supported the role of conscientiousness in prediction of school performance, whereas in a longitudinal study Shiner (2000) has shown that academic conscientiousness in childhood is predictive of both academic achievement and conduct ten years later. In organizational settings, reviews provided by Barrick and Mount (1991), Tett, Jackson, and Rothstein (1991), Ones, Viwesvaran, and Schmidt (1993), and Salgado (1997), have led to the conclusion that Conscientiousness is consistently related to job performance criteria (cf. Hogan & Ones, 1997). In health behavior research, Conscientiousness has been shown to play an important role in predicting a range of important outcomes such as longevity (Friedman, Tucker, Schwartz, Martin *et al.*, 1995), smoking (Hampson, Andrews, Barckley, Lichtenstein, & Lee, 2000), mammography utilization (Schwartz, Taylor, Willard, Siegel, Lamdan, & Moran, 1999), physical fitness (Hogan, 1989), and lower risky health behavior (Lemos-Giraldez & Fidalgo-Aliste, 1997; Vollrath, Knoch, & Cassano, 1999). In the area of antisocial behavior, Conscientiousness plays a role as well. Heaven (1996) reported Conscientiousness to be negatively related to vandalism, and Clower and Bothwell (2001) found Conscientiousness to be negatively related to inmate recidivism.

Emotional Stability and Neuroticism

The first inventory measuring neurotic tendencies is Woodworth's (1917) Personal Data Sheet, developed during World War I to assess the ability of soldiers to cope with military stresses. Being emotionally stable has been considered a requirement in such demanding situations as there are in the airforce (cf. Henmon, 1919) and the police force (cf. Graf, 1924). Thurstone and Thurstone (1930) developed a neurotic inventory called "A Personality Schedule" to assess the neurotic tendencies of university freshmen. Their inventory was in part based on Woodworth's (1917) instrument. As one of the "Big Two", Neuroticism, often also referred to as Anxiety, had been observed by Wiggins (1968) most notably in the works of Eysenck (1957), Cattell (1957), Guilford (1959), and Gough (1957).

Neuroticism has been found relevant as a predictor of school attainment (e.g., Entwistle & Cunningham, 1968; Eysenck & Cookson, 1969). At a university level, high neurotic students are probably handicapped as compared to low neurotics. In the organizational context, Emotional stability turned out to be a good predictor of job performance and job satisfaction (Judge & Bono, 2001) and of higher status in social groups (Anderson, John, Keltner, & Kring, 2001). In the social context, Neuroticism has been found detrimental to commitment in a relationship (Kurdek, 1997) and to the level of marital satisfaction (Karney & Bradbury, 1997). McCullough *et al.* (2001) found that Neuroticism was positively related to vengefulness. In the clinical situation, there is strong evidence of the relevance of Neuroticism in the assessment of personality disorders (cf. Schroeder, Wormworth, & Livesley, 1992). Neuroticism correlates significantly with various measures of illness (cf. Costa & McCrae, 1987; Friedman & Booth-Kewley, 1987). There is evidence that Neuroticism is involved in processes described in illness behavior models (e.g. Larsen, 1992). It is a strong predictor of psychological distress (Ormel & Wohlfartf, 1991), predicts both positive and negative mood (David, Green, Martin, & Suls, 1997), and it is associated with higher interest in social comparison and with less favorable reactions in cancer patients (Van der Zee, Oldersma, Buunk, & Bos, 1998).

Intellect and Openness to Experience

Feelings are usually running highest for the Fifth of the Big Five (De Raad & Van Heck, 1994). This refers to its naming but also to its origin and its relevance as a personality trait factor. In a sense, discussions with respect to this factor incorporate the various points of criticism that are expressed over the Big Five as a model. While several candidates for factor five have been suggested, including Culture (Tupes & Christal, 1961; Norman, 1963), Intelligence (Borgatta, 1964), Intellectance (Hogan, 1983), and Imagination (Saucier, 1994), the main dispute over the Fifth of the Big Five concerned the lexical versions of factor five, on the one hand, and on the other hand, Openness to Experience as developed for the NEO-PI (Costa & McCrae, 1985).

In assessment situations it has been mainly the Openness to Experience conception that established the relevance and significance of the Fifth of the Big Five. This factor may be relevant in psychiatry and clinical psychology. Aspects of Openness to Experience seem to be related to several disorders (Costa & Widiger, 1994) and to high-risk health behavior (Booth-Kewley & Vickers, 1994). In the more task-oriented contexts the relevance of the Fifth has also been pointed out. In contexts of learning and education, Openness to Experience has been related to learning strategies. Learning strategies possibly mediate a relationship between Openness to Experience and grade point average (cf. Blickle, 1996). In organizational settings, Openness to Experience has been associated with increased creative behavior (George &

Zhou, 2001) and job performance (Bing & Lounsbury, 2000; Dollinger & Orf, 1991; Salgado, 1997), and it was negatively related to level of salary (Seibert & Kraimer, 2001). Mak and Tran (2001) provided evidence of the relevance of Openness to Experience for intercultural social self-efficacy. Clower and Bothwell (2001) found low Openness to Experience to be related to inmate recidivism.

Facets of the Big Five

The Big Five factors represent a broad level of personality structure, in which generality is emphasized at the cost of specificity. There is no guarantee that those broad factors do exhaust all significant personality dimensions. While there is evidence that some specific personality dimensions can be conveniently accommodated within the Big Five framework, and others can be understood as facets of the Big Five or as combinations of them (Johnson & Ostendorf, 1993), there is discussion over whether some other specific dimensions (e.g., honesty, reciprocity, morality) may be placed within the Big Five framework (see Paunonen & Jackson, 2000; Saucier & Goldberg, 1998).

Two main approaches, the so called hierarchical and the circumplex approaches, have been proposed to model the different levels of specificity versus generality, in particular in terms of the distinction between facets and factors (Perugini, 1999). Both approaches recognize that the Big Five factors are better thought of as broad personality dimensions subsuming several more specific dimensions. These specific dimensions or facets can be either considered as hierarchically nested in the Big Five or as blends of the Big Five.

Under the *hierarchical* approach facets are often considered as first order factors, and the Big Five as second order factors. The NEO-PI-R, for example, specifies six facets for each of the five factors, and the BFQ specifies two facets per factor. Even though facets can have some secondary and tertiary loadings, they are supposed to load primarily on a specific Big Five factor and, as such, to represent the specific personality traits that form the core of the more general Big Five factor.

The *circumplex* approach represents a finer-grained configuration distinguishing 90 segments in the so-called Abridged Big Five Circumplex (AB5C; Hofstee *et al.*, 1992). In this model, facets are constituted as blends of two factors, based on the observation that many traits are most adequately described by two substantial loadings instead of just one. The 90 segments include 10 segments each containing traits that load on only one of the factor poles, and 80 segments containing the blends of the factor poles with all the poles of the other four factors. The flavor of each separate Big Five factor is given by both the two factor-pure facets and by the 16 facets based on blends. Because of its explicit representation of the trait domain, this circumplex model provides an excellent starting point for the development of personality assessment instruments.

Notwithstanding the differences in orientation and emphasis, under both approaches a distinction is drawn between Big Five factors and their facets. One intriguing question is therefore whether there is any utility in assessing both. This question is considered here from three perspectives: theoretical, structural, and predictive.

Theoretically, the role of facets is very important. The specific spectrum of each Big Five factor is not easily conveyed at the broader (factor) level. While definitions of each of the five factors are readily available and much research has been produced on linking those factors to an impressive range of criteria, knowledge of the specific facets of each factor allows for a finer-grained understanding of the personality lexicon and such understanding facilitates criteria-linkage. As argued by Saucier and Ostendorf (1999), a representation combining broad and narrow constructs offers a good compromise between efficiency (or parsimony) and fidelity. Moreover, the theoretical structure is much clearer and likely to contribute to an increased understanding of the functioning of personality dimensions. In fact, although the psychological mechanisms linked to a broad personality dimension can be also specified at a general level, it is at the facet level that this specification can be accomplished best. For example, self-regulation is central to Conscientiousness, but it is likely to be especially important for facets such as Organization rather than Perfectionism. Furthermore, a specification of both facets and broader factors allows for a better understanding of the dynamics of a personality profile: except for people with extreme scores, usually there is substantial variation in the contribution of each facet of a factor to the overall factor score.

Structurally, there is hardly any difference in the overall Big Five structure when adding facets to the factors. The advantage is that adding facets provides for a stratification of the universe of traits, which can be used to develop assessment instruments that are balanced as regards representative sampling of items from this universe (cf. De Raad & Hendriks, 1997). The Five Factor Personality Inventory, for example, makes use of this property in order to provide a Big Five structure that is balanced as regards the representation of both pure factors and blends.

At the *predictive* level, the situation is less clear-cut. Some researchers have argued that the assessment of broad factors is preferable over narrower facets, especially in situations where the criteria to be predicted are also broad and complex (Ones & Viswesvaran, 1996). Others have argued that the specific variance accounted for by narrower facets possibly increases the prediction of relevant criteria, even when those criteria are broad and complex (Paunonen, 1998; Paunonen & Ashton, 2001). Facets can uniquely contribute because they may contain reliable variance that is not shared with the broader trait to which they belong but that is shared with some relevant criteria. It is just an empirical matter whether this addition would be useful. Paunonen and Ashton (2001) have produced evidence that this is indeed the case. They compared broad Big Five factors with their facets in terms of predictive power across a broad range of behavioral criteria. The results clearly demonstrated a predictive gain with the addition of carefully selected facets to broad factors.

It may be wise for researchers to consider using facets in addition to the Big Five factors. The potential benefit of using facets often outweighs the costs, and the theoretical and practical gains seem sufficient enough to justify in most cases such a more demanding choice. When feasible, researchers might pay specific attention to the lower-level features of the Big Five and select those that would be most approp-

riate for the given research question. The attention does not need to be unduly restricted to the Big Five dimensions: there are research contexts where other specific
dimensions could be relevant. However, a measure of the Big Five should be routi-
nely used, as this would guarantee scientific progress and cumulative knowledge.

Trait assessment instruments

There are some obvious and striking differences between the Big Five and related
assessment instruments that are generally of interest. One of the pertinent characteristics is the number of items and the amount of time necessary to fill them out.
Since this information is not always specified, we generalize the average on the basis of the known figures, yielding about six to seven items filled out per minute. This
would, for example, be about ten minutes for the brief 50-item BFMS or the 60-item
nonverbal FF-NPQ, 15 minutes for the FFPI, 20 minutes for the HiPIC, 25 minutes
for the TPQue, 35 minutes for the NEO-PI-R, and 45 minutes for the GPI and the
ACL. The average internal consistency of the Big Five and related scales across the
instruments in this volume is just over .80. In general there are somewhat higher
values with increasing number of items, and lower values with decreasing number of
items, with favorable exceptions, for example, for the FF-NPQ and the FFPI.
Reasons for choosing a certain instrument may depend on various considerations,
such as amount of time available, costs of the instrument, difficulty of item-
formulation, context of use, validity-information, etc. In the following paragraph,
some characteristic features of the various instruments in this volume are reviewed,
without trying to provide a systematic overview. The readers are urged to go to the
relevant and to make their own comparison.

Big Five trait-markers

Possibly the most direct way to arrive at an instrument assessing the Big Five is to
select trait-variables as *markers* of the Big Five, on the basis of their loadings on
those factors. This could yield assessment instruments comparable to that of Norman
(1963). Simply taking the first *n* highest loading trait-variables per factor might do
the job. A frequently used marker list to measure the Big Five is the one described in
Norman (1963). The list is based on earlier work by Cattell (1947). Other lists have
been often produced either as a stand-alone effort or as a by-product of psycholexical studies. For the history of this and of similar constructs from the same period, as
well as for a comprehensive coverage of many psycholexical studies, see De Raad
(2000).
     Saucier and Goldberg (this volume) review ten potential criteria that might be
used to select markers. They indeed emphasize criteria consistent with the factor
analytic strategy of selecting items with high loadings on the targeted factor and low
loadings on other factors. Most of their criteria are consistent with classical test the-

ory, and some are more consistent with item response theory (IRT). Goldberg (1992) developed a list of 100 'unipolar' markers for the Big Five, which is to be considered as illustrative of some of those criteria. The alphabetical list can be found as Appendix A in Goldberg (1992), together with an instruction and a rating scale for self-description. In his 1992 article Goldberg concludes: "It is to be hoped that the availability of this easily administered set of factor markers will now encourage investigators of diverse theoretical viewpoints to communicate in a common psychometric tongue". This list of Big Five markers necessarily carries the restrictions that are inherent in utilizing the single language of American English and the corresponding Big Five structure as a standard for other languages. Saucier and Goldberg (this volume) also discuss criteria such as brevity, orthogonality and differentiation, and they provide illustrative examples of the application of those criteria.

Big Five inventories, questionnaires, and adjective scales

Many instruments have been developed to assess the Big Five factors. Notwithstanding the fact that those instruments, of which the majority is presented in this volume, purport to assess essentially the same constructs, they differ in various respects. They may highlight the particulars of a specific language or culture (e.g., NEO-PI-R in Icelandic), focus on assessing specific age groups (e.g., HiPIC), emphasize alternative media of communication (e.g., NPQ) or specific uses in the assessment process (e.g., SIFFM), provide a different theoretical perspective (e.g., a dyadic interactional perspective), or are especially detailed about certain psychometric issues (e.g., Kashiwagi, this volume).

Costa and McCrae's (1985; 1992) NEO-PI-R is the most frequently used personality questionnaire to assess the Big Five. Although it has been influenced by and geared towards the early formulation of the Big Five model (Norman, 1963), it has not been developed within the psycholexical tradition. The development of the N (Neuroticism), E (Extraversion), and O (Openness to Experience) scales started with Costa and McCrae's (1976) cluster analyses of 16PF scales, the intercorrelations of which led to the NEO. After taking knowledge of an early Big Five formulation, Costa and McCrae added Agreeableness and Conscientiousness to their model, assuming that their N, E, and O captured the first three of the Big Five. The NEO-PI (Costa & McCrae, 1985) included scales to assess six facets of Neuroticism, Extraversion, and Openness to Experience. Only the 240-item NEO-PI-R (Costa & McCrae, 1992) also included six facets of Agreeableness and Conscientiousness.

A use of the Big Five in which an optimal coverage of the semantics of the Big Five system was realized, can be found in the development of the Five Factor Personality Inventory (FFPI; Hendriks, 1997; Hendriks, Hofstee, & De Raad, 1999). Use was made of the fine-grained AB5C-segmentation of the trait sphere, a system that can be conceived of as an *empirically* based partitioning into facets, the majority of which containing a semantically more or less coherent cluster of traits. These facet clusters were used as the starting-point for item generation. A pool of 914 items that was agreed upon to represent the AB5C system, was made available with approximately identical phrasings in Dutch, German, and English. Items were only accepted for the final pool if clear, unambiguous translations in those languages could be found. The final instrument is trilingual in nature and it is pruned to 100 items. The items have a simple and easy to understand behavioral format, put in third person singular which makes them suitable for both other-ratings and self-ratings.

The Big Five Questionnaire (BFQ) has been developed for the assessment of the Five Factor Model of personality traits using a top down approach, that is by first defining the five dimensions, then the most important facets for each factor, and finally by producing items to assess these constructs (Caprara, Barbaranelli, Borgogni, & Perugini, 1993). The BFQ was developed alongside the first psycholexical study in the Italian context (Caprara & Perugini, 1994) and took into account some of the original findings, especially for the definition of the first factor. In fact, in the BFQ the first factor is defined as Energy, which is also based on a careful scrutiny of the adjectives defining factor I in the psycholexical study.

Research on the structure of childhood traits is scarce. As part of an international research project (Kohnstamm *et al.*, 1998) Mervielde and De Fruyt assembled an extensive list of items by which parents describe their school-age children. That pool of items, the classification of which took largely place within the confines of Big Five categories, ultimately led to the development of the HiPIC, the Hierarchical Personality Inventory for Children.

Especially to clinicians and to researchers in the domain of personality disorders, semi-structured interviews are at times preferred over self-report because they allow the evaluation of the practitioner to be included in the assessment. The SIFFM was developed to provide such an interview-based measure. The measure was designed to assess both adaptive and maladaptive characteristics related to Big Five traits. The SIFFM is especially meant as a complement to a Big Five self-report, mainly because self-reports may be affected by current mood-states and by other self related biases, especially in clinical settings.

A controversy with respect to verbal self- and other-ratings is that they may reflect consistencies in language rather than consistencies in observed behavior. For this reason, Paunonen, Ashton, and Jackson (2001) developed an instrument that did not make use of verbal items, but included cartoon-like pictures, in which a person performs specific behaviors in specific situations. Paunonen and Jackson (1979) initially developed a nonverbal item pool for a person perception study and aiming to represent traits of Murray's (1938) system of needs. From this item pool a subset of items was selected to form the Nonverbal Personality Questionnaire (NPQ). With a few exceptions items were selected from the NPQ to form the shorter FF-NPQ, measuring each of the Big Five factors.

A common practice among practitioners and researchers doing cross-cultural work is to transport personality inventories developed in one country to another country of interest. The issue involved is expressed in Berry's distinction between emic and etic structures (1969). Imposing a personality trait structure developed in one language (emic) as "universally applicable" (etic) in another language is not without danger. The Global Personality Inventory (GPI) involved input from some ten teams of consultants and researchers from around the world, with quick consensus reached on the importance of the Big Five structure, and more rounds of input needed to reach consensus at the facet level. All the teams participated in the production of an item-pool. The items of a long and first version of the GPI was translated into nine languages and data were collected in many diverse countries to be used for the selection of the final set of GPI items.

The Traits Personality Questionnaire is a questionnaire that is heavily influenced by the NEO-PI-R in the construction stage Starting from an a priori conception of the Big Five model of personality, in particular the NEO-PI-R, an item-pool was constructed for the development of the TPQue to be used to assess sub-scales and factor scales of the Big Five in Greek language. A relatively large set of items was used in a pilot study, and the final list of items was selected on the basis their being optimal markers of scales and sub-scales.

A major part of the Big Five domain is of an interpersonal character; particularly the factors Extraversion and Agreeableness represent traits and behaviors with strong interpersonal connotations. Wiggins (1979) used a category of approximately 800 interpersonal trait terms, stemming from psycholexical research of traits, for an initial description of an interpersonal taxonomy. A two-dimensional circumplex model was used for representational purposes. These two dimensions are strongly related to the E and A factors of the Big Five model. After the development of the Interpersonal Adjective Scales measuring the two dimensions, a revision followed in the IASR. He latter instrument was revised not only to provide a short-form measure of the IAS, but also to include the three remaining Big Five dimensions.

Very often researchers would like to use a Big Five measure, and ask for the briefest form possible. Brief and adequate measures are not easily realized. The Big Five Marker Scales (BFMS) form an exception. Developed from a set of trait adjectives common to two independent trait taxonomies in Italian, markers for each of the Big Five in Italian were selected for which very reasonable psychometric characteristics could be established. These Italian Big Five markers have been iteratively selected using an emic-etic analytic strategy. Besides representing a quick overall measure of the Big Five, the BFMS provides a structure into which the whole spectrum of the personality lexicon can be represented. The resulting taxonomy shares much with the AB5C system, although it differs in a few details, and it can be used also for robust comparisons across cultural contexts at the facets level.

The Japanese Adjective List (JAL) for the Big Five contains a final set of 105 adjectives that are optimally measuring the Big Five in the Japanese context. Kashiwagi has carefully adopted a sophisticated factor analytic approach and is detailed in arguing why this approach leads to an optimal structure. While the procedure is certainly not standard, it does represent a fine example of how psychometrically sound techniques can be fruitfully applied to select best markers of the Big Five.

Questionnaires related to or shaped after the Big Five

The impact of the Big Five factors have been such that researchers often clarify the relations of their own alternative trait models with the Big Five. A few such alternative models have been proposed, such as a Big Three (Peabody & Goldberg, 1989), a Big Six (Jackson, Ashton, & Tomes, 1996), a Big Seven factor model (Almagor, Tellegen, & Waller, 1995) and an alternative Five Factor model (Zuckerman, 1994). All these models share features with the Big Five but differ too. In addition, some classic personality inventories originally developed to measure some other personality dimensions and still widely used throughout the world have been molded after the Big Five.

The HPI (Hogan & Hogan, this volume) has a conceptual foundation in the Socioanalytic theory that combines interpersonal theory and evolutionary theory. One of the unique characteristics of the HPI is that it has been developed using data from working adults, and it is designed to be especially apt for use in occupational settings. Although the Big Five model was used as the starting-point for the construction of the inventory, it was concluded that seven dimensions were necessary to describe the data. Those seven dimensions can be easily aligned with the Big Five, either directly or as a combination of them. This allows re-interpreting existing data in light of the Big Five as well as to compare findings. Emotional Stability, Agreeableness, and Conscientiousness of the Big Five can be identified in HPI Adjustment, Likeability, and Prudence. Extraversion can be retraced in both HPI Ambition and Sociability, and Intellect/Openness to Experience is represented in both HPI Intellectance and School Success.

The Six Factor Personality Questionnaire (SFPQ; Jackson & Tremblay, this volume) is developed using scales of the Personality Research Form (PRF), a questionnaire constructed for the assessment of personality variables largely based on the work of Murray. Three of the six factors are identified as Extraversion, Agreeableness, and Openness to Experience. One departure is the Independence factor which name is related to the opposite pole of Neuroticism. The other departure is found in the two factors Methodicalness and Industriousness, which can be seen as a division of Conscientiousness.

Zuckerman's alternative five-factorial model (ZKPQ) does not show a one-to-one correspondence with the Big Five. Yet, four of the ZKPQ factors can be readily interpreted in the Big Five framework. Big Five Intellect/Openness to Experience is not represented; instead the activity and energy facets of Big Five Extraversion have obtained more emphasis in a separate Activity factor, which seems to more in line with the biological orientation of the ZKPQ.

One of the most classical personality questionnaires, the 16PF, provides in its fifth edition five second-order factors which can be easily understood as variants of the Big Five. The 16PF came about as a final result to represent substantial parts of the original Allport and Odbert (1936) list of trait terms. That long list of several thousands of terms was represented at an intermediate stage by a list of 171 trait terms. A further reduction of the latter list was used as input for the development of the 16PF. The adult version of the 16PF has been evaluated in different settings, while alternative forms have been developed for specific contexts. In addition, versions have been developed for age groups younger than 16.

The Adjective Check List (ACL) is developed for use especially in research situations. FormyDuval Hill, Williams, and Bassett (this volume) describe how the ACL can be scored to assess the Big Five dimensions. The ACL started with a substantial number of Cattell's list of 171 trait terms and to that selection other items were added to represent relevant concepts from Freud, Jung, Mead, and Murray.

An articulated situation is offered for the MMPI, which is one of the most used personality inventory for psychopathological assessment, originally developed in the '40s and recently refurbished (MMPI-2). Harkness and McNulty (1994) have developed the so-called PSY-5 constructs starting from a pool of symptoms and characteristics of both normal and dysfunctional personality functioning leading to the identification of 60 major topics in human personality. These fundamental topics have been used to generate five higher order aggregates having some resemblance with the Big Five. The PSY-5 scales can be obtained after ad hoc coding of the 567 MMPI-2 items. Among these scales, there is a higher representation of emotionally-laden constructs or, whereas the factors Conscientiousness and especially Openness to Experience (or Intellect) are less well covered.

The PPQ originated from Kline's work on personality and from his attempt to offer a Big Five based instrument for the occupational context. Unfortunate circumstances, especially the early death of Paul Kline, have influenced the further testing and the PPQ properties and its availability to the research community. However, Barrett's description (this volume) of the PPQ possibly opens up avenues for further research with the instrument.

Final comment

Because the Big Five model has acquired the status of a reference-model, its uses can be expanded to those of systems of classification and clarification for descriptive vocabularies that are not developed from a Big Five perspective, in order to evaluate the comprehensiveness of the trait-semantics of those vocabularies. Moreover, the model is expected to play an important role in modern theory building, due to the fact that its five main constructs capture so much of the subject matter of personality psychology. A recurrent issue in this volume is the further specification of abstract and general factors. Many of the assessment instruments described in this volume enable to assess facets in addition to factor scales. Part of the specification procedures might profit well from paying attention to systematic reviews of situational features.

Many more instruments along the main Big Five theme will be developed in the near future, as translations of existing instruments or as instruments that are completely developed within particular languages. Especially efforts may be expected to specify facets of the Big Five that can be cross-culturally validated. The issue of *cross-cultural generalizability* is a recurrent one in the recent history of the Big Five. After an initial period where the Big Five have emerged in so many different languages and cultures, there is now more awareness of subtle differences that may exist between factors recovered in lingually different psycholexical studies. Whereas a core of consensus among the basic features seems to be agreed upon, there are still differences of opinion concerning the number of factors, rotational variants, culture-specific factors, and so on. Some authors have argued that a Big Three model may represent a cross-culturally more generalizable structure of personality (e.g., Peabody & Goldberg, 1989; Di Blas, Forzi, & Peabody, 2000; cf. Peabody & De Raad, 2000). Curiously, one of the Big Two – historically strong – dimensions, Neuroticism, is not emphasized in that system; that discrepancy deserves special attention. The few studies psycholexical studies where the cross-cultural generalizability has been tested (De Raad, Perugini, & Szirmák, 1997; De Raad, Perugini, Hřebičková, & Szarota, 1998; Hofstee, Kiers, De Raad, Goldberg, & Ostendorf, 1997) have produced an "annotated" Big Five at least. On the other hand, questionnaires developed within one culture, and validated in other cultures (e.g., NEO-PI-R, FFPI) have generally given impressive evidence supporting the stability of the Big Five. Once again, the emic-etic distinction plays quite a role in determining what the answer is to the issue of cross-cultural generalizability. Studies in more and different languages may add to this discussion; the African and the South American continents, Arabic countries, and traditional communities with preserved languages, have not participated yet.

Another issue concerns the *sufficiency* of the Big Five. Whereas we believe that the Big Five is a reasonably agreed upon system and for now the best working hypothesis, and that it is important to use them in as many research contexts as possible, it is by no means obvious that they are sufficient. For instance, a general factor related to Morality and Honesty tends to appear in several psycholexical studies when data are reanalyzed (Ashton & Lee, 2001; Ashton, Lee, & Son, 2000). More research in different languages should provide a test in case; perhaps in some years researchers may need to reconsider their ideas about a Big Five personality system. In this respect, the Big Five model is better conceived of as a starting point for further research, instead of as an arrival point.

Trait structures from different languages differ, and so do assessment instruments, imported or not. This conclusion is not dramatic; it is a challenge to cross-cultural research-programs to isolate and identify what is valid across cultural borders, and to specify the particulars of the different cultures. A lot has yet to be done. The Big Five factor model has shown to be highly prolific in the construction of assessment instruments, notwithstanding the fact that its significance has only been recognized during the last decade of the twentieth century. Moreover, the Big Five factors are far from definitive, and the derived assessment instruments deserve constant attention and an open eye for new facets and features to be included, in the model as well as in its assessment.

References

Adkins, G., Martin, P., & Poon, L.W. (1996). Personality traits and states as predictors of subjective well-being in centenarians, octogenarians, and sexagenarians. *Psychology & Aging, 11*, 408-416.

Allport, G.W., & Odbert, H.S. (1936). Trait-names: A psycho-lexical study. *Psychological Monographs, 47* (1, Whole No. 211).

Almagor, M., Tellegen, A., & Waller, N.G. (1995). The Big Seven model: A cross-cultural replication and further exploration of the basic dimensions of natural language trait descriptors. *Journal of Personality and Social Psychology, 69*, 300-307.

Anderson, C., John, O.P., Keltner, D., & Kring, A.M. (2001). Who attains social status? Effects of personality and physical attractiveness in social groups. *Journal of Personality & Social Psychology, 81*, 116-132.

Angleitner, A., & Ostendorf, F. (1994). Temperament and the Big Five factors of personality. In C.F. Halverson, Jr., G.A. Kohnstamm, & R.P. Martin (Eds.), *The developing structure of temperament and personality from infancy to adulthood* (pp. 69-90). Hillsdale, New Jersey: Lawrence Erlbaum.

Asendorpf, J.B., & Wilpers, S. (1998). Personality effects on social relationships. *Journal of Personality & Social Psychology, 74*, 1531-1544.

Ashton, M.C., & Lee, K. (2001). A theoretical basis for the major dimensions of personality. *European Journal of Personality, 15*, 327-353.

Ashton, M.C., Lee, K., & Son, C. (2000). Honesty as the sixth factor of personality: Correlations with Machiavellianism, primary psychopathy, and social adroitness. *European Journal of Personality, 14*, 359-368.

Astington, E. (1960). Personality assessment and academic performance in a boys' grammar school, *British Journal of Educational Psychology, 30*, 225-236.

Barrick, M.R., & Mount, M.K. (1991). The Big Five personality dimensions and job performance: A meta-analysis, *Personnel Psychology, 44*, 1-26.

Bernardin, H.J., Cooke, D.K., & Villanova, P. (2000). Conscientiousness and agreeableness as predictors of rating leniency. *Journal of Applied Psychology, 85*, 232-236.

Bernard, L.L. (1924). *Instinct: A study in Social Psychology.* New York: Henry Holt and Company.

Berry, J. (1969). On cross-cultural comparability. *International Journal of Psychology, 4*, 119-128.

Bing, M.N., & Lounsbury, J.W. (2000). Openness and job performance in U.S.-based Japaneses manufacturing companies. *Journal of Business and Psychology, 14*, 515-522.

Blickle, G. (1996). Personality traits, learning strategies, and performance. *European Journal of Personality, 10*, 337-352.

Blickle, G. (1997). Argumentativeness and the facets of the Big Five. *Psychological Reports, 81*, 1379-1385.

Booth-Kewley, S., & Vickers, R. R. (1994). Associations between major domains of personality and health behavior. *Journal of Personality, 62*, 281-298.

Borgatta, E.F. (1964). The structure of personality characteristics. *Behavioral Science, 9*, 8-17.

Bosworth, H.B., Feaganes, J.R., Vitaliano, P.P., Mark, D.B., & Siegler, I.C. (2001). Personality and coping with a common stressor: Cardiac catheterization. *Journal of Behavioral Medicine, 24,* 17-31.

Bouchard, T.J., Jr. (1993). Genetic and environmental influences on adult personality: evaluating the evidence. In J. Hettema & I.J. Deary (Eds.), *Foundations of Personality* (pp. 15-44). The Netherlands: Kluwer Academic Publishers.

Buss, D.M. (1991). Evolutionary personality psychology. *Annual Review of Psychology, 42,* 459-491.

Buss, D.M. (1996). Social adaptation and five major factors of personality. In J.S. Wiggins (Ed.), *The Five-Factor Model of Personality: Theoretical Perspectives* (pp. 180-207). New York: The Guildford Press.

Caprara, G. V., Barbaranelli, C., Borgogni, L., & Perugini, M. (1993). The "Big Five Questionnaire": A new questionnaire to assess the Five Factor Model. *Personality and Individual Differences, 15,* 281-288.

Caprara, G.V., & Perugini, M. (1994). Personality described by adjectives: Generalizability of the Big Five to the Italian lexical context. *European Journal of Personality, 8,* 357-369.

Cattell, R.B. (1947). Confirmation and clarification of primary personality factors, *Psychometrika, 12,* 197-220.

Cattell, R.B. (1957). *Personality and Motivation Structure: Structure and Measurement.* Yonkers-on-Hudson, NY: World Book.

Cattell, R.B., Cattell, M.D., & Johns, E. (1984). *Manual and norms for the High School Personality Questionnaire (HSPQ).* Champaign, IL: Institute for Personality and Ability Testing.

Clower, C.E., & Bothwell, R.K. (2001). An exploratory study of the relationship between the Big Five and inmate recidivism. *Journal of Research in Personality, 35,* 231-237.

Costa, P.T., Jr., & McCrae, R.R. (1976). Age differences in personality structure: A custer analytic approach. *Journal of Gerontology, 31,* 564-570.

Costa, P.T., Jr., & McCrae, R.R. (1985). *The NEO Personality Inventory Manual,* San Diego: Psychological Assessment Resources.

Costa, P.T., Jr., & McCrae, R.R. (1987). Neuroticism, somatic complaints, and disease: Is the bark worse than the bite? *Journal of Personality, 55,* 299-316.

Costa, P.T., Jr. & McCrae, R.R. (1992). *Revised NEO Personality Inventory (NEO PI-RTM) and NEO Five-Factor Inventory (NEO-FFI) professional manual.* Odessa, FL: Psychological Assessment Resources.

Costa, P.T., Jr., & Widiger, T.A. (Eds.). (1994). *Personality disorders and the five-factor model of personality.* Washington, DC: American Psychological Association.

David, J.P., Green, P.J., Martin, R., & Suls, J. (1997). Differential roles of neuroticism, extraversion, and event desirability for mood in daily life: An integrative model of top-down and bottom-up influences. *Journal of Personality & Social Psychology, 73,* 149-159.

Dembroski, T.M., & Costa, P.T., Jr. (1987). Coronary-prone behavior: Components of the Type A pattern and hostility. *Journal of Personality, 55,* 211-235.

DeNeve, K.M., & Cooper, H. (1998). The happy personality: A meta-analysis of 137 personality traits and subjective well-being. *Psychological Bulletin, 124,* 197-229.

De Raad, B. (2000). *The Big Five Personality Factors: The Psycholexical Approach to Personality.* Göttingen: Hogrefe & Huber Publishers.

De Raad, B., & Doddema-Winsemius, M. (1999). Instincts and Personality. *Personality and Individual Differences, 27,* 293-305.

De Raad, B., & Hendriks, A.A.J. (1996). A psycholexical route to content-coverage in personality assessment. *European Journal of Psychological Assessment, 13*, 85-98.

De Raad, B., Hendriks, A.A.J., & Hofstee, W.K.B. (1992). Towards a refined structure of personality traits. *European Journal of Personality, 6*, 301-319.

De Raad, B., Perugini, M., & Szirmák, Z. (1997). In pursuit of a cross-lingual reference structure of personality traits: Comparisons among five languages. *European Journal of Personality, 11*, 167-185.

De Raad,B., Perugini, M., Hřébičková, M., & Szarota, P. (1998). Lingua franca of personality: Taxonomies and structures based on the psycholexical approach. *Journal of Cross-Cultural Psychology, 29*, 212-232.

De Raad, B., & Schouwenburg, H.C. (1996). Personality in learning and education: A review. *European Journal of Personality, 10*, 303-336.

De Raad, B., & Van Heck, G.L. (Eds.) (1994). The fifth of the Big Five. *European Journal of Personality, 8*, Special Issue.

Di Blas, L., Forzi, M., & Peabody, D. (2000). Evaluative and descriptive dimensions from Italian personality factors. *European Journal of Personality, 14*, 279-290.

Digman, J.M. (1997). Higher-order factors of the Big Five. *Journal of Personality and Social Psychology, 73*, 1246-1256.

Dollinger, S. J., & Orf, L. A. (1991). Personality and performance in "personality": Conscientiousness and Openness. *Journal of Research in Personality, 25*, 276-284.

Entwistle, N.J., & Cunningham, S. (1968). Neuroticism and school attainment - a linear relationship? *Journal of Educational Psychology, 38*, 123-132.

Eysenck, H.J. (1957). *The Dynamics of Anxiety and Hysteria*. London: Routledge and Kegan Paul.

Eysenck, H.J. (1992). The definition and measurement of psychoticism. *Personality and Individual Differences, 13*, 757-785.

Eysenck, H.J., & Cookson, D. (1969). Personality in primary school children: ability and achievement. *British Journal of Educational Psychology, 39*, 109-122.

Friedman, H.S., & Booth-Kewley, S. (1987). The "disease-prone personality": A meta-analytic view of the construct. *American Psychologist, 42*, 539-555.

Friedman, H.S., Tucker, J.S., Schwartz, J.E., Martin, L.R., et al (1995). Childhood conscientiousness and longevity: Health behaviors and cause of death. *Journal of Personality & Social Psychology, 68*, 696-703.

George, J.M., & Zhou, J. (2001). When openness to experience and conscientiousness are related to creative behavior: An interactional approach. *Journal of Applied Psychology, 86*, 513-524.

Goldberg, L. R. (1992). The development of markers of the Big-Five factor structure. *Psychological Assessment, 4*, 26-42.

Gough, H.G. (1957). *Manual for the California Psychological Inventory*. Palo Alto, Calif.: Consulting Psychologists Press.

Graf, O. (1924). Das Ausleseverfahren bei der Bayerischer Schutzpolizei [Method of selection of the Bavarian police]. *Psychotechnisches Zeitschrift, 4*, 109-113; 163-169.

Graziano, W.G., & Eisenberg, N. (1997). Agreeableness: a dimension of personality. In: R. Hogan, J. Johnson & S. Briggs (Eds.), *Handbook of Personality Psychology* (pp. 795-824). San Diego, CA: Academic Press.

Guilford, J.P. (1959). *Personality*. New York: McGraw-Hill.

Guilford, J.P., & Braly, K.W. (1930). Extroversion and introversion. *Psychological Bulletin, 27*, 96-107.

Hampson, S.E., Andrews, J.A., Barckley, M., Lichtenstein, E., & Lee, M.E. (2000). Conscientiousness, perceived risk, and risk-reduction behaviors: A preliminary study. *Health Psychology, 19,* 496-500.

Harkness, A.R., & McNulty, J.L. (1994). The personality psychopathology five (PSY-5): Issue from the pages of a diagnostic manual instead of a dictionary. In S. Strack & M. Lorr (Eds.), *Differentiating Normal and Abnormal Personality* (pp. 291-315). New York: Springer.

Havill, V., Allen, K., Halverson, C.F., & Kohnstamm, G.A. (1994). Parents' use of Big Five categories in their natural language descriptions of children. In C.F. Halverson, Jr., G.A. Kohnstamm, & R.P. Martin (Eds.), *The Developing Structure of Temperament and Personality from Infancy to Adulthood.* Lawrence Erlbaum: Hillsdale, New Jersey.

Heaven, P. (1996). Personality and self-reported delinquency: Analysis of the 'Big Five' personality dimensions. *Personality and Individual Differences, 20,* 47-54.

Hendriks, A.A.J. (1997). *The construction of the Five-Factor Personality Inventory (FFPI).* Doctoral Dissertation, University of Groningen, The Netherlands.

Hendriks, A.A.J., Hofstee, W.K.B., & De Raad, B. (1999). The Five-Factor Personality Inventory (FFPI). *Personality and Individual Differences, 27,* 307-325.

Henmon, V.A.C. (1919). Air service tests of aptitude for flying. *Journal of Applied Psychology, 3,* 103-109.

Henss, R. (1995). Das Fünf-Faktoren-Modell der Persönlichkeit bei der Beurteilung van Gesichtern [The Five-Factor model of personality in judging faces]. *Report Psychologie, 20,* 28-39.

Hofstee, W.K.B. (2001). Intelligence and personality: Do they mix? In J.M. Collis & S. Messick (Eds.), *Intelligence and Personality: Bridging the gap in theory and measurement* (pp. 43-60). Mahwah, New Jersey: Lawrence Erlbaum.

Hofstee, W. K. B., De Raad, B., & Goldberg, L. R. (1992). Integration of the Big Five and circumplex approaches to trait structure. *Journal of Personality and Social Psychology, 63,* 146-163.

Hofstee, W.K.B., Kiers, H.A.L., De Raad, B., Goldberg, L.R., & Ostendorf, F. (1997). Comparison of Big Five structures of personality traits in Dutch, English, and German. *European Journal of Personality, 11,* 15-31.

Hogan, R.T. (1983). A socioanalytic theory of personality. In M. Page (Ed.), *Nebraska Symposium on Motivation - Current Theory and Research,* Vol. 30 (pp. 58-89). Lincoln: University of Nebraska Press.

Hogan, J. (1989). Personality correlates of physical fitness. *Journal of Personality & Social Psychology, 56,* 284-288.

Hogan, J., & Ones, D.S. (1997). Conscientiousness and integrity at work. In R. Hogan, J. Johnson, & S. Briggs (Eds.), *Handbook of Personality Psychology* (pp. 849-870). San Diego, CA: Academic Press.

Jackson, D.N., Ashton, M.C., & Tomes, J.L. (1996). The six-factor model of personality: Facets from the Big Five. *Personality and Individual Differences, 21,* 391-402.

Jensen-Campbell, L.A. & Graziano, W.G. (2001). Agreeableness as a moderator of interpersonal conflict. *Journal of Personality, 69,* 323-362.

John, O.P., & Srivastava, S. (1999). The Big Five trait taxonomy: History, Measurement, and theoretical perspectives. In L.A. Pervin & O.P. John (Eds.), *Handbook of Personality: Theory and Research* (pp. 102-138). New York: The Guilford Press.

Johnson, J.A., & Ostendorf, F. (1993). Clarification of the five-factor model with the Abridged Big Five Dimensional Circumplex. *Journal of Personality & Social Psychology, 65,* 563-576.

Judge, T.A., & Bono, J.E. (2001). Relationship of core self-evaluations traits--self-esteem, generalized self-efficacy, locus of control, and emotional stability--with job satisfaction and job performance: A meta-analysis. *Journal of Applied Psychology*, *86*, 80-92.

Judge, T.A., Martocchio, J.T., & Thoresen, C.J. (1997). Five-factor model of personality and employee absence. *Journal of Applied Psychology*, *82*, 745-755.

Jung, C.G. (1917). *On the Psychology of the Unconscious*. Princeton, NJ: Standard Edition.

Karney, B.R., & Bradbury, T.N. (1997). Neuroticism, marital interaction, and the trajectory of marital satisfaction. *Journal of Personality & Social Psychology*, *72*, 1075-1092.

Kohnstamm, G.A., Halverson, C.F., Jr., Mervielde, I., & Havill, V.L. (1998). Analyzing parental free descriptions of child personality. In G.A. Kohnstamm, C.F. Halverson, Jr., I. Mervielde & V.L. Havill (Eds.), *Parental descriptions of child personality: developmental antecedents of the Big Five?* (pp. 1-9). Mahwah, NJ: Erlbaum.

Kohnstamm, G.A., Slotboom, A., & Elphick, E. (1993). *Dutch parents' free descriptions of child characteristics: a search for the onset of the five factor structure in adult perceptions*. Unpublished manuscript, University of Leyden, The Netherlands.

Kurdek, L.A. (1997). Relation between neuroticism and dimensions of relationship commitment: Evidence from gay, lesbian, and heterosexual couples. *Journal of Family Psychology*, *11*, 109-124.

Larsen, R.J. (1992). Neuroticism and selective encoding and recall of symptoms: evidence from a combined concurrent-retrospective study. *Journal of Personality and Social Psychology*, *62*, 480-488.

Lemos Giraldez, S., & Fidalgo Aliste, A.M. (1997). Personality dispositions and health-related habits and attitudes: A cross-sectional study. *European Journal of Personality*, *11*, 197-209.

Lieberman, M.D., & Rosenthal, R. (2001). Why introverts can't always tell who likes them: Multitasking and nonverbal decoding. *Journal of Personality and Social Psychology*, *80*, 294-310.

Lower, C.E., & Bothwell, R.K. (2001). An exploratory study of the relationships between the Big Five and inmate recidivism. *Journal of Research in Personality*, *35*, 231-237.

Mak, A.S., & Tran, C. (2001). Big Five personality and cultural relocation factors in Vietnamese Australian students' intercultural social self-efficacy. *International Journal of Intercultural Relations*, *25*, 181-201.

McCrae, R.R., & John, O.P. (1992). An introduction to the Five-Factor model and its applications. *Journal of Personality*, *60*, 175-215.

McCullough, M.E., Bellah, C.G., Kilpatrick, S.D., & Johnson, J.L. (2001). Vengefulness: relationships with forgiveness, rumination, well-being, and the Big Five. *Personality and Social Psychology Bulletin*, *27*, 601-610.

Miller, T.R. (1991). The psychotherapeutic utility of the Five-Factor Model of personality: A clinician's experience. *Journal of Personality Assessment*, *57*, 415-433.

Murray, H.A. (1938). *Explorations in personality*. New York: Oxford Press.

Neuman, G.A., & Wright, J. (1999). Team effectiveness: Beyond skills and cognitive ability. *Journal of Applied Psychology*, *84*, 376-389.

Norman, W.T. (1963). Toward an adequate taxonomy of personality attributes: replicated factor structure in peer nomination personality ratings. *Journal of Abnormal and Social Psychology*, *66*, 574-583.

Ones, D. S., & Viswesvaran, C. (1996). Bandwidth-fidelity dilemma in personality measurement for personnel selection. *Journal of Organizational Behavior, 17*, 609-626.

Ones, D.S., Viswesvaran, C., & Schmidt, F.L. (1993). Comprehensive meta-analysis of integrity test validities: findings and implications for personnel selection and theories of job performance. *Journal of Applied Psychology, 78*, 679-703.

Ormel, J., & Wohlfarth, T. (1991). How neuroticism, long-term difficulties, and life situation change influence psychological distress: A longitudinal model. *Journal of Personality & Social Psychology, 60*, 744-755.

Paunonen, S.V. (1998). Hierarchical organization of personality and prediction of behavior. *Journal of Personality and Social Psychology, 74*, 538-556.

Paunonen, S.V., Ashton, M.C. (2001). Big Five factors and facets and the prediction of behavior. *Journal of Personality & Social Psychology, 81*, 524-539.

Paunonen, S.V., Ashton, M.C. & Jackson, D.N. (2001). Nonverbal assessment of the Big Five personality factors. *European Journal of Personality, 15*, 3-18.

Paunonen, S.V., & Jackson, D.N. (1979). Nonverbal trait inference. *Journal of Personality and Social Psychology, 37*, 1645-1659.

Paunonen, S.V., & Jackson, D.N. (2000). What is beyond the Big Five? Plenty! *Journal of Personality, 68*, 821-835.

Peabody, D., & De Raad, B. (2000). The substantive nature of psycholexical personality factors: A comparison across languages. Paper presented at the 10th European Conference on Personality, Cracow: Poland.

Peabody, D., & Goldberg, L.R. (1989). Some determinants of factor structures from personality trait-descriptors. *Journal of Personality and Social Psychology, 57*, 552-567.

Perugini, M. (1999). A proposal for integrating hierarchical and circumplex modelling in personality. In I. Mervielde, I. Deary, F. De Fruyt, and F. Ostendorf (Eds.), *Personality psychology in Europe*, Vol. 7 (pp. 85-99). Tilburg, The Netherlands: Tilburg University Press.

Salgado, J.F. (1997). The five factor model of personality and job performance in the European Community. *Journal of Applied Psychology, 82*, 30-43.

Saucier, G. (1994). Trapnell versus the lexical factor: more ado about nothing? *European Journal of Personality, 8*, 291-298.

Saucier, G., & Goldberg, L. R. (1998). What is beyond the Big Five? *Journal of Personality, 66*, 495-524.

Saucier, G., & Ostendorf, F. (1999). Hierarchical subcomponents of the Big Five personality factors: A cross-language replication. *Journal of Personality & Social Psychology, 76*, 613-627.

Scheier, M.F. & Carver, C.S. (1987). Dispositional optimism and physical well-being: the influence of generalized outcome expectancies on health. *Journal of Personality, 55*, 169-210.

Schroeder, M.L., Wormworth, J.A., & Livesley, W.J. (1992). Dimensions of personality disorder and their relationships to the Big Five dimensions of personality. *Psychological Assessment, 4*, 47-53.

Schuerger, J.M., & Kuna, D.L. (1987). Adolescent personality and school performance: A follow-up study. *Psychology in the Schools, 24*, 281-285.

Schwartz, M.D., Taylor, K.L., Willard, K.S., Siegel, J.E., Lamdan, R.M., & Moran, K. (1999). Distress, personality, and mammography utilization among women with a family history of breast cancer. *Health Psychology, 18*, 327-332.

Seibert, S.E., & Kraimer, M.L. (2001). The Five-Factor Model of personality and career success. *Journal of Vocational Behavior, 58*, 1-21.

Shiner, R.L. (2000). Linking childhood personality with adaptation: Evidence for continuity and change across time into late adolescence. *Journal of Personality & Social Psychology, 78*, 310-325.

Siegler, I.C., & Brummett, B.H. (2000). Associations among NEO personality assessments and well-being at mid-life: Facet-level analyses. *Psychology & Aging, 15*, 710-714.

Smith, G.M. (1967). Usefulness of peer ratings of personality in educational research. *Educational and Psychological Measurement, 27*, 967-984.

Smith, T.W., & Williams, P.G. (1992). Personality and health: Advantages and limitations of the Five-Factor model. *Journal of Personality, 60*, 395-423.

Steel, G.D., Suedfeld, P., Peri, A., & Palinkas, L.A. (1997). People in high latitudes: the 'Big Five' personality characteristics of the circumpolar sojourner. *Environment and Behavior, 29*, 324-347.

Strelau, J., Angleitner, A., Bantelmann, J., & Ruch, W. (1990). The Strelau Temperament Inventory Revised (STR-R): Theoretical considerations and scale development. *European Journal of Personality, 4*, 209-235.

Ten Berge, M., & De Raad, B. (2001). The construction of a joint taxonomy of traits and situations. *European Journal of Personality, 15*, 253-276.

Ten Berge, M., & De Raad, B. (in press). The structure of situations from a personality perspective. *European Journal of Personality*.

Tett, R.P., Jackson, D.N., & Rothstein, M. (1991). Personality measures as predictors of job performance: a meta-analytic review. *Personnel Psychology, 44*, 703-742.

Thurstone, L.L., & Thurstone, T.G. (1930). A neurotic inventory. *Journal of Social Psychology, 1*, 3-30.

Tupes, E.C., & Christal, R.C. (1961). *Recurrent Personality Factors Based on Trait Ratings* (USAF ASD Technical Report, No. 61-97). U.S. Air Force, Lackland Air Force Base, TX.

Van Dam, K. (1996). Persoonlijkheidswaarneming in het selectie-interview [Personality perception in the selection-interview]. *Gedrag en Organisatie, 9*, 1-14.

Van der Zee, K., Oldersma, F., Buunk, B.P., & Bos, D. (1998). Social comparison preferences among cancer patients as related to neuroticism and social comparison orientation. *Journal of Personality & Social Psychology, 75*, 801-810.

Vinchur, A.J., Schippmann, J.S., Switzer, F.S. III, & Roth, P.L. (1998). A meta-analytic review of predictors of job performance for salespeople. *Journal of Applied Psychology, 83*, 586-597.

Vollrath, M., Knoch, D., & Cassano, L. (1999). Personality, risky health behaviour, and perceived susceptibility to health risks. *European Journal of Personality, 13*, 39-50.

Wanberg, C.R., Kanfer, R., & Banas, J.T. (2000). Predictors and outcomes of networking intensity among unemployed job seekers. *Journal of Applied Psychology, 85*, 491-503.

Watson, D., & Clark, L.A. (1997). Extraversion and its positive emotional core. In R. Hogan, J. Johnson & S. Briggs (Eds.), *Handbook of Personality Psychology* (pp. 767-793). Academic Press: San Diego, CA.

Wiggins, J.S. (1968). Personality structure. *Annual Review of Psychology, 19*, 293-350.

Wiggins, J.S. (1979). A psychological taxonomy of trait-descriptive terms: The interpersonal domain. *Journal of Personality and Social Psychology, 37*, 395-412.

Wiggins, J.S. (1991). Agency and Communion as conceptual coordinates for the understanding and measurement of interpersonal behavior. In L.W.M. Grove & D. Cicchetti (Eds.), *Thinking clearly about psychology. Vol. 2: Personality and Psychopathology* (pp. 89-113). Minneapolis: University of Minnesota Press.

Wiggins, J.S. (Ed.) (1996). The Five-Factor Model of personality: Theoretical perspectives. New York: The Guilford Press.

Wiggins, N., Blackburn, M., & Hackman, J.R. (1969). Prediction of first-year graduate success in psychology: peer ratings. *The Journal of Educational Research*, *63*, 82-85.

Woodworth, R.S. (1917). *Personal Data Sheet.* Chicago: Stoelting.

Wolfe, R.N., & Johnson, S.D. (1995). Personality as a predictor of college performance. *Educational and Psychological Measurement*, *55*, 177-185.

Zuckerman, M. (1994). An alternative five factor model of personality. In C.F. Halverson, G.A. Kohnstamm, & R.P. Martin (Eds.), *The developing structure of temperament and personality from infancy to adulthood* (pp. 53-68). New York: Erlbaum.

ASSESSMENT METHODOLOGY

Chapter 2

Assessing the Big Five: Applications of 10 psychometric criteria to the development of marker scales

Gerard Saucier
Lewis R. Goldberg

Introduction

A factor is a parsimonious reduction of many observed variables into one hypotheti-cal variable, accomplished within a particular set of data. The Big Five personality factor structure (Goldberg, 1981; Saucier & Goldberg, 1996a, 1996b) involves five orthogonal (i.e., mutually uncorrelated) factors that capture the five largest sources of variance shared by the variables in fairly representative assemblages of personal-ity-attribute descriptors in a number of languages (e.g., English, German, Polish, Czech, Turkish). Whether the Big Five is the optimal cross-culturally generalizable taxonomic structure for human personality is still a matter of controversy (see Saucier & Goldberg, in press), but it is clearly a very useful structure.

Once a useful set of factors like the Big Five is discovered, it is expedient to ex-tend them beyond the particular set of data in which they were first located. How might one do so? One option would be to readminister the entire set of variables that led to the factors and repeat the analysis in new samples. But in the case of factors based on large numbers of variables (like the Big Five), this is quite inconvenient. Instead, it would be desirable to discover a relatively small set of variables that will consistently produce the structure a set of factor "markers."

This chapter describes various marker sets developed by the authors for the Big Five and related structures. We present these marker sets within a broader concep-tual framework, reviewing 10 diverse psychometric criteria by which marker sets can be developed and evaluated. Because constructing a set of factor markers is typically an item-reduction exercise (i.e., selecting an optimal set of items from a

Big Five Assessment, edited by B. De Raad & M. Perugini. © 2002, Hogrefe & Huber Publishers.

larger item pool), we focus on the item selection process. The principles and issues we discuss are important to personality-test construction in general, in most cases applying also to scales that are not factor-analytically derived as are Big Five scales.

To conserve space, we will generally provide a summary of our scale development procedures, and then refer the reader to published articles on these marker sets; in the case of our new unpublished marker sets we will provide more detail.

Item phrasing: Two widely recognized basics

Criterion 1: Clearly understandable items

Unless one has an explicit interest in collecting responses to ambiguous stimuli (as in projective instruments), the meaning of an item should be relatively unambiguous to the respondents. Assuming one's stimuli include words, a clear and easy to understand item is one that uses familiar rather than difficult vocabulary, and simple phrases lacking conjunctions which make items "double-barrelled." Indeed, from this standpoint single words (e.g., adjectives) might be considered superior, but they have one important limitation. Single words are often polysemous (i.e., they have multiple meanings) and thus somewhat ambiguous; a good item subdues rather than aggravates this tendency.

Those items that meet various other criteria we describe later, such as being highly associated with other items or having high loadings on factors, tend to be clear and unambiguous ones. At the outset of item selection, however, the investigator may save much time and effort by identifying and eliminating the most unclear and difficult items. In lexical studies that have led to the Big Five structure, this elimination process has been built into the initial process of reducing the number of variables from thousands to hundreds in preparation for data collection.

Criterion 2: Balanced keying

Imagine that all of the items indexing an attribute were formulated so that the keyed response (the one that contributes to a high rather than a low score) involved the same response option (e.g., "True" rather than "False") or were at the same end of a rating scale. In this case, the content of the scale will be inextricably confounded with individuals' preferences to use one or the other end of the rating scale (i.e., response "acquiescence"). In general, each of the scales in an optimal marker set should have an equal number of items representing the presence of an attribute and either its opposite attribute, if possible, or its absence[1]. Balanced-keyed scales possess one kind of desirable method-heterogeneity (Nunnally & Bernstein, 1994, p. 313). As we shall see, the balanced-keying desideratum presents a challenge in some domains (e.g., Neuroticism) where it is difficult to find or formulate a large number of candidate items representing the lack (or opposite) of that particular attribute.

The importance of balanced keying suggests that optimal measures should be developed not from single items but rather from parcels of items, each parcel consisting of an equal number of items keyed in each direction. Because acquiescence would then not contribute significantly to factors, factor analysis of parcels should be preferable to analyses of single items. One could use the sum of responses to pairs of opposite-keyed items (with scores not reflected) as an index of acquiescence; this index may be a useful covariate, inasmuch as acquiescence variance can affect the factor structure (Hofstee, Ten Berge, & Hendriks, 1998). Without balanced keying, acquiescence is likely to be confounded with item content and with social-desirability responding (Hofstee *et al.*, 1998). Marker sets described by Saucier (2000b), described later in this article, make use of parcels.

Incorporating desirable elements of diverse scale-construction strategies

Goldberg (1972; Hase & Goldberg, 1967) described three general strategies of test construction, labeled Intuitive, Internal, and External. In the Internal (or factor-analytic) strategy, items loading most highly on a factor are selected for the scale measure of the factor. Only the internal structure of the initial item pool determines item selection and keying direction, although the labeling of the scales developed by this strategy rests on the test constructor's personal judgment. Because marker sets are by definition based on factors, it is the Internal strategy that we will emphasize in this chapter. However, the Internal strategy used alone can lead to limitations in the resulting scales. Elements of the two other strategies can make an incremental contribution to marker set construction, as seen in our next two criteria.

---

[1] At a more technical level, it should be apparent that balanced keying will not guarantee perfect balance between the two types of items, since the correlations among the items of each type will affect the variance associated with each of those half-scales; differences in these correlational patterns can lead to differences in the relative weights of the half-scales in the composite measure. Nonetheless, balanced keying will generally provide at least some rough control of this problem.

Criterion 3: Intuitive fit between item and construct

Goldberg (1972) noted that:

... the very characteristic of both the External and Internal strategies that gives them their power also provides their Achilles' Heel: namely, their dependence upon — and vulnerability to — characteristics of the particular samples used in their construction. The Intuitive strategy, in contrast, is minimally dependent on sample-specific characteristics; only at the stage of scale "purification" (e.g., discarding items with low correlations with scale scores) do sample characteristics have any chance to enter the scale construction process (p. 49-50).

Goldberg (1972) found that Intuitive scales, those developed solely from judgments about the item content, turned out to be of comparable validity to scales developed by other strategies, a finding replicated by Burisch (1978; see Burisch, 1984a). Indeed, Ashton and Goldberg (1973) found that the average psychology student was able to construct scales as reliable and valid as well-known External scales constructed by a far more expensive and time-consuming process.

What gives the Intuitive approach its strength? Ashton and Goldberg (1973) noted that face validity and empirical validity should converge when there are conditions of mutual trust between subjects and investigators, as in typical self-reports under anonymous conditions (though not necessarily when there is something to gain by deception). Under such research conditions, it has long been known that the more directly the content of the items corresponds to the content of the construct, the better is the measure; and alternatively the more "subtle" are the items (in terms of the scoring keys), the less robust are those items across different subject samples and assessment contexts (Goldberg & Slovic, 1967; Jackson, 1971; Norman, 1963).

What's the take-home message for developers of marker scales? There is much to gain by ensuring that the items relate to one's intuitive or theoretical understanding of the content of the dimension in question. Items that do not have this relation are more prone to be reflecting artifacts, or chance characteristics of the sample at hand. Thus, the Intuitive approach provides some assurance against faulty reliance on sample-specific characteristics.

Criterion 4: Suitable bandwidth

Hase and Goldberg (1967) described the External strategy as one in which the items are selected on the basis of their associations with some external criterion (e.g., peer ratings, job performance). In one version of this strategy, the test constructor initially attempts to locate two distinct groups of subjects who differ in some significant manner (e.g., schizophrenics vs. normals, lawyers vs. people in general, males vs. females) or who fall at each of the two poles of a personality trait (as determined, for example, by peer ratings). The test items are then administered to members of both criterion groups, and those items that differentiate most strongly between the groups are retained for the scale. In the pure form of this strategy, only the empirically discovered discriminating power of the item determines item selection for a scale, and the scale is typically labeled in terms of the criterion groups used. Common characteristics of scales developed from the External strategy are their heterogeneity in content, which results in rather low intercorrelations among the items; to ensure high Alpha coefficients for the resulting scales, the scales must be quite long.

As already noted, two studies (Hase & Goldberg, 1967; Ashton & Goldberg, 1973) failed to find any validity advantages for External scales. However, Goldberg (1972) found that the External strategy appears to produce a broader bandwidth instrument — that is, one valid for a broader array of criteria — though one with slightly lower fidelity for the most predicable criteria. The slight advantage in bandwidth must be due to these less homogeneous scales including some personologically relevant variance that is not included in the scales developed by the Internal and Intuitive strategies. Although we do not typically advocate the use of the External strategy, these findings suggest an important caution for developers of marker sets. To the extent that an investigator seeks to maximize homogeneity, he/she may be unknowingly compromising validity, especially with respect to any additional criteria beyond those that may be originally anticipated (Loevinger, 1954).[2]

One application of the External strategy of scale construction that has been used to develop marker scales relies on the selection of items with particularly strong correlations between self and peer descriptions of the target person. For example, in the development of their Five-Factor Personality Inventory (FFPI) Hendriks, Hofstee, and De Raad (1999) used self-peer agreement as a primary (external) criterion for item selection. To the extent that marker items selected using this criterion are not particularly univocal indicators of the factors they were selected to approximate, this strategy can lead to high inter-scale associations, as is true of the FFPI scales.

Representative sampling is an alternative approach that promotes the selection of content with broad bandwidth. Loevinger (1957) suggested that in any measure "the various areas or subareas of content should be represented in proportion to their life-importance" and noted that Cattell, an early advocate of the lexical approach, "assumed that life-importance could be judged by dictionary representation" (p. 659). Representative sampling of items from some domain of content is no different in principle from representative sampling of subjects from some population of interest. In both cases, one must select the strata, regions, or facets that one wants to sample, and then one selects the individual persons or items within each class on a quasi-random basis. For the representative sampling of items, one may attempt to include representatives of as wide a range of variables as one can locate. To the extent to which one can locate a full range of facets in the domain, one can sample broadly,

---

[2] In this chapter, we focus on bandwidth at the scale level. Broad item-level bandwidth (i.e., the extent to which a single item captures a broad array of content) might lead to an increase rather than a decrease in scale homogeneity. Broad items might be constructed using broad, familiar descriptive concepts (e.g., Is good, Is attractive) or, more problematically given our Criterion 1, by joining several forms of content by conjunctions (e.g., Is kind and generous and humble).

and thus one's measure should be associated with a wider range of potential criterion variables.

Representative sampling is consonant with the goal of "content validation." Content validation is appropriate to situations where two conditions hold: (a) validity depends greatly on the adequacy with which a specified domain of content is sampled and (b) the measure must stand by itself as an adequate measure of what it is supposed to measure, with no ultimate gold-standard criterion ever likely to become available to serve in its validation. Content validation generally involves reference to a standard source or to relatively objective expert views (which might be represented in the literature). One example of an attempt to provide a representative sample of constructs from the scientific literature is the set of six facet scales targeted at each of the five factors included in the NEO-PI-R (Costa & McCrae, 1992).

A study by Peabody (1987) exemplifies a representative-sampling approach. He began with an item pool of 571 personality adjectives derived from previous research (e.g., Goldberg, 1982; Norman, 1967). These terms were reduced systematically to a set of 53 bipolar pairs, which were included as a representative set in the studies by Peabody and Goldberg (1989). Similarly, Saucier (in press) developed 100 representative parcels based on 500 very high frequency adjectival person-descriptors in English. Pairs of terms whose highest correlation (positive or negative) was with each other were supplemented by additional terms as needed to increase Alpha. A marker set derived from Saucier's representative set of parcels is described later in this chapter.

Goldberg's (1990) 133 clusters provides another illustration of Big Five factor markers based on representative sampling. The starting point was a set of 1,431 personality adjectives that Norman in unpublished research had classified into 75 categories. Using criteria of (a) lexicographically documented synonymity and (b) relatively homogeneous social-desirability values, Goldberg (1990, Study 2) reduced the terms to 479, grouped into 133 clusters[3]. In a further study leading to a revised set of 100 clusters, Goldberg used perhaps the most common item-selection criterion — that of internal consistency — our next topic.

---

[3] The criterion of homogeneous desirability values is related to a criterion of homogeneous response means (similar desirability values tend to lead to similar means), and is highly compatible with the criterion of maximizing internal consistency. This is because variables with similar means have a higher maximum intercorrelation than do variables with differing means. However, this criterion is not harmonious with aspects of modern test theory that critique "parallelism" (e.g., sets of nearly redundant items) and put a premium on scales whose items have a wide range of difficulty levels (with the response-mean parameter being analogous to difficulty level). One could argue, as we do later, that there is advantage in using the short homogeneous parcel (rather than the item) as a basic unit, and aggregating parcels having a range of difficulty levels (response means) into the marker scale.

Criteria consonant with classical test theory

Criterion 5: Maximizing internal consistency

Virtually all psychologists have been taught that a desirable feature of any measure is high reliability (the relative absence of measurement error). Internal consistency is the most commonly employed form of reliability, and it is typically estimated by Coefficient Alpha. Alpha is a function of scale length (the longer the higher) and homogeneity (the average intercorrelation among the items in a scale).[4] Naturally, then, maximizing Coefficient Alpha has been widely used as an item-selection criterion. Using contemporary data-analysis software, one can easily identify and cull out those items whose corrected item-total correlations are sufficiently low that their removal increases the value of Alpha in the sample under study.[5] We will refer to this common strategy as "Alpha-maximizing."

Application: Goldberg's (1990) 100 custers

Goldberg's (1990, Study 3) creation of 100 clusters illustrates the Alpha-maximizing approach. The 133 clusters developed in Goldberg's Study 2 included a

---

[4] There appear to be two prime reasons for the relative emphasis on internal consistency over retest stability: (a) unlike internal consistency coefficients, retest stability coefficients are influenced by extraneous elements like carryover effects and practice effects as well as the length of time between measurements; (b) the assumption that all personality attributes must ideally be stable over time can be questioned. However, one could conceivably use retest stability as an item selection criterion, particularly if one wished to favor stable over unstable attributes. Obviously, for attributes that are temporary states (e.g., emotions) retest stability would be expected to be moderate. If one focuses on internal consistency, an alternative to Alpha is Omega (Zinbarg, Yovel, Revelle, & McDonald, 2000) which is a function of average general factor loading more than average intercorrelation.

[5] In the simplest IRT (item response theory) model, the one-parameter-logistic (1PL) model, item difficulty levels are allowed to vary, but item-discrimination indices are constrained to be equal. The nearest equivalents in classical measurement approaches to IRT item-discrimination indices are either the corrected item-total correlation or the loading of an item on a factor that represents the attribute. Accordingly, a good scale under the 1PL model has some analogy to a scale in which all the items have similarly high corrected item-total correlations, or similarly high loadings on a common factor. A scale whose items discriminate equally well has some distinct virtues. When these items are subjected to reliability analysis, it will be impossible to improve the internal consistency of the scale by deleting any item. Moreover, if these items were subjected to a factor analysis, they would have the maximum possible tendency to cluster together on a single factor, both in replications as well as in the original sample.

few single-term categories (of uncertain reliability) and a few clusters with low internal consistency coefficients. In new samples of data using the 479 adjectives included in the 133 clusters, Goldberg eliminated the single-term categories, and iteratively eliminated the least homogeneous items from a number of other clusters (i.e., those with the lowest item-total correlations); a few new synonym sets were developed from the items that were no longer included in the remaining clusters (again based mainly on the Alpha-maximizing criterion). The result was a set of 100 clusters based on 339 adjectives.[6]

As would be expected, the Alpha values of the new 100 clusters were higher than those from the initial set of 133 scales. In general, Alpha values based on original responses are higher than those based on ipsatized responses (i.e., cases Z-scored so that each respondent has a mean of 0 and a variance of 1 across all of the items), because individual differences in response biases tend to increase indices of internal consistency. Using ipsatized data, the Alpha values for the 100 clusters averaged .61, as compared to .48 for the initial 133 scales. The items included in these 100 clusters, along with the scale reliabilities, are available in an earlier report (Goldberg, 1990, Table 3).

The 100 clusters have the advantage of a high degree of representative sampling: A wide array of personality attributes is included. Another advantage is that the clusters can be used as lower-level facets in their own right, affording an abundance of information for predictive purposes. One disadvantage is that no cluster included reverse-keyed items. Another is that 339 adjectives must be administered in order to provide scores for the Big Five factors. Moreover, one has no guarantee that the five derived factor scores would be the same in different subject samples, partly because some of the clusters have complex associations with the Big Five factors, and some have only weak relations with any of them. In other words, these are a richly detailed but not an efficient set of factor markers. In subsequent work, Goldberg (1992) developed more efficient (albeit less representative) marker sets by applying two other widely used item-selection criteria, to which we now turn.

Criterion 6: Factor saturation (high loadings on the targeted factor)

This criterion is central to the Internal strategy of scale construction (Goldberg, 1972). The rationale is clear-cut. A set of markers for a factor is designed to represent that factor. What more efficient way to represent the factor than with the items that have the highest loadings on (or extension correlations with) that factor?

High internal consistency is a necessary but not a sufficient indicator of unidimensionality (Zinbarg, Yovel, Revelle, & McDonald, 2000). However, Criteria 5 (Internal consistency) and 6 (Factor saturation) generally tend to converge, most strongly so in the special case of a structure that properly has only one factor. The first unrotated factor has the maximum internal consistency of any possible linear

---

[6] However, eliminating items based on a internal consistency criterion can capitalize on chance in a way similar to stepwise regression analyses, and thus both procedures share this potential liability.

combination of the items analyzed. Factor scores on this single factor are highly related to a scale derived from the highest loading items, and thus either can be used to index individual differences on that factor. MacDonald (1999) notes that a "(psychometrically) homogeneous test is one whose items measure just one attribute in common — a common factor," a supposition that can be tested by "seeing if the responses to them fit the single factor model" (p. 78). In a simplified scale-construction approach, one might merely utilize Criteria 5 and 6, which are already highly convergent. Our next criteria can each be seen as a way of correcting for the limitations of this simplified approach.

Criterion 7: Factor discrimination (low loadings on other factors)

In a factor structure like the Big Five that includes more than one factor, those variables having high loadings on each factor can be distinguished from one another by the relative magnitude of their loadings on the other factors. Some variables may have high loadings on one or more of the other factors; variables with such high "complexity" with respect to the factors may be viewed as factorial "blends" or as "interstitial" variables. Some variables may have low loadings on all of the other factors that are retained; variables with such extreme "simplicity" with respect to the factors might be thought of as factorially "univocal" or as "factor-pure." This low-divergent-loadings criterion tends to enhance the unidimensionality of the set of variables associated with each factor.

If one combines Criteria 6 (Factor saturation) and 7 (Factor discrimination), one selects those items that simultaneously load most highly, and most univocally, on a given factor. These are the variables that conform most directly to the factor rotation concept of "simple structure," as they capture the distinct features of the factor most directly. The most efficient set of factor markers are these univocal variables, and they are the ones that are most likely to produce across-sample replicability of the factor structure. That is, factor markers consisting of univocal items can be expected to reproduce the original factor structure in replication studies more surely than those with either low or complex associations with the factors.

We note one caveat about univocal variables, to which we shall return later: Other things being equal, the more univocal are the variables included in a marker set, the more homogeneous and narrow are they likely to be. But, as indicated by our Criterion 4, the bandwidth of one's markers constitutes an important property of any marker set. To the extent to which one desires a broad-bandwidth instrument, perhaps by the representative sampling of lower-level facets, one will usually go beyond extremely univocal variables, which can be homogeneous but narrow in content reference.[7]

---

[7] Criterion 7 can be related to the Stylistic strategy of scale construction (Hase & Goldberg, 1967) as exemplified in the development of social-desirability scales. Big Five scales tend to have their favorable poles associated, suggesting that the intercorrelations reflect a single desirability factor. Thus, the "low loadings" criterion tends to minimize the influence of this stylistic factor.

Application: Goldberg's (1992) 100 unipolar markers

Although the 100 clusters from Goldberg (1990) have the advantage of providing markers with an unusually broad bandwidth, they require the administration of 339 adjectives, and thus they are hardly a maximally efficient marker set. In constructing some more efficient sets of Big Five markers, Goldberg (1992) took into account all of the criteria that we have heretofore discussed. Among the marker sets described in that article was a set of 100 unipolar factor markers that has since become widely used.

From a pool of 566 reasonably common personality-descriptive adjectives, Goldberg selected 116 terms having high loadings on one factor and, relative to other candidate terms for that factor, relatively low loadings on the other factors (Criteria 6 and 7). The initial set of 116 terms was reduced to 100 using the internal-consistency criterion (Criterion 5), as well as a criterion of replicability in their factor loadings across three samples of subjects. In order to make the marker sets relatively equal in size, 20 terms were selected for each factor.[8] In order to reduce the effect of individual differences in response scale usage, 10 items were selected for the positive and 10 for the negative pole of each factor, with the exception of Factor IV (Emotional Stability) where a dearth of suitable positive items led to a mix of 6 positive and 14 negative items.

Goldberg (1992) showed that each of the five 20-item subsets of these 100 markers, when considered as separate scales, yielded highly reliable scores: The mean (across factors) Alpha coefficients ranged from .85 to .93 depending on the data set, with all of the coefficients above .80 in each data set. Partly because of these favorable psychometric properties, this marker set has been widely used to index the Big Five factors. However, there are at least three potential problems with this marker set, each of which has led to the development of different types of new markers. First of all, many investigators desire to include some markers of each of the Big Five domains in an extensive battery of other measures, but they balk at devoting the testing time needed to administer all 100 items; for these purposes, shorter and thus more efficient marker sets are needed. In addition, although the Big Five factors are orthogonal conceptually (and when operationalized via orthogonal rotations), the five scales scored from the 100 markers are typically at least slightly interrelated; less highly related marker sets would be desirable in some contexts. These problems are addressed by additional criteria for item-selection that we will discuss shortly.

Another problem with Goldberg's (1990) 100 markers involves the nature of the items themselves. Because single trait-descriptive adjectives encode behaviors at such a high level of abstraction, they are often difficult to translate precisely from

---

[8] Note that if one's goal was an even more complete equality of the scale variances, one might have had to select slightly different numbers of items for each of the five factors.

one language to another. That is, although it is often possible to locate a term in each of the two languages that refers to much the same type of behavior, the two terms may differ in their social-desirability value (Hofstee, 1990). More behaviorally specified item formats (such as the items included in the International Personality Item Pool; Goldberg, 1999) could turn out to be far easier to translate with precision. One way of addressing this problem is illustrated in the following application.

Applying these criteria to an alternative item format

Goldberg (1999) reported the development of an Internet collaboratory for the advancement of personality measurement, based on an item format pioneered by Hendriks, Hofstee, and De Raad (1999). This International Personality Item Pool (IPIP) now includes nearly 2,000 items, each a short verbal statement describing some aspect of one's thoughts, feelings, or behaviors (e.g., Act wild and crazy; Don't care about rules; Sense others' wishes; Have a soft heart). Preliminary personality scales have been developed from the IPIP to measure the 45 bipolar facets from the A-bridged Big Five-dimensional Circumplex model (AB5C) of Hofstee, De Raad, and Goldberg (1992). Table 1 lists the number of items keyed in each direction, the mean item intercorrelation, and the Coefficient Alpha reliability estimate for each of these 45 AB5C marker scales; the items included in each scale are listed in Goldberg (1999). Most of these scales include about 10 items, with mean intercorrelations around .25 and Alpha coefficients around .80.

The coordinates for the AB5C model were based on Goldberg's (1992) 100 unipolar markers. Therefore, the 45 bipolar IPIP-AB5C facet scales can be regarded as a translation of an adjectival Big Five marker set into a more behaviorally specified item format, by means of an application of "uniform" sampling. Uniform sampling of a semantic space is a characteristic of the "circumplex" tradition (e.g., Wiggins, 1980) in which the locations of variables in two dimensions are projected onto a circular representation, and then exemplar items are selected at equally spaced locations around the circle. In uniform sampling, regions where variables are densely concentrated are systematically undersampled whereas more sparsely populated interstitial regions are oversampled (Goldberg, 1992), thus contrasting markedly with representative sampling.

As markers of the broad Big Five domains, one could use the five IPIP scales measuring the factor-pure AB5C facets. However, each of these IPIP scales includes only items that are more highly associated with their narrow facet than with any of the other facets, and such items may not necessarily be optimal measures of the five domains alone. Moreover, those scales are targeted at the Big-Five factor structure of phenotypic personality attributes (Saucier & Goldberg, 1996b), not at McCrae and Costa's (1996) Five-Factor Model of personality traits, which differ to some degree in how the factors are conceptualized. Some investigators may prefer to measure the constructs in the latter model rather than (or in addition to) those in the former one. Consequently, we have developed IPIP-based measures of both models.

Table 1. Characteristics of the 45 preliminary IPIP scales targeted at the AB5C facets

AB5C Facet	Provisional Label	No. of Items	Mean Item r	Coef. Alpha
Factor I				
I+/I+ vs. I-/I-	Gregariousness	4 + 6 = 10	.34	.83
I+/II+ vs. I-/II-	Friendliness	5 + 5 = 10	.37	.85
I+/III+ vs. I-/III-	Assertiveness	9 + 3 = 12	.20	.75
I+/IV+ vs. I-/IV-	Poise	5 + 5 = 10	.31	.82
I+/V+ vs. I-/V-	Leadership	5 + 5 = 10	.31	.82
*I+/II- vs. I-/II+	Provocativeness	8 + 3 = 11	.19	.72
I+/III- vs. I-/III+	Self-Disclosure	8 + 2 = 10	.26	.78
I+/IV- vs. I-/IV+	Talkativeness	8 + 2 = 10	.35	.84
*I+/V- vs. I-/V+	Sociability	3 + 7 = 10	.16	.66
Factor II				
II+/II+ vs. II-/II-	Understanding	5 + 5 = 10	.30	.81
II+/I+ vs. II-/I-	Warmth	9 + 2 = 11	.33	.84
*II+/III+ vs. II-/III-	Morality	5 + 7 = 12	.18	.73
II+/IV+ vs. II-/IV-	Pleasantness	6 + 6 = 12	.22	.76
*II+/V+ vs. II-/V-	Empathy	5 + 4 = 9	.20	.70
*II+/I- vs. II-/I+	Cooperation	2 + 10 = 12	.18	.73
*II+/III- vs. II-/III+)	Sympathy	6 + 6 = 12	.20	.74
*II+/IV- vs. II-/IV+	Tenderness	9 + 4 = 13	.18	.74
II+/V- vs. II-/V+	Nurturance	6 + 7 = 13	.16	.71
Factor III				
III+/III+ vs.III-/III-	Conscientiousness	6 + 7 = 13	.19	.75
III+/I+ vs. III-/I-	Efficiency	5 + 6 = 11	.30	.83
*III+/II+ vs. III-/II-	Dutifulness	6 + 7 = 13	.21	.78
III+/IV+ vs. III-/IV-	Purposefulness	5 + 7 = 12	.27	.81
III+/V+ vs. III-/V-	Organization	9 + 3 = 12	.23	.78
*III+/I- vs. III-/I+	Cautiousness	5 + 7 = 12	.21	.77
*III+/II- vs. III-/II+	Rationality	8 + 6 = 14	.13	.67
III+/IV- vs. III-/IV+	Perfectionism	7 + 2 = 9	.26	.76
III+/V- vs. III-/V+	Orderliness	7 + 3 = 10	.27	.78
Factor IV				
IV+/IV+ vs. IV-/IV-	Stability	5 + 5 = 10	.37	.86
IV+/I+ vs. IV-/I-	Happiness	5 + 5 = 10	.34	.84
IV+/II+ vs. IV-/II-	Calmness	4 + 6 = 10	.33	.83
IV+/III+ vs. IV-/III-	Moderation	4 + 6 = 10	.24	.76
IV+/V+ vs. IV-/V-	Toughness	4 + 8 = 12	.29	.84
IV+/I- vs. IV-/I+	Impulse Control	2 + 9 = 11	.24	.78
IV+/II- vs. IV-/II+	Imperturbability	2 + 7 = 9	.37	.84
*IV+/III- vs. IV-/III+	Cool-headedness	0 +10 = 10	.21	.73
*IV+/V- vs. IV-/V+	Tranquility	7 + 4 = 11	.22	.76
Factor V				
V+/V+ vs. V-/V-	Intellect	6 + 5 = 11	.27	.81
V+/I+ vs. V-/I-	Ingenuity	6 + 3 = 9	.37	.84
*V+/II+ vs. V-/II-	Reflection	8 + 2 = 10	.26	.75
*V+/III+ vs. V-/III-	Competence	8 + 0 = 8	.26	.74
V+/IV+ vs. V-/IV-	Quickness	7 + 3 = 10	.37	.84
*V+/I- vs. V-/I+	Introspection	10 + 2 = 12	.18	.71
V+/II- vs. V-/II+	Creativity	5 + 5 = 10	.30	.81
V+/III- vs. V-/III+	Imagination	5 + 5 = 10	.27	.78
*V+/IV- vs. V-/IV+	Depth	7 + 2 = 9	.27	.77
	Mean		**.26**	**.78**

Note: All analyses are based on the responses of 501 adult subjects from the Eugene-Springfield Community Sample; These scales have been augmented with items from other AB5C facets.

Specifically, we have developed both 50-item (10 items per domain) and 100-item (20 items per domain) scales to measure the five domains in each of the two models (Goldberg, 1997).

Over 500 adult participants from a community sample completed both the 240-item NEO-PI-R and an initial set of 1,252 IPIP items (Goldberg, in press); the IPIP items were administered in three separate questionnaires over a three-year period of time, and the NEO inventory was administered on another occasion during the same time period. Each of the participants had previously completed an inventory of 360 trait-descriptive adjectives which included Goldberg's (1992) 100 unipolar Big-Five factor markers. The five orthogonal factor scores from the 100 markers (based on ipsatized data) served as the criteria for the Big-Five constructs, and scores on the five 48-item domain scales from the NEO-PI-R served in that role for the Five-Factor (NEO) model. Responses to all of the IPIP items were first correlated with each of the criterion indices, and the items were then categorized by their highest correlations. Initial scales were developed using the most highly related items in each category, and if necessary these scales were then refined by internal consistency analyses (Criterion 5, maximizing Alpha).

Table 2 presents some characteristics of the new IPIP scales for the Big-Five domains, including the number of positively and negatively keyed items in each scale, its mean item intercorrelation, its Coefficient Alpha reliability estimate, and its correlation with the orthogonal factor scores derived from the Big-Five adjective markers. On average, the shorter scales had a mean item intercorrelation of .34, an Alpha of .84, and a correlation of .67 with the factor markers (.81 when corrected for unreliability); the longer scales had a mean item intercorrelation of .31, an Alpha of

Table 2. Characteristics of the Preliminary IPIP Scales Measuring the Big Five Domains

Big Five Domain	Number of Items	Mean Item Intercorrelation	Coefficient Alpha	Correlation with Markers
Shorter Scales				
I. Extraversion	5 + 5 = 10	.40	.87	.73 [.84]
II. Agreeableness	6 + 4 = 10	.31	.82	.54 [.66]
III. Conscientiousness	6 + 4 = 10	.29	.79	.71 [.90]
IV. Emot. Stability	2 + 8 = 10	.38	.86	.72 [.84]
V. Intellect	7 + 3 = 10	.34	.84	.67 [.80]
Total/Mean	**26 +24 = 50**	**.34**	**.84**	**.67 [.81]**
Longer Scales				
I. Extraversion	10 +10 = 20	.34	.91	.76 [.84]
II. Agreeableness	14 + 6 = 20	.28	.88	.57 [.65]
III. Conscient.	11 + 9 = 20	.27	.88	.74 [.84]
IV. Emot. Stability	4 +16 = 20	.35	.91	.74 [.81]
V. Intellect	13 + 7 = 20	.32	.90	.69 [.77]
Total/Mean	**52 +48 = 100**	**.31**	**.90**	**.70 [.78]**

Note: Values in brackets are correlations corrected for unreliability; these may be underestimates, given that the reliabilities of the factor markers were assumed to be the same as those of their corresponding IPIP scales.

.90, and correlated .70 with the markers (.78 when corrected). The items included in each of these new Big-Five scales are provided on the IPIP Website.

Table 3 presents the corresponding values for the new IPIP scales measuring the constructs in the Five-Factor (NEO) model, including the correlations with the 48-item NEO domain scales. On average, the shorter scales had a mean item intercorrelation of .33, an Alpha of .82, a correlation with the NEO domains of .77 (.90 when corrected); the longer scales had a mean item intercorrelation of .30, an Alpha of .89, and a mean correlation of .81 (again .90 when corrected). The items included in each of these new FFM scales are also provided at the IPIP Website.

There are no common items among the scales within each scale set, although all of the items in the 10-item scales are included in their 20-item counterparts. The part-whole correlations between the shorter and the longer scales were: .95, .94, .95, .96, and .96 for the Big Five constructs, and .95, .92, .96, .95, and .96 for the Five-Factor (NEO) constructs, both sets in Big Five order. The average of the intercorrelations among the scales based on the Big-Five constructs, presented in Table 4, were very slightly lower than for those based on the Five-Factor (NEO) constructs. When corrected for attenuation due to the scale unreliabilities, the across-set convergence was essentially perfect ($r = 1.00$) for the Extraversion, Conscientiousness, and Emotional Stability (Neuroticism) constructs; the corrected correlations for the Agreeableness scales were .79 (.84) and for Intellect/Openness they were .83 (.86).

Table 3. Characteristics of the preliminary IPIP scales measuring the NEO domain constructs

NEO Domain	Number of Items	Mean Item Intercorrelation	Coefficient Alpha	Correlation with NEO
Shorter Scales				
I. Neuroticism	5 + 5 = 10	.37	.86	.82 [.92]
II. Extraversion	5 + 5 = 10	.38	.86	.77 [.88]
III. Openness	5 + 5 = 10	.33	.82	.79 [.91]
IV. Agreeableness	5 + 5 = 10	.27	.77	.70 [.85]
V. Conscientiousness	5 + 5 = 10	.31	.81	.79 [.92]
Total/Mean	25 +25 = 50	.33	.82	.77 [.90]
Longer Scales				
I. Neuroticism	10 +10 = 20	.33	.91	.86 [.93]
II. Extraversion	10 +10 = 20	.35	.91	.79 [.88]
III. Openness	10 +10 = 20	.29	.89	.83 [.92]
IV. Agreeableness	10 +10 = 20	.23	.85	.78 [.90]
V. Conscientiousness	10 +10 = 20	.31	.90	.80 [.88]
Total/Mean	50 +50 = 100	.30	.89	.81 [.90]

Note: Values in brackets are correlations corrected for unreliability. The Coefficient Alpha reliability values for the 48-item NEO domain scales were: N = .93; E = .89; O = .91; A = .89; and C = .91.

Table 4. Correlations among and between the preliminary IPIP scales measuring the domain constructs from the Big Five and the Five Factor (NEO) Models

	I/E	II/A	III/C	IV/N	V/O
I/E	.93 (.96)	.28 (.39)	.07 (.17)	.18 (.27)	.35 (.40)
II/A	.15 (.22)	.63 (.73)	.11 (.17)	.21 (.23)	.17 (.18)
III/C	.24 (.28)	.22 (.21)	.81 (.87)	.15 (.15)	.03 (.07)
IV/N	-.35 (-.38)	-.43 (-.41)	-.36 (-.40)	-.89(-.93)	.13 (.20)
V/O	.36 (.37)	.11 (.09)	.01 (.05)	-.08 (-.09)	.69 (.77)

Note: Correlations among the IPIP Big Five domain scales are presented above the main diagonal, correlations among the IPIP Five Factor (NEO) domain scales are below the diagonal, and correlations between the corresponding scales in each set are listed **in bold** in the diagonal. (Correlations based on the 20-item scales are listed in parentheses after the values for the 10-item scales.) Factor I = Extraversion; Factor II = Agreeableness; Factor III = Conscientiousness; Factor IV = Emotional Stability (versus Neuroticism); and Factor V = Intellect/Openness to Experience.

Criterion 8: Scale brevity, or keeping it short and sweet

In measurement, brevity imparts efficiency, and thus brevity is generally desirable (Burisch, 1984b). We noted the value of item brevity with respect to our first criterion, but Criterion 8 addresses scale brevity. For some research, teaching, and assessment purposes, even a 100-item inventory, such as the marker set from Goldberg (1992), is too lengthy. However, because any abbreviated measure almost inevitably suffers from a loss of reliability compared to the full measure, there is a recurring cost involved in the creation of a "short form" of a longer measure. To minimize this cost, one must attempt to conserve internal consistency while culling items. By doing so, however, one could easily precipitate a decline in validity even though Alpha is relatively constant, because the scale is being made overly narrow and homogeneous (Loevinger, 1954). Smith, McCarthy, and Anderson (2000) discuss other potential problems in short-form development, stressing that short forms (a) be developed only on well-validated measures, (b) preserve the content coverage and subfactors of the longer form, (c) protect reliability, (d) demonstrate overlapping variance with the longer form when administered independently, (e) show a factor structure similar to that of the longer form, (f) have demonstrated validity and high correct classification rates in independent samples, and (g) show meaningful savings in time or resources.

What is the absolute minimum number of items that should constitute a scale? *One* item is certainly too few; internal consistency is not easily estimated and balanced keying is impossible. On the other hand, in unusual cases where the construct being measured is highly familiar (or "schematized") to respondents, unidimensional, and primarily subjective in content, one item could be adequate (Robins *et al*, 2001). Although *two*-item scales have neither of the disadvantages of one-item scales, internal consistency tends to be purchased at the cost of extreme narrowness of breadth. With *three*-item scales, unbalanced keying is again a problem. Thus, *four*-item scales seem to be a practical minimum in most cases. Such mini-scales have been referred to as "testlets," "item parcels," "homogeneous item composites," "factored homogeneous item dimensions," and the like; and they have been used as the basic building blocks for longer scales by Comrey (1988), Hogan and Hogan (1995), and Saucier (2001; in press).

It may be, however, that the fewer items one selects from a large item-pool, the greater is the likelihood that their selection will have capitalized on chance characteristics of the derivation sample, leading to decreased internal consistency in new samples. Moreover, a high Coefficient Alpha in a four-item scale is typically only possible if the content is highly focused and narrow, so marker sets commonly include more than four items. And, internal consistency is not the only reason for including more items. Nunnally and Bernstein (1994, p. 16) suggest that data from single items are ordinal, but aggregates of these items are more readily treated at the interval level of measurement. A scale including 8 or 10 items is likely to generate scores with a more Gaussian distribution than would a scale consisting of only four items.

Application: Saucier's Big Five Mini-Markers

Saucier (1994) scrutinized the performance of each of Goldberg's (1992) 100 unipolar markers in 12 data sets, searching for those items that loaded most highly on the expected factor in virtually all analyses. After selecting an initial set of eight items for each factor based on this "factor purity" criterion, revisions were made to (a) increase user-friendliness by reducing the number of negations beginning with the prefix "un-," (b) decrease the number of root-negation pairs (e.g., Kind-Unkind) so as to lessen any overnarrowing of content, and (c) increase the correlation of the brief scales with the original 100 unipolar marker scales. After 9 such item-substitutions, the final 40-item set included eight items for each factor. In the case of Factors I (Extraversion), II (Agreeableness), and III (Conscientiousness) there were four items for each pole of the factor. In the case of Factors IV (Emotional Stability) and V (Intellect/Imagination) a dearth of suitable terms led to the selection of six terms at one pole (low Emotional Stability, high Intellect) and two at the other pole.

Internal consistency estimates for the five Mini-Marker scales were provided by Saucier (1994) in four data sets. The 20 Alpha coefficients ranged from .69 to .86, averaging around .80; these coefficients were generally about .07 lower than those for the longer 100 markers set. There are indications, however, that validity is comparable with that for the longer marker set (Dwight, Cummings, & Glenar, 1998). As would be expected from scales with lower internal consistency, Saucier (1994) noted that the Mini-Markers had lower inter-scale correlations than did the 100 unipolar markers from which they were derived. For example, the mean inter-scale correlations for the 100 markers which averaged .19 in raw data and .10 in ipsatized data were reduced in the Mini-Markers to .15 in raw data and .09 in ipsatized data. Are inter-scale correlations of this size acceptable? Could they be reduced further by purposeful scale-construction procedures?

Criterion 9: Mutual orthogonality among marker scales

In his critique of the Big Five model, Block (1995) pointed out that although the model is based on orthogonal factors, the five factors are normally operationalized with scales that are at least somewhat interrelated. In self-ratings, Goldberg's (1992) unipolar markers have intercorrelations as high as .37, and in peer ratings as high as .58.[9] Indeed, Digman (1997) was able to develop second-order factors on the basis of the intercorrelations among the scales within various five-factor marker sets. Even in data sets where the average intercorrelation is low, the correlation between a pair of markers can be quite high, and one such high correlation alone is enough to call into question the assumption of five "orthogonal" factors.

Orthogonal factors are not necessarily better than oblique factors. But orthogonal factors are an advantageous feature of the Big Five model for at least two reasons. First, when one is mapping a domain of variables, as when one is mapping a physical landscape, orthogonal axes provide a superior coordinate system for locating points on the map. Second, as Jackson (1971) noted, "if one wishes to maximize the predictability of a battery, entirely uncorrelated tests would be appropriate" (p. 246). Orthogonal predictors are more efficient in multiple-regression analyses because they minimize multicollinearity and maximize discriminant validity.

It has long been known that marker scales based on orthogonal factors are not necessarily themselves mutually orthogonal (e.g., Cattell & Tsujioka, 1964). Recognition of non-orthogonality in marker scales has prompted some statistical remedies, such as (a) the ipsatization of the original response data, which tends to lower scale intercorrelations, and (b) the use of orthogonal (e.g., varimax) factor scores (Goldberg, 1992). Ipsatizing within sets of items that do not have balanced keying with respect to content can lead to inadvertently discarding content variance. Moreover, the most common form of ipsatizing, the use of standard (Z) scores, controls for between-subject differences in spread (variance) as well as central tendency (mean); while this practice has been explicitly recommended by Goldberg (1990; 1992), it has recently been criticized by Hofstee *et al.* (1998).

The most direct method for assuring orthogonality is to use orthogonal factor scores instead of scale scores. One limitation of this procedure is that the factors derived de novo on each occasion are less uniform across samples than are scale scores. Perhaps as a consequence, most users of Big Five markers use simple (but correlated) scale scores based on raw data, eschewing both types of statistical remedies. Accordingly, a close approximation to orthogonality would be a desirable feature in a Big Five marker set.

---

[9] Nor are high inter-scale correlations confined to lexical studies or adjective stimuli. The Revised NEO Personality Inventory (NEO-PI-R) has domain-scale intercorrelations as high as -.53 in self-ratings (Costa & McCrae, 1992).

Table 5. The orthogonal subset of the 100 unipolar markers (Ortho-40): Reliabilities and interscale correlations

	Derivation Samples			Cross-Validation Sample
	Self	Liked Peer	Pooled Peer	Community Sample
Coefficient Alpha				
I	.84	.86	.86	.81
II	.73	.79	.92	.71
III	.86	.87	.89	.85
IV	.70	.62	.70	.72
V	.71	.72	.83	.74
Interscale Correlations				
I-II	.03	.02	-.10	.03
I-III	-.07	-.12	-.08	.04
I-IV	.00	.02	-.17	.05
I-V	.03	.06	-.13	.10
II-III	.11	.15	.19	.12
II-IV	-.05	.03	.30	.19
II-V	.04	.21	.40	.06
III-IV	-.03	.09	.14	.13
III-V	.08	.06	.28	.06
IV-V	-.06	-.04	.10	-.03
Mean Correlation				
Ortho-40	.01	.05	.09	.07
100 Markers	.13	.24	.27	.25
40 Mini-Markers	.11	.18	.26	.22

Note: Sample sizes: Self = 320; Liked Peer = 316; Pooled Peer = 205; Community Sample = 1,125. All analyses used the original (non-ipsatized) response data. The 40 Ortho items: I = Bold, Extraverted, Talkative, Unrestrained vs. Introverted, Quiet, Reserved, Shy; II = Kind, Sympathetic, Undemanding, Warm vs. Cold, Demanding, Harsh, Unsympathetic; III = Efficient, Neat, Organized, Systematic vs. Careless, Disorganized, Sloppy, Unsystematic; IV = Unenvious, Unexcitable vs. Anxious, Emotional, Fearful, Fretful, Nervous, Touchy; V = Artistic, Complex, Creative, Deep, Introspective, Philosophical vs. Simple, Unreflective.

The application of Criterion 7, emphasizing low divergent loadings, tends to suppress inter-scale associations but not necessarily to remove them. If most of the potential marker items for a factor are associated in the same direction with another factor, simply choosing those items with the lowest divergent loadings will not serve to guarantee unrelated marker sets. To remove the inter-scale correlations, one must select marker items whose correlations with each of the other factors are balanced with respect to sign. Then, because scale scores that are uncorrelated in a derivation sample may not be uncorrelated in a new sample, one must demonstrate that the approximation to orthogonality persists when the scale scores are intercorrelated in a new sample.

Application: The "Ortho-40" markers

Table 5 provides an illustration of the results of using orthogonality as a criterion for item selection. The 100 items in Goldberg's set of unipolar markers were scrutinized in the self- and peer-rating data sets used in Goldberg's (1992) Study 4. Items that contributed most to the positive scale intercorrelations were removed until eight items remained per scale (with some priority given to maintaining balanced keying). This 40-item subset is labeled the Ortho-40. Coefficient Alpha reliability averages about .10 lower than for the 100-marker scales, and about .03 lower than for the Mini-Marker subset (also based on 40 items). But inter-scale correlations are dramatically lower than for either of the other two sets, on average about .15 lower per pair of scales. The highest inter-scale correlations are in the Pooled Peer sample, where the general evaluation factor has a powerful effect on these coefficients; in this extreme case, whereas one correlation in the 100 Markers reached .58 (Factors II and IV), the highest correlation in the Ortho-40 was .40 (Factors II and V). Overall, the Ortho-40 sacrifices some internal consistency in order to gain greater mutual orthogonality. The Ortho-40 subset demonstrates that the Big Five are not oblique by necessity; if one has a sufficiently large item pool, it should be possible to develop a set of marker scales that are virtually unrelated.

Another illustration of the application of Criterion 9 is provided by Saucier's (2000a) new Modular Markers, which have inter-scale correlations that are comparable to those of the Ortho-40, but with higher reliabilities. However, these Modular Markers were developed using an additional criterion, which must first be introduced.

Considerations congruent with newer forms of measurement theory

None of the criteria offered so far are inconsistent with classical test theory (McDonald, 1999). However, from the standpoint of item response theory (e.g., Embretson & Reise, 2000) these criteria, which tend toward maximizing Alpha and homogenizing item difficulties, could lead to scales with a tendency to "parallelism"[10] Strictly parallel items have the same difficulty levels (e.g., mean response) and discrimination (e.g., item-total correlation) parameters; redundant items thus tend to be parallel. A set of relatively redundant items will have a high degree of internal consistency. But a set of such items is problematic because it is likely to be overly narrow, which may decrease validity (see Criterion 4 regarding bandwidth). And it may distinguish well among individuals at one level of the broader construct but not at other levels. For example, a marker scale for Extraversion formed from the three items "Talks too much", "Can't stop talking", and "Chatters away even if no one is listening" might effectively distinguish extreme extraverts from both moderate extraverts and introverts, but would probably do a poor job of distinguishing between the latter two groups. Nonetheless, this set of items should exhibit substantial internal consistency. A peaked, or kurtotic, test maximizes reliability (Lord, 1952), and can be expected to show high levels of consistency across samples in exploratory factor analyses.

---

[10] Criterion 4, stressing broad bandwidth, is the most likely exception, since a measure of a broad attribute is unlikely to result from a set of redundant items.

Our final criterion is derived from aspects of item response theory (IRT), which has been widely applied to measures of ability and aptitude but has not yet had a major impact on personality measurement. Unfortunately, IRT analyses require relatively large samples and seem better suited to relatively specific, homogeneous content than the heterogeneous constructs of the sort personality psychologists have emphasized (Nunnally & Bernstein, 1994, p. 434). However, without adopting a full-scale IRT approach, one can still borrow at least one important IRT scale-construction criterion.[11]

Criterion 10: Equidiscrimination (discriminating at diverse levels)

A contribution of IRT is its emphasis upon selecting items with a spread of difficulty levels in order to discriminate among (i.e., effectively differentiate) individuals at a variety of levels of the attribute. If one wanted to measure individual differences in the ability to solve arithmetic problems, one would not restrict one's questions to a single level of difficulty (e.g., only addition of single-digit integers, or alternatively only multiplication of twelve-digit numbers). Instead, one would include items covering a range of difficulty levels to allow the measure to discriminate very high ability from moderate ability, and very low ability from mere mediocrity. Tests that include a wide range of item difficulty levels provide more information, and thus have broader bandwidth.

In personality measurement, item difficulty levels index the "difficulty" respondents are likely to have in admitting to, ascribing, or agreeing with the content of the item, as indicated by inter-item variations in the response means. Items that are easy to endorse will tend to discriminate well only between those who are very low and moderately low on the attribute, whereas items that are difficult to endorse will tend to discriminate well only between those who are very high and moderately high on the attribute. Items with more intermediate response-means are prone to discriminate well in the middle of the attribute distribution, but not at either extreme. In most cases, classical item-selection procedures lead to a bias toward selecting items of intermediate difficulty (Nunnally & Bernstein, 1994, p. 329).

One would expect that *any* item selection procedure that works to diversify the content of the selected items will work against parallelism, and in favor of discrimination at diverse levels of the attribute. Thus, five-factor measures like the NEO-PI-R domain scales (Costa & McCrae, 1992) or Johnson's (2000) IPIP-NEO short-form, which build up the score for a factor from subscales with diverse content, are

---

[11] Minimizing differential item functioning (DIF; also sometimes referred to as item bias) is another scale-construction criterion prominent in IRT deserving of more attention and study with respect to personality measurement. DIF exists whenever two items differ between groups in their parameters (e.g., discrimination, difficulty level). As Nunnally and Bernstein (1994) advise, "one should choose items whose parameters are most similar across groups, whether these parameters are defined classically or through IRT. This is especially true when the groups differ in gender or ethnicity" (p. 417). One might divide one's data into subsamples based on gender or ethnicity and (a) eliminate items with relatively poor discrimination in any subsample, or (b) retain those items that show the smallest differences in parameters between subsamples.

unlikely to be characterized by parallelism. However, the relative discriminatory power of these measures at differing levels of the attribute remains to be demonstrated.

A measure that discriminates well across levels of the latent attribute is most needed when important practical decisions are made about people based on their scores on a measure, and thus highly reliable distinctions at all levels of the attribute are necessary; this criterion would be particularly valuable for any measure that is used in a wide variety of selection situations. To the extent that factor markers are used only for locating other variables, rather than locating individuals, such a criterion may be less necessary. Nonetheless, because markers scales that were originally developed for the purpose of locating variables (e.g., Goldberg, 1992) have then become widely used as measures of individual differences, it may be sensible to incorporate this criterion into marker construction from the onset.

To develop measures that discriminate well at various levels of the latent attribute, Nunnally (1967) proposed a simple item-selection procedure for what he called the equidiscriminating (EQD) test. An EQD measure can be constructed by selecting items based on their characteristics at multiple cutoff levels. On the basis of the frequency distribution of the underlying attribute (e.g., the factor scores for a broad factor), one selects cutpoints between fractions of the distribution. For example, one can select one-third of the items to differentiate the top 25 per cent of the sample from the bottom 75 per cent, another third to differentiate the top half of the sample from the lower half, and a final third to discriminate the bottom 25 per cent of the sample from the top 75 per cent (Nunnally & Bernstein, 1994, p. 330). Then, one selects some items that served best to differentiate individuals above each cutpoint from those below it. There are other ways to reach the same equidiscriminating end result, of course, including procedures specific to IRT, but Nunnally's procedure may be the simplest to implement.

Application: Modular markers

Saucier (in press) created a new set of marker scales for the Big Five, as well as scales for broader structures of one and two factors based on studies of natural-language descriptors. The label "Modular Markers" for these scales is based on the flexible use of item parcels serving in marker sets for the development of scales at more than one hierarchical level. These new scales were constructed so as to simultaneously achieve three major objectives — relative orthogonality (Criterion 9), higher internal consistency (Criterion 5) than was obtained with the Ortho-40, and improved equidiscrimination (Criterion 10) than previous marker sets.

The initial item pool consisted of 100 representative parcels, plus 21 supplementary item parcels, also of two to four adjectives (Saucier, in press). For each of the Big Five factors, the distribution of factor scores based on analyses of personality-

Table 6. The factor loadings of the 32 parcels in the set of Modular Markers

	II	III	I	IV-	V
Kindness	.77*	.26	.03	.00	-.22
Warmth	.73*	.20	.30	.08	.17
Sympathy	.73*	.21	.11	.18	.30
Agreeableness	.65*	.08	-.08	-.06	.26
Sensitivity	.60*	.16	.09	.43	.26
Toughness	-.64*	.04	.09	.10	.06
Slyness	-.55*	-.09	.13	.09	.16
Criticalness	-.47*	.05	.05	.25	.17
Demandingness	-.47*	.19	.22	.31	.11
Efficiency	.23	.79*	.03	-.11	.10
Organization	.07	.77*	-.04	-.05	-.01
Perfectionism	-.04	.71*	-.07	.12	.19
Decisiveness	.00	.55*	.21	-.31	.15
Caution	.21	.50*	-.31	.19	.10
Ambition	.08	.39*	.32	.03	.18
Forgetfulness	-.02	-.57*	-.01	.26	.01
Talkativeness	-.06	-.08	.70*	.11	-.13
Sociability	.35	.20	.66*	-.05	-.07
Assertiveness	-.37	.27	.62*	-.03	.20
Spontaneity	.18	-.16	.51*	.26	.31
Adventurousness	-.03	-.05	.47*	-.03	.34
Restraint	.10	.15	-.71*	.10	.07
Shyness	.11	-.08	-.66*	.23	.11
Fretfulness	-.16	-.20	-.22	.65*	-.08
Anxiety	-.20	-.12	-.01	.63*	-.02
Emotional Excitability	.18	-.06	.39	.59*	.08
Jealousy/Envy	-.34	-.20	.02	.55*	-.11
Hyperdevotedness	.13	.12	-.14	.48*	.09
Analytical Inquiry	.01	.15	-.02	.05	.81*
Reflectiveness	.20	.11	-.16	.07	.65*
Intellectuality	.11	.32	.09	-.12	.52*
Unconventionality	-.24	-.41	.21	-.03	.41*

Note: $N = 1,620$. Coefficients are varimax-rotated factor loadings; I = Extraversion (Dynamism); II = Agreeableness (Altruism vs. Antagonism); III = Conscientiousness (Self-Regulation); IV = Emotional Stability (reflected: Anxiety); V = (Autonomous) Intellect;* = Highest loading for each variable.

descriptive adjectives in 14 data sets (Saucier, 2001) was dichotomized around cut-points at the 16.67, 33.33, 50, 66.67, and 83.33 percentiles of the distribution.[12] For each factor, each of the 121 candidate parcels was correlated with each dichotomy.

The three highest-correlating parcels for each dichotomy were retained as part of the initial version of the marker scale. This initial version was revised so as to further reduce scale intercorrelations and also to better maximize correlations with the criterion factor scores.

---

[12] The 33.33 and 66.67 cutpoints did not have incremental usefulness beyond the other three cutpoints, and thus it was not necessary to use them in this instance.

Table 7. The Modular Markers: Reliabilities and Interscale Correlations

	Derivation Samples			Cross-Validation Sample
	Self	Liked Peer	Pooled Peer	Community Sample
Coefficient Alpha				
I	.88	.89	.91	.84
II	.82	.86	.94	.83
III	.85	.88	.91	.86
IV	.79	.75	.80	.82
V	.77	.75	.87	.82
Interscale Correlations				
I-II	-.11	-.07	-.02	-.01
I-III	.11	.04	-.03	.22
I-IV	-.06	-.05	-.10	.08
I-V	.13	.26	.15	.20
II-III	.01	.12	-.01	.05
II-IV	-.09	.04	.28	.28
II-V	.02	.00	.21	-.21
III-IV	.01	.13	.09	.23
III-V	.04	.02	.23	.03
IV-V	.00	.00	.18	-.02
Mean Correlation				
Modular Markers	.01	.05	.10	.08
100 Markers	.13	.24	.27	.25
40 Mini-Markers	.11	.18	.26	.22
Ortho-40 mean	.01	.05	.09	.07

Note: Sample sizes: Self = 320; Liked Peer = 316; Pooled Peer = 205; Community Sample = 592; All analyses used the original (non-ipsatized) response data.

The end result was the set of parcels presented in the Appendix: 7 parcels (20 items) for Extraversion, 9 parcels (22 items) for Agreeableness, 7 parcels (18 items) for Conscientiousness, 5 parcels (16 items) for Emotional Stability, and 4 parcels (14 items) for Intellect. Factor analyses of the 32 parcels (from 90 adjectives) making up the Big Five marker set indicated that the parcels reproduced the desired factors quite faithfully with either varimax or quartimax rotated solutions. The varimax solution for a combined sample of 1,620 ratings is presented in Table 6.

Table 7 provides Big Five Modular Marker scale intercorrelations, using original (non-ipsatized) responses in five samples; the comparable values for Goldberg's (1992) 100 Markers are also provided. The 100 Markers have roughly the same level of average inter-scale correlations as do most previous Big Five marker sets (e.g., Benet-Martinez & John, 1998; Costa & McCrae, 1992) — about .20. In contrast, the Modular Markers have an average inter-scale correlation of only about .05, similar to that of the Ortho-40 set presented earlier. The highest single inter-scale correlation found in any sample was only .28 (compared to .40 for the Ortho-40). However, the Alpha reliability coefficients of the Modular Marker scales are higher than those for the Ortho-40 by about .05 on average, as one would expect given their greater length (90 items instead of 40). These comparisons suggest that the Modular Markers may be slightly superior to the Ortho-40 as a set of mutually orthogonal marker scales.

The Modular Markers, with 90 adjectives, are of roughly comparable length to

Table 8. The Mini-Modular markers (3M40): Reliabilities and interscale correlations

	Derivation Samples			Cross-Validation Sample
	Self	Liked Peer	Pooled Peer	Community Sample
Coefficient Alpha				
I	.82	.84	.85	.77
II	.71	.76	.89	.71
III	.76	.75	.84	.76
IV	.67	.63	.71	.72
V	.67	.64	.80	.73
Interscale Correlations				
I-II	.02	.05	.01	.09
I-III	.03	-.04	-.06	.19
I-IV	-.05	-.09	-.17	.06
I-V	.09	.15	.07	.14
II-III	.01	.08	-.04	.10
II-IV	-.05	.04	.26	.24
II-V	.00	.10	.24	-.10
III-IV	.03	.09	.06	.18
III-V	-.02	-.02	.08	-.04
IV-V	-.02	.06	.17	.08
Mean Correlation				
3M40	.01	.04	.06	.10
Ortho-40	.01	.05	.09	.07
100 Markers	.13	.24	.27	.25
40 Mini-Markers	.11	.18	.26	.22

Note: Sample sizes: Self = 320; Liked Peer = 316; Pooled Peer = 205; Community Sample = 592 for the 3M40 scales and 1,125 for the other marker sets. All analyses used the original (non-ipsatized) response data. The 3M40 items: I = Assertive, Playful, Sociable, Talkative vs. Quiet, Reserved, Shy, Withdrawn; II = Kind, Sentimental, Sympathetic, Tolerant vs. Cold, Critical, Demanding, Harsh; III = Cautious, Efficient, Meticulous, Organized, Perfectionistic vs. Absent-minded, Disorganized, Indecisive; IV = Unenvious, Unexcitable vs. Anxious, Emotional, Fearful, Fretful, High-strung, Nervous; V = Complex, Intellectual, Nonconforming, Philosophical, Unconventional vs. Conventional, Unintellectual, Unreflective.

the 100 Markers, but they were developed using different criteria, reflecting differing priorities. The 100 Markers were constructed with an emphasis on Criteria 5 through 7 (Alpha maximization, Factor saturation, and Discrimination), and as would be expected their reliabilities are slightly higher than for their Modular Markers counterparts, which were developed with more emphasis on Criteria 9 and 10. However, the use of a representative set of item parcels at the first stage of scale construction gives the Modular Markers some kinship to Goldberg's (1990) 133 and 100 clusters which we described earlier, with more emphasis on Criterion 4 than was true for the 100 Markers. Many of the parcels in the Modular Markers have balanced keying, which was true for none of Goldberg's (1990) clusters.

What if one were to apply the brevity criterion (Criterion 8) to the Modular Markers, and seek an abbreviated set? Table 8 provides internal consistency estimates and inter-scale correlations for a set of 40 Mini-Modular-Markers (3M40). This reduced set of adjectives was developed by selecting from the 90 Modular Markers a subset of items that (a) retained the highest-loading items with (b) about equal numbers having positive and negative loadings on each of the other factors, (c) while maintaining a spread of response means on each scale, with some secondary attention also to (d) maintaining balanced keying, (e) representing as many of the 32 parcels as feasible, and (f) excluding items where doing so increased the internal consistency of the scale. Bases (a) through (f) correspond to our Criteria 6, 9, 10, 2, 4, and 5, respectively.

Compared to the full set of 90 Modular Marker items, inter-scale correlations for the 3M40 are about the same on average. But internal consistency is lower (almost .10 per scale on average) than for the longer marker set. Compared to the Ortho-40 described earlier, the inter-scale correlations are similar, but the Alpha coefficients for the 3M40 scales are slightly lower (generally by less than .05). The lower internal consistency is due to the higher degree of representative sampling in the 3M40 scales. Although the two marker sets have nearly identical items for Emotional Stability, on the other factors the 3M40 scales appear to be broader in content reference, primarily because the item pool in the Modular Markers has more breadth than that found in the 100 Markers on which the Ortho-40 was based. For example, the 3M40's scale for Intellect has "unconventionality" content that is lacking in the Ortho-40 version (as well as the 100 Markers). Representative sampling does not maximize Coefficient Alpha, although it may heighten validity with respect to a broad array of criteria. Indeed, Saucier (in press) reported that the Ortho-40, Modular Markers, and 3M40 Big Five marker sets demonstrated validities as high as the 100 unipolar markers of Goldberg (1992) and the NEO-FFI (Costa & McCrae, 1992) even though their Alpha coefficients were generally lower.

Integrating diverse psychometric criteria for item selection

Scale construction can serve any of many possible masters, but these masters can lead us in divergent directions. One might attempt to create marker scales based on all of the 10 criteria we have discussed, without realizing the extent to which some of these criteria are in conflict with each other. For example, maximizing the Coefficient Alpha of a scale can be done at the expense of (a) maximizing the spread of item difficulties and (b) brevity. If such Alpha-maximization involves narrowing the content of the scale, validity could be attenuated over what it might otherwise be. If one seeks a representative sampling of variables in one's marker set, one is unlikely to achieve relatively orthogonal markers for orthogonal factors; and likewise, if one achieves orthogonal markers, it is probably at the expense of representative sampling. Uniform sampling, such as that used in the development of circumplex scales (e.g., Saucier, Ostendorf, & Peabody, 2001; Wiggins, 1980), will also tend to conflict with representativeness, not to mention brevity.

Thus, in most cases it will not be practical to apply all the criteria we have described to the construction of a single scale. We suggest that, instead, the criteria be integrated into a measurement paradigm in which each of the criteria is applied somewhere, but not necessarily everywhere. For example, one might build an initial set based on representative sampling of the domain, then select markers as a subset of this representative sample. One might utilize Alpha-maximizing approaches in creating item parcels but temper this standard with the "discrimination at diverse levels" criterion in aggregating the parcels into measures of broader attributes, whose mutual orthogonality could be systematically maximized if factor-orthogonality is important. Although these procedures are more complex, the simultaneous consideration of diverse psychometric goals should lead to higher quality measures than might otherwise be achieved.

Recommendations

We have presented a variety of English-language marker sets targeted at the Big Five. These marker sets differ with respect to the original item pool as well as the criteria used in constructing them. Which is the best marker set? With respect to predictive validity, Saucier (in press) compared all of the adjectival marker sets we have presented (except the 100 clusters) and found no meaningful differences; surprisingly, the 40-item marker sets appeared to have validities equivalent to those with more than twice as many items. The 100 unipolar markers and the Mini-Markers are especially geared toward factorial replicability — generating an intended structure in exploratory factor analysis of the constituent items. Due to their length, the 100 markers, and then the Modular Markers, typically have the highest Alpha coefficients, and thus would provide the most precise differentiation of individuals. On the other hand, the Mini-Markers, Ortho-40, and 3M40 all require less than half as much subject time as these more reliable marker sets. Finally, if one wishes to have more mutually orthogonal scale scores, one would choose the Modular Markers, Ortho-40, or 3M40.

From another perspective, the 100 unipolar markers combine high Alpha coefficients with factorial replicability. The Mini-Markers combine factorial replicability with brevity. The Modular Markers have more breadth and relative mutual orthogonality, although Alphas are not quite as high as those for the 100 Markers. Both the Ortho-40 and 3M40 combine brevity and mutual orthogonality; based on the way that the item pool from which each was derived, the Ortho-40 is likely to have more factorial replicability and the 3M40 more breadth.

These all appear to be good marker sets, but there is no single "best" one. Instead, what is best depends on how the investigator weights and values the various scale-development criteria. This is consonant with the overarching theme in our chapter: Trade-offs arise in the scale construction process that usually prevent one from generating a single perfect scale for a construct. We do tend to favor, however, scales that were developed taking a larger number of important criteria into account (such as the Modular Markers and its short form, the 3M40), on the grounds that these scales are less likely to have an "Achilles heel"; they are more balanced with respect to their virtues. Similarly, we encourage other investigators to take a broader view of scale construction, and to integrate a diverse range of useful criteria into the scale-construction process.

Author's note

Work on this article was supported by Grant MH-49227 from the National Institute of Mental Health, U.S. Public Health Service. The authors are enormously indebted to Michael Ashton, Kimberly Anne Barchard, Ira Bernstein, Michael Browne, Matthias Burisch, A. Timothy Church, Robyn M. Dawes, Herbert Eber, Candan Ertubey, David Evans, Willem K. B. Hofstee, Eric Knowles, John Loehlin, Susan D. Long, Roderick P. McDonald, Richard Robins, Oya Somer, Lynne Steinberg, Krista Trobst, Erika Westling, Jerry S. Wiggins, and Richard Zinbarg for their thoughtful comments and suggestions.

References

Ashton, S.G., & Goldberg, L.R. (1973). In response to Jackson's challenge: The comparative validity of personality scales constructed by the external (empirical) strategy and scales developed intuitively by experts, novices, and laymen. *Journal of Research in Personality, 7,* 1-20.

Benet-Martínez, V., & John, O.P. (1998). *Los Cinco Grandes* across cultures and ethnic groups: Multitrait multimethod analyses of the Big Five in Spanish and English. *Journal of Personality and Social Psychology, 75,* 729-750.

Block, J. (1995). A contrarian view of the five-factor approach to personality description. *Psychological Bulletin, 117,* 187-215.

Burisch, M. (1978). Construction strategies for multiscale personality inventories. *Applied Psychological Measurement, 2,* 97-111.

Burisch, M. (1984a). Approaches to personality inventory construction: A comparison of merits. *American Psychologist, 39,* 214-227.

Burisch, M. (1984b). You don't always get what you pay for: Measuring depression with short and simple versus long and sophisticated scales. *Journal of Research in Personality, 18,* 81-98.

Cattell, R.B., & Tsujioka, B (1964). The importance of factor-trueness and validity, versus homogeneity and orthogonality, in test scales. *Educational and Psychological Measurement, 24,* 3-30.

Comrey, A.L. (1988). Factor-analytic methods of scale development in personality and clinical psychology. *Journal of Consulting and Clinical Psychology, 56,* 754-761.

Costa, P.T., Jr., & McCrae, R.R. (1992). *Revised NEO Personality Inventory (NEO PI-R) and NEO Five-Factor Inventory (NEO-FFI) professional manual.* Odessa, FL: Psychological Assessment Resources.

Digman, J. M. (1997). Higher-order factors of the Big Five. *Journal of Personality and Social Psychology, 73,* 1246-1256.

Dwight, S.A., Cummings, K.M., & Glenar, J.L. (1998). Comparison of criterion-related validity coefficients for the Mini-Markers and for Goldberg's markers of the Big Five personality factors. *Journal of Personality Assessment, 70,* 541-550.

Embretson, S.E., & Reise, S.P. (2000). *Item response theory for psychologists*. Mahwah, NJ: Erlbaum.

Goldberg, L.R. (1972). Parameters of personality inventory construction and utilization: A comparison of prediction strategies and tactics. *Multivariate Behavioral Research Monograph, 7*, No. 72-2.

Goldberg, L.R. (1981). Language and individual differences: The search for universals in personality lexicons. In L. Wheeler (Ed.), *Review of personality and social psychology* (Vol. 2, pp. 141-165). Beverly Hills, CA: Sage.

Goldberg, L.R. (1982). From Ace to Zombie: Some explorations in the language of personality. In C.D. Spielberger, & J. N. Butcher (Eds.), *Advances in Personality Assessment* (Vol. 1: pp. 203-234). Hillsdale, NJ.: Erlbaum.

Goldberg, L. R. (1990). An alternative "Description of personality": The Big-Five factor structure. *Journal of Personality and Social Psychology, 59*, 1216-1229.

Goldberg, L.R. (1992). The development of markers for the Big-Five factor structure. *Psychological Assessment, 4*, 26-42.

Goldberg, L.R. (1997). *The Development of Five-Factor Domain Scales from the IPIP Item Pool*. Unpublished manuscript. Oregon Research Institute; Eugene, OR 97403; USA.

Goldberg, L.R. (1999). A broad-bandwidth, public-domain, personality inventory measuring the lower-level facets of several five-factor models. In I. Mervielde, I. Deary, F. De Fruyt, & F. Ostendorf (Eds.), *Personality Psychology in Europe, Vol. 7* (pp. 7-28). Tilburg, The Netherlands: Tilburg University Press.

Goldberg, L.R. (in press). The comparative validity of adult personality inventories: Applications of a consumer-testing framework. In S. R. Briggs, J. M. Cheek, & E. M. Donahue (Eds.), *Handbook of Adult Personality Inventories*. New York: Plenum.

Goldberg, L.R., & Slovic, P. (1967). The importance of test item content: An analysis of a corollary of the deviation hypothesis. *Journal of Counseling Psychology, 14*, 462-472.

Hase, H.D., & Goldberg, L.R. (1967). Comparative validity of different strategies of constructing personality inventory scales. *Psychological Bulletin, 67*, 231-248.

Hendriks, A.A.J., Hofstee, W.K.B., & De Raad, B. (1999). The Five-Factor Personality Inventory (FFPI). *Personality and Individual Differences, 27*, 307-325.

Hofstee, W.K.B. (1990). The use of everyday personality language for scientific purposes. *European Journal of Personality, 4*, 77-88.

Hofstee, W.K.B., Ten Berge, J.M.F., & Hendriks, A.A.J. (1998). How to score questionnaires. *Personality and Individual Differences, 25*, 897-909.

Hofstee, W.K.B., De Raad, B., & Goldberg, L.R. (1992). Integration of the Big-Five and circumplex approaches to trait structure. *Journal of Personality and Social Psychology, 63*, 146-163.

Hogan, R., & Hogan, J. (1995). *Manual for the Hogan Personality Inventory*. Tulsa, OK: Hogan Assessment Systems.

Jackson, D.N. (1971). The dynamics of structured personality tests: 1971. *Psychological Review, 78*, 229-248.

Johnson, J.A. (2000). *Developing a short form of the IPIP-NEO: A report to HGW Consulting*. Unpublished manuscript. Department of Psychology, University of Pennsylvania, DuBois PA.

Loevinger, J. (1954). The attenuation paradox in test theory. *Psychological Bulletin, 51*, 493-504.

Loevinger, J. (1957). Objective tests as instruments of psychological theory. *Psychological Reports, 3*, 635-694.

Lord, F.M. (1952). The relationship of the reliability of multiple choice items to the distribution of item difficulties. *Psychometrika, 18*, 181-194.

McCrae, R.R., & Costa, P.T., Jr. (1998). Toward a new generation of personality theories: Theoretical contexts for the Five-Factor Model. In J. S. Wiggins (Ed.). *The Five-Factor Model of Personality: Theoretical Perspectives* (pp. 51-87). New York: Guilford.

McDonald, R.P. (1999). *Test theory: A unified treatment.* Mahwah, NJ: Erlbaum.

Norman, W.T. (1963). Relative importance of test item content. *Journal of Consulting Psychology, 27*, 166-174.

Norman, W.T. (1967). *2800 personality trait descriptors: Normative operating characteristics for a university population.* Department of Psychology, University of Michigan, Ann Arbor, MI.

Nunnally, J.C. (1967). *Psychometric theory.* New York: McGraw-Hill.

Nunnally, J.C., & Bernstein, I.H. (1994). *Psychometric theory* (3rd ed.). New York: McGraw-Hill.

Peabody, D. (1987). Selecting representative trait adjectives. *Journal of Personality and Social Psychology, 52*, 59-71.

Peabody, D., & Goldberg, L.R. (1989). Some determinants of factor structures from personality-trait descriptors. *Journal of Personality and Social Psychology, 57*, 552-567.

Robins, R.W., Hendin, H.M., & Trzesniewski, K. H. (2001). Measuring global self-esteem: Construct validation of a single-item measure and the Rosenberg self-esteem scale. *Personality and Social Psychology Bulletin, 27*, 151-161.

Saucier, G. (1994). Mini-markers: A brief version of Goldberg's unipolar Big-Five markers. *Journal of Personality Assessment, 63*, 506-516.

Saucier, G. (2001). *What is more replicable than the Big Five? Broader factors in English-language personality adjectives.* Manuscript submitted for publication.

Saucier, G. (in press). Orthogonal markers for orthogonal factors: The case of the Big Five. *Journal of Research in Personality.*

Saucier, G., & Goldberg, L.R. (1996a). Evidence for the Big Five in analyses of familiar English personality adjectives. *European Journal of Personality, 10*, 61-77.

Saucier, G., & Goldberg, L.R. (1996b). The language of personality: Lexical perspectives on the five-factor model. In J. S. Wiggins (Ed.). *The five-factor model of personality: Theoretical perspectives* (pp. 21-50). New York: Guilford.

Saucier, G., & Goldberg, L.R. (2001). Lexical studies of indigenous personality factors: Premises, products, and prospects. *Journal of Personality, 69*, 847-879.

Saucier, G., Ostendorf, F., & Peabody, D. (2001). The non-evaluative circumplex of personality adjectives. *Journal of Personality, 69*, 537-582.

Smith, G.T., McCarthy, D.M., & Anderson, K.G. (2000). On the sins of short-form development. *Psychological Assessment, 12*, 102-111.

Wiggins, J.S. (1980). Circumplex models of interpersonal behavior. In L. Wheeler (Ed.), *Review of personality and social psychology* (Vol. 1, pp. 265-294). Beverly Hills, CA: Sage.

Zinbarg, R.E., Yovel, I., Revelle, W., & McDonald, R.P. (2000). *Beyond Alpha: Coefficients of generalizability and the internal structure of tests.* Unpublished manuscript. Department of Psychology; Northwestern University (Evanston, IL 60208-2710; USA).

Appendix. The 32 parcels included in the Big Five modular markers

Spontaneity:	Impulsive, Spontaneous, Playful (.65, .59)
Talkativeness:	Talkative, (-) Quiet (.61,.77)
Sociability:	Sociable, (-) Unsociable, (-) Withdrawn (.73$_b$, .78)
Assertiveness:	Dominant, Assertive, Forceful,(-) Timid (.68$_a$, .75)
Adventurousness:	Daring, Adventurous, (-) Unadventurous (.77$_a$, .78)
Shyness:	Shy, Bashful (.83, .81)
Restraint:	Inhibited, Reserved, Restrained (.52$_c$, .62)
Warmth:	Warm, (-) Cold (.64, .73)
Sympathy:	Sympathetic, Compassionate (.75,.78)
Sensitivity:	Sensitive, Sentimental (.48, .66)
Kindness:	(-) Cruel, Kind (.56, .66)
Agreeableness:	Agreeable, Tolerant, Lenient (.52$_a$, .65)
Toughness:	Rough, Tough, Stern, Harsh (.58$_b$, .73)
Criticalness:	Critical, (-) Uncritical (.44$_a$, .63)
Demandingness:	Demanding, (-) Undemanding (.53$_a$, .70)
Slyness:	Sly, Cunning, Shrewd (.59$_c$, .69)
Organization:	Organized, (-) Disorganized (.80, .82)
Caution:	Careful, Cautious (.70,.77)
Ambition:	Ambitious, (-) Unambitious (.78, .71)
Decisiveness:	Decisive, (-) Indecisive (.58$_b$, .66)
Efficiency:	Efficient, (-) Inefficient, (-) Careless (.70, .69)
Perfectionism:	Perfectionistic, Exacting, Meticulous, Precise (.74$_c$, .75)
Forgetfulness:	Forgetful, Absent-minded, Scatterbrained (.73$_b$, .76)
Jealousy/Envy:	Jealous, Possessive, Envious, (-) Unenvious (.67, .76)
Emotional Excitability:	Excitable, Emotional, (-) Unexcitable (.63$_a$, .72)
Anxiety:	Anxious, Nervous, High-strung (.73$_a$, .63)
Fretfulness:	Fretful, Fearful (.43$_a$, .54)
Hyperdevotedness:	Overloyal, Overprotective, Overconscientious, Oversentimental (.70$_g$, .61$_d$)
Intellectuality:	Intellectual, (-) Unintellectual (.70, .71)
Analytical Inquiry:	Philosophical, Deep, Complex, Analytical (.67$_b$, .70)
Reflectiveness:	Introspective, Contemplative, (-) Unreflective (.57$_a$, .73)
Unconventionality:	(-)Traditional, (-) Conventional, Unconventional, Nonconforming, Rebellious (.76, .74)

Note: ESPS = Eugene-Springfield Community Sample combined with college peer-rating sample, $N = 901$; ABCD - Combined college-student samples A, B, C, and D, $N = 1,028$. Coefficients in parentheses are, respectively, coefficient alpha in ESPS and ABCD; subscript letters indicate sample size for all items in parcel, a – $N = 694$, b – $N = 596$, c – $N = 592$, d – $N = 841$, e – $N = 823$.

BIG FIVE INVENTORIES AND QUESTIONNAIRES

Chapter 3

Validity and utility of the Revised NEO Personality Inventory: Examples from Europe[1]

Paul T. Costa, Jr.
Robert R. McCrae
Friðrik H. Jónsson

Introduction

The Revised NEO Personality Inventory (NEO-PI-R; Costa & McCrae, 1985, 1992b) was the first published questionnaire designed specifically to assess the Five-Factor Model (FFM) of personality. In the late 1970s, our research using a variety of questionnaire measures had led us to the conclusion that many traits could be organized in terms of three factors: Neuroticism (N), Extraversion (E), and Openness to Experience (O; Costa & McCrae, 1980). At the same time, Goldberg's (1981) lexical studies suggested that five factors were needed to account for traits named in the English language. Research comparing his structure with ours (McCrae & Costa, 1985) convinced us that we needed to add Agreeableness (A) and Conscientiousness (C) factors to our model, and we developed scales to measure them.

The resulting instrument has become the most widely used measure of the FFM, or "Big Five," as Goldberg (1993) and others working in the lexical tradition usually call this model. The NEO-PI-R differs from most adjective-based operationalizations of the FFM chiefly in two respects. First, Factor V in the lexical tradition is usually called *Intellect*, and emphasizes self-reported cognitive abilities; the corresponding NEO-PI-R factor is called *Openness to Experience*, and covers a broader range of constructs (McCrae, 1994). Second, most adjective measures assess only the five broad factors, whereas the NEO-PI-R was designed from its inception as a hierarchical instrument (Costa & McCrae, 1995). Six specific traits, or facets, were selected

[1] Portions of this chapter were presented at "Cultural Diversity and European Integration", the first Joint European Conference of the International Association for Cross-Cultural Psychology and the International Test Commission, Graz, Austria, June 28 - July 2, 1999.

Table 1. Characteristics of the Revised NEO Personality Inventory (NEO-PI-R)

Scales: Five domains (Neuroticism, Extraversion, Openness to Experience, Agreeableness, Conscientiousness) and thirty facet scales, six per factor. Factors can be scored using factor weights (Costa & McCrae, 1992b, Table 2).

Description: 240-item (30-40 min.) questionnaire developed through rational and factor analytic methods. Responses range from *Strongly Disagree* to *Strongly Agree*, and scales are balanced to control for acquiescence. Form S is used for self-reports; Form R for observer ratings. Both paper-and-pencil and computer versions are available; the latter offers an interpretive report. A 60-item (10 min.) short form, the NEO Five-Factor Inventory (NEO-FFI), assesses only the five domains. *Your NEO Summary* provides feedback to respondents.

Appropriate Populations: The NEO-PI-R was developed for use by college students and adults. It has been used extensively in both normal and clinical populations, for research and in clinical and industrial/organizational applications. Recent research suggests it can be used in adolescents as young as 12 (De Fruyt, Mervielde, Hoekstra, & Rolland, 2000), although modification of some items would be advisable. Form R has been used to rate individuals who are incapacitated or deceased.

Reliability: Internal consistency estimates for the domains range from .86 to .93; for the facets, from .56 to .87; correlations between NEO-FFI and NEO-PI-R domains range from .77 to .92 (Costa & McCrae, 1992b). Two-year retest reliabilities range from .83 to .91 for domains and from .64 to .86 for facets (McCrae, Yik, Trapnell, Bond, & Paulhus, 1998).

Validity: The NEO-PI-R has been used in over a thousand published studies and has demonstrated longitudinal stability, predictive utility, and consensual validation. Self/spouse and self/peer correlations range from .34 to .73 (Costa & McCrae, 1992b). NEO-PI-R factors have been related to most alternative measures of the Five-Factor Model, and facet scales have shown specific validity net of the five factors (McCrae & Costa, 1992).

Cross-Cultural Generalizability: In addition to the European versions reviewed here, the NEO-PI-R or NEO-FFI has been translated into Hebrew, Arabic, Persian, Marathi, Telegu, Thai, Malay, Indonesian, Filipino, Chinese, Japanese, Korean, Shona, Xhosa, and Southern Sotho. Analyses of translations have provided evidence of generalizability (McCrae, 2001).

Location: The NEO-PI-R is available from Psychological Assessment Resources, P. O. Box 998, Odessa, FL 33556., U.S.A., and on the web at www.parinc.com

to represent each factor — for example, Trust, Straightforwardness, Altruism, Compliance, Modesty, and Tender-Mindedness are the facets of A. Facets were selected on the basis of a review of the personality literature, and these distinctions have proven useful in a variety of contexts (e.g., Jang, McCrae, Angleitner, Riemann, & Livesley, 1998).

In research conducted chiefly in North America, the NEO-PI-R has shown longitudinal stability, heritability, and consensual validation (Costa & McCrae, 1992a). A substantial body of studies supports the hypothesis that the FFM covers the full range of personality traits (McCrae, 1989): Although some specific traits, such as physical attractiveness, may lie beyond the scope of the FFM, there is as yet no consensus on any additional major factors (but see Cheung & Leung, 1998; Piedmont, 2000; and Waller, 1999 for some candidate factors). Details on the development of the instrument and evidence of its construct validity are provided elsewhere (Costa & McCrae, 1995, in press; Costa, McCrae & Dye, 1991; McCrae & Costa, 1983; Piedmont, 1998). An overview is provided in Table 1.

Beginning in the 1990s, researchers around the world began to translate and adapt the NEO-PI-R (or its short form, the NEO Five-Factor Inventory or NEO-FFI). Research using these translations showed that the FFM structure is universal (McCrae & Costa, 1997), and that similar age (McCrae *et al.*, 1999) and gender (Costa, Terracciano, & McCrae, 2001) differences are found across a wide variety of cultures, including those of Africa and Asia. In this article we will review some of the studies conducted using European versions of the NEO-PI-R and consider some of the practical and theoretical implications of this research. European translations are of particular interest because Europe is a center of personality research, and the variety of languages and cultures provides a good test of the generalizability of the instrument.

A new personality inventory in the Old World

According to the Sagas, the Old and New Worlds were first bridged by an Icelander named Bjarni Herjolfsson around the year 986 A.D., when his ship overshot Greenland and drifted to within sight of new shores. He did not land, but passed on his tale (and his ship) to the better-known Leif Ericsson (Brøndsted, 1965). In this article we describe a different bridge between the two Worlds: Just a thousand years after Bjarni's sighting, the NEO-PI-R was published in America (Costa & McCrae, 1985), and it has quickly spread throughout Europe.

It is, of course, a mere conceit to suppose that Europe and America are really different Worlds. Contemporary psychology draws as much on Freud, Pavlov, and Piaget as it does on James, Allport, and Skinner. In particular, the multivariate trait psychology on which the NEO-PI-R is based was heavily influenced by the methods and findings of the British school, from Galton to Cattell (Costa & McCrae, 1976) and Eysenck (Costa & McCrae, 1986). The FFM was initially discovered in analyses of English language trait terms (Goldberg, 1993), but at least four of the factors have also been found in lexical analyses of a number of other European languages (De Raad, Perugini, Hřebíčková, & Szarota, 1998). There is thus every reason to expect that the NEO-PI-R should work well in Europe.

Table 2 summarizes the present status of the instrument in Europe, including a few translations currently in progress. *Authorized* translations have been approved for research use on the basis of review of an independent back-translation; *validated* translations have been used in research and shown some degree of empirical support. Dutch, German, French, Polish, and other versions have been published (Borkenau & Ostendorf, 1993; Hoekstra, Ormel, & De Fruyt, 1996; Rolland, 1998; Zawadzki, Strelau, Szczepaniak, & Śliwińska, 1997), and a British adaptation of the English version is distributed by The Test Agency. The other completed translations are currently available by license from the American publisher, Psychological Assessment Resources.

Hambleton (1994) has discussed guidelines for adapting psychological tests across cultures. He notes that "the expertise and experience of translators is perhaps the most crucial aspect of the entire process of adapting instruments" (p. 235), and argues that translators should have familiarity not only with both languages, but also

Table 2. European translations of the NEO-FFI and NEO-PI-R by language family

Language	Version	Translator[a]	Status
Altaic			
Turkish	NEO-FFI	D. Sunar	Validated
	NEO-PI-R	S. Gülgöz	Validated
Indo-European			
Albanian			
Albanian	NEO-FFI	D. R. Carney	In progress
Germanic			
Danish	NEO-PI-R	H. Hansen	Validated
Dutch/Flemish	NEO-PI-R	H. Hoekstra	Published
German	NEO-FFI	P. Borkenau	Published
	NEO-PI-R	A. Angleitner	Published
Icelandic	NEO-PI-R	F. H. Jónsson	Validated
Norwegian	NEO-PI-R	Ø. Martinsen	Validated
	NEO-PI-R	L. Eriksen	Validated
Swedish	NEO-FFI	B. Hagberg	Authorized
	NEO-PI-R	H. Bergmann	Validated
Greek			
Greek	NEO-PI-R	E. Besevegis	In progress
Romance			
French	NEO-PI-R	J. -P. Rolland	Published
Italian	NEO-PI-R	G. V. Caprara	Validated
Portuguese	NEO-PI-R	M. P. de Lima	Published
Romanian	NEO-FFI	S. Borza	In progress
Spanish	NEO-FFI	J. F. Salgado	Validated
	NEO-PI-R	M. Avia	Published
Slavic			
Bulgarian	NEO-PI-R	N. Alexandrova	In progress
Croatian	NEO-PI-R	I. Marušić	Validated
Czech	NEO-FFI	M. Hřebíčková	Published
Polish	NEO-FFI	J. Strelau	Published
	NEO-PI-R	J. Siuta	Authorized
Russian	NEO-FFI	M. Bodunov	Authorized
	NEO-PI-R	V. Oryol	Validated
Serbian	NEO-PI-R	G. Knežević	Validated
Slovak	NEO-PI-R	I. Ruisel	In progress
Semitic			
Maltese	N domain	A. Borg	Authorized
Uralic			
Estonian	NEO-PI-R	J. Allik	Validated
Finnish	NEO-PI	L. Pulkkinen	Validated
Hungarian	NEO-PI-R	Z. Szirmák	Validated

[a]Many translations are the work of teams; only the corresponding author is listed here.

with the constructs of interest and the process of test construction. In practice, this means that translation should be entrusted not simply to competent bilinguals, but to bilingual personality psychologists. All the European translations were made by personality psychologists; usually teams of translators were involved. Studies using European translations were conducted by European psychologists, knowledgeable about the test-taking experience and motivation of their subjects. Standard guidelines for translating the NEO-PI-R are available from the authors.

Hambleton also lists a series of guidelines for establishing the interpretability of scores. It should be noted that use of a personality measure within a culture should be based on considerations of construct validity; whereas use of a personality measure across cultures requires, in addition, demonstration of scalar equivalence — that is, evidence that the same raw scores indicate the same levels of the trait in the different cultures (Van de Vijver & Leung, 1997). The amount of within-culture validity evidence varies across European translations, but in general, experience in Europe suggests that careful translations of the NEO-PI-R by qualified psychologists yield versions that consistently demonstrate construct validity. There is much less direct evidence to date on the scalar equivalence of these versions to the American NEO-PI-R, but exploratory analyses again suggest that good translations of the NEO-PI-R are likely to produce at least rough equivalence (McCrae, 2001).

The entries in Table 2 have been organized by language family, and it is clear that most European languages are represented. In terms of numbers of speakers, the major omissions are Belorussian and Ukrainian, and most citizens of those countries are sufficiently fluent in Russian to use that version (personal communication, Z. Simakhodskaya, April 24, 1999). Lettish and Gaelic translations would complete the roster of branches of Indo-European. A Basque translation would add another language family; unfortunately, being an extinct language, an Etruscan version is probably out of reach.

Without denying the value of indigenous constructs and measures, there is obviously much to recommend the use of the same instrument in many different cultures. Findings in one culture can suggest hypotheses for research in others; cultures themselves can be compared in terms of a common metric. The NEO-PI-R has frequently been chosen for this role because it claims to be comprehensive, and thus to provide a basis for systematic evaluations of personality.

The Icelandic NEO-PI-R

We illustrate the process of translating, validating, and interpreting the NEO-PI-R by considering the Icelandic version. Iceland is an island with a population of a quarter million. The original settlers — Norwegians and their Celtic slaves — arrived just over a thousand years ago and soon converted to Christianity. The Icelandic language, derived from Old Norse, has remained largely unchanged since that time; the Sagas of the 12th Century can still be read by modern Icelanders. Between 1262 and 1904 Iceland was ruled by Norwegian and Danish kings, and it continues to show strong Scandinavian influences. In other respects, Icelanders resemble Americans — for example, in the high value they set on individualism (Jónsson & Ólafsson, 1991).

A few prior studies have examined personality variables in Icelandic groups. Hart, Hofmann, Edelstein, and Keller (1997) assessed personality in Icelandic children and found resilient, overcontrolled, and undercontrolled types resembling those found in American children. Bjoergvinsson and Thompson (1994) replicated the North American factor structure of the Basic Personality Inventory (Jackson, 1989) in a sample of Icelandic teenagers. Sigurdsson and Gudjonsson (1995) showed that drug-dependent prisoners scored lower on measures of socialization and higher on measures of Neuroticism and Psychoticism than other Icelandic prisoners. These findings suggest the hypothesis that personality variables function much the same in Icelandic and American samples. Experience with the Icelandic NEO-PI-R constitutes a further test of that hypothesis.

The translation was made by FHJ and two students, following procedures suggested by the test authors. During the translation, all items in each facet were grouped together to emphasize the construct of interest instead of the literal wording of each item. A back-translation into English was made by a State Authorized Court Interpreter unfamiliar with the NEO-PI-R. RRM reviewed the back-translation and identified 19 questionable items — 7.9 per cent of the total. For example, the English Item 20, "I am easy-going and lackadaisical," was initially back-translated as "I am calm and carefree," suggesting low N rather than the intended low C. Problems in the back-translation itself appeared to account for four of the questionable items; the remainder were reworded in Icelandic and back-translated again — Item 20 now appeared as "I am ambitionless and indifferent," clearly low C — and this final version was reviewed and authorized.

Similar procedures have been followed in all authorized translations, and most back-translations have been judged about 90 per cent accurate on the first review. This speaks well of the skill of the translators and the care they took in crafting their translations, but it also suggests that personality constructs themselves are rather easily conveyed in many different languages.

In a series of studies, the Icelandic NEO-PI-R was administered to 337 men and women, aged 18 to 67. Most were psychology or social science students or their parents or friends. All volunteered, and all were tested individually, either in the laboratory or at home. Coefficient alphas for the five domains ranged from .83 to .91; for the 30 8-item facet scales, they ranged from .48 for O6: Openness to Values to .81 for N3: Depression, with a median of .68. This value is only slightly lower than the American median value of .71, and comparable to values found in German, Italian, and Croatian versions (McCrae et al., 1999). High internal consistency, which often means only item redundancy (Cooper, 1998), has never been a priority in NEO-PI-R scale development.

When five factors are extracted from intercorrelations of the 30 facet scales in this Icelandic sample, varimax rotation yields a clear replication of the American factor structure, with factor congruence coefficients all .96 or .97. Table 3 reports a very slightly better fit from a targeted rotation (McCrae, Zonderman, Costa, Bond, & Paunonen, 1996). All facets load at least .40 on the intended factor, and all except E3: Assertiveness have their highest loading there. The similarity of secondary loadings can be evaluated by variable congruence coefficients, all of which exceed chance levels. At least by internal criteria, the individual facet scales show conver-

Table 3. Factor structure of the Icelandic NEO-PI-R

NEO-PI-R Facet	Procrustes Rotated Principal Component					Variable Congruence
	N	E	O	A	C	
Neuroticism						
N1: Anxiety	**.84**	-.15	-.03	-.01	-.05	.98**
N2: Angry Hostility	**.63**	.05	-.01	**-.49**	.01	.99**
N3: Depression	**.80**	-.27	.00	.02	-.18	.98**
N4: Self-Consciousness	**.71**	-.21	-.17	.24	-.11	.96**
N5: Impulsiveness	**.42**	.34	-.02	-.27	-.35	.99**
N6: Vulnerability	**.74**	-.08	-.15	.04	-.32	.99**
Extraversion						
E1:Warmth	-.14	**.73**	.27	.32	.16	.99**
E2: Gregariousness	-.14	**.77**	-.07	.10	.01	.98**
E3: Assertiveness	-.38	**.41**	.27	**-.45**	.22	.98**
E4: Activity	-.10	**.55**	.11	-.20	.31	.97**
E5: Excitement Seeking	.02	**.55**	.00	-.18	-.13	.95**
E6: Positive Emotions	-.14	**.74**	.16	.10	.14	.99**
Openness to Experience						
O1: Fantasy	.16	.21	**.60**	-.10	-.21	.99**
O2: Aesthetics	.23	.13	**.65**	.17	.10	.98**
O3: Feelings	.28	**.44**	**.56**	.08	.19	.98**
O4: Actions	-.30	.21	**.64**	-.01	-.05	.99**
O5: Ideas	-.09	-.02	**.72**	-.06	.13	.99**
O6: Values	-.23	.07	**.65**	.13	-.04	.92*
Agreeableness						
A1: Trust	-.34	**.44**	.13	**.46**	.05	.95**
A2: Straightforwardness	.00	-.08	-.19	**.68**	.09	.97**
A3: Altruism	-.03	.39	.08	**.55**	.24	.98**
A4: Compliance	-.16	-.09	-.06	**.74**	-.10	.99**
A5: Modesty	.35	-.12	-.15	**.62**	.02	.97**
A6: Tender-Mindedness	.09	.09	.33	**.56**	-.12	.90*
Conscientiousness						
C1: Competence	**-.41**	.24	.27	-.12	**.56**	.96**
C2: Order	.08	-.01	-.15	-.05	**.72**	.97**
C3: Dutifulness	-.08	.03	-.09	.22	**.69**	.97**
C4:Achievement Striving	-.06	.21	.06	-.04	**.79**	.99**
C5: Self-Discipline	-.24	.05	.01	.09	**.85**	.97**
C6: Deliberation	-.08	-.31	-.14	.26	**.52**	.96**
Factor Congruence	*.98**￼*	*.97**￼*	*.96**￼*	*.97*	*.98**￼*	*.97**￼*

Note: N = 337. Loadings over .40 in absolute magnitude are given in boldface. *Congruence higher than 95% of rotations from random data. **Congruence higher than 99% of rotations from random data.

gent and discriminant validity, and the structure of personality traits in Iceland seems to be the same as in America.

Is this a function of the similar value systems or Germanic languages of these two cultures? Probably not. Table 4 summarizes results of European tests of factor replicability; high congruences are found in every culture so far examined. While this is good news for personality psychologists, it is no longer really news, nor is it a unique property of the NEO-PI-R. The universality of the FFM has been demonstrated

Table 4. Factor congruence coefficients comparing NEO-PI-R translations to the American normative structure

Sample (N)	Procrustes-rotated principal component				
	N	E	O	A	C
Dutch (1,305)	.98	.97	.94	.97	.98
German (1,324)	.97	.96	.97	.98	.97
Norwegian (379)	.96	.96	.94	.96	.97
French (447)	.97	.96	.94	.96	.97
Italian (697)	.97	.95	.96	.97	.97
Portuguese (2,000)	.98	.94	.89	.97	.97
Croatian (719)	.97	.96	.95	.97	.97
Russian (178)	.96	.95	.95	.94	.96
Serbian (422)	.96	.97	.95	.97	.97
Estonian (711)	.96	.97	.96	.97	.97

Note: Data from Hoekstra *et al.*, 1996; Kallasmaa, Allik, Realo, & McCrae, 2000; Knežević, Radović, & Opačić, 1997; Martin *et al.*, 1997; McCrae & Costa, 1997; McCrae, Costa *et al.*, 1996; Rolland, Parker, & Stumpf, 1998; personal communication, H. Nordvik, May 5, 1999.

often, using different instruments (Paunonen *et al.*, 1996) as well as different cultures (McCrae & Costa, 1997).

Given the demonstration of factorial validity in Icelandic, there is a strong temptation to proceed immediately to an interpretation of mean levels. Do these descendants of the Vikings show the high levels of irascibility, excitement seeking, and arrogance, and the low impulse control that we might attribute to their fierce ancestors (Magnusson, 1960)? Figure 1 shows mean NEO-PI-R profiles plotted against American adult norms. Men and women show very similar patterns, suggesting that gender differences in the American norms are preserved in Iceland. Overall, these Icelanders appear to be high in N, E, and O, and low in A and C; examination of facet scales show that they are also high in N2: Angry Hostility and E5: Excitement Seeking, and low in A5: Modesty and C5: Self-Discipline. It does appear that modern Icelanders have something of the temperament of Vikings.

But that conclusion is many steps ahead of the supporting evidence. To begin with, there is a powerful alternative hypothesis, because the pattern of high N, E, and O, and low A and C is familiar to students of adult development. Table 5 summarizes cross-sectional age trends from adolescence through middle age in ten European nations; although relatively modest in magnitude, the effects are generally significant in these large samples, and the direction of the effects is uniform. Perhaps the Icelanders depicted in Figure 1 share the temperament, not of Vikings, but of adolescents and young adults[1]. In fact, the median age in this sample is 23. This example can serve as a reminder that any interpretation of national character

---

[1]The Vikings known to history were probably rowdy in part because they were young; life expectancy was short in the Middle Ages. Those who lived longer, like the eponymous hero of *Njal's Saga*, probably developed more maturity and self-restraint

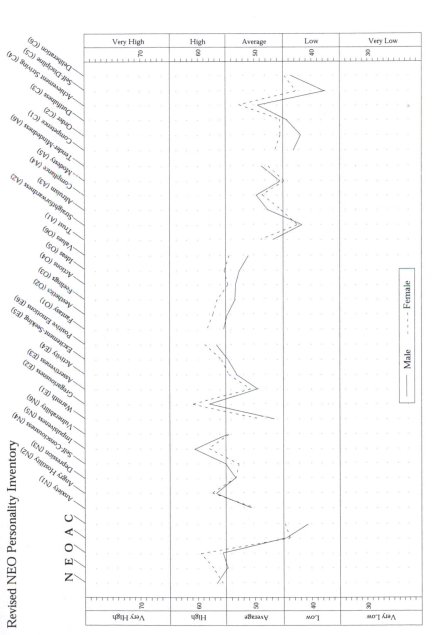

Figure 1. Mean NEO-PI-R scores for Icelandic men (solid line) and women (dashed line), plotted on American adult within-gender norms. Profile form reproduced by special permission of the Publisher, from the Revised NEO Personality Inventory, by Paul T. Costa, Jr., and Robert R. Mc-Crae. Copyright 1978, 1985, 1989, 1992 by PAR, Inc. Further reproduction is prohibited without permission of PAR, Inc.

should be based on nationally representative samples, which this clearly is not. Plausible as the age interpretation is, it is by no means certain that it is correct. Plotting Icelandic data on American profile sheets presumes that raw scores are strictly comparable (Van de Vijver & Leung, 1997), and that has not yet been demonstrated. Perhaps the most direct way to test the equivalence of scale scores is through studies of bilinguals who complete two versions of a scale. Bilingual studies would probably be easy in Iceland, where English is widely spoken, but they have not yet been conducted. In fact, the only bilingual equivalence study conducted in Europe that we have been able to identify compared Estonian and Russian versions of the NEO-PI-R. Konstabel (1999) showed high cross-language correlations (medians of .88 and .81 for domains and facets, respectively), but significant (though small) mean level differences for two domains and several facets. Experience with bilingual studies in non-European languages (McCrae, Yik, Trapnell, Bond, & Paulhus, 1998; Piedmont & Chae, 1997) suggests that this is likely to be a typical result: Different language versions of the NEO-PI-R yield very similar, but not identical, mean values. Where cultural differences in mean levels are the focus of interest, bilingual studies would seem to be essential.

NEO-PI-R research in Europe

In addition to bilingual studies, interpretation of the Icelandic NEO-PI-R would be enhanced by studies of cross-observer agreement, correlations with other scales and inventories, and research on personality development. We can probably anticipate

Table 5. Cross-Sectional Adult Age Trends in Five Domains

Sample	Domain				
	N	E	O	A	C
Turkish (511)	Down	Down	Down	Up	Up
British (540)	Down	Down	*n.s.*	*n.s.*	Up
Dutch/Flemish	Down	Down	Down	Up	*n.s.*
German (3,442)	Down	Down	Down	Up	Up
Italian (690)	*n.s.*	Down	Down	Up	Up
Portuguese (1,880)	Down	Down	Down	Up	Up
Spanish (764)	Down	Down	Down	*n.s.*	Up
Croatian (702)	*n.s.*	Down	Down	Up	Up
Czech (912)	Down	Down	Down	Up	Up
Russian (297)	*n.s.*	Down	Down	Up	Up
Estonian (598)	*n.s.*	Down	Down	Up	Up

Note: From Costa *et al.*, 2000; McCrae *et al.*, 1999; McCrae *et al.*, 2000, personal communication, F. De Fruyt, May 27, 1999.

the results of those studies, however, by examining research conducted elsewhere in Europe.

One of the unusual features of the NEO-PI-R is the provision of parallel self-report and observer rating forms. Agreement across methods of measurement constitutes one of the most powerful forms of evidence for the validity of personality scales, and American studies have shown substantial self/spouse, self/peer, and peer/peer agreement (Costa & McCrae, 1992b). Using the 60-item NEO-FFI in a German sample, Riemann, Angleitner, and Strelau (1997) reported self/peer and Spearman-Brown corrected peer/peer correlations ranging from .49 to .65 for the five domains. Zawadzki and colleagues (1997) showed uncorrected peer/peer correlations of .26 to .53 in a Polish sample; they also showed self/peer correlations ranging from .36 to .66. Ongoing analyses in Russian (T. Martin, personal communication, June 4, 1999) and Norwegian (personal communication, Ø. Martinsen, May 28, 1999) samples show significant self/partner agreement for the domains and most of the facets of the full NEO-PI-R.

Both self- and peer-reports have been used in behavior genetic studies. One of the first studies on the heritability of factors beyond N and E utilized Swedish translations of brief O, A, and C scales (Bergeman *et al.*, 1993). Zawadzki and colleagues (1997) used the NEO-FFI in a Polish sample of 546 pairs of twins, aged 17 to 64, to examine heritability of the five factors. All five were significantly heritable when self-reports were examined (h^2s = .30 to .57), and all but Agreeableness were heritable in peer ratings (h^2s = .52 to .71). Riemann and colleagues (1997) used German self-reports and peer ratings to estimate heritability of latent variables; increased precision of measurement from the combined assessments led to much higher estimates of heritability, ranging from .66 to .79. In an unusual cross-cultural behavior genetics study, Jang *et al.* (1998) showed that NEO-PI-R facets were equally heritable in German and Canadian twin samples.

In both the U.S. and Europe, the NEO-PI-R has begun to be used extensively in industrial/organizational contexts. De Fruyt and Mervielde (1997) showed that NEO-PI-R scores predicted vocational interests in a Belgian sample. Furnham, Crump, and Whelan (1997) reported that NEO-PI scales correlated meaningfully with British assessors' ratings of managerial capacity. Salgado and Rumbo (1994) demonstrated that the Conscientiousness scale of the Castilian NEO-FFI predicted job aspiration and performance among financial service managers. Martinsen (personal communication, May 28, 1999) showed personality profile differences associated with occupational groups in Norway: Artists were high in Openness, nurses in Agreeableness.

A number of articles have examined relations between NEO-PI-R scales and other personality measures. Some of these studies replicate associations previously reported in American samples — for example, with public and private self-consciousness (Realo & Allik, 1998) or the Eysenck scales (Avia *et al.*, 1995). Others have examined convergence between the NEO-PI-R and indigenous measures of the five factors — for example, in Italian (Caprara, Barbaranelli, Borgogni, & Perugini, 1993) and Dutch (Hendriks, Hofstee, & De Raad, 1999). Perhaps most interesting, however, are those that relate the NEO-PI-R to constructs of European origin. These studies speak to the comprehensiveness of the FFM and to the comparability of more or less independent conceptual systems.

Strelau and Zawadzki (1995), for example, operationalized the Regulative Theory of Temperament in an instrument called the Formal Characteristics of Behavior — Temperament Inventory (FCB-TI). The Regulative Theory of Temperament is an elaboration of Pavlovian concepts, and the FCB-TI measures Briskness, Perseverance, Sensory Sensitivity, Emotional Reactivity, Endurance, and Activity. Although Perseverance and Endurance sound as though they are forms of Conscientiousness, correlations with the Polish NEO-FFI show that they are related, in different directions, chiefly to N. Perseverance, which might better be labeled Perseveration, refers to a rigid repetition of behavior and is associated with high N. Endurance refers to low arousability in the face of stimulation, and is related chiefly to low N. Openness, which is sometimes missing in lexical analyses (De Raad *et al.*, 1998), is at least partially represented in the FCB-TI in the form of Sensory Sensitivity; Agreeableness, however, is unrelated to any of these temperamental variables.

Future directions

It should soon be possible to administer the NEO-PI-R, or at least the NEO-FFI, to any European. All available data suggest that the instrument works reasonably well in translation, and indeed, that findings from one country are usually generalizable to others (cf. Salgado, 1997). Recent trends toward political and economic unity in Europe seem to be paralleled by the demonstration of psychological unity, at least at the level of enduring dispositions.

On a practical level, the availability of a common instrument should facilitate both research and application. Use in I/O psychology has already been mentioned; the FFM and the NEO-PI-R also have promising roles in clinical psychology and psychiatry (Anderson, Barnes, Patton, & Perkins, 1999; Matthews, Saklofske, Costa, Deary, & Zeidner, 1998; Petot, 1994), behavioral medicine (Lemos-Giráldez & Fidalgo-Aliste, 1997), and educational and political psychology (Blickle, 1996; Riemann, Grubich, Hempel, Mergl, & Richter, 1993; Schouwenburg & Kossowska, 1999).

At a more theoretical level, the NEO-PI-R should be especially valuable in cross-cultural psychology. In this context, it is well to recall that European languages extend well beyond the boundaries of Europe. The Russian NEO-PI-R has been used to examine acculturation of immigrants in the United States (Simakhodskaya, 2000); the English version has been used to compare Black and White college students in South Africa (Heuchert, Parker, Stumpf, & Myburgh, 2000); research on the validity of the Portuguese version in Brazil is underway. The translations listed in Table 1 offer useful tools for comparisons around the world.

Two other research topics are of particular interest to us. First, although a good deal can be learned about personality development from cross-sectional comparisons of age differences across cultures (McCrae *et al.*, 1999), the stability of individual differences can only be addressed by longitudinal studies. Only a handful of such studies have been conducted outside the U.S. (e.g., Thomae, 1976), and they did not use measures of the FFM. A body of parallel studies in several different cultures using the NEO-PI-R over, say, a ten-year interval would be enormously informative about the course of adult personality development. A Russian longitudinal study of self-reports and observer ratings is currently underway (Martin, Costa, Oryol, Ruka-vishnikov, & Senin, in press).

Finally, there is keen interest today in studies of the molecular genetics of personality. Because genetic influences appear to be similar across cultures (Jang *et al.*, 1998), such studies might be done anywhere. But early findings have proven difficult to replicate (Ball *et al.*, 1997), probably because so many hundreds of genes influence personality that finding any one is a daunting task. New strategies are needed and are likely to work best in highly homogeneous populations where genetic noise is minimized. Sardinia provides one such opportunity, and research including the Italian version of the NEO-PI-R is currently being planned. Another opportunity, of course, is in Iceland, and as we have seen, the Icelandic NEO-PI-R is ready for use there.

References

Anderson, R., Barnes, G., Patton, D., & Perkins, T. (1999). Personality in the development of substance abuse. In I. Mervielde, I. Deary, F. De Fruyt, & F. Ostendorf (Eds.), *Personality psychology in Europe* (Vol. 7, pp. 141-158). Tilburg, The Netherlands: Tilburg University Press.

Avia, M.D., Sanz, J., Sánchez-Bernardos, M.A., Martínez-Arias, M.R., Silva, R., & Graña, J. L. (1995). The Five-Factor Model—II. Relations of the NEO-PI with other personality variables. *Personality and Individual Differences, 19*, 81-97.

Ball, D., Hill, L., Freeman, B., Eley, T.C., Strelau, J., Riemann, R., Spinath, F.M., Angleitner, A., & Plomin, R. (1997). The serotonin transporter gene and peer-rated neuroticism. *NeuroReport, 8*, 1301-1304.

Bergeman, C.S., Chipuer, H.M., Plomin, R., Pedersen, N.L., McClearn, G.E., Nesselroade, J.R., Costa, P.T., Jr., & McCrae, R.R. (1993). Genetic and environmental effects on openness to experience, agreeableness, and conscientiousness: An adoption/twin study. *Journal of Personality, 61*, 159-179.

Bjoergvinsson, T., & Thompson, A.P. (1994). Psychometric properties of an Icelandic translation of the Basic Personality Inventory: Cross-cultural invariance of a three-factor solution. *Personality and Individual Differences, 31*, 47-56.

Blickle, G. (1996). Personality traits, learning strategies, and performance. *European Journal of Personality, 10*, 337-352.

Borkenau, P., & Ostendorf, F. (1993). *NEO-Fünf-Faktoren Inventar (NEO-FFI) nach Costa und McCrae: Handanweisung*. Göttingen: Hogrefe.

Brønsted, J. (1965). *The Vikings* (K. Skov, Trans.). London: Penguin.

Caprara, G.V., Barbaranelli, C., Borgogni, L., & Perugini, M. (1993). The "Big Five Questionnaire": A new questionnaire to assess the five factor model. *Personality and Individual Differences, 15*, 281-288.

Cheung, F.M., & Leung, K. (1998). Indigenous personality measures: Chinese examples. *Journal of Cross-Cultural Psychology, 29*, 233-248.

Cooper, C. (1998). Why many personality scales may be trivial. In J. Bermúdez, B. de Raad, J. de Vries, A.M. Pérez-García, A. Sánchez-Elvira, & G.L. van Heck (Eds.), *Personality psychology in Europe* (Vol. 6, pp. 33-39). Tilburg, The Netherlands: Tilburg University Press.

Costa, P.T., Jr., & McCrae, R.R. (1976). Age differences in personality structure: A cluster analytic approach. *Journal of Gerontology, 31*, 564-570.

Costa, P.T., Jr., & McCrae, R.R. (1985). *The NEO Personality Inventory manual*. Odessa, FL: Psychological Assessment Resources.

Costa, P.T., Jr., & McCrae, R.R. (1986). Major contributions to personality psychology. In S. Modgil & C. Modgil (Eds.), *Hans Eysenck: Consensus and controversy* (pp. 63-72, 86, 87). Barcombe Lewes Sussex, England: Falmer.

Costa, P.T., Jr., & McCrae, R.R. (1992a). Four ways five factors are basic. *Personality and Individual Differences, 13*, 653-665.

Costa, P.T., Jr., & McCrae, R.R. (1992b). *Revised NEO Personality Inventory (NEO-PI-R) and NEO Five-Factor Inventory (NEO-FFI) professional manual*. Odessa, FL: Psychological Assessment Resources, Inc.

Costa, P.T., Jr., & McCrae, R.R. (1995). Domains and facets: Hierarchical personality assessment using the Revised NEO Personality Inventory. *Journal of Personality Assessment, 64*, 21-50.

Costa, P.T., Jr., & McCrae, R.R. (in press). The Revised NEO Personality Inventory (NEO-PI-R). In S.R. Briggs, J.M. Cheek, & E.M. Donahue (Eds.), *Handbook of adult personality inventories*. New York: Plenum.

Costa, P.T., Jr., McCrae, R.R., & Dye, D.A. (1991). Facet scales for Agreeableness and Conscientiousness: A revision of the NEO Personality Inventory. *Personality and Individual Differences, 12*, 887-898.

Costa, P.T., Jr., McCrae, R.R., Martin, T.A., Oryol, V.E., Senin, I.G., Rukavishnikov, A.A., Shimonaka, Y., Nakazato, K., Gondo, Y., Takayama, M., Allik, J., Kallasmaa, T., & Realo, A. (2000). Personality development from adolescence through adulthood: Further cross-cultural comparisons of age differences. In V.J. Molfese & D. Molfese (Eds.), *Temperament and personality development across the life span* (pp. 235-252). Hillsdale, NJ: Erlbaum.

Costa, P.T., Jr., Terracciano, A., & McCrae, R.R. (2001). Gender differences in personality traits across cultures: Robust and surprising findings. *Journal of Personality and Social Psychology, 81*, 322-331.

De Fruyt, F., & Mervielde, I. (1997). The Five-Factor Model of personality and Holland's RIASEC interest types. *Personality and Individual Differences, 23*, 87-103.

De Fruyt, F., Mervielde, I., Hoekstra, H.A., & Rolland, J.-P. (2000). Assessing adolescents' personality with the NEO-PI-R. *Assessment, 7*, 329-345.

De Raad, B., Perugini, M., Hřebíčková, M., & Szarota, P. (1998). Lingua franca of personality: Taxonomies and structures based on the psycholexical approach. *Journal of Cross-Cultural Psychology, 29*, 212-232.

Furnham, A., Crump, J., & Whelan, J. (1997). Validating the NEO Personality Inventory using assessor's ratings. *Personality and Individual Differences, 22*, 669-675.

Goldberg, L.R. (1981). Language and individual differences: The search for universals in personality lexicons. In L. Wheeler (Ed.), *Review of personality and social psychology* (Vol. 2, pp. 141-165). Beverly Hills, CA: Sage.

Goldberg, L.R. (1993). The structure of phenotypic personality traits. *American Psychologist, 48*, 26-34.

Hambleton, R.K. (1994). Guidelines for adapting educational and psychological tests: A progress report. *European Journal of Psychological Assessment, 10*, 229-244.

Hart, D., Hofmann, V., Edelstein, W., & Keller, M. (1997). The relation of childhood personality types to adolescent behavior and development: A longitudinal study of Icelandic children. *Developmental Psychology, 33*, 195-205.

Hendriks, A.A.J., Hofstee, W.K.B., & De Raad, B. (1999). The Five-Factor Personality Inventory. *Personality and Individual Differences, 27*, 307-325.

Heuchert, J.W.P., Parker, W.D., Stumpf, H., & Myburgh, C.P.H. (2000). The Five-Factor Model in South African college students. *American Behavioral Scientist, 44*, 112-125.

Hoekstra, H.A., Ormel, J., & De Fruyt, F. (1996*). Handleiding NEO Persoonlijkheidsvragenlijsten NEO-PI-R en NEO-FFI [Manual for NEO Personality Inventories NEO-PI-R and NEO-FFI]*. Lisse, The Netherlands: Swets & Zeitlinger.

Jackson, D.N. (1989). *Basic Personality Inventory manual*. Port Huron, MI: Sigma Assessment Systems.

Jang, K.L., McCrae, R.R., Angleitner, A., Riemann, R., & Livesley, W.J. (1998). Heritability of facet-level traits in a cross-cultural twin sample: Support for a hierarchical model of personality. *Journal of Personality and Social Psychology, 74*, 1556-1565.

Jónsson, F.H., & Ólafsson, S. (1991). *Lífsskoðun í nútímalegum þjóðfélögum [Values in modern societies]*. Reykjavík: Félagsvísindastofnun.

Kallasmaa, T., Allik, J., Realo, A., & McCrae, R.R. (2000). The Estonian version of the NEO-PI-R: An examination of universal and culture-specific aspects of the Five-Factor Model. *European Journal of Personality, 14*, 265-278.

Knežević, G., Radović, B., & Opačić, G. (1997). An evaluation of the "Big Five Model" of personality through an analysis of the NEO-PI-R Personality Inventory. *Psihologija, 1-2*, 3-24.

Konstabel, K. (1999). *A bilingual retest study of the Revised NEO Personality Inventory: A comparison of Estonian and Russian versions*. Unpublished Master's Thesis, University of Tartu.

Lemos-Giráldez, S., & Fidalgo-Aliste, A.M. (1997). Personality dispositions and health-related habits and attitudes: A cross-sectional study. *European Journal of Personality, 11*, 197-209.

Magnusson, M. (1960). Introduction. In M. Magnusson & H. Pálsson (Eds.), *Njal's saga*. New York: Penguin.

Martin, T.A., Costa, P.T., Jr., Oryol, V.E., Rukavishnikov, A.A., & Senin, I.G. (in press). Applications of the Russian NEO-PI-R. In R.R. McCrae & J. Allik (Eds.), *The Five-Factor Model across cultures*. Dordrecht, The Netherlands: Kluwer Academic Publishers.

Martin, T.A., Draguns, J.G., Oryol, V.E., Senin, I.G., Rukavishnikov, A.A., & Klotz, M.L. (1997, August). *Development of a Russian-language NEO-PI-R*. Paper presented at the Annual Convention of the American Psychological Association, Chicago, IL.

Matthews, G., Saklofske, D.H., Costa, P.T., Jr., Deary, I.J., & Zeidner, M. (1998). Dimensional models of personality: A framework for systematic clinical assessment. *European Journal of Psychological Assessment, 14*, 36-49.

McCrae, R.R. (1989). Why I advocate the five-factor model: Joint analyses of the NEO-PI and other instruments. In D.M. Buss & N. Cantor (Eds.), *Personality psychology: Recent trends and emerging directions* (pp. 237-245). New York: Springer-Verlag.

McCrae, R.R. (1994). Openness to Experience: Expanding the boundaries of Factor V. *European Journal of Personality, 8,* 251-272.

McCrae, R.R. (2001). Personality traits and culture: Exploring intercultural comparisons. *Journal of Personality, 69,* 819-846.

McCrae, R.R., & Costa, P.T., Jr. (1983). Joint factors in self-reports and ratings: Neuroticism, Extraversion, and Openness to Experience. *Personality and Individual Differences, 4,* 245-255.

McCrae, R.R., & Costa, P.T., Jr. (1985). Updating Norman's "adequate taxonomy": Intelligence and personality dimensions in natural language and in questionnaires. *Journal of Personality and Social Psychology, 49,* 710-721.

McCrae, R.R., & Costa, P.T., Jr. (1992). Discriminant validity of NEO-PI-R facet scales. *Educational and Psychological Measurement, 52,* 229-237.

McCrae, R.R., & Costa, P.T., Jr. (1997). Personality trait structure as a human universal. *American Psychologist, 52,* 509-516.

McCrae, R.R., Costa, P.T., Jr., Lima, M.P., Simões, A., Ostendorf, F., Angleitner, A., Marušić, I., Bratko, D., Caprara, G.V., Barbaranelli, C., Chae, J.-H., & Piedmont, R.L. (1999). Age differences in personality across the adult life span: Parallels in five cultures. *Developmental Psychology, 35,* 466-477.

McCrae, R.R., Costa, P.T., Jr., Ostendorf, F., Angleitner, A., Hřebíčková, M., Avia, M.D., Sanz, J., Sánchez-Bernardos, M.L., Kusdil, M.E., Woodfield, R., Saunders, P.R., & Smith, P.B. (2000). Nature over nurture: Temperament, personality, and lifespan development. *Journal of Personality and Social Psychology, 78,* 173-186.

McCrae, R.R., Costa, P.T., Jr., Piedmont, R.L., Chae, J.-H., Caprara, G.V., Barbaranelli, C., Marušič, I., & Bratko, D. (1996, November). *Personality development from college to midlife: A cross-cultural comparison*: Paper presented at the Annual Convention of the Gerontological Society of America, Washington, DC.

McCrae, R.R., Yik, M.S.M., Trapnell, P.D., Bond, M.H., & Paulhus, D.L. (1998). Interpreting personality profiles across cultures: Bilingual, acculturation, and peer rating studies of Chinese undergraduates. *Journal of Personality and Social Psychology, 74,* 1041-1055.

McCrae, R.R., Zonderman, A.B., Costa, P.T., Jr., Bond, M.H., & Paunonen, S.V. (1996). Evaluating replicability of factors in the Revised NEO Personality Inventory: Confirmatory factor analysis versus Procrustes rotation. *Journal of Personality and Social Psychology, 70,* 552-566.

Paunonen, S.V., Keinonen, M., Trzebinski, J., Forsterling, F., Grishenko-Rose, N., Kouznetsova, L., Chan, D.W. (1996). The structure of personality in six cultures. *Journal of Cross-Cultural Psychology, 27,* 339-353.

Petot, J.-M. (1994). L'intérêt clinique du modèle de personnalité en cinq facteurs [Clinical interest of the Five-Factor Model of personality]. *Revue Européenne de Psychologie appliquée, 44,* 57-63.

Piedmont, R.L. (1998). *The Revised NEO Personality Inventory: Clinical and research applications.* New York: Plenum.

Piedmont, R.L. (1999). Does spirituality represent the sixth factor of personality? Spiritual Transcendence and the Five-Factor Model. *Journal of Personality, 67,* 985-1013.

Piedmont, R.L., & Chae, J.H. (1997). Cross-cultural generalizability of the five-factor model of personality: Development and validation of the NEO-PI-R for Koreans. *Journal of Cross-Cultural Psychology, 28,* 131-155.

Realo, A., & Allik, J. (1998). The Estonian Self-Consciousness Scale and its relation to the Five-Factor Model of Personality. *Journal of Personality Assessment, 70,* 109-124.

Riemann, R., Angleitner, A., & Strelau, J. (1997). Genetic and environmental influences on personality: A study of twins reared together using the self- and peer report NEO-FFI scales. *Journal of Personality, 65*, 449-475.

Riemann, R., Grubich, C., Hempel, S., Mergl, S., & Richter, M. (1993). Personality and attitudes towards current political topics. *Personality and Individual Differences, 15*, 313-321.

Rolland, J. P. (1998). *NEO-PI-R: Inventaire de Personnalité-Révisé (Adaptation française) [NEO-PI-R: Revised Personality Inventory (French adaptation)]*. Paris: Les Editions du Centre de Psychologie Appliquée.

Rolland, J.P., Parker, W.D., & Stumpf, H. (1998). A psychometric examination of the French translations of the NEO-PI-R and NEO-FFI. *Journal of Personality Assessment, 71*, 269-291.

Salgado, J.F. (1997). The Five-Factor Model of personality and job performance in the European Community. *Journal of Applied Psychology, 82*, 30-43.

Salgado, J.F., & Rumbo, A. (1994). *Personality and job performance in financial services managers*. Unpublished manuscript, University of Santiago de Compostela.

Schouwenburg, H.C., & Kossowska, M. (1999). Learning styles: Differential effects of self-control and deep-level information processing on academic achievement. In I. Mervielde, I. Deary, F. De Fruyt, & F. Ostendorf (Eds.), *Personality psychology in Europe* (Vol. 7, pp. 263-284). Tilburg, The Netherlands: Tilburg University Press.

Sigurdsson, J.F., & Gudjonsson, G.H. (1995). Personality characteristics of drug-dependent offenders. *Nordic Journal of Psychiatry, 49*, 33-38.

Simakhodskaya, Z. (2000, August). *Russian Revised NEO-PI-R: Concordant validity and relationship to acculturation*. Paper presented at the 108th Convention of the American Psychological Association, Washington, DC.

Strelau, J., & Zawadzki, B. (1995). The Formal Characteristics of Behaviour-Temperament Inventory (FCB-TI): Validity studies. *European Journal of Personality, 9*, 207-229.

Thomae, H. (Ed.). (1976). *Patterns of aging: Findings from the Bonn Longitudinal Study of Aging*. Basel: S Karger.

Van de Vijver, F.J.R., & Leung, K. (1997). *Methods and data analysis for cross-cultural research*. Thousand Oaks, CA: Sage.

Waller, N.G. (1999). Evaluating the structure of personality. In C.R. Cloninger (Ed.), *Personality and psychopathology* (pp. 155-197). Washington, DC: American Psychiatric Press.

Zawadzki, B., Strelau, J., Szczepaniak, P., & Śliwińska, M. (1997). *Inwentarz Osobowości NEO-FFI Costy i McCrae (Adaptacja polska) [NEO-FFI Personality Inventory of Costa and McCrae (Polish adaptation)]*. Warsaw: Pracownia Testów Psychologicznych.

Chapter 4

The Five-Factor Personality Inventory: Assessing the Big Five by means of brief and concrete statements

A. A. Jolijn Hendriks
Willem K. B. Hofstee
Boele De Raad

Introduction

The Five-Factor Personality Inventory (FFPI; Hendriks, 1997; Hendriks, Hofstee, & De Raad, 1999a, 1999b; Hendriks, Hofstee, De Raad, & Angleitner, 1995) is a questionnaire for assessing a person's standing on the Big Five dimensions Extraversion, Agreeableness, Conscientiousness, Emotional Stability, and Autonomy. The FFPI consists of 100 brief and concrete behaviorally descriptive statements in the third person singular (e.g., takes charge, avoids company, takes others' interests into account). This item format can be used for other-ratings as well as self-ratings. In the latter case, it may stimulate the subject to take a more objective perspective. Ratings are made on a 5-point scale ranging from *not at all applicable* to *entirely applicable*. A person's position on each of the five dimensions is calculated by taking differentially weighted sums of all his or her 100 item responses (Hofstee, Ten Berge, & Hendriks, 1998). This scoring procedure according to rotated principal components maximizes internal consistency reliability and amount of variance explained (Ten Berge & Hofstee, 1999).

History and rationale of the FFPI

The FFPI has been developed within the psycholexical paradigm (e.g., De Raad,

Big Five Assessment, edited by B. De Raad & M. Perugini. © 2002, Hogrefe & Huber Publishers.

2000; Digman, 1990; Goldberg, 1981, 1990; John, 1990; John, Angleitner, & Ostendorf, 1988). In the psycholexical paradigm it is assumed that all behavioral differences that people encounter in their daily interactions become "sedimented" in everyday language (Cattell, 1943, p. 483; Goldberg, 1981). In other words, eventually, people will have words to talk about these differences. Dictionaries record the most commonly used language units. Research on personality traits discriminating people or groups of people thus starts from an unabridged dictionary. The first systematic scan for personality-descriptive terms has been carried out by Allport and Odbert (1936), who recognized 4,504 stable traits among a total list of 17,953 terms that can "...distinguish the behavior of one human being from that of another" (p. 24). It was not until the early 1940's however that, gradually, insight was gained in the underlying structure of personality traits. After the pioneer studies of Cattell (1943, 1945, 1947) and Fiske (1949), subsequent studies like those of Tupes and Christal (1961), Norman (1963), and Goldberg (1981, 1982) provided the foundations of what became known as the "Big Five" (Goldberg, 1981) or "Five-Factor Model" (FFM; McCrae & Costa, 1997)[1]. Progress was made more rapidly since computers became available enabling more sophisticated techniques of large-scale data analysis like principal components (factor) analysis. In the last two decades, trait taxonomic research has been carried out by many researchers in many different countries. The real break-through of the FFM came about when factor solutions proved to be stable across methods of data collection and analysis (Goldberg, 1990; Peabody & Goldberg, 1989) and the model appeared not to be confined to sets of trait-adjectives, but was found to hold also in the domain of personality questionnaires (Digman, 1990; Digman & Inouye, 1986; Ostendorf & Angleitner, 1992) and temperament inventories (Angleitner & Ostendorf, 1994).

At present, the FFM is the most widely used working hypothesis of personality structure (McCrae & Costa, 1997), notwithstanding the fact that the model has been seriously criticized regarding number and nature of the factors (e.g., Block, 1995; Eysenck, 1991; McAdams, 1992; Paunonen & Jackson, 2000). Among psycholexical psychologists consensus has been reached on four of the five factors, generally labeled: Extraversion, Agreeableness, Conscientiousness, and Emotional Stability (or, conversely, Neuroticism). The fifth factor is still in dispute, even among psycholexical psychologists (De Raad & Van Heck, 1994). This least replicable factor has been labeled variously as Culture, (Tupes & Christal, 1961), Intellect (Goldberg, 1992; Ostendorf, 1990), Openness to Experience (Costa & McCrae, 1992), and Creativity or Imagination (Saucier, 1992). Recently, Autonomy has become another serious candidate (Hendriks, 1997; Hendriks *et al.*, 1999b; Perugini & Ercolani, 1998; Rodríguez-Fornells, Lorenzo-Seva, & Andrés-Pueyo, 2001).

---

[1] One of our reviewers suggested to refrain from using the "Big Five" and "FFM" interchangeably. We feel however that there are no qualitative differences between the five-factorial model associated with studies based on the psycholexical approach to personality and the one operationalized in the NEO-PI-R, calling for distinctive names. As Goldberg (1993) already notes, there are many more similarities than dissimilarities.

In the last decade, an increasing number of instruments to measure the Big Five personality dimensions became available, as is illustrated by the contents of this book. The FFPI may be considered as a serious challenge to this set of instruments, for several reasons. Firstly, the FFPI has a direct link to the psycholexical approach to personality, by being based largely on the Abridged Big-Five Dimensional Circumplex model of personality traits (AB5C model; Hofstee & De Raad, 1991; Hofstee, De Raad, & Goldberg, 1992). Secondly, the FFPI is a broadly applicable instrument, because of its item format and wording. Thirdly, the FFPI is parsimonious in comparison with most of the alternative Big Five questionnaires. Finally, the FFPI has been developed interactively in the Dutch, American-English, and German languages, to enhance translatability and, therefore, its chances on cross-cultural applicability.

At the time that we constructed the FFPI, the majority of the instruments developed especially to measure the Big Five were lists of trait-descriptive adjectives (cf. Briggs, 1992). Examples are the Five Personality Factors Test (5PFT; Elshout & Akkerman, 1975), the Standard Personality Adjective Checklist (SPEL; Hofstee, Brokken, & Land, 1981), Goldberg's Big Five adjective markers (Goldberg, 1990, 1992), and the Interpersonal Adjective Scale Revised for Big Five (IAS-R-B5; Trapnell & Wiggins, 1990). Those specifically defined Big Five inventories available (e.g., the revised NEO-Personality Inventory [NEO-PI-R] of Costa & McCrae, 1992; the Big Five Inventory [BFI] of John, Donahue, & Kentle, 1991) or under construction (the Big Five Questionnaire [BFQ] of Caprara, Barbaranelli, Borgogni, & Perugini, 1993) consisting of personality-descriptive phrases still showed many items containing trait-adjectives (BFQ; NEO-PI-R) or, even, revolving around trait-adjectives (BFI). Trait-adjectives are inherently abstract, because they summarize behavior. As a consequence, they do not make up the best constituents of a questionnaire to be administered to subjects with a wide range of educational levels. For the FFPI, we wrote items that convey trait meaning in statements as briefly, simply, and concretely as possible. To this purpose, guidelines (Hofstee, 1991) were taken into account, to ensure creating items that would be applicable to a wide variety of subjects and settings, and would elicit ratings as objectively as possible. Items that were selected to constitute the FFPI contain no negations and were all found to be comprehensible by subjects with a low level of education.

Currently, most researchers adhere to a hierarchical conception of the FFM. Each of the five more abstract dimensions (e.g., Extraversion) is taken to subsume a number of mid-level personality traits or "facets" (e.g., assertiveness, activity). Instruments according to a hierarchical model are characterized by rational scale construction. Because they are not rooted in factor analysis (Block, 1995; Saucier & Ostendorf, 1999), the proposed number and nature of the facets may differ widely. The NEO-PI-R (Costa & McCrae, 1992), for instance, comprises 30 facets (240 items), six facets per Big Five factor (labeled: Neuroticism, Extraversion, Openness to Experience, Agreeableness, and Conscientiousness). Alternatively, the BFQ (Caprara *et al.*, 1993) has only two facets per Big Five factor (labeled: Emotional Stability, Energy, Openness, Friendliness, and Conscientiousness). Empirical scale construction would rather suggest three to four facets or "subcomponents" per Big

Five factor (Saucier & Ostendorf, 1999). In fact, a hierarchical model is at odds with the simplicity and parsimoniousness originally searched for by psycholexical psychologists. By conceiving the Big Five as a dimensional model (see below), a comparable amount of descriptive specification can be reached while staying within the five-dimensional trait space. With only a 100 items, the FFPI yields scores on the Big Five factors as well as facet scores. These facet scores specify a persons' position on distinct subclusters of traits of (pairwise combinations of) the Big Five. Differently from facet scores in a hierarchical model, however, FFPI facet scores do not account for additional variance over and above variance explained by the Big Five. Their rationale lies in the applied context only.

Several authors point at the necessity to construct measures that encompass lower levels of specification than the Big Five, to enlarge the power of the FFM to predict important life criteria (e.g., Ashton, Jackson, Paunonen, Helmes, & Rothstein, 1995; Robertson & Callinan, 1998). It is much more efficient, however, to use the FFM primarily as an integrative structure in which other and more "dedicated" instruments (measuring, e.g., sensation seeking, workplace delinquency, or proactive personality) can be empirically positioned and compared than to try to encompass all lower levels of trait description that might help to enlarge the predictive validity of the FFM (cf. Hurtz & Donovan, 2000). Very likely, reliable and valid narrow measures will almost always outperform the broader personality dimensions in predictive power (e.g., Ashton, 1998; Crant & Bateman, 2000).

Questionnaires are notoriously difficult to translate into other languages. When items need to be adapted for each language version, comparability of results among versions becomes questionable. As regards the FFPI, translatability of the items into at least two other languages (American-English and German) was taken as a prerequisite for item selection, in addition to good psychometric properties. Our aim was to deliver a Big Five questionnaire that would be internationally applicable.

Development of the FFPI

Sources for item production

Point of departure for item production was the AB5C model of personality traits (Hofstee & De Raad, 1991; Hofstee *et al.*, 1992). The AB5C model integrates the classical Big Five simple-structure model and two-dimensional circumplex models (Wiggins, 1979). The AB5C model takes into account that most traits appear to be "blends" of two of the Big Five factors rather than factor-pure representatives: apart from a high (primary) loading on one factor, these traits have substantial (secondary) loadings on a second factor. In a simple-structure model traits are assigned to the one factor on which they load highest. In a circumplex-model, traits are ordered along the boundary of a circle according to their loadings on two orthogonal factors.

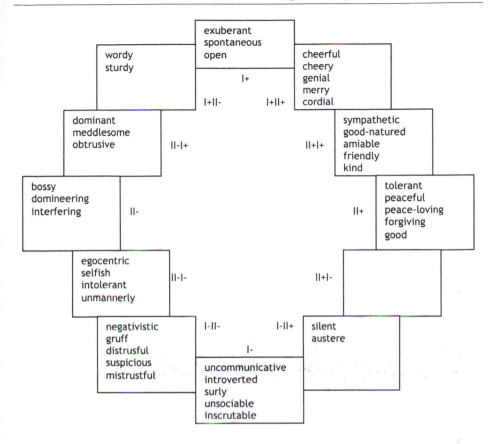

Figure 1. The I x II (Extraversion x Agreeableness) circumplex from Hendriks (1997)

Pairwise combinations of the orthogonal Big Five factors yield ten ($1/2n[n-1] = 10$, with $n = 5$) such two-dimensional slices, or circumplexes, of the five-dimensional trait space. Each circumplex is divided in 12 circle segments (facets) of 30° each, each containing those traits that have their primary and secondary loadings (approximately) in common (for further details, see Hofstee *et al.*, 1992). In the Netherlands, 1,203 traits (Brokken, 1978) were assigned to the AB5C-facets according to their two highest loadings (De Raad, Hendriks, & Hofstee, 1992; Hofstee & De Raad, 1991). Figure 1 shows the I x II (Extraversion x Agreeableness) circumplex as an example.

The AB5C model totals to 90 facets ($n[n-1]$, with $n = 10$ factor poles), as opposite poles of the same factor cannot be paired by definition. All 65 well-filled facets were taken as a point of departure for writing items. The content of a facet is to be understood in a recursive way: by taking the shared meaning of the traits it contains, while contrasting it to its opposite cluster and centering it between its two neighboring clusters. Facet I+II+ (cheerful, cheery, genial, merry, cordial), for example, yielded

Table 1. Guidelines for item production

- Phrase items in the third person singular
- Phrase items in observable terms
- Avoid modifiers
- Avoid suggestive wording
- Avoid difficult words and expressions
- Avoid negations
- Avoid idiom
- Avoid racist, sexist, ethnocentric and androcentric expressions
- Avoid items mainly consisting of a personality-descriptive adjective, noun, or their combination
- Avoid specification
- Use proper Dutch

Note: Hofstee (1991).

the following items, among others: radiates joy, makes people feel welcome, gets along well with others. Based on the AB5C model, a total of 909 items were written.

In addition, 136 items were written taking the list of 1,557 personality-descriptive verbs (De Raad, Mulder, Kloosterman, & Hofstee, 1988) as a point of departure (for details, see Hendriks, 1997). Examples are: insults people, cheers people up. Personality-descriptive verbs add meaning that is not found in trait-adjectives (De Raad, 1992; De Raad *et al.*, 1988).

Finally, 266 additional items were written to cover Intellect. This strategy was chosen to gear the item pool to the American and German trait structures. For, the Dutch Factor V is Rebelliousness or Spirit, rather than Intellect (Hofstee & De Raad, 1991). The initial Dutch item pool thus consisted of (909 + 136 + 266 =) 1,311 sentence items.

Procedure for item production

Items were written in three consecutive teams of five to ten members, roughly in correspondence with the three sources for item production: the AB5C model, personality-descriptive verbs, and trait-adjectives referring to Intellect. Team members independently produced items, which were discussed in team sessions as to whether they fulfilled the guidelines for item production (Hofstee, 1991) and the meaning of the segments. The guidelines for item production address an item's outline and phrasing (Table 1). They served the purpose of creating items for an instrument that can be used for a broad range of educational levels, avoids discrimination of certain people or groups of people, and, last but not the least, elicits ratings as objectively as possible. Teams as a whole decided whether items should be kept, adapted, or rejected for the initial Dutch item pool.

Establishing the final item pool

The 1,311 sentence items were translated into American-English (in cooperation with Lewis R. Goldberg from the Oregon Research Institute) and German (by Alois Angleitner and his team from the University of Bielefeld). Only those items were retained for which good translations could be found in both languages; in the process, items were slightly adapted if necessary. Eventually, 914 items defined the final, trilingual, item pool.

Item selection

Item selection was carried out in two steps. In the first stage of the project, self- and other-ratings were collected on the 914 sentence items and 225 personality-descriptive adjectives representing the Dutch five-dimensional trait space. Subjects were 153 first-year students and 14 staff members of psychology. They rated themselves and were rated by two to four others who knew the target person well. All ratings were made on a 5-point scale running from *much less than others* to *much more than others*. For the large majority (133) of subjects, we received a complete set of one self- and four other-ratings. Because the adjective-based Big Five factor structure in self-ratings and other-ratings appeared highly similar (cf. Ostendorf, 1990), self- and other-ratings were pooled, to increase precision and generalizability. The total sample consisted of 790 raters, about twice as many women as men, aged 15-80 years ($M = 28$ years, $SD = 12.5$ years). A principal components analysis (PCA) followed by varimax rotation was performed to establish the dimensionality of the item pool and we examined the relationship between the sentence items and trait-adjectives (Big Five) structures. The scree plot clearly indicated that five factors should be retained for rotation. Correlations calculated between subjects' scores on the five varimax-rotated sentence-based factors and the five varimax-rotated adjective-based factors amounted to .89, .88, .92, .85, and .88 for Factor I to Factor V, respectively. The off-diagonal values were essentially zero, except for the one indicating the relationship between sentence-based Factor V and adjective-based Factor IV (0.14). Each sentence item was assigned to one of the 90 AB5C facets according to its largest projection in Big Five space, i.e. its two highest correlations with the five adjective-based factors (e.g., see De Raad *et al.*, 1992; Hofstee *et al.*, 1992). In practice, it means postmultiplying the matrix of correlations (factor loadings) by a matrix containing the proper sines and cosines (available from the first author) and identifying the largest (positive or negative) values. Largest projections (AB5C facet loadings) appeared to range from -.66 to .71, with a median absolute value of .47. The sentence items covered the AB5C model quite well: only 10 facets were found empty (see Hendriks, 1997, Table 7). For each sentence item, we established the correlation between self-ratings and the averaged (per target) other-ratings. These self-(mean)peer validities ranged from -.08 to .66, with a mean and median value of .33.

Based on their projections and self-(mean)peer validities, as well as data on comprehensibility, observability, and social desirability of the items (for details, see Hendriks, 1997) as secondary criteria for item selection, a preselection of 284 sentence items was made. We chose those items that showed the largest projections and highest validities, and, in addition, were found comprehensible, observable, and not too socially (un)desirable. Ratings on comprehensibility (1 = *perfectly comprehensible,* 3 = *totally incomprehensible*) were provided by 45 students from a local school for lower professional training (low level of education). Ratings on observability (1 = *not or hardly observable to others,* 5 = *clearly observable to others*) and social desirability (1 = *very negatively,* 2 = *negatively,* 3 = *neutral,* 4 = *positively,* 5 = *very positively*) were provided by two samples of (90%) university students (*N* = 43 for observability and *N* = 48 for social desirability) from a wide variety of disciplines.

The 284 sentence items included 125 items (25 per factor) for each of two parallel instruments, and another 34 items that were part of the Acquiescence scale (see below, correction for acquiescence). For both versions, items were selected such that secondary loadings were balanced as much as possible; for instance, if two III+IV+ items were selected, two III+IV- items were also selected. However, the spread of the sentence items across the AB5C model did not allow to follow this procedure in full. Therefore, items were selected such that correlations to be expected between the five scales were roughly the same for both versions of the instruments.

Additional data were collected on the 284 sentence items and 225 trait-adjectives. Subjects were 125 first-year students of psychology. With the exception of eight of them, each target gave a self-rating and was rated by two to four others who knew the target person well. All ratings were made on a 5-point scale running from *not at all applicable* to *totally applicable.* The total sample consisted of 606 raters, almost twice as many women as men, aged 15-86 years (*M* = 28 years, *SD* = 13.5 years). This data set was combined with the one (*N* = 790) already available, resulting in a total of 1,311 raters after deletion of subjects with too many missing values (≥ 3%) or suspect response profiles (following L. R. Goldberg, personal communication, November 23, 1994). We considered a subject's response profile suspect if this subject's item responses consisted of long series of identical (extreme) values, or if the difference between synonym and antonym correlation for this subject was less than .70. Following Goldberg (ibid.), we computed a subject's synonym correlation across 40 (quasi) synonym pairs (8 per factor; correlation between the items of a pair on average: .62), and his/her antonym correlation across 40 (quasi) antonym pairs (8 per factor; correlation between the items of a pair on average: -.50), from the 914 items making up the final item pool. Compared to Goldberg ("We then culled subjects if they provided ... a synonym correlation less than .40 or an antonym correlation larger than -.30"), we used a less strict rule for culling: (synonym correlation minus antonym correlation) < (.40 - [-.30] =) .70. We substituted the scale midpoint ("3") for missing values in cases showing less than 3 per cent missing item responses.

Prior to further analyses, a check was performed on the appropriateness of pooling the two data sets. In the first stage of the project, a comparative instruction had been used, while in the second stage of the project, an applicability instruction was used. It is quite conceivable that a rater finds certain behavior descriptions *applicable* ("4" under the applicability instruction) to a target person, while he or she would hesitate to state that the same descriptions apply *more* ("4" under the comparative instruction) to this target person than to others. The intra-individual spreads across items may thus differ significantly depending on the type of instructions given to raters. Furthermore, other-ratings tend to be more extreme than self-ratings (Hendriks, 1997, p. 15). Indeed, a two-way analysis of variance, with Rater and Instruction as the independent variables and subjects' intra-individual spreads across the 284 sentence items as the dependent variable, showed significant main effects for Rater ($F[1,1307] = 13.37$, $p < .001$) and Instruction ($F[1,1307] = 461.27$, $p < .001$); no interaction effect was found. Other-ratings yielded more variance than self-ratings and the applicability instruction yielded more variance than the comparative instruction. Thus, prior to further analyses, we corrected subjects' raw scores by dividing them by the standard deviation of the condition (self- or other-rating, comparative or applicability instruction).

A PCA followed by varimax rotation performed on the 284 sentence items yielded five factors, according to the scree test, indicating that the five-factor structure was recovered in this selection of 284 items from the pool of sentence items. Congruence coefficients phi between the sentence-based factors and the adjective-based Big Five structure amounted .91, .91, .92, .89, and .70 between varimax-rotated factors, and .93, .92, .91, .94, and .88 after procrustes rotation to optimal agreement, for Factors I to V, respectively. We further examined the relationship between the Dutch sentence-based structure and the one established in a large American sample ($N = 766$), kindly made available by L. R. Goldberg. These two data sets had 260 sentence items in common. Congruence coefficients for varimax-rotated factors (based on 260 items) amounted to .94, .89, .87, .89, and .91 for Factors I to V, respectively. Additional measures for quantifying fit between matrices of factor loadings (McCrae, Zonderman, Costa, Bond, & Paunonen, 1996) supported our conclusion that the Dutch and American factor structure of the sentence items were remarkably similar. The overall congruence appeared .90 after varimax rotation and .91 after procrustes rotation to optimal agreement. At the level of items phi coefficients ranged from .38 to .99, with a median value of .94; only 16 per cent of the sentence items had values below .85, which value is taken to indicate factor congruence (Haven & Ten Berge, 1977).

Given the similarity between the Dutch and American structures, we decided to take the AB5C facet positions of the items in the American structure into account in the final item selection. To establish the final position of the axes, a two-sided procrustes rotation to optimal agreement was performed; the consensus matrix of the Dutch and American structures was varimax-rotated once more (Kiers, 1997). Each sentence item was assigned to one of the 90 AB5C facets according to its largest projection.

Table 2. Mean values of the 100 FFPI items on the criteria for item selection

		N items	M	(Sd)	Range	Md
			AB5C-facet projection:[a]			
I	Extraversion	20	0.64	(0.05)	0.52-0.70	0.65
II	Agreeableness	20	0.62	(0.07)	0.46-0.74	0.63
III	Conscientiousness	20	0.61	(0.06)	0.52-0.71	0.62
IV	Emotional Stability	20	0.64	(0.06)	0.53-0.71	0.64
V	Autonomy	20	0.57	(0.06)	0.47-0.69	0.58
			Self-(mean)peer validity:			
I	Extraversion	20	0.51	(0.06)	0.41-0.65	0.50
II	Agreeableness	20	0.40	(0.09)	0.27-0.57	0.41
III	Conscientiousness	20	0.47	(0.09)	0.32-0.62	0.46
IV	Emotional Stability	20	0.44	(0.09)	0.29-0.61	0.45
V	Autonomy	20	0.37	(0.09)	0.22-0.55	0.38
			Comprehensibility:[b]			
I	Extraversion	20	1.01	(0.02)	1.00-1.04	1.00
II	Agreeableness	20	1.01	(0.01)	1.00-1.04	1.02
III	Conscientiousness	20	1.01	(0.02)	1.00-1.04	1.00
IV	Emotional Stability	20	1.02	(0.02)	1.00-1.07	1.01
V	Autonomy	20	1.01	(0.02)	1.00-1.07	1.02
			Observability:[c]			
I	Extraversion	20	3.76	(0.47)	2.81-4.33	3.70
II	Agreeableness	20	3.82	(0.39)	3.00-4.51	3.79
III	Conscientiousness	20	3.72	(0.43)	2.74-4.53	3.68
IV	Emotional Stability	20	3.37	(0.48)	2.63-4.42	3.34
V	Autonomy	20	3.61	(0.31)	3.21-4.21	3.52
			Social Desirability:[d]			
I	Extraversion	20	3.17	(0.85)	2.04-4.27	3.05
II	Agreeableness	20	3.04	(1.02)	1.83-4.27	3.02
III	Conscientiousness	20	3.10	(0.72)	1.88-4.40	3.21
IV	Emotional Stability	20	3.02	(0.85)	1.85-4.23	2.67
V	Autonomy	20	3.06	(0.85)	1.90-4.08	3.25

Note: From Hendriks (1997). [a]Absolute values. [b]1 = Perfectly comprehensible, 3 = Totally incomprehensible. [c]1 = Not or hardly observable to others, 5 = Clearly observable to others. [d]1 = Very negative, 5 = Very positive.

Selecting items for two parallel versions of the instrument appeared hardly feasible. Instead of two less optimal versions, we decided to construct one version containing the best items in terms of the primary and secondary criteria. Several item sampling plans were considered (Hendriks, 1997; Hendriks *et al.*, 1999b). Eventually, we decided to select 20 good items per factor (having their primary loading on that factor), to be well spread across the different facets of a factor in order to avoid redundancy. The following criteria for item selection were applied: AB5C facet loading (projection) , comprehensibility ($\leq$ 1.07, on a scale from 1 *perfectly comprehensible* to 3 *totally incomprehensible*), self-(mean)peer validity, observability, and nonextreme social desirability. Observability and nonextreme social desirability served as marginal criteria. Variety of item content was a requirement that led to the rejection of otherwise good items. Table 2 gives an overview of the values of the 100 selected items on the different criteria. Table 3 gives an overview of the spread of the 100 FFPI items across the AB5C model.

FFPI scale scores obtained by unit weighing of the item responses are correlated

Table 3. Spread of the 100 FFPI items across the AB5C Model

	I+	I-	II+	II-	III+	III-	IV+	IV-	V+	V-	
I+	1		4	3		1	2		6		
I-		4	1				1	6		2	
II+	3	2	3		2		1		1		
II-		1		4		1		1		1	
III+					4					1	
III-	1			1		3	1		1		
IV+	3						2		2		
IV-		2		2	1			2		5	
V+	2		2		2	2	3				
V-		1			1	3		1		1	
	10	10	10	10	10	10	10	10	10	10	100

Note: From Hendriks (1997). Column headings denote the primary loading of a factor, row headings denote the secondary loading of a factor. AB5C facet I+II+, for instance, is represented by 3 items.

up to .50, due to shared secondary loadings of the items. Therefore, orthogonalized scale scores (factor scores) are the preferred units of analysis. A stand-alone (Pascal) scoring program that calculates a person's uncorrelated factor scores from his or her 100 item responses can be obtained from the first author. The (five) factors are labeled: Extraversion, Agreeableness, Conscientiousness, Emotional Stability and Autonomy. In spite of the purposeful overrepresentation of Intellect-items in the pool of 914 sentence items and the list of 225 trait-adjectives, neither the trait-adjective based nor the sentence-based (five-)factor solutions showed Intellect to be the core meaning of the fifth factor. The core meaning of the five factors and examples of items are given in Table 4.

Table 4. Bipolar core meaning of the FFPI factors and examples of items (in italics)

EXTRAVERSION

Talkative	Silent
Loves to chat	Uncommunicative
Laughs aloud	Avoids contacts with others

AGREEABLENESS

Mild	Bossy
Tolerant	Egocentric
Is willing to make compromises	*Imposes his/her will on others*

CONSCIENTIOUSNESS

Systematic	Undisciplined
Precise	Sloppy
Does things according to a plan	*Acts without planning*

EMOTIONAL STABILITY

Can take his/her mind off his/her problems	Gets overwhelmed by emotions
Is always in the same mood	Is easily moved to tears
	Is easily hurt

AUTONOMY

Can easily link facts together	*Follows the crowd*
Wants to form his/her own opinions	Copies others
Analyses problems	Agrees to anything

The concept of (personal) autonomy stems from political philosophy and has to do with making one's *own* choices (Metaal, 1992). The underlying idea of the concept of autonomy is self-control and independence (Haworth, 1986). An autonomous person "subjects the norms with which he or she is confronted to critical evaluation and then proceeds to reach practical decisions by way of independent and rational reflection" (Young, 1986, p. 10). Riesman, Denney, and Glazer (1950, p. 301) define autonomous people as questioners. According to these authors, "The 'autonomous' are those who on the whole are capable of conforming to the behavioral norms of their society ... but who are free to choose whether to conform or not" (p. 287). Within psychology, autonomy is a less well-defined concept (Metaal, 1992): it is referred to among others as a developmental endpoint (Erikson, 1968, pp. 107-114), a basic need (Murray, 1938, p. 82), and a causality orientation, referring to the perceived source of initiation and regulation of behavior (Deci & Ryan, 1985). One way or another, autonomy is considered an important concept in almost all fields of psychology. These fields include clinical and developmental psychology (e.g., Bekker, 1993; Clark, Steer, Beck, & Ross, 1995; Mills, 1994; Ryff, 1989), educational psychology (e.g., Cronbach, 1977, pp. 51 ff.; Wong, 2000), health psychology (e.g., Knee & Zuckerman, 1998), organizational psychology (e.g., Breaugh & Becker, 1987), personality psychology (e.g., Deci & Ryan, 1987; Paunonen, Jackson, & Keinonen, 1990), and social psychology (e.g., Deci & Ryan, 1987). Several instruments contain an Autonomy scale: the Edwards Personal Preference Schedule (EPPS; Edwards, 1954), the Personality Research Form (PRF; Jackson, 1984), the Interpersonal Dependency Inventory (Hirschfeld *et al.*, 1977), the Adjective Checklist (ACL; Gough & Heilbrun, 1983), the General Causality Orientations Scale (Deci & Ryan, 1985), the Nonverbal Personality Questionnaire (NPQ; Paunonen *et al.*, 1990), and the Autonomy Scale (Bekker, 1993). As compared to these other instruments, FFPI-Autonomy may come closest to the dominant conception of autonomy in political philosophy (Metaal, 1992) in which critical reflection is the core meaning.

Correction for acquiescence

Acquiescence variance in trait ratings may seriously disturb the factor structure of personality traits and should therefore be removed (Hofstee *et al.*, 1998). Acquiescent responding is a tendency to an "excentric" scale usage, which manifests itself through a deviation from the scale's midpoint (e.g., "3" on a 5-point scale) of a person's mean score on a sizeable number of pairs of items that are opposite in meaning (e.g., warm vs. cold, friendly vs. unfriendly). Acquiescence variance can be reliably established if a questionnaire contains enough (e.g., 25-30) such pairs, spread across this questionnaire's domains of content (Hendriks, 1997). Hendriks *et al.* (1999b) found that in normal samples the Acquiescence factor may account for well over eight per cent of the variance in trait ratings. At all stages of the project of the construction of the FFPI, PCAs were performed on the "acquiescence-corrected" item responses. Correction took place by subtracting a person's mean score on an

Acquiescence scale from all of this person's raw item responses. Recently, more sophisticated techniques for correction, such as partialling, became available (Ten Berge, 1999). The Pascal scoring program mentioned above yields factor scores that are free of acquiescence variance.

Psychometric properties of the FFPI

Reliability

Internal consistency

The internal consistency reliability (Cronbach's α) of the FFPI factors proved to be good (Table 5). At the time the FFPI was constructed, Hendriks (1997) found α-reliabilities of .83 for Autonomy and .89 for the other four factors. In a variety of Dutch and one Flemish normal population samples ($N = 104$ to $N = 2,494$), mean αs ranged from .81 for Autonomy to .86 for Extraversion and Conscientiousness (Hendriks *et al.*, 1999b). Comparable values were found in normal population samples ($N = 97$ to $N = 678$) of 11 other cultures (Hendriks,

Table 5. Reliability of the FFPI factors

Study	Sample	Rating	N	FFPI				
				I	II	III	IV	V
Internal consistency (α)								
Hendriks, 1997	Normal	Self/other[a]	1,311	.89	.89	.89	.89	.83
Hendriks, 2000	Patient	Self	237	.85	.82	.82	.81	.77
Hendriks *et al.*, 1999b[b,c]	Normal	self/other	104-2,494	.86	.84	.86	.85	.81
Hendriks, Perugini *et al.*, 2001[b,c]	Normal	Self	97-678	.87	.84	.84	.84	.79
Hendriks *et al.*, 2001	Patient	Self	105	.86	.80	.82	.85	.78
Perugini & Ercolani, 1998	Normal	Self	137	.89	.85	.83	.89	.83
Perugini & Ercolani, 1998	Normal	Other	226	.90	.86	.85	.91	.84
Rodriguez *et al.*, 2001	Normal	Self	567	.84	.84	.84	.82	.78
				—	—	—	—	—
On average:				.87	.84	.84	.86	.80
Test-retest								
Hendriks, 1997	Normal	Self/other[a]	178	.79	.79	.83	.82	.79
Hendriks *et al.*, 1999b	Normal	Self	1,768	.79	.74	.77	.75	.76
				—	—	—	—	—
On average:				.79	.77	.80	.79	.78

Note: I = Extraversion, II = Agreeableness, III = Conscientiousness, IV = Emotional Stability, V = Autonomy. [a]Combined. [b]Averaged values. [c]After procrustes rotation to the Dutch target structure.

Perugini *et al.*, 2001). In a sample of 237 Dutch (non-psychiatric) hospital patients, α ranged from .77 for Autonomy to .85 for Extraversion (Hendriks, 2000). In a sample of 105 German inpatients and outpatients with psychopathology, α ranged from .78 for Autonomy to .86 for Extraversion (Hendriks, Ostendorf, & Dieckmann, 2001). Others (Costa, Yang, & McCrae, 1998; Van Kampen, 2000; Van der Zee, Buunk, Sanderman, Botke, & Van den Bergh, 1999) who used the FFPI factor scores in their studies report only the internal consistency reliabilities of the scale scores, which are generally good.

Test-retest

The FFPI showed good levels of stability (Table 5). Across a six-months time span, correlations ($N = 178$) between factor scores were found of .79, .79, .83, .82, and .79 for Extraversion, Agreeableness, Conscientiousness, Emotional Stability, and Autonomy, respectively (Hendriks, 1997). Across a one-year time span, we found test-retest correlations ($N = 1,768$) of .79, .74, .77, .75, and .76 for Extraversion, Agreeableness, Conscientiousness, Emotional Stability, and Auton-omy, respectively (Hendriks *et al.*, 1999b). The latter are based on only 50 items (10 per factor), thus underestimating the true values.

Validity

Convergent validity

Overall, FFPI Extraversion, Agreeableness, Conscientiousness, and Emotional Stability showed good levels of convergent validity with their respective coun-terparts in other Big-Five measures such as the NEO-PI-R (Costa & McCrae, 1992; Dutch translation: Hoekstra, Ormel, & De Fruyt, 1996), the Berkeley Personality Profile (BPP; Harary & Donahue, 1994), the Big Five Inventory (BFI; John *et al.*, 1991), Goldberg's Big Five adjective markers (Goldberg, 1992), and the Short Adjective Checklist to measure Big Five (SACBIF; Perugini & Leone, 1996). An overview is given in Table 6. Across studies, convergent correlations average to .74 for Extraversion, .60 for Agreeableness, .73 for Conscientiousness, .71 for Emotio-nal Stability. In Dutch ($N = 125$) and Flemish ($N = 105$) samples, convergent correlations with the NEO-PI-R were on average .79 (.80 and .77, respectively) for Extraversion, .65 (.69, .61) for Agreeableness, .78 (.75, .81) for Conscientiousness, and -.75 (-.83, -.67) for Emotional Stability (Hendriks *et al.*, 1999b; see also Hen-driks, 1997). Costa *et al.* (1998) report convergent validities between NEO-PI-R and FFPI in an American sample that are somewhat lower; in their study, however, the mean interval between administrations of the two instruments was 3.1 years, thus correlations partly indicate stability values. Substantial correlations for Extraversion, Agreeableness, Conscientiousness, and Emotional Stability were also found between FFPI and BPP (Hendriks *et al.*, 1999b), BFI (Rodríguez-Fornells *et al.*, 2001),

Golberg's markers and SACBIF (Perugini & Ercolani, 1998), and the 4-Dimensional Personality Test (Van Kampen, 1996), a Big Five related instrument. Autonomy is clearly less convergent with its FFM counterpart factors: correlations with Intellect (Perugini & Ercolani, 1998) or Openness to Experience (Costa *et al.*, 1998; Hendriks, 1997; Hendriks *et al.*, 1999b; Perugini & Ercolani, 1998; Rodríguez-Fornells *et al.*, 2001) appear to be .40 at best.

Autonomy seems to be a broader construct than Intellect and Openness to Experience, also encompassing "leadership": apart from being related to Need for Cognition — alike Intellect and Openness — and Capacity for Managing New Situations — alike Openness — Autonomy showed unique additional relationships with Self Awareness, (non-)Sensitivity to Others, and Generalized Self-Efficacy (Perugini & Ercolani, 1998). Rodríguez-Fornells *et al.* (2001) found Autonomy to be related to non-impulsive risk taking.

Criterion validity

Up to now, self-peer agreement figures are the sole indices of criterion validity available (Table 6). We compared self-ratings to the mean of two to four other-ratings and found correlations ($N = 260$) between factor scores of .73 for Extraversion, .70 for Agreeableness, .70 for Conscientiousness, .68 for Emotion-al Stability, and .54 for Autonomy (Hendriks, 1997; Hendriks *et al.*, 1999b). Perugini and Ercolani (1998) compared self-ratings to (a) one other-rating and (b) the mean of five other-ratings. In the former case, correlations ($N = 112$) between factor scores ranged from .33 for Autonomy to .54 for Emotional Stability. In the latter case, correlations ($N = 23$) ranged from .45 for Autonomy to .77 for Conscientiousness.

Predictive validity

There is a growing body of evidence that personality pathology can be seen as the extremes of normal variation (e.g., Bagby *et al.*, 1999; Costa & McCrae, 1990; Deary, Peter, Austin, & Gibson, 1998; Miller, Lynam, Widiger, & Leukefeld, 2001; Soldz, Budman, Demby, & Merry, 1993; Trull, 1992). In Big Five space, Emotional Stability and Extraversion are the two most important factors for explaining variance in personality disorders. However, instruments (questionnaire or structured interview), samples (normal or clinical), and type of rating (e.g., self- or clinician's) play a role in precisely which relationships are found between the Big Five and personality disorders (Soldz *et al.*, 1993). In self-ratings, all FFPI factors appeared significantly and meaningfully related to personality disorders, as measured by the VKP (Duijsens, 1996), a self-report questionnaire; predominantly, however, relationships were found for Emotional Stability, Extraversion and Conscientiousness (Hendriks *et al.*, 1999b). These relationships are summarized in Table 6 by the ones for the DSM-IV and ICD-10 total scores (total number of criteria met) and are briefly discussed below. For each factor, results are presented in the order from strongest to weakest relationships.

Table 6. Validity of the FFPI factors

Study	Measure	Rating	N	FFPI				
				I	II	III	IV	V
Convergent								
Costa et al., 1998	NEO-PI-R	Self	116	.71	.52	.65	-.57	.32
Hendriks et al., 1999b	NEO-PI-R	Self[a]	88-102	.79	.65	.78	-.75	.40
	BPP	Self	315	.83	.58	.78	-.81	.41
Perugini & Ercolani, 1998	Goldberg-markers	Self/Other[b]	249	.60	.59	.72	.62	.41
	SACBIF	Self/Other[b]	249	.70	.62	.74	.70	.35
	Self Awareness	Self	137	-	-	-	-	.59
	SO	Self	137	-	-	-	-	-.38
	CMNS	Self	137	-	-	-	-	.41
	NC	Self	137	-	-	-	-	.33
	GSE	Self	137	-	-	-	-	.34
Rodríguez et al., 2001	BFI	Self	350	.74	.59	.74	-.74	.48
Van Kampen, 2000	4DPT	Self	104	.78	-.64	.73	-.81	-
On average:[c]				.74	.60	.73	.71	.40
Criterion								
Hendriks et al., 1999b	2-4 others[a]	Self	260	.73	.70	.70	.68	.54
Perugini & Ercolani, 1998	1 other	Self	112	.52	.39	.51	.54	.33
	5 others[a]	Self	23	.48	.63	.77	.53	.45
On average:				.58	.57	.66	.58	.44

Predictive			N	I	II	III	IV	V
Adema et al., 2000								
	MDLS	Self	193	-.19				.39
	RDLS	Self	193			.34		-.32
	ADLS	Self	193		.28			
	UDLS	Self	193			-.34		
De Fruyt, 1997								
	WFS	Self	105				.38	-.24
	Weeping as Coping	Self	105				-.41	-.35
	Positive effect	Self	105	.28			.31	-.27
Hendriks et al., 1999b								
	DSM-IV total	Self	143	-.29		-.23	-.38	
	ICD-10 total	Self	143	-.26		-.20	-.42	
Nauta & Sanders, 2000								
	Contending	Self	77		-.31		-.31	
	Avoiding	Self	77					-.40
Van der Zee et al., 1999								
	Downw. identific.	Self	112	0.19			-.44	
	Upward identific.	Self	112	0.19				
	Upward contrast	Self	112	0.26				
	Physical well-being	Self	112	0.22			.22	
	Depression	Self	112				-.52	
	Uncertainty	Self	112				-.48	
	Mastery	Self	112				.48	

Note: I = Extraversion, II = Agreeableness, III = Conscientiousness, IV = Emotional Stability, V = Autonomy. BPP = Berkeley Personality Profile, SACBIF = Short Adjective Checklist to measure Big Five, SO = Sensitivity to Others, CMNS = Capacity for Managing New Situations, NC = Need for Cognition, GSE = Generalized Self-Efficacy, BFI = Big Five Inventory, 4DPT = 4-Dimensional Personality Test, MDLS = Meaning directed learning style, RDLS = Reproduction directed learning style, ADLS = Application directed learning style, UDLS = Undirected learning style, WFS = Weeping frequency score, Weeping as Coping = Weeping as a coping style, Positive effect = Experiencing positive effects of weeping, DSM-IV total and ICD-10 total = total number of criteria met, Contending = Imposing one's preferred solution on the other party, Avoiding = A (temporal) withdrawel from the conflict issue. [a]Averaged values. [b]Combined. [c]Absolute values.

Emotional Stability showed significant negative correlations ($|.17| \leq r \leq |.49|$, mean $r = -.36$) with the anxious, depressive, borderline, dependent, impulsive, avoidant, paranoid, histrionic, and anankastic (obsessive-compulsive) disorders. These disorders share mainly the feature of overactions to internal and external stimuli. Extraversion showed significant negative correlations ($|.17| \leq r \leq |.39|$, mean $r = -.27$) with the avoidant, schizoid, anxious, depressive, schizotypal, passive aggressive, dependent, obsessive-compulsive, and paranoid disorders. These disorders have mainly social withdrawal in common. Conscientiousness showed significant negative correlations ($|.17| \leq r \leq |.36|$, mean $r = -.24$) with the schizotypal, antisocial (dissocial), histrionic, borderline, passive aggressive, narcissistic, and impulsive disorders. These disorders share features of unreliability and lack of self-discipline. Autonomy showed significant correlations with the avoidant ($r = -.36$), anxious ($r = -.24$), and dependent ($r = -.22$) disorders. Finally, Agreeableness showed significant correlations with the narcissistic ($r = -.25$), dissocial ($r = -.24$), and histrionic ($r = -.19$) disorders. In FFPI other-ratings, generally the same, but weaker, relationships were found, albeit that Extraversion was related to a lesser number of disorders than in self-ratings.

In comparison with other Big-Five measures, some of the FFPI factors seem to tap slightly different aspects of behavior. For instance, FFPI Disagreeableness refers primarily to seeing to one's own needs first and taking advantage of other people, rather than antagonistic features like vindictiveness and lack of trust that are part of NEO Disagreeableness. Thus, not surprisingly, we found Agreeableness to be (negatively) related to the narcissistic but not the paranoid and borderline disorders. FFPI Unconscientiousness includes irresponsibility and neglect, next to lacking orderliness, planfulness, and discipline. This may explain why we found Conscientiousness weakly negatively related to disorders that can be said to have some maladjustment in common: the schizotypal, antisocial, borderline, histrionic, and narcissistic disorders. However, finding these relationships with Conscientiousness is not uncommon.

Adema, Van der Zee, and Van der Molen (2000) examined the relationship between personality and learning styles in a sample of 193 second-year students of psychology. They found significant zero-order correlations for all five FFPI factors. In accordance with expectations, particularly Conscientiousness and Autonomy appeared significant predictors, Autonomy primarily to the meaning directed learning style (e.g., "I check whether the conclusions of the authors flow logically from the facts on which they were based"), Conscientiousness to the reproduction directed (e.g., "I line up the most important facts and learn these by heart") and undirected learning styles (e.g., "I have little faith in my own study-capabilities"), see Table 6. These are meaningful relationships: whereas Conscientiousness refers primarily to working hard and systematically, Autonomy encompasses analytical engagement (Hendriks, 1997). Unexpectedly, Emotional Stability contributed at the level of subcomponents (not reported in Table 6): emotionally unstable students tended to use an undirected regulation strategy, being insecure about their own directions but unable to benefit from others' directions. Conceivably, strong feelings of anxiety inhibit proper thinking and listening to others. Also unexpected,

Agreeableness appeared associated with the application directed learning style (e.g., "If I have the possibility to choose, I especially take courses that seem useful for my future vocation"). This relationship may be sample specific: most psychology students are oriented to study subjects that are of practical use and score high on Agreeableness.

De Fruyt (1997) examined the relationship between personality and adult crying in a sample of 105 second-year students of psychology and their relatives. Except for Autonomy (no counterpart), almost identical correlations were found with FFPI and NEO-PI-R factors. As regards the FFPI, Emotional Stability and Autonomy were found to be associated with weeping frequency and weeping as a coping style; Extraversion and Emotional Stability proved to be associated with experiencing positive effects of weeping (Table 6). Emotionally unstable subjects and subjects low on Autonomy weeped and perceived weeping as a coping style significantly more often than emotionally stable subjects and subjects high on Autonomy; relationships were statistically significant even after partialling gender and age. Being overwhelmed by emotions is one of the characteristics of people scoring low on Emotional Stability. And, as far as crying is induced by situations one cannot handle, people high on Autonomy will be less likely to find themselves in such situations than people low on Autonomy. Emotionally stable and extraverted subjects experienced more positive effects and relief after crying than unstable and introverted subjects. No significant associations were found on experiencing negative effects of weeping. It is quite conceivable that positive feelings vanish when crying becomes more of a habit (unstable subjects). Extraverts are in general more positive and more comfortable with expressing their feelings than are introverts.

Nauta and Sanders (2000) examined the relationship between style of negotiation behavior and the Big Five personality factors as operationalized in the FFPI in a sample of 77 managers and employees in 11 manufacturing companies. A combination of high extraversion and high agreeableness appeared significantly positively associated with problem solving behavior. A combination of high extraversion and low agreeableness appeared significantly positively associated with contending behavior (imposing one's preferred solution on the other party). However, unexpectedly, the strongest associations were found for Emotional Stability and Autonomy (Table 6). Emotional Unstability (Neuroticism) inhibited contending behavior. Autonomy inhibited avoiding behavior (a [temporal] withdrawal from the conflict issue). Albeit unexpected, these are meaningful relationships, demonstrating the construct validity of the FFPI factors. Contending behavior, or competition, may be unattractive to individuals who are emotionally unstable, because such situations may upset them. Avoiding behavior in negotiations may contain an element of not grasping a conflict issue, or lacking the intellectual skills to approach an issue (Nauta & Sanders, 2000, p. 152).

Van der Zee *et al.* (1999) examined the relationship between social comparison processes and the Big Five personality factors as operationalized in the FFPI in a sample of 112 patients with various forms of cancer. Personality, social comparison processes, and physical and psychological (depression, uncertainty, and mastery) well-being were assessed at the beginning of treatment; physical and psychological well-being were assesed again at the end of treatment. As expected, Neuroticism (Emotional Unstability) was associated with downward identification, i.e. identification with fellow patients who were doing worse. And, as expected, Extraversion was associated with both upward and downward identification, indicating that extraverts identify themselves with others more than introverts. Unexpectedly, however, Extraversion was most strongly associated with upward contrasting, i.e. comparing oneself to others who are doing better ("When I think about others who are doing better than I am, I sometimes feel frustrated about my situation", see Van der Zee *et al.*, ibid.). But this, initially counterintuitive, finding could be explained also by a general tendency of extraverts to be oriented to the external world: to compare to others and strive for what others have achieved (cf. ambition). Neuroticism showed significant relationships with psychological well-being at the end of treatment, even after controlling for the level of psychological well-being at the beginning of treatment. A relationship between Neuroticism and psychological well-being is a well established finding (Costa & McCrae, 1992; Matthews, Saklofske, Costa, Deary, & Zeidner, 1998).

To summarize, most authors (Adema *et al.*, 2000; De Fruyt, 1997; Nauta & Sanders, 2000; Van der Zee *et al.*, 1999) experienced some unexpected results. Still, all found meaningful relationships, providing evidence for the construct validity of the FFPI.

Cross-cultural generalizability

The FFPI has been translated into 17 languages as yet. Hendriks, Perugini and others (2001) examined the cross-cultural generalizability of the FFPI in 13 European and non-European nations. The data set encompassed representatives of the Germanic (Belgium, England, Germany, the Netherlands, USA), Romance (Italy, Spain), and Slavic (Croatia, Czech Republic, Slovakia) branches of the Indo-European languages, as well as Semito-Hamitic (Israel) and Altaic (Hungary, Japan) language families. All samples except the smallest one ($N = 97$) showed clear five-factor structures. High congruence coefficients were found between each sample structure and Dutch and American large-sample reference structures (mean congruence values ϕ are given in Table 5). More than 80 per cent of the items were equally stable within each country. The internal consistencies of the five factors were generally good, as is illustrated by the mean αs after procrustes rotation to the Dutch reference structure (.87, .84, .84, .84, .79, for I to V), given in Table 5.

The FFPI in practice

The FFPI can be used for self-ratings and other-ratings equally well. In case of self-ratings, the third-person item format invites the subject to take an objective perspective. Completion of the FFPI will take a subject 10-15 minutes. The FFPI can be administered in private or in classroom settings. Its use is restricted to psychologists and other disciplines licensed for psychodiagnostics.

Subjects and samples

The FFPI is suitable for subjects of approximately 12 years of age and older (Szirmák, 2001). An education completed at the level of primary school should be sufficient. All items of the FFPI fulfill the criterion of scoring below 1.07 on a 3-point scale ranging from 1 (*perfectly comprehensible*) to 3 (*totally incomprehensible*), as judged by 45 students from a local school for lower professional training, Groningen, the Netherlands.

In the oldest age group, subjects may need personal assistance in the correct use of the rating scale: some people in homes for the elderly tended to answer the items with "yes" or "no" (Scheirs, Vingerhoets, & Hendriks, 1997). A good criterion for whether or not assistance is needed might be a person's living circumstances: if subjects are able to take care of their daily living themselves, they should also be able to complete the FFPI without any assistance.

The FFPI is primarily meant for use in samples from the normal population. Preliminary findings suggest that the FFPI is reliable and valid also in samples of patients with physical complaints (Hendriks, 2000). Concerning its use with patients with psychiatric complaints, additional research is needed (Hendriks, Ostendorf *et al.*, 2001).

Instructions

Instructions are the same for self- and other-ratings: "The enclosed list contains personality traits. Please fill in behind each trait the amount to which this trait is applicable to the above named person. Choices are: 1 (*not at all applicable*), 2 (*little applicable*), 3 (*only moderately applicable*), 4 (*largely applicable*), 5 (*entirely applicable*). (Followed by an example). "If you are in doubt, please compare the person to be rated with others you know well. Please don't skip traits". In case of self-ratings, "yourself" is mentioned as the "person to be rated".

For (non-psychiatric) patients, it is advised to let the general instructions be preceded by a situation-specific instruction, such as the following for hospital patients (self-ratings): "Please let your answers *not* be influenced by your current condition resulting from your illness or any other reason for having been hospitalized. What this questionnaire is about is how you came to know yourself in the course of your lifetime." (Hendriks, 2000).

Scoring

The FFPI is scored according to rotated principal components (Hofstee *et al.*, 1998), which means that item weights are used to calculate a person's (five) uncorrelated factor scores from his or her 100 item responses. In research settings, a paper-and-pencil version of the FFPI is probably the one most widely used. Still, computerized scoring can and should take place; it takes less than two minutes to enter the 100 item responses onto a computer. As mentioned before, a stand-alone (Pascal) scoring program is obtainable from the first author, but for scientific research purposes only. This scoring program makes use of the matrix of item weights B established in a large and representative Dutch sample ($N = 2,494$). In the near future, this B will be replaced by the matrix of item weights established in a cross-national validation study in 13 countries (Hendriks, Perugini *et al.*, 2001). If a data set contains missing values, the scoring program substitutes a person's mean score (rounded to the nearest integer value) across the nonmissing items, separately for each factor pole, prior to calculating factor scores. To a total of 50 per cent of the item responses (5 per factor pole) may be missing; however, with an increasing number of missing item responses, factor scores should be interpreted with caution.

A computerized version of the FFPI or mail-in scoring service for the paper-and-pencil version will become available from a commercial publisher upon completion of the manual in a particular language, which is, up to now, only the case in the Netherlands. Then specific information like *facet* scores can also be easily obtained. A disadvantage is that, once commercially published (like in the Netherlands), the FFPI can no longer be obtained for free. Note, however, that the utility of facet scores lies in the applied context only. Facet scores (e.g., V+I+) contain no specific variance over and above the variance accounted for by the two pertaining factors (i.e. Autonomy and Extraversion). Thus, for correlational research purposes, the five factor scores suffice.

Anchored scores

The FFPI-scoring device produces compatible anchored factor scores (Hofstee & Hendriks, 1998). These are standardized scores anchored at the scale midpoint: they preserve absolute information. Whereas regular or standard factor scores are centered at the mean of the population ($M = 0$, $SD = 1$), the mean of compatible anchored factor scores (anchored scores) in a population may deviate considerably from zero, in a positive (socially desirable) direction ($M > 0$, $SD = 1$). The difference may be illustrated by the following example. Imagine a person who fills in a set of Extraversion/Introversion items and scores on average "3.5" on a 5-point scale (Introversion items reflected). If the mean score of his/her fellow-subjects is higher, our subject would be reported to be slightly introverted (below the mean), relative to the others. With anchored scores, our subject would be reported to be slightly extraverted (scoring slightly above the scale midpoint). Compatible anchored factor scores and regular factor scores show the same factor structure: they are linear transformations, differing by only a constant, namely the mean anchored score (for details, see Hofstee & Hendriks, 1998). In other words, the two types of factor scores do not make a difference in findings in correlational research. The surplus value of anchored factor scores lies in the applied context.

Contexts

Like any other personality questionnaire, the FFPI can be used for (1) scientific research at the level of groups of people and (2) diagnostic purposes at the level of the individual. Concerning the latter, applied, purposes, one should think primarily of contexts in which it is in the interest of the client to be well advised, like in counseling or educational and vocational guidance; much more than in the former contexts, in the selection context convergent information from other measures (e.g., assessment center) is needed. In clinical practice, one may think of matching treatments to personalities (Miller, 1991).

In clinical contexts, the need for additional ratings next to a patient's self-rating, e.g., from family members or others who know the patient well, might be self-evident. But also more generally, mean scores across a number of raters are to be preferred to one self- or other-rating, because averaging across raters reduces error variance (Hofstee, 1994).

An application that explicitly asks for a number of raters is the assessment of "ideal" personality profiles, e.g., for specific professions, treatments, or occupations. The procedure would be that 5 to 10 experts complete the FFPI with the ideal student, patient, applicant, or whatever is the focus of interest in mind. Ratings are averaged across raters. Such profiles may help in clarifying expectations, conditions, or preconceived opinions on the part of the provider (educational institute, inpatient's or outpatient's clinic, employer). They may thus offer additional information (e.g., to students) or a point of departure for further discussion (e.g., definition of job requirements). When relevant, empirical and ideal profiles could be matched, e.g., by calculating their Euclidian distance in five-space (Hofstee, 1999): $\sqrt{([I_i - I_e]^2 + [II_i - II_e]^2 + [III_i - III_e]^2 + [IV_i - IV_e]^2 + [V_i - V_e]^2)}$, with subscripts "e" denoting the individual's factor score and "i" the ideal factor score.

Translations of the FFPI

The FFPI has been translated into the following languages: Brazilian-Portuguese, Chinese, Croatian, Czech, (American- and UK-)English, German, Greek, Hebrew, Hungarian, Italian, Japanese, Norwegian, Polish, Rumanian, Slovakian, Spanish, and Swedish. Colleagues who would be interested in one of these versions or in producing a translation into a language not yet mentioned may contact the first author.

Existence of norms

As yet, norms (Hendriks *et al.*, 1999a) are available in the Netherlands only. They can be obtained from the publisher.

Conclusion

The psychometric properties of the FFPI in normal population samples are well-established by now. Reliability and construct validity proved to be good to excellent and were found to be remarkably stable across a variety of samples in many different countries. Preliminary findings in patient samples are promising. Certainly, additional data need to be collected on predictive (criterion) validity. Furthermore, the instruments' validity in specific settings (e.g., the selection context) needs to be explored. The FFPI is a relatively "young" instrument and building the nomological network takes time. Given the results so far, however, our expectations are high.

References

Adema, J., Van der Zee, K.I., & Van der Molen, H.T. (2000, July). *Exploring the relationship between learning styles and personality*. Paper presented at the 10th European Conference on Personality, Cracow, Poland.

Allport, G.W., & Odbert, H.S. (1936). Trait-names: A psycho-lexical study. *Psychological Monographs, 47* (1, Whole No. 211).

Angleitner, A., & Ostendorf, F. (1994). Temperament and the Big Five factors of personality. In C.F. Halverson, Jr., G.A. Kohnstamm, & R.P. Martin (Eds.), *The developing structure of temperament and personality from infancy to adulthood* (pp. 69-90). Hillsdale, NJ: Lawrence Erlbaum Associates.

Ashton, M.C. (1998). Personality and job performance: The importance of narrow traits. *Journal of Organizational Behavior, 19*, 289-303.

Ashton, M.C., Jackson, D.N., Paunonen, S.V., Helmes, E., & Rothstein, M.G. (1995). The criterion validity of broad factor scales versus specific facet scales. *Journal of Research in Personality, 29*, 432-442.

Bagby, R.M., Costa, P.T., Jr., McCrae, R.R., Livesley, W.J., Kennedy, S.H., Levitan, R.D., Levitt, A.J., Joffe, R.T., & Young, L.T. (1999). Replicating the five factor model of personality in a psychiatric sample. *Personality and Individual Differences, 27*, 1135-1139.

Bekker, M.H.J. (1993). The development of an Autonomy scale based on recent insights into gender identity. *European Journal of Personality, 7*, 177-194.

Block, J. (1995). A contrarian view of the Five-Factor approach to personality description. *Psychological Bulletin, 117*, 187-215.

Breaugh, J.A., & Becker, A.S. (1987). Further examinations of the Work Autonomy Scales: Three studies. *Human Relations, 40*, 381-400.

Briggs, S.R. (1992). Assessing the Five-Factor Model of personality description. *Journal of Personality, 60*, 253-293.

Brokken, F.B. (1978). *The language of personality.* Unpublished doctoral dissertation. University of Groningen, The Netherlands.

Caprara, G.V., Barbaranelli, C., Borgogni, L., & Perugini, M. (1993). The "Big Five Questionnaire": A new questionnaire to assess the Five Factor Model. *Personality and Individual Differences, 15*, 281-288.

Cattell, R.B. (1943). The description of personality: Basic traits resolved into clusters. *Journal of Abnormal and Social Psychology, 38*, 476-506.

Cattel, R.B. (1945). The description of personality: Principals and findings in a factor analyses. American Journal of Psychology, 58, 69-90.

Cattell, R.B. (1947). Confirmation and clarification of primary personality factors. *Psychometrika, 12*, 197-220.

Clark, D.A., Steer, R.A., Beck, A.T., & Ross, L. (1995). Psychometric characteristics of revised Sociotropy and Autonomy Scales in college students. *Behavior Research and Therapy, 33*, 325-334.

Costa, P.T., Jr., & McCrae, R.R. (1990). Personality disorders and the five-factor model of personality. *Journal of Personality Disorders, 4*, 362-371.

Costa, P.T., Jr., & McCrae, R.R. (1992). *NEO PI-R: Professional Manual.* Odessa, FL: Psychological Assessment Recources.

Costa, P.T., Jr., Yang, J., & McCrae, R.R. (1998). Aging and personality traits: Generalizations and clinical implications. In I.H. Nordhus, G.R. VandenBos, S. Berg, & P. Fromholt (Eds.), *Clinical geropsychology* (pp. 33-48). Washington, DC: American Psychological Association.

Crant, J.M., & Bateman, T. (2000). Charismatic leadership viewed from above: The impact of proactive personality. *Journal of Organizational Behavior, 21*, 63-75.

Cronbach, L.J. (1977). *Educational Psychology* (3rd ed.). New York: Harcourt Brace Jovanovich.

Deary, I.J., Peter, A., Austin, E., & Gibson, G. (1998). Personality traits and personality disorders. *British Journal of Psychology, 89*, 647-661.

Deci, E.L., & Ryan, R.M. (1985). The General Causality Orientations scale: Self-determination in personality. *Journal of Research in Personality, 19*, 109-134.

Deci, E.L., & Ryan, R.M. (1987). The support of autonomy and the control of behavior. *Journal of Personality and Social Psychology, 53*, 1024-1037.

De Fruyt, F. (1997). Gender and individual differences in adult crying. *Personality and Individual Differences, 22*, 937-940.

De Raad, B. (1992). The replicability of the Big Five personality dimensions in three word-classes of the Dutch language. *European Journal of Personality, 6*, 15-29.

De Raad, B. (2000). *The Big Five personality factors: The psycholexical approach to personality.* Göttingen: Hogrefe & Huber.

De Raad, B., Hendriks, A.A.J., & Hofstee, W.K.B. (1992). Towards a refined structure of personality traits. *European Journal of Personality, 6*, 301-319.

De Raad, B., Mulder, E., Kloosterman, K., & Hofstee, W.K.B. (1988). Personality-descriptive verbs. *European Journal of Personality, 2*, 81-96.

De Raad, B., & Van Heck, G.L. (Eds.) (1994). The fifth of the Big Five. *European Journal of Personality, 8*, Special Issue.

Digman, J.M. (1990). Personality structure: Emergence of the five-factor model. In M. R. Rosenzweig & L.W. Porter (Eds.), *Annual Review of Psychology* (Vol. 41, pp. 417-440). Palo Alto, CA: Annual Reviews.

Digman, J.M., & Inouye, J. (1986). Further specification of the five robust factors of personality. *Journal of Personality and Social Psychology, 50*, 116-123.

Duijsens, I.J. (1996). *Assessment of personality disorders: Construction, reliability and validity of the VKP self-report*. Lisse: Swets & Zeitlinger.

Edwards, A.L. (1954). *Edwards Personal Preference Schedule, Manual*. New York: Psychology Corporation.

Elshout, J.J., & Akkerman, A.E. (1975). *Vijf-Persoonlijkheidsfactoren Test (5PFT): Handleiding* [Five Personality Factors Test: Manual]. Nijmegen: Berkhout.

Erikson, E.H. (1968). *Identity, youth and crisis*. New York: Norton and Company.

Eysenck, H.J. (1991). Dimensions of personality: 16, 5 or 3?-Criteria for a taxonomic paradigm. *Personality and Individual Differences, 12*, 773-790.

Fiske, D.W. (1949). Consistency of the factorial structures of personality ratings from different sources. *Journal of Abnormal and Social Psychology, 44*, 329-344.

Goldberg, L.R. (1981). Language and individual differences: The search for universals in personality lexicons. In L. Wheeler (Ed.), *Review of personality and social psychology* (Vol. 2, pp. 141-165). Beverly Hills, CA: Sage.

Goldberg, L.R. (1982). From Ace to Zombie: Some explorations in the language of personality. In C.D. Spielberger & J.N. Butcher (Eds.), *Advances in Personality Assess-ment* (Vol. 1, pp. 203-234). Hillsdale, NJ: Erlbaum.

Goldberg, L.R. (1990). An alternative "Description of Personality": The Big-Five factor structure. *Journal of Personality and Social Psychology, 59*, 1216-1229.

Goldberg, L.R. (1992). The development of markers of the Big-Five factor structure. *Psychological Assessment, 4*, 26-42.

Goldberg, L.R. (1993). The structure of phenotypic personality traits. *American Psychologist, 48*, 26-34.

Gough, H.G., & Heilbrun, A.B. (1983). *The Adjective Checklist, Manual*. Palo Alto, CA: Consulting Psychologists Press.

Harary, K., & Donahue, E. (1994). *Who do you think you are? Explore your many-sided self with the Berkeley Personality Profile*. San Francisco: Harper.

Haven, S., & Ten Berge, J.M.F. (1977). Tucker's coefficient of congruence as a measure of factorial invariance: An empirical study. *Heymans Bulletins, 290* EX. Department of Psychology, University of Groningen.

Haworth, L. (1986). *Autonomy. An essay in philosophical psychology and ethics*. New Haven: Yale University Press.

Hendriks, A.A.J. (1997). *The construction of the Five-Factor Personality Inventory*. Unpublished doctoral dissertation, University of Groningen, The Netherlands.

Hendriks, A.A.J. (2000). *The validity and reliability of the FFPI for assessing hospital (in)patients' personality profiles*. Manuscript submitted for publication.

Hendriks, A.A.J., Hofstee, W.K. B., & De Raad, B. (1999a). *Handleiding bij de Five-Factor Personality Inventory (FFPI)* [The Five-Factor Personality Inventory: Professional Manual]. Lisse: Swets Test Publishers.

Hendriks, A.A.J., Hofstee, W.K.B., & De Raad, B. (1999b). The Five-Factor Personality Inventory (FFPI). *Personality and Individual Differences, 27*, 307-325.

Hendriks, A.A.J., Hofstee, W.K.B., De Raad, B., & Angleitner, A. (1995). *The Five-Factor Personality Inventory (FFPI)*. Unpublished manuscript, Department of Psychol- ogy, University of Groningen, The Netherlands.

Hendriks, A.A.J., Ostendorf, F., & Dieckmann, A. (2001). *The reliability and construct validity of the FFPI in a sample of inpatients and outpatients with psychopathology*. Manuscript in preparation, Academic Medical Center/University of Amsterdam.

Hendriks, A.A.J., Perugini, M., Angleitner, A., Ostendorf, F., Johnson, J.A., De Fruyt, F., Hrebícková, M., Murakami, T., Bratko, D., Conner, M., Nagy, J., Nussbaum, S., Rodrí-guez-Fornells, A., & Ruisel, I. (2001). *The Five-Factor Personality Inventory: Cross-cultural generalizability across 13 countries.* Manuscript submitted for publication.

Hirschfeld, R.M.A., Klerman, G.L., Gough, H.G., Barrett, J., Korchin, S.J., & Chodoff, P. (1977). A measure of interpersonal dependency. *Journal of Personality Assessment, 41,* 610-618.

Hoekstra, H.A., Ormel, J., & De Fruyt, F. (1996). *Handleiding bij de NEO Persoonlijkheids Vragenlijsten NEO-PI-R en NEO-FFI* [NEO Personality Inventories NEO-PI-R and NEO-FFI: Professional Manual]. Lisse: Swets Test Publishers.

Hofstee, W.K.B. (1991). *Richtlijnen voor het schrijven van vragenlijstitems* [Guidelines for writing inventory items]. Internal note. Department of Personality and Educational Psychology, University of Groningen, The Netherlands.

Hofstee, W.K.B. (1994). Who should own the definition of personality? *European Journal of Personality, 8,* 149-162.

Hofstee, W.K.B. (1999). Big-Five-profielen van persoonlijkheidsstoornissen: Psychodia-gnostisch gereedschap [Big Five profiles of personality disorders: Psychodiagnostic tools]. *De Psycholoog, 9,* 381-384.

Hofstee, W.K.B., Brokken, F.B., & Land, H. (1981). Constructie van een Standaard Persoonlijkheids Eigenschappen Lijst (SPEL) [Construction of a Standard List of Personality Traits (SPEL)]. *Nederlands Tijdschrift voor de Psychologie, 36,* 443-452.

Hofstee, W.K.B., & De Raad, B. (1991). Persoonlijkheidsstructuur: De AB5C-taxonomie van Nederlandse eigenschapstermen [Personality structure: The AB5C taxonomy of Dutch trait terms]. *Nederlands Tijdschrift voor de Psychologie, 46,* 262-274.

Hofstee, W.K.B., De Raad, B., & Goldberg, L.R. (1992). Integration of the Big Five and circumplex approaches to trait structure. *Journal of Personality and Social Psychology, 63,* 146-163.

Hofstee, W.K.B., & Hendriks, A.A.J. (1998). The use of scores anchored at the scale midpoint in reporting individuals' traits. *European Journal of Personality, 12,* 219-228.

Hofstee, W.K.B., Ten Berge, J.M.F., & Hendriks, A.A.J. (1998). How to score questionnaires. *Personality and Individual Differences, 25,* 897-909.

Hurtz, G.M., & Donovan, J.J. (2000). Personality and job performance: The Big Five revisited. *Journal of Applied Psychology, 85,* 869-879.

Jackson, D.N. (1984). *Personality Research Form, Manual* (3rd ed.). Port Huron, MI: Sigma Assessment Systems.

John, O.P. (1990). The 'Big Five' factor taxonomy: Dimensions of personality in the natural language and in questionnaires. In L.A. Pervin (Ed.), *Handbook of Personality: Theory and research* (pp. 66-100). New York: Guilford.

John, O.P., Angleitner, A., & Ostendorf, F. (1988). The lexical approach to personality: A historical review of trait taxonomic research. *European Journal of Personality, 2,* 171-203.

John, O.P., Donahue, E.M., & Kentle, R.L. (1991, July). *The "Big Five" Inventory: Versions 4a and 54.* Technical Report. Berkeley, CA: Institute of Personality Assessment and Research.

Kiers, H.A.L. (1997). Techniques for rotating two or more loading matrices to optimal agreement and simple structure: A comparison and some technical details. *Psychometri-ka, 62,* 545-568.

Knee, C.R., & Zuckerman, M. (1998). A nondefensive personality: Autonomy and Control as moderators of defensive coping and self-handicapping. *Journal of Research in Personality, 32*, 115-130.

Matthews, G., Saklofske, D.H., Costa, P. T., Jr., Deary, I.J., & Zeidner, M. (1998). Dimensional models of personality: A framework for systematic clinical assessment. *European Journal of Psychological Assessment, 14*, 36-49.

McAdams, D.P. (1992). The five-factor model in personality: A critical appraisal. *Journal of Personality, 60*, 329-361.

McCrae, R.R., & Costa, P.T., Jr. (1997). Personality structure as a human universal. *American Psychologist, 52*, 509-516.

McCrae, R.R., Zonderman, A.B., Costa, P.T., Jr., Bond, M.H., & Paunonen, S.V. (1996). Evaluating replicability of factors in the Revised NEO Personality Inventory: Confirmatory factor analysis versus Procrustes rotation. *Journal of Personality and Social Psychology, 70*, 552-566.

Metaal, N. (1992). *Persoonlijke autonomie. Een psychologische studie naar alledaagse verklaringen* [Personal autonomy. A psychological study of ordinary explanations]. Lisse: Swets & Zeitlinger.

Miller, D.M., Lynam, D.R., Widiger, T.A., & Leukefeld, C. (2001). Personality disorders as extreme variants of common personality dimensions: Can the Five-Factor Model adequately represent psychopathy? *Journal of Personality, 69*, 253-276.

Miller, T.R. (1991). The psychotherapeutic utility of the Five-Factor Model of personality: A clinician's experience. *Journal of Personality Assessment, 57*, 415-433.

Mills, J.K. (1994). Interpersonal dependency correlates and locus of control orientation among obese adults in outpatient treatment for obesity. *The Journal of Psychology, 128*, 667-674.

Murray, H.A. (1938). *Explorations in personality*. New York: Oxford University Press.

Nauta, A., & Sanders, K. (2000). Interdepartmental negotiation behavior in manufacturing organizations. *International Journal of Conflict Management, 11*, 135-161.

Norman, W.T. (1963). Toward an adequate taxonomy of personality attributes: Replicated factor structure in peer nomination personality ratings. *Journal of Abnormal and Social Psychology, 66*, 574-583.

Ostendorf, F. (1990). *Sprache und Persönlichkeitsstruktur: Zur Validität des Fünf-Faktoren-Modells der Persönlichkeit* [Language and personality structure: Towards the validity of the five-factor model of personality]. Regensburg: Roderer.

Ostendorf, F., & Angleitner, A. (1992). On the generality and comprehensiveness of the Five-Factor model of personality. Evidence for five robust factors in questionnaire data. In G-V. Caprara & G.L. Van Heck (Eds.), *Modern personality psychology. Critical reviews and new directions*. New York: Harvester Wheatsheaf.

Paunonen, S.V., & Jackson, D.N. (2000). What is beyond the Big Five? Plenty! *Journal of Personality, 68*, 821-835.

Paunonen, S.V., Jackson, D.N., & Keikonen, M. (1990). The structured nonverbal assessment of personality. *Journal of Personality, 58*, 481-502.

Peabody, D., & Goldberg, L.R. (1989). Some determinants of factor structures from personality-trait descriptors. *Journal of Personality and Social Psychology, 57*, 552-567.

Perugini, M., & Ercolani, A.P. (1998). Validity of the Five Factor Personality Inventory (FFPI): An investigation in Italy. *European Journal of Psychological Assessment, 14*, 234-248.

Perugini, M., & Leone, L. (1996). Construction and validation of a Short Adjectives Checklist to measure Big Five (SACBIF). *European Journal of Psychological Assessment, 12*, 33-42.

Riesman, D., Denney, R., & Glazer, N. (1950). *The lonely crowd. A study of the changing American character.* New Haven: Yale University Press.

Robertson, I., & Callinan, M. (1998). Personality and work behaviour. *European Journal of Work and Organizational Psychology, 7*, 321-340.

Rodríguez-Fornells, A., Lorenzo-Seva, U., & Andrés-Pueyo, A. (2001). Psychometric properties of the Spanish adaptation of the Five-Factor Personality Inventory. *European Journal of Psychological Assessment, 17*, 145-153.

Ryff, C.D. (1989). Happiness is everything, or is it? Explorations on the meaning of psychological well-being. *Journal of Personality and Social Psychology, 57*, 1069-1081.

Saucier, G. (1992). Openness versus Intellect: Much ado about nothing? *European Journal of Personality, 6*, 381-386.

Saucier, G., & Ostendorf, F. (1999). Hierarchical subcomponents of the Big Five personality factors: A cross-language replication. *Journal of Personality and Social Psychology, 76*, 613-627.

Scheirs, J., Vingerhoets, A., & Hendriks, J. (1997). Hoe zit het nou echt met dat Brabantse karakter? De Brabantse persoonlijkheid bezien door een psychologische bril [What are the facts concerning the Brabant character? Inspecting Brabant personality through psychological spectacles]. *Brabants Heem, 49*, 81-90.

Soldz, S., Budman, S., Demby, A., & Merry, J. (1993). Representation of personality disorders in circumplex and five-factor space: Explorations with a clinical sample. *Psychological Assessment, 5*, 41-52.

Szirmák, Z. (2001). *The Big Five in young adolescence.* Manuscript in preparation, Free University of Berlin.

Ten Berge, J.M.F. (1999). A legitimate case of component analysis of ipsative measures, and partialling the mean as an alternative to ipsatization. *Multivariate Behavioral Research, 34*, 89-102.

Ten Berge, J.M.F., & Hofstee, W.K.B. (1999). Coefficients alpha and reliabilities of unrotated and rotated components. *Psychometrika, 64*, 83-90.

Trapnell, P.D., & Wiggins, J.S. (1990). Extension of the Interpersonal Adjectives Scales to include the Big Five dimensions of personality. *Journal of Personality and Social Psychology, 59*, 781-790.

Trull, T.J. (1992). DSM-III-R personality disorders and the Five-Factor model of personality: An empirical comparison. *Journal of Abnormal Psychology, 101*, 553-560.

Tupes, E.C., & Christal, R.E. (1961). Recurrent personality factors based on trait ratings. Technical Report ASD-TR-61-97, Lackland Air Force Base, TX: U.S. Air Force. Republished in *Journal of Personality, 60*, 225-251 (1992).

Van der Zee, K.I., Buunk, B.P., Sanderman, R., Botke, G., & Van den Bergh, F. (1999). The Big Five and identification-contrast processes in social comparison in adjustment to cancer treatment. *European Journal of Personality, 13*, 307-326.

Van Kampen, D. (1996). *Basic personality factors from clinical/theoretical perspective.* Unpublished doctoral dissertation, Vrije Universiteit, Amsterdam, The Netherlands.

Wiggins, J.S. (1979). A psychological taxonomy of trait-descriptive terms: The interpersonal domain. *Journal of Personality and Social Psychology, 37*, 395-412.

Wong, M.M. (2000). The relations among causality orientations, academic experience, academic performance, and academic commitment. *Personality and Social Psychology Bulletin, 26*, 315-326.

Young, R. (1986). *Personal autonomy: Beyond negative and positive liberty*. The Hague: Croom Helm.

Chapter 5

Studies of the Big Five Questionnaire

Claudio Barbaranelli
Gian Vittorio Caprara

Introduction

The Big Five Questionnaire has been developed for the assessment of the Big Five Model of personality traits (BFM) using a rational-based, or "top down" approach, that moves from theoretically defined personality dimensions to identify the appropriate items representing measures of them (see Burisch, 1984). According to this approach, once the Big Five were identified as the high-order, most recurrent factors of personality, facets or subdimensions were identified from a scanning of the pertinent literature, and sentence-items were produced to assess these constructs. Compared to other sentence-based questionnaires developed for measuring the Big Five (e.g., NEO Personality Inventory, Costa & McCrae, 1985; 1992; Hogan Personality Inventory, Hogan, 1986), the BFQ presents some special features. First, it represents a relatively parsimonious and economical measure of the Big Five in terms of number of facets referred to in each primary dimension, and in terms of number of sentences produced. Second, it includes a scale designed to measure social desirability. Furthermore, a major distinctive feature with regards to the Big Five "orthodoxy" concerns the definition of Factor I. Although the more common label for the first factor of the Big Five has been "Extraversion", we preferred to use the label "Energy". This claim does not repose on a mere linguistic preference, rather it derives from a close scrutiny of the adjectives found under Factor I in psycho-lexical studies (e.g., Caprara & Perugini, 1994; Goldberg, 1990; 1992; see also John, 1989; 1990), as well as from careful consideration of the meanings actually conveyed by the words "extraversion" and "extravert". Adjectives such as active, dynamic, energetic, lively, vigorous are usually found under Factor I. Moreover, in Webster's (1974) unabridged dictionary of American English one may find under *extraversion* "an attitude in which a person directs his/her interest to phenomena outside him-herself rather than to his/her own experience and feelings" (p. 652), and under *extravert* "a person whose interest is more in his/her environment and in other people than in

Big Five Assessment, edited by B. De Raad & M. Perugini. © 2002, Hogrefe & Huber Publishers.

him-herself, a person who is active and expressive" (p. 652).

While it still holds that few personality constructs have remained as controversial and as productive of research over the years as extraversion-introversion (Carrigan, 1960), we believe that research does not benefit from a dimension which often does not distinguish "ease in interpersonal relationships" from "activity, vigor, energy". Ultimately, "Energy" seemed more appropriate to convey the character of vigor, activity and strength of Factor I, as well as to capture important aspects of personality that other taxonomies have considered under the labels of "activity" and "level of activity" (see, e.g., Buss & Plomin, 1984; Comrey, 1980; Guilford, 1975; Hogan, 1986; Murray, 1938; Strelau, 1983; Zuckerman, 1994; Zuckerman, Kuhlman, Thornquist, & Kiers, 1991). Research on the biological basis of personality suggests the importance of the distinction between temperamental-constitutional features and social features of the construct of Extraversion (Eaves, Eysenck, & Martin, 1989; Eysenck, 1990). Likely, such a distinction would help clarify the patterns of genetic and environmental correlates found in Extraversion as well as its psycho-physiological correlates (Eaves *et al.*, 1989). Accordingly, the BFQ Energy factor was defined to emphasize the dynamic-energetic aspects of Factor I, and to mark better its distinction from Factor II. However, this emphasis did not underscore the interpersonal features of Factor I, that are still considered in many of the items included in the Energy scales, and are explicitly acknowledged in one of its facet scales, namely Dominance.

The BFQ contains five domain scales and ten facet scales, plus a Lie scale designed to measure social desirability and the tendency to distort meanings of the scores. Table 1 presents short definitions of the domain and facet scales of the BFQ.

Table 1. Domain and facets scale of the BFQ

Domain Scales	Facet Scales
Energy: Level of activity, vigour, sociability, talkativeness, assertiveness and dominance, competitiveness, leadership	*Dynamism:* Activity and enthusiasm *Dominance:* Assertiveness and self-confidence
Friendliness: Friendly complience vs. hostility, trust, prosocialness	*Cooperativeness:* Altruism, empathy, generosity, unselfishness *Politeness:* Kindness, civility, docility and trust
Conscientiousness: self-regulation in both its proactive and inhibitory aspects	*Scrupulousness:* Dependability, orderliness and precision *Perseverance:* Capability of fulfilling one's own tasks and commitments, tenaciousness, persistence
Emotional Stability: Capability of controlling one's own emotional reactions, absence of negative affects, psychological well-being	*Emotion Control:* Absence of anxiety, depression and vulnerabililiy, mood stability *Impulse Control:* Capability of controlling irritation, discontent, and anger
Openness: Broadness of cultural interests, tolerance toward differences, need and search for novelty	*Openness to Culture:* Intellectual curiosity, interest in being informed, appreciation of culture *Openness to Experiences:* Openness to novelty, tolerance of values, interest toward diverse people, habits and life-styles

Table 2. Rotated factor matrices (Comrey Tandem Criteria II) in the Italian normative sample

BFQ Facet Scales	Factors				
	E	F	C	S	O
Dynamism	.76	.24	.03	.00	.26
Dominance	.60	-.27	.21	.01	.18
Cooperativeness	.05	.63	.12	.00	.26
Politeness	.05	.71	-.04	.18	.09
Scrupulousness	-.07	.00	.74	.00	-.05
Perseverance	.46	.06	.51	.08	.24
Emotion Control	.16	-.04	.03	.80	.08
Impulse Control	-.11	.24	.06	.82	.03
Openness to Culture	.06	.10	.28	.07	.64
Openness to Experiences	.26	.18	-.05	.03	.69
% of explained variance	12.5	11.3	9.5	13.6	11.3

Note. E = Energy; F = Friendliness; C = Conscientiousness; S = Emotional Stability; O = Openness; N = 9,333.

Each facet scale contains 12 items; in order to control for possible acquiescence response set half the items are positively phrased with respect to the scale name and half are negatively phrased. The Lie (L) scale contains 12 items which are all positively phrased. For each of the 132 items in the questionnaire, the respondent has a 5-choice answer scale that ranges from complete disagreement (1 = very false for me) to complete agreement (5 = very true for me).

The psychometric properties of the BFQ have been repeatedly validated in Italian samples (see Caprara *et al.*, 1993; Caprara, Barbaranelli, & Livi, 1994). Table 2 summarizes the factorial structure of the BFQ on the normative sample that comprises 9,333 subjects (50.5 % females, 49.5 % males) aged from 16 to 84 years old (M = 38.5, SD = 15.7). This solution was obtained by the least-squares principal factor method as implemented in the Comrey program for factor analysis (Comrey, 1973; Comrey & Lee, 1992). The scree test of eigenvalues (Cattell & Vogelmann, 1977) was used as a tool for establishing the number of factors that were present in the solution. The factors were rotated using the Tandem Criteria for orthogonal analytic rotation (Comrey, 1967). In comparison with other rotation methods the Tandem Criteria permits one to obtain factor solutions which are more "clean" and more fitted to the observed correlations among variables (Lee & Comrey, 1979). The solution presented in table 2 is in line with what expected: all the BFQ facet-scales present high loadings on the intended factor, and low loadings on the other factors, with the exception of Perseverance. Finally, Cronbach's alpha values of the different scales ranged from .74 to .90.

Cross-Cultural validity of the BFQ

The BFQ has been translated into different languages. While French, Spanish, and Slovenian versions have already been published, validation studies are in progress for German, English, Dutch, Swedish, Czech, Greek, and Hungarian.

The generalizability of the BFQ across four different countries (Italy, USA, Spain, and Germany) was proved in a recent study where multiple multivariate methods such as Simultaneous Component Analysis, Exploratory, and Confirmatory Factor Analyses were used (Caprara, Barbaranelli, Bermudez, Maslach, & Ruch, 2000). In this study, two kinds of analyses have been performed: An analysis at the level of the single sentences that are used to assess the constructs (item-level analysis), and an analysis at the level of the aggregates of items that define sub-dimensions or facets for the Big Five (scale-level analysis). The results of the item-level analysis evidenced that the items were greatly congruent in measuring the same constructs across countries (i.e., structural equivalence), although they showed some differential functioning in the different countries (i.e., item bias). In the same study, scale-level analyses showed that the Italian, American, German, and Spanish versions of the BFQ have factor structures that are fully comparable. Because the pattern of relationships among the BFQ facet-scales is basically the same in the four different countries, different data analysis strategies (Simultaneous Components Analysis, Exploratory Factor Analysis, Confirmatory Factor Analysis) converge in pointing to a substantial equivalence among the constructs that these scales are measuring.

Table 3 shows results from factor analyses on the 4 different samples. These analyses have been carried out on the facet scales using all the items that turned out *not* be affected by item bias. Congruence coefficients (Tucker, 1951) among the different solutions ranged from .94 to .99. Cronbach's alpha ranged from .74 to .85 in the American sample, from .73 to .87 in the Spanish sample, and from .65 to .85 in the German sample.

Construct validity of the BFQ: Correlations with other instruments

The construct validity of the BFQ has been examined in various studies by correlating its scales with: a) the scales of other Big Five markers such as the NEO-PI (Costa & McCrae, 1985) and the NEO-PI-R (Costa & McCrae, 1992); b) the scales of questionnaires measuring concurrent personality taxonomies such as the Eysenck Personality Questionnaire (EPQ; Eysenck & Eysenck, 1976), the Comrey Personality Scales (CPS; Comrey, 1995), Cattell's 16PF — Form A (Cattell, Eber, & Tatsuoka, 1970), the Multidimensional Personality Questionnaire (MPQ; Tellegen, 1982); c) scales measuring important criterion variables such as the Wechsler Adult Intelligence Scale (WAIS; Wechsler, 1981), and the scales of perceived psychological well-being (PPWB; Ryff, 1989). Table 4 summarizes the findings obtained in these studies.

Table 3. Rotated pattern matrices (Principal Axis Factoring followed by Oblimin rotation) in Italian, American, Spanish and German samples

BFQ Facet Scale	Energy				Friendliness				Conscientiousness				Emotional Stability				Openness			
	ITA	USA	SPA	GER	ITA	USA	SPA	GER	ITA	USA	SPA	GER	ITA	USA	SPA	GER	ITA	USA	SPA	GER
Dynamism	67	76	50	62	24	21	44	37	02	02	01	-08	00	01	-02	03	22	08	18	07
Dominance	65	57	64	66	-32	-17	-07	-12	18	38	09	20	02	-02	-01	-03	07	-04	-05	01
Cooperativeness	04	05	-19	-07	60	51	52	57	17	-01	19	00	03	05	-08	-05	21	28	37	31
Politeness	11	11	-04	03	67	72	69	57	-01	04	00	-06	09	09	04	07	02	-09	-01	-01
Scrupulousness	-13	-13	03	-16	-01	02	-06	-02	76	62	57	64	-03	-06	-01	00	-11	11	-12	-02
Perseverance	35	32	28	29	-01	-03	06	11	44	61	54	57	07	10	04	02	19	14	18	13
Emotion Control	15	28	06	14	-07	-14	01	03	02	-12	-01	01	85	81	81	83	04	06	01	05
Impulse Control	-13	-18	-16	-12	11	14	04	05	13	07	11	07	75	79	81	84	02	-02	-01	03
Openness to Culture	-15	-03	-01	01	-05	-10	01	-08	23	10	20	15	06	02	-01	08	67	72	59	62
Openness to Experiences	23	20	26	25	12	25	13	10	-03	01	01	-11	-03	00	03	-05	64	52	62	68
% Explained Variance	12.6	13.1	9.6	11.4	10.6	10.3	11.1	9.3	9.9	10.5	8.1	8.5	13.4	13.4	13.4	14.3	11.9	10.3	11.6	10.9

Note: Loadings of facets referring to the same factor are in *italics*; ITA = Italy (*N* = 2,324), USA = United States (*N* = 2,324), SPA = Spain (*N* = 741), GER = Germany (*N* = 1,121); Decimal points have been omitted.

Table 4. Correlations of BFQ domain scales with scales of other instruments

	BFQ scales					
	Energy	Friendli-ness	Conscien-tiousness	Emotional Stability	Openness	Lie Scale
NEO-PI (N = 288)						
N Neuroticism	-.37**	-.29**	-.17**	-.80**	-.21**	-.28**
E Extraversion	.71**	.29**	.13*	ns	.36**	-.12*
O Openness to Experience	.27**	.33**	ns	ns	.65**	ns
A Agreeableness	ns	.66**	ns	.21**	.13*	.18**
C Conscientiousness	.31**	ns	.63**	.12*	ns	.23**
NEO-PI-R (N = 695)						
N Neuroticism	ns	.15**	.23**	-.78**	ns	-.18**
E Extraversion	.67**	-.28**	.23**	-.23**	.23**	ns
O Openness to Experience	.36**	.09*	ns	-.16**	.68**	-.16**
A Agreeableness	.36**	.58**	ns	-.12**	.30**	.11**
C Conscientiousness	.09*	ns	.73**	-.19**	ns	.28**
EPQ (N = 186)						
P Psychoticism	ns	-.26**	-.36**	ns	ns	ns
E Extraversion	.63**	.39**	ns	.23**	.26**	.36**
N Neuroticism	-.25**	-.21*	ns	-.75**	-.21*	-.26**
L Lie Scale	ns	.29**	.30**	.32**	ns	.50**
CPS (N = 288)						
T Trust	ns	.47**	ns	.24**	ns	ns
O Orderliness	-.13*	ns	.47**	ns	-.26**	.18**
C Social Conformity	ns	ns	ns	ns	-.31**	.21**
A Activity	.66**	.20**	.42**	.27**	.32**	.15*
S Emotional Stability	.34**	.26**	ns	.71**	.14*	.15*
E Extraversion	.74**	.24**	.12*	.17**	.38**	.24**
M Masculinity	.20**	ns	ns	.38**	.19**	.16**
P Empathy	ns	.57**	ns	.12*	.19**	ns
R Response Bias	.20**	ns	ns	.20**	ns	.16**
V Validity	ns	.34**	.15*	.18*	ns	.37**
MPQ (N = 375)						
NA Negative Affect	ns	-.30**	ns	-.48**	-.18**	ns
PA Positive Affect	.66**	.27**	.36**	ns	.29**	.25**
CT Constraint	-.14*	ns	.43**	.15*	-.22**	.21**
16PF (N = 608)						
A Outgoing	.21**	.19**	.14**	ns	ns	.08*
B Bright	ns	ns	.10**	ns	.14**	-.14**
C Emotionally Stable	.34**	.19**	.17**	.48**	.20**	.26**
E Assertive	.46**	-.19**	.10**	-.17**	.13**	-.17**
F Happy-go-lucky	.51**	.28**	.10**	.11**	.29**	ns
G Conscientious	.08*	.10**	.43**	.08*	ns	.19**
H Venturesome	.63**	.26**	.19**	.32**	.21**	.15**

I Tender Minded	-.24**	.20**	ns	-.10**	.09*	ns
L Suspicious	ns	-.26**	ns	-.30**	ns	-.32**
M Imaginative	ns	.15**	ns	.13**	.27**	ns
N Shrewd	-.20**	ns	ns	ns	-.18**	.17**
O Apprehensive	-.37**	-.13**	-.21**	-.59**	-.20**	-.22**
Q1 Experimenting	.16**	ns	ns	.11**	.20**	-.11**
Q2 Self-sufficient	-.23**	-.30**	-.12**	-.12**	ns	ns
Q3 Compulsive	.12**	.10**	.39**	.32**	ns	.27**
Q4 Tense	-.24**	-.25**	-.15**	-.72**	-.18**	-.37**
FB Fake Bad	-.13**	-.31**	-.15**	-.24**	-.21**	ns
FG Fake Good	.24**	.18**	.34**	.38**	.12**	.30**
WAIS (N = 76)						
IQ-V Verbal IQ	ns	ns	ns	.23*	.40**	ns
IQ-P Performance IQ	ns	ns	-.23*	ns	.27*	ns
PPWB (N = 985)						
Dominance-Satisfaction	.37**	.08*	.35**	.35**	.15**	.37**
Positive relations	.22**	.50**	.14**	.24**	.30**	ns
Autonomy	.30**	-.14**	.22**	.25**	.32**	.09**
Self-acceptance	.27**	.08*	.19**	.44**	.26**	.11**
Search for Novelty	.43**	.22**	.22**	.22**	.54**	-.09**
Sense of growth	.22**	.16**	.28**	.08*	.26**	.08*

Note: * $p < .05$; ** $p < .01$; ns = statistically non significant.

As can be seen in Table 4, BFQ scales showed a clear-cut pattern of correlations with the scales contained in the various instruments examined. In particular, *Energy* was positively and highly correlated with the various extraversion scales, but also with scales related to activity, assertiveness, venturesomeness, and positive affect. *Friendliness* was positively correlated with scales related to agreeableness, trust, empathy, and positive relations with others. *Conscientiousness* was positively correlated with scales related to conscientiousness, orderliness, activity, and constraint. *Emotional Stability* was negatively correlated with the various neuroticism scales, and with scales measuring apprehensiveness, tension, and negative affectivity, but was positively correlated with scales measuring emotional stability and self-acceptance. *Openness* was positively correlated with scales measuring openness to experience, search for novelty, and with verbal IQ. Finally, the *Lie* scale was positively correlated with the other social desirability scales and with response bias scales. These results confirm both the convergent and the discriminant validity of BFQ scales.

Construct validity of the BFQ: Multitrait-Multimethod analyses

In a recent multitrait-multimethod (MTMM) study Barbaranelli and Caprara (2000)

Table 5. Rotated factor matrix of BFQ - Other ratings (Varimax orthogonal rotated solution)

BFQ Facets Scales	Factors				
	E	F	C	S	O
Dynamism	.77	.29	.03-	.01	.25
Dominance	.69	-.25	.12	-.06	.18
Cooperativenes	.07	.76	.15	.04	.23
Politeness	-.02	.65	.01	.32	.02
Scrupulousness	-.04	.03	.77	.01	.08
Perseverance	.40	.18	.58	-.03	.18
Emotion Control	.07	.05	-.04	.73	.05
Impulse Control	-.19	.28	.09	.88	.01
Openness to Culture	.16	.06	.37	.08	.51
Openness to Experiences	.33	.22	.05	.01	.62
% of explained variance	14.0	13.2	11.2	14.2	8.4

Note: E = Energy; F = Friendliness; C = Conscientiousness; S = Emotional Stability; O = Openness; *N* = 1,200.

examined the construct validity of the Big Five using the BFQ and the so called BFO[1] ("Big Five Observer", Caprara, Barbaranelli, & Borgogni, 1994), an adjective based measure of the Big Five. Both instruments were used for collecting self-report and other-ratings. In particular, 200 subjects (100 males and 100 females) described their own personality on the BFQ and on the BFO, and they were rated by 6 acquaintances (for a total of 1200 other-ratings) with the same instruments. Before describing the results of the MTMM study we believe it is useful to present some results related to psychometric characteristics of the BFQ — other-ratings, as well as of the BFO.

Table 5 presents the results of an exploratory factor analysis conducted on the BFQ — other-ratings with the aim of examining its internal validity. The expected factor structure was confirmed, Cronbach's alpha coefficients of the scales ranged from .77 to .89, Tucker congruence coefficients with the *BFQ — self-report* factor

---

[1] The BFO has been designed to measure the personality traits comprised by the five factor model by means of 40 pairs of bipolar adjectives (8 pairs for each of the 5 factors). The adjectives were selected from the psycholexical study in the Italian language conducted by Caprara and Perugini (1994), who identified a list of 492 Italian adjectives as being useful to describe personality. The most representative adjectives for each factor were identified by three expert judges using a "cluster sampling" approach (see Goldberg, 1992). Then, for each one of the five factors the eight adjectives presenting the higher corrected item-total correlation coefficient were selected, and opposite adjectives for them were identified using a Thesaurus of the Italian language (Gabrielli, 1977). Following Goldberg and Kilowski (1985) we believed that bipolar adjectives could clarify the intrinsic ambiguity of several terms by specifying the dimension being measured, so that no terms in a pair of opposites would be interpreted in isolation and idiosyncratically. Each of the 40 pairs of opposite adjectives was rated on a 7 point scale. To control for acquiescence, the first presented adjective in half of the pairs goes in the direction of the dimension measured (e.g., Dominant/Submissive), while in the remaining pairs the order of presentation of the adjectives is reversed (e.g., Introverted/Extraverted).

Table 6. Factor structure for the BFO Self Report and Other Ratings

	Self-Report					Other Ratings				
	I	II	III	IV	V	I	II	III	IV	V
Energy										
Dominant/Submissive	.03	.13	**.36**	.45	-.34	-.10	.07	-.33	**.42**	.48
Introverted/Extraverted	-.01	-.06	**.70**	.05	.21	.07	-.06	.23	**.70**	.06
Leader/Pawn	.04	.11	**.40**	.49	-.28	-.01	.08	-.21	**.42**	.53
Bold/Timid	.09	.03	**.61**	.31	-.18	.08	-.07	-.08	**.60**	.35
Retiring/Sociable	.03	.01	**.66**	-.01	.40	.10	.01	.42	**.65**	.04
Silent/Talkative	-.05	-.02	**.71**	.07	.31	-.01	.00	.35	**.68**	.09
Energetic/Unenergetic	.06	.41	**.49**	.18	-.02	.01	.45	-.01	**.44**	.27
Clumsy/Self-Confident	.14	.16	**.62**	.28	.06	.14	.07	.09	**.65**	.24
Friendliness										
Cold/Warm	-.13	-.08	.30	.10	**.46**	-.04	.02	**.52**	.26	.00
Selfless/Selfish	.06	.20	.06	.05	**.46**	.19	.17	**.55**	.02	.13
Hostile/Friendly	.10	-.01	.30	.04	**.62**	.14	.08	**.65**	.34	.01
Trusty/Suspicious	.31	-.11	.17	.00	**.33**	.29	-.05	**.39**	.18	.16
Rude/Gentle	.18	.22	.03	.06	**.62**	.24	.29	**.63**	.04	-.02
Indulgent/Severe	.21	-.21	-.09	-.14	**.40**	.30	-.12	**.46**	-.07	-.02
Tolerant/Intolerant	.34	-.06	-.08	.06	**.46**	.38	.01	**.51**	-.13	.05
Unfair/Fair	.01	.27	.04	.15	**.52**	.02	.27	**.54**	.07	.15
Conscientiousness										
Careful/Careless	.02	**.63**	.05	.09	-.01	.12	**.59**	.03	-.06	.15
Scrupulous/Lax	-.05	**.68**	-.06	.07	-.06	.01	**.67**	-.03	-.08	.12
Well Organized/Disorganized	.04	**.70**	.01	-.12	-.07	.21	**.63**	-.01	-.14	-.04
Lazy/Hard-working	.09	**.62**	.34	-.07	.11	.10	**.64**	.16	.33	-.08
Tired/Tireless	.16	**.44**	.47	-.02	.10	.07	**.53**	.09	.45	-.06
Weak willed/Self-disciplined	.08	**.63**	.28	.07	.23	.02	**.67**	.26	.20	.06
Negligent/Conscientious	.05	**.57**	-.05	.14	.37	.02	**.61**	.31	.02	.09
Undependable/Reliable	.07	**.48**	-.09	.19	.29	.07	**.46**	.31	-.05	.22
Emotional Stability										
Anxious/Serene	**.74**	-.07	.11	.09	-.03	**.73**	-.03	.01	.24	.02
Stable/Instable	**.50**	.40	-.01	.12	-.01	**.56**	.31	.04	-.04	.16
Patient/Impatient	**.53**	.18	-.13	-.05	.29	**.58**	.19	.32	-.15	-.01
Nervous/At ease	**.82**	-.05	-.01	-.01	.15	**.81**	.04	.16	.06	-.10
Relaxed/Tense	**.80**	-.03	.01	.11	-.02	**.77**	-.02	.02	.04	.05
Satisfied/Unsatisfied	**.47**	.18	.24	.11	.04	**.46**	.19	.10	.23	.21
Worrying/Calm	**.80**	.03	-.06	.02	.15	**.79**	.07	.14	.02	-.09
Vulnerable/Resistant	**.48**	.21	.31	.06	-.06	**.41**	.25	-.03	.37	.07
Openness										
Original/Conventional	.05	-.13	.16	**.61**	-.05	.02	-.07	.05	.14	**.64**
Unintelligent/Intelligent	-.02	.12	.08	**.54**	.24	-.10	.22	.36	.08	**.38**
Not Receptive/Receptive	-.10	.08	.22	**.40**	.20	-.09	.22	.32	.22	**.50**
Informed/Uninformed	.14	.18	.01	**.57**	-.01	.13	.28	.09	-.04	**.58**
Creative/Uncreative	.10	.07	.15	**.52**	.09	.07	.15	.09	.15	**.57**
Dull/Sharp	-.02	.17	.03	**.54**	.33	-.10	.31	.32	.08	**.36**
Innovating/Traditional	.08	-.25	.11	**.48**	.02	.05	-.10	.07	.12	**.63**
Uncultured/Cultured	-.01	.09	-.06	**.65**	.21	-.03	.24	.27	-.01	**.50**
% of Explained Variance	9.8	9.5	9.2	8	8	10.1	9.9	9.3	9.3	8.2

Note: These are Varimax-rotated principal components for 1,576 subjects (self-report) and 1,350 raters (other ratings); Loadings on the intended factor are boldface.

structure ranged from .97 to .99, and the correlation coefficients with the same scales of the *BFQ - self report* ranged from .53 to .72.

Table 6 presents the factor structure of the BFO in self-report and in other ratings. Congruence coefficients among these two solutions ranged from .88 to .95. Cronbach's alpha reliability coefficients ranged from .69 to .82 in self-report, and from .72 to .83 in other-ratings. Correlations among self-report and other-ratings ranged from .47 to .70.

The aforementioned multitrait-multimethod study matched two "response mode" (sentence based questionnaire and list of adjectives) and two sources of information or raters (self report and other ratings). The 20x20 multitrait-multimethod matrix derived from these measures has been analyzed via Structural Equation Models (Bollen, 1989) according to the criteria proposed by Widaman (1985), Marsh (1989) and Bagozzi (1994): In particular, four different models have been compared. In all these models, global fit indexes (such as the chi-square statistic, the Comparative Fit Index, and the Root Mean Squared Residual; see Bollen & Long, 1993) resulted moderate; convergent validity was supported by the high loadings of scales measuring the same trait; discriminant validity was supported by low correlations among the different traits; method variance and error variance resulted moderate or low.

Among the different models examined, one turned out to be particularly interesting. This model was called CFA-RARE ("Confirmatory Factor Analysis — Rater/Response mode" model) because it distinguished between two different kinds of method factors: *rater* (self and other) and *response mode* (questionnaire and list of adjectives). Table 7 presents a summary of parameter estimates for this model.

Trait factor loadings were all significant, suggesting that the measures are good indicators of their respective trait factors, thus supporting high convergent validity. Loadings on the *"response mode"* method factors (i.e., questionnaire and adjective list) generally turned to be low except for *Openness to Experience* and for *Friendliness*: this means that the influence of response mode is relevant only for these two factors. Loadings on the *"rater"* method factors (self-report and other-ratings) evidenced that the effect of *self-report* method factor was relevant for Energy, Conscientiousness and Openness, while the effect of *other ratings* method factor was relevant for Friendliness and for Emotional Stability. Residual variance was significant but moderate for all scales, suggesting a low to moderate percentage of variance due to unique factors or to error of measurement. Finally, discriminant validity was confirmed by low correlations between the traits, that were all lower than .30 with the exception of Openness to Experience with Energy ($r = .54$, $p < .001$), Emotional Stability with Friendliness ($r = .32$, $p < .001$), and Conscientiousness with Openness to Experience ($r = .37$, $p < .001$).

From the results presented in Table 7 it is possible to partition the variance of each personality factor into variance due to the trait measured (which reflects the convergence of the four different scales used for measuring each trait), variance due to response mode, and rater method factors (which reflects the particular method used to assess the traits), and residual variance (which reflects a combination of specific variance and measurement error). Overall, 66 per cent of *Energy* variance was explained by the trait factor, 4 per cent by response mode, 8 per cent by raters, while

Table 7. Traits and methods loadings for the Rater-Response Mode model

	Traits					Methods				
	E	A	C	S	O	Qu	Ad	Se	Ot	rv
Questionnaire Self Report										
Energy	.73					.16		.45		.23
Friendliness		.65				.33		.06		.46
Conscientiousness			.69			.30		.30		.35
Emotional Stability				.88		.01		.05		.23
Openness					.40	.69		.46		.15
Adjective List Self Report										
Energy	.72						.17	.35		.32
Friendliness		.65					.37	.11		.42
Conscientiousness			.73				.22	.36		.29
Emotional Stability				.78			.26	.10		.32
Openness					.54		.17	.61		.31
Questionnaire Other Ratings										
Energy	.93					.20			-.02	.10
Friendliness		.83				-.01			.41	.14
Conscientiousness			.80			.29			.17	.24
Emotional Stability				.76		-.09			.54	.14
Openness					.73	.41			.09	.29
Adjective List Other Ratings										
Energy	.85						.26		.05	.21
Friendliness		.67					.45		.40	.18
Conscientiousness			.80				.24		.20	.27
Emotional Stability				.67			.31		.55	.15
Openness					.72		.42		.14	.28

Note: E = Energy, F = Friendliness, C = Conscientiousness, S = Emotional Stability, O = Openness; Qu = Questionnaire, Ad = Adjectives list, Se = Self report, Ot = Other ratings, rv = residual variance; All coefficients are significant at .05 level or higher, except those in italics; Results are from the standardized solution.

22 per cent was residual variance; 50 per cent of *Friendliness* variance was explained by the trait factor, 11 per cent by response mode, 9 per cent by raters, and 30 per cent was residual variance; 57 per cent of *Conscientiousness* variance was explained by the trait factor, 7 per cent by response mode, 7 per cent by raters, while 29 per cent was residual variance; 60 per cent of *Emotional Stability* variance was explained by the trait factor, 4 per cent by response mode, 15 per cent by raters, while 21 per cent was residual variance; 38 per cent of *Openness* variance was explained by the trait factor, 22 per cent by response mode, 15 per cent by rater, while 26 per cent was residual variance. In general, trait variance was very high for all factors with the exception of Openness, method variance (i.e., response mode plus rater) was high for Openness and low for all the other factors. Residual variance was moderate. On average, 54 per cent of variance was explained by traits, 10 per cent by response mode, 11 per cent by raters, and 25 per cent was residual variance.

The personality of voters and of consumers

The BFQ in the domain of political behavior

In a recent study Caprara, Barbaranelli, and Zimbardo (1999) explored new relationships between basic personality profiles of voters and their choice of political party affiliation. The Italian political system has recently moved from extreme, ideologically distinctive parties to complex coalitions ("Center-Left" and "Center-Right" coalitions). We found significant evidence for the utility of the Big Five Model of Personality in distinguishing voter party identification. More than 2000 Italian voters who identified themselves as belonging either to "Center-Left" or "Center-Right" political coalitions differed systematically on several personality dimensions measured by the Big Five Questionnaire.

In particular, using a MANCOVA design, significant relationships were found between three of the five factors of the Big Five scales and the political orientation of the participants in the investigation. Those voters identified as supporting the Center-Right showed higher scores than the Center-Left voters in Energy; $F(1,1942) = 21.64$, $p < .001$. In addition, they were also slightly higher on Conscientiousness; $F(1,1942) = 5.58$, $p < .05$. The voters of Center-Left showed highly significant scores on Friendliness, $F(1,1942) = 20.07$, $p < .001$, as well as on Openness, $F(1,1942) = 19.80$, $p < .001$. No difference between these two groups of voters emerged for Emotional Stability, $F(1,1942) = 1.44$, $p = .23$. Figure 1 shows the personality profiles of the two voter groups, expressed as T-scores for each of the five domains of the BFQ. It is noteworthy that the differences in personality traits due to

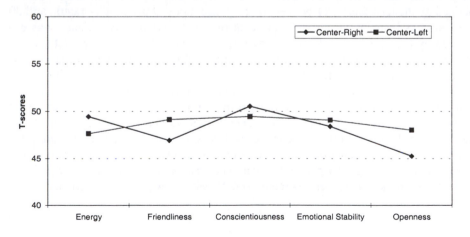

Figure 1. Personality profiles of Italian electors on the BFQ.

political partisanship are still significant after controlling for several demographic variables.

Finally, through a logistic regression we examined the impact of personality traits in respect to political choice (center left vs. center right). None of the demographic variables considered (gender, age, and education) entered into the final regression equation, which was highly significant. The only variables that had significant impact on political preference were four of the BFQ domain scales, namely Energy ($r = -.12, p < .001$), Friendliness ($r = .06, p < .001$), Openness ($r = .13, p < .001$), and also Conscientiousness ($r = -.05, p < .001$). The equation allowed the correct classification of 61.4 per cent of Center-Left voters, 57.6 per cent of Center-Right voters, with an overall hit rate of 59.5 per cent. These results are quite surprising since only personality had a significant impact on political preference, while none of the demographic variables had an impact on party choice behavior once the personality effects were partialled out.

The BFQ in the domain of consumer behavior

With the aim of extending the use of the Big Five to domains different from those usually considered in personality research, we started to investigate the role of the Big Five in respect to consumer behavior and habits. About 5,000 adults, representative of the Italian national population, were administered a short version of the BFQ along with a survey-questionnaire aimed at investigating their consumption and purchasing habits and behaviors. We focused our attention especially on the following variables: a) the propensity to make one's own purchase in supermarkets, malls, hard discounts, and the like; b) the time spent in watching television; c) the books read in the past year; d) the topics preferred in newspapers; e) the propensity toward purchasing life insurances, and to invest into pension funds; f) the propensity toward savings (by means of Government stocks, stocks, investment funds, passbooks, bank current accounts). Background variables such as gender, age and education have been controlled for.

The pattern of high scores on Friendliness, Openness, and Conscientiousness appeared to be associated with the propensity toward making one's own purchase in supermarkets, malls, hard discounts, and the like. This pattern reveals a profile of a consumer who is trustful, open to innovation, scrupulous, and methodical. The pattern of high scores on Conscientiousness and Openness and low scores on Emotional Stability was associated to the time spent in watching television. This pattern reveals a profile of a user who actively searches for novelty, is scrupulous but somewhat impulsive. The pattern of high scores on Friendliness and Openness was associated to the books read in the past year.

The different topics preferred in newspapers corresponded to different personality patterns. In fact, subjects who preferred topics such as fashion, health, and the like showed high scores on Friendliness and Conscientiousness, but low scores on Emotional Stability. Subjects who preferred topics such as politics, culture, and economics showed high scores on Openness. Subjects who preferred topics such as shows, sports, and comics showed low score an all the Big Five, but especially on Openness.

The pattern of high scores on Energy, Openness, and Conscientiousness was associated to the propensity toward purchasing life insurances, and to invest into pension funds, revealing the profile of a consumer who is scrupulous, active, and positively oriented toward novelty. Finally, a pattern of high scores on Friendliness, Openness, and Conscientiousness was associated to the propensity toward savings (by means of Government stocks, stocks, investment funds, pass-books, bank current accounts), revealing the profile of a consumer who is scrupulous, trustful, and positively oriented toward novelty.

These results prove the utility of broad personality dimensions as indicators of consumer habits which may open new perspectives to marketers, as well as other contexts where personality variables might be useful for the prediction and explanation of behavior. The Big Five turned out to be substantially and differentially associated to diverse behavioral habits while controlling for background demographic variables such as gender, age, and education. These findings suggest that in the marketing domain a close scrutiny of personality patterns associated to specific behaviors, habit, and preferences may be important for the identification of specific targets for specific products, as well as for a communication strategy that takes into account the different individual inclinations.

Describing personality in late childhood and early adolescence

To assess the Big Five in late childhood through self-report as well as through parent and teacher ratings, we constructed a new questionnaire, the "Big Five Questionnaire – Children" (BFQ-C), consisting of 65 items, 13 for each of the five factors (Barbaranelli, Caprara, & Rabasca, 1998; Barbaranelli, Caprara, Rabasca, & Pastorelli, 2001).

Factor analyses on self-report and other ratings of elementary and junior high school children confirmed the expected Big Five structure. Factor solutions showed a high degree of congruence. There was a moderate although significant convergence between self-reports, parent, and teacher ratings. However, several differences emerged regarding the composition of the factors in the different solutions. In particular, the two dimensions that presented the higher differences across the different data sets were Conscientiousness and Intellect/Openness, especially when considering the rater and the age group. The two basic components of Conscientiousness (i.e., the proactive and the inhibitive; see McCrae & John, 1992) tended to emerge in separate factors, especially in self-report and teacher ratings of elementary school children. While the items related to the proactive component (perseverance and hardworking) tended to load on the Intellect/Openness factor, the items related to the inhibitive component (orderliness and scrupulousness) tended to define a narrow but distinct factor. Intellect/Openness items, in turn, tended to define two separate clusters: one cluster related to academic performance, which was found to be associated with proactive Conscientiousness, and another cluster related to Openness to Experience, which was found to be associated with Energy/Extraversion. These results mainly confirm earlier results obtained by Peabody and Goldberg (1989), who further differentiated "controlled" and "expressive" features of Intellect/Openness, and by Mervielde *et al.* (1995) who noticed the tendency of the "controlled" form of Intellect/Openness to cluster with Conscientiousness markers.

The correlations between the Big Five and different criteria considered for the validation of the BFQ-C were significant and high. Intellect/Openness and Conscientiousness were the more important personality correlates of *Academic Achievement* across different informants, with correlations ranging from .39 to .66. These two traits were also the more important correlates of Externalization Behavioral Problems as measured by the Child Behavior Checklist (Achenbach & Edelbrock, 1983; 1986), with correlations ranging from -.29 to -.41. Finally, Emotional Instability turned out to be the more relevant correlate of Internalization as measured by the Child Behavior Checklist (Achenbach & Edelbrock, 1983; 1986), with correlations ranging from .28 to .42. These results replicate what has been found in other studies that used different instrument for assessing the Big Five in childhood (e.g., John, Caspi, Robins, Moffit, & Stouthamer-Loeber, 1994; Mervielde *et al.*, 1995). Finally, the BFQ-C factors showed high and clear-cut correlations with the three factors of the Eysenck taxonomy as measured by the Junior Personality Questionnaire (JPQ; S.B.G. Eysenck, 1965). In particular, JPQ Extraversion was positively correlated with Energy/Extraversion, r (931) = .45, p < .001, with Intellect /Openness, r (931) = .24, p < .001, and with Friendliness, r (931) = .18, p < .001. JPQ Neuroticism was positively correlated with Emotional Instability, r (931) = .54, p < .001, and negatively correlated with Intellect/Openness, r (931) = -.20, p < .001, and with Energy/Extraversion, r (931) = .-18, p < .001. Finally, JPQ Psychoticism was negatively correlated with Conscientiousness, r (931) = -.29, p < .001, Friendliness, r (931) = -.26, p < .001, and Intellect/Openness, r (931) = -.23, p < .001, and positively correlated with Emotional Instability, r (931) = .29, p < .001. This pattern of correlations was mostly consistent with those found on adult subjects (e.g., Caprara, Barbaranelli, Borgogni, & Perugini, 1993; McCrae & Costa, 1985).

In light of these results, the BFQ-C may be considered to provide a comprehensive personality instrument to investigate systematically the origins and the development of relevant individual differences in children in relation to adjustment and maladjustment. As the BFQ-C can be used either as a self-report instrument, or as an instrument for collecting ratings from teachers and parents, it offers notable advantages in educational and counseling settings. The personality dimensions of the Big Five model are grounded into the lexicon people use in everyday life, and therefore the BFQ-C is probably easily understandable also by laypeople, fostering communications among parents, teachers, and counselors.

Conclusion

The studies reviewed here confirm the validity of the Big Five Questionnaire across different countries and languages as well as across different raters, response formats and applied settings. The Big Five dimensions are highly correlated with other inventories and appropriate external criteria. The BFQ-C developed for late childhood/ early adolescence furthermore attests to the possibility of extending this model for describing personality to earlier ages than the ones more usually considered.

All these findings also support the practical value of the Big Five Model. In fact, the convergence among self-report and other ratings shows that this model, capitalizing on the language that people use in everyday life, provides a lexicon (i.e., a *common* set of markers) which may enhance interjudge agreement and reduce interjudge variability (see McCrae & Costa, 1987). In this regard, a better accuracy of personality descriptions and greater consensus can be achieved (see Funder, Kolar, & Blackman, 1995; Kenny, Albright, Malloy, & Kashy, 1994), as *self-other agreement* (i.e., how an individual's view of him/her self and the view another person has of that individual are in agreement), and *other-other agreement* (i.e., how two independent judges are in agreement in relation to a particular individual) can be maximized.

While the Big Five cover relevant domains of personality, they are specific enough to differentiate among specific aspects of the personality, providing the elements for articulate fine-grained descriptions of personality. Indeed, they might provide a compass to map individual differences into a common reference structure (Ozer & Reise, 1994). Results from our studies in which the BFQ was used for investigating voters' and consumers' personality further extend what have been found in other fields such as organizational and industrial psychology (Barrick & Mount, 1991; Tett, Jackson, & Rothstein, 1991), educational psychology (Graziano & Ward, 1992; John et al., 1994), behavioral medicine (Dembrowski & Costa, 1987; Siegman et al., 1987), psychopathology (Widiger & Trull, 1992). Those studies confirm that the Big Five are not mathematical artifacts derived from non-generalizable data sets, but they have clearly behavioral counterparts in the real world.

As we acknowledge that much debate on Big Five limitations and merits is still going on, we do not hesitate to state again that the strength of the Big Five Model is in its "practical" value: The Five Factors in fact might represent "a well-substantiated and agreed-upon framework for the structure of personality" (Briggs, 1992, p. 254) to be used to provide a common language for research and assessment in personality psychology, and ultimately to generate new findings.

References

Achenbach, T.M., & Edelbrock, C. (1983). *Manual for Child Behavior Checklist and Revised Child Behavior Profile*. Burlington, VT: University of Vermont Press.

Achenbach, T. M., & Edelbrock, C. (1986). *Manual for the teacher's report form and teacher version of the child behavior profile*. Burlington, VT: University of Vermont Press.

Bagozzi, P. (1994). The evaluation of structural equation models and hypothesis testing. In R. Bagozzi (Ed.), *Principles of marketing research* (pp. 386-422). Cambridge, MA: Blackwell.

Barbaranelli, C., & Caprara, G.V. (2000). Measuring the Big Five in Self Report and Other Ratings: A Multitrait-Multimethod study. *European Journal of Psychological Assessment, 16*, 29-41.

Barbaranelli, C., Caprara, G.V., & Rabasca, A. (1998). *BFQ-C. Big Five Questionnaire Children. Manuale*. Firenze: O.S., Organizzazioni Speciali.

Barbaranelli, C., Caprara, G.V., Rabasca, A., & Pastorelli, C. (2001). *A questionnaire for measuring the Big Five in late childhood*. Paper submitted for publication.

Barrick, M.R., & Mount, M.K. (1991). The big five personality dimensions and job performance: A meta-analysis. *Personnel Psychology, 44*, 1-26.

Bollen, K.A (1989). *Structural Equations with Latent Variables*. New York: John Wiley & Sons.

Bollen, K.A., & Long, S.J. (1993). *Testing Structural Equation Models*. Newbury Park, CA: Sage Publications.

Briggs, S. (1992). Assessing the Five Factor model of personality description. *Journal of Personality, 60*, 254-293.

Burisch, M. (1984). Approaches to personality inventory construction: A comparison of merits. *American Psychologist, 35*, 863-872.

Buss, A.H., & Plomin, R. (1984). *Temperament: Early developing personality traits*. Hillsdale, NJ: Lawrence Erlbaum Associates.

Caprara, G.V., Barbaranelli, C., Bermudez, J., Maslach, C., & Ruch, W. (2000). Multivariate methods for the comparison of factor structures in cross-cultural research: An illustration with the Big Five Questionnaire. *Journal of Cross-Cultural Psychology, 31*, 301-328.

Caprara, G. V., Barbaranelli, C., & Borgogni, L. (1994). *BFO: Big Five Observer. Manuale*. Firenze: OS, Organizzazioni Speciali.

Caprara, G.V., Barbaranelli, C., Borgogni, L., & Perugini, M. (1993). The Big Five Questionnaire: A new questionnaire for the measurement of the five factor model. *Personality and Individual Differences, 15*, 281-288.

Caprara, G.V., Barbaranelli, C., & Livi, S. (1994). Mapping personality dimensions in the big five model. *European Journal of Applied Psychology, 44*, 9-16.

Caprara, G.V., Barbaranelli, C., & Zimbardo, P. (1999). Personality profiles and political parties. *Political Psychology, 20*, 175-197.

Caprara, G.V., & Perugini, M. (1994). Personality described by adjectives: Generalizability of the "Big Five" to the Italian lexical context. *European Journal of Personality 8*, 357-369.

Carrigan, P. (1960). Extraverion-Introversion as a dimension of personality: A reappraisal. *Psychological Bulletin, 57,* 329-360.

Cattell, R.B., Eber, H.W., & Tatsuoka, M.M. (1970). *The handbook for the Sixteen Personality Factor Questionnaire.* Champaign, IL: Institute for Personality and Ability Testing.

Cattell, R. B., & Vogelmann, S. (1977). A comprehensive trial of the scree and KG criteria for determining the number of factors. *Multivariate Behavioral Research, 12,* 289-325.

Comrey, A.L. (1967). Tandem criteria for analytic rotation in factor analysis. *Psychometrika, 32,* 143-154.

Comrey, A.L. (1973). *A first course in factor analysis* (1st ed.). New York: Academic Press.

Comrey, A.L. (1980). *Handbook for the interpretation of the Comrey Personality Scales.* San Diego, CA: EdITS Publishers.

Comrey, A.L. (1995). *Handbook and manual for the interpretation of the Comrey Personality Scales.* San Diego, CA: EdITS Publishers.

Comrey, A.L., & Lee, H.B. (1992). *A first course in factor analysis* (2nd ed.). Hillsdale, NJ: Lawrence Erlbaum Associates.

Costa, P.T., Jr., & McCrae, R.R. (1985). *The NEO Personality Inventory manual.* Odessa, FL: Psychological Assessment Resources.

Costa, P.T., Jr., & McCrae, R.R. (1992). *Revised NEO Personality Inventory (NEO-PI-R) and NEO Five-Factor Inventory (NEO-FFI) professional manual.* Odessa, FL: Psychological Assessment Resources.

Dembroski, T.M., & Costa, P.T., Jr., (1987). Coronary prone behavior: components of the type A pattern and hostility. *Journal of Peronality, 55,* 211-235.

Eaves, L., Eysenck, H., & Martin, N. (1989). *Genes, culture and personality.* London: Academic press.

Eysenck, H.J. (1990). Biological dimensions of personality. In L.A. Pervin (Ed.), *Handbook of personality: theory and research* (pp. 244-276). New York: Guilford.

Eysenck, H.J., & Eysenck, S.B.G. (1976). *Manual for the Eysenck Personality Questionnaire.* San Diego, CA:EdITS.

Eysenck, S.B.G. (1965). *Manual for the Junior Eysenck Personality Inventory.* San Diego: Educational and Industrial Testing Service.

Funder, D. C., Kolar, D.C., & Blackman, M.C. (1995). Agreement among judges of personality: Interpersonal relations, similarity, and acquaintanceship. *Journal of Personality and Social Psychology, 69,* 656-672.

Gabrielli, A. (1977). *Dizionario dei sinonimi e dei contrari.* [Dictionary of synonyms and antonyms]. Milano: Istituto Editoriale Italiano.

Goldberg, L.R. (1990). An alternative "Description of personality": The Big Five factor structure. *Journal of Personality and Social Psychology, 59,* 1216-1229.

Goldberg, L.R. (1992). The development of the markers of the Big-Five factor structure. *Psychological Assessment, 4,* 26-42.

Goldberg, L.R., & Kilkowski, J.M. (1985). The prediction of semantic consistency in self-descriptions: Characteristics of persons and of terms that affect the consistency of response to synonym and antonym pairs. *Journal of Personality and Social Psychology, 48,* 82-98.

Graziano, W.G., & Ward, D. (1992). Probing the Big Five in adolescence: Personality and adjustment during a developmental transition. *Journal of Personality, 60,* 425-439.

Guilford, J.P. (1975). Factors and factors of personality. *Psychological Bulletin, 82,* 802-814.

Hogan, R. (1986). *Hogan Personality Inventory manual,* Minneapolis, MN: National Computer Systems.

John, O.P. (1989). Towards a taxonomy of personality descriptors. In D.M. Buss & N. Cantor (Eds.), *Personality psychology: Recent trends and emerging directions* (pp. 261-271). New York: Springer Verlag.

John, O.P. (1990). The "big five" factor taxonomy: Dimensions of personality in natural language and in questionnaires. In L.A. Pervin (Ed.), *Handbook of personality: theory and research* (pp. 66-100). New York: Guilford.

John, O.P., Caspi, A., Robins, R.W., Moffit, T.E. & Stouthamer-Loeber, M. (1994). The "Little Five": Exploring the nomological network of the Five-Factor Model of personality in adolescent boys. *Child Development, 65,* 160-178.

Kenny, D.A., Albright, L., Malloy, T.E., & Kashy, D.A. (1994). Consensus in interpersonal perception: Acquaintance and the Big Five. *Psychological Bulletin, 116,* 245-258.

Lee, H.B., & Comrey, A.L. (1979). Distortions in a commonly used factor analysis procedure. *Multivariate Behavioral Research, 14,* 301-321.

Marsh, H.W. (1989). Confirmatory factor analysis of multitrait-multimethod data: Many problems and a few solutions. *Applied Psychological Measurement, 13,* 335-361.

McCrae, R.R., & Costa, P.T., Jr. (1985). Comparison of EPI and Psychoticism scales with measures of the Five Factor model of Personality. *Personality and Individual Differences, 6,* 587-597.

McCrae, R.R., & Costa, P.T., Jr. (1987). Validation of the five factor model of personality across instrument and observers. *Journal of Personality and Social Psychology, 52,* 81-90.

McCrae, R.R., & John, O.P. (1992). An introduction to five factor model and its applications. *Journal of Personality, 60,* 175-215.

Mervielde, I., Buyst, V., & De Fruyt, F. (1995). The validity of the Big-Five as a model for teachers' ratings of individual differences among childrens aged 4-12 years. *Personality and Individual Differences, 18,* 525-534.

Murray, H.A. (1938). *Explorations in personality.* New York: Oxford University Press.

Ozer, D.J., & Reise, S.P. (1994). Personality assessement. *Annual Review of Psychology, 45,* 357-388.

Peabody, D., & Goldberg, L.R. (1989). Some determinants of factor structures from personality-trait descriptors. *Journal of Personality and Social Psychology, 57,* 552-567.

Ryff, C. D. (1989). Happiness is everything, or is it? Exploring on the meaning of psychological well-being. *Journal of Personality and Social Psychology, 57,* 1069-1081.

Siegman, A.W., Dembroski, T.M. & Ringel, N. (1987). Components of hostility and severity of coronary artery disease. *Psychosomatic Medicine, 49,* 127-135.

Strelau, J. (1983). *Temperament, personality and activity.* New York: Academic Press.

Tellegen, A. (1982). *Brief Manual for the Differential Personality Questionnaire.* University of Minnesota.

Tett, R.P., Jackson, D.N., & Rothstein, M. (1991). Personality measures as predictors of job performance: A meta-analytic review. *Personnel Psychology, 44,* 703-742.

Tucker, L.R. (1951). *A method for synthesis of factor analysis studies.* (Personnel Research Section Report No. 984). Washington, D.C.: Dept. of the Army.

Webster (1974). Webster's unabridged dictionary. Springfield, MA: Merrian-Webster Inc.

Wechsler, D. (1981). *Manual for the Wechsler Adult Intelligence Scale.* NY: Psychological Corporation.

Widaman, K.F. (1985). Hierarchical nested covariance structure models for multitrait-multimethod data. *Applied Psychological Measurement, 9,* 1-26.

Widiger, T.A., & Trull, T.J. (1992). Personality and Psychopathology: An application of the Five-Factor Model. *Journal of Personality, 60,* 363-393.

Zuckerman, M. (1994). An alternative Five-Factor Model for personality. In C.F. Halverson, G.H. Kohnstamm, and R.P. Martin (Eds.), *The developing structure of temperament and personality* (pp. 53-68). Hilsdale, NJ: Lawrence Erlbaum Associates

Zuckerman, M., Kuhlman, D.M., Thornquist, M., & Kiers, H. (1991). Five (or three) robust questionnaire scale factors of personality without Culture. *Personality and Individual Differences, 9,* 939-941.

Chapter 6

Assessing children's traits with the Hierarchical Personality Inventory for Children

Ivan Mervielde
Filip De Fruyt

Introduction

Despite clear evidence that the FFM is useful to describe personality differences in children (Digman, 1963; Digman & Inouye, 1986; John, Caspi, Robins, Moffit, & Stouthamer-Loeber, 1994; Kohnstamm, Halverson, Mervielde, & Havill, 1998; Mervielde, Buyst, & De Fruyt, 1995; Mervielde & De Fruyt, 2000; 2001), there are relatively few inventories that are specifically designed to assess children's personality. In line with the lexical tradition, the validity of the FFM for younger age groups has been mainly demonstrated in studies using personality descriptive adjectives, using parents, caregivers, or teachers as informants (De Fruyt & Furnham, 2000; Kohnstamm *et al.*, 1998; Mervielde & De Fruyt, 2001). However, it remains to be established whether trait adjectives form the most appropriate level to conduct developmental studies on individual differences. Apart from using adjectives in inventories for children, other major questions are whether the trait-sediment for children is simply a subset of the adult trait-sediment, whether there is something specific for children that is never caught by adult trait-selections, and whether (some) "adult" adjectives have a specific "child" understanding as well.

Behavior varies with age, and a personality inventory should ideally tap such developments. The thinking about characteristics of people — young and old — probably takes place in terms of rather abstract words, such as trait adjectives. However, dictionaries do not include references to the adequacy of adjectives to describe differences in particular groups, such as age or normal versus clinical groups. Sentence items might be more suitable to describe age-specific behavior, because they refer to less abstract qualities of behavior.

Trait adjectives culled from dictionaries further reflect the passive rather than the

Big Five Assessment, edited by B. De Raad & M. Perugini. © 2002, Hogrefe & Huber Publishers.

active personality descriptive vocabulary, and hence do not take into account the frequency of use of personality descriptors in everyday discourse. Although frequency of use is implicit in the lexical hypothesis, it has not been studied systematically. Raters may spontaneously use and prefer a sentence item format, rather than trait adjectives, for self- and peer descriptions. De Raad (1985) found evidence of rather low frequency of use of adjectives in spontaneous talk. Finally, except for a limited number of studies on personality-descriptive verbs (De Raad, Mulder, Kloosterman, & Hofstee, 1988) and nouns (De Raad & Hoskens, 1990), the lexical tradition heavily relies on the study of trait adjectives. Sentence items could be an alternative to assess age and group-specific individual differences, eventually resulting in different factor solutions.

Elphick, Slotboom, and Kohnstamm (1997) described three different strategies to assess the FFM in non-adult age groups. The *first*, most commonly applied approach uses an adult FFM measure for assessing children's or adolescents' traits. Parker (1997; 1998), for example, demonstrated that the NEO-FFI could be easily administered to gifted adolescents. More recently, De Fruyt, Mervielde, Hoekstra, and Rolland (2000) showed that the more comprehensive NEO-PI-R is also structurally invariant in more heterogeneous samples of adolescents. Alternatively, item phrasing and/or rating instructions of adult personality inventories are sometimes slightly adapted to make them more suitable for childhood or adolescent personality assessment, such as for the Junior Eysenck Personality Inventory (Eysenck, 1965).

A *second* strategy derives FFM scores from childhood or adolescent inventories that are constructed to primarily operationalize another personality model than the FFM. Items and scales are rearranged in order to form reliable markers for the FFM dimensions. John *et al.* (1994) and Van Lieshout and Haselager (1994) derived five-factor scores from a re-analysis of Block's California Child Q-set (CCQ; Block & Block, 1980). Similarly, Judge, Higgins, Thoresen, and Barrick (1999) studied trait rank-order continuity across the life-span derived from an FFM rescaling of Q-sort data. The major drawback of this method is that these five-factor measures largely depend on the theoretical framework of the original instrument, and hence are at best proxies of FFM dimensions.

Finally, another approach is a bottom-up strategy, directed to the construction of a new and specific FFM inventory assessing children's or adolescents' traits. This *third* strategy first necessitates a careful analysis of the full range of personality differences that can be reliably observed in the target age group(s). The rationale behind this approach is that the kind and number of traits assessed should closely mirror the observable personality differences among individuals of the target age group. The Hierarchical Personality Inventory for Children (HiPIC; Mervielde & De Fruyt, 1999) was constructed along such a bottom up approach. The present chapter describes its rationale, construction, and application for the assessment of personality traits of children aged 6 to 12 years.

Development

Describing the childhood personality domain

The challenge to describe the range of childhood personality traits was taken up by an international research team, examining the content and structure of parental free descriptors of children aged 3 to 12 years (Kohnstamm *et al.,* 1998). This international consortium, with teams from Belgium, China, Germany, Greece, USA, Poland, and The Netherlands, included developmental and personality psychologists interested to examine the developmental antecedents of the adult Big Five.

In order to sample the range of personality differences observable in children across different cultures, all research teams applied the same procedure, interviewing parents and asking them to describe what they thought was characteristic for their child. Third year psychology students served as interviewers and were instructed to give only neutral prompts to elicit further description, without additional constraints. Interviews were tape-recorded and transcribed verbatim afterwards. The Flemish team, for example, collected descriptors from 427 parents this way, describing children of 3 to 13 years. However, in the subsequent phases, only the descriptors of children aged 5 to 13 years were used, because the primary objective was to focus on primary school age.

The transcribed interviews were further segmented into small personality descriptive utterances, which were subsequently assigned to a personality descriptive category system. This personality descriptive lexicon explicitly referred to the five factors, with eight additional categories derived from the temperament and developmental literature, tentatively labeled as Independence (VI), Mature for age (VII), Illness, handicaps, and health (VIII), Rhythmicity (IX), Gender appropriate behavior (X), Physical attractiveness (XI), Cuddliness and clinging behavior (XII), Relationships with siblings and parents (XIII), and finally a rest category for descriptors that could not be classified (XIV). The first five main categories were further structured in subcategories. The category system partly followed the FFM, but did not preclude that other dimensions outside the FFM would emerge (Kohnstamm *et al.,* 1995). The 427 interviews with Flemish parents provided a total pool of 9,607 descriptors (for details, see Kohnstamm *et al.,* 1998). Between 70 and 80 per cent of all parental free descriptors could be classified as instances of the Big Five in all cultures (Kohnstamm *et al.,* 1998). The distribution of Flemish descriptors across the 14 categories of the lexicon is described in Table 1. Mervielde (1998) further demonstrated that 68 per cent of all parents referred to at least four of the Big Five categories, whereas less than 10 per cent referred to only two or to just one category.

Table 1. Percentage of classified descriptors across coding categories

	Category-label	%
1	Extraversion	27.0
2	Agreeableness	19.4
3	Conscientiousness	8.4
4	Emotional stability	9.4
5	Openness to experience/Intellect	12.9
6	Independence, Ability to do things independently	3.5
7	Mature for age	2.4
8	Illness, handicaps, and health	0.6
9	Rhythmicity of eating, sleeping, etc.	0.9
10	Gender appropriate, physical attractiveness	0.9
11	School performance, attitudes toward school	4.0
12	Contact comfort, desire to be cuddled, clinging	1.7
13	Relations with siblings and parents	4.3
14	Ambiguous phrases and descriptions that cannot be coded elsewhere	4.5

However, the classification results only tentatively underscore the comprehensiveness and saliency of the FFM categories, because they just reflect a classification process, rather than providing insight into the dimensions underlying individual differences assembled with a free description procedure.

From free descriptors to items

To further structure the categorised Flemish descriptors, homogeneous groups of similar and content related descriptions were formed within each category by teams of five judges. Judges did not receive a priori guidelines about the optimal number or the breadth of these groups. This classification procedure was only applied to main categories or subcategories with more than one per cent of the total number of descriptors. The production of content related groups and the subsequent assignment of descriptors was carefully checked and supervised by two research assistants. About 100 groups of 'synonym' -free descriptions were identified for the age groups 5 to 7, 8 to 10 and 11 to 13[1], roughly comparable across age-groups. For example, a Conscientiousness' subcategory 'Carefulness – negative', was further split into four groups, i.e. 'orderly-neat', 'precise', 'good attention span-attentive', and 'responsible-reliable', including 18, 23, 16, and 17 free descriptions, respectively, for children aged 8 to 10 years. A detailed overview of the Flemish free descriptor groups can be found elsewhere (Mervielde & De Fruyt, 1999).

Although the sampled free descriptions cover a wide range of behaviours characteristic of school-age children, they cannot be used directly as questionnaire items because their grammatical structure is very divergent, hampering a uniform interpretation of their meaning. Moreover, many of the descriptors are trait adjectives or adjectives form the descriptive core of the sentences. The primary objective of the

---

[1] We primarily focused on primary school age. Clustering of descriptors for the age group 2 to 4 years will be accomplished later on.

Flemish project was to construct an inventory with sentence items, referring to concrete observable behaviour, rather than compiling a list with trait adjectives. Rules developed for the construction of an adult five-factor inventory, the FFPI (Five-Factor Personality Inventory; Hendriks, 1997), were adopted for the production of behavioural items, in order to streamline the format of all items. Each of the items was formulated in the third person verb form (e.g., "keeps emotions and thoughts for oneself", "has a limited vocabulary"), did not contain a trait adjective and was formulated in a direct form avoiding negations.

We started with the production of items for the 100 descriptor-groups that were identified for the children aged 8 to 10 years. For each of the homogeneous groups of free descriptors of this age-level, two to four items were written based on the content of that group. Items for the age-levels 5 to 7 and 11 to 13 were produced according to a similar procedure, with the objective of maximising the number of common items for the three age-levels, based on a comparison of the content of the homogeneous groups for different age-levels. This strategy resulted in initial item sets with 240 items for age 5 to 7, 282 items for age 8 to 10, and 234 items for age 11 to 13. One hundred and twenty-two items were common to the three age-groups.

Delineating the domain structure

The resulting item sets were given to adult raters (one or both parents + teachers) who had to provide ratings of children's behavior on a five-point scale, anchored as follows: (1) Almost not characteristic, (2) Little characteristic, (3) More or less characteristic, (4) Characteristic, and (5) Very characteristic. Scores given by the two or three adult raters (parents/teachers) were averaged, in order to increase the reliability of the rating and to limit the influence of any particular rater perspective. Preliminary principal component analyses at the item level indicated that for each age-level, the first five principal components tended to group items according to each of the FFM categories that were used to sort the free descriptors. The correspondence of the structure of the initial pool of behavioural items with the "lexical Big Five" was further checked for age groups 5 to 7 and 8 to 10. For both age-levels additional ratings of each child were available on the B5BBS-25, an instrument with 25 bipolar scales marking the five factors (B5BBS-25; Mervielde, 1992), selected from Goldberg's Big Five adjective markers (Goldberg, 1989). In addition, ratings on trait adjectives culled from the free descriptions were available. Observers provided ratings on 143 trait adjectives for age-level 5 to 7 years and on 152 adjectives for age-level 8 to 10 years. A joint principal component analysis of the components extracted from the behavioural items, with ratings of the same children on the B5BBS-25 (Mervielde, 1992) scales and five components extracted from ratings on trait adjectives confirmed the correspondence between the principal components extracted from the behavioural item sets and the Big Five as conceived in the lexical approach. Therefore it was decided to systematically extract and rotate five components to construct age-specific questionnaires, assessing broad and more specific traits.

Table 2. Phases for the selection of items and the composition of clusters and facets

Step	Construction phase	Method of item selection
1	Scales 1	Group items into scales based on the free description cluster that was used to write them (100 clusters →100 scales)
2	Scales 2	Compute alpha reliability for each scale: - put items that lower alpha into single-item scale - split scales with alpha < .60 into single-item scales
3	Scales 3	Principal component analysis of all scales: - extract and varimax rotate 5 components - drop scales with communalities < .30
4	Scales 4	Reassign single-item scales to multi–item scales based on correlation analysis
5	Scales 5	Principal component analysis of all scales: - extract and varimax rotate 5 components - assign scales to the highest loading component
6	Facets 1	Principal component analysis of items within each of the 5 components: - extract and rotate (Oblimin) 2 to 7 components - assign items to facets based on the PC-analyses
7	Facets 2	Compute alpha reliability for each facet: - remove items that lower alpha - re-assign some items based on correlational analysis
8	Facets 3	Principal component analysis of all facets: - extract and varimax rotate 5 components - remove facets with low communalities
9	Facets 4	Select 8 items for each facet based on: - item-total correlation - contribution to simple structure
10	Facets 5	Compute alpha reliability for each facet
11	Facets 6	Principal component analysis of facets

For each age-level, items were first grouped into scales based on the free description group that was used to produce them. Cronbach alpha coefficients for each scale were computed, and items that lowered the alpha's were re-assigned to single-item scales. In addition, multi-item scales with alpha's < .60 were also split into single-item scales. Multi- and single-item scales were then submitted to a new principal component analysis per age-level, followed by varimax rotation of five components.

Scales with communalities < .30 were dropped. Single-item scales from the previous phase were reassigned to the highest correlating multi-item-scale. A final principal component analysis of all scales per age-level was conducted, retaining five varimax-rotated factors. The items primarily loading on each component defined the item domain of analysis for constructing facets within these particular components. An outline of the different steps to define the content domains is presented in the top section of Table 2.

Constructing facets within domains

To infer a facet structure within each of the five components, all items primarily loading on a particular component were submitted to principal component analysis, followed by oblimin rotation of two to seven components. A similar procedure was followed to investigate the domain structure of each age group. The number of components to be retained within a domain was determined by a combination of criteria, including inspection of the scree plot, the total amount of explained variance, communalities of the items, and the number of items loading on within-domain factor. Oblimin rotation was preferred, given the substantial variance shared by items, primarily loading on the same component in the domain analysis.

Items were subsequently assigned to facets based on the results of the principal component analyses. Alpha reliabilities for the resulting facets were computed, and items were removed that lowered the alpha's and re-assigned to new facets based on their intercorrelation pattern. A new principal component analysis of the facets was then conducted to remove facets with low communalities. For each facet, 8 items were selected based on their item-total correlation and on their contribution to simple structure. The alpha reliabilities of the final selection of 8 items per facet were computed, followed by principal component analysis of the facet scales. The different steps in the facet construction process are described in the bottom section of Table 2.

The final number of items for each of the facets was restricted to 8 in order to avoid too lengthy questionnaires. Inspection of the reliabilities and of average inter-item correlations shows that the facets are homogeneous with alpha reliabilities ranging from .85 to .94 for the youngest age group, from .86 to .95 for the middle group, and from .85 to 93 for the oldest children. Given the rather high average inter-item correlations, one can be fairly sure that the contents of the items belonging to a given facet are highly similar. Constructing facets always entails a difficult choice between bandwidth and fidelity. Bandwidth was emphasized initially, because broad sets of categories and clusters were used to organise parental free descriptions and to write items for the initial item pools per age group. Homogeneity of content within a facet was emphasized in the aggregation process of descriptor-groups and of items into facets to come up with reliable facet scales with a stable and replicable position within the personality descriptive model. By shifting the emphasis from bandwidth to fidelity the content validity may be reduced somewhat, but this is the price to be paid for a stable facet structure.

The 11-step construction procedure outlined in Table 2 led to three questionnaires with a rather similar structure, covering behavioural differences observable in children 5 to 7, 8 to 10, and 11 to 13. Nineteen different facets were delineated from the parental free descriptions across the three age groups, with 17 facets being similar across ages. Two facets could not be recovered in each age group, namely Altruism and Independence. The Altruism facet was only prominent in the age groups 5 to 7 and 11 to 13, while Independence was only represented in the descriptors of children aged 8 to 10.

The common 17 facets demonstrated to have stable primary loading patterns in the FFM framework across ages, although some of the domain labels had to be adapted to accommodate a broader spectrum of traits observable in children.

The composition of the first childhood domain factor, Conscientiousness, was the same across the three age groups, including the facets Achievement Striving, Order, Perseverance and Concentration. Three of these facets are closely related to facets defined in the NEO-PI-R (Costa & McCrae, 1992). Order and Achievement Striving have an identical label, while Perseverance is closely related to Self-discipline, described as "refers to the ability to begin tasks and carry them through to completion despite boredom and other distractions" (Costa & McCrae, 1992, p. 18). Finally, Concentration as such is not included in the adult NEO-PI-R model but it may be related to Dutifulness and to Deliberation. The greater emphasis on Concentration may further reflect a major concern of parents judging children.

The second childhood domain factor, related to Agreeableness, contains a broad spectrum of facets — including Altruism, Dominance, Egocentrism, Compliance, and Irritability — belonging to different factors in adult FFM operationalizations. Facets are more evaluatively negative in nature here, referring to characteristics of the "easy versus difficult child" as conceived in the temperament literature. To distinguish this broader content from the adult Agreeableness factor, the factor was labelled as Benevolence, including typical adult Agreeableness facets such as Compliance, Egocentrism, and Altruism, but also facets that are primarily related to other Big Five factors in adults such as Dominance and Irritability. Dominance primarily loads on the Extraversion domain in adults, whereas Irritability is more related to Neuroticism. Possible reasons for this broader domain content are that the Benevolence factor refers to a sort of Externalizing factor, also represented in the Child Behavior Checklist (CBCL; Achenbach, 1991; see also later in this chapter for the empirical relationship). In addition, the broader spectrum may also result from using parents as primary informants for both defining and rating the personality domain. The traits captured by the Benevolence factor are conceptually related to "manageability of the child" and may hence reflect a dimension with a strong socially evaluative connotation for caregivers.

The third childhood domain factor, Extraversion, is composed of the same four facets at each age level, namely Shyness, Expressiveness, Optimism, and Energy, all having clear counterparts in the adult personality literature. However, the facets' loadings on the domain vary across age. Shyness is the highest loading facet for age 5 to 7, while Energy is the highest loading facet for the oldest group. Optimism is apparently linked to the Positive emotions facet of Extraversion as measured by the NEO-PI-R, while Expressiveness refers to the open expression of emotions and to talkativeness.

The fourth childhood domain factor is called Imagination. In the Big Five literature the related factor has been variously interpreted as Intellect, Culture, or Openness to Experience. However, none of these labels seem to adequately represent the common core among the Creativity, Curiosity, and Intellect facets that emerged in the present research for each of the three age groups. In agreement with a proposal by Saucier (1992) the label Imagination was chosen, referring to both Creativity and Intellect.

Finally, the smallest factor in terms of the number of facets is Emotional Stability, including Anxiety as a factor-pure marker, and Self-confidence with a secondary loading on Extraversion. Independence was only recovered from the item set for age group 8 tot 10, and it also covaried with three other domains. Parallel to findings of the lexical approach (Goldberg, 1993), it seems that the Emotional Stability factor is also more restricted in content than the four others when analyzing free descriptions.

A common inventory for 6 to 12

Although the objective was the construction of three different age-specific questionnaires, the large number of similar facets across age groups is indicative for the high degree of overlap among the three questionnaires. More than half the items were common to the three instruments and even more were common to two of the three. This correspondence is of course the result of our policy to start from a highly common set of categories and descriptor-groups to cover the content of free parental descriptions. In addition, items that were already part of another age-specific questionnaire were preferentially selected to assess similar traits in another age group in order to further strengthen the common core.

Focussing on the common core rather than on the diversity across age groups has several advantages. From a practical point of view, there is a limit to the degree of differentiation. The validation of factors and facets for age-specific questionnaires requires many studies, and an equally differentiated set of age-specific criterion measures may not be available. Moreover, for research purposes it is often difficult to collect data from sufficient numbers of subjects within a specific age-group. For individual diagnosis, narrow age-ranges require separate norms for each age group. Finally, comparison across age levels is only feasible for the common set of items that may turn out to have yet a divergent structure. That common structure may be biased by an unequal distribution of items and/or facets from one particular item-set. Because quantitative comparison of mean levels and structure across age groups has to be based on a set of common items, emphasising a broad common core of items seems to be the most adequate strategy for research purposes as well as for diagnostic applications.

Mervielde and De Fruyt (1999) computed Tucker congruence coefficients between the factor matrices of the three age groups, over the set of 17 facets common to the three instruments, in order to empirically examine the relationships between the three age-specific questionnaires. The congruencies between age group 5 to 7 and 8 to 10 varied from .95 to .98. For the age groups 8 to 10 and 11 to 13 coefficients ranged from .94 to .99. The congruence between the two most distant groups (5 to 7 and 11 to 13) ranged from .90 to .97. Although by dropping the non-common facets, Altruism and Independence, the congruence coefficients overestimate the true degree of correspondence. The fact that all observed congruencies are higher than .90, nevertheless confirms that there is a high degree of similarity among the three age-specific questionnaires. For this reason, but also for the development of an instrument applicable to a reasonably broad age range, it was decided to merge the three questionnaires into one instrument, targeted at the primary school age (6 to 12 years).

The final inventory included the 17 common facets, together with Altruism that was common to age groups 8 to 10 and 11 to 13. Independence as a facet was dropped because it only emerged from the analyses of age group 8 to 10. To decide which items were to be included for each of the 18 facets, the following rules were adopted. Items loading on a given facet in each of the three age-specific questionnaires were retained for the final version. Then, items that were common to two of the three age-groups were added. If at that stage the total number of 8 items was not reached, items were added that were specific to the youngest age group. By pooling all averaged ratings across samples, it was possible to compute new facet scores for each of the 18 facets based on 6 to 8 items. A principal component analysis of the facet scales, followed by Varimax rotation, clearly confirmed the presumed structure of the integrated HiPIC scales, suggesting that 80.7 per cent of the variance was explained by the first five rotated components.

Table 3. HiPIC domains, facets and sample items

Domains/facets	Sample item
Conscientiousness	
Achievement motivation	wants to shine at everything
Concentration	works with sustained attention
Perseverance	perseveres until the goal is achieved
Orderliness	leaves everything lying around (RK)
Benevolence	
Egocentrism	finds it hard to share with others
Irritability	is quick to take offence
Compliance	obeys without protest
Dominance	acts the boss
Altruism	defends the weak
Extraversion	
Shyness	tries to establish contact with new class-fellows (RK)
Optimism	sees the sunny side of things
Expressiveness	keeps feelings and thoughts to him/herself (RK)
Energy	has an excess of energy
Emotional Stability	
Anxiety	is quick to worry about things
Self-confidence	takes decisions easily (RK)
Imagination	
Creativity	derives pleasure from creating things
Curiosity	likes to learn new things
Intellect	is quick to understand things

Note: RK = reversed keyed item

Instrument characteristics

The final Hierarchical Personality Inventory for Children (HiPIC; Mervielde & De Fruyt, 1999) includes 144 items, 8 items per facet, assessing 18 facets hierarchically structured under the domains. The production process of the inventory was directed at an adequate and psychometric sound representation of the content enclosed in parental free descriptors, empirically aggregated to more reliable facets and domains. An overview of the hierarchical structure and a sample item per facet are presented in Table 3.

Structural replicability

The common HiPIC version was given to the parents of a new sample of 719 twins and their siblings aged between 5 and 13 (De Fruyt & Mervielde, 1998). Both parents provided independent ratings of the children. Ratings were averaged across parents, and the facet scales were subsequently submitted to principal component analysis. The factor loading matrices for the total sample, and for boys and girls separately, are presented in Table 4. Inspection of these matrices shows that the HiPIC structure is highly replicable in an independent new sample, with all facet scales loading on the expected components. Moreover, the factor structure proves invariant for boys and girls, with only minor deviations in primary and secondary loading patterns. The alpha reliabilities parallel the coefficients found in the construction samples, all ranging between .81 (Self-confidence) to .92 (Orderliness), with mean inter-item correlations varying between .36 (Self-confidence) and .58 (Orderliness). These psychometric findings have been recently confirmed in studies with both clinical and non-clinical subjects (Mus, 2000; Van Leeuwen, 2000; Van Hoecke, 2000; Vanoutrive, 2001) that included the HiPIC as part of their assessment battery. In all studies, the assumed factor structure was clearly replicated, underscoring adult findings that the FFM is also useful to conceive individual differences in clinical samples (Costa & Widiger, 1994).

Convergent and discriminant validities across observers

De Fruyt and Vollrath (submitted) recently examined the convergent and discriminant validities across parents in a combined Flemish ($N = 104$) and Swiss ($N = 205$) sample. A comparison of the maternal and paternal correlational pattern in the total Flemish and Swiss sample enables an analysis of the convergent and discriminant validity of the HiPIC domain and facet scales across observers. At the domain level, the median convergent correlation of paternal and maternal factor scores was .74, with a discriminant median validity across observers and domains of .02. The

Table 4. HiPIC factor loading matrix, after varimax rotation

	Conscientiousness			Unbenevolence			Extraversion			Imagination			Instability		
	T	M	F	T	M	F	T	M	F	T	M	F	T	M	F
C: Order	**.86**	**.87**	**.84**	-.20	-.16	-.24	-.07	-.05	-.07	-.06	-.04	-.06	.08	.06	.09
C: Concentration	**.85**	**.85**	**.84**	-.16	-.14	-.16	-.15	-.14	-.17	.24	.24	.26	-.17	-.21	-.16
C: Perseverance	**.85**	**.83**	**.87**	-.25	-.26	-.23	-.01	.02	-.01	.11	.15	.06	-.07	-.10	-.05
C: Achievement striving	**.83**	**.84**	**.82**	.09	.06	.14	.14	.14	.15	.33	.32	.35	.05	.05	.02
B: Egocentrism	-.14	-.14	-.13	**.89**	**.89**	**.88**	-.08	-.05	-.12	-.03	-.05	-.01	.17	.17	.18
B: Irritability	-.20	-.18	-.20	**.76**	**.75**	**.77**	.15	.15	.15	-.01	-.01	-.01	.39	.38	.41
B: Dominance	.11	.09	.11	**.75**	**.76**	**.76**	.37	.36	.35	.15	.17	.16	-.19	-.18	-.23
B: Compliance	.48	.48	.47	**-.74**	**-.73**	**-.76**	-.01	.04	-.04	-.05	-.07	-.01	.02	.04	-.02
B: Altruism	.12	.07	.11	**-.62**	**-.65**	**-.57**	.45	.40	.53	.21	.24	.22	.26	.25	.23
E: Expressiveness	-.01	-.01	-.07	.13	.11	.19	**.76**	**.75**	**.74**	.32	.34	.36	.03	.02	-.04
E: Shyness	.04	.08	.03	.04	.03	.04	**-.75**	**-.71**	**-.75**	-.07	-.12	-.08	.31	.33	.33
E: Energy	-.07	.01	-.05	.18	.16	.17	**.72**	**.75**	**.76**	.01	-.06	.03	.00	.06	.00
E: Optimism	.03	.05	.00	-.32	-.33	-.30	**.66**	**.66**	**.65**	.31	.23	.40	-.24	-.26	-.25
I: Creativity	.03	.03	.02	-.12	-.10	-.13	.14	.11	.16	**.83**	**.82**	**.84**	-.01	-.05	.01
I: Curiosity	.25	.30	.28	.10	.05	.11	.27	.24	.30	**.78**	**.80**	**.75**	-.07	-.05	-.05
I: Intellect	.41	.40	.43	.11	.09	.14	.13	.12	.12	**.67**	**.67**	**.66**	-.30	-.29	-.32
S: Anxiety	.07	.03	.07	.13	.10	.17	-.08	-.06	-.08	-.02	-.04	.01	**.91**	**.92**	**.90**
S: Self-confidence	.21	.23	.20	.05	.04	.06	.40	.39	.37	.31	.32	.30	**-.74**	**-.73**	**-.76**

Note: Primary loadings are printed in bold; T = total sample; M = boys; F = girls

median convergent validity coefficients for the facet scales of each HiPIC domain were .70, .65, .77, .65, and .74 for Extraversion, Benevolence, Conscientiousness, Stability, and Imagination, respectively. The semi-convergent validity across observers for a domain is indicated by the absolute median validity coefficients across observers for the facets in a domain, without the correlations on the diagonal. For example, paternal Creativity (I1) ratings were correlated with maternal Intellect (I2) and Curiosity (I3) ratings; paternal Intellect (I2) ratings with maternal Creativity (I1) and Curiosity ratings (I3); and finally, paternal Curiosity (I3) with maternal Creativity (I1) and Intellect (I2) ratings. The absolute validity coefficients should be taken, because for three of the five HiPIC domains, facet-labels refer to opposite poles of the same domain. Provided the unequal number of facets per domain, there are 12 such correlations for Extraversion, and 20, 12, 2, and 6 for Benevolence, Conscientiousness, Stability, and Imagination, respectively. The absolute median semi-convergent validities were .34, .33, .55, .43, and .40, respectively, and were about .20 to .30 lower than the convergent coefficients. Finally, the discriminant validities for the facets in a domain are indicated by the absolute median correlation between the facets of a domain and all facets of the other HiPIC domains. For example, paternal E1, E2, E3, and E4 ratings were correlated with all maternal B-, C-, S- and I-facet ratings and vice versa. There are 112 such discriminant correlations for the E-domain and 130, 112, 64, and 90 for B, C, S, and I, respectively. The absolute median discriminant validities for these domains were .12, .12, .14, .13, and .15.

In summary, the convergent validities were substantially higher than the semi-convergent validities, as they should be, and the absolute median discriminant validities were in-between .12 and .15. Ideally, they should be close to zero, but rater biases and social evaluative meaning contribute to the intercorrelation pattern. All in all, these analyses underscore the convergent, semi-convergent, and discriminant validities of the facets.

Temporal stability

De Fruyt and Mervielde (2000) investigated the stability of the HiPIC traits across a three-year interval in a longitudinal twin-family study, including parental ratings of twins and siblings. Stability coefficients for the domains, not corrected for unreliability, ranged from .59 (Emotional Stability) to .76 (Imagination). The stability coefficients for the Conscientiousness, Extraversion, Benevolence, and Imagination facets were roughly comparable across domains, with those for Emotional Stability being about .10 lower. The domains had slightly higher stability coefficients than the facets. Stability coefficients of domains and facets were further comparable across fathers and mothers.

Construct validity

Although the HiPIC was primarily conceived as an observer inventory, it is also useful as a self-rating instrument for adolescents aged between 12 and 15. De Fruyt *et al.* (2000) examined the interrelationships between self-reported HiPIC and NEO-PI-R adolescent ratings, demonstrating absolute correlation coefficients between .70 and .74 between four of the corresponding domain scales, and a smaller correlation between the Openness to Experience and Imagination domains ($r = .45$). Moreover, facets with similar content or conceptually related labels in the two inventories correlated in the .60 to .70 range, underscoring the construct validity of the HiPIC facets. Tucker congruence coefficients for self- and parental ratings on the HiPIC demonstrated to be on average .95, ranging between .87 and .98.

Van Leeuwen (2000) investigated the relationships with the Child Behavior Checklist (CBCL; Achenbach, 1991; Verhulst, Van der Ende, & Koot, 1996) in a population study on parenting behavior, demonstrating that (un)Benevolence correlates .53 and Conscientiousness -.32 with Externalizing behavior, while (un)Stability correlated .49 and Extraversion -.21 with Internalizing scores. The correlations with the remaining domains were all below |.20|. These findings underscore the external validity of the HiPIC domains, suggesting that the CBCL and HiPIC include common variance.

Finally, the HiPIC scales proved also useful for person-centered descriptive analyses. De Fruyt and Mervielde (2000) clustered HiPIC raw domain scores[2], first according to Ward's method followed by a hierarchical K-Means cluster analysis. The resulting clusters clearly corresponded to prototypes previously described in person-centered analyses of other FFM measures (Asendorpf & Van Aken, 1999). Comparable to Asendorpf and Van Aken (1999), the resilients had an overall well-adjusted profile, whereas the undercontrollers had on average substantially lower Benevolence and Conscientiousness scores. The overcontrollers had on average high Neuroticism, but lower Extraversion scores.

Conclusions

In sum, the HiPIC can be considered as a most comprehensive personality inventory today assessing individual differences in children. The instrument is broadly applicable in both research and professional practice when a detailed assessment of individual differences of children is requested. Its 144 short and grammatically similarly phrased items, are grouped into 18 facets, hierarchically structured under five broad domain factors. The HiPIC can be used as an observer inventory by parents and

---

[2] We usually compute factorscores for the HiPIC domains, except otherwise specified. Raw domain scores are sumscores derived from aggregation of facets (after reversing the order when facets are oppositionally keyed).

teachers, but can also be used for self-reports by adolescents aged between 12 and 15. It takes about 15 to 20 minutes to fill out, and instructions are kept simple and are kept to a minimum, asking informants to examine whether each item can be considered as characteristic for the child on a five-point scale. The scoring and the computation of facet and domain scores are preferably done automatically to minimize keying and computation errors. For a subset of items, raw scores have to be reversed to key them in line with the facet label. After reversing, facet scores can be easily computed through aggregation of the 8 item scores. Usually factor scores are computed as indicators of the five domains, starting from a principal component analysis of the 18 facets, and are hence independent from each other. Detailed instructions on administration, scoring, and interpretation, and different norm sets, including norms for population and clinical samples, are available from the authors. Preliminary English and German translations of the instrument are currently used in different research projects. The HiPIC will be commercially available by the beginning of 2002, distributed by a European Test Publisher. Colleagues interested to use the instrument for research or other purposes in the meantime are requested to contact one of the authors.

The availability of an inventory assessing primary and secondary order traits in primary school children fills a gap in current personality development research and assessment practice. Furthermore, the rationale behind the construction of the HiPIC extends the lexical approach of personality description, investigating the structure of the active and age-specific personality descriptive vocabulary. The analysis of the parental free descriptions strikingly parallels Shiner's (1998) literature search for the most important constructs to describe individual differences in children. Both the empirical and the conceptual analysis of children's individual differences do not reveal important dimensions outside the five-factor framework and thus extend and confirm the results from the lexical approach starting from trait adjectives. Although the labels for two of the five HiPIC domains are different from the adult Big Five, the previous analyses have demonstrated that they can be conceptually and empirically related to the adult factors. Longitudinal research will ultimately demonstrate whether these dimensions and facets can be considered as developmental precursors of the adult dimensions and their lower level traits.

Finally, we hope that the development of the HiPIC may further contribute to an increased attention for childhood individual differences in assessment practice. The wealth of instruments assessing adult traits compared to the relatively few instruments applicable for childhood personality description enclosed in this volume, illustrates the need for a specific, robust and comprehensive inventory primarily designed for childhood personality assessment. We are therefore looking forward to suggestions and experiences of both researchers and practitioners with the application of the HiPIC.

Acknowledgements

The construction of the HiPIC was accomplished with financial support from Grant No. OZF-0112792 from the Ghent University and from a NATO Collaborative Research Grant (941239) awarded to I. Mervielde. The cross-validation data were obtained from The Flemish Longitudinal Twin and Family study, accomplished with financial support from the Flemish Fund of Scientific Research (Grant No. OZF-0112792) awarded to Ivan Mervielde. Filip De Fruyt held a position as post-doctoral research fellow of the Flemish Fund of Scientific Research during the preparation of this chapter.

References

Achenbach, T.M. (1991). *Manual for the Child Behavior Checklist/4-18 and 1991 Profile.* Burlington, VT: University of Vermont, Department of Psychiatry.

Asendorpf, J.B., & Van Aken, M.A.G. (1999). Resilient, overcontrolled, and undercontrolled personality types in childhood: Replicability, predictive power and the trait-type issue. *Journal of Personality and Social Psychology, 77*, 815-832.

Block, J., & Block, J.H. (1980). *The California Child Q-set.* Palo Alto, CA: Consulting Psychologists Press.

Costa, P.T., Jr., & McCrae, R.R. (1992). *NEO PI-R. Professional manual.* Odessa, FL: Psychological Assessment Resources·

Costa, P.T., Jr., & Widiger, T.A. (Eds.). (1994). *Personality disorders and the five-factor model of personality.* Washington, DC: American Psychological Association.

De Fruyt, F., & Furnham, A. (2000). Advances in the assessment of the Five-Factor Model. *Psychologica Belgica, 40*, 51-75.

De Fruyt, F., & Mervielde, I. (1998). Contrast effects and parental ratings of twins' personality. In H. Devine-Wright, *Conference abstracts of the 9th European Conference on Personality*, (pp. 74-75). University of Surrey.

De Fruyt, F., & Mervielde, I. (2000). *A behavior genetic analysis of stability and change from childhood to adolescence.* Paper presented at the XXVIIth International Congress of Psychology, 23-28 July, Stockholm Sweden.

De Fruyt, F., & Mervielde, I. (2000). *A person-centred analysis of multiple traits across age groups and different five-factor measures.* Paper presented at the 1st Expert Workshop on Personality Psychology, 29 October – 1 November, Ghent Belgium.

De Fruyt, F., & Vollrath, M. (submitted). *Inter-parent agreement on higher and lower level traits in two countries: Effects of parent and child gender.*

De Fruyt, F., Mervielde, I., Hoekstra, H.A., & Rolland, J.-P. (2000). Assessing adolescents' personality with the NEO PI-R. *Assessment, 7*, 329-345.

De Raad, B., & Caljé, H. (1990). Personality in the context of conversation: Person-talk scenarios replicated. *European Journal of Personality, 1*, 19-36.

De Raad, B., Mulder, E., Kloosterman, K., & Hofstee, W.K.B. (1988). Personality-descriptive verbs. *European Journal of Personality, 2,* 81-96.

De Raad, B., & Hoskens, M. (1990). Personality-descriptive nouns. *European Journal of Personality, 2,* 131-146.

Digman, J.M., & Inouye, J. (1986). Further specification of the five robust factors of personality. *Journal of Personality and Social Psychology, 50,* 116-123.

Digman, J.M. (1963). Principal dimensions of child personality as inferred from teachers' judgements. *Child Development, 34,* 43-60.

Elphick, E., Slotboom, A.-M., & Kohnstamm, D. (1997). Personality judgments by parents of young adolescents. *Nederlands Tijdschrift voor de Psychologie, 52,* 151-162.

Eysenck, S. (1965). *Manual of the Junior Eysenck Personality Inventory.* London: Hodder & Stoughton.

Goldberg, L.R. (1989). *Standard markers of the Big-Five factor structure.* Paper presented at the Invited Workshop on Personality Language. The Netherlands: University of Groningen.

Goldberg, L.R. (1993). The structure of phenotypic personality traits. *American Psychologist, 48,* 26-34.

Hendriks, A.A.J. (1997). *The construction of the Five-Factor Personality Inventory (FFPI).* Unpublished doctoral dissertation. University of Groningen, The Netherlands.

John, O. P., Caspi, A., Robins, R. W., Moffit, T. E., & Stouthamer-Loeber, M. (1994). The "Little Five": Exploring the nomological network of the Five-Factor Model of personality in adolescent boys. *Child Development, 65,* 160-178.

Judge, T.A., Higgins, C.A., Thoresen, C.J., & Barrick, M.R. (1999). The Big Five personality traits, general mental ability, and career success across the life span. *Personnel Psychology, 52,* 621-652.

Kohnstamm, G.A., Halverson, C.F., Jr., Mervielde, I., & Havill, V.L. (Eds.). (1998). *Parental descriptions of child personality: Developmental antecedents of the Big Five?.* Mahwah, NJ: Erlbaum.

Mervielde, I. (1992). The B5BBS-25: A Flemish set of bipolar markers for the Big Five personality factors. *Psychologica Belgica, 32,* 195-210.

Mervielde, I. (1998). Validity of results obtained by analyzing free personality descriptions. In G. A. Kohnstamm, C. F. Halverson, Jr., I. Mervielde, & V. L. Havill (Eds.), *Parental descriptions of Child Personality: Developmental antecedents of the Big Five?* (pp. 189-203). Mahwah, NJ: Erlbaum.

Mervielde, I., & De Fruyt, F. (1999). Construction of the Hierarchical Personality Inventory for Children (HiPIC). In I. Mervielde, I. Deary, F. De Fruyt, & F. Ostendorf (Eds.), *Personality psychology in Europe* (pp. 107-127). Tilburg University Press.

Mervielde, I., & De Fruyt, F. (2000). The "Big Five" personality factors as a model for the structure of children's peer nominations. *European Journal of Personality, 14,* 91-106.

Mervielde, I., & De Fruyt, F. (2001). Personal versus common personality language. In R. Riemann, F. Ostendorf, & F. Spinath (Eds.), *Personality and temperament: Genetics, evolution, and structure* (pp. 185-207). Lengerich: Papst Scientific Publishers.

Mervielde, I., Buyst, V., & De Fruyt, F. (1995). The validity of the Big Five as a model for teachers' ratings of individual differences in children aged 4 to 12. *Personality and Individual Differences, 18,* 525-534.

Mus, A. (2000). *Persoonlijkheidstrekken van pesters en gepeste kinderen: de rol van individuele verschillen bij het optreden van psychosomatische klachten.* [Traits of bullies and victims: The role of individual differences in psychosomatic complaints]. Unpublished undergraduate thesis. Ghent University.

Parker, W.D. (1997). An empirical typology of perfectionism in academically talented children. *American Educational Research Journal, 34*, 545-562.

Parker, W.D. (1998). Birth-order effects in the academically talented. *Gifted Child Quarterly, 42*, 29-38.

Parker, W. D., & Stumpf, H. (1998). A validation of the five-factor model of personality in academically talented youth across observers and instruments. *Personality and Individual Differences, 25*, 1005-1025.

Saucier, G. (1992). Openness versus intellect: Much ado about nothing? *European Journal of Personality, 5*, 381-386.

Shiner, R.L. (1998). How shall we speak of children's personalities in middle childhood? A preliminary taxonomy. *Psychological Bulletin, 124*, 308-332.

Van Hoecke, E., Baeyens, D., De Fruyt, F., Van Laecke, E., Raes, A., Hoebeke, P., & Van de Walle, J. (2001). *Personality traits of children with voiding problems.* Paper to be presented at the Conference of the International Children's Continence Society, April 26-29, Aarhus, Denmark.

Van Leeuwen, K. (2000). *Deficits in parenting skills as an indicator of behavior problems with children and youth. Development of a screeningsinstrument for the Flemish community.* Ghent University: Department of Psychology.

Van Lieshout, C.F.M., & Haselager, G.J.T. (1994). The Big Five personality factors in Q-sort descriptions of children and adolescents. In C.F., Halverson, G.A., Kohnstamm, & R.P., Martin (1994). *The developing structure of temperament and personality from infancy to adulthood* (pp. 293-318). Hillsdale, NJ: Erlbaum.

Vanoutrive, M. (2001). *Persoonlijkheid en depressie: een empirisch onderzoek bij jongeren van 10 tot 15 jaar en hun moeders.* [personality and depression: An empirical study in adolescents aged 10 tot 15 and their mothers]. Ghent University: Unpublished undergraduate thesis.

Verhulst, F.C., Van der Ende, J., & Koot, H.M. (1996). *Handleiding voor de CBCL/4-18.* Erasmus Universiteit Rotterdam, Afdeling Kinder- en Jeugdpsychiatrie.

Chapter 7

The Structured Interview for the Five Factor Model of Personality (SIFFM)

Timothy J. Trull
Thomas A. Widiger

Introduction

The *Structured Interview for the Five Factor Model of Personality* (SIFFM; Trull &
Widiger, 1997) is a semi-structured interview to assesses adaptive and maladaptive
variants of traits relevant to the Five-Factor Model of personality (FFM). As readers
of this volume know, the FFM consists of the following bipolar trait dimensions: (1)
Neuroticism (vs. emotional stability); (2) Extraversion (vs. introversion); (3) Openness to Experience (vs. closedness to experience); (4) Agreeableness (vs. antagonism); and (5) Conscientiousness (vs. negligence) (McCrae & Costa, 1990). Each of
these broad domains can also be differentiated into underlying facets (i.e., primary
or first-order personality traits).

There are a number of reasons why we developed a semi-structured interview for
the assessment of the FFM. Much of our research and clinical work has focused on
personality disorders (e.g., Trull, 1995; Trull & Widiger, 1991; Trull, Widiger, &
Guthrie, 1990; Widiger, Mangine, Corbitt, Ellis, & Thomas, 1995; Widiger &
Sanderson, 1997). However, empirical research, and our own clinical experiences,
has led us to prefer the FFM as a model of personality disorder, as well as of normal
personality functioning (Trull, 1992; 2000; Widiger, 2000; Widiger & Trull, 1992).
Why this preference? We believe that the FFM offers many advantages over existing
models of personality disorder.

No doubt, the diagnosis of DSM-IV personality disorders is of substantial clinical
and social importance (Widiger & Sanderson, 1997). Disorders of personality functioning have been recognized since the beginning of medicine and within each edition of the major diagnostic manuals of mental disorders because many patients do
appear to present with problems that are best understood as resulting from long-
standing maladaptive personality traits (Livesley, 2001; Millon *et al.*, 1996). For

Big Five Assessment, edited by B. De Raad & M. Perugini. © 2002, Hogrefe & Huber Publishers.

example, persons who have met the various diagnostic criterion sets for Antisocial Personality Disorder have been shown to be at significant risk for unemployment, impoverishment, injury, violent death, substance and alcohol abuse, incarceration, recidivism (parole violation), and significant relationship instability (Robins, Tipp, & Przybeck, 1991; Stoff, Breiling, & Maser, 1997). Dependent personality traits have been shown to be associated with excessive and maladaptive efforts to maintain relationships and with a vulnerability to episodes of depression in response to interpersonal loss (Blatt & Zuroff, 1992; Bornstein, 1992; Santor & Zuroff, 1997). Narcissistic personality traits have been associated with the occurrence of antagonistic, aggressive, and even violent reactions to threats and injuries to self-esteem (Bushman & Baumeister, 1998; Rhodewalt, Madrian, & Cheney, 1998). Borderline Personality Disorder has been associated with a wide variety of maladaptive outcomes (e.g., death by suicide, relationship instability, personal distress, and eating, mood, substance, and dissociative disorders) that often have substantial public health costs (Gunderson, 1984; Linehan & Heard, 1999). Personality disorders also influence significantly the occurrence, expression, course, and/or treatment of most other mental disorders (Shea, Widiger, & Klein, 1992) as well as themselves being the focus of therapeutic interventions (Perry, Banon, & Ianni, 1999; Sanislow & McGlashan, 1998).

However, personality disorders are among the most problematic to diagnose (Maser, Kaelber, & Weise, 1991; Perry, 1992; Widiger & Coker, in press; Zimmerman, 1994). For example, because of the polythetic nature of the diagnostic criteria for the DSM-IV personality disorders, there is great heterogeneity among persons who receive the same personality disorder diagnosis (Trull, 2000; Widiger, 1993). Thus, two individuals diagnosed with Borderline Personality Disorder may present with different combinations of symptoms and different clinical presentations. Second, the DSM-IV makes an arbitrary distinction between personality disorders and "normal" personality functioning (Widiger & Corbitt, 1994). No rationale or empirical support has ever been provided for the most of the personality disorder diagnostic thresholds, and these arbitrary thresholds result in a significant loss of information. Finally, the comorbidity or co-occurrence among personality disorder diagnoses is substantial (Oldham *et al.*, 1992; Trull, 2000; Widiger & Rogers, 1989) and inconsistent with "the categorical perspective that Personality Disorders represent qualitatively distinct clinical syndromes" (APA, 1994, p. 633). It is not clear how much more clinically useful information is garnered by listing three or four diagnoses (the average number of personality disorder diagnoses received by individual patients) that are themselves overlapping and still inadequate in characterizing all of the important adaptive and maladaptive personality traits that are present within each individual patient. The inclusion of new personality disorder diagnoses within the APA diagnostic manual is unlikely to occur (Pincus, Frances, Davis, First, & Widiger, 1992), yet many also feel that the DSM-IV does not provide enough coverage of maladaptive personality traits that will often be the focus of clinical treatment (Westen & Arkowitz-Westen, 1998; Widiger, 1993).

An FFM alternative: The SIFFM

A dimensional, quantitative assessment of personality traits can address many of these limitations of the DSM-IV personality disorder diagnoses (Costa & Widiger, in press). This is the approach of the SIFFM. The traits that are assessed by the SIFFM are those identified within the dimensional Five-Factor Model (FFM) or Big Five Model (BFM) of personality, as described by Costa and McCrae (1992), Digman (1990), Goldberg (1992), Tellegen and Waller (in press), and others. There are alternative dimensional models of personality (e.g., Benjamin, 1993; Clark, 1993; Cloninger, Svrakic, & Przybeck, 1993; Millon & Davis, 1994), but we believe that the Big Five Model (BFM) and, more specifically, the FFM have certain features that result in significant advantages over these alternatives (Costa & Widiger, 1994; in press; Trull, 2000; Wiggins, 1996).

First, compared to the DSM-IV, which is theoretically diverse, the BFM/FFM is more theoretically neutral. These models do not represent the personal or theoretical views of any theorist. Rather, their derivation was based on the idea that the most important personality traits could be identified by sampling trait terms that appeared most frequently within the natural language. A second advantage is the substantial empirical support for the BFM/FFM, much more support than has been provided for the DSM-IV description of personality disorders. Finally, the BFM/FFM is much more comprehensive than the DSM-IV classification. The BFM/FFM, in a fairly succinct way, provides a description of a wide range of both adaptive and maladaptive personality traits. Rather than being a listing of relatively obscure traits that have little relevance, the BFM/FFM traits include major normal and abnormal personality traits that have been the subject of much research and clinical attention.

Development of the SIFFM

The SIFFM was developed in order to provide an interview measure of the Five-Factor Model of personality. Although several self-report measures exist for this purpose, no structured interview to assess the Big Five or FFM has ever been developed. Previously, we discussed the desire and need for an interview instrument that assesses the Five-Factor Model (Widiger & Costa, 1994; Widiger & Trull, 1992, 1997). An interview-based measure is important for several reasons. First, there is a great deal of concern that self-report inventory scores may be significantly affected by current mood state. Although interview based scores may not be completely immune from such an influence, their format (which allows for clarifications and additional probes) suggests that interviews may be less susceptible to the influence of temporary mood states. Second, many mental health professionals seem to prefer

Table 1. Domains and facets of personality assessed by the Structured Interview for the Five-Factor Model of Personality (SIFFM)

Neuroticism	Anxiety; Hostility; Depression; Self-Consciousness; Impulsiveness; Vulnerability
Extraversion	Warmth; Gregariousness; Assertiveness; Activity; Excitement Seeking; Positive Emotions
Openness to Experience	Fantasy; Aesthetics; Feelings; Actions; Ideas; Values
Agreeableness	Trust; Straightforwardness; Altruism; Compliance; Modesty; Tendermindedness
Conscientiousness	Competence; Order; Dutifulness; Achievement Striving; Self-Discipline; Deliberation

interview-based measures of personality and psychopathology (Rogers, 1995). For example, the discrepancy between self-report inventory and interview-based scores is well-documented (Perry, 1992; Zimmerman, 1994). When faced with such a discrepancy, clinicians and clinical researchers will often assume that interview-based assessments are likely to be more valid because the assessment occurred face-to-face and because there were opportunities for follow-up questions and probes (Perry, 1992). Finally, in order to establish the construct validity of these personality dimensions and traits, instruments using different modes of assessment (other than self-report) are necessary. Therefore, from both a clinical and research perspective, an interview assessing the personality traits that are included in the Five-Factor Model of Personality is needed and, for some clinicians and researchers, can at times be a preferred method of assessment.

Currently, the most frequently used self-report measure of the Five-Factor Model of personality is the Costa and McCrae (1992) NEO-PI-R (Briggs, 1992; Widiger & Trull, 1997). An attraction of the SIFFM is that it was coordinated closely with the NEO-PI-R. The interview questions included within the SIFFM are probes for the assessment of the domains and facets of the FFM as described and assessed by the NEO-PI-R. However, the SIFFM also attempts to assess systematically both the normal/adaptive and abnormal/maladaptive variants of the personality traits that comprise the Five-Factor Model of personality. The SIFFM includes questions that specifically target features indicative of maladaptive variants of each of the 30 facets of the NEO-PI-R. Because our interview assesses adaptive and maladaptive levels of personality traits, we believe that the SIFFM will appeal to clinicians and researchers who are interested in evaluating individuals for personality pathology.

Format of the SIFFM, scoring, and interpretation

The SIFFM assesses the five domains of personality functioning that represent the Five-Factor Model (FFM) of personality. Table 1 presents an overview of the domains and facets of personality assessed by the SIFFM.

Table 2. Example of three SIFFM items and anchor points for scoring

9.	Do you consider yourself to be a depressed person? **IF YES:** Do you often feel worthless, lonely, or blue? How long do these periods last? How often do you feel happy?)
	0 **NO**; does not consider self a depressed person.
	1 **YES**; considers self a depressed person; feels down a significant amount of the time.
	2 **YES**; considers self a depressed person; rarely (if ever) feels happy; depressive periods last a long time.
29.	Do you prefer to do most activities with other people or alone? **IF WITH OTHER PEOPLE:** Are you rarely by yourself?
	0 Prefers to do most activities alone
	1 Prefers to do most activities with other people
	2 Rarely alone
32.	Do you have many friends? **IF NO:** Do you have any close friends or confidants?
	2 **YES**; does have many friends
	1 **NO**; does not have many friends
	0 **NO**; does not have any close friends or confidants

Length

The SIFFM contains 120 interview items, and requires approximately 1 hour to administer. The SIFFM contains 4 initial probes for each of the 30 facets covered in the Five-Factor Model of personality (i.e., 24 probes for each of the five major domains of the FFM).

Instructions

Scores on the SIFFM reflect the degree to which a particular personality trait is present. Therefore, the interviewer provides appropriate instructions for answering SIFFM items, such that respondents' answers reflect their "usual selves." Specifically, the following instructions are provided:

"There are no "right" or "wrong" answers to the questions I will be asking you. The questions deal with how you see yourself and how others may see you. It is important that you give your honest opinion and that your answer reflect the way you usually are. That is, answer the questions in a way that describes your "usual self."

Further, because the level of a personality trait is being assessed, it is important that interviewers ask for examples of behavior that demonstrate the trait in question, when appropriate. The SIFFM questions are relatively straightforward, and one can generally trust that the respondents have adequately understood them and that their responses can be taken at face-value. However, a potential advantage of semi-structured interviews relative to self-report inventories is the opportunity to ask for examples and illustrations of the respondents' opinions and self-descriptions to ensure that they have in fact adequately understood the intention and meaning of the test items. In many places throughout the interview, we prompt the interviewer to ask for examples. However, the interviewer should feel free to ask for examples throughout the interview in order to collect more information on the trait.

Format for rating interview responses

Answers for each SIFFM item are rated on a 3-point scale (0, 1, 2), that is ordinal in nature. A higher score indicates that the trait in question is present to a greater degree. For example, a score of "1" on the SIFFM question #9 assessing the facet of depression indicates that the respondent considers his-/herself to be a "depressed person" and feels worthless, lonely, or blue a significant amount of time (see Table 2). A score of "2" on this interview item indicates that in addition to considering his-/herself to be a depressed person, the respondent rarely feels happy and the depressive periods may last for quite some time. Therefore, in this example, a higher score indicates a greater degree or severity of trait depression.

Our choice of a 3-point scale allows for variability in scores and is the direct result of pilot testing different response formats. In these preliminary studies, highly reliable scores for SIFFM items were obtained using a 3-point rating scale.

Scoring SIFFM items

The administration and scoring of individual SIFFM responses is relatively straightforward. Each SIFFM item follows a similar format. An initial (probe) question is posed, and more questions may or may not be asked depending on the response to this initial question. For example, Table 2 presents SIFFM item #9. The initial probe question is, "Do you consider yourself to be a depressed person?" If the respondent's answer is "No" or strongly suggests a negative answer (e.g., "Only on very rare occasions"), the interviewer records this response and then moves on to the next SIFFM item. On the other hand, if a "Yes" or positive response is offered, the interviewer proceeds to the next set of questions that are enclosed in parentheses. In our example, SIFFM item #9 (Depression), the interviewer would then ask, "Do you often feel worthless, lonely, or blue? How long do these periods last? How often do you feel happy?"

Under each set of questions for each item are the scores (0, 1, 2) and operational guidelines for each possible score. The scoring of SIFFM responses is facilitated by the provision of descriptions of responses necessary to receive each of the three possible scores. These guidelines also serve to prompt the interviewer to ask additional questions of the respondent in order to obtain the information necessary to provide the most accurate score. The interviewer simply matches the answer(s) to each item with the appropriate descriptor and then circles that score.

Two additional comments regarding administration and scoring are warranted. First, although a positive ("Yes") response to the initial probe question typically indicates that the interviewer should proceed to additional questions for each item, this is not always the case. To cite two examples, the probe question for SIFFM item #29 (Gregariousness) is "Do you prefer to do most activities with other people or alone?" Obviously, this is not a yes/no question. In this case, as indicated in the text that is in bold and in all capital letters (**IF WITH OTHER PEOPLE**), the interviewer proceeds if the respondent's answer indicates that he or she prefers to do most activities with other people. A second example is SIFFM item #32 (Gregariousness). The probe question is, "Do you have many friends?" In this case, a "No" response will lead the interviewer to proceed to the additional questions.

This brings up the second issue. Because we attempted to provide a relative balance of questions that assess high versus low levels of the trait in question, the order of the scores for SIFFM items is sometimes reversed. For example, note that the order of the scores for item #32 is 2, 1, 0 instead of 0, 1, 2. This reverse-order is necessary because this item assesses low levels of the trait in question — in this case, the trait of gregariousness. A "Yes" answer to the probe ("Do you have many friends?") indicates relatively higher levels of gregariousness and warrants a score of "2." However, a "No" to the probe followed by a response indicating no close friends or confidants would earn a score of "0." To simplify matters (so reverse-score algorithms do not have to be employed at a later stage in scoring, and so the meaning of individual item scores as recorded in the interview booklet is clear), we provided the appropriate score next to the respective scoring guideline.

Calculating SIFFM facet and domain scores

SIFFM facet and domain scores are calculated by adding up the relevant item scores. Because SIFFM items are organized by domain and facet, these calculations are fairly simple. In the interview booklet, the four items on each page make up a facet score. For example, SIFFM items #1 through #4 target the Neuroticism facet of Anxiety. The sum of the obtained scores for these four items is the Anxiety facet score. The sum of the facet scores for Anxiety, Angry Hostility, Depression, Self-Consciousness, Impulsiveness, and Vulnerability is the Neuroticism domain score.

Most test manuals provide "normative" data so that obtained scores can be compared to the mean scores of various groups of respondents (e.g., community residents, clinic outpatients, etc.). In the case of the SIFFM, we did not provide normative data for several reasons. First, very large and representative samples are necessary to support this approach. For example, in order to obtain a representative sample of community residents, it is necessary to sample large numbers of randomly selected individuals who represent demographic features in the same proportions as those found in the population at large. Needless to say, this is a tremendous undertaking that can only be approximated at best. Further, this requires a great deal of time and expense — especially in the case of a structured interview. Only one semi-structured interview for mental, psychiatric disorders has obtained normative data (i.e., the interview used in the National Institute of Mental Health epidemiological research), due in large part to the costs of such a data collection (Rogers, 1995). In addition, in many cases, these community-based samples are significantly different from the individuals sampled for a particular study. For example, the economic and racial backgrounds of a sample of urban, inner-city participants are unlikely to be similar to those from a U.S. Census-matched normative group. For these and other reasons, we (along with others) advocate the collection of "local norms" if the clinician or researcher prefers to contrast obtained scores with mean scores from a normative or comparison group.

A second reason why we have not collected or presented normative data concerns the way the SIFFM was constructed. One of the major distinguishing features of this interview is that maladaptivity or dysfunction associated with these personality traits is assessed in the SIFFM items. Because of this feature, SIFFM scores to some extent reflect not only the level of a personality trait but also the degree to which it is problematic. This is quite different from the typical self-report inventory where high scores suggest high levels of the trait in question but do not necessarily indicate dysfunction. For example, two individuals may obtain the exact same high score on a measure of the trait of altruism; however, for one individual this level of the trait is adaptive whereas for the other it is maladaptive (i.e., he or she may have been exploited or "used" by others). SIFFM scores reflect not only the degree to which the trait is present, but also suggest the level of dysfunction that accompanies the trait in question, irregardless of the normative frequency or prevalence of the respective dysfunction within a particular population.

Interpretation

There are several possible ways to interpret SIFFM scores. At the item level, scores and the corresponding scoring guidelines can be examined to make inferences regarding the intensity and dysfunctionality of a trait. Because there are 120 items and individual item scores are less reliable than composite scores (i.e., facet or domain scores), the exclusive use of this interpretive strategy is not recommended nor is it likely to be practical. We recommend that item-level interpretation be used only when facet or domain scores raise the possibility of dysfunction.

Regarding the interpretation of *SIFFM facet scores* (sum of four SIFFM item scores), we offer the following guidelines:

Scores 0 to 2:   salient LOW level of trait
Scores 3 to 5:   MODERATE level of trait
Scores 6 to 8:   salient HIGH level of trait

These ranges are based on the following rationale: *salient LOW level* scores are defined at the lower end (score = 0) by *four item scores of 0* and at the upper end (score = 2) by *at least two item scores of 0 and no item score > 1*; and *salient HIGH level* scores are defined at the lower end (score = 6) by *at least two item scores of 2 and no item score < 1* and at the upper end (score = 8) by *four item scores of 2*. Although there are alternative ways of obtaining facet scores in these ranges, these general guidelines should be useful in identifying the level of a facet trait endorsed by the interview respondent.

For salient low and salient high levels, some degree of dysfunction is suggested but not necessarily indicated. For example, salient high levels of Trust (a facet of Agreeableness) could be adaptive (e.g., person has faith in good intentions of others, readily discusses personal insecurities, problems, and vulnerabilities with others, and is able to place a dependence on and faith in others), but a maladaptive variant would involve being excessively gullible or naive, failing to recognize that some persons should not be trusted, and failing to take practical cautions with respect to personal safety or property. Similarly, salient low levels of Trust could be adaptive (e.g., person is reasonably or effectively skeptical or dubious regarding proposals or intentions of others) but a maladaptive variant would involve being paranoid and suspicious of most persons, readily perceiving malevolent intentions within benign, innocent remarks, and often becoming involved in arguments with friends, colleagues, or associates due to an unfounded belief that he or she is being mistreated, exploited, or victimized. As discussed below, the judgement of dysfunction should be based on an examination of an individual's responses to SIFFM items that specifically assess for impairment.

Regarding the interpretation of *SIFFM domain scores* (sum of 24 SIFFM item scores), the following guidelines are offered:

Scores 0 to 12:	salient LOW level of trait
Scores 13 to 35:	MODERATE level of trait
Scores 36 to 48:	salient HIGH level of trait

These ranges are based on the following rationale: *salient LOW level* scores are defined at the lower end (score = 0) by *24 item scores of 0* and at the upper end (score = 12) by *at least 12 item scores of 0 and no item score > 1*; and *salient HIGH level* scores are defined at the lower end (score = 36) by *at least 12 item scores of 2 and no item score < 1* and at the upper end (score = 48) by *24 item scores of 2*. Again, there are alternative ways of obtaining scores in these ranges. However, these general guidelines should be useful in identifying the level of a domain trait endorsed by the interview respondent.

We want to emphasize that these cutoff guidelines are rationally-based. Therefore, future research is necessary to empirically evaluate their utility. Further, it is important to note that the Salient Low or Salient High score designations do not necessarily indicate maladaptivity or dysfunction, only that it is more likely. The judgement of maladaptivity or dysfunction should be made based on an individual's responses to SIFFM items that specifically assess for dysfunction.

Critical facets and items

As noted previously, the SIFFM taps a wide range of maladaptive and adaptive personality features. In contrast to most FFM instruments, the SIFFM contains many items that assess maladaptive features associated with major personality traits. For example, maladaptive variants of antagonism and introversion are well assessed by the NEO-PI-R (Costa & McCrae, 1992) but perhaps not all of the maladaptive variants of agreeableness or extraversion are equally well represented (Widiger & Costa, 1994). The weaker representation of maladaptive agreeableness and extraversion relative to antagonism and introversion (respectively) in the NEO-PI-R is probably consistent with the extent to which traits of agreeableness and extraversion are in fact generally or typically more adaptive than traits of antagonism and introversion (respectively). Nevertheless, the SIFFM attempts to provide a more comprehensive and systematic assessment of the maladaptive variants of all of the poles of the five domains of the FFM in order to increase the potential utility and applicability of the FFM for clinical settings in which the maladaptive variants of agreeableness and extraversion (for example) are of considerable importance and interest.

Further, many of the interview's items assess personality features that are directly relevant to the DSM-IV personality disorders (APA, 1994). Those traits that are most relevant to the individual DSM-IV personality disorders are highlighted in Table 3. This table summarizes hypothesized SIFFM facet-personality disorder relationships for each of the 10 official DSM-IV personality disorders.

As a further clinical aid, we compiled a list of those SIFFM items that are *directly* relevant to the criteria for each of the official DSM-IV personality disorders. These SIFFM items explicitly tap DSM-IV personality disorder symptoms, and therefore have high face validity. The clinician may choose to view these as "critical items" for each personality disorder. These items are listed in the SIFFM manual (Trull & Widiger, 1997).

Keep in mind two points, however. The SIFFM was not designed to directly assess *all* criteria of the DSM-IV personality disorders. Many of the personality traits relevant to the DSM-IV personality disorders are assessed with SIFFM items, but the SIFFM is not directly keyed to DSM-IV personality disorder criteria. Second, the potential advantage of the SIFFM is that it provides more comprehensive coverage of maladaptive personality traits than DSM-IV personality disorder assessment instruments. The SIFFM taps many maladaptive features that are not considered in the DSM-IV personality disorder diagnostic system. For example, SIFFM item #68 (an Openness to Ideas item) asks:

Would you say that your ideas are rather traditional or old-fashioned?
(IF YES: Are you reluctant to consider new or alternative ideas of other cultures or perspectives?)

Clearly, being "closed" to ideas regarding different lifestyles, perspectives, or cultures can be maladaptive. Such a trait may cause problems in relationships with others both within and outside of an occupational context. However, this maladaptive personality feature is not directly tied to any DSM-IV personality disorder.

We hope these examples point out the broad range of personality traits that are assessed by SIFFM items. Because of the SIFFM's comprehensiveness, SIFFM interview scores are clinically informative from both a formal diagnostic (i.e., DSM-IV) as well as a more general assessment perspective.

Development of the SIFFM

As mentioned previously, the SIFFM targets the FFM constructs that are assessed by

Table 3. Summary of SIFFM trait and DSM-IV personality disorder relationships

SIFFM Facet	Schizoid	Schizotypal	Paranoid	Avoidant	Dependent	Obsessive Compulsive	Histrionic	Narcissistic	Borderline	Antisocial
Neuroticism										
Anxiety		H	H	H	H				H	L
Hostility	L		H		L	H	H	H	H	H
Depression				H	H			L	H	L
Self-Consciousness	L	H		H			H	H		L
Impulsiveness									H	H
Vulnerability		H		H	H		H	H/L	H	L
Extraversion										
Warmth	L				H	L	H		H	
Gregariousness	L	L		L	H		H		H	
Assertiveness				L	L	H		H	H	
Activity	L			L	L	H	H			
Excitement Seeking				L		L	H			H
Positive Emotions	L		L			L	H	H/L		
Openness to Experience										
Fantasy		H				L	H	H	H	
Aesthetics		H				L				
Feelings	L	L				L	H		H	
Actions		H		L		L	H			
Ideas		H	L			L	L			
Values		H	L			L				
Agreeableness										
Trust		L	L		H		H		L	L
Straightforwardness					H		L		L	L
Altruism					H	L	L	L		L
Compliance			L		H	L			L	L
Modesty				H	H			L		L
Tendermindedness			L		H		H	L		L
Conscientiousness										
Competence				L	L	H		H		
Order						H				L
Dutifulness						H				L
Achievement Striving						H		H	L	L
Self-Discipline						H	L			L
Deliberation					L	H	L		L	L

Note: H = high on the trait, L = low on the trait.

were generated by five researchers with backgrounds in clinical psychology and the FFM. In response to feedback indicating difficulties in the administration or under-standing of any items or in the scoring of item responses, modifications to the wor-ding of items were made. In some cases, items were deleted or added at this initial stage of development. The first formal empirical examination of the SIFFM items involved the administration of a preliminary 169-item version to both clinical and nonclinical samples. This initial version included approximately 6 items per facet, reverse-scored items, and items targeting maladaptive levels of the traits.

The criteria we used to determine which items to retain for the final version of the SIFFM included: (a) high corrected-item total correlation (high internal consis-tency); (b) item score correlation with its targeted NEO-PI-R facet and domain score (convergent validity), and relative lack of correlation with non-targeted NEO-PI-R facets and domain scores (discriminant validity); (c) reasonable variability in item scores as indicated by an examination of item means and standard deviations; and (d) encouraging factor loadings based on the results of a series of 30 principal axis factor analyses that included all items targeting a specific facet, the corresponding NEO-PI-R facet score, and non-targeted domain scores from the NEO-PI-R. Based on these criteria, we selected four SIFFM items for each of the 30 facets of the FFM. The final version of the SIFFM includes 120 items: four items for each facet, 24 items for each domain. Further, 32 of the items were reverse-scored.

Psychometric properties of the SIFFM

Reliability

Three types of reliability have been examined: inter-rater reliability, internal consis-tency, and test-retest reliability.

Inter-rater reliability

The degree to which interview responses can be scored reliably is of utmost impor-tance. A slick, crafty interview that cannot be scored reliably will not be useful to clinicians or to researchers. Fortunately, all studies that have evaluated the inter-rater reliability of SIFFM scores have reported very encouraging results. Trull *et al.* (1998) reported high inter-rater reliability coefficients for independent ratings of interview audio-tapes in samples of 187 undergraduates and of 46 outpatients re-ceiving treatment for a psychological condition. The undergraduates were inter-viewed by advanced undergraduate students, graduate students in clinical psychol-ogy, and a licensed clinical psychologist, while the outpatients were interviewed by graduate students in clinical psychology and a licensed clinical psychologist. Audio-tapes of 35 per cent (66 of 187) of the SIFFM interviews with undergraduates and of

43 per cent (20 of 46) of the SIFFM interviews with outpatients were reviewed and scored independently by a reliability checker. Intraclass correlation coefficients (ICCs; Shrout & Fleiss, 1979) were calculated comparing the independent ratings of the scores on each of the 30 SIFFM facets as well as on each of the five SIFFM domain scores. The ICCs for almost all domains and facets were exceptionally high (i.e., greater than .90), and the reliability values for the undergraduate and clinical participants, respectively, did not differ significantly.

The inter-rater reliability of SIFFM scores has also been evaluated in two other studies, one assessing clinical outpatients and one assessing undergraduate participants. Trull, Vieth, Wolfenstein, and Burr (2002) administered the SIFFM to 52 outpatients (40 women, 12 men; M age = 36.00 [14.4]) drawn from several community-based health clinics. Thirty of these audio-taped SIFFM interviews were reviewed and scored independently by a reliability checker. Inter-rater reliability indices (ICCs) were excellent for both SIFFM domain scores (all ICCs = .99) and SIFFM facet scores (range = .94 to 1.00).

Trull *et al.* (2002) also reported on the inter-rater reliability of SIFFM scores in a sample of 150 college undergraduates (75 men, 75 women; M age = 18.41 [0.75]). Ninety-three of these participants had scored above threshold on a measure of Borderline Personality Disorder features, suggesting the presence of BPD pathology. Thirty-eight of the 150 audio-taped SIFFM interviews were reviewed and scored independently by a reliability checker. All SIFFM domain ICCs were .99, and the ICCs for SIFFM facet scores ranged from .93 to 1.00.

Internal consistency

Trull *et al.* (1998) computed Cronbach's alpha coefficient for each SIFFM domain scale in their undergraduate sample and clinical sample, separately. For the undergraduate sample, the internal consistency coefficients ranged from .71 (Agreeableness) to .84 (Neuroticism and Extraversion), while in the clinical sample the range was from .72 (Agreeableness) to .97 (Neuroticism and Extraversion). Although, as expected (given that internal consistency is at least partially a function of item length), SIFFM facet internal consistencies were lower, most of the values for these two samples were in the acceptable range.

In a sample of 52 clinical outpatients, Trull *et al.* (2002) reported that the median internal consistency coefficient (alpha) for SIFFM domains was .74 while the median alpha for SIFFM facet scores was .62. In the sample of 150 college students described above, Trull *et al.* (2002) reported that the median internal consistency coefficient for SIFFM domains was .77 while the median alpha for SIFFM facet scores was .60.

Table 4. Test-retest reliabilities and stability indices for SIFFM domain and facet scales (*N* = 44)

SIFFM Scale	Pearson Correlation *r*	Intraclass Correlation ICC
Neuroticism	.82	.81
Anxiety	.82	.65
Hostility	.71	.71
Depression	.78	.78
Self-Consciousness	.75	.75
Impulsiveness	.61	.59
Vulnerability	.69	.67
Extraversion	.93	.93
Warmth	.90	.90
Gregariousness	.85	.85
Assertiveness	.85	.85
Activity	.77	.77
Excitement Seeking	.70	.70
Positive Emotions	.81	.81
Openness to Experience	.89	.89
Fantasy	.83	.83
Aesthetics	.87	.87
Feelings	.78	.78
Actions	.58	.58
Ideas	.78	.78
Values	.81	.81
Agreeableness	.88	.88
Trust	.75	.75
Straightforwardness	.78	.78
Altruism	.81	.81
Compliance	.66	.66
Modesty	.64	.63
Tendermindedness	.75	.75
Conscientiousness	.90	.90
Competence	.78	.78
Order	.87	.87
Dutifulness	.65	.65
Achievement Striving	.64	.64
Self-Discipline	.79	.79
Deliberation	.69	.68

Test-retest reliability

To date, only one study has examined the test-retest reliability of SIFFM scores. Trull *et al.* (1998) reported the results of a small test-retest study of SIFFM scores. Participants were 44 undergraduate students who completed the SIFFM on two occasions separated by two weeks. As indicated in Table 4, Pearson correlations and

Table 5. Correlations between SIFFM facet scores and corresponding NEO-PI-R facet scores

SIFFM Facet	N = 233 All Subjects	N = 187 Undergrad	N = 46 Clinic
Neuroticism			
Anxiety	.59	.50	.67
Hostility	.63	.60	.68
Depression	.71	.64	.68
Self-Consciousness	.68	.60	.71
Impulsiveness	.41	.37	.51
Vulnerability	.63	.49	.65
Extraversion			
Warmth	.59	.59	.45
Gregariousness	.47	.39	.63
Assertiveness	.81	.79	.81
Activity	.60	.58	.48
Excitement Seeking	.58	.51	.53
Positive Emotions	.71	.64	.61
Openness to Experience			
Fantasy	.62	.61	.65
Aesthetics	.63	.67	.39
Feelings	.36	.49	.30
Actions	.39	.45	.33
Ideas	.57	.62	.49
Values	.29	.26	.14
Agreeableness			
Trust	.70	.72	.65
Straightforwardness	.60	.61	.41
Altruism	.42	.41	.54
Compliance	.54	.54	.51
Modesty	.42	.37	.35
Tendermindedness	.38	.36	.37
Conscientiousness			
Competence	.53	.51	.52
Order	.77	.74	.84
Dutifulness	.27	.23	.35
Achievement Striving	.67	.65	.68
Self-Discipline	.72	.71	.71
Deliberation	.63	.62	.68

ICCs for the SIFFM domain scores were very high (range = .81 to .93), as were the reliability indices for facet scores in this sample (average r for facet scores = .76, average ICC = .75).

Validity

The validity of SIFFM scores has been examined in several studies. Perhaps the most obvious validity assessment involves an examination of the relations between SIFFM domain and facet scores and corresponding scores from the NEO-PI-R. Trull *et al.* (1998) reported that SIFFM domain and NEO-PI-R domain scores were highly related to each other. Specifically, combining the clinical and nonclinical samples, the convergent validity coefficients for the Neuroticism, Extraversion, Openness,

Agreeableness, and Conscientiousness domains were .77, .84, .65, .75, and .82, respectively. In general, SIFFM facet score correlations with corresponding facet scores from the NEO-PI-R were in the moderate to high range. These convergent validity results were replicated across clinical and nonclinical samples. Table 5 presents these correlations.

Axelrod, Widiger, Trull, and Corbitt (1997) reported the convergent and discriminant validity coefficients for an initial draft of the SIFFM's assessment of the facets of Agreeableness. Each of the respective Agreeableness facet scales from the NEO-PI-R and SIFFM obtained significant positive correlations. Most of the discriminant validity coefficients were statistically insignificant, and in no case was a discriminant validity coefficient of the same magnitude as the corresponding convergent validity coefficient.

Personality disorder scores

Because SIFFM scores are believed to reflect maladaptive levels of major personality traits (and because personality disorders are purported to be comprised of maladaptive personality traits), SIFFM scores should be significantly related to personality disorder scores. Trull *et al.* (1998) evaluated the pattern of correlations between SIFFM scores and scores on a self-report measure of DSM-III-R personality disorders (the PDQ-R; Hyler & Rieder, 1987) in the combined sample of clinical and nonclinical participants ($N = 232$). Results indicated the majority of personality disorder constructs were positively correlated with SIFFM Neuroticism scores, negatively correlated with SIFFM Extraversion scores, and negatively correlated with SIFFM Conscientiousness scores. These results are consistent with expectations based on an understanding of the FFM and with previous studies that examined the relations between personality disorder constructs and scores from alternative FFM measures (e.g., see Costa & McCrae, 1990; Soldz *et al.*, 1993; Trull, 1992). Table 6 presents the zero-order correlations between SIFFM scores and PDQ-R symptom counts.

Axelrod *et al.* (1997) demonstrated that a differentiation among the DSM-III-R personality disorders (APA, 1987) can be obtained at the facet level of the FFM. They indicated that DSM-III-R Antisocial, Borderline, Narcissistic, Paranoid, and Passive-Aggressive personality disorders all correlated significantly with the broad domain of Antagonism (ranging in value from .26 to .50), but each of these personality disorders could also be distinguished with respect to which facets of Antagonism are primarily involved. For example, the Narcissistic Personality Disorder was primarily negatively related to the facet of Modesty (i.e., arrogance), Tender-Mindedness (i.e., tough-mindedness), and Altruism (i.e., exploitation), whereas the Paranoid Personality Disorder was primarily negatively related to just the facet of Trust (i.e., suspiciousness and paranoia). Low Tender-Mindedness (i.e., tough-mindedness) was evident in the Antisocial and Narcissistic personality disorders but not in the Borderline, Paranoid, or Passive-Aggressive personality disorders. Low Modesty (i.e., arrogance) related only to the Narcissistic Personality Disorder.

Table 6. Correlations between SIFFM facet scores and PDQ-R personality disorder symptom counts (N = 232)

SIFFM Facet	Schizoid	Schizotypal	Paranoid	Avoidant	Dependent	Obsessive Compulsive	Passive Aggressive	Self Defeating	Histrionic	Narcissistic	Borderline	Antisocial	Sadistic
Neuroticism	.28	.53	.42	.66	.57	41	.50	56	.47	.39	.62	.18	.07
Anxiety	.13	.41	.26	.43	.43	.25	.28	.38	.37	.29	.52	.09	.07
Hostility	.20	.43	.43	.42	.34	.36	.46	.40	.33	.40	.58	.26	.22
Depression	.29	.37	.27	.54	.51	.31	.34	.51	.35	.23	.45	.05	-.05
Self-Consc	.24	.47	.43	.70	.49	.30	.35	.44	.31	.27	.41	.12	.03
Impulsiveness	.10	.27	.09	.16	.17	.24	.34	.23	.33	.29	.36	.36	.20
Vulnerability	.25	.39	.31	.56	.53	.34	.42	.49	.40	.26	.43	.00	-.08
Extraversion	-.46	-.29	-.28	-.65	-.29	-.20	-.31	-.30	-.07	-.10	-.25	.02	.08
Warmth	-.44	-.32	-.37	-.57	-.13	-.21	-.26	-.27	-.03	-.15	-.26	-.09	-.06
Gregariousn	-.35	-.01	-.08	-.33	.11	-.01	-.04	-.01	.23	.14	.02	.13	.11
Assertiveness	-.23	-.24	-.19	-.52	-.35	-.11	-.24	-.17	-.07	-.12	-.18	-.10	.04
Activity	-.36	-.25	-.14	-.45	-.21	-.13	-.23	-.24	-.06	-.06	-.23	.03	.11
Excite Seek	-.29	-.07	-.06	-.40	-.25	-.09	-.10	-.16	-.07	.06	.02	.23	.27
Positive Emo	-.41	-.35	-.35	-.54	-.36	-.31	-.44	-.43	-.25	-.24	-.42	-.05	-.09
Openness	.04	.31	.01	.14	.07	.16	.21	.23	.24	.20	.28	.15	.10
Fantasy	.02	.34	.03	.16	.17	.24	.29	.25	.36	.36	.28	.12	.16
Aesthetics	.12	.24	.04	.19	.00	.06	.16	.11	.04	.09	.15	.07	-.02
Feelings	-.08	.11	.01	.19	.30	.11	.12	.22	.35	.06	.23	-.06	-.09
Actions	-.21	-.08	-.18	-.27	-.22	-.18	-.12	-.11	-.14	-.05	-.01	.20	.12
Ideas	.23	.37	.11	.23	.03	.23	.22	.23	.15	.18	.20	.10	.08
Values	.11	.18	.01	.03	.00	.14	.12	.15	.13	.11	.20	.14	.10
Agreeableness	-.08	-.13	-.32	.02	.24	-.14	-.20	.08	.02	-.23	-.12	-.27	-.38
Trust	-.27	-.39	-.54	-.31	-.02	-.26	-.29	-.27	-.13	-.29	-.34	-.21	-.24
Straightforw	.06	-.12	-.14	-.03	.04	-.12	-.26	-.02	-.10	-.28	-.16	-.25	-.37
Altruism	-.11	-.08	-.20	-.01	.16	-.12	-.16	.11	-.05	-.13	-.02	-.18	-.13
Compliance	-.02	.01	-.16	.06	.19	-.06	-.08	.05	.11	-.05	-.09	-.08	-.21
Modesty	.17	.18	.06	.27	.20	.05	.13	.26	.03	-.11	.18	-.04	-.16
Tender Mind	-.08	-.05	-.15	.11	.28	.03	-.05	.15	.20	.00	.00	-.21	-.29
Conscientiousness	-.19	-.26	-.05	-.26	-.26	-.17	-.46	-.19	-.23	-.17	-.35	-.24	-.02
Competence	-.14	-.28	-.15	-.29	-.32	-.21	-.39	-.24	-.30	-.22	-.39	-.21	-.09
Order	-.04	-.03	.07	-.12	-.14	-.06	-.22	-.06	-.03	-.03	-.04	.00	.11
Dutifulness	-.11	-.11	-.17	-.11	.00	-.02	-.10	-.03	-.15	-.02	-.26	-.24	-.04
Achmt Strv	-.23	-25	-.07	-.26	-.27	-.12	-.39	-.21	-.15	-.05	-.21	-.27	.02
Self-Discipl	-16	-.24	-.04	-.24	-.29	-.24	-.45	-.21	-.25	-.21	-.32	-.11	.00
Deliberation	-09	-13	.09	.00	.04	.00	-.23	.00	-.06	-.10	-.17	-.19	-.11

Trull, Widiger, and Burr (2001) provided a more comprehensive and thorough study of the importance of considering the underlying facets of each of the domains of the FFM, testing in particular the predictions of Trull and Widiger (1997; see Table 3 of this chapter) regarding which FFM lower-order traits (i.e., facets) are most highly related to individual personality disorder constructs. Trull *et al.* (2001) evaluated specific/unique associations by controlling for personality disorder comorbid symptoms (i.e., partialling out symptoms of non-targeted personality disorders). In general, results supported the predictions of Trull and Widiger (1997) in that many of the significant relations between facets and personality disorder constructs held, even after controlling for comorbid personality disorder symptoms. For example, both the Dependent and Avoidant Personality Disorders (which are highly comorbid in clinical settings; Oldham *et al.*, 1992) correlated highly with the broad domain of Neuroticism. However, the Dependent Personality Disorder was associated primarily and uniquely with the Neuroticism facets of Depression and Vulnerability, whereas the Avoidant Personality Disorder was associated primarily and uniquely with the Neuroticism facet of Self-Consciousness. Similarly, whereas both the highly comorbid Avoidant and Schizoid personality disorders correlated highly with Introversion, each could again be differentiated with respect to particular facets of Introversion. Schizoid Personality Disorder was associated primarily and uniquely with low Positive Emotions (along with low Gregariousness and low Warmth). Avoidant Personality Disorder, on the other hand, was associated primarily and uniquely with low Assertiveness and low Excitement-Seeking (along with low Gregariousness), consistent with the expected differentiations of these personality disorders at the facet level (Trull & Widiger, 1997).

Peer report of FFM traits

Another method of establishing the validity of SIFFM scores involved the collection of peer/collateral data on the FFM. Trull *et al.* (1998) obtained peer reports of FFM traits on a sample of 55 undergraduates who also completed the SIFFM. For each participant, a male and a female peer (each of whom reported knowing the participant well and for at least two years) completed the NEO-FFI (Costa & McCrae, 1992), an inventory that yields scores on the five major dimensions of the FFM. Each peer NEO-FFI was standardized according to the gender norms corresponding to the sex of the target. A mean peer NEO-FFI score for each domain was computed by averaging the scores from the two peers for each participant. Zero-order correlations between participant's SIFFM scores and the mean peer NEO-FFI T scores were calculated. Convergent validity coefficients for FFM domains were .52 (Neuroticism), .67 (Extraversion), .32 (Openness), .39 (Agreeableness), and .47 (Conscientiousness). These convergent validity coefficients were higher than off-diagonal values in the corresponding rows and columns, suggesting that observer ratings of FFM traits converged on the same trait domains as assessed by the SIFFM.

Incremental validity

Several studies have assessed the incremental validity of SIFFM scores in predicting personality disorder symptoms. If the SIFFM, indeed, does a better job of tapping into maladaptive variants of major personality traits, one would expect that SIFFM scores could account for significant amounts of variance in personality disorder scores above and beyond what could be accounted for by popular measures of major personality traits.

Using a combined sample of clinical and nonclinical participants ($N = 232$), Trull *et al.* (1998) examined the incremental validity of SIFFM domain scores in predicting DSM-III-R personality disorder symptom scores as assessed by the PDQ-R. In a series of hierarchical regressions (using each personality disorder symptom score as the criterion, respectively), Trull *et al.* assessed the ability of SIFFM domain scores to predict PDQ-R scores once NEO-PI-R domain scores had been entered into the regression model. Results indicated that in all cases except for Paranoid, Obsessive Compulsive, and Narcissistic PDQ-R scores, SIFFM domain scores demonstrated incremental validity. The ability of SIFFM facets (hypothesized to be most highly related to the target personality disorder; see Table 3) to show incremental validity over the NEO-PI-R domain scores in predicting personality disorder scores on the PDQ-R was evaluated in a series of hierarchical regressions (Trull & Widiger, unpublished data). Results suggested that the block of respective SIFFM facets accounted for a significant amount of the variance in the targeted personality disorder score over and above what could be accounted for by the NEO-PI-R domain scores in all cases except for Obsessive Compulsive personality disorder. These results are presented in Table 7.

Trull *et al.* (2002) reported on a series of incremental validity analyses that focused on the ability of SIFFM scores to account for variance DSM-IV Borderline, Antisocial, and Histrionic symptom counts (as assessed by a semi-structured diagnostic interview) above and beyond what could be accounted for by Temperament scores (i.e., Negative Temperament, Positive Temperament, Disinhibition) from the SNAP (Clark, 1993). Subjects included both clinical and nonclinical participants (combined; $N = 202$). In the first series of analyses, SIFFM domain scores accounted for a significant amount of additional variance in Borderline ($\Delta R^2 = .09$, $p < .0001$), Antisocial ($\Delta R^2 = .06$, $p < .005$), and Histrionic ($\Delta R^2 = .12$, $p < .0001$) symptom counts, over and above that accounted for by SNAP Temperament scores. Using this same combined sample, a second series of analyses examined the incremental validity of selected SIFFM facets believed to be most relevant to each of the three personality disorders, respectively (see Trull & Widiger, 1997), over SNAP scales purported to assess each personality disorder (Clark, 1993). Once again, the block of SIFFM facet predictors showed significant predictive ability over and above SNAP scores in accounting for variance in Borderline ($\Delta R^2 = .04$, $p < .05$), Antisocial ($\Delta R^2 = .06$, $p < .05$), and Histrionic ($\Delta R^2 = .16$, $p < .0001$) symptom counts.

These incremental validity studies, however, should not be understood as suggestions that the SIFFM would provide a better or more valid assessment of the FFM than the NEO-PI-R. We expect that further research, particularly studies within the general population and community, would indicate that the NEO-PI-R provides a more reliable and valid assessment of the FFM than the SIFFM, and may even do so for some purposes within clinical settings (Widiger & Trull, 1997). The ideal use of the SIFFM will be as a supplement to, rather than as a replacement of, the NEO PI-R. This is particularly the case in instances where there are concerns regarding potential distortions to respondents' answers secondary to mood states or when there is a particular need for using a semi-structured interview methodology.

Table 7. Hierarchical regressions assessing the incremental validity of select SIFFM facets in predicting targeted Axis II personality disorders.

Criterion Symptom Count	Step/Predictors	df	ΔR^2 (adjusted)	$F\Delta$	Significant SIFFM Predictors
Paranoid (PR)	1. NEO domains	5,226	.44	37.66***	
	2. SIFFM PR-facets	8,218	.04	3.11**	Trust (---)
Schizotypal (ST)	1. NEO domains	5,226	.34	24.50***	
	2. SIFFM ST-facets	11,215	.10	4.99***	Self-Consciensness (+++), Feelings (-), Indeas (++)
Schizoid (SZ)	1. NEO domains	5,226	.24	15.33***	
	2. SIFFM SZ-facets	7,219	.03	2.33*	Positive Emotions (-)
Histrionic (HI)	1. NEO domains	5,226	.31	21.74***	
	2. SIFFM HI-facets	18,208	.17	4.99***	Gregariousness (+++), Excitement Seeking (---), Fantasy (+), Feelings (+++), Altruism (-) Tendermindedness (+)
Narcissistic (NA)	1. NEO domains	5,226	.32	22.51***	
	2. SIFFM NA-facets	12,214	.05	2.62**	Assertiveness (-), Fantasy (+++)
Borderline (BD)	1. NEO domains	5,226	.44	37.02***	
	2. SIFFM BD-facets	15,211	.07	3.29***	Anxiety (+), Hostility (++), Impulsiveness (+)
Antisocial (AT)	1. NEO domains	5,226	.20	12.48***	
	2. SIFFM AT-facets	18,208	.12	3.21***	Impulsiveness (++), Excitement Seeking (+++) Achievement Striving (--), Self Discipline (+)
Avoidant (AV)	1. NEO domains	5,226	.63	79.37***	
	2. SIFFM AV-facets	11,215	.05	4.22***	Self-Consciousness (+++)
Dependent (DP)	1. NEO domains	5,226	.48	42.81***	
	2. SIFFM DP-facets	16,210	.06	2.77***	Depression (+), Gregariousness (++), Assertiveness (--)
Obsessive Compulsive (OC)	1. NEO domains	5,226	.24	15.52***	
	2. SIFFM OC-facets	20,206	.03	1.53	

Note: see Table 3 for listing of SIFFM facets relevant to each personality disorder.

Summary

The SIFFM was designed as an interview-based assessment of both adaptive and maladaptive features related to the personality traits included in the FFM. The SIFFM will be attractive to clinicians and researchers who prefer interview-based assessments or who would like to employ an assessment measure that will complement the NEO-PI-R. To date, data obtained regarding the reliability and validity of SIFFM scores have been encouraging. The SIFFM is easy to administer and to score. Further, scores derived from the SIFFM have been shown to be related to other measures of personality traits and measures or DSM personality disorders in a pattern that would be expected given a knowledge of these traits and disorders. Finally, several studies have demonstrated that, by virtue of the measure's design, SIFFM scores appear to tap into maladaptive variants of personality traits that may not be assessed by other alternative personality measures. Although these results are indeed promising, more research is needed to assess the validity and utility of the SIFFM.

References

American Psychiatric Association. (1987). *Diagnostic and statistical manual of mental disorders* (3rd ed., rev. ed.). Washington, DC: American Psychiatric Association.

American Psychiatric Association. (1994). *Diagnostic and statistical manual of mental disorders* (4th ed.). Washington, DC: American Psychiatric Association.

Axelrod, S.R., Widiger, T.A., Trull, T.J., & Corbitt, E.M. (1997). Relations of five-factor model antagonism facets with personality disorder symptomatology. *Journal of Personality Assessment, 69*, 297-313.

Benjamin, L. S. (1993). *Interpersonal diagnosis and treatment of personality disorders.* New York: Guilford.

Blatt, S.J., & Zuroff, D.C. (1992). Interpersonal relatedness and self-definition: Two prototypes for depression. *Clinical Psychology Review, 12*, 527-562.

Bornstein, R.F. (1992). The dependent personality: developmental, social, and clinical perspectives. *Psychological Bulletin, 112*, 3-23.

Briggs, S.R. (1992). Assessing the five-factor model of personality description. *Journal of Personality, 60*, 253-293.

Bushman, B.J., & Baumeister, R.F. (1998). Threatened egotism, narcissism, self-esteem, and direct and displaced aggression: does self-love or self-hate lead to violence? *Journal of Personality and Social Psychology, 75*, 219-229.

Clark, L.A. (1993). Personality disorder diagnosis: Limitations of the Five-Factor Model. *Psychological Inquiry, 4*, 100-104.

Cloninger, C. R., Svrakic, D. M., Przybeck, T. R. (1993). A psychobiological model of temperament and character. *Archives of General Psychiatry, 50*, 975-990.

Costa, P. T., Jr., & McCrae, R. R. (1990). Personality disorders and the five-factor model of personality. *Journal of Personality Disorders, 4*, 362-371.

Costa, P.T., Jr., & McCrae, R.R. (1992). *Revised NEO Personality Inventory (NEO-PI-R) and NEO Five-Factor Inventory (NEO-FFI) professional manual.* Odessa, FL: Psychological Assessment Resources.

Costa, P.T., Jr., & Widiger, T.A. (Eds). (1994). *Personality disorders and the five-factor model of personality.* Washington, DC: American Psychological Association.

Costa, P.T., Jr., & Widiger, T.A. (Eds). (in press). *Personality disorders and the five-factor model of personality* (2nd ed.). Washington, DC: American Psychological Association.

Digman, J.M. (1990). Personality structure: Emergence of the five-factor model. *Annual Review of Psychology, 41*, 417-440.

Goldberg, L.R. (1992). The development of markers of the Big Five factor structure. *Psychological Assessment, 4*, 26-42.

Gunderson, J.G. (1984). *Borderline personality disorder.* Washington, DC: American Psychiatric Press.

Hyler, S.E., & Rieder, R.O. (1987). *Personality Diagnostic Questionnaire-Revised (PDQ-R).* New York: Author.

John, O.P. (1990). The "Big Five" factor taxonomy: Dimensions of personality in the natural language and in questionnaires. In L.A. Pervin (Ed.), *Handbook of personality: Theory and research* (pp. 66-100). NY: Guilford.

Linehan, M.M., & Heard, H. (1999). Borderline personality disorder: Costs, course, and treatment outcome. In N. Miller & K. Magruder (Eds.), *The cost-effectiveness of psychotherapy: A guide for practitioners, researchers, and policy-makers* (pp. 291-305). NY: Oxford University Press.

Livesley, W.J. (Ed.). (2001). *Handbook of personality disorders.* NY: Guilford.

Maser, J.D., Kaelber, C., & Weise, R.E. (1991). International use and attitudes toward DSM-III and DSM-III-R: Growing consensus in psychiatric classification. *Journal of Abnormal Psychology, 100*, 271-279.

McCrae, R.R., & Costa, P.T., Jr. (1990). *Personality in adulthood.* New York: Guilford.

Millon, T., & Davis, R.D. (1994). Millon's evolutionary model of normal and abnormal personality: Theory and measures. In S. Strack & M. Lorr (Eds.), *Differentiating normal and abnormal personality* (pp. 79-113). NY: Springer.

Millon, T., Davis, R.D., Millon, C.M., Wenger, A.W., Van Zuilen, M.H., Fuchs, M., & Millon, R.B. (1996). *Disorders of personality. DSM-IV and beyond.* NY: John Wiley & Sons.

Oldham, J.M., Skodol, A.E., Kellman, H.D., Hyler, S.E., Rosnick, L., & Davies, M. (1992). Diagnosis of DSM-III-R personality disorders by two semistructured interviews: Patterns of comorbidity. *American Journal of Psychiatry, 149*, 213-220.

Perry, J.C. (1992). Problems and considerations in the valid assessment of personality disorders. *American Journal of Psychiatry, 149*, 1645-1653.

Perry, J.C., Banon, E., & Ianni, F. (1999). Effectiveness of psychotherapy for personality disorders. *American Journal of Psychiatry, 156*, 1312-1321.

Pincus, H., Frances, A., Davis, W., First, M., & Widiger, T. (1992). DSM-IV and new diagnostic categories: Holding the line on proliferation. *American Journal of Psychiatry, 149*, 112-117.

Rhodewalt, F., Madrian, J.C., & Cheney, S. (1998). Narcissism, self-knowledge, organization, and emotional reactivity: the effect of daily experience on self-esteem and affect. *Personality and Social Psychology Bulletin, 24*, 75-87.

Robins, L.N., Tipp, J., & Przybeck, T.R. (1991). *Antisocial personality.* In L.N. Robins & D.A. Regier (Eds.), Psychiatric disorders in America (pp. 258-290). New York: Free Press.

Rogers, R. (1995). *Diagnostic and structured interviewing: A handbook for psychologists.* Odessa, FL: PAR.

Sanislow, C.A., & McGlashan, T.H. (1998). Treatment outcome of personality disorders. *Canadian Journal of Psychiatry, 43*, 237-250.

Santor, D.A., & Zuroff, D.C. (1997). Interpersonal responses to threats of status and interpersonal relatedness: effects of dependency and self-criticism. British *Journal of Clinical Psychology, 36*, 521-541.

Shea, M. T., Widiger, T. A., & Klein, M. H. (1992). Comorbidity of personality disorders and depression: Implications for treatment. *Journal of Consulting and Clinical Psychology, 60*, 857-868.

Shrout, P.E., & Fleiss, J.L. (1979). Intraclass correlations: Uses in assessing rater reliability. *Psychological Bulletin, 86*, 420-428.

Soldz, S., Budman, S., Demby, A., & Merry, J. (1993). Representation of personality disorders in circumplex and Five-Factor space: Explorations with a clinical sample. *Psychological Assessment, 5*, 41-52.

Stoff, D.M., Breiling, J., & Maser, J.D. (Eds.). (1997). *Handbook of antisocial behavior.* NY: Wiley.

Tellegen, A., & Waller, N.G. (in press). Exploring personality through test construction: Development of the Multidimensional Personality Questionnaire. In S.R. Briggs & J.M. Cheek (Eds.), *Personality measures: Development and evaluation* (Vol. 1). Greenwich, CT: JAI Press.

Trull, T.J. (1992). DSM-III-R personality disorders and the Five-Factor Model of personality: An empirical comparison. *Journal of Abnormal Psychology, 101*, 553-560.

Trull, T. J. (1995). Borderline personality disorder features in nonclinical young adults 1. Identification and validation. *Psychological Assessment, 7*, 33-41.

Trull, T.J. (2000). Dimensional models of personality disorder. *Current Opinion in Psychiatry, 13*, 179-184.

Trull, T. J., Vieth, A. Z., Wolfenstein, M., & Burr, R. (2002). *Incremental validity of the SIFFM.* Unpublished manuscript.

Trull, T. J., & Widiger, T. A. (1991). The relationship between borderline personality disorder criteria and dysthymia symptoms. *Journal of Psychopathology and Behavioral Assessment, 13*, 91-105.

Trull, T. J., & Widiger, T. A. (1997). *SIFFM: Structured Interview for the Five-Factor Model of Personality.* Odessa, FL: PAR.

Trull, T. J., Widiger, T. A., & Burr, R. (2001). A structured interview for the assessment of the five-factor model of personality: Facet-level relations to the Axis II personality disorders. *Journal of Personality, 69*, 175-198.

Trull, T. J., Widiger, T. A., & Guthrie, P. (1990). The categorical versus dimensional status of borderline personality disorder. *Journal of Abnormal Psychology, 99*, 40-48.

Trull, T.J., Widiger, T.A., Useda, J.D., Holcomb, J., Doan, B-T., Axelrod, S.R., Stern, B.L., & Gershuny, B.S. (1998). A structured interview for the assessment of the five-factor model of personality. *Psychological Assessment, 10*, 229-240.

Westen, D., & Arkowitz-Westen, L. (1998). Limitations of Axis II in diagnosing personality pathology in clinical practice. *American Journal of Psychiatry, 155*, 1767-1771.

Widiger, T.A. (1993). The DSM-III-R categorical personality disorder diagnoses: A critique and an alternative. *Psychological Inquiry, 4*, 75-90.

Widiger, T.A. (2000). Personality disorders in the 21st century. *Journal of Personality Disorders, 14*, 3-16.

Widiger, T.A., & Coker, L.A.. (in press). Assessing personality disorders. In J. N. Butcher (Ed.), *Clinical personality assessment. Practical approaches* (2nd ed.). New York: Oxford University Press.

Widiger, T.A., & Corbitt, E.M. (1994). Normal versus abnormal personality from the perspective of the DSM. In S. Strack & M. Lorr (Eds.), *Differentiating normal and abnormal personality* (pp. 158-175). New York: Springer.

Widiger, T. A., & Costa, P.T. Jr. (1994). Personality and personality disorders. *Journal of Abnormal Psychology, 103*, 78-91.

Widiger, T.A., Mangine, S., Corbitt, E.M., Ellis, C.G., & Thomas, G.V. (1995). *Personality disorder interview-IV: A semistructured interview for the assessment of personality disorders*. Odessa, FL: Psychological Assessment Resources.

Widiger, T., & Rogers, J. (1989). Prevalence and comorbidity of personality disorders. *Psychiatric Annals, 19*, 132-136.

Widiger, T.A., & Sanderson, C.J. (1997). Personality disorders. In A. Tasman, J. Kay, & J.A. Lieberman (Eds.), *Psychiatry* (Vol., 2, pp. 1291-1317). Philadelphia, PA: W.B. Saunders.

Widiger, T.A., & Trull, T.J. (1992). Personality and psychopathology: an application of the five-factor model. *Journal of Personality, 60*, 363-393.

Widiger, T.A., & Trull, T.J. (1997). Assessment of the five-factor model of personality. *Journal of Personality Assessment, 68*, 228-250.

Wiggins, J.S., (1996). *The five-factor model of personality: Theoretical perspectives*. New York: Guilford.

Zimmerman, M. (1994). Diagnosing personality disorders. A review of issues and research methods. *Archives of General Psychiatry, 51*, 225-245.

Chapter 8

The nonverbal asssessment of personality: The NPQ and the FF-NPQ

Sampo V. Paunonen
Michael C. Ashton

Introduction

The purpose of this chapter is to describe the development of two novel measures of personality characteristics. The first measure is called the Nonverbal Personality Questionnaire (NPQ) and the second is the Five-Factor Nonverbal Personality Questionnaire (FF-NPQ). What makes these two measures novel is that they do not employ verbal item content. Nonverbal stimuli are used as items instead, in an otherwise standard paper-and-pencil personality questionnaire.

Nonverbal personality assessment

Nonverbal measures of personality have existed for many years. Examples include the popular Rorschach inkblot test and the Thematic Apperception Test (TAT). Those measures, however, are different from the ones to be described in this chapter. Whereas the Rorschach and the TAT are both unstructured, in the sense that examinees are allowed to generate open-ended verbal responses to the items, the NPQ and FF-NPQ are structured measures. This means that a person completing the tests must choose his or her responses to each nonverbal item from a series of alternatives or response options.

There are some obvious advantages to a nonverbal measure of personality. One advantage is for cross-cultural personality research — the fact that item translation is not necessary for using such measures in different cultures and language groups means that one impediment to such cross-cultural research has been removed. (For the NPQ and FF-NPQ, the instruction page has verbal content that would, of course, require translation.) A related advantage is that any differences found across cultures

Big Five Assessment, edited by B. De Raad & M. Perugini. © 2002, Hogrefe & Huber Publishers.

in the psychometric properties of the nonverbal measure cannot be attributed to poor item translations. In contrast, if different reliabilities were found across cultures on a verbal personality scale, the difference could partly be due to translated items that misrepresent the personality construct. Another advantage of a nonverbal measure of personality is the possible application to respondents for whom verbal items pose certain difficulties. We refer to individuals with reading difficulties, people with a short attention span, young children, and those with a poor grasp of the language.

The NPQ initially arose out of some research in which we created illustrated behavioral acts as stimulus materials for a study in person perception (Paunonen & Jackson, 1979). Those nonverbal stimuli were re-worked into the form of a self-report personality questionnaire. That initial questionnaire was then revised into the present NPQ. The FF-NPQ was subsequently developed to measure the Big Five personality factors using nonverbal items of the type found in the NPQ. In fact, most of the items of the FF-NPQ were selected from the NPQ.

Construction of the NPQ

In our study of person perception (Paunonen & Jackson, 1979), we required a set of behavioral acts, being exemplars of common personality traits, that could be used to describe a person, but without words. Visual depictions of behavior were thus needed. An artist was consequently commissioned to draw some 200 cartoon-like pictures of a person performing specific behaviors in specific situations. The illustrated behaviors were each intended to portray one of 17 traits in Murray's (1938) system of needs, with between 9 and 14 behavior scenarios each. Such needs, or traits, include Affiliation, Dominance, Nurturance, and so on, and are measured by more traditional verbal personality inventories, such as Jackson's (1984) Personality Research Form (PRF).

It occurred to us in preparing the materials for our person perception study that the nonverbal items used in that research might also be useful as self-report items in a paper-and-pencil personality inventory format. To this end, we prepared an initial 202-item nonverbal personality questionnaire, which is the basis of the current NPQ, having 17 trait scales and an Infrequency validity scale. An example nonverbal item, depicting thrill-seeking behavior, can be seen in a reproduction of side one of the NPQ Instructions and Rating Form page shown in Figure 1. Other examples of the NPQ items can be found in some of the articles cited in this chapter (Paunonen, Ashton, & Jackson, 2001; Paunonen & Jackson, 1979; Paunonen, Jackson, & Keinonen, 1990; Paunonen, Keinonen, Trzebinski, Forsterling, Grishenko-Rose, Kouznetsova, & Chan, 1996).

NONVERBAL PERSONALITY QUESTIONNAIRE

Instructions and Rating Form

Attached is a **Picture Booklet** containing a series of illustrations depicting a *central figure* (the one with the *hair* drawn in) performing specific behaviors in certain situations.

Please look at each illustration and rate the *likelihood that you would engage in the type of behavior* shown.

Using the **Rating Form** on the other side of this page, record your responses by selecting an appropriate number from the 7-point rating scale. Consider the example below:

Example

> *7* - **extremely likely** that I would perform this type of behavior
> *6* - **very likely** that I would perform this type of behavior
> *5* - **moderately likely** that I would perform this type of behavior
> *4* - **neither likely nor unlikely** that I would perform this type of behavior
> *3* - **moderately unlikely** that I would perform this type of behavior
> *2* - **very unlikely** that I would perform this type of behavior
> *1* - **extremely unlikely** that I would perform this type of behavior

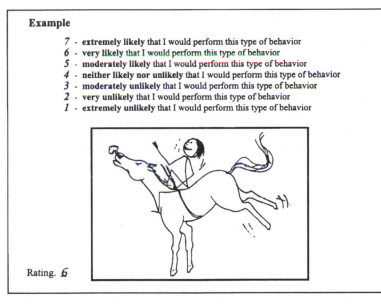

Rating. *6*

In this example the person has responded that it would be *very likely* that he/she would engage in the kind of activity in which the central figure is engaging. Your own response might have been different.

In a similar manner, consider each illustration in the **Picture Booklet** and estimate the likelihood that you would engage in the type of behavior depicted by the central figure.

Please respond to every picture and record your response on the 7-point rating scales on the back of this page. Do not mark the **Picture Booklet** or any other materials.

Turn Page Over . . .

Figure 1. Instructions and Rating Form page (obverse side) of the Nonverbal Personality Questionnaire.

Table 1. Nonverbal Personality Questionnaire trait scale names and descriptions

Achievement	Aspires to accomplish difficult tasks; responds positively to competition.
Affiliation	Enjoys being with friends and people in general; is sociable.
Aggression	Enjoys combat and argument; easily annoyed; likes to "get even."
Autonomy	Abhors restraints, confinements, or restrictions imposed by people or places; is independent.
Dominance	Attempts to influence or direct other people; enjoys the role of leader.
Endurance	Is willing to work long hours; does not give up easily.
Exhibition	Wants to be the center of attention; enjoys having an audience.
Impulsivity	Tends to act on the "spur of the moment;" is emotionally volatile.
Nurturance	Gives sympathy and comfort to those in need; assists others whenever possible.
Order	Keeps personal effects and surroundings neat and organized.
Play	Enjoys games, sports, social activities, and other amusements.
Sentience	Notices smells, sounds, sights, tastes, and textures; maintains an aesthetic view of life.
Social Recognition	Is concerned about reputation and what other people think; seeks their esteem and approval
Succorance	Frequently seeks sympathy, protection, love, and advice
Thrill-seeking	Enjoys exciting or dangerous activities; not overly concerned with personal safety.
Understanding	Is intellectually curious and reflective; wants to understand many areas of knowledge.

Note in Figure 1 the instruction to respondents in completing the NPQ; they are asked to estimate "the likelihood that you would engage in the type of behavior shown," using a seven-point rating scale. They are not asked whether they have ever performed the depicted behavior, or even whether they are likely to perform the behavior exactly as illustrated. Instead, the rating instructions emphasize the idea of each behavior item in the questionnaire as being an exemplar of a class or domain of behaviors. Also note the central character in each item is intended to be sex-neutral, so that both men and women can identify with the depicted behaviors.

As will be outlined in the following sections, the final NPQ form represents a 136-item subset of the 202 nonverbal items we initially created (Paunonen & Jackson, 1979), the items being keyed on 16 of the 17 original trait domains plus Infrequency. (The Infrequency scale contains items that are likely to be endorsed only by someone who is completing the questionnaire thoughtlessly. One such item, for example, shows a person drinking poison.) The 16 personality traits measured by the NPQ are shown in Table 1. Note that the verbal PRF also measures those same traits, among a few others. The NPQ, in fact, was first conceived as a nonverbal counterpart to the verbal PRF.

Initial NPQ item analysis

In our first analysis of the nonverbal personality items, we administered the 202-item pool to four groups of respondents (Paunonen *et al.*, 1990). All four samples consisted of university undergraduates, three of them samples of Canadian students and one group of students at the University of Helsinki. All samples but one (a Canadian sample) also completed the verbal PRF measures of Murray's (1938) system of needs. Because the PRF measures the same traits as does the NPQ (Table 1), we could use the former as a criterion for validating the latter.

On the whole, we found the psychometric properties of the experimental nonverbal scales to be acceptable in that study (Paunonen *et al.*, 1990). In all four samples, the internal consistency reliability coefficients were good, with an overall mean of .71. This is relatively high considering the scales each had only 11.2 items on average. The convergent validities of the nonverbal and verbal measures of the same traits averaged .49 over the different scales and the three respondent samples having criterion data.

It should be noted at this point that the convergent validities between the nonverbal and verbal measures of the same traits should not necessarily be expected to be too high. The reason is that the nonverbal depictions of behavior, by their very nature, can only refer to observable actions of people. Verbal depictions of behavior, in contrast, can refer to unobservable behaviors such as wishes, preferences, and sentiments. Therefore, some of the PRF trait scales refer to behaviors that are not represented in the corresponding NPQ trait scales, a fact that will tend to attenuate their intercorrelations.

Our next step was to eliminate some of the least psychometrically desirable nonverbal items from the 202-item questionnaire. Our target was to have eight items in each trait scale. Thus, we used a sequential ranking procedure to select items. This involved ordering the items on a trait scale according to some psychometric property and eliminating those items that failed to meet a minimum standard. The remaining items were then ordered with reference to some other psychometric property. If more than eight items survived the various psychometric hurdles, the overall best eight items were chosen for the final 136-item NPQ. Our sequential, stepwise item selection procedure in illustrated in Figure 2.

The revised nonverbal inventory

The nonverbal Abasement scale was deleted in the very earliest stages of test construction because of its generally poor item and scale properties, particularly in the Finnish sample. The remaining 16 scales (plus Infrequency) were each shortened to eight items using the procedures shown in Figure 2. Despite shortening the scales' lengths by about 30 per cent on average, the mean reliability computed on the item analysis samples (described above) was .70, a value not much less than the .71 mean reliability of the longer nonverbal scales. This illustrates an important psychometric point: shorter scales are not necessarily less reliable than are longer scales. A few of the items in the longer scale could actually be contributing very little to the reliability of the measure, or even detracting from it, because of their poorer psychometric properties relative to other scale items (see also Paunonen, 1984; Paunonen & Jackson, 1985).

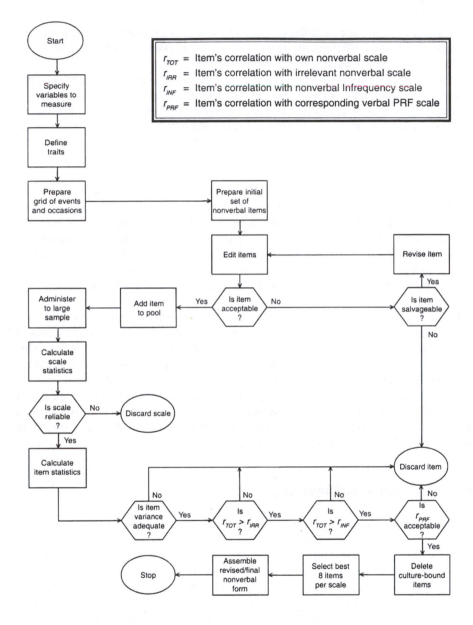

Figure 2. Flowchart of the construction of the Nonverbal Personality Questionnaire. From "The structured nonverbal assessment of personality," by S. V. Paunonen, D. N. Jackson, & M. Keinonen, 1990, *Journal of Personality, 58,* p. 491. Copyright 1990 by Blackwell Publishers.

Poor items included in a scale do not just affect its reliability, but they also can attenuate the scale's convergent validity. That is, shorter scales can also be more valid than the longer scales of which they are a part. Indeed, for the present NPQ scales, their convergent validities with the PRF criterion scales generally improved after the nonverbal scales were shortened to eight items each. The mean correlation between revised scales of the NPQ and the PRF for three respondent samples was .52, slightly higher than the .49 mean validity computed for the longer scales.

Another test of the validity of a personality measure that is sometimes applied is to correlate self-ratings on the measure with peer ratings of the respondents. This was possible in this study (Paunonen *et al.*, 1990) because one of the Canadian samples included both types of data. Specifically, the subjects in that sample completed the NPQ items in a self-report format and a peer report format. (In the latter format, respondents were asked to judge a nonverbal item on the likelihood that the peer being rated would perform the type of behavior illustrated.) Note that the subjects rating each other in that study were not all of high acquaintanceship. In fact, they were measured beforehand on mutual acquaintanceship and then assigned into dyads representing eight different levels of familiarity. Each person in each dyad then rated both self and peer on all 136 NPQ items.

Figure 3 shows the mean self-peer trait correlations on the NPQ as a function of degree of acquaintanceship. Also shown is a comparable graph for self-peer correlations on the verbal PRF trait scales (see Paunonen, 1989, for more details about these peer ratings). Both graphs show a generally linear increase in rater accuracy as acquaintanceship increases. Note that the average level of correlation for the nonverbal scales is about .21, which is not much less than the average correlation of .24 for the longer and more established PRF scales. Although neither of these two mean values seems very high, one must remember that they include varying levels of target-rater acquaintanceship. At the highest levels of acquaintanceship, self-peer correlations are in the neighborhood of .40, both for the verbal and the nonverbal scales. We consider this to be more than satisfactory given that (a) the NPQ scales are quite short with only eight items each, and (b) the Revised NEO Personality Inventory (NEO-PI-R) domain scales show an average self-peer correlation of around .43, and they have 48 items each (Costa & McCrae, 1992, p. 50).

Cross-cultural evaluations of the NPQ

Since its construction, we have administered the NPQ to respondents in several different countries. In all cases, we were interested in the generalizability of the NPQ's psychometric properties. Our particular concern was with the nonverbal scales' reliabilities, criterion validities, and factor structure across cultures.

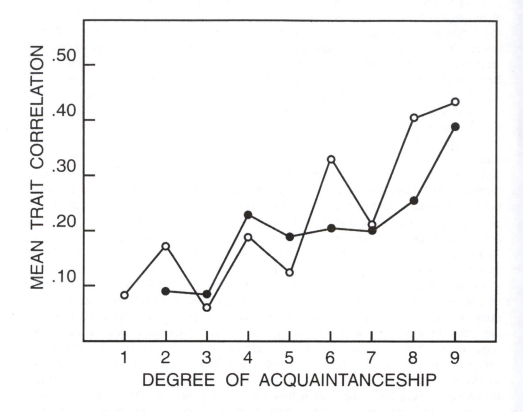

Figure 3. Mean self-peer trait correlation on Nonverbal Personality Questionnaire scales (filled circles) and Personality Research Form scales (open circles), as a function of degree of acquaintanceship. From "The structured nonverbal assessment of personality," by S. V. Paunonen, D. N. Jackson, & M. Keinonen, 1990, *Journal of Personality, 58*, p. 497. Copyright 1990 by Blackwell publishers.

Psychometric properties

In a study reported by Paunonen, Jackson, Trzebinski, and Forsterling (1992), our primary goal was to provide a multimethod cross-cultural evaluation of personality structure. We were interested particularly in seeking evidence for the Five-Factor Model of personality, using both verbal and nonverbal data collected in different countries. At the same time, our purpose was to evaluate the factorial validity of the NPQ scales. Any new omnibus measure of personality must, in general, fit into the trait nomological network established by existing measures of the same constructs (Loevinger, 1957). That is, the personality factors underlying a new measure should reproduce that factors underlying an established measure. If the factors are different, then one can reasonably question the construct validity of the new personality instrument.

Recall that the NPQ was designed to measure most of the same traits measured by the PRF. Also recall that the NPQ scales have shown acceptable levels of correlation with corresponding PRF scales. However, the non-corresponding scales should also correlate with roughly the same pattern in the two inventories. Thus, the intercorrelations among the NPQ scales should be approximately the same as the intercorrelations among the PRF scales. This is the issue of the nonverbal inventory's factor structure, referred to above, which bears on the issue of its construct validity. And, factor analysis is a method perfectly suited for addressing those issues.

In this study (Paunonen *et al.*, 1992), we evaluated NPQ data from respondents in four countries: Canada, Finland (these two samples were the same as those used by Paunonen *et al.*, 1990), Poland, and Germany. Criterion scores on the PRF scales were also available for the three European groups. The NPQ internal consistency reliabilities were good, with an overall mean of .67 (Canada = .65, Finland = .70, Poland = .65, Germany = .67). The mean NPQ-PRF convergent validity for the corresponding trait scales in the three European samples was .46 (Finland = .50, Poland = .40, Germany = .47), a value slightly lower than the .52 reported by Paunonen *et al.* (1990). Discriminant validity estimates were also computed for the NPQ trait scales as the mean absolute heterotrait correlation. These mean values were .16, .14, and .15, for Finland, Poland, and Germany, respectively. Those discriminant validities were, of course, appropriately low.

Results of factor analyses of the four samples' verbal and nonverbal personality data were remarkably consistent. In each analysis, we found five factors using the scree test. Furthermore, when those factors were rotated to a common orientation in the factor space (in this case, the PRF factor structure reported by Skinner, Jackson, & Rampton, 1976; cf. Ashton, Jackson, Helmes, & Paunonen, 1998; Jackson, Paunonen, Fraboni, & Goffin, 1996) using an orthogonal Procrustes transformation (Schönemann, 1966), the solutions were quite similar. The NPQ-PRF factor comparisons for corresponding dimensions yielded a mean coefficient of congruence of .85, averaged across all within-country factor comparisons. There was no tendency for any one country to have higher factor convergence than another, in general, or for any one factor to have higher convergence. And, only one NPQ-PRF factor comparison (for the Polish sample on what was labeled the Aesthetic-Intellectual factor by Skinner *et al.*, 1976) failed our significance test of the congruence coefficient based on random data (see Paunonen, 1997). All of the within-country and between-country factor congruence coefficients are reproduced in Table 2.

Another important result of this study (Paunonen *et al.*, 1992) was in the nature of the factors we discovered in the cross-cultural data with both the verbal and the nonverbal personality inventories. Those factors clearly resembled the traditional Big Five personality dimensions. In fact, they had high congruence coefficients with independent factors discovered by Costa and McCrae (1988) in PRF data, which those authors interpreted as strongly suggesting the Big Five. The mean congruence

Table 2. Coefficients of congruence between corresponding factors derived from responses to the Personality Research Form (PRF) and the Nonverbal Personality Questionnaire (NPQ) in four countries

	Factor				
Comparison	Academic Orientation	Aesthetic-Intellectual	Autonomy	Aggression	Social Control
PRF—NPQ Canada	.91	.78	.92	.84	.88
PRF—NPQ Finland	.83	.89	.90	.86	.89
PRF—NPQ Poland	.85	.61	.80	.72	.90
PRF—NPQ Germany	.90	.83	.93	.74	.92
Canada—Finland PRF	.96	.90	.97	.92	.91
Canada—Poland PRF	.94	.93	.95	.93	.96
Canada—Germany PRF	.97	.94	.96	.92	.97
Finland—Poland PRF	.92	.82	.95	.88	.94
Finland—Germany PRF	.95	.84	.97	.89	.89
Poland—Germany PRF	.95	.95	.96	.93	.95
Canada—Finland NPQ	.93	.98	.97	.99	.97
Canada—Poland NPQ	.93	.96	.90	.96	.95
Canada—Germany NPQ	.93	.96	.92	.80	.97
Finland—Poland NPQ	.93	.93	.89	.95	.91
Finland—Germany NPQ	.94	.95	.86	.76	.95
Poland—Germany NPQ	.91	.95	.86	.82	.92

Note: Factor labels from the Skinner *et al.* (1976) solution. From "Personality structure across cultures: A multimethod evaluation," by S. V. Paunonen, D. N. Jackson, J. Trzebinski, & F. Forsterling, 1992, *Journal of Personality and Social Psychology, 62,* p. 452. Copyright 1992 by the American Psychological Association.

coefficient between the present factors and the Costa and McCrae Big Five was .83 for our NPQ data and .92 for our PRF data, averaged across factors and countries. The slightly lower mean convergence for the nonverbal data notwithstanding (due, no doubt, to different behaviors represented in the nonverbal and verbal items), these results suggest that the Big Five factors do not depend on the explicit use of language in the measurement of personality.

Replicated psychometric properties

In another study (Paunonen *et al.*, 1996), we collected more cross-cultural data with the NPQ. Specifically, we administered the inventory to respondents in Canada, Finland, Poland, Germany, Russia, and Hong Kong. (For the four countries already referred to earlier in this chapter, new samples of subjects were obtained). Also administered to respondents was the verbal PRF questionnaire as a criterion measure. The goal of this study was to evaluate the replicabilities of the NPQ psychometric properties discovered in previous studies. Of particular interest was the inclusion in this study of the Chinese city-state of Hong Kong.

The internal consistency reliabilities for the NPQ were, averaged across scales, .75 for the Canadian sample, .67 for the four European samples, and .61 for the Chinese sample. A similar ordering of reliabilities was found for the PRF verbal scales. We speculated that these cultural differences in reliability could reflect some problems with the translation of the NPQ rating instructions and/or the PRF verbal items, particularly into Chinese. Alternatively, the cultural differences could reflect a less than optimal applicability of the traits or items to respondents in non-North American cultures.

The NPQ scale validities also showed some cultural differences. The convergent validities were quite good only in the Canadian sample, averaging .51 across scales. Validities were more moderate in the four European samples, with a mean of .39, and relatively low in the Chinese sample, with a mean of .28. These cultural differences could, again, indicate that the translations of the verbal criteria into languages other than English may have been suboptimal for some of the scales in some of the cultures. Or, the differences in validities might suggest that North American traits or their behavior-in-situation exemplars do not necessarily apply to other cultures, particularly to a Chinese culture. We have more to say about these possibilities later in this chapter.

To evaluate the factor structure of the NPQ, the 16 personality scales in each data set were intercorrelated and factored by the method of principal components. Eigenvalue and scree criteria indicated between four and six factors across the four countries. Five factors, however, seemed to provide an adequate and satisfactory solution in all cases. Thus, five factors were extracted and then rotated with a Procrustes transformation (Schönemann, 1966) to the Big Five target structure presumably underlying the PRF traits, as reported by Costa and McCrae (1988). The results of those orthogonal factor rotations showed very good convergences, in general, for corresponding NPQ dimensions across the four cultures. The mean congruence coefficient calculated across all culture-culture factor comparisons was .90. The comparable mean value for the PRF data was slightly lower at .83.

Another cross-cultural investigation of the psychometric properties of the NPQ was recently conducted by Lee, Ashton, Hong, and Park (2000) with 221 university student respondents in South Korea. The internal-consistency reliabilities of the NPQ scales in that sample averaged .71. This mean value is noticeably higher than the mean reliability of .61 that was reported in another East Asian culture, Hong Kong (see above). Lee *et al.* factor-analyzed the NPQ scales, rotating the factors to a Big Five solution using an orthogonal Procrustes rotation. The resulting factors showed high and statistically significant congruence coefficients with the PRF Big Five factors identified by Costa and McCrae (1988), ranging from .79 to .94.

Meta-analysis of NPQ factors

In a recent study, we sought once again to evaluate the generalizability of the NPQ scales' psychometric properties across different cultures (Paunonen, Zeidner, Engvik, Oosterveld, & Maliphant, 2000). In this case, however, we wanted to extend our analyses to new cultures not used in the past, including a Middle Eastern culture. Also, we decided to use a meta-analytic approach to resolving the factor structure of the NPQ scales, which is designed to produce a composite structure that best represents all of the countries assessed. To this end, we applied a meta-analytic technique for factor analysis proposed by Becker (1996).

Respondents in this study (Paunonen *et al.*, 2000) were university students in Canada, England, the Netherlands, Norway, and Israel. All subjects were administered the nonverbal items of the NPQ and the verbal items of the PRF. The NPQ reliabilities were, on the whole, quite good considering that the scales consist of only eight items each. The mean internal consistency coefficients, averaged across the 16 NPQ scales, ranged from .72 for the English sample to .65 for the Israeli sample. The range of NPQ-PRF convergent validities, averaged across corresponding trait scales, was from .48 for the Norwegian data to .27 for the Israeli data. The relatively low mean validity for the Israeli sample is equivalent to the validity reported for the NPQ scales in the Chinese sample we described earlier (Paunonen *et al.*, 1996).

The NPQ scales next were intercorrelated and factored by the method of principal components. Not only did we analyze the data independently by country, but we also followed Becker's (1996) procedure for combining those data in one meta-analysis. Essentially, a weighted means procedure is used to aggregate the countries' individual product-moment intercorrelations matrices into a single pooled matrix. The variable intercorrelations are then disattenuated for unreliability before factoring, so that the resultant structure is not affected by differential errors in the measurements.

Five factors were extracted from the NPQ trait scores in the pooled data, accounting for 83.8 per cent of the scales' variance. The factors were then rotated to a target matrix using an orthogonal Procrustes procedure (Schönemann, 1966). The target chosen represented the factor structure matrix of the PRF traits presented by Costa and McCrae (1988) and interpreted by them as representing the Big Five. The results of the present meta-factor analysis for the combined NPQ data sets are shown in Table 3.

The NPQ meta-factor solution shown in Table 3 is very clear with regard to the Big Five, and we think most will agree with our choice of factor labels. Only two traits loaded more highly on a factor other than that targeted for the variable — Dominance tended to load the Extraversion factor instead of its targeted Agreeableness factor, and Understanding tended to define Conscientiousness somewhat more than its intended Openness to Experience factor. Note that the NPQ version of Neuroticism, being defined by Social Recognition and Succorance, is somewhat restricted to a dependence on others for acceptance and emotional support. This stands in contrast to the traditional version of Neuroticism, which is related more to anxiety and depressed mood. This is an issue we address again in the development of the FF-NPQ, described in the following sections.

The results of this study (Paunonen *et al.*, 2000) are largely consistent with other cross-cultural findings we have reported for the NPQ. Some of the implications of this consistency are that (a) the nonverbal personality scales have good reliability, criterion validity, and factorial validity; (b) the scales are applicable across many

Table 3. Procrustes rotated meta-factors of combined Nonverbal Personality Questionnaire (NPQ) data from 5 countries

Factor	Factor				
NPQ scale	E	A	C	N	O
Extraversion (E)					
Affiliation	*.74*	.44	.12	.32	.23
Exhibition	*.80*	-.29	-.16	.13	.25
Play	*.68*	-.50	.03	.04	.15
Agreeableness (A)					
Nurturance	.50	*.61*	.35	.21	.33
Aggression	.20	*-.80*	-.27	.27	.03
Dominance	.65	*-.34*	.24	.21	.39
Conscientiousness (C)					
Achievement	.23	-.19	*.74*	.26	.46
Endurance	.21	-.06	*.71*	-.15	.56
Order	.03	.22	*.70*	.45	.02
Impulsivity	.47	-.42	*-.54*	.40	.26
Neuroticism (N)					
Social recognition	.40	-.47	.24	*.64*	.00
Succorance	.10	.20	-.09	*.83*	.25
Openness to Experience (O)					
Autonomy	.12	.00	.08	-.09	*.93*
Thrill-seeking	.39	-.41	-.08	-.29	*.66*
Sentience	.18	.41	.17	.43	*.65*
Understanding	-.06	-.09	.61	.20	*.56*

Note: Targeted loadings in italics. From "The nonverbal assessment of personality in five cultures," by S. V. Paunonen, M. Zeidner, H. Engvik, P. Oosterveld, & R. Maliphant, 2000, *Journal of Cross-Cultural Psychology, 31*, p. 232. Copyright 2000 by Western Washington University.

cultures and can be used for cross-cultural personality assessments; and (c) the structure of personality has some generality across cultures and, furthermore, (d) that structure tends to support the well-known Five-Factor Model of personality.

Construction of the FF-NPQ

Although the NPQ provides psychometrically sound measures of a wide array of personality trait variables, we realized that in some settings a nonverbal measure of a few broad personality dimensions might be desired. To provide such a measure, we decided to construct a new questionnaire that would assess personality variation only at the broad level of abstraction represented by the Big Five factors. That new questionnaire is known as the Five-Factor Nonverbal Personality Questionnaire (FF-NPQ; Paunonen *et al.*, 2001).

Overview of the FF-NPQ

The FF-NPQ contains 60 nonverbal items that measure, with 12 items each, the Big Five personality factors of Extraversion, Agreeableness, Conscientiousness, Neuroticism, and Openness to Experience. Those items, with a few exceptions to be discussed below, were selected from the longer 136-item NPQ to represent each of the Big Five factor domains. In completing the FF-NPQ, essentially the same rating instructions are given respondents as those shown in Figure 1 for the NPQ. Because of its short length of 60 items, most people finish the five-factor inventory in about 10 minutes.

Item selection strategy

Our first task in constructing the FF-NPQ (see Paunonen *et al.*, 2001) was to decide which NPQ trait scales should contribute to the item pool for each nonverbal Big Five factor measure. We initially considered the possibility of assigning traits to factors based on the NPQ meta-factor analysis reported in Table 3. We noticed, however, that those factors might represent somewhat unorthodox rotations (from the point of view of the conventional Five-Factor Model) of some of the Big Five axes. For example, the NPQ Understanding scale, which might normally be viewed as a univocal marker of Openness to Experience, loaded slightly more highly on Conscientiousness than on Openness. We decided, therefore, to verify the relevance of each NPQ trait scale to the traditional Big Five domains by correlating those scales with known markers of the Big Five structure; specifically, we correlated the NPQ scales with the scales of the NEO Five-Factor Inventory (NEO-FFI; Costa & McCrae, 1992).

Correlations between the NPQ and NEO-FFI scales were calculated on a sample of 304 Canadian university student respondents (112 men, 192 women). Using a .30 correlation as a threshold for assigning an NPQ scale to a Big Five domain, we then made the following trait-factor assignments: Affiliation, Dominance, and Exhibition were assigned to Extraversion; Nurturance and (low) Aggression were assigned to Agreeableness; Achievement, Endurance, (low) Impulsivity, and Order were assigned to Conscientiousness; Succorance alone was assigned to Neuroticism; and Autonomy, Sentience, and Understanding were assigned to Openness to Experience. Three NPQ scales, Thrill-Seeking, Social Recognition, and Play, did not correlate .30 or above with any NEO-FFI scale, and were thus excluded from the FF-NPQ item selection process.

For each Big Five domain, we wished to create a new, 12-item, nonverbal factor scale by selecting items from the relevant set of 8-item NPQ trait scales. However, in the case of the Neuroticism domain, the only eligible NPQ scale was Succorance, so the eight items of that scale, and no others, were automatically included in the

Table 4. Means and standard deviations for FF-NPQ scales in a Canadian sample

FF-NPQ scale	Full sample (N = 304)		Men (N = 112)		Women (N = 192)	
	Mean	SD	Mean	SD	Mean	SD
Extraversion	48.9	11.9	48.9	12.2	48.9	11.7
Agreeableness	64.4	11.3	58.3	11.3	67.9	9.7
Conscientiousness	56.4	10.7	53.0	10.5	58.3	10.4
Neuroticism	33.3	7.7	31.0	7.7	34.7	7.5
Openness to Experience	57.3	11.1	54.1	10.4	59.1	11.2

Note: All item responses recorded on 7-point rating scales; Each FF-NPQ scale has 12 items, except Neuroticism with 8; FF-NPQ = Five-Factor Nonverbal Personality Questionnaire. From "Nonverbal assessment of the Big Five personality factors," by S. V. Paunonen, M. C. Ashton, & D. N. Jackson, 2001, *European Journal of Personality, 15,* p. 8. Copyright 2001 by John Wiley & Sons.

FF-NPQ Neuroticism scale. For the remaining four Big Five domains, we pooled the items from the relevant NPQ trait scales, and then calculated corrected item-total correlations for each of the preliminary Big Five measures, retaining the best items. Besides considering item-total correlations in our item selection procedure, we deleted any item that showed a higher correlation with the total score on another Big Five domain, and also excluded items that depicted behaviors whose cross-cultural generality seemed to be less than desirable.

The final composition of each FF-NPQ factor scale, in terms of the constituent NPQ trait scales and the numbers of items selected therefrom (in parentheses), was as follows. Extraversion: Affiliation (3), Dominance (3), Exhibition (6); Agreeableness: Nurturance (5), Aggression (7, reverse-keyed); Conscientiousness: Achievement (4), Endurance (3), Order (5); Neuroticism: Succorance (8); Openness to Experience: Autonomy (3), Sentience (4), Understanding (5). Note that the version of the FF-NPQ which we evaluated in this study (Paunonen *et al.*, 2001) had only 56 items in total. Since that study, the Neuroticism scale has been revised and lengthened from 8 to 12 items, a procedure we describe later in this chapter.

Psychometric properties

We evaluated the psychometric properties of the 56-item FF-NPQ inventory within the derivation sample of 304 Canadian respondents described above. First, we considered the scale means and standard deviations, which are shown in Table 4. These values indicate that the scale means were relatively close to the hypothetical scale midpoints (32 for Neuroticism, 48 for all other scales), and that the standard deviations were close to one-sixth of the possible range of scores (56 - 8 = 48 for Neuroticism, 84 - 12 = 72 for all other scales). Women averaged about a standard deviation higher than men on Agreeableness, and about half of a standard deviation higher than men on Conscientiousness, Neuroticism, and Openness to Experience. Women and men showed approximately equal mean scores on Extraversion.

Table 5 summarizes some of the other psychometric properties of the FF-NPQ factor scales in our sample. The internal-consistency reliabilities of the scales (Table

Table 5. Psychometric properties of FF-NPQ scales in a Canadian sample

FF-NPQ scale	Internal consistency (*N* = 304)	Correlation with NEO-FFI (*N* = 304)	Self-peer correlation (*N* = 96)
Extraversion	.81	.53	.45
Agreeableness	.82	.59	.40
Conscientiousness	.79	.50	.41
Neuroticism	.75	.45	.39
Openness to Experience	.82	.55	.38

Note: FF-NPQ = Five-Factor Nonverbal Personality Questionnaire; NEO-FFI = NEO Five-Factor Inventory.

5, column 1) were quite good, ranging from .75 to .82, and averaging .80; even the eight-item Neuroticism scale had a respectable reliability. Correlations between the FF-NPQ scales and their NEO-FFI counterparts (Table 5, column 2) revealed fairly high levels of convergent validity for the FF-NPQ. Those correlations ranged from .45 to .59, and the average convergence of .52 is not much different from values normally obtained between different sets of verbal markers of the Big Five (e.g., Costa & McCrae, 1992, p. 54). In contrast, none of the discriminant correlations between FF-NPQ and NEO-FFI scales exceeded .25, and the mean absolute value was an appropriately low .14 (see Paunonen *et al.*, 2001).

A subset of 96 students in the sample of 304 respondents completed the FF-NPQ in both a self-report and peer report format. We were thus able to correlate each of these 96 participants' self-report scores on the FF-NPQ scales with peer report scores on the same scales. These calculations revealed that the five convergent correlations between self and peer, shown in column 3 of Table 5, ranged from .38 to .45, with a mean of .41. This value compares favorably with the .43 correlation between self- and peer report scores on the much longer, 48-item NEO-PI-R domain scales (Costa & McCrae, 1992, p. 50). The self-peer discriminant correlations for the FF-NPQ scales were quite low, with an average value of only .08, and with no correlation exceeding .16.

Most respondents in the FF-NPQ validation sample also completed the Behavior Report Form (Paunonen, 1993; 1998; Paunonen & Ashton, 2001b), a self-report measure designed to assess criteria of some social significance, such as traffic violations and alcohol consumption, that might have underlying personality determinants. Across 14 such criteria, each assessed only as a single item, the mean multiple correlation yielded by the five FF-NPQ factor scales as predictors was .25, which exactly equaled the corresponding value obtained by the five NEO-FFI factor scales as predictors (see Paunonen *et al.*, 2001, Table 6). Thus, the estimated external criterion validity of the new nonverbal FF-NPQ measures of the Big Five was equal to that of established verbal measures of the same constructs.

Table 6. Psychometric properties of FF-NPQ scales in international samples

FF-NPQ scale	Internal consistency	Correlation with PRF
Extraversion	.75	.54
Agreeableness	.72	.50
Conscientiousness	.71	.50
Neuroticism	.64	.35
Openness to Experience	.77	.50

Note: Each coefficient is the average of seven countries' results (*N* = 90-113); FF-NPQ = Five-Factor Nonverbal Personality Questionnaire. PRF = Personality Research Form.

Cross-cultural evaluations

Given that the NPQ has shown good psychometric properties in various cultures, the prospects for the cross-cultural applicability of the FF-NPQ seems promising. We conducted an initial investigation of the FF-NPQ across cultures (Paunonen *et al.*, 2001) using archival data from samples of respondents already described in this chapter. They included 701 university students (447 women, 254 men) in Canada, England, Finland, Germany, Norway, Poland, and Russia. All of the participants completed the nonverbal NPQ scales, from which FF-NPQ scores could be calculated, in addition to the verbal PRF scales (some of the latter were in an abbreviated form).

Our results showed that the means and standard deviations for men and women on the FF-NPQ scales for the international samples were close to the values reported for the normative Canadian sample. Furthermore, as shown in column 1 of Table 6, internal-consistency reliabilities, averaged across countries, were quite satisfactory, ranging from .64 to .77 for the five scales. The mean internal-consistency reliabilities, averaged across the five scales, varied slightly by country, ranging from .66 in Finland to .79 in England. The FF-NPQ scale intercorrelations were relatively small, with no correlations exceeding .39, and with a mean absolute correlation of .22; these values tended to be similar across the individual countries in this data set.

We calculated correlations between the FF-NPQ nonverbal measures of the Big Five and verbal measures of the Big Five that were constructed from the PRF scales. To construct each PRF-based Big Five measure, we simply summed the PRF scales whose NPQ counterparts had provided items for the corresponding FF-NPQ factor measure (as described in an earlier section). Convergent correlations between the PRF and FF-NPQ measures of the Big Five, shown in column 2 of Table 6, ranged from .35 to .54, with an average of .48. The average convergent correlation differed a bit by country, ranging from .40 in Finland to .55 in Norway and in England. We consider these values to be quite satisfactory considering (a) the relatively short length of the nonverbal factor scales, and (b) the fact that the verbal and nonverbal scales undoubtedly measure somewhat different aspects of the same personality constructs. The discriminant correlations between PRF and FF-NPQ scales were generally small in the international data, with none exceeding .26, having a mean absolute correlation of .10, and being similar in size across countries.

Postscript

The psychometric performance of the FF-NPQ, as evaluated in Canadian and European data, appears to be quite good in all respects (Paunonen *et al.*, 2001). The nonverbal scales have appropriate means and standard deviations, good reliabilities, acceptable levels of convergent and discriminant validity, and are predictive of specific behavior criteria. It was clear in some of those results, however, that the weakest FF-NPQ scale of the five was Neuroticism, which generally showed slightly lower reliabilities and convergent correlations than did the other four factor scales. This was probably due to the brevity of the Neuroticism scale (8 items, versus 12 items for the other scales) and, in the case of the convergent correlations with the NEO-FFI variables, perhaps due also to the limited range of content in this scale (i.e., being related only to the need for succorance).

To improve the psychometric quality of the FF-NPQ Neuroticism scale, we have since commissioned the drawing of new nonverbal items, and conducted item trials based on a new respondent sample. Specifically, 13 new items were drawn to represent a few different aspects of behavior related to nonclinical neuroticism (e.g., phobias, depression, etc.). Those items were then administered to 178 Canadian university students, along with the other 56 FF-NPQ items and the NEO-FFI.

Our intent was to select the 12 best Neuroticism items from the set of 13 new items plus 8 existing items. To this end, we factored the 21 items to determine if there was any tendency of the items to cluster into correlated facets of Neuroticism. We found that 14 of the items strongly defined four factors, with three or four items on each factor. Those four factors were clearly related to phobic behavior, paranoia, depression, and the need for succorance, respectively. Therefore, we decided to select the best three items for each of these four facets to be included in our revised 12-item Neuroticism factor scale.

When scored as separate three-item scales, the four Neuroticism facet scales all intercorrelated positively, ranging from .31 to .44 with the mean of .36. When all 12 items were combined into an overall Neuroticism factor scale, its reliability in our sample of respondents was .81. Furthermore, the factor scale's correlation with the NEO-FFI Neuroticism scale was .57. Our revised 12-item Neuroticism scale, therefore, now has psychometric properties very similar to those of the other 12-item FF-NPQ scales (see Table 5 and Table 6).

Directions for future research

In this chapter, we have described the conceptualization and development of two new and novel questionnaires designed to measure the traits and the factors of personality. The questionnaires are the NPQ and FF-NPQ, and what makes them novel is the fact that their items do not contain verbal content, and yet they are structured in the sense that respondents must choose their item responses from a list of alternatives. The empirical data we reviewed support the construct validity of the new nonverbal scales. In general, they have shown good levels of reliability, criterion validity, and factorial validity, both in North American and non-North American respondent samples.

As we mentioned in the Introduction, a nonverbal measure of personality has utility for certain applications. In particular, cross-cultural studies and the assessment of different linguistic groups come to mind. But our enthusiasm for the NPQ and FF-NPQ questionnaires notwithstanding, we feel it is necessary to delineate some important limitations in the use of those measures. These limitations pertain to (a) the culture-freeness of the nonverbal items, (b) the use of imported or foreign measures of personality in different cultures, and (c) the universality and comprehensiveness of the Five-Factor Model of personality structure.

On culture-free personality items

The data presented in this chapter, which largely support cross-cultural applications of the NPQ and FF-NPQ, should not be interpreted as a claim for the culture-freeness of the nonverbal items. The nonverbal items certainly are not culture-free, and they may not even be culture-reduced. In fact, many of those items have culture-specific referents. Furthermore, some of the items clearly are most relevant to Western, educated, middle-class respondents. One item, for example, shows a person cooking a meal for friends on a manufactured outdoor grill, and another item shows someone enjoying a modern art exhibit in a museum. This content specificity may explain why some of the NPQ scales showed lower levels of reliability and validity in some non-Western samples (Paunonen *et al.*, 1996, 2000).

Some of the nonverbal items are clearly not likely to be endorsed by certain groups. And the reasons might not just be cultural, but could include political, geographic, or economic factors as well. For example, even very aggressive people in some totalitarian countries might be unwilling to endorse the NPQ Aggression item showing a person yelling at a police officer who is writing a traffic ticket. Highly sentient respondents living in a desert environment might, despite their level of that need, tend to rate as an improbable behavior the Sentience item showing a person lying on a beach at the seaside. And, poor people everywhere are not likely to endorse the Social Recognition item showing a person buying an expensive watch.

We do not intend to portray the NPQ or FF-NPQ as completely culture-free. A truly culture-free personality instrument might resemble something like the Rorschach inkblot test. With such unstructured measures, a respondent's interpretation of an ambiguous image is thought to be symptomatic of some latent personality trait. But even such abstract nonverbal items have had problems in proving their culture-fairness (see Frijda & Jahoda, 1966). Nonetheless, it is our belief that the NPQ and FF-NPQ personality measures can be useful for research and assessment in many different cultural contexts.

On imported measures of personality

People have long been interested in the issue of the consistency of human behavior across cultures. Different questions related to this issue have been asked (see Paunonen, 2000). Do people engage in the same behaviors in different cultures? If those behaviors represent latent personality traits, are those traits themselves consistent across cultures? And, if such traits are organized in a structured personality network, is that organization a universal one? In answering questions like these, researchers will often export their favorite measure of personality for use in other (i.e., foreign) cultures. This is what we did when we used the NPQ and FF-NPQ in the cross-cultural studies described in this chapter.

The present cross-cultural data were remarkably consistent in the studies we have reviewed here. In another article (Paunonen & Ashton, 1998), we have argued that such consistency supports the generality of personality traits and trait behaviors across cultures. In other words, it would be hard to argue that the traits or behaviors are not relevant to a culture if the imported measures show good levels of reliability, criterion validity, and factorial validity in that culture. But even if the psychometric properties of the imported measures were substantially different across cultures, that would not necessarily mean that the constructs are not relevant to those cultures.

What if one were to find that the same personality instrument administered in two different cultures yielded different results? Does that mean that the personality variables assessed using the imported measure are not relevant to one or both of those cultures? Not necessarily. There are many reasons why a personality inventory will yield different psychometric properties in different cultures. These reasons include item translation problems (not relevant, of course, to the NPQ or FF-NPQ), response style involvement, test format issues, criterion-related difficulties, and more (see Paunonen & Ashton, 1998). But even if such methodological reasons can be discounted as the cause of the psychometric differences, can it be claimed that the constructs measured are not relevant to the cultures assessed and, therefore, that the use of an imported measure is at fault?

It is generally believed that a personality measure can fail in a culture because (a) the items used are not relevant to the people in the culture, or (b) the trait itself is not relevant to that culture. Regarding the first point, there is no question that the behavior exemplars of a trait vary from one culture to another and, ideally, different versions of the test should reflect that variation. The second point, the notion that the personality trait itself is nonexistent in a culture, is a much more elusive idea. If a trait exists in one culture but not in another it must mean that, in the latter culture, no postulated trait-relevant behaviors occur.

It is our view that, although trait exemplars might very well be different in different cultures, most (if not all) of the postulated latent traits of personality exist in those cultures, and could be found with a proper program of construct validation (see Paunonen, 2000). However, the items in an imported personality measure, including the NPQ and the FF-NPQ, might not be relevant to the respondents in a particular culture, making it appear as if some of the personality constructs are at fault.

We agree, in general, with those who caution against the thoughtless adoption of foreign measurement devices in cross-cultural research. Our reasons, however, have more to do with problems concerning the relevance of the test items to cultures, rather than with problems concerning the relevance of the personality constructs underlying those items. It is our suspicion that well-developed personality measures, measures that have demonstrable levels of construct validity across diverse cultures, will reveal that there are few personality traits that are not general to those cultures. Thus, we maintain that the constructs measured by the NPQ and FF-NPQ are relevant to most, if not all, cultures, even though some of their items might not be.

On the Five-Factor Model of personality structure

As its name implies, the Five-Factor Nonverbal Personality Questionnaire was developed in accordance with the Five-Factor Model of personality structure. The dimensions of personality measured by FF-NPQ, the Big Five, are ubiquitous, having been identified in many disparate cultures, using many different personality assessment instruments, by many independent researchers. Moreover, the data reviewed in this chapter support our claim that the FF-NPQ scales do a reasonable job at measuring those personality dimensions. This being said, our present test construction efforts should not be interpreted as suggesting that measurement of the Big Five factors alone is sufficient for adequate personality assessment.

We have reported, in several studies (Ashton, 1998; Ashton, Jackson, Paunonen, Helmes, & Rothstein, 1995; Paunonen, 1998; Paunonen & Ashton, 2001a; Paunonen & Ashton, 2001b; Paunonen & Nicol, 2001; Paunonen, Rothstein, & Jackson, 1999), the fact that the Big Five factors of personality do a reasonably good job of predicting criterion behaviors of some social significance (e.g., smoking behavior, alcohol consumption, grade point average). However, those studies have also shown that one can do better if one also considers behavior variation that is not part of any Big Five factor.

Where does one find behavior variation independent of the Big Five factors? In at least two places. First, there are traits and dimensions of personality that lie largely beyond the Big Five factors' sphere of influence. For instance, there is the sixth big factor of personality reported by Ashton, Lee, and Son (2000), and the 10 or so lower level traits described by Paunonen and Jackson (2000), none of which fit well within the factor space of the Big Five. Second, we can find such variation in the traits that are facets of the Big Five factors, but with Big Five variance partialed out. That is, a Big Five factor's constituent traits invariably contain significant amounts of trait-specific variance. And our empirical results clearly indicate that that specific variance, which by definition is independent of the traits' common variance, is often predictive of some criterion variables of interest, sometimes adding substantially to the accuracy of prediction equations based on Big Five factors alone (e.g., see Paunonen & Ashton, 2001b).

In summary, by considering only the Big Five factors as predictors of behavior, one sacrifices optimal levels of behavior predictability. As a consequence, one also sacrifices a commensurate amount of behavior understanding. Our recommendation is that, when the assessment circumstances will allow, measurement of the Big Five factors of personality should be supplemented with an assessment of the individual Big Five facet variables.

Author's note

The preparation of this chapter was supported by the Social Sciences and Humanities Research Council of Canada Research Grant 410-98-1555 to Sampo V. Paunonen.

References

Ashton, M.C. (1998). Personality and job performance: The importance of narrow traits. *Journal of Organizational Behavior, 19*, 289-303.

Ashton, M.C., Jackson, D.N., Helmes, E., & Paunonen, S.V. (1998). Joint factor analysis of the Personality Research Form and the Jackson Personality Inventory: Comparisons with the Big Five. *Journal of Research in Personality, 32*, 243-250.

Ashton, M.C., Jackson, D. N., Paunonen, S.V., Helmes, E., & Rothstein, M.G. (1995). The criterion validity of broad factor scales versus specific trait scales. *Journal of Research in Personality, 29*, 432-442.

Ashton, M.C., Lee, K., & Son, C. (2000). Honesty as the sixth factor of personality: Correlations with Machiavellianism, primary psychopathy, and social adroitness. *European Journal of Personality, 14*, 359-368.

Becker, G. (1996). The meta-analysis of factor analyses: An illustration based on the cumulation of correlation matrices. *Psychological Methods, 1*, 341-353.

Costa, P.T., Jr., & McCrae, R.R. (1988). From catalog to classification: Murray's needs and the five-factor model. *Journal of Personality and Social Psychology, 55*, 258-265.

Costa, P.T., Jr., & McCrae, R.R. (1992). *Revised NEO Personality Inventory (NEO-PI-R) and NEO Five-Factor Inventory (NEO-FFI) professional manual*. Odessa, FL: Psychological Assessment Resources, Inc.

D'Andrade, R.G. (1974). Memory and the assessment of behavior. In H. Blalock (Ed.), *Measurement in the Social Sciences* (pp. 159-186). Chicago: Aldine-Atherton.

Frijda, N., & Jahoda, G. (1966). On the scope and methods of cross-cultural research. *International Journal of Psychology, 1*, 109-127.

Jackson, D.N. (1984). *Personality Research Form manual*. Port Huron, MI: Research Psychologists Press.

Jackson, D.N., Paunonen, S.V., Fraboni, M., & Goffin, R.D. (1996). A five-factor versus a six-factor model of personality structure. *Personality and Individual Differences, 20*, 33-45.

Lee, K., Ashton, M.C., Hong, S., & Park, K.B. (2000). Psychometric properties of the Nonverbal Personality Questionnaire in Korea. *Educational and Psychological Measurement, 60,* 131-141.

Loevinger, J. (1957). Objective tests as instruments of psychological theory [Monograph]. *Psychological Reports, 3,* 635-694.

Murray, H.A. (1938). *Explorations in personality.* New York: Oxford Press.

Paunonen, S.V. (1984). Optimizing the validity of personality assessments: The importance of aggregation and item content. *Journal of Research in Personality, 18,* 411-431.

Paunonen, S.V. (1989). Consensus in personality judgments: Moderating effects of target-rater acquaintanceship and behavior observability. *Journal of Personality and Social Psychology, 56,* 823-833.

Paunonen, S.V. (1993, August*). Sense, nonsense, and the Big Five factors of personality.* Paper presented at the annual meeting of the American Psychological Association, Toronto, Ontario.

Paunonen, S.V. (1997). On chance and factor congruence following orthogonal Procrustes rotation. *Educational and Psychological Measurement, 57,* 33-59.

Paunonen, S.V. (1998). Hierarchical organization of personality and prediction of behavior. *Journal of Personality and Social Psychology, 74,* 538-556.

Paunonen, S.V. (2000). Construct validity and the search for cross-situational consistencies in personality. In R.D. Goffin & E. Helmes (Eds.), *Problems and solutions in human assessment: Honoring Douglas N. Jackson at seventy* (pp. 123-140). Norwell, MA: Kluwer.

Paunonen, S.V., & Ashton, M.C. (1998). The structured assessment of personality across cultures. *Journal of Cross-Cultural Psychology, 29,* 150-170.

Paunonen, S.V., & Ashton, M.C. (2001a). Big Five predictors of academic achievement. *Journal of Research in Personality, 35,* 78-90.

Paunonen, S.V., & Ashton, M.C. (2001b). Big Five factors and facets and the prediction of behavior. *Journal of Personality and Social Psychology, 81,* 524-539.

Paunonen, S.V., Ashton, M.C., & Jackson, D.N. (2001). Nonverbal assessment of the Big Five personality factors. *European Journal of Personality, 15,* 3-18.

Paunonen, S.V., & Jackson, D.N. (1979). Nonverbal trait inference. *Journal of Personality and Social Psychology, 37,* 1645-1659.

Paunonen, S.V., & Jackson, D.N. (1985). The validity of formal and informal personality assessments. *Journal of Research in Personality, 19,* 331-342.

Paunonen, S.V., & Jackson, D.N. (2000). What is beyond the Big Five? Plenty! *Journal of Personality, 68,* 821-835.

Paunonen, S.V., Jackson, D.N., & Keinonen, M. (1990). The structured nonverbal assessment of personality. *Journal of Personality, 58,* 481-502.

Paunonen, S.V., Jackson, D.N., Trzebinski, J., & Forsterling, F. (1992). Personality structure across cultures: A multimethod evaluation. *Journal of Personality and Social Psychology, 62,* 447-456.

Paunonen, S.V., Keinonen, M., Trzebinski, J., Forsterling, F., Grishenko-Rose, N., Kouznetsova, L., & Chan, D.W. (1996). The structure of personality in six cultures. *Journal of Cross-Cultural Psychology, 27,* 339-353.

Paunonen, S.V., & Nicol, A.A.M. (2001). The personality hierarchy and the prediction of work behaviors. In R. Hogan & B.W. Roberts (Eds.), *Personality psychology and the workplace* (pp. 161-191). Washington, DC: American Psychological Association.

Paunonen, S.V., Rothstein, M.G., & Jackson, D.N. (1999). Narrow reasoning about the use of broad personality measures in personnel selection. *Journal of Organizational Behavior, 20*, 389-405.

Paunonen, S.V., Zeidner, M., Engvik, H., Oosterveld, P., & Maliphant, R. (2000). The non-verbal assessment of personality in five cultures. *Journal of Cross-Cultural Psychology, 31*, 220-239.

Schönemann, P.H. (1966). A generalized solution of the orthogonal Procrustes problem. *Psychometrika, 31*, 1-16.

Shweder, R.A. (1975). How relevant is an individual difference theory of personality? *Journal of Personality, 43*, 455-485.

Skinner, H.A., Jackson, D.N., & Rampton, G.M. (1976). The Personality Research Form in a Canadian context: Does language make a difference? *Canadian Journal of Behavioral Science, 8*, 156-168.

Chapter 9

The Global Personality Inventory (GPI)

Mark J. Schmit
Jenifer A. Kihm
Chet Robie

Introduction

The Global Personality Inventory (GPI) is a measurement tool specifically developed for work-related use by psychologists working in or with organizations. It was designed for applications such as pre-employment selection, developmental assessment, coaching, and succession management. It was originally developed for internal use at an international consulting firm, Personnel Decisions International (PDI). As part of a recent merger/acquisition deal, the instrument became the property of ePredix, Inc., though PDI is still the primary user of the tool, using it in assessment center work around the world. It will soon be widely available for purchase and use by practitioners; academic uses are currently permitted and encouraged (contact nigel.dalton@epredix.com).

The development plan of the GPI included two major ways in which "global" would apply to the final instrument. First, it was designed to be an omnibus measure of personality based on the Big-Five factor structure. Second, the GPI was developed using an atypical approach that involved psychologists from around the world contributing to the construct development, item writing, and pilot testing. Statistical methods were used to create a final version of the test that showed scale invariance across-cultures. In these ways, the GPI is truly a global measurement tool. The original development of the GPI was reported in Schmit, Kihm, and Robie (2000)[1].

[1] A large portion of this paper is reprinted from Schmit MJ, Kihm JA, Robie C. (2000). Development of a Global Measure of Personality. *Personnel Psychology, 53(1)*, 153-193. Reprinted with permission from *Personnel Psychology*.

Big Five Assessment, edited by B. De Raad & M. Perugini. © 2002, Hogrefe & Huber Publishers.

The approach to measurement

Personality tests have typically been developed in a single country and are then transported to other countries, an approach known as an imposed-etic strategy (Berry, 1969). The best measures have very good psychometric evidence to support the use and interpretation of the measures for many different applications in the home country of the original development studies. Once a measure has proven useful in its home country, an effort often begins to translate the measure for use in other countries. Many personality tests have been developed in the United States and were then transported through translated measures to other countries in this manner (e.g., MMPI, CPI, 16PF). There is evidence that this approach has been relatively successful in providing measurement instruments that demonstrate similar psychometric properties across cultures.

A good example is provided by Costa and McCrae's NEO-PI-R, a measure based on the Five-Factor Model of personality. Recent evidence provided by these researchers suggests that the NEO-PI-R may be useful in differentiating individual differences in personality across cultures (see McCrae & Costa, 1997, for a review). The instrument has been found to show similar psychometric properties in several countries around the world (e.g., China, Korea, Russia, Germany, Holland, Israel, Philippines, Japan, and Portugal). Several other measures have enjoyed similar success (e.g., California Psychological Inventory (CPI); Sixteen Personality Factor Questionnaire (16PF); Occupational Personality Questionnaire (OPQ); Minnesota Multiphasic Personality Inventory (MMPI); see Katigbak, Church, & Akamine, 1996, for a review).

Despite the apparent transportability of a measure across cultural lines, there are some caveats to this approach. First, items developed in a particular country might better represent the construct being measured than items written in a different country that were translated to the language of the import country. That is, personality may not be different across cultures, but expressions of personality are highly likely to differ (Church & Katigbak, 1988). Second, exported instruments are often changed significantly as they are transported from country to country, leaving one uncertain about the comparability of measures being used across different language versions (Hambleton & Kanjee, 1995). Finally, many instruments developed for clinical use have limited coverage and adaptability to work done by applied psychologists in work contexts. Thus, we designed a strategy for developing a measure of personality to be used by applied psychologists world-wide that involved psychologists from many cultures in all phases of the development process, including construct identification and definition, item development, instrument translation, data collection, construct equivalence studies, and validation.

The design of our development effort was fashioned after models that have attempted to combine both etic and emic approaches to develop a derived etic measure (Berry, 1989; Davidson, Jaccard, Triandis, Morales, & Diaz-Guerrero, 1976; Triandis, Malpass, & Davidson, 1971). An emic approach is taken from within a culture, while an etic approach examines many cultures from a perspective outside the cultural systems (Berry, 1969; Pike, 1966). Combining the approaches in test development has been shown to lead to the most useful common, or universal, measure (Berry, 1989; Church & Katigbak, 1988).

In the development of our new cross-cultural measure of personality, we also attempted to use all of the methods that have been designated as best practices in such an effort. Accordingly, we used the *International Guidelines for Adapting Educational and Psychological Tests* (Hambleton, 1994; Hambleton & Kanjee, 1995) as benchmarks for each step of our development process. The objective was to develop a measure with a cleaner factor structure, better reliability, less differential item and test functioning, and ultimately better validity for the inferences made from the measure when used by applied psychologists than tests developed and transported by less rigorous methods.

There are several reasons why a common measure of personality for use in multiple countries might be highly desirable. An international industrial-organizational psychology consulting firm (such as Personnel Decisions International; PDI) that uses personality measures for the assessment of employees in client organizations is an example of an organization that would seek a common measure to be used in its offices around the world. This measure could be used for selection, development, coaching, and feedback purposes. For a firm such as this, a common measure with strong psychometric properties across cultures would allow the firm to establish norms at local, country, continent, and global levels. Having these types of norms could facilitate cross-cultural assignment and development of executives. Common administration systems and software could be developed around such a measure. Many other administrative issues could be resolved with a common measure.

Most important, however, is the potential gain in the ability to do cross-cultural research and comparisons of individuals. Currently, applied psychologists typically use transported instruments that have been modified in multiple ways across multiple instruments. Thus, cross-cultural research and cross-cultural applications are limited. When cross-cultural research is conducted with instruments demonstrating varying degrees of moderate to low psychometric quality, including differential item and test functioning across cultures, mean differences between cultures, or inferences made about differences or variations of scores of individuals from different cultures are tenuous at best and usually are not interpretable at all.

In the remainder of this chapter, the development of a global personality inventory (i.e., the Global Personality Inventory; GPI) will be described. This instrument is intended to be a measure of personality that will prove useful in the practices of one particular world-wide provider of industrial-organizational psychological applications and services. However, the process we undertook and the methods we employed in developing this instrument should prove useful as a model in developing any instrument that measures a common set of constructs that can be employed in many different locations throughout the world.

Instrument development

An international group of GPI development teams was assembled. These teams included consultants and researchers affiliated with the above-mentioned international consulting firm from around the world, in addition to external researchers from various universities (see acknowledgements). The roles of external, academic researchers were defined to include providing content and research expertise, providing access to research samples, making methodological recommendations, and partnering with consultant team members on presentations and papers to be delivered at professional conferences and published in academic journals. Ten teams were assembled with a total of 70 team members, most of whom were Ph.D. or Masters level psychologists. All of the consulting firm's current global offices had representatives on these teams. Psychologists on the teams were from the USA, UK, France, Belgium, Sweden, Germany, Spain, Netherlands, China, Japan, Singapore, Korea, Argentina, and Columbia.

A personality measure to be used worldwide should be well grounded in personality theory. In addition, we believed that a theory of job performance should be kept in mind during the development, as the intended application of the instrument was to be focused on the work life of respondents. This stage of development was driven by theory, previous research, and rational thought, rather than by sheer empirical data. The outcome of this development phase was to be a conceptual model including the constructs to be measured by the GPI. In addition, construct definitions were to be developed in this stage which would serve as the basis for item writing.

Selection of broad models to structure the GPI

Personality model

The personality model of choice today, among both personality and industrial-organizational researchers, is the Five-Factor Model of personality. The Five Factors include Extroversion, Agreeableness, Conscientiousness, Emotional Stability, and Openness to Experience. Some researchers have suggested that the model is both too broad and not fully representative of human personality (e.g., Hough, 1998). This may or may not be true, but this does not limit its usefulness as an organizing taxonomy for conceptual variables at a level below the Five Factors. There is much greater agreement among researchers that applied measurement of personality can be very useful at a level below the Five Factors (Paunonen, 1998). At this level, facets of the larger Five Factors can be thought of as being both primarily and secondarily related to higher level variables. That is, a facet that is primarily related to Extroversion may be secondarily related to Conscientiousness. Desire for Achievement/Advancement is a good example of this type of facet because it has been found to load on both the Extroversion and Conscientiousness factors (Hough, 1998). Linking measures of GPI facets to the Five Factor model was thought to be a prudent method for developing construct validity evidence for the instrument. Additionally, having a broad factor structure would allow for scales to be combined into broad predictor composites, as broad predictor composites have been found to be very useful in predicting broad criteria, such an overall performance (Ones & Viswesvaren, 1996).

Another reason for using the Five Factor Model as an organizing taxonomy is the large base of research that exists for this model. Costa and McCrae, of the National Institute on Aging, have shown the model to fit almost all of the major personality inventories used today. In addition, recent evidence provided by these researchers suggests that the Five Factor model is invariant across cultures (McCrae & Costa, 1997). The model has been found to hold in several countries with very diverse cultural differences around the world (e.g., United States, China, Korea, Russia, Germany, Holland, Israel, Philippines, Japan, and Portugal).

Job performance model

The GPI will be used primarily in the context of work, and therefore, we wanted to keep in mind a model of job performance throughout the development process. Years of research at PDI have resulted in several variations of a model of job performance (cf. Davis, Hellervik, Skube, Geblein, & Sheard, 1996). The core performance factors of this model are highly consistent with current research suggesting core job performance elements for most jobs (e.g., Campbell, Gasser, & Oswald, 1996; Campbell, McCloy, Oppler, & Sager, 1993). Thus, the core performance factors of these models were used as an organizing structure for how the personality constructs relate to work behaviors. The development teams used the core model as a starting point and made slight modifications through consensus to arrive at the final performance model. The core performance factors included: Administrative, Thinking, Interpersonal, Leadership, Work Orientation, Self-Management, and Motivation.

Conceptual development of facet constructs for the GPI

Conceptual development of facet scales

A literature review was conducted, gathering information on all facet scales that have been linked to the Five Factor model. Particular attention was paid to those scales previously used in a work context. During the literature review we also sought to identify any international papers describing the conceptual and empirical linkages of facets to the Big Five. A review of the major personality inventories used today in business and industry was also conducted (e.g., California Psychological Inventory

(CPI), Sixteen Personality Factor Questionnaire (16PF), Occupational Personality Questionnaire (OPQ), Myers-Briggs Type Indicator (MBTI), Hogan Personality Inventory (HPI), NEO-Personality Inventory (NEO-PI)). From these reviews, a list of potential facet constructs was developed and conceptually defined. An initial set of 29 facets and definitions were created.

World-wide conceptual input

The organizing models (i.e., personality and performance), construct list, and definitions developed from the literature search were then sent to our global teams for review. They were instructed to search their own local literature for alternative models, facet to Big Five links, and construct definitions. The team members were also asked to use their own experience as individual assessors to identify potential personality constructs or syndromes that they have found to be empirically or clinically tied to work successes and failures. They were referred to the job performance model as a starting point for thinking about predictor constructs. Input on both the Five Factor personality model and the performance model used as the organizing structures was also sought. Finally, they were asked to critique the list of 29 previously developed facets and definitions for construct coverage, cultural appropriateness, and consistency with the literature.

A global consensus was quickly reached that both the Five Factor model of personality and the broad performance model were appropriate for cross-cultural use. The only modification was made to the performance model where the Work Orientation factor was divided into two orientations, Collective and Individual Orientation, consistent with cultural differences. This distinction followed the Hofstede (1980) conception of these differences. Thus, the distinction of collectivism versus individualism refers to the dependence on others versus the independence from others.

Several rounds of input were required to reach consensus on constructs at the facet level. For each round of input, two subject matter experts received the development team feedback and incorporated it into the definitions and models. Development teams were then asked whether the changes were appropriate for the construct as defined in their own cultures. Consensus was sought after each round of revisions before moving on to the next round.

In the first round of construct input, each of the ten teams provided detailed critiques and suggestions for improving the initial set of facets. This input was used to build a second set of facet constructs theoretically linked to both the Big Five model of personality and a PDI job performance model. This set of facet constructs and definitions was then submitted to the teams for further review. This second round of reviews produced substantially less input, yet none-the-less important. A major addition that was suggested in the second round of reviews was the incorporation of management failure or derailing constructs. The description of these constructs suggested that the constructs would differ in two significant ways from the previously proposed constructs. First, it was clear that these constructs were not pure trait constructs (i.e., not uni-dimensional), but were instead composites of trait constructs (i.e., multi-dimensional) representing syndromes. And second, they were constructs that represented underlying mechanisms that would trigger behaviors outside the realm of behaviors considered "normal" in the work place. In other words, these were constructs that could lead to, or are associated with, dysfunctional work behaviors. Thus, it was determined that the items to be used in measuring these constructs would be more extreme in nature than those used in traditional measures of normal adult personality.

Two additional constructs, Impressing and Self-awareness/Self-insight, were added in the third round of reviews that represent similar trait composites. The Impressing scale was added as a measure similar to social desirability measures. It was defined as a syndrome where individuals who possess high levels of this characteristic are likely to try to impress others in many situations, including the testing situation. Thus, it was thought to be a multi-dimensional measure of substance, not just responding style (cf. McCrae & Costa, 1983). The second multi-dimensional construct of Self-awareness/Self-insight was defined consistent with Buss' conception of this set of characteristics that he felt clearly went beyond the scope of the Five Factor model of personality (Buss & Finn, 1987).

In summary, the second round of global construct reviews resulted in a set of 33 revised and new facet constructs at the trait level and four management failure constructs. This set of constructs was then submitted once again to the GPI development teams. Input from the third round of reviews led to a final set of 32 facet constructs linked to the Five Factor model, five management failure constructs, and two additional compound trait composites (see Table 1 for the final set of constructs). This set was submitted back to the teams and final approval of the conceptual model was reached by consensus.

Item development for construct scales

The goal in the development of a personality inventory for PDI to use worldwide was to create a set of scales with common items that will be useful in any culture, both today and in the future. As noted earlier, a combined emic and etic approach was used.

Item format

The type of item format(s) to be used on the GPI was explored at this point in the development process. A literature review was conducted to identify potential item types and the advantages and disadvantages of each. Alternatives studied included statements, paired statements, adjectives, bipolar adjectives, and adjective triads. In addition, how the items were to be scaled was explored at this point (e.g., T/F or Likert-Type scaling). Based on the review, it was decided that general statement type items would be developed and scaled with a 5-point Likert-type scale, ranging from Strongly Agree to Strongly Disagree. This decision was based on the desire to have relatively short scales with good variability. Other formats such as true/false or forced choice did not appear to fit this objective.

Development of items for each construct

Each GPI development team was asked to hold a planning meeting for item writing. In these meetings the teams discussed the task and how the team would accomplish the task. Team leaders were asked to make item-writing assignments capitalizing on the strengths of each member in the group. That is, persons with the best knowledge of a particular construct were to be assigned to write items for that construct. After items had been written, the teams were asked to reassemble to discuss and edit the items. Each team was asked to write six to eight items per construct for the 39 constructs.

Several item writing guidelines were given to the teams. Below is the text of the instructions given to the teams:

When writing items:
a) All items should be written in the first person - e.g., "I am ..." "I like..." "For me..." etc.;
b) All items should be written in such a way that they do not contain phrases that are culture bound. The California Personality Inventory (CPI) item that asks about preferences for Abraham Lincoln versus George Washington is a good example of a culture bound item;
c) Items should be written to target a single underlying personality construct. Think about your item from the perspective of the test-taker. Think to yourself: "When a person responds to my item, what construct are they trying to portray information about in their response?" Remember also that this measure will be used in employment-related interventions. This may slightly change the way respondents think about your item. Again, try to think of how the context presses both the response and the construct being portrayed by the respondent. You should think about both the personality construct the item should measure and the performance construct(s) related to the personality construct. In other words, what performance construct(s) should be predicted by the scale and items in it?;
d) When you write personality items, think about someone you know who is very high or low on the trait for which you are writing items. Think about the beliefs, attitudes, behaviors, mannerisms, feelings, and desires that this person projects as a result of the trait. Do some people watching...you will learn a great deal about personality and individual differences associated with specific traits. Think back on your experiences in assessments;
e) Keep items fairly short and direct;
f) Consult with academic partners if you feel they can help you in the item writing process. Consult textbooks on personality testing, psychometrics, and personality theory for additional help;

g) Write the items in your native language first. Then, translate them to English. Get agreement from your team about whether the essence of the item was translated properly. This is a very important step. Everyone should agree that the item is translated properly or it should be dropped.

An attempt was made to keep the guidelines to a minimum so as not to structure the task to the point that creativity would suffer. The development teams wrote a total of 3,012 items. Obviously this number of items had to be reduced before empirical data could be collected.

The first step in the reduction process involved a subject matter expert review of the items. A group of 12 development team members, who were considered to be personality and cross-cultural experts, met to reduce the set of items. The goal was to reduce the number of items to 20 items per facet. Several criteria were used in the reduction process. *First*, items were dropped if they were deemed to be related to more than one of the facets. *Second*, items were dropped if they were deemed to be items that were inappropriate for any particular level of employees (particularly, we were looking for items that would be appropriate for executive level test-takers, as well as other levels of employees in organizations). *Third*, items were dropped if they contained phrases or words that appeared to be very culture specific. *Fourth*, items that were deemed likely to have significant translation problems were dropped. *Fifth*, items were chosen to cover all aspects of the definition of the facet (e.g., clearly redundant items were reduced to the best one item of the redundant set). *Sixth*, an attempt was made to include a relatively equal number of items from each culture represented by the item writers. That is, a stratified sample of items from across the cultures represented was sought as an outcome. (We felt that this was core to developing scales that would operate effectively across cultures. Within a scale, small subtleties within different cultures might be detected by items developed in that culture, but as a whole, the scale would operate similarly across all cultures.) *Finally*, job performance factors were considered in the selection of items. Items with that were deemed unlikely to be related to job performance or might be found to be offensive to test-takers in a work context were excluded.

At least three subject matter experts examined the items written for each facet and made recommendations for items to be dropped. Based on consensus of the subject matter experts, a pool of 802 items was identified as meeting the criteria for item inclusion. Next, the items were randomized and three subject matter experts sorted the items back into the facet categories. Items were retained if all three experts sorted the items into the same category. A total of 79 items were dropped as a result of this process, leaving a pool of 723 remaining items.

The 723 items, along with construct definitions, were then sent back to the development teams for review. The teams were asked to review the items using the same inclusion/exclusion criteria the subject matter experts used. In particular, they were instructed to identify items that they believed would not translate well into their language or were not congruent with the measurement of the construct of interest in their culture. They were also asked to make editorial suggestions on the list of items. As a result of this review, 216 items were dropped from the pool of 723, leaving 507 items. Many of the 507 items were modified slightly to fulfill the editorial requests. At this point, the initial, or Alpha, version of the test had been solidified. It contained 39 scales (32 trait scales and 7 syndrome scales) with 13 items each.

Item translation

The Alpha version of the GPI was translated from English into nine languages, British, German, French, Spanish, Dutch, Swedish, Japanese, Chinese, and Korean. The item translation process followed a series of steps and included several review processes. First a team consisting of a translator, editor, desktop publisher, and project manager was assembled. The English documents went to the translator first. When he/she completed the translation, it was sent to the editor who read through it, made comments, corrections, and suggestions. The editor then returned the documents with his/her recommendations to the original translator. The translator made any necessary adjustments in the text and sent the translation to be typeset. When the layout was completed, the document was returned to the translator to make certain text was not lost or misplaced during the typesetting process. All translators and editors were accredited translators. Additionally, they were all native speakers of the language in which they work, all were educated specifically in translation, and all were tested for competency. They were not, however, psychologists. Therefore, once the translator approved the final version, the items were sent back to our psychologists on the GPI development teams. The items were reviewed by bilingual psychologists on our development teams and edited once again, if warranted.

The development teams took various approaches to ensure the quality of the translations. In all cases, at least two psychologists compared the original English version of the items to the translated version. These reviewers looked for linguistic correctness and psychological fidelity of the translated item with the original item.

In China and Japan, a much more complex process was used because of the more complex nature of their languages and dissimilarity from English. In China, a double translation process was conducted. The translation process described above was conducted in the US, while a similar process was conducted in China. Then a bilingual Chinese psychologist and his team of graduate students reviewed both sets of translations against each other and against the original English version. They made editorial and content changes based on these reviews.

In Japan, two bilingual psychologists compared the initial translation to the English version. After corrections were made and checked, two bilingual native English speakers did a back translation and then a separate bilingual psychologist compared the back translation to the original English version and further edits were made. The translations were then reviewed and revised by the original review team plus a third person for objectivity.

After all the development teams had finished reviewing and revising the translations, the materials were sent back to the original translation team. The editor and desktop publisher then put the translated items into a booklet form. When the layout was completed, the document was returned again to the original translator to make certain text was not lost or misplaced during the typesetting process. When the translator approved the final version, it was determined that the alpha version of the GPI was ready to go to the initial data collection phase.

Item testing

The goals of the item testing phase of the GPI development project were to develop a test: a) of manageable length (i.e., no more than 10 items per scale), b) that functions similarly across cultures, c) consisting of a common set of items in all language versions, and d) that is able to differentiate among individuals with different performance potential within and across levels of employees in organizations. Both traditional and modern statistical methods were used in this process. Item response theory (IRT) analyses were among the techniques used in the item testing. Essentially, the purpose of the IRT analyses was to identify items and scales that measured the same things, in the same way, for individuals from different cultures with the same true scores on a construct.

Data collection

Data were collected in many samples throughout the world to maximize the heterogeneity both within and across cultures. Within cultures, we tested individuals across as many different levels of employees as possible. Across cultures, we collected data in as many diverse countries as possible. These countries included China, Japan, Singapore, Indonesia, Sweden, United Kingdom, Netherlands, Belgium, France, Switzerland, Spain, Colombia, and the United States. Given that the primary clients of PDI are middle management and higher executives, over-sampling was conducted for these sub-groups. Samples sources include primarily MBA or other students with work experience, local community samples, and individuals recruited by the GPI development team members (e.g., friends, relatives, and clients). The total sample consisted of over 2,000 individuals, with just over 50 per cent from the middle management level and above.

The three largest samples were from the United States ($N = 303$), China ($N = 432$), and Spain ($N = 463$). These three samples were used for the majority of the item testing analyses. In addition to being the three largest samples, we felt these samples represented sufficiently distinct cultures that allowed us to identify those items that negatively affect comparability across cultures.

Data analysis

For practical purposes we decided that the final scales would have no more than 10 items, and fewer if possible. Therefore, our first step was to reduce the 39 scales from 13 items to 10 items each. Scale reliability estimates (Cronbach's coefficient alpha) and item-total correlations were calculated for all scales and items separately for each set of data. The three items with the lowest item-total correlations across the three samples were dropped. Results from the three sets of analyses were remarkably similar. Identifying the three worst items was very straightforward. Additionally, two scales, Goal-Directed Thinking and Conformance, had very low internal consistency in all three country samples, even after the three items were dropped. These scales were flagged for possible exclusion in the final test.

Next, the data from the three countries were each split into 39 separate data sets (117 data sets in total). Each of these data sets contained data from one scale and one culture only. This was done so that we could treat each scale as a separate, unidimensional test for item response theory (i.e., IRT) analysis — a requirement for most IRT models (Thissen & Steinberg, 1988). For this project, we used Samejima's (1969) graded response model. This model is appropriate for responses made on Likert-format scales, which is the scale format used in the GPI. The graded response model describes the relation of an item to an underlying psychological construct with a slope (i.e., discrimination) parameter (a), that indicates the strength of the relation of an item with a construct, and threshold parameters (b_i), that represent response endorsement probabilities.

Item parameters were calculated for each item in all three samples and test scores were created for all subjects using these item parameters. Test information curves were then produced to visually examine the usefulness of the IRT scoring algorithm based on these item parameters. When using the full response scale (five response options), the test information curves were not normal and difficult to interpret. We thought this might be due to unstable parameter estimates for the extreme responses (i.e., strongly disagree and strongly agree) in the three smallish samples. To test this conjecture, we collapsed the raw data from a five-point response scale to a three-point response scale by grouping strongly agree and agree responses together and strongly disagree and disagree responses together. The middle, or neutral, response was not changed. New parameter estimates and subject test scores were created. New test information curves were produced. The new curves appeared to be much more normal and the parameter estimates more stable. Chi-square fit statistics that quantify the difference between observed data and the data reproduced by the estimating item parameters suggested that the three-option scoring actually fit the data better for graded response model purposes than the five-option scoring (see Drasgow, Levine, Tsien, Williams, & Mead, 1995, for a full explication of this method). In fact, using this method to gauge the fit of the data to the IRT model, all of the scales (including the trait composite scales) using 3-point scoring fit the assumptions of the IRT model at levels greater than those evidenced in other published studies using this same method on Likert-type personality data (cf. Zickar & Drasgow, 1996; Zickar & Robie, 1999). All further IRT-based analyses conducted to test for differential item and test functioning (i.e., cross-cultural differences) were based on parameter estimates from the collapsed data sets.

Differential item and differential test functioning

Differential item functioning (DIF) refers to the situation in which a particular item has different response functions for different groups of people such that an individual from one group has a different expected probability of choosing a particular option than an individual from another group, even though the two individuals possess the same level of the trait (θ) being examined (Camilli & Shepard, 1994). For example, if an individual from Spain who possesses a particular level of a trait (e.g., $\theta = 1.50$) has a different probability of choosing the most positive option for an item measuring that trait (e.g., Adaptability) compared to an individual from the US with the identical θ, then that item would be said to evidence DIF.

Differential test functioning (DTF) is the scale-level analog to DIF, and refers to differences in expected total test or scale scores by individuals with equal standings on the latent trait but who belong to different subpopulations (Drasgow & Hulin, 1990). Analysis of both DIF and DTF is important. The presence of several items displaying DIF, which can cancel each other, may not be indicative of serious measurement bias at the scale level. Furthermore, when using personality data for making personnel selection decisions, decision-makers almost always rely on information at the scale-level. Nevertheless, item-level differential functioning remains important to study because knowing the item properties (e.g., different discrimination parameters or different endorsement parameters) that contribute to scale-level differential functioning is helpful for eliminating DTF.

The US sample served as the reference group for all analyses. The Chinese and Spanish samples were compared to the US sample separately to determine whether DTF was present for any scale in either cross-cultural comparison. For those scale comparisons that evidenced DTF, we sought to determine which items were contributing to these differences.

Before conducting analyses to assess DTF, we linked measurement (θ) scales between the reference (US) and focal (Spanish or Chinese) groups. Such linking puts the item parameters on the same scale, which is necessary to estimate the θ difference between the groups of respondents and to appropriately test for DIF/DTF. Linking of θ metrics was done using Equate 2.1 (Baker, 1997), which estimates a set of linear equating constants that are used to convert one set of item parameters to the metric of another set of item parameters (Baker, 1992).

DIF statistics were computed using DFITP4 (Raju, 1998). The DIF statistic, NCDIF, tests for non-compensatory DIF among all items (Raju, Van der Linden, & Fleer, 1995; Flowers, Oshima, & Raju, 1999). When testing for non-compensatory DIF, one assumes that all other items in the scale are free from DIF (i.e., DIF in one item cannot cancel out DIF in another item). Additionally, DFITP4 computes compensatory DIF (CDIF) estimates for each item within a test (i.e., an individual GPI scale). DTF is the sum of these compensatory item-level DIF statistics (Raju *et al.*,

Table 1. Differential item (DIF) and test (DTF) functioning results of the initial version of the GPI

Scale	U.S. vs. Spain		U.S. vs. China		Both Comparisons	
	# DIF	# DTF	# DIF	# DTF	# DIF	# DTF
Agreeableness						
Conformance (8)	7 (6)	1 (1)	7 (6)	2 (2)	6 (4)	0 (0)
Consideration (10)	3 (3)	1 (1)	5 (4)	3 (2)	3 (3)	0 (0)
Empathy (8)	3 (3)	1 (1)	3 (3)	1 (1)	1 (1)	0 (0)
Interdependence (9)	7 (6)	2 (2)	7 (7)	1 (1)	7 (6)	1 (1)
Openness (9)	6 (4)	3 (3)	6 (4)	1 (0)	4 (2)	0 (0)
Thought Agility (10)	6 (4)	1 (1)	4 (4)	2 (2)	3 (1)	0 (0)
Trust (10)	5 (3)	7 (7)	6 (6)	2 (2)	2 (2)	1 (1)
Conscientiousness						
Attention to Detail (10)	6 (5)	6 (5)	5 (5)	3 (3)	4 (3)	3 (2)
Dutifulness (9)	5 (5)	2 (2)	6 (6)	0 (0)	4 (4)	0 (0)
Responsibility (8)	2 (2)	2 (2)	4 (4)	1 (1)	2 (2)	1 (1)
Work Focus (10)	5 (4)	1 (1)	9 (7)	1 (1)	4 (2)	0 (0)
Extroversion						
Adaptability (8)	5 (5)	3 (3)	7 (6)	0 (0)	5 (4)	0 (0)
Competitiveness (9)	5 (3)	1 (1)	6 (6)	0 (0)	2 (1)	0 (0)
Desire for Achievement (9)	5 (4)	3 (3)	7 (7)	5 (1)	4 (3)	2 (1)
Desire for Advancement (10)	5 (4)	4 (4)	7 (6)	2 (2)	3 (2)	1 (1)
Energy Level (10)	6 (5)	4 (4)	5 (4)	1 (1)	3 (3)	1 (1)
Influence (10)	5 (4)	1 (1)	7 (2)	3 (3)	5 (1)	1 (1)
Initiative (10)	6 (2)	0 (0)	7 (6)	2 (2)	5 (1)	0 (0)
Risk-Taking (10)	7 (2)	2 (1)	10 (9)	1 (1)	7 (2)	1 (0)
Sociability (10)	7 (7)	7 (7)	8 (7)	2 (2)	5 (5)	1 (1)
Taking Charge (10)	5 (3)	4 (4)	8 (6)	0 (0)	4 (2)	0 (0)
Neuroticism						
Emotional Control (9)	6 (5)	5 (4)	8 (7)	0 (0)	5 (4)	0 (0)
Negative Affectivity* (9)	6 (5)	3 (3)	6 (4)	1 (1)	4 (1)	0 (0)
Optimism (10)	7 (6)	1 (1)	8 (7)	3 (2)	5 (4)	0 (0)
Self-Confidence (9)	8 (7)	2 (1)	7 (6)	4 (4)	6 (4)	1 (0)
Stress Tolerance (10)	6 (6)	7 (5)	5 (5)	1 (1)	4 (4)	1 (1)
Openness to Experience						
Goal-Directed Thinking (8)	5 (5)	0 (0)	3 (3)	1 (1)	2 (2)	0 (0)
Independence (10)	7 (6)	6 (5)	6 (6)	3 (3)	4 (3)	3 (3)
Innovativeness/Creativity (10)	6 (5)	2 (2)	7 (5)	2 (1)	4 (3)	0 (0)
Social Astuteness (9)	4 (4)	1 (1)	7 (5)	2 (2)	4 (3)	0 (0)
Thought Focus (9)	2 (2)	2 (2)	5 (3)	1 (1)	1 (1)	0 (0)
Vision (9)	5 (4)	2 (2)	6 (4)	2 (2)	3 (2)	0 (0)
Trait Composites						
Ego-Centered* (9)	8 (6)	2 (2)	9 (9)	0 (0)	8 (6)	0 (0)
Impressing* (8)	7 (5)	7 (7)	8 (6)	2 (1)	7 (5)	2 (1)
Intimidating* (9)	6 (5)	2 (1)	7 (5)	8 (8)	5 (3)	2 (1)
Manipulating* (10)	7 (6)	4 (4)	8 (5)	0 (0)	6 (4)	0 (0)
Micro-Managing* (10)	7 (6)	1 (1)	6 (5)	3 (3)	4 (3)	0 (0)

Passive-Aggressive* (8)	8 (8)	0 (0)	6 (5)	3 (1)	6 (5)	0 (0)
Self-Awareness/Self-Insight (10)	7 (7)	2 (2)	3 (3)	2 (2)	3 (3)	1 (1)

Note: Number of items in each scale after dropping items based on classical test theory analyses in parentheses after scale name. *High scores on these scales are undesirable. # DIF = number of items in each scale that evidenced significant differential item functioning. # DTF = number of items needed to be dropped to make DTF non-significant (numbers in parentheses are based on less stringent differential functioning criteria — see *Differential item and test functioning* section of the chapter).

1995; Flowers *et al.*, 1999). Raju *et al.* (1995) proposed a $\chi 2$ test for assessing the statistical significance of the observed DTF index; the degrees of freedom for this index equal to N_F - 1, where N_F is the number of examinees in the focal group. Raju (personal communication, October 12, 1998) currently recommends using a cut-off of 0.096 on the DTF index for scales composed of items with five options (0.010 has traditionally been used with 3-point scales; see Fleer, 1993; Flowers, 1995). Scales with DTF values above this cut-off that also have significant $\chi 2$ values at a $p < .01$ level are said to evidence DTF. Raju's (personal communication, October 12, 1998) cutoffs for both DIF and DTF are based on an analytical formulation that is intended to identify items and tests (i.e., scales) that evidence DIF or DTF which is of practical significance. Analyses in the current study were conducted first using the 0.010 DTF cut-off and then a more liberal 0.096 cut-off. We looked at this more liberal cut-off because the data underlying the collapsed data was a 5-point scale (we report results for both cut-offs in Table 1).

An iterative process, involving several rounds of parameter estimation and linking, was used to identify which items had DIF (Candell & Drasgow, 1988). Items that exhibited DIF (a $\chi 2$ with a $p \le .01$ and a NCDIF value ≥ 0.010 in the first set of analyses; a $\chi 2$ with a $p \le .01$ and a NCDIF value ≥ 0.096 in the second set of analyses) were removed from the analyses and equating constants were re-computed without the items that evidenced DIF. Using these new equating constants, NCDIF statistics were re-computed. If additional items exhibited DIF at this stage, another iteration was continued with a new linking. This iterative process continued until no new items with DIF were identified.

Table 1 shows the result of DIF and DTF analyses. The values under the #DIF column indicate the number of items within that scale that evidence DIF using a NCDIF criterion of .010, which we had used in our first round of analyses. The values in parentheses are the same indicator, but with the less stringent criterion of 0.096. When looking at NCDIF, regardless of the criterion used, a large number of individual items evidence DIF. Yet, when combined into a scale, the actual number of items that appear to be causing bias at the test level is minimal (based on CDIF). The number of items that contribute to DTF, based on CDIF are listed in the column labeled #DTF. This also represents the number of items that would need to be deleted from the scale to remove DTF. In most cases this is a very small number. When both the Spain v. US and China v. US analyses are considered simultaneously (last two columns), in only a few cases did any one item contribute to DTF in both comparisons. These analyses provide strong evidence that, at the scale level, the GPI can function similarly across cultures, using the same item set.

Table 2. Descriptive statistics for the final form of the GPI in the U.S., Spain, and China

Scale	U.S. (N = 303)			Spain (N = 463)			China (N = 432)		
	α	M	SD	α	M	SD	α	M	SD
Agreeableness									
Consideration (10)	.80[a]	7.40[a]	1.13[a]	.76[a]	7.44[a]	1.18[a]	.79[a]	6.98[b]	1.16[a]
Empathy (7)	.70[a]	4.81[a]	.87[a]	.62[a]	4.73[a]	.86[a]	.69[a]	4.75[a]	.80[a]
Interdependence (8)	.71[a]	3.98[a]	1.06[a]	.78[b]	4.54[b]	1.19[a]	.64[a]	4.39[c]	.94[b]
Openness (7)	.65[a]	4.34[a]	.87[a]	.64[a]	4.31[a]	.96[b]	.64[a]	3.89[b]	.90[a,b]
Thought Agility (9)	.73[a,b]	6.48[a]	.93[a]	.67[a]	6.30[b]	.97[a]	.75[b]	6.52[a]	.92[a]
Trust (7)	.76[a]	4.93[a]	.89[a]	.71[a]	4.32[b]	1.08[b]	.59[b]	4.57[c]	.80[a]
Conscientiousness									
Attention to Detail (9)	.77[a]	5.52[a]	1.25[a]	.76[a]	5.74[a]	1.21[a]	.66[b]	5.90[c]	.95[b]
Dutifulness (8)	.69[a]	4.81[a]	.96[a]	.67[a]	4.28[b]	1.02[a]	.64[a]	5.09[c]	.90[b]
Responsibility (7)	.77[a]	5.29[a]	.87[a]	.73[a]	4.77[b]	.95[b]	.55[b]	5.08[c]	.67[c]
Work Focus (9)	.70[a]	5.34[a]	1.17[a]	.73[a]	4.60[b]	1.27[a]	.65[a]	5.29[a]	1.00[b]
Extroversion									
Adaptability (8)	.67[a]	4.93[a]	.98[a,b]	.55[b]	4.51[b]	1.00[a]	.55[b]	4.36[b]	.89[b]
Competitiveness (8)	.82[a]	3.96[a]	1.35[a]	.76[b]	3.22[b]	1.29[a]	.62[c]	4.54[a]	.93[b]
Des. for Ach. (8)	.80[a]	5.52[a]	1.12[a]	.68[b]	4.76[b]	1.04[a]	.72[b]	5.08[c]	.98[a]
Des. for Adv. (7)	.72[a]	3.78[a]	1.08[a]	.65[a]	3.56[b]	.99[b]	.70[a]	4.19[c]	.96[b]
Energy Level (9)	.81[a]	5.26[a]	1.33[a]	.75[b]	4.59[b]	1.33[a]	.76[b]	4.99[c]	1.21[a]
Influence (9)	.80[a]	5.51[a]	1.16[a]	.75[b]	4.67[b]	1.19[a]	.80[a]	5.70[c]	1.12[a]
Initiative (9)	.77[a]	5.56[a]	1.14[a,b]	.78[a]	5.07[b]	1.24[a]	.71[b]	5.17[b]	1.00[b]
Risk-Taking (9)	.81[a]	5.48[a]	1.22[a]	.79[a]	5.55[a]	1.32[b]	.73[b]	5.01[b]	1.14[a]
Sociability (9)	.86[a]	5.57[a]	1.61[a]	.75[b]	5.46[a]	1.37[b]	.73[b]	5.23[b]	1.17[c]
Taking Charge (10)	.88[a]	6.21[a]	1.58[a]	.85[b]	5.01[b]	1.69[a]	.81[b]	6.04[a]	1.32[b]

Neuroticism

Emotional Control (7)	.79[a]	4.03[a]	1.15[a]	.75[a,b]	3.29[b]	1.23[a]	.70[b]	3.99[a]	.99[b]
Neg. Affectivity* (7)	.66[a]	2.07[a]	.92[a,b]	.60[a,b]	2.68[b]	.98[a]	.54[b]	3.13[c]	.84[b]
Optimism (9)	.79[a]	5.96[a]	1.18[a]	.76[a]	5.46[b]	1.36[b]	.67[b]	5.44[b]	1.03[c]
Self-Confidence (7)	.68[a]	4.91[a]	.81[a]	.70[a]	3.92[b]	.97[b]	.63[a]	4.75[c]	.78[a]
Stress Tolerance (8)	.81[a]	4.29[a]	1.32[a]	.70[b]	3.49[b]	1.14[b]	.67[b]	4.25[a]	.98[b]

Openness to Experience

Independence (8)	.67[a]	4.35[a]	1.00[a]	.66[a]	4.46[a]	1.06[a]	.65[a]	4.63[b]	.98[a]
Inno./Creativity (9)	.86[a]	5.92[a]	1.33[a]	.81[b]	5.91[a]	1.25[a,b]	.81[b]	5.63[b]	1.14[b]
Social Astuteness (8)	.68[a]	4.78[a]	.93[a]	.65[a]	4.63[b]	.96[a]	.70[a]	4.92[c]	.91[a]
Thought Focus (7)	.70[a]	4.69[a]	.82[a]	.73[a]	4.24[b]	.91[a]	.75[a]	4.53[c]	.83[a]
Vision (9)	.78[a]	5.81[a]	1.12[a]	.80[a]	5.08[b]	1.29[b]	.82[a]	5.61[c]	1.16[a]

Trait Composites

Ego-Centered* (7)	.64[a]	3.31[a]	.94[a]	.64[a]	2.89[b]	.98[a]	.61[a]	3.72[c]	.88[a]
Impressing* (7)	.54[a]	3.66[a]	.80[a]	.42[a]	3.86[b]	.82[a]	.45[a]	4.64[c]	.69[b]
Intimidating* (7)	.65[a]	2.09[a]	.94[a]	.57[a]	2.67[b]	.98[a]	.42[b]	3.34[c]	.79[b]
Manipulating* (10)	.72[a]	3.72[a]	1.22[a]	.76[a]	3.64[a]	1.49[b]	.74[a]	4.61[b]	1.33[a]
Micro-Managing* (7)	.75[a]	2.41[a]	.99[a]	.60[b]	2.51[a]	.90[a,b]	.50[c]	3.40[b]	.81[b]
Pass.-Aggressive* (7)	.64[a]	2.84[a]	.93[a]	.52[b]	3.07[b]	.93[a]	.63[a]	3.76[a]	.92[a]
S. Aware / SI (9)	.79[a]	6.53[a]	1.08[a]	.78[a]	5.70[b]	1.35[b]	.75[a]	6.49[a]	.96[a]

Note: Number of items for each scale are in parentheses. Each item is scored $1 = 0$, $2 = .25$, $3 = .5$, $4 = .75$, $5 = 1$. *High scores on these scales are undesirable. Values with the same superscript are not statistically different ($p < .05$) for across-sample comparisons.

Final scale decisions

After the DIF iterations were complete, we had many pieces of item- and scale-level information on which to base our decisions about final scale composition. This information included item parameter estimates (a and b_i), DIF and DTF values, and more traditional test information, such as means, standard deviations, item-total correlations, and internal consistency estimates. See Table 2. We used a holistic approach to make final decisions. The criteria we used to guide our decisions are detailed below.

The first criterion we set was that retained items should have a-parameters greater than 0.50. Items with a-parameters below this criterion offer little discrimination among test-takers. Another criterion we used was that retained items should not have extreme b-parameters (those above or below four). Such items discriminate best for those with very extreme levels of a trait, which is not common among working adults. Additionally, we considered all items on a scale simultaneously, with respect to their b-parameters. We wanted items that, when combined, measure the full range of the trait well (i.e., we wanted a series of items with b-parameters that allowed us to measure the trait well within ± three standard deviations).

In addition to using IRT item parameter-related criteria, we also considered the DIF and DTF information. We sought to keep items that did not contribute to DTF, and that did not exhibit excessive NCDIF in one or both cultural comparisons. Additionally, we avoided keeping items that were identified by the DFITP4 program as those to be dropped in order to eliminate DTF.

Lastly, throughout several rounds of dropping and adding items based on the IRT-based criteria listed above, we examined item-total correlations and internal consistency statistics. The final scales contained a minimum of seven items and a maximum of ten items, contained items that had acceptable item-total correlations in the US, Spanish, and Chinese samples, and had acceptable internal consistency. The previously identified problematic scales of Goal-Directed Thinking and Conformance did not attain an acceptable level of psychometric adequacy by dropping particularly poor items. After examining both the item statistics and correlations with other scales, consensus was reached among the GPI development teams that these two constructs were both multi-dimensional and redundant with other content of the GPI. Thus, these scales were dropped from the GPI. The final version of the GPI contained 37 scales and 300 items. Sample items are included in Appendix B.

After the new scales were established, internal consistency estimates were calculated for the final 37 scales using data from all other countries than the US, Spain, or China. These countries are: England, Colombia, US (for those who speak English as a second language), Sweden, France, Japan, Germany, Singapore, and The Netherlands. In general, alpha values for the scales in these cultures were acceptable, as most were in the .70s and .80s ranges (See Table 3).

For all of the language versions used to generate these alphas, item-total correla-

Table 3. Internal reliability estimates for GPI scales in diverse cultural samples

Scale	N's	USA English as 2nd Lang.	England	The Netherlands	Sweden	France	Germany	Japan	Singapore	Columbia
		93	60	28	30	244	122	101	102	101
Adaptability (8)		.65	.79	.72	.60	.59	.65	.79	.74	.65
Attention to Detail (9)		.81	.80	.83	.80	.78	.71	.79	.93	.82
Competitiveness (8)		.62	.79	.70	.69	.83	.65	.77	.75	.70
Consideration (10)		.83	.92	.70	.83	.80	.72	.84	.86	.85
D. for Achievement (8)		.76	.80	.75	.77	.80	.75	.85	.85	.82
D. for Advancement (7)		.64	.74	.75	.78	.78	.70	.64	.77	.72
Dutifulness (8)		.65	.80	.34	.75	.68	.61	.76	.73	.75
Emotional Control (7)		.71	.80	.60	.62	.71	.75	.78	.77	.73
Empathy (7)		.74	.82	.76	.82	.70	.73	.68	.83	.75
Energy-Level (9)		.76	.80	.75	.81	.75	.74	.79	.84	.76
Impressing (7)		.52	.69	.05	.65	.49	.41	.51	.64	.64
Independence (8)		.73	.71	.52	.65	.69	.56	.66	.68	.71
Influence (9)		.77	.83	.89	.79	.80	.76	.83	.82	.75
Initiative (9)		.74	.85	.79	.83	.78	.71	.84	.83	.82
Innovativeness (9)		.83	.91	.68	.87	.83	.79	.89	.85	.85
Interdependence (8)		.77	.80	.62	.76	.76	.69	.72	.69	.81
Negative Affectivity (7)		.63	.71	.58	.62	.57	.32	.64	.67	.70
Openness (7)		.62	.76	.72	.61	.73	.70	.76	.68	.79
Optimism (9)		.76	.84	.66	.78	.80	.68	.85	.83	.78
Responsibility (7)		.77	.89	.80	.45	.69	.66	.79	.87	.87
Risk-Taking (9)		.79	.85	.87	.83	.82	.81	.78	.83	.80
Self-Awareness (9)		.82	.82	.78	.77	.74	.82	.84	.86	.91
Self-Confidence (7)		.71	.78	.61	.59	.72	.45	.76	.79	.87
Sociability (9)		.83	.86	.83	.87	.77	.74	.89	.80	.75
Social Astuteness (8)		.75	.78	.56	.75	.73	.60	.78	.81	.73
Stress Tolerance (8)		.76	.84	.73	.80	.74	.68	.85	.78	.72
Taking Charge (10)		.83	.90	.88	.88	.86	.79	.87	.89	.82
Thought Agility (9)		.82	.91	.80	.78	.75	.67	.86	.82	.80
Thought Focus (7)		.68	.85	.80	.54	.76	.74	.76	.82	.83
Trust (7)		.72	.81	.64	.72	.64	.59	.76	.67	.65
Vision (9)		.79	.86	.71	.82	.75	.65	.81	.83	.83
Work Focus (9)		.79	.76	.76	.79	.76	.74	.82	.77	.81
Ego-Centered (7)		.64	.64	.52	.58	.71	.45	.59	.61	.57
Intimidating (7)		.66	.64	.56	.55	.56	.48	.54	.65	.49
Manipulation (10)		.79	.79	.71	.71	.82	.63	.81	.74	.72
Micro-managing (7)		.69	.74	.63	.55	.63	.50	.62	.60	.55
Passive-Aggressive (7)		.56	.69	.71	.79	.53	.46	.67	.60	.50

Note: The values in parentheses next to the scale names indicate the number of items in each scale

tions were examined in an effort to identify aberrant results across the versions. For items that had adequate item-total correlations in most language versions but did not in one or two, we examined the items for possible translation problems. Translator-psychologist meetings were used to identify both grammatical and cultural translation problems. The translator would back translate the item to English and the psychologist would work with the translator to arrive at a translation that captured the original psychological content of the item. Nearly all identified items were changed in at least some small way in an effort to improve their psychometric quality. These items are flagged for future analyses when additional data are available for the latest edition of the items and scales to which they belong.

Scale validation

Comparability of factor structure across cultures

To this point in the test development, our focus has been on the item- and scale-level. However, we were also interested in exploring whether the factor structure was similar across the cultures studied and whether it conformed to the Big Five structure. We utilized targeted Procrustes techniques instead of CFA (i.e., confirmatory factor analytic) techniques because of some of the disadvantages of CFA, including technical difficulties in the estimation of some models (McCrae, Zonderman, Costa, Bond, & Paunonen, 1996) and the tendency in CFA for several substantively different models to fit any given data set at a similar level (MacCaullum, Wegener, Vchino, & Fabrigan, 1993).

Before conducting the factor analyses, we excluded from analysis any trait composite scale because each of these scales is composed of constructs that are both-within and external to what most researchers would conceive of as the bounds of the Big Five factor structure (Ego-centered, Manipulating, Intimidating, Micromanaging, Passive-aggressive, Impressing, Self-awareness/Self-insight). Out of the 37 remaining scales, we used 30 for the Procrustes analysis. We always used the principal components, varimax-rotated factor structure from the American sample as the target matrix and rotated the principal components, varimax-rotated factor structures from the Spanish and Chinese samples to that matrix. Three-, four-, five-, six-, and seven-factor solutions were computed in this manner and congruence coefficients were calculated (see McCrae *et al.*, 1996, for specifics on the methodology). As can be seen from Table 4, the factor structures were stable for the three-, four-, and five-factor solutions (i.e., all factor congruence coefficients at or above approximately .90, cf. Paunonen, 1997), but became unstable at six and seven factors. Given that we hypothesized and were interested in the five-factor solution, we will concentrate on this interpretation of the data.

Table 4. Factor congruence coefficients with the American normative structure

Number of Factors	Congruence Coefficients						
3 (U.S. vs. Spain)	.97	.93	.97				
3 (U.S. vs. China)	.97	.92	.95				
4 (U.S. vs. Spain)	.97	.96	.96	.94			
4 (U.S. vs. China)	.97	.93	.91	.91			
5 (U.S. vs. Spain)	.98	.94	.95	.94	.92		
5 (U.S. vs. China)	.95	.91	.92	.91	.89		
6 (U.S. vs. Spain)	.97	.95	.80	.91	.96	.75	
6 (U.S. vs. China)	.95	.90	.81	.88	.91	.70	
7 (U.S. vs. Spain)	.98	.93	.96	.97	.96	.84	.89
7 (U.S. vs. China)	.97	.86	.91	.92	.92	.67	.84

Note: Principal components, Varimax-rotated. Final form of the GPI was used with trait composites removed. For the five-factor solution, Factor 1 = Extroversion, Factor 2 = Neuroticism, Factor 3 = Agreeableness, Factor 4 = Conscientiousness, Factor 5 = Openness to Experience.

Factor loadings for each of the five-factor Procrustes solutions are displayed in Table 5. The factor loadings were highly consistent with the authors' a priori hypotheses. Although some degree of secondary loadings were evidenced, these results are consistent with the level of equivalence found with the NEO-PI-R across cultures (Costa & McCrae, 1997; McCrae *et al.*, 1996). Moreover, the item congruence coefficients, which index the degree to which the items fit the factor structure, averaged .95 in the U.S. versus Spain comparison (range = .77 to .99) and .92 in the U.S. versus China comparison (range = .82 to 1.00). As with the factor congruence coefficients, item congruence coefficients above .90 are generally considered to be evidence of a good fit of the model to the data (Paunonen, 1997). Using Paunonen's (1997) monte-carlo generated equation of congruence prediction (p. 52), all of the item and factor congruence coefficients were above the 95 per cent confidence limit of what might be expected if one factored randomly-generated data and attempted to fit a model with the same number of variables and factors.

The confirmation of a Five Factor model underlying the GPI provides robust evidence for construct validity of the measure. Further, the facet level loading results are highly consistent with previous measures of the Big Five, suggesting that this cross-cultural measure of personality is likely to perform at least as well as instruments developed and transported with an imposed-etic strategy.

We subsequently conducted similar analyses in which we used the original, five-factor, principal components, varimax-rotated factor structure from the original American sample as the target matrix and rotated the principal components, varimax-rotated factor structures from three other samples to that matrix. These three other samples were: (1) a random, stratified sample of respondents from U.S. households ($N = 988$), (2) a sample of individuals who participated in PDI assessments for developmental purposes ($N = 946$), and (3) a sample of individuals who participated in PDI assessments for promotion/selection purposes ($N = 1,069$). The distribution of age across the organizational samples was similar in both mean level and dispersion (promotion/selection $M = 39.47$ and $SD = 8.44$; development $M = 41.06$ and $SD = 7.01$). The U.S. normative sample was both older ($M = 52.79$) and approximately

Table 5. Factor loadings for factors in the normative American structure and the Spanish and Chinese versions of the GPI rotated to the normative American structure

Scale	Factor														
	A			C			E			N			O		
	US	Sp	Ch	US	Sp	Ch	US	Sp	Ch	US	Sp	Ch	US	Sp	Ch
Agreeableness															
Consideration	81	79	67	19	14	39	10	-01	29	-01	06	-03	06	16	-05
Empathy	77	67	60	06	10	26	-03	05	25	-03	10	12	33	45	37
Interdependence	52	47	60	04	11	14	12	-06	02	24	32	33	-26	-30	-03
Openness	45	49	40	12	14	-10	10	-08	26	41	46	53	03	03	04
Thought Agility	60	57	44	20	18	35	10	17	27	17	16	22	40	35	35
Trust	38	53	46	00	00	30	06	10	04	59	28	39	-11	-48	-36
Conscientious															
Att. to Detail	14	27	24	74	72	70	13	24	11	-26	10	-19	13	27	19
Dutifulness	10	18	48	71	68	57	02	06	-08	06	-02	06	00	07	10
Responsibility	14	30	20	69	68	67	08	20	19	25	20	22	16	12	07
Work Focus	01	04	04	72	79	52	18	24	13	29	20	51	04	06	29
Extroversion															
Adaptability	25	23	21	-14	-29	-29	47	46	59	51	37	13	14	26	22
Competitiveness	-19	-39	-15	20	16	16	65	63	70	-13	-07	15	05	03	-02
Des. for Ach.	11	10	07	29	28	27	70	68	74	16	05	12	30	27	29
Des. for Adv.	-08	-14	-13	15	20	13	66	65	62	-10	-16	-27	16	05	08
Energy Level	13	15	06	15	20	07	65	59	54	35	32	44	-03	16	30
Influence	24	16	46	-06	12	08	69	65	40	13	09	29	29	43	52
Initiative	19	23	43	23	28	15	73	70	54	14	15	20	18	26	38
Risk-Taking	10	16	-07	-17	-30	-19	68	57	74	30	29	09	11	21	00
Sociability	43	47	42	-21	-08	-22	58	44	53	17	35	27	-13	-19	-06
Taking Charge	01	-06	23	03	10	05	77	75	52	08	04	29	25	33	45

Neuroticism															
Emot. Control	-07	-17	00	12	20	26	-03	-09	-01	**72**	**73**	**68**	12	37	28
Neg. Aff. *	-16	**-41**	-19	-15	-04	-23	-08	-08	09	**-69**	**-46**	**-68**	07	25	16
Optimism	26	21	35	12	-03	14	**45**	**44**	**51**	**59**	**63**	**47**	02	04	04
Self-Confidence	05	04	10	23	27	**41**	**44**	**54**	**56**	**50**	38	35	38	37	15
Stress Tolerance	-11	-31	-08	-03	-01	01	15	11	23	**82**	**80**	**79**	04	27	06
Openness to Experience															
Independence	-31	-18	-16	15	-10	16	15	19	27	-32	-19	**-49**	**57**	**64**	37
Inno./Creativity	21	37	24	-24	02	-05	38	**52**	**61**	34	19	22	**50**	**40**	**45**
Soc. Astuteness	36	23	34	17	16	10	30	36	34	-19	02	-08	**40**	**61**	**59**
Thought Focus	14	20	25	08	21	12	24	38	**40**	20	19	30	**77**	**62**	**64**
Vision	17	15	20	18	28	16	38	33	**42**	01	00	21	**66**	**65**	**70**

Note: Varimax-rotated principal components. Decimal points are omitted. Loadings greater than .40 in absolute value are in boldface. *High scores on this scale are undesirable. A = Agreeableness, C = Conscientiousness, E = Extroversion, N = Neuroticism, O = Openness. US = American sample (N = 463), Sp = Spanish sample (N = 303), Ch = Chinese sample (N = 432).

Table 6. Factor loadings for factors in various GPI samples rotated to the original normative American structure

	Factor														
	A			C			E			N			O		
Scale	UN	DV	PS	UN	DV	PS	UN	DV	PS	UN	DV	PS	UN	DV	PS
Agreeableness															
Consideration	79	83	72	30	19	32	-05	09	05	09	05	13	05	00	07
Empathy	77	76	79	13	17	17	01	11	15	16	02	-01	31	27	18
Interdependence	56	53	35	-04	05	00	20	06	-09	27	30	54	-27	-07	23
Openness	54	32	59	-03	05	14	09	24	25	43	47	20	07	-01	-16
Thought Agility	62	50	64	15	22	19	18	08	07	23	29	26	39	41	31
Trust	43	44	33	18	09	11	05	01	-01	49	50	65	-33	-12	04
Conscientious.															
Att. to Detail	21	09	34	73	75	70	09	04	15	-12	-19	-26	31	16	-01
Dutifulness	25	31	10	65	57	60	00	03	06	13	08	28	-07	10	15
Responsibility	26	19	26	70	64	57	16	24	26	22	26	40	14	12	18
Work Focus	07	-01	15	72	69	67	20	19	21	22	36	28	19	09	16
Extroversion															
Adaptability	25	25	36	-20	-25	-21	46	43	62	48	42	27	23	21	-02
Competitiveness	-23	-25	-36	-04	14	14	73	69	57	04	-02	15	-01	-05	10
Des. for Ach.	11	10	13	23	29	27	71	71	66	13	16	31	38	28	29
Des. for Adv.	-06	-09	-12	03	15	18	73	68	64	-11	-08	-02	09	18	10
Energy Level	03	15	08	17	14	19	60	67	64	27	30	36	18	04	07
Influence	24	28	07	06	08	06	70	65	56	12	12	29	31	31	53
Initiative	27	27	29	18	18	20	74	70	59	15	15	22	27	22	32
Risk-Taking	-02	03	08	-24	-26	-28	66	64	65	19	26	24	27	27	17
Sociability	50	44	37	-03	-04	09	49	55	44	24	21	27	-19	-24	-12
Taking Charge	00	09	-05	12	17	05	77	70	62	14	13	26	21	34	46

Neuroticism															
Emot. Control	04	03	21	02	18	20	02	-02	33	**74**	**71**	39	23	27	-07
Neg. Aff. *	-23	-35	-21	-18	-18	-17	-07	-11	-12	**-64**	**-58**	**-70**	23	17	06
Optimism	36	38	**41**	19	08	21	30	**45**	**51**	**62**	**50**	**40**	12	-04	-01
Self-Confidence	-04	05	09	32	29	38	**49**	**53**	**50**	37	34	31	33	34	24
Stress Tolerance	-11	-16	00	-03	06	09	11	06	36	**83**	**79**	**58**	09	03	-21
Openness to Experience															
Independence	**-41**	-32	-16	14	01	05	08	09	32	-30	-39	**-66**	**57**	**44**	06
Inno./Creativity	26	17	31	02	-10	-07	**48**	**43**	39	24	25	23	**51**	**56**	**53**
Soc. Astuteness	35	**44**	32	18	16	18	37	36	**46**	-01	-01	04	**44**	34	39
Thought Focus	14	16	22	15	08	06	**43**	31	33	20	29	24	**65**	**69**	**66**
Vision	19	21	17	18	12	08	**44**	36	33	01	15	20	**62**	**70**	**73**

Note: Varimax-rotated principal components. Decimal points are omitted. Loadings greater than .40 in absolute value are in boldface. *High scores on this scale are undesirable. A = Agreeableness, C = Conscientiousness, E = Extroversion, N = Neuroticism, O = Openness. UN = Updated Normative sample (N = 988), DV = Development sample (N = 946), SL = Promotion/Selection sample (N = 1,069).

twice as diverse in age (*SD* = 15.19) than either of the organizational samples. The organizational samples were composed of approximately 70-75 per cent males whereas normative sample was composed of approximately 50-55 per cent males. The organizational samples were predominantly managerial whereas the normative sample contained a range of job levels.

Factor loadings for these five-factor Procrustes solutions are displayed in Table 6. For the U.S. normative and PDI developmental samples, the factor and item congruence coefficients were above .90. However, for the promotion/selection sample, the Neuroticism factor congruence coefficient was .88 and the Openness factor congruence coefficient was .82. Also for this sample, the item (in this context, scale) congruence coefficient were .55 for Interdependence, .62 for Emotional Control, and .62 for Independence.

These results are not unexpected as research has shown that high stakes testing situations, such as when one is taking a test for promotion or selection purposes, tend to degrade the construct validity of personality measures (Schmit & Ryan, 1993). It unlikely that the degradation of construct validity evidenced in the promotion/selection sample seriously affects decisions that are made from the instrument in that context. In fact, a recent study by Robie (2000), comparing the scale score means and standard deviations from the above organizational samples, found very small average differences (less than 1/5 of one standard deviation) and very similar standard deviations across the two samples. Moreover, item-level IRT analyses comparing incumbent and applicant responses to a personality measure that the GPI is partially based upon found little differential item or test functioning (Robie, Zickar, & Schmit, in press).

Current validation studies

Several additional validation studies are either still being conducted or have been completed. These studies are briefly described here.

Reliability and related issues

A study of the reliability of the GPI has been conducted at two large US universities using undergraduate students (Ryan, Robie, Schmit, & Uhlmann, 2000). Trait measures should be internally consistent and highly consistent across time. For the IRT analyses in the development study, response options were collapsed from five to three because of the distributions of responses in the available samples. While we have left the number of response options at five in the current version of the GPI, 2-, 3-, and 5-point response scales have been compared in this large sample student study to identify the level at which the optimal information is gained and least error introduced. The total number of participants in this study was approximately 300 with approximately 100 participants per response scale.

Participants in the Ryan *et al.* (2000) study were asked to fill out the GPI twice with the administrations separated by two weeks. Results indicated that scale scores from the 5-point response scale were more internally consistent ($M\alpha_{T1} = .73$; $M\alpha_{T2} = .77$), more stable across time ($M_r = .78$), and less skewed than the scale scores from the other two response scale formats. No differences emerged in the amount of missing data evidenced for or participant reactions to the various formats. The results of the Ryan *et al.* (2000) study suggest that the present use of the 5-point response format is probably best practice for this particular personality measure.

Criterion-related validity

Several studies are being conducted to compare various performance criteria with GPI scales across cultures and management levels. The job performance model used in the development of the GPI was used in the development of criterion measure for these studies. Our research plan also includes the comparison of a common criterion measure across cultures using similar techniques that were used for predictor evaluation. Appendix A shows the expected relationships between GPI facet scales and job performance factors.

Initial results from four concurrent validation studies are provided in Table 7. The four samples were all from middle management jobs, including HR Managers and Division Managers (both in Retail), Distribution Center Management, and Managers in a State agency (public sector). As the total N of the samples is relatively small, correlations are reported at the broadest level. GPI facet scales were combined in unit-weighted composites at the Big Five level, while criterion ratings were aggregated to form a single, overall performance composite. Because the criterion measures differed slightly from study to study, criterion scores were standardized within study before aggregation. Consistent with previous meta-analytic work (e.g., Barrick & Mount, 1991), the results showed Conscientiousness and Extroversion factors to have the strongest relationship to overall performance. In addition, the remaining three predictor composites were related to overall job performance, but at relatively lower levels.

GPI scale scores, 360 feedback, and other assessment center data are currently being collected. These data will provide further criterion-related validity evidence for inferences made using the GPI. To date, we have examined the relations between the GPI (scored at the Big Five level) and scales (averaged across boss, peer, and

Table 7. Correlation of Big Five predictor composite scores and overall job performance

	M	SD	Overall Job Performance
Overall Job Performance	1.49	6.49	—
Extraversion	55.78	9.49	$r = .30^*$
Agreeableness	34.68	4.99	$r = .22^*$
Conscientiousness	22.98	3.62	$r = .25^*$
Neuroticism	22.79	2.91	$r = .14$
Openness to Experience	24.98	3.58	$r = .17^*$

Note: *One-tailed test, significant at $p < .05$. All correlations are uncorrected. $N = 198$.

subordinate ratings) on a 23-scale PDI 360-degree feedback instrument called the Executive Success Profile (ESP; Hezlett, Ronnkvist, Holt, & Sloan, 1997; definitions of each scale can be found in Appendix C) for 115 executives (54%) and middle managers (35%) from a variety of organizations who participated for developmental purposes. The sample was predominantly Caucasian (95%), male (83%), and middle-aged (M = 43.01, SD = 6.65). Agreeableness and Neuroticism on the GPI were not significantly related (α = .05) to any of the ESP scales. Conscientiousness on the GPI was significantly related (α = .05) to the following ESP scales: Building Organizational Relationships (r = .20), Fostering Open Dialogue (r = .19), and Drive for Stakeholder Success (r = .21). Extroversion on the GPI was significantly related (α = .05) to the following ESP scales: Visionary Thinking (r = .26), Global Perspective (r = .26), Shaping Strategy (r = .27), Driving Execution (r = .27), Empowering Others (r = .24), Influencing and Negotiating (r = .26), High Impact Delivery (r = .20), Entrepreneurial Risk Taking (r = .29), Cross-functional Capability (r = .24), Industry Knowledge (r = .23), Business Situation Versatility (r = .27), and Leading Continuous Improvement (r = .29). Lastly, Openness on the GPI was significantly related (α = .05) to the following ESP scales: Visionary Thinking (r = .31), Global Perspective (r = .33), Shaping Strategy (r = .25), Driving Execution (r = .20), High Impact Delivery (r = .19), Entrepreneurial Risk Taking (r = .31), Industry Knowledge (r = .26), Business Situation Versatility (r = .25), and Leading Continuous Improvement (r = .26).

We also examined the correlations of the GPI trait composite scales with the ESP scales for this organizational sample. The following GPI trait composite scales were not significantly related (α = .05) to any of the ESP scales: Ego-Centered, Micro-Managing, and Passive-Aggressive. The GPI Impressing scale was significantly related (α = .05) to the Adaptability scale on the ESP (r = .21). The GPI Self-Awareness/Self-Insight scale was significantly related (α = .05) to the Financial Acumen scale on the ESP (r = -.19). The GPI Intimidating scale was significantly related (α = .05) to the following ESP scales: Visionary Thinking (r = .22), Financial Acumen (r = .22), and Entrepreneurial Risk Taking (r = .20). The GPI Manipulation scale was significantly *positively* related (α = .05) to every ESP scale with an average r = .26 *except* Financial Acumen and Inspiring Trust!

The Manipulation trait scale may be akin to the Machiavellian factor that has been found in lexical (i.e., Big Five) studies as a sixth factor (Ashton, Lee, & Son, 2000). Wilson, Near, and Miller (1996; 1998) describe Machiavellianism as a set of manipulative strategies of social conduct and suggest that it is actually an adaptive characteristic in some situations but not others. Wilson *et al.* (1996; 1998) also state that those who score high on Machiavellianism are often charming and attractive in short-term social interactions. Perhaps many raters in 360-degree feedback contexts only observe the ratees in the context of these short-term interactions; it is important to understand that 360-degree feedback systems are not designed to provide a true measure of performance but, instead, the perceptions of various constituencies regarding a given person's performance. Thus, it is uncertain from this data whether one is to infer that Machiavellianistic forms of behavior are truly adaptive for man-

Table 8. Correlations among Big Five composities and syndrome scales

	M	SD	2	3	4	5	6	7	8	9	10	11	12
1. Extroversion	47.26	9.02	.31*	.26*	.51*	.68*	.48*	.19*	.20*	.31*	.08*	-.17*	.34*
2. Agreeableness	31.55	4.23		.41*	.36*	.23*	-.11*	.28*	-.35*	-.23*	-.36	-.23*	.43*
3. Conscientiousness	22.93	2.98			.30*	.37*	.06	.45*	-.11*	-.21*	.07	-.10*	.56
4. Neuroticism	20.77	3.01				.43*	.13*	.19*	-.08*	-.02	-.19*	-.19*	.54
5. Openness to Experience	24.62	3.88					.46*	.23*	.20*	.33*	.26*	.09*	.39*
6. Ego-Centered	3.06	1.02						.19*	.37*	.54*	.42*	.19*	.08
7. Impressing	3.98	.77							-.02	.07	.16*	.18*	.23*
8. Intimidating	2.27	.90								.43*	.43*	.22*	-.13*
9. Manipulating	3.62	1.33									.40*	.39	-.12*
10. Micro-Managing	2.70	.87										.33*	-.11*
11. Passive-Aggressive	2.98	.94											-.16*
12. Self-Awareness/Self-Insight	6.51	1.07											

Note: *One-tailed test, significant at $p < .05$; All correlations are uncorrected; $N = 461$

Table 9. Example GPI Scale Norm Differences Among Different Populations

Scale (# of items)	General Population N = 461		Individual Contributors N = 252		Middle Managers N = 289		Executives N = 140	
	M	SD	M	SD	M	SD	M	SD
Desire for Advancement (7)	3.20	1.04	3.30	1.15	3.89	1.15	4.38	1.01
Influence (9)	5.07	1.13	5.08	1.19	6.04	1.10	6.22	1.03
Risk Taking (9)	4.77	1.34	5.17	1.38	5.87	1.35	6.01	1.22
Taking Charge (10)	5.80	1.68	5.88	1.51	7.07	1.29	7.57	1.01
Responsibility (7)	5.45	0.77	5.45	0.92	5.58	0.88	5.48	0.80

agers and executives, or are simply an effective means of appearing to be effective. Interestingly, the profile of an individual who scores high on the Manipulation scale tends to be someone who is high on Desire for Advancement ($r = .20$), Independence ($r = .20$), and Negative Affectivity ($r = .45$) and low on Dutifulness ($r = -.31$), Interdependence ($r = -.23$), Responsibility ($r = -.23$), Stress Tolerance ($r = -.21$), and Trust ($r = -.35$). Clearly, this is not an entirely positive picture!

Construct validity

We are currently collecting data in order to compare GPI scale scores to other well-established personality measures. In addition, a study of self-other responses to the GPI is being conducted. In this study, individuals who complete the GPI will have significant others in their lives complete the same measure about them. These studies will provide further evidence for the construct validity of the GPI scales.

Some additional information about the construct validity of the trait composite and syndrome scales in the GPI is provided in Table 8. The table includes correlations among the Big Five trait composites and the syndrome scales from data collected from the general population norm group noted in the next section.

General population and specific norms

Studies have been conducted to collect both general and management population norms for the United States. Similar normative data has been collected for other countries and regions as well. The general population data were based on a stratified sample from random U.S. households. The data represent all working adults at all levels in organizations. The final group included approximately 1000 adults. More specific norms are currently being collected for executive, middle managers (managers of managers), and individual contributors. Table 9 contains a sample of GPI scales and norms from the four populations. These data illustrate that the facet scales presented are detecting differences across levels that might be expected. There are mean differences across levels for the Desire for Advancement, Influence, Taking Charge, and Risk Taking scales; for each scale, the higher in the organization, the higher the mean score. However, the Responsibility scale does not vary across levels, as might be expected. Many of the other scales in the GPI also reflect past findings with similar constructs and are consistent with theoretical expectations providing further support for the construct validity of the instrument.

Summary

There are two features of the GPI that make it unique among previously developed personality measures. First, the measure was not developed in a specific country and then transported to others. Rather, it was developed with input from around the world. Second, applied psychologists developed the measure explicitly for work-related applications.

The development and validation of the GPI followed a method that truly took a global approach. The methods included both rational and empirical techniques. We started with input from many cultures, both in the development of constructs and in the operationalization of those constructs in the item content. Statistical methods were used with data from several cultures in order to optimize the possibility that the GPI would be a test that can be useful to applied psychologists in many, if not all, cultures. Both item-level and scale-level construct validity were established using traditional and modern psychometric methods. Current research is focused on building criterion-related validity and additional construct validity evidence for the inferences to be made with the GPI. Again, a multi-cultural approach is being followed. We believe this global approach will result in a measure that is useful to applied psychologists in many cultures.

Applied psychologists who wish to interpret scores across cultures need a common framework provided by a tool in which they can have confidence that scores mean the same thing in different cultures. For example, if a psychologist in Japan wishes to assess a Japanese manager for potential assignment in the US, he or she could compare the scores of that manager to both Japanese and US managers to identify how the manager stacks up in each group. Armed with this information, the psychologist can make decisions about the compatibility and potential for success as a manager in the US management culture, in addition to providing information important for coaching prior to the transitions. The GPI provides the common framework necessary for this and many other applications of cross-cultural assessment because the evidence for the construct validity of the tool across cultures is strong.

The second feature of the GPI is that it was developed specifically for work-related uses (e.g., selection, development, coaching, etc.). Personality and performance models were considered both in the conceptual development of the GPI's content and in the writing and selection of items. Applied psychologists from many cultures came to consensus on what constituted successful performance at work. They also came to consensus on what personality constructs were important to measure in order to better understand the behaviors and predictors of behaviors in those performance constructs. Further, during the item writing process, the psychologists were asked to think about both the predictor and criterion space when writing the items. The result was that a work context was either specifically mentioned in many items or at least implied. Previous research has shown the possible advantages of such an approach (Schmit, Ryan, Stierwalt, & Powell, 1995). While it is still an empirical question with limited support to date, we believe that GPI will be a useful tool in the prediction of work-related behavior across cultures.

References

Ashton, M.C., Lee, K., & Son, C. (2000). Honesty as the sixth factor of personality: Correlations with Machiavellianism, primary psychopathy, and social adroitness. *European Journal of Personality, 14,* 359-369.

Baker, F.B. (1992). Equating tests under the graded response model. *Applied Psychological Measurement, 16,* 87-96.

Baker, F.B. (1997). *Equate 2.1: Computer program for equating two metrics in item response theory* [computer program]. Madison: University of Wisconsin, Laboratory of Experimental Design.

Barrick, M.R., & Mount, M.K. (1991). The Big Five personality dimensions and job performance: A meta-analysis. *Personnel Psychology, 44,* 1-26.

Berry, J.W. (1969). On cross-cultural comparability. *International Journal of Psychology, 4,* 199-128.

Berry, J.W. (1989). Imposed etics-emics-derived etics: The operationalization of a compelling idea. *International Journal of Psychology, 24,* 721-735.

Buss, A.H., & Finn, S.E. (1987). Classification of personality traits. *Journal of Personality & Social Pscyhology, 52,* 432-444.

Camilli, G., & Shepard, L.A. (1994). *Methods for identifying biased test items.* Thousand Oaks, CA: Sage.

Campbell, J.P., Gasser, M.B., & Oswald, F.L. (1996). The substantive nature of job performance variability. In K. R. Murphy (Ed.), *Individual differences and behavior in organizations.* San Francisco, CA: Jossey-Bass.

Campbell, J.P., McCloy, R.A., Oppler, S.H., & Sager, C.E. (1993). A theory of performance. In N. Schmitt & W.C. Borman (Eds.), *Personnel selection in organizations.* San Francisco, CA: Jossey-Bass.

Candell, G.L., & Drasgow, F. (1988). An iterative procedure for linking metrics and assessing item bias in item response theory. *Applied Psychological Measurement, 12,* 253-260.

Church, A.T., & Katigbak, M.S. (1988). The emic strategy in the identification and assessment of personality dimensions in a non-western culture: Rationale, steps, and a Philippine illustration. *Journal of Cross-Cultural Psychology, 19,* 140-163.

Davidson, A., Jaccard, J., Triandis, H.C., Morales, M.L., & Diaz-Guerrero, R. (1976). Cross-cultural model testing: Toward a solution of the etic-emic dilemma. *International Journal of Psychology, 1,* 1-13.

Drasgow, F., & Hulin, C.L. (1990). Item response theory. In M.D. Dunnette & L.M. Hough (Eds.), *Handbook of industrial & organizational psychology* (2nd ed.,Vol. 1, pp. 577-636). Palo Alto, CA: Consulting Psychologists Press.

Drasgow, F., Levine, M.V., Tsien, S., Williams, B., & Mead, A.D. (1995). Fitting polytomous item response theory models to multiple-choice tests. *Applied Psychological Measurement, 19,* 143-165.

Fleer, P.F. (1993). *A Monte Carlo assessment of a new measure of item and test bias.* Unpublished dissertation, Illinois , Illinois Institute of Technology, Chicago, IL.

Flowers, C.P. (1995). *A monte carlo assessment of DFIT with polytomously-scored unidimensional tests.* Unpublished dissertation, Georgia State University, Atlanta, GA.

Flowers, C.P., Oshima, T.C., & Raju, N.S. (1999). A description and demonstration of the polytomous-DFIT framework. *Applied Psychological Measurement, 23,* 309-326.

Hambleton, R.K. (1994). Guidelines for adapting educational and psychological tests: A progress report. *European Journal of Psychological Assessment, 10,* 229-244.

Hambleton, R.K., & Kanjee, A. (1995). Increasing the validity of cross-cultural assessments: Use of improved methods for test adaptations. *European Journal of Psychological Assessment, 11,* 147-157.

Hezlett, S.A., Ronnkvist, A.M., Holt, K.E., & Sloan, E.B. (1997). *The Executive Success Profile technical summary.* Minneapolis, MN: Personnel Decisions International.

Hofstede, G. (1980). *Culture's consequences: International differences in work-related values.* Beverly Hills, CA: Sage.

Hough, L.M. (1998). Personality at work: Issues and evidence. In M. Hakel (Ed.), *Beyond multiple choice: Evaluating Alternatives to traditional testing for selection* (pp. 131-159). Hillsdale, NJ: Erlbaum Associates, Inc.

Katigbak, M.S., Church, A. T., & Akamine, T.X. (1996). Cross-cultural generalizability of personality dimensions: Relating indigenous and imported dimensions in two cultures. *Journal of Personality and Social Psychology, 70,* 99-114.

MacCallum, R.C., Wegener, D.T., Vchino, B.N., & Fabrigan, L.R. (1993). The problem of equivalent models in applications of covariance structure analysis. *Psychological Bulletin, 114,* 185-1999.

McCrae, R.R., & Costa, P.T., Jr. (1983). Social desirability scales: More substance than style. *Journal of Consulting & Clinical Psychology, 51,* 882-888.

McCrae, R.R., & Costa, P.T., Jr. (1997). Personality trait structure as a human universal. *American Psychologist, 52,* 509-516.

McCrae, R.R., Zonderman, A.B., Costa, P.T., Jr., Bond, M.H., & Paunonen, S.V. (1996). Evaluating replicability of factors in the revised NEO personality inventory: Confirmatory factor analysis versus Procrustes rotation. *Journal of Personality and Social Psychology, 70,* 552-566.

Ones, D.S., & Viswesvaran, C. (1996). Bandwidth-fidelity dilemma in personality measurement in personnel selection. *Journal of Organizational Behavior, 17,* 609-626.

Paunonen, S.V. (1997). On chance and factor congruence following orthogonal Procrustes rotation. *Educational and Psychological Measurement, 57,* 33-59.

Paunonen, S.V. (1998). Hierarchical organization of personality and prediction of behavior. *Journal of Personality and Social Psychology, 74,* 538-556.

Pike, K.L. (1966). *Language in relation to a unified theory of the structure of human behaviour.* The Hague: Mouton.

Raju, N. (1998). *DFITP4: A Fortran program for calculating DIF/DTF* [Computer program]. Chicago: Illinois Institute of Technology.

Raju, N.S., Van der Linden, W.J., & Fleer, P.F. (1995). IRT-based internal measures of differential functioning of items and tests. *Applied Psychological Measurement, 19,* 353-368.

Robie, C. (2000). *Faking and personality measurement.* Minneapolis, MN: Personnel Decisions International.

Robie, C., Zickar, M.J., & Schmit, M.J. (in press). Measurement equivalence between applicant and incumbent groups: An IRT analysis of personality scales. *Human Performance.*

Ryan, A.M., Robie, C., Schmit, M.J., & Uhlmann, R.A. (2000). *Number of response options and personality testing in selection contexts*. Manuscript submitted for publication.

Samejima, F. (1969). Estimation of latent ability using a response pattern of graded scores. *Psychometrika Monographs, 34,* (Suppl. 17).

Schmit, M.J., & Ryan, A.M. (1993). The Big Five in personnel selection: Factor structure in applicant and nonapplicant populations. *Journal of Applied Psychology, 78,* 966-974.

Schmit, M.J., Ryan, A.M., Stierwalt, S.L., & Powell, A.B. (1995). Frame-of-reference effects on personality scale scores and criterion-related validity. *Journal of Applied Psychology, 80,* 607-620.

Thissen, D., & Steinberg, L. (1988). Data analysis using item response theory. *Psychological Bulletin, 104,* 385-395.

Triandis, H.C., Malpass, R.S., & Davidson, A. (1971). Cross-cultural psychology. *Biennial Review of Anthropology,* 1-84.

Wilson, D. S., Near, D., & Miller, R. R. (1996). Machiavellianism: A synthesis of the evolutionary and psychological literatures. *Psychological Bulletin, 119,* 285-299.

Wilson, D.S, Near, D.C., & Miller, R.R. (1998). Individual differences in Machiavellianism as a mix of cooperative and exploitative strategies. *Evolution & Human Behavior, 19,* 203-212.

Zickar, M.J., & Drasgow, F. (1996). Detecting faking on a personality instrument using appropriateness measurement. *Applied Psychological Measurement, 20,* 71-87.

Zickar, M.J., & Robie, C. (1999). Modeling faking good on personality items: An item-level analysis. *Journal of Applied Psychology, 84,* 551-563.

Appendix A: Performance Factors and GPI Personality Facets

This is a model of PDI Performance Factors and associated GPI traits and trait composites. The assumption is that individuals with relatively better scores (i.e., in the desired direction) on traits associated with a performance factor will indeed perform better in parts of their work that fall into these factor categories.

I. Administrative Factor

1. Attention to Detail - This is a measure of the tendency to be exacting and precise. This is a trait characterized by: a desire for accuracy, neatness, thoroughness, and completeness; the ability to spot minor imperfections or errors; and a meticulous approach to performing tasks.

2. Work Focus - This is a measure of the tendency to be self-disciplined in one's approach to work. This is a trait characterized by: efficient work habits; being planful and organized; being focused on the process of task implementation; being able to concentrate on what is most important at the moment; not being distracted easily by other's or one's own boredom; and not procrastinating on tasks that are unpleasant or not very exciting.

II. Thinking Factor

1. Thought Agility - This is a measure of the tendency to be open both to multiple ideas and to using alternative modes of thinking. It is a measure of divergent thinking that is focused on the input and processing of information. This is a trait characterized by: thought flexibility; the ability to think things through by looking at many perspectives; the desire to draw out ideas from others; and a willingness to consider other's ideas along with one's own.

2. Innovativeness/Creativity - This is a measure of the tendency to produce unique and original things. It is a measure of divergent thinking that is focused on the generation and output of unique ideas and expressions of ideas. This trait is characterized by: being inventive; being imaginative; being expressive of ideas and feelings through original and unique output.

3. Thought Focus - This is a measure of the tendency to understand ambiguous information by analyzing and detecting the systematic themes in the data. It is a measure of convergent thinking that is focused on the input and processing of information. This is a trait characterized by: analytical and logical thinking ability; the ability to find patterns in data that may seem initially unsystematic or ambiguous; a desire to focus on finding a single best answer rather than proposing multiple possibilities; a preference for objective rather than subjective input; and a desire to use a systematic approach to guide thinking.

4. Vision - This is a measure of the tendency to have foresight in one's thinking. This trait is characterized by: the ability to visualize outcomes, the tendency to think in a holistic manner; taking into account all variables that will effect future events; the tendency to take a long range perspective in one's thinking; and the ability to anticipate future needs, problems, obstacles, eventualities, and outcomes.

III. Leadership Factor: Facilitating Traits and Derailing Trait Composites

   A. Facilitating Traits

   1. Taking Charge - This is a measure of the tendency to take a leadership role. This trait is characterized by: a desire to direct the activities of others; an ability to mobilize others to take action; a desire to take a leadership role; a desire to step forward when there is no clear leader; and a willingness to take responsibility for guiding others' actions.

   2. Influence - This is a measure of the tendency to get others to view and do things in a certain way. This trait is characterized by: being persuasive; negotiating well; impacting the thoughts and actions of others; gaining support and commitment from others; being diplomatic; and using tact.

   B. Derailing Trait Composites

   1. Ego-Centered - This is a measure of the tendency to be self-centered and appear egotistical. This is a trait composite characterized by: appearing overly involved with and concerned about one's own well being and importance; an inflated evaluation of personal skills and abilities; appearing condescending to others; and an attitude of entitlement to position and rewards.

   2. Manipulation - This is a measure of the tendency to be self-serving and sly. This trait composite is characterized by: a tendency to try to cover up mistakes; the ability to protect oneself by shifting blame onto others; carefully sharing information to serve one's own purpose to the detriment of others; and a willingness to take advantage of others.

   3. Micro-Managing - This is a measure of the tendency to over-manage once a person has advanced to higher levels of management. This trait composite is characterized by: staying involved in too many decisions rather than passing on responsibility; doing detailed work rather than delegating it; and staying too involved with direct reports rather than building teamwork among the staff.

   4. Intimidating - This is a measure of the tendency to use power in a threatening way. This syndrome is characterized by: acting cold and aloof; an abrasive approach to others, a bullying style; and the use of knowledge or power to create fear in or subdue others.

   5. Passive-Aggressive - This is a measure of the tendency to avoid confronting others, conveying acceptance or cooperation and yet appearing to behave in uncooperative and self-serving ways. This trait is characterized by: communicating or implying cooperation, conveying acceptance by lack of objection, or expressing support for another person's idea, but behaving in contradictory ways that serve ones self-interest or potentially undermines the efforts of others who are possible threats.

IV. Interpersonal Factor

   1. Sociability - This is a measure of the tendency to be highly engaged by any social situation. This trait is characterized by: being friendly; a desire to be involved

in situations with high opportunity for interpersonal interaction; an enjoyment of other people's company; and a need to interact with others frequently throughout the day.

2. Consideration - This is a measure of the tendency to express care about other's well being. This trait is characterized by: showing concern for others; demonstrating compassion, warmth, and sensitivity towards others' feelings and needs; and supporting or taking care of others in need.

3. Empathy - This is a measure of the tendency to understand what others are experiencing and to convey that understanding to them. This trait is characterized by: a desire to listen to, understand, and accept others' problems or opinions; an ability to understand the practical and emotional needs of others; an ability to communicate to others the understanding of their experiences; an ability to respond to others in a way that is non-judgmental and respects them as unique human beings and full contributors to society; an ability to "feel with" as opposed to "feel for" others; and a capacity to identify with others on an emotional level.

4. Trust - This is a measure of the tendency to believe that most people are good and well-intentioned. This trait is characterized by: a belief in the goodness of people; a belief that most people are trustworthy; and not being skeptical or cynical about the nature of peoples' intentions and behaviors.

5. Social Astuteness - This is a measure of the tendency to accurately perceive and understand the meaning of social cues and use that information to accomplish a desired goal. This trait is characterized by: an ability to detect social cues and interpret how these social cues are related to the underlying motives of other people; a desire to understand how others might act based on their intentions, motivations, and concerns; and an ability to read and respond to the positions of others in a given situation.

V. Work Orientation

  A. Individualism Traits

    1. Independence - This is a measure of the tendency to be autonomous. This trait is characterized by: a preference to make decisions without input from others; a preference to not be dependent on others; and a desire to not be closely supervised or work in an interdependent group or organization.

    2. Competitiveness - This is a measure of the tendency to evaluate one's own performance in comparison to others. This trait is characterized by: a desire to do better than others in many ways; an enjoyment of situations that can lead to a clear winner and loser; and a preference for an environment in which people are differentiated by accomplishments that come at a cost to others.

    3. Risk-Taking - This is a measure of the tendency to take chances based on limited information. This trait is characterized by: an enjoyment of situations with uncertainty; being entrepreneurial; deriving personal satisfaction from making decisions based on limited information; and being adventurous.

    4. Desire for Advancement - This is a measure of the tendency to be ambitious in the advancement of one's career or position in organizational hierarchy. This trait is

characterized by: a desire to get to the top levels of organizational hierarchy; a determination to succeed in one's chosen career path; a preference for advancement potential over job security; and a continual desire to get ahead of where one is currently in work and life in general.

B. Collectivism Traits

1. Interdependence – This is a measure of the tendency to work well with others. This trait is characterized by: an ability to perform well in groups; a desire to work closely with others on shared work; active cooperation with others; a desire to build supportive networks of communication; flexible cooperation in conflict resolution situations; and a preference to work toward the goals of the group rather than individual goals.

2. Dutifulness - This is a measure of the tendency to be filled with a sense of moral obligations. This trait is characterized by: a desire to do what is right; the practice of good business ethics; a desire to meet moral and legal obligations; and an adherence to a set of commonly held or societal laws.

3. Responsibility – This is a measure of the tendency to be reliable and dependable. This trait is characterized by: a willingness to behave in expected and agreed upon ways; following through on assignments and commitments; keeping promises; and accepting the consequences of one's own actions.

VI. Self-Management Factor

1. Adaptability - This is a measure of the tendency to be open to change and considerable variety. This trait is characterized by: a willingness to change one's approach; being flexible; a willingness to adjust to constraints, multiple demands, and adversity; and demonstrating versatility in handling different types of people and situations.

2. Openness - This is a measure of the tendency to accept and respect the individual differences of people. This trait is characterized by: an understanding of the uniqueness of all people; a desire to understand different cultures, values, opinions, and belief systems; a mind set that all people have value; and an openness to the possibility that all human differences must not be either bad or good.

3. Negative Affectivity - This is a measure of the tendency to be generally unsatisfied with many things, including but not limited to work. This trait is characterized by: a tendency to be unsatisfied with one's position, organization, pay, and other aspects of work; a general negative attitude; and a general dissatisfaction with one's life events and surroundings.

4. Optimism - This is a measure of the tendency to believe that good things are possible. This trait is characterized by: showing high spirits in just about any situation; being happy, joyful, and excited about things; and demonstrating enthusiasm in challenging situations.

5. Emotional Control - This is a measure of the tendency to be even-tempered. This trait is characterized by: the ability to stay calm and collected when confronted with adversity, frustration or other difficult situations; an ability to avoid defensive reactions or hurt feelings as a result of others' comments; an ability to be emotion-

ally unaffected by external events that one has no control over; and not showing extreme positive or negative mood swings.

6. Stress Tolerance - This is a measure of the tendency to endure typically stressful situations without undue physical or emotional reaction. This trait is characterized by: being free from anxieties; not worrying excessively; demonstrating a relaxed approach to stressful situations; and an ability to tolerate stress imposed by other people or circumstances.

7. Self-Confidence - This is a measure of the tendency to believe in one's own abilities and skills. This trait is characterized by: a tendency to feel competent in several areas; a tendency to demonstrate an attitude that one can succeed in endeavors; and a belief that one is capable and self-determined.

8. Impressing - This is a measure of the tendency to try to make a good impression on others. This trait is characterized by: a desire to please others; a tendency to tell people what they want to hear; the use of flattery and craftiness to manipulate the impressions held by others; being cautious not to expose one's true self image; and not being frank and forthcoming.

9. Self-Awareness/Self-Insight - This is the tendency to be aware of one's strengths and weaknesses. This trait is characterized by: self-insight into one's motives, needs, and values; an ability to avoid self-deception regarding strengths and weaknesses; an understanding of one's limitations; and the tendency to study and understanding one's own behavior.

VII. Motivation Factor

1. Energy Level - This is a measure of the tendency to be highly active and energetic. This trait is characterized by: a need to keep busy doing something at all times; a preference for a fast-paced lifestyle; and a tendency to avoid inactive events or situations.

2. Initiative - This is a measure of the tendency to take action in a proactive, rather than reactive, manner. This trait is characterized by: a desire to take action where others might take a wait-and-see approach; a desire to find ways to get things started; a desire to volunteer to take on new responsibilities; and a willingness to take on new or additional challenges.

3. Desire for Achievement - This is a measure of the tendency to have a strong drive to realize personally meaningful goals. This trait is characterized by: being challenged by difficult goals; being energized by accomplishing goals; a desire to work hard to achieve goals; taking satisfaction from doing something difficult; and pushing one's self outside of one's comfort zone to achieve a goal.

Appendix B: GPI Personality Facets and Sample Items

Scale	Sample Item
Agreeableness	
Consideration	I like to do little things for people to make them feel good.
Empathy	I take other people's circumstances and feelings into consideration before making a decision.
Interdependence	I tend to put group goals first and individual goals second.
Openness	I do not have to share a person's values to work well with that person.
Thought Agility	I think it is vital to consider other perspectives before coming to conclusions.
Trust	I believe people are usually honest with me.
Conscientiousness	
Attention to Detail	I like to complete every detail of tasks according to the work plans.
Dutifulness	I conduct my business according to a strict set of ethical principles.
Responsibility	I can be relied on to do what is expected of me.
Work Focus	I prioritize my work effectively so the most important things get done first.
Extroversion	
Adaptability	For me, change is exciting.
Competitiveness	I like to win, even if the activity isn't very important.
Desire for Achievement	I prefer to set challenging goals, rather than aim for goals I am more likely to reach.
Desire for Advancement	I would like to attain the highest position in an organization someday.
Energy Level	When most people are exhausted from work, I still have energy to keep going.
Influence	People come to me for inspiration and direction.
Initiative	I am always looking for opportunities to start new projects.
Risk-Taking	I am willing to take big risks when there is potential for big returns.
Sociability	I find it easy to start up a conversation with strangers.
Taking Charge	I actively take control of situations at work if no one is in charge.
Neuroticism	
Emotional Control	Even when I am very upset, it is easy for me to control my emotions.
Negative Affectivity	I am easily displeased with things at work.
Optimism	My enthusiasm for living life to its fullest is apparent to those with whom I work.
Self-Confidence	I am confident about my skills and abilities.
Stress Tolerance	I worry about things that I know I should not worry about.
Openness to Experience	
Independence	I tend to work on projects alone, even if others volunteer to help me.
Innovativeness/Creativity	I work best in an environment that allows me to be creative and expressive.
Social Astuteness	I know what is expected of me in different social situations.
Thought Focus	I quickly make links between causes and effects.
Vision	I can often foresee the outcome of a situation before it unfolds.
Trait Composites	
Ego-Centered	I have often wondered how others would manage without me.
Impressing	It is always best to keep important people happy.
Intimidating	It is sometimes necessary to criticize others openly and publicly for their poor performance.
Manipulating	People can serve as excellent tools for getting what you want or need.
Micro-Managing	Delegation weakens the power of a leader.
Passive-Aggressive	There are times I say I will cooperate when I know I will not do it.
Self-Awareness/Self-Insight	I know what motivates me.

Appendix C: ESP Scales and Definitions

1. Thinking Factor

   a. Season Judgment: Applies broad knowledge and seasoned experience when addressing complex issues; defines strategic issues clearly despite ambiguity; takes all critical information into account when making decisions; makes timely, tough decisions.

   b. Visionary Thinking: Has a clear vision for the business or operation; maintains a long-term, big-picture view; foresees obstacles and opportunities; generates breakthrough ideas.

   c. Financial Acumen: Understands the meaning and implications of key financial indicators; manages overall financial performance (income statement and balance sheet); uses financial analysis to evaluate strategic options and opportunities.

   d. Global Perspective: Keeps abreast of important trends that impact the business or organization (technological, competitive, social, economic, etc.); understands the position of the organization within a global context.

2. Strategic Management Factor

   a. Shaping Strategy: Develops distinctive strategies to achieve competitive advantage; translates broad strategies into specific objectives and action plans; aligns the organization to support strategic priorities.

   b. Driving Execution: Assigns clear authority and accountability; directs change while maintaining operating effectiveness; integrates efforts across units and functions; monitors results; tackles problems directly and with dispatch.

3. Leadership Factor

   a. Attracting and Developing Talent: Attracts high caliber people; develops teams and talent with diverse capabilities; accurately appraises the strengths and weaknesses of others; provides constructive feedback; develops successors and talent pools.

   b. Empowering Others: Creates a climate that fosters personal investment and excellence; nurtures commitment to a common vision and shared values; gives people opportunity and latitude to grow and achieve; promotes collaboration and teamwork.

   c. Influencing and Negotiating: Promotes ideas and proposals persuasively; shapes stakeholder opinions; projects a positive image; works through conflicts; negotiates win/win solutions.

   d. Leadership Versatility: Plays a variety of leadership roles (e.g., driving, delegating, supporting, coaching) as appropriate; adapts style and approach to match the needs of different individuals and teams.

4. Interpersonal Factor

    a. Building Organization Relationships: Cultivates an active network of relationships inside and outside the organization; relates well to key colleagues (i.e., bosses, peers, direct reports); stays in touch with employees at all levels.

    b. Inspiring Trust: Establishes open, candid, trusting relationships; treats all individuals fairly and with respect; behaves in accord with expressed beliefs and commitments; maintains high standards of integrity.

5. Communication Factor

    a. Fostering Open Dialogue: Promotes a free flow of information and communication throughout the organization (upward, downward, and across); listens actively; encourages open expression of ideas and opinions.

    b. High Impact Delivery: Delivers clear, convincing, and well-organized presentations; projects credibility and poise even in highly visible, adversarial situations.

6. Motivation Factor

    a. Drive For Stakeholder Success: Sets and pursues aggressive goals; drives for results; demonstrates a strong commitment to organizational success; works to do what is best for all stakeholders (customers, shareholders, employees, etc.).

    b. Entrepreneurial Risk Taking: Champions new ideas and initiatives; identifies new business opportunities and makes them a reality; fosters innovation and risk taking.

7. Self-Management Factor

    a. Mature Confidence: Realistically appraises own strengths and weaknesses; shares credit and visibility; maintains and projects confidence, even when not supported by others.

    b. Adaptability: Maintains a positive outlook, resisting stress and working constructively under pressure; responds resourcefully to change and ambiguity.

    c. Career and Self-direction: Conveys a clear sense of personal goals and values; manages time efficiently; pursues continuous learning and self-development.

8. Breadth and Depth Factor

    a. Cross-functional Capability: Understands the role and interrelationships of each organizational function (e.g., marketing, sales, operations, finance, human resources); has experience and skill in managing across functional and organizational lines.

    b. Industry Knowledge: Knows what it takes to be successful in this industry; has a thorough knowledge of this industry's history, customers, and competitive environment.

    c. Business Situation Versatility: Knows how to size up and meet the challenges of different business situations (e.g., start-up, fast growth, steady state, turnaround, close-down, merger/acquisition).

    d. Leading Continuous Improvement: Initiates, directs, and sustains efforts to ensure continuous learning and improvement throughout the organization.

Chapter 10

The Traits Personality Questionnaire (TPQue)

Ioannis Tsaousis

Introduction

The Traits Personality Questionnaire (TPQue) is a comprehensive measure in Greek language of the five major dimensions of personality and of the most important traits that define each of them. The constructs of the TPQue were formed according to the content and structure of the NEO-PI-R of Costa and McCrae (1992). We considered the NEO-PI-R as a more adequate instrument for the development of a comprehensive personality trait inventory in comparison to other tests and models of trait personality theory, including the work of Eysenck, Cattell, Guilford. We took this model as starting-point not only because of its comprehensiveness but also because of its being so well documented. According to Costa and McCrae (1992) their model comprises five main *domains* that "...give a quick grasp of the major features", and 30 facets that "...allow more detailed analysis of the particular forms in which these major domains are expressed" (p. 39). Under this perspective, it could be argued that there is a direct link between the NEO-PI-R and the TPQue, since the conceptual definitions provided by Costa and McCrae (1992), for their NEO-PI-R, constitute the theoretical framework of the five factor scales and the 30 sub-scales of the TPQue.

The development of the TPQue

Two main approaches have been adopted to construct the factor scales and the factor sub-scales that constitute the TPQue: a *deductive* as well as an *inductive* technique. Following the deductive approach, questionnaire items were written to reflect the a priori model of personality. Following this principal, all the items in the TPQue were written to reflect behavior, habitual responses, and trait dispositions of the five-factor model of personality. Following the inductive approach, data were collected

Big Five Assessment, edited by B. De Raad & M. Perugini. © 2002, Hogrefe & Huber Publishers.

and reduced to establish the simplest, most parsimonious statistical solution. For this purpose, exploratory as well as confirmatory factor analyses were used; these methods were expected to provide a brief and comprehensive factor structure model.

The developmental stages of the TPQue included three phases: the first phase included the generation of the items, the pilot study and the item analysis; the second phase included the psychometric evaluation (reliability and validity) of the newly developed questionnaire, and finally, the third phase included the standardization procedure (development of norms).

Item generation

The first step was the development of the items. During this stage we focused on determining the factor scales and sub-scales of the Concept Model and on writing appropriate items to measure them. Since the main objective of the present questionnaire was to tap the specific ethnic and cultural characteristics of the Greek population as they are sedimented in the Greek language, the adaptation of the conceptual definitions provided in the NEO-PI-R could not directly be used as a departure point for the development of items. For this reason, a taxonomic study was carried out in order to identify Greek adjectives that conceptualize the factor scales and sub-scales of the Greek instrument.

For each of the 30 NEO-PI-R sub-scales that constitute the theoretical framework of the Greek questionnaire, positive and negative definitive adjectives were identified in a Greek Thesaurus (Sakellariou, 1991). The following procedure was followed: first, the main adjective for each sub-scale (the corresponding translation of Costa & McCrae's facet name) was established (e.g., Warm, Vulnerable, Modest) and their synonyms (e.g., friendly, sensitive, humble) and antonyms (e.g., aloof, hard, boastful) were identified; subsequently, synonyms and antonyms of those earlier synonyms and antonyms were collected, and so on until a sufficient number of adjectives in both categories (positive and negative) was established.

These clusters of synonyms and antonyms (approximately 15-20 per sub-scale) formed the basic item pool, from which items for each sub-scale were written. A total of 600 items were written that might be used to measure the 30 sub-scales and the 5 factor scales of the TPQue, which was at least one statement for each adjective. Following certain exclusion criteria (ambiguity, negations, idiomatic expressions, suggestive formulations, sexist or ethnocentric formulations, etc.) the best 360 items were selected. To investigate whether each of the selected items reflected the conceptual definition of each sub-scale, ratings from 20 judges were obtained, using a 5-point rating scale ranging from 1 (not representative at all) to 5 (very representative). The results revealed that only 6 of the 360 selected items were not representative of the construct they intended to measure. Although the results suggested that these items should be eliminated, we decided to keep them in the pilot study to see how they would react in the field test. As expected, all six items were eliminated in subsequent construction stages.

Apart from the resulting 360 items, the initial pool of TPQue items contained an additional 30 items intended to measure *lying* and *social desirability* responses. The two scales each comprised 15 items which were mainly elicited from corresponding scales of well-known inventories such as MMPI-L and -K scales (Hathaway & McKinley, 1983), EPQ-L scale (Eysenck & Eysenck, 1975), Edwards Social Desirability scale (Edwards, 1957), etc. At the end of this stage, the total number composing the initial pool of TPQue items was 390.

Pilot study

The 390 items were used in a pilot-study in order to reduce the number and to create the final version of the TPQue. The subject sample consisted of 138 students (17-32 years of age), recruited from various universities in Greece. Participants were asked to indicate to what extent items apply to self, using a 4-point 'Likert' scale form, ranging from 0 (strongly disagree) to 3 (strongly agree). It was decided that the neutral option should be left out at this stage, in order to force individuals to choose one of the other remaining categories, hence eliminating the effect of central tendency.

Item analysis

The first step in item selection was the development of a *marker set of items* for each sub-scale and each factor scale separately. Markers form a core cluster of items which is closely related to other items for the scale, but not closely related to items for other scales or sub-scales. The advantage of using a marker set in this initial stage of item selection is that overlap between items from various sub-scales is controlled, and also that relative independence between factor scales is ensured, this being one of the assumptions of the conceptual model.

Three stages can be distinguished in the development of each set of *sub-scale markers*: First, all the items relating to each sub-scale (12 items per sub-scale) were collected and their mean scores from the pilot study estimated. Second, using Principal Component Analysis, all the items with mean scores between 1 and 2 were factor analyzed. Finally, four items (two with the highest positive and two with the highest negative loading, to control for the acquiescence effect) from the generated factor analytic solutions were chosen, and a marker set of items for each of the 30 sub-scales was composed.

The next step was to develop *factor markers* for each of the five factor scales, following the same procedure. First, all items that had been used in the sub-scale markers for each factor (6 sub-scales x 4 items = 24 items) were collected (forming an initial item pool for each factor scale), and factor analyzed (Principal Components). Then, two items (one with the highest positive and one with the highest negative loading) from each sub-scale marker were selected, generating a factor marker scale of 12 equally balanced positive and negative items for each factor scale (6 sub-scales x 2 items =12 items).

Subsequently, each factor marker scale was correlated with the remaining factor marker scales, together with variables such as the L scale, SDR scale, sex, and age, in order to investigate the relationship of each scale with its own items, and to eliminate items that were highly correlated with other scales. Additionally, in order to improve the cohesiveness of each factor marker scale, the two items with the lowest correlations (one positive and one negative) were identified and replaced with the two items with the highest correlations, which were elicited from the remaining 12 items rejected from the initial item pool of each factor marker scale.

In the final step, each item was correlated with every scale, and each scale was correlated with every other scale within the same factor, as well as with scales from different factors. Items were only selected if they were highly correlated with the scale under construction, and of low correlation with the other scales or sub-scales.

Description of the TPQue

The TPQue consists of 180 items measuring the five broad dimensions of personality, and thirty specific sub-scales, which correspond to the most influential traits of the five domains. Each factor scale consists of 36 items, including 6 items per sub-scale. Additionally, it contains two independent scales (consisting of 13 items each) measuring lying and social desirability responses (Tsaousis, 1996), giving a total number of 206 items. Item responses are recorded on a 5-point scale ranging from *strongly disagree* (1) to *strongly agree* (5), indicating to what extent individuals agree or disagree with the content of the items; the estimated completion time is approximately 30 minutes.

The most important characteristics that define each of the TPQue factor scales, are presented next. Table 1 presents examples of items for each of the 30 TPQue sub-scales.

Extraversion

People who score high on this TPQue factor scale are sociable, like going to social events such as parties, etc., and generally feel very comfortable when they are amongst others. They like talking a lot, are optimists, active, and like facing new adventures, and, generally speaking, are considered as warm and enjoyable people. People who tend to score low on this scale are reserved (without meaning unfriendly), independent (rather than followers), and evenpaced (rather than sluggish). They are usually shy when meeting new people, but this is not an indication that they suffer from social anxiety. Finally, they are not as enthusiastic as extraverts are, which, however, does not mean that they are pessimistic or unhappy.

Table 1. Examples of items for TPQue sub-scales

Sub-Scales	Items
Extraversion Sub-scales	
Warmth (E1)	I usually get involved emotionally in my friends' problems
Gregariousness (E2)	I do not like going to parties (R)
Assertiveness (E3)	Very often I take on the responsibility of organizing the activities of my company
Activity (E4)	I consider myself an active and energetic person
Excitement Seeking (E5)	Usually, I try to avoid daring situations (R)
Positive Emotions (E6)	I consider myself an optimistic person
Neuroticism Sub-scales	
Anxiety (N1)	Many people think of me as a person who does not feel afraid easily".
Angry Hostility (N2)	Quite often I get mad with others
Depression (N3)	I think that I feel sad more often than other people do
Self - Consciousness (N4)	I have no problem going into a class that is full of people, who have already started a discussion
Impulsiveness (N5)	I believe that I am a person who can control their emotions (R)
Vulnerability (N6)	Sometimes I feel so helpless, that I ask someone else to help me
Openness Sub-Scales	
Fantasy (O1)	I consider myself a person with a rich, active imagination
Aesthetics (O2)	Reading literature bores me (R)
Feelings (O3)	Sometimes I feel guilty about things that happen around me, about which I do nothing to change (e.g. poverty, misery, etc.)
Actions (O4)	I like to taste traditional dishes from various countries (R)
Ideas (O5)	I think of my self as open minded
Values (O6)	I am among those who believe that there is not always only one truth
Agreeableness Sub-Scales	
Trust (A1)	Most of the people I know are good and honest
Straightforwardness (A2)	Flattering people is a good way of asking them to do what you want them to (R)
Altruism (A3)	When somebody needs me, I always help them
Compliance (A4)	I consider my self as competitive person (R)
Modesty (A5)	I prefer not speaking about myself
Tender-Mindedness (A6)	I find it essential to be aware of social policy issues
Conscientiousness Sub-Scales	
Competence (C1)	Sometimes, I feel completely useless (R)
Order (C2)	I find a well organized life-style with pre-scheduled activities fits my personality perfectly
Dutifulness (C3)	I usually avoid giving promises, because I know that I rarely keep them (R)
Achievement Striving (C4)	I like to put goals in my life, and work hard to achieve them
Self - Discipline (C5)	When I am dealing with a task, I concentrate on it until I finish
Deliberation (C6)	Very often people tell me that I am frivolous

Note: items marked with (R) are reversely scored

Neuroticism

High scorers on this factor scale are usually people that live stressful lives, who are very anxious about all their dealings with day-to-day life, and generally worry about matters too much; they have the tendency to experience fear more frequently than other people do, are unable to resist their cravings or urges, and are vulnerable, and because of this, they experience depressive emotions and are very sensitive to ridicule. People who score low on this factor scale are usually characterized by emotional stability; they are relaxed most of the time, rarely get upset, and under stressful or dangerous situations they keep their nerves calm; they do not worry about things that are going to happen in the future, and generally feel secure and self-satisfied.

Openness to experience

People who score high on this scale are open-minded, look forward to learning and discovering new things, and see every new experience as a challenge to their abilities. They have a very active imagination, and frequently use it to escape from reality. They appreciate art as an aspect that enriches their inner world, and experience both happiness and sadness with very strong emotions. Low scorers on this factor scale do not like changes, prefer the old and well-established ways of doing things, and have more conservative ideas than high scorers; they are not interested in art, and consider people with an active imagination immature; they prefer to keep their feet on the ground, and their emotional responses are usually muted.

Agreeableness

Individuals who score high on this scale are people who usually care about others and try to help all in need; they are modest and inclined to forgive easily even when they have been hurt, and they trust everyone, since they believe that most people have good intentions; they are straightforward and sincere, and if something annoys them, they prefer to discuss it directly with the person responsible, rather than accuse him/her behind his/her back. People who score low on this scale are egocentric in their behavior, highly antagonistic rather than cooperative with their colleagues or friends, and most of the time they are skeptical of others' intentions; they like to manipulate others for their own gains, and consider flattering as a skill that helps in achieving their goals; they rarely forget someone who has hurt or blamed them, and they can sometimes be very cruel or cynical.

Conscientiousness

High scorers on this scale are confident about their capabilities, are dutiful, and strictly adhere to their ethical principles and moral obligations; order plays an essential role in their life, and as such they are very well organized, and they think very carefully before acting; they tend to control their desires or impulses, whilst highly motivated to get the job done; they are ambitious, make plans and place goals, and work hard to achieve them. People who score low on this scale do not have self-control over their behavior, desire or disagreements; they rarely keep their promises, hate order, and prefer not making future plans for their life; many people consider them as unreliable, lazy, and lax.

Reliability of the TPQue

To investigate the TPQue's reliability, the indices of internal consistency and test-retest reliability were estimated. Furthermore, in order to investigate the stability of each scale over time, the differences of the mean scores obtained from two separate administrations were compared, using the *t* criterion for related samples.

Internal consistency

Cronbach's alphas were computed for each factor scale and sub-scale of the TPQue. Table 2 gives coefficient alphas for the factor scales and sub-scales along with their standard error of measurement (Sem).

The TPQue factor scales have coefficient alphas ranging from .78 to .89. Most of the individual sub-scales have internal consistencies ranging from .51 to .80, which are acceptable for scales with only six items (Cattell & Kline, 1977). However, six sub-scales (E1, N5, O5, A2, A3, and A6) have lower alphas (ranging from .34 to .48), suggesting a broader mix of items or lower homogeneity.

Test-retest reliability

Test-retest data were collected from a sample of 125 individuals, who were tested over a time interval of 4 weeks. As shown in Table 3, the test-retest correlations for factor scales ranged from .89 to .95 ($p < .01$), and reliability correlations for the sub-scales ranged from .72 to .91 ($p < .01$). In both cases, the results indicate the stability of all the TPQue factor scales and sub-scales.

Table 2. Internal consistency for TPQue factor scales and sub-scales (*N* = 1,054)

	Alpha	*M*	*SD*	*SEM* (raw)	*SEM* (T)
Factor Scales					
Extraversion (E)	.88	122.40	17.16	5.94	3.47
Neuroticism (N)	.89	112.25	18.97	6.29	3.32
Openness (O)	.83	126.48	15.70	6.47	4.12
Agreeableness (A)	.78	118.44	13.07	6.13	4.69
Conscientiousness (C)	.88	115.07	17.43	6.04	3.47
Sub-Scales					
Warmth (E1)	.48	20.57	3.40	2.45	9.52
Gregariousness (E2)	.68	21.08	4.13	2.34	5.66
Assertiveness (E3)	.71	19.19	4.16	2.24	5.39
Activity (E4)	.65	19.98	3.72	2.20	5.19
Excitement Seeking (E5)	.62	20.32	3.65	2.25	6.16
Positive Emotions (E6)	.62	21.26	3.84	2.37	6.16
Anxiety (N1)	.75	19.94	4.66	2.33	5.00
Angry Hostility (N2)	.75	19.36	4.61	2.30	5.00
Depression (N3)	.73	18.93	4.39	2.28	5.20
Self-Consciousness (N4)	.66	17.96	4.34	2.53	5.83
Impulsiveness (N5)	.37	19.36	3.38	2.69	7.94
Vulnerability (N6)	.79	16.69	4.93	2.26	4.58
Fantasy (O1)	.70	22.39	4.15	2.27	5.48
Aesthetics (O2)	.80	22.10	4.47	2.12	4.47
Feelings (O3)	.51	21.36	3.57	2.50	7.00
Actions (O4)	.59	20.46	3.89	2.49	6.40
Ideas (O5)	.34	19.80	3.41	2.77	8.12
Values (O6)	.69	20.10	4.50	2.51	5.57
Trust (A1)	.57	20.85	3.37	2.21	6.56
Straightforwardness (A2)	.37	18.60	3.34	2.65	7.94
Altruism (A3)	.45	19.69	3.06	2.27	7.42
Compliance (A4)	.64	18.70	4.00	2.40	6.00
Modesty (A5)	.63	19.20	3.97	2.41	6.08
Tender-Mindedness (A6)	.47	21.40	3.17	2.31	7.28
Competence (C1)	.61	20.16	3.64	2.27	6.24
Order (C2)	.68	17.89	4.82	2.73	5.66
Dutifulness (C3)	.53	18.85	3.63	2.49	6.86
Achievement Striving (C4)	.61	20.22	3.76	2.34	6.24
Self-Discipline (C5)	.59	19.03	3.70	2.37	6.40
Deliberation (C6)	.68	18.91	4.05	2.29	5.66

Note: SEM (raw) = Standard error of measurement for raw data, SEM (T) = Standard error of measurement for T scores.

Table 3. Test-retest reliability coefficients for TPQue factor scales and sub-scales (*N* = 125)

	1st Testing		2nd Testing		Test-retest	SEM	
	M	*SD*	*M*	*SD*	Reliability	Raw	T
Factor Scales							
Extraversion (E)	122.40	17.16	122.87	16.39	.91	5.15	3.00
Neuroticism (N)	112.25	18.97	107.10	19.34	.95	4.24	2.24
Openness (O)	126.48	15.70	130.36	15.77	.93	4.15	2.65
Agreeableness (A)	118.44	13.07	117.58	12.83	.89	4.33	3.32
Conscientiousness (C)	115.07	17.43	113.89	16.80	.93	4.61	2.65
Sub-Scales							
Warmth (E1)	20.57	3.40	21.03	2.87	.72	1.80	5.29
Gregariousness (E2)	21.08	4.13	21.02	3.79	.83	1.70	4.12
Assertiveness (E3)	19.19	4.16	19.40	4.14	.89	1.38	3.32
Activity (E4)	19.98	3.72	19.51	3.60	.85	1.44	3.87
Excitement Seeking (E5)	20.32	3.65	20.20	3.38	.85	1.41	3.87
Positive Emotions (E6)	21.26	3.84	21.70	3.78	.87	1.38	3.61
Anxiety (N1)	19.94	4.66	18.78	4.74	.89	1.55	3.32
Angry Hostility (N2)	19.36	4.61	18.39	4.60	.87	1.66	3.61
Depression (N3)	18.93	4.39	17.55	4.44	.86	1.64	3.74
Self-Consciousness (N4)	17.96	4.34	16.62	4.20	.86	1.62	3.74
Impulsiveness (N5)	19.36	3.38	19.49	3.10	.79	1.55	4.58
Vulnerability (N6)	16.69	4.93	16.27	4.98	.91[a]	1.48	3.00
Fantasy (O1)	22.39	4.15	22.87	3.96	.84	2.62	4.00
Aesthetics (O2)	22.10	4.74	23.48	3.69	.84	2.99	4.00
Feelings (O3)	21.63	3.57	22.25	3.28	.73[a]	1.86	5.20
Actions (O4)	20.46	3.89	20.59	3.95	.85	1.51	3.87
Ideas (O5)	19.80	3.41	20.08	3.58	.80	1.52	4.47
Values (O6)	20.10	4.50	21.10	4.68	.91	1.35	3.00
Trust (A1)	20.85	3.37	21.52	3.22	.79[a]	1.54	4.58
Straightforwardness (A2)	18.60	3.34	18.67	3.04	.80	1.49	4.47
Altruism (A3)	19.69	3.06	18.94	2.94	.78[a]	1.44	4.69
Compliance (A4)	18.70	4.00	18.84	3.91	.83	1.65	4.12
Modesty (A5)	19.20	3.97	18.74	3.70	.80	1.77	4.47
Tender-Mindedness (A6)	21.40	3.17	20.87	2.81	.77[a]	1.52	4.80
Competence (C1)	20.16	3.64	20.29	3.54	.82	1.54	4.24
Order (C2)	17.89	4.82	18.04	4.43	.90	1.52	3.16
Dutifulness (C3)	18.85	3.63	18.30	3.47	.81[a]	1.58	4.36
Achievement Striving (C4)	20.22	3.76	19.93	3.59	.85	1.46	3.87
Self-Discipline (C5)	19.03	3.70	18.76	3.55	.84	2.34	4.00
Deliberation (C6)	18.91	4.05	18.57	3.95	.86	1.52	3.74

Note: 1st Testing = first administration, 2nd Testing = second administration after 4 weeks, *SEM* (raw) = Standard error of measurement for raw data, *SEM* (T) = Standard error of measurement for T scores, [a] = significant differences between scores from the two administrations.

Table 4. Inter-correlations among Factor Scales of the TPQue

	N	O	A	C
E	-.35 **	.39 **	.07 *	.20 **
N		-.07 **	.03	-.38 **
O			.19 **	-.04
A				.17 **

Note: E = Extraversion, N = Neuroticism, O = Openness to Experience, A = Agreeableness, C = Conscientiousness; $p < 0.05$; ** $p < 0.01$

Finally, when the stability of the mean scores of the five scales was investigated, all factor scales, showed remarkable stability over time, since the mean scores from the two administrations did not differ significantly. When the sub-scales' mean scores from the two administrations were tested, only 6 sub-scales (N6, O3, A1, A3, A6, and C3) were found to differ significantly (Table 3).

Relationships among the TPQue factor scales

The degree of overlap between factor scales was an obvious consideration to be dealt with during the construction stages of the TPQue, as was the good internal consistency and the psychological meaningfulness of all scales. As mentioned earlier, in the development procedure we tried to build up relatively independent factor scales out of items keyed to one and only one scale, in order to avoid artifactual correlations. This was successful to some extent. No factor scale was highly correlated with any another. However, in some cases, where the relativeness of the concepts was very close, there was some overlap. Table 4 shows the inter-correlations among TPQue factor scales.

Validity of the TPQue

There are several methods of exploring validity, and TPQue provides evidence to support most of them. More specifically, there is evidence available to support *content validity, construct validity* and *factorial validity* of the measure.

Content validity

According to Haynes, Richard, and Kubany (1995), *content validity* is the degree to which elements of an assessment instrument are relevant to and representative of the targeted construct for a particular assessment purpose. The relevance of a measure refers to the appropriateness of its elements for the targeted construct and function of assessment (Ebel & Frisbie, 1991; Guion, 1977; Messick, 1993). The representativeness of an instrument refers to the degree to which its elements are proportional to the facets of the targeted construct (Lynn, 1986; Nunnally & Bernstein, 1994; Suen & Ary, 1989). TPQue demonstrates its content validity by providing evidence for its two basic components: representativeness and relevance.

In Costa and McCrae's (1992) NEO-PI-R, representativeness is addressed by identifying six distinct facets to sample each domain and by selecting non-redundant items to measure each facet. Since TPQue uses the same hierarchical organization as in the NEO-PI-R (Kline, 1993), the representativeness of its sub-scales is also assumed. In terms of the relevance of the items in measuring the targeted constructs, independent judges were used in order to decide whether the written items reflect what they are trying to measure.

For this purpose, 20 judges were used to evaluate the relativeness of the selected items to the targeted constructs, using a 5-point scale (1: *not representative at all*, 5: *very representative*). Then, the mean score for each item was estimated, and the items with a mean score above 3.5 were selected. Finally, all 180 items were found to meet the specified cut off point, suggesting that TPQue items are highly related to the constructs they measure.

Convergent and discriminant validity of the TPQue

A usual step in scale development involves the concurrent validation process in which the new scale is correlated with other scales that are posited to tap similar processes. More specifically, TPQue factor scales were correlated with the Eysenck Personality Questionnaire — EPQ (Eysenck & Eysenck, 1975; Demetriou, 1986), the 16 Personality Factors Questionnaire, Form C — 16PF-C (Cattell, Eber, & Tatsuoka, 1970), Observer ratings for Openness, Agreeableness, and Conscientiousness Scales, the Minnesota Multiphasic Personality Inventory — MMPI (Hathaway & McKinley, 1983), Self Directed Search — SDS (Holland, Fritzsche, & Powell, 1985), Job Satisfaction Scale — JSS (Warr, Cook, & Wall, 1979), and Organizational Culture Inventory — OCI (Cooke & Lafferty, 1989). Table 5 presents evidence for convergent and discriminant validity of the factor scales of the TPQue.

The TPQue and Eysenck's EPQ

At the top of Table 5 correlations between TPQue and EPQ scales are provided. As can be seen from the results, the TPQue Neuroticism (N) and Extraversion (E) factor scales were correlated highly with the corresponding EPQ N and E dimensions. Additionally, the TPQue Agreeableness (A) and Conscientiousness (C) factor scales were correlated negatively with the EPQ Psychoticism (P) scale, a result which is consistent with Eysenck's argument that P is a blend of low C and A (Eysenck, 1992).

Table 5. Correlation coefficients of the TPQue Factor Scales with various criterion scales

Criterion Scales	TPQue E	TPQue N	TPQue O	TPQue A	TPQue C
EPQ (N = 88)					
Extraversion	.82*	-.35*	.32*	-.12	.19
Neuroticism	-.36*	.69*	-.19	-.08	-.13
Psychoticism	.10	-.06	-.10	-.44*	-.28*
16PF (N = 83)					
Self- Reliance (Q2)	-.40**	.09	-.15	.04	-.02
Tension (Q4)	-.10	.55**	.04	-.10	-.12
Openness to Change (Q1)	.21	-.22	.49**	.01	.11
Perfectionism (Q3)	-.12	-.40**	-.25**	.23*	.53**
Observer ratings (N = 86)					
Openness			.42*	.14	.08
Agreeableness			.14	.53*	.26
Conscientiousness			.08	.07	.33*
MMPI (N = 76)					
Hypochondriasis (Hs)	-.42**	.39**	-.24	.03	-.07
Depression (D)	-.51**	.57**	-.40**	.06	-.15
Hysteria (Hy)	-.44**	.37**	-.31*	-.02	-.07
Psychopathic Deviate (Pd)	-.11	.39**	-.02	-.02	-.02
Masculinity-Femininity (Mf)	-.14	.16	.22	.25	.10
Paranoia (Pa)	-.35**	.64**	-.15	-.01	-.30*
Psychasthenia (Pt)	-.44**	.75**	-.28*	-.14	-.45**
Schizophrenia (Sc)	-.48**	.69**	-.25	-.15	-.51**
Hypomania (Ma)	.07	.36**	.17	-.13	-.28*
Social Introversion-Extroversion (Si)	-.56	.61**	-.31*	.05	-.30*
SDS (N = 152)					
Realistic	.23**	-.25**	.004	-.06	.10
Investigative	.16*	-.28**	.24**	-.05	.23**
Artistic	.03	.11	.40**	-.03	-.12
Social	.20*	.10	.21**	.14	.07
Enterprising	.43**	-.24**	-.18*	-.28**	.27**
Conventional	.17*	-.14	-.18*	-.20*	.23**
JSS (N = 222)	.14*	-.24**	-.15*	-.04	.18**
OCI (N = 157)					
Humanistic/Helpful	.17	-.17	-.07	.44**	.25**
Affiliation	.10	-.13	-.09	.39**	.22*
Achievement	.01	-.08	-.18	-.02	.21*
Self-Actualization	-.16	-.02	-.05	-.22*	-.03
Approval	-.12	.06	-.01	-.10	.06
Conventionality	-.02	.03	-.10	-.20*	-.13
Dependence	.01	.06	-.09	.04	.03
Avoidance	-.02	.06	-.07	-.27**	-.05
Oppositional	-.05	-.01	-.06	-.29**	.03
Power	.01	-.01	-.09	-.07	.19*
Competitive	.15	-.28**	.01	.29**	.30**
Perfectionism	.01	-.04	-.11	.20*	.35**

Note: EPQ = Eysenck Personality Questionnaire, 16PF = 16 Personality Factors Questionnaire, MMPI = Minnesota Multiphasic Personality Inventory, SDS = Self Directed Search, JSS = Job Satisfaction Scale, OCI = Organisational Culture Inventory; * $p < 0.05$; ** $p < 0.01$

The TPQue and Cattell's 16PF

Table 5 also provides correlations between the TPQue factor scales and the 16PF second order scales. The correlations were in the direction and generally of the magnitude predicted. In particular, the TPQue N, O, and C factor scales were positively correlated with Tension (Q4), Openness to Change (Q1), and Perfectionism (Q3) scales, respectively, while the TPQue E factor scale was negatively correlated with the Self-Reliance (Q2) scale.

The TPQue and Observers ratings

Another study involved the correlation of three of the TPQue factor scales — Openness (O), Conscientiousness (C), and Agreeableness (A) — with corresponding ratings obtained from observers (friends and relatives), who were called to give ratings for the people who had previously completed the TPQue. As shown in Table 5, all factor scales were positively correlated with the corresponding observers' ratings, and two of them, the O and A factor scales, were substantial in magnitude.

The TPQue and MMPI

In another study, the TPQue factor scales were correlated with MMPI scales. As can be seen from the results presented in Table 5, the TPQue N factor scale was correlated positively with almost all MMPI scales (except the Masculinity/Femininity scale). This result is consistent with the theory that people prone to experience negative emotions show higher levels of psychopathological symptoms (Avia, Sanchez-Bernardos, Martinez-Arias, Silva, & Grana, 1995). Additionally, as expected, many of the MMPI clinical scales were negatively correlated with the TPQue E factor scale, a result which is consistent with the idea of Extraversion as a dimension of positive emotions (Wiggins & Pincus, 1989). The remaining TPQue factor scales showed specific relations with MMPI clinical scales, consistent with theoretical predictions. For example, the TPQue O factor scale was correlated negatively with MMPI Depression (D), Hysteria (Hy), Psychasthenia (Pt) and Social Introversion-Extroversion (Si) scales, while the TPQue C factor scale was correlated negatively with Paranoia (Pa), Psychasthenia (Pt), Schizophrenia (Sc), Hypomania (Hy), and Introversion-Extroversion (Si) scales. All the above findings are consistent with previous research comparing scores on these measures (Avia *et al.*, 1995; Costa, Busch, Zonderman, & McCrae, 1986; Costa & McCrae, 1990).

The TPQue and Holland's SDS

Correlations of the TPQue factor scales with Holland's RIASEC vocational interest model are also presented in Table 5. Consistent with our expectations, the TPQue E factor scale was correlated positively with Enterprising and Social types, while the

TPQue N factor scale was correlated negatively with Investigative, Realistic, Social, and Conventional types. Furthermore, the TPQue O factor scale was mainly positively correlated with the Artistic type, as predicted, while the TPQue A factor scale was correlated negatively with both Enterprising and Conventional types. Finally, the TPQue C factor scale was correlated positively with the Investigative, Enterprising, and Conventional types. These findings are consistent with the existing literature (Costa, McCrae, & Holland, 1984; De Fruyt & Mervielde, 1997; Tokar & Swanson, 1995).

The TPQue and JSS

In Table 5, correlations between TPQue factor scales and JSS are also provided. As expected, the TPQue E and C factor scales were correlated positively with job satisfaction (Diener, 1996; Robertson, Baron, Gibbons, MacIver, & Nyfield, 2000; Salgado, 1997), while the TPQue N and O factor scales were correlated negatively (Nikolaou, in press) with the same construct.

The TPQue and OCI

The TPQue factor scales were also correlated with OCI scales. There are numerous significant associations between the TPQue personality dimensions and concepts measured by the OCI. For example, the TPQue A factor scale was correlated positively with the Humanistic/Helpful and Affiliation scale, and negatively with Oppositional and Avoidance scales, as expected. Similarly the TPQue C factor scale was found to be positively correlated with Perfectionism, Competitive, Achievement, and Power scales, amongst others. Most of the other correlations were interpretable within the Big Five context.

Additionally, almost all 30 convergent correlations between the factors and the corresponding sub-scale scores ranged from .44 (N3) to .96 (O2), with a median of .71. Only two sub-scales appear to have very low correlations with their factor scores; these are A3 and C1. By contrast, the majority of the 150 discriminant correlations (93.3 %) were below .38.

Factor structure

Since TPQue is intended to represent the five-factor model of personality, one obvious test of its adequacy is how well its internal structure corresponds to the predictions of the model. There are at least two levels at which the factor structure of the TPQue can be examined: at the item level and at the sub-scale level.

The TPQue consists of 180 items that define 30 six-item sub-scales grouped into five-factor scales. Would an item factor analysis recover these scales? When five varimax-rotated principal components were extracted, the majority of them corresponded to the hypothesized factors. A total of 144 of the 180 items (80 %) had their largest loading on the intended factor. For the 36-item factor scales, 32 E items,

Table 6. Factor structure of the TPQue Factor Scales and sub-scales and congruences for Factor scales and sub-scales after Procrustes rotation to the normative American Structure

TPQue sub-scales	N	E	O	A	C	Variable Congruence
Extraversion sub-scales						
Warmth	-.02	**.64**	.28	.51	.01	.97**
Gregariousness	-.24	**.72**	-.01	-.07	.04	.97**
Assertiveness	-.32	**.53**	.28	-.29	.34	.99**
Activity	-.17	**.62**	.19	-.27	.26	.93**
Excitement Seeking	-.20	**.65**	.27	-.17	.19	.84
Positive Emotions	-.21	**.72**	.20	-.13	.05	.93**
Neuroticism sub-scales						
Anxiety	**.87**	-.01	-.06	-.00	.02	.99**
Angry Hostility	**.67**	.18	.08	**-.42**	-.00	.95**
Depression	**.81**	-.18	-.04	.10	-.14	.97**
Self-Consciousness	**.53**	-.38	-.26	.29	-.17	.86*
Impulsiveness	**.40**	.39	.04	-.17	**-.35**	.99**
Vulnerability	**.79**	-.10	-.15	.05	-.29	.98**
Openness sub-scales						
Fantasy	.13	.08	**.61**	.12	-.16	.90*
Aesthetics	.04	.06	**.66**	.20	.16	.99**
Feelings	.26	.29	**.52**	.34	-.01	.85
Actions	-.11	.31	**.57**	-.07	.03	.96**
Ideas	-.08	.19	**.68**	-.13	.09	.95**
Values	-.15	-.11	**.65**	-.10	-.20	.95**
Agreeableness sub-scales						
Trust	-.08	**.43**	-.11	**.54**	-.04	.81
Straightforwardness	.00	.13	**.26**	**.33**	.16	.62
Altruism	.11	.38	.01	**.56**	.10	.94**
Compliance	-.02	-.09	.04	**.78**	-.11	.97**
Modesty	.15	-.20	.02	**.56**	.05	.92*
Tender-Mindedness	.19	.32	.17	**.58**	.28	.91*
Conscientiousness sub-scales						
Competence	-.38	.13	.01	.02	**.70**	.98**
Order	-.03	-.08	-.20	.14	**.57**	.96**
Dutifulness	.-09	-.03	.00	.27	**.74**	.99**
Achievement Striving	-.04	.13	.01	-.03	**.76**	.97**
Self-Discipline	-.17	.06	.06	.08	**.82**	.96**
Deliberation	-.21	-.24	-.04	.14	**.66**	.99**
Factor Congruencies	**.95****	**.94****	**.92****	**.91****	**.95****	**.93****

Note: N = Neuroticism, E = Extraversion, O = Openness to Experience, A = Agreeableness, C = Conscientiousness; * Congruence higher than that of 95% rotations from random data; ** Congruence higher than that of 99 % rotations from random data.

28 N items, 25 O items, 24 A items, and 33 C items had their highest loading on the intended factor.

Furthermore, to determine the extent to which the five-factor model emerged from the sample, a principal components analysis and an orthogonal Procrustes rotation were performed on the 30 TPQue sub-scales. The loadings on the five factors, which accounted for 56.33 per cent of the variance, are shown in Table 6.

As shown in Table 6 each sub-scale has its highest loading on the intended factor, and where large secondary loadings appear, they are appropriate and meaningful. For example, E1 (Warmth) has a large positive loading on A (.51), because warm people are generally sympathetic to others and eager to help them. Likewise, N5 (Impulsiveness) has a large negative secondary loading on C, because people with low self-control are characterized by the inability to manage their impulses or desires. The above results are also consistent with findings from other cross-cultural studies (Pulver, Allik, Pulkkinen, & Hamalainen, 1995).

Moreover, in order to check whether the factor analytic results corresponded to the conceptual model, factor scores were computed for the principal factor solution, and then correlated with the 'theoretical' scores on the five scales, which were obtained by summing the scores from their related items (Caprara, Barbaranelli, Borgoni, & Perugini, 1993; Costa & McCrae, 1992; Gudjonsson & Sigurdsson, 1999). The correlations were .89, .92, .81, .83, and .91, for E, N, O, A, and C, respectively. The results revealed that there was a substantial overlap between the factor scores and their 'theoretical' scores, which is another indication of the structural validity of the questionnaire.

Factorial invariance in the TPQue is a necessary, though not sufficient, criterion for judging the success with which the instrument reflects the model. For this reason, the stability of the factor structure across different samples was also examined. Separate factor analyses were conducted for males and females (Tsaousis, 1999) as well as for non-applicants, job applicants, and employees (Tsaousis & Nikolaou, in press), and congruence coefficients (Harman, 1976) were calculated between the contrasted pairs[1]. The results justified the high stability of the factorial structure of the TPQue, since the same five factors were found in each group, and all the congruence coefficients were above the critical value of .90 (Harman, 1976).

Given this convergence of the results of exploratory factor analysis, it seemed highly recommendable to apply the method of confirmatory factor analysis (CFA) to provide yet another check on the factor structure.

The models

Several factor structures were theoretically possible, based on either the 30 scales or the 5 factors. In this CFA, seven different models were tested:

Model A: **Null model:** This model had no common factors between the 30 TPQue sub-scales. It was used as a baseline for the other models.

Model B: **One factor model:** This model assumed that all the sub-scales were loaded onto a single factor.

---

[1] Congruence coefficient is a statistical idex that allows the extent of similarity of dissimilarity between two sets of factors obtained from different samples or solutions to be determined.

Model C: **TPQue model:** This model was obtained by fixing all factor loadings for the 30 sub-scales to the varimax-rotated values obtained in our exploratory factor analysis. Each TPQue scale was an indicator only of its Big Five structure, and no secondary loadings were allowed.

Model D: **TPQue secondary loadings model:** This model was obtained by imposing the primary loadings of Model C in addition to the 26 secondary loadings found to be .20 or higher in the validimax factor structure solution from the exploratory factor analysis[2].

Model E: **Standard Orthogonal model:** This model represents the most parsimonious model with the five factor theory. Each sub-scale was loaded only on the intended factor (no secondary loadings), and no parameters were pre-estimated, but were left to vary freely.

Model F: **Oblique model:** This model resulted from the imposition of ten additional constrains on the parameters of model E. In particular, the TPQue five factors were allowed to intercorrelate with each other.

Model G: **Modification index model:** Finally, this model was derived from the program's modification suggestion in order to obtain a better fit. Thus, three additional constrains were added to the parameters of model E. Firstly, O and C factors were allowed to be correlated. Secondly, the error terms of C4: Achievement Striving and O1: Fantasy, were allowed to be correlated with A and C factors, respectively.

Table 7 displays the CFA results and reports absolute, relative and parsimonious indices of fit that comprehensively evaluate the fit of the different models computed.

As Jöreskog and Sorbom (1993) have noted, the use of chi-square as a central χ^2-statistic is based on the assumption that the model holds exactly in the population. This assumption, however, is unreasonable and almost unattainable in most empirical research (Jöreskog & Sorbom, 1993; Loehlin, 1992; Bollen, 1989; Church & Burke, 1994). A consequence of this assumption is that models that hold approximately in the population will be rejected in large samples. Thus, with models so complex as personality models, in particular the Big Five, this statistic is not expected to provide a good fit of data. For this reason, other indices will be concentrated on, which, as literature has indicated, are less conservative and independent of sample size.

The first two models constitute control models against the five TPQue models examined. Table 7 shows that according to the statistics of all goodness-of-fit indices (absolute, relative, or parsimonious) it is not possible to accept both models. Furthermore, all indices appear to have values worse than those of any of the subsequent models. Model C, which was based on the exploratory factor solution, pro-

---

[2] For the E factor, secondary loadings were included for the sub-scales of Angry Hostility, Depression, Self-Consciousness, Impulsiveness, Vulnerability, Actions, Ideas, Compliance, Modesty, Competence, and Achievement Striving; for the N factor, loadings for Competence and Deliberation; for the O factor loadings for Warmth, Excitement-Seeking and Modesty; for the A factor, loadings for Warmth, Gregariousness, Angry Hostility, Feelings, and Dutifulness; and for C factor, loadings for Assertiveness, Impulsiveness, Vulnerability, Values, and Tender-Mindedness.

Table 7. Overall fit Indices for the TPQue factor scales and sub-scales

Models	Absolute Indices			Relative Indices			Parsimony Index
	χ^2	df	χ^2/df	TLI	NFI	CFI	PNFI
Model A: Null	2387.77	435	5.49	.88	.86	.88	.81
Model B: One factor	1791.22	409	4.39	.91	.89	.91	.79
Model C: TPQue	1453.17	430	3.38	.93	.91	.94	.85
Model D: Second. loadings	1781.95	431	4.14	.91	.90	.92	.83
Model E: Orthogonal	1260.01	405	3.11	.94	.93	.95	.81
Model F: Oblique	1164.20	395	2.94	.94	.93	.96	.80
Model G: Modification Index	1194.97	403	2.97	.95	.93	.95	.81

Note: TLI = Tucker-Lewis Index; *NFI* = Normed Fit Index; *CFI* = Normed Noncentrality Fit Index; *PNFI* = Parsimonious Normed-Fit Index.

vided a rather acceptable fit, with the ratio of chi-square to degrees of freedom (χ^2/df) less than four (3.38). Most importantly, all three relative indices (*TLI, NFI,* and *CFI*) together with the Parsimonious Normed-Fit Index (*PNFI*) also prvided acceptable values, indicating good fit (.93, .91, .94, and .85, respectively). This result reconfirms the factor structure of the TPQue, as revealed by the exploratory factor analysis. In fact, it provides another strong argument in supporting the hypothesis that the TPQue Concept Model is a measure of the Big Five model.

In an attempt to improve the above model and to get a better fit to the data, Model D was developed, including 26 secondary factor loadings, besides the primary loadings from Model C. Unfortunately, this model proved to be worse than the previous model ($\chi^2/df = 4.14$, *TLI* = .91, *NFI* = .90, *CFI* = .92, and *PNFI* = .83). Model C appeared to be significantly superior to Model D: χ^2_D (1781.95) - χ^2_C (1453.17) = χ^2_{Diff} (1) = 328.95, *p* < .0001.

In Model E, a five factor orthogonal solution, almost all the parameters of the model were left to run freely, instead of specifying the factor loadings for each sub-scale (as in Model C). Only the first sub-scale's regression weight for each factor was fixed at 1.0, in order to identify the model and to set the metric for the factor variances. This model also provided a good fit to the data ($\chi^2/df = 3.11$, *TLI* = .94, *NFI* = .93, *CFI* = .95, and *PNFI* = .81), and in fact resulted in a significant improvement over the two previous models: χ^2_C (1453.17) - χ^2_E (1260.01) = χ^2_{Diff} (25) = 193.16, *p* < .0001, and χ^2_C (1781.95) - χ^2_E (1260.01) = $\chi^2_{Diff.}$(26) = 521.94, *p* < .0001.

Model F, where the factor scales were allowed to be intercorrelated between each other, had the most parsimonious fit with all indices suggesting good fit ($\chi^2/df = 2.94$, *TLI* = .94, *NFI* = .93, *CFI* = .96, and *PNFI* = .80). Again this model was significantly superior to Model E: χ^2_E (1260.01) - χ^2_F (1164.20) = $\chi^2_{Diff.}$(10) = 95.81, *p* < .0001.

Finally, although Model G, as suggested by the AMOS modification index facility, possessed a better fit than models C and E, ($\chi^2/df = 2.97$, *TLI* = 95, *NFI* = .93, *CFI* = .95, and *PNFI* = .81), it did not provide an improvement over the F model.

In summary, whereas almost all TPQue models proved to fit the data well, the most parsimonious was the model with all its factor scales intercorrelated to each other (Model F). The above results can be interpreted in two ways: on the one hand, there is enough evidence to support the claim that confirmatory factor analysis indeed reconfirmed the results obtained by exploratory factor analysis, which claimed the TPQue Concept Model to be indeed a Big Five model. On the other hand, CFA analysis demonstrated that the best fit to the data was achieved when all five factor scales were correlated to each other.

This result is consistent with the theory of Big Five, in the sense that it is not possible for personality factors not to be correlated to each other, since they constitute dimensions of the same construct. For example, circumplex studies suggest that the personality domain may be better represented as a continuum of personality distinctions, rather than as a set of clearly separable dimensions (Wiggins, 1979; Kiesler, 1983; Saucier, 1992). It is also consistent with the Concept Model of the TPQue, which suggests that its five factor scales are all correlated with each other to some extent.

Standardization of the TPQue — Norms

Participants

The normative sample on which the TPQue profile forms are based consists of 1,054 students, of whom 868 were recruited from 7 Greek universities in the country, and 186 from two high schools (a private school in Athens and a public school in the province of Messinia). The mean age of the participants was 19.9 years ($SD = 4.32$), of which 410 (39 %) were male and 644 (61 %) female Greek students. This proportion is very close to the proportion of male and female students studying at Greek universities (41 % and 59 % respectively)[3]. The average male student was 20.04 years ($SD = 4.81$) whereas the average female student was 19.8 years ($SD = 3.99$). Details of the sample participated in the standardization procedure are provided in Table 8.

---

[3] Source: Minister of Education (1992). Personal correspondence.

Table 8. TPQue normative sample in terms of region and faculty (*N*=1,054)

Institutes	Combined Sample		Males		Females	
Region						
University of Crete	429	(40.7)	133	(32.4)	296	(46.0)
University of Athens	82	(7.8)	26	(6.3)	56	(8.7)
University of Patras	93	(8.8)	17	(4.1)	76	(11.8)
University of Macedonia	32	(3.0)	15	(3.6)	17	(2.6)
Panteios University	85	(8.1)	27	(6.6)	58	(9.0)
S . E . L . E . T . E	69	(6.5)	55	(13.4)	14	(2.2)
Ziridis High School	92	(8.7)	58	(14.1)	34	(5.3)
Kalamata High School	94	(8.9)	37	(9.0)	57	(8.9)
Various Universities	78	(7.5)	42	(10.5)	36	(5.5)
Total	1054	*(100%)*	410	*(100%)*	644	*(100%)*
Faculty						
Classical Studies	308	(29.2)	49	(12.0)	259	(40.1)
Social Sciences	414	(39.2)	135	(33.0)	279	(43.2)
Science	272	(25.7)	189	(46.1)	83	(12.8)
Other	60	(5.9)	37	(8.9)	23	(3.9)
Total	1054	*(100%)*	410	*(100%)*	644	*(100%)*

Note: University of Crete is dispersed in 3 different cities, Chania, Rethymno, and Irakleio. The above mentioned figure of 429 students contains samples from all the three cities in the following proportion: Chania: 62 (5.8 %), Rethymno: 214 (20.3 %), and Irakleio: 153 (14.6 %); The figures in the brackets represent the percentage of the sample

Norms of the TPQue

Although the TPQue was initially standardized for a college age population, it has also been successfully used in other population groups. It shows the same factor structure in student and non-student respondents as well as clinical and non-clinical respondents, and has been extensively validated for women as well as men. TPQue provides norms for college age population (Tsaousis, 1999), occupational population — applicants as well as employees — (Tsaousis & Nikolaou, in press), clinical population (Tsaousis & Semkou, 1999), and high school student population (Tsaousis, 1996). TPQue uses two different normative systems, Percentiles and *T* scores. Additional norms are being developed for other groups at the present time.

Descriptive characteristics of the TPQue

The means and standard deviations of all TPQue factor scales and sub-scales in both the total sample and in the male and female sub-samples are given in Table 9; *t*-tests were also conducted to investigate whether there were significant differences between males and females on all scales. The results indicate that females obtained higher scores than males in Neuroticism [t (1052) = -8.62, p < .0001], Openness [t (1052) = -5.94, p < .0001], Agreeableness [t (1052) = -6.89, p < .0001] and Con-

Table 9. Means and Standard Deviations for TPQue Factor scales and sub-scales

	Males (N=410)		Females (N=644)		Combined (N=1,054)	
	M	SD	M	SD	M	SD
Factor Scales						
Extraversion	122.93	17.18	122.06	17.15	122.40	17.16
Neuroticism	106.14	17.68	116.14 *	18.74	112.25	18.96
Openness to Experience	122.93	15.37	128.73 *	15.49	126.48	15.69
Agreeableness	115.04	12.38	120.61 *	13.05	118.44	13.07
Conscientiousness	112.97	17.97	116.40 *	16.95	115.07	17.43
Extraversion Sub-scales						
Warmth	19.88	3.49	21.00 *	3.28	20.57	3.40
Gregariousness	20.92	4.13	21.19	4.13	21.08	4.13
Assertiveness	19.56	4.02	18.96 *	4.23	19.19	4.16
Activity	20.55	3.71	19.62 *	3.69	19.98	3.72
Excitement -Seeking	20.87	3.76	19.97 *	3.54	20.32	3.65
Positive Emotions	21.15	3.77	21.32	3.89	21.26	3.84
Neuroticism Sub-scales						
Anxiety	18.78	4.41	20.67 *	4.67	19.94	4.66
Angry Hostility	18.37	4.44	19.99 *	4.60	19.36	4.61
Depression	17.80	4.10	19.65 *	4.43	18.93	4.39
Self-Consciousness	17.26	4.25	18.41 *	4.33	17.96	4.34
Impulsiveness	18.92	3.33	19.64 *	3.39	19.36	3.38
Vulnerability	15.00	4.76	17.77 *	4.74	16.69	4.93
Openness Sub-scales						
Fantasy	21.96	4.26	22.66 *	4.08	22.39	4.15
Aesthetics	20.43	5.05	23.16 *	4.21	22.10	4.74
Feelings	20.51	3.42	22.35 *	3.49	21.63	3.57
Actions	19.99	3.79	20.75 *	3.93	20.46	3.89
Ideas	20.02	3.37	19.66	3.43	19.80	3.41
Values	20.02	4.57	20.15	4.46	20.10	4.50
Agreeableness Sub-scales						
Trust	20.79	3.37	20.89	3.37	20.85	3.37
Straightforwardness	18.04	3.31	18.96 *	3.31	18.60	3.34
Altruism	19.24	3.00	19.97 *	3.06	19.69	3.06
Compliance	18.00	3.84	19.14 *	4.05	18.70	4.01
Modesty	18.67	3.90	19.53 *	3.97	19.20	3.96
Tender-Mindedness	20.31	3.07	22.11 *	3.03	21.41	3.17
Conscientiousness Sub-Scales						
Competence	20.32	3.80	20.05	3.52	20.16	3.64
Order	17.15	5.00	18.36 *	4.64	17.89	4.82
Dutifulness	18.28	3.59	19.21 *	3.61	18.85	3.63
Achievement Striving	19.88	3.78	20.44 *	3.73	20.22	3.76
Self-Discipline	18.58	3.86	19.33 *	3.57	19.04	3.70
Deliberation	18.76	3.95	19.01	4.12	18.91	4.05

Note: * Significant differences between males and females at $p < 0.05$.

scientiousness [t (1052) = -3.13, p < .001], while there were no significant differences between males and females in Extraversion [t (1052) = .81, ns]. The results are consistent with studies where other personality inventories have been used (e.g., Costa & McCrae, 1992; Eysenck & Eysenck, 1975).

Summarizing, the Traits Personality Questionnaire (TPQue) contains 206 items, requires approximately a fifth-grade reading level, and provides evidence of sound psychometric properties across different samples. Research evidence suggests that the TPQue is already beginning to prove its utility not only as a research tool but also in a number of applied settings, including personal development counseling, vocational guidance, personnel selection and appraisal. Although some of its subscales need revision in order to improve its effectiveness in measuring the Big Five constructs, the measure appears to be a useful measurement tool for assessing 'normal' personality. Finally, although we already have evidence for discriminant and convergent validity, experimental studies are needed to provide more concurrent validity information, especially with other Big Five scales when these are available in the Greek language.

References

Avia, D., Sanz, J., Martínez-Arias, R., Silva, F., & Graña, J. (1995). The five factor model-II. Relations of the NEO-PI with other personality variables. *Personality and Individual Differences, 19*, 81-97.

Bollen, K.A. (1989). *Structural equations with latent variables*. New York: John Wiley and Sons.

Caprara, G.-V., Barbaranelli, C., Borgogni, L., & Perugini, M. (1993). The "Big Five Questionnaire": A new questionnaire to assess the five factor model. *Personality and Individual Differences, 15*, 281-288.

Cattell, R.B., Eber, H.W., & Tatsuoka, M.M. (1970). *Handbook for the Sixteen Personality Factor Questionnaire* (3rd ed.). Champaing, Illinois: Institute for Personality and Ability Testing.

Cattell, R.B., & Kline, P. (1977). *The scientific analysis of personality and motivation*. New York: Academic Press.

Church, T., & Bruke, J.P. (1994). Exploratory and Confirmatory tests of big five and Tellegen's three and four-dimensional models. *Journal of Personality and Social Psychology, 66*, 93-114.

Cooke, R.A., & Lafferty, J.C. (1989). *Organizational Culture Inventory*. Plymouth, MI: Human Synergistics.

Costa, P.T., Jr., & McCrae, R.R. (1990). Personality disorders and the five-factor model of personality. *Journal of Personality Disorders, 4*, 362-371.

Costa, P. T., Jr., & McCrae, R.R. (1992). *NEO PI-R. Professional Manual*. Odessa, Florida: Psychological Assessment Resources, Inc.

Costa, P. T., Jr., McCrae, R.R., & Holland, J.L. (1984). Personality and vocational interests in an adult sample. *Journal of Applied Psychology, 3*, 390-400.

Costa, P.T., Jr., Bush, C.M., Zonderman, A.B., & McCrae, R.R. (1986). Correlations of MMPI factor scales with measures of the five factor model of personality. *Journal of Personality Assessment, 50*, 640-650.

De Fruyt, F. & Mervielde, I. (1997). The five-factor model of personality and Holland's RIASEC interest types. *Personality and Individual Differences, 23*, 87-103.

Demetriou, C.E. (1986). Το ερωτηματολόγιο προσωπικότητας EPQ (Eysenck Personality Questionnaire): στάθμιση στον ελληνικό πληθυσμό, ενήλικο και παιδικό [The Eysenck Personality Questionnaire (EPQ): standardization in the Greek adult and child population]. *Εγκέφαλος, 23*, 41-54.

Diener, E. (1996). Traits Can Be Powerful, but Are Not Enough: Lessons from Subjective Well-Being. *Journal of Research in Personality, 30*, 389-399.

Ebel, R.L., & Frisbie, D.A. (1991). *Essentials of educational measurement* (5th ed.). Englewood Cliffs, NJ: Prentice-Hall.

Edwards, A.L. (1957). *The social desirability variable in personality assessment and research.* New York: Dryden Press.

Eysenck, H.J. (1992). Four Ways Five Factors are not Basic. *Personality and Individual Differences, 6*, 667-673.

Eysenck, H.J., & Eysenck, S.B.G. (1975). *The Eysenck Personality Questionnaire.* Sevenoaks: Hodder & Stoughton.

Gudjonsson, G.H., & Sigurdsson, J.F. (1999). The Gudjonsson Confession Questionnaire-Revised (GCQ-R): Factor structure and its relationship with personality. *Personality and Individual Differences, 27*, 953-968.

Guion, R.M. (1977). Content validity-The source of my discontent. *Applied Psychological Measurement, 1*, 1-10.

Harman, H.H. (1976). *Congruent and Prescribed Factor Solution. In Modern Factor Analysis.* Chicago: University Chicago Press.

Hase, H.D., & Goldberg, L.R. (1967). The comparative validity of different strategies of deriving personality inventory scales. *Psychological Bulletin, 67*, 231-248.

Hathaway, S.R., & McKinley, J.C. (1983). *The Minnesota Multiphasic Personality Inventory manual.* New York: The Psychological Corporation.

Haynes, N.S., Richard, S.D., & Kubany, S.E. (1995). Content validity in psychological assessment: a functional approach to concepts and methods. *Psychological Assessment, 7*, 238-247.

Holland, J.L., Fritzsche, B.A., & Powell, B. (1985). *The Self-Directed Search (SDS): Technical Manual.* Odessa, FL.: Psychological Assessment Resources, Inc.

Jöreskog, K., & Sorbom, D. (1993). *LISREL 8: Structural equation modelling with the SIMPLIS command language.* Chicago, IL: SSI.

Kiesler, D.J. (1983). The 1982 interpersonal circle: A taxonomy for complementarity in human transactions. *Psychological Review, 90*, 185-214.

Kline, P. (1993). *The handbook of psychological testing.* London: Routledge.

Loehlin, J.C. (1987). Heredity, environment, and the structure of the California Psychological Inventory. *Multivariate Behavioral Research, 22*, 137-148.

Lynn, M.R. (1986). Determination and quantification of content validity. *Nursing Research, 35*, 382-385.

Messick, S. (1993). Validity. In R.L. Linn (Ed.), *Educational measurement.* Phoenix: American Council on Education and Oryx Press.

Nikolaou, I. (in press). The Five-Factor Model of Personality and Work Behaviour in Greece. *European Journal of Work and Organisational Psychology.*

Nunnally, J.C., & Bernstein, I.H. (1994). *Psychometric theory* (3rd ed.). New York: McGraw-Hill.

Pulver, A., Allik, J., Pulkkinen, L., & Hamalainen, M. (1995). A Big-Five personality inventory in two non-indo-European languages. *European Journal of Personality, 9,* 109-124.

Robertson, I.T., Baron, H., Gibbons, P., MacIver, R., & Nyfield, G. (2000). Conscientiousness and managerial performance. *Journal of Occupational and Organizational Psychology, 73,* 171-180.

Sakelariou, X. (1991). Λεξικό συνωνύμων: Αντιθέτων-παραγώγων, συνθέτων και επιθέτων της δημοτικής [Thesaurus: synonyms, antonyms, formations and adjectives of the modern Greek language (5th ed). Athens: Sideris].

Salgado, J.F. (1997). The five factor model of personality and job performance in the European Community. *Journal of Applied Psychology, 82,* 30-43.

Saucier, G. (1992). Benchmarks: Integrating affective and interpersonal circles with the Big-Five personality factors. *Journal of Personality and Social Psychology, 62,* 1025-1035.

Suen, H.K., & Ary, D. (1989). *Analyzing quantitative observation data.* Hillsdate, NJ: Erlbaum.

Tokar, D.M., & Swanson, J.L. (1995). Evaluation of the correspondence between Holland's vocational personality typology and the five-factor model of personality. *Journal of Vocational Behavior, 46,* 89-108.

Tsaousis, I. (1996). *The psychometric assessment of personality in Greek speaking population.* Unpublished doctoral dissertation, University of London - Goldsmith's College, London, U.K.

Tsaousis, I. (1999). The Trait Personality Questionnaire: A Greek Measure for the Five Factor Model. *Personality and Individual Differences, 26,* 262-274.

Tsaousis, I., & Semkou, A. (1999). *The Traits Personality Questionnaire (TPQue). More evidence on construct validity: A comparison with MMPI.* Paper presented at 5th European Congress of Psychological Assessment, Patras, Greece.

Tsaousis, I., & Nikolaou, I. (in press). The stability of the five factor model across samples. *International Journal of Selection and Assessment .*

Warr, P., Cook, J., Wall, T. (1979). Scales for the measurement of some work attitudes and aspects of psychological well - being. *Journal of Occupational Psychology, 52,* 129-148.

Wiggins, J.S. (1979). A psychological taxonomy of trait-descriptive terms: The interpersonal domain. *Journal of Personality and Social Psychology, 37,* 395- 412.

Wiggins, J.S., & Pincus, A. (1989). Conceptions of personality disorders and dimensions of personality. Psychological Assessment: *A Journal of Consulting and Clinical Psychology, 1,* 305-316.

BIG FIVE ADJECTIVE SCALES

Chapter 11

The Interpersonal Adjective Scales: Big Five Version (IASR-B5)

Jerry S. Wiggins
Krista K. Trobst

Introduction

"The five-factor model provides a larger framework in which to orient and interpret the circumplex, and the interpersonal circle provides a useful elaboration about aspects of two of the five factors" (McCrae & Costa, 1989, p. 593).

Recent research in personality structure has emphasized both five-factor and circumplex structural models (e.g., Wiggins & Pincus, 1992) and, as the opening quotation from McCrae and Costa makes clear, these two models are seen as complementary rather than competitive (see Figure 1). The Interpersonal Adjective Scales — Revised: Big Five Version (IASR-B5) were constructed to provide ". . . a *highly efficient* instrument for combined circumplex and five-factor assessment" (Trapnell & Wiggins, 1990, p. 781, emphasis added).

As discussed elsewhere (Wiggins, 1995), the Interpersonal Adjective Scales are embedded in a conceptual framework that has its origins in five venerable traditions: (1) the lexical tradition (John, Angleitner, & Ostendorf, 1988), (2) the interpersonal theory tradition in clinical psychology and psychiatry (Kiesler, 1996), (3) the traditions of order and facet analysis (Guttman, 1966), (4) the social exchange and impression management traditions (Carson, 1969), and (5) the multivariate-trait tradition (Wiggins & Trapnell, 1997). Over time, the scales have been modified for different purposes and their names changed to reflect these modifications: the Interpersonal Adjective Scales were first (IAS; Wiggins, 1979), followed by the revised Interpersonal Adjective Scales (IAS-R; Wiggins, Trapnell, & Phillips, 1988), and by the extension of the Interpersonal Adjective Scales to include the Big Five dimensions of personality (IASR-B5; Trapnell & Wiggins, 1990).

Big Five Assessment, edited by B. De Raad & M. Perugini. © 2002, Hogrefe & Huber Publishers.

Five Factor Model   **Circumplex Model**

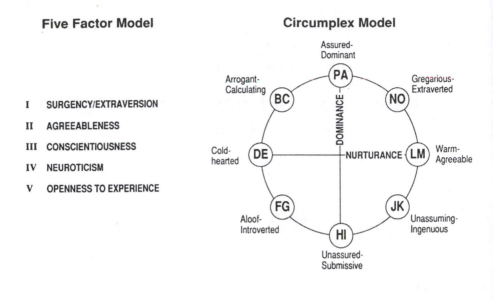

I   SURGENCY/EXTRAVERSION

II   AGREEABLENESS

III   CONSCIENTIOUSNESS

IV   NEUROTICISM

V   OPENNESS TO EXPERIENCE

Figure 1. Five-factor model of personality and circumplex model of interpersonal behavior (from Trapnell & Wiggins, 1990, page 782).

Interpersonal Adjective Scales (IAS)

The Interpersonal Adjective Scales (IAS) were conceived at Oregon Research Institute during the 1970s in a collaborative project with Lewis R. Goldberg. Briefly, Goldberg (1977) had developed his well known *lexical* taxonomy of trait descriptive terms, with adjectives classified according to word usage in self- and other-description, and he was encouraging other investigators to develop alternative taxonomies for comparative purposes. With the help of other investigators at ORI[1], Wiggins developed a *psychological* taxonomy of trait-descriptive terms which was conceptually based (rather than based solely on word meanings). The universe of content here was the 18,125 terms classified by Norman (1967) and further developed by Goldberg (1977). In our taxonomy, what had previously been considered by Goldberg to be a taxon of "stable biophysical traits" was further differentiated into interpersonal traits, material traits, temperamental traits, social roles, character, and mental predicates (Wiggins, 1979). Within the category of approximately 800 interpersonal trait terms, an initial taxonomy was developed with reference to the writings of Timothy Leary (1957). The measurement model adopted to represent this category of traits was the circumplex model of Louis Guttman (1954).

---

[1] James M. Kilkowski and Alexander Galvin.

In the circumplex model, variables are arrayed in a circular fashion around the two orthogonal bipolar axes of dominance/submissiveness and nurturance/coldness. A series of initial attempts to develop circumplex measures for the interpersonal categories described by Leary (1957) were unsuccessful due to notable gaps in coverage and a lack of bipolarity among certain categories presumably located opposite to one another on Leary's circle (Wiggins, 1979, pp. 400-402). Revision of the original Leary categories and new item selection procedures resulted in eight 16-item genuinely bipolar categories. This 128-item version was called the Interpersonal Adjective Scales (IAS) and its empirical circumplex structure was among the best reported in the literature up to that time (Wiggins, Steiger, & Gaelick, 1981).

Interpersonal Adjective Scales — Revised (IAS-R)

The IAS was revised in order to: (a) provide a short-form measure that would make it more convenient for investigators to include the IAS in test batteries and (b) ensure that the two circumplex dimensions were orthogonal to the remaining three dimensions (i.e., Neuroticism, Conscientiousness, and Openness) of the Big Five factors of personality research (Wiggins *et al.*, 1988). With respect to the latter goal, both published and unpublished feedback from colleagues had suggested appropriate modifications. For example, Peabody and Goldberg (1989) had suggested that the ambitious (P) *versus* lazy (H) contrast is not strictly interpersonal in nature and McCrae (personal communication, September 4, 1986) had indicated that a joint factor analysis of the IAS and the NEO-PI confirmed that the IAS ambitious scale was most strongly associated with the NEO Conscientiousness domain. Furthermore, Kiesler (1983) had previously indicated that the P *versus* H contrast was best interpreted as assured (P) *versus* unassured (H). Our revision of IAS-R substantiated Kiesler's interpretation and was in accord with the suggestions of Peabody and Goldberg and with those of McCrae (although the IAS-R P vs. H dimension continues to demonstrate a moderate association with the achievement striving facet of the NEO-PI-R; Costa & McCrae, 1995). The structure of the 64-item version of IAS (IAS-R) is illustrated in Figure 2. This version has been shown to meet the strong geometric and substantive assumptions involved when classifying persons into typological categories (Wiggins, Phillips, & Trapnell, 1989). It is also the version that is available as a commercial test (Wiggins, 1995).

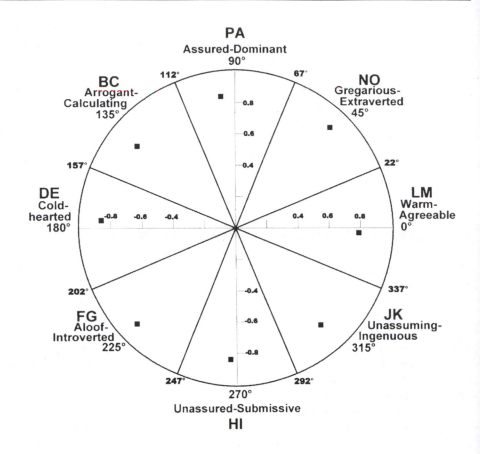

Figure 2. Circumplex structure of revised IAS (from Wiggins, 1995, page 4).

Interpersonal Adjective Scales - Big Five Version (IASR-B5)

Scale construction

Our recognition that the Dominance and Nurturance coordinates of the interpersonal circumplex are rotational variants of the Extraversion and Agreeableness dimensions of the five-factor model (e.g., McCrae & Costa, 1989) led us to construct an adjectival Big Five version of the Interpersonal Adjective Scales (IASR-B5; Trapnell & Wiggins, 1990). Once again, scale construction was based on Goldberg's (1977) seminal item pool of 1,710 trait-descriptive adjectives that was derived from the dictionary studies of Allport and Odbert (1936) and of Norman (1967). We used the portion of Goldberg's data set that included ratings of self-applicability of each of the 1710 adjectives by 187 university undergraduates. Homogeneous clusters of items relating to neuroticism ($N = 30$), conscientiousness ($N = 25$), and openness to experience ($N = 44$) were selected from this data set that were identical to or close synonyms of adjectives found to have high factor loadings in previous factor-analytic studies (e.g., Goldberg, 1985; McCrae & Costa, 1985). These three clusters were supplemented by items not included in the 1,710 item list (primarily negations of high loading items) and the total item set was administered to two new samples of 581 and 360 undergraduates. The 10 highest loading positive and the 10 highest loading negative items were retained within each factor (see Trapnell & Wiggins, 1990).

Three 20-item balanced scales of neuroticism, conscientiousness, and openness to experience, together with our previously developed circumplex measure of dominance and nurturance, constitute the final version of IASR-B5. It should be noted that in the present version of the IASR-B5 (available from the authors) the first 64 items are identical in format, item order, and glossary to the those found in the commercial version of the IAS. Thus, all findings with respect to the eight octant scales and circumplex of IAS-R (e.g., Wiggins, 1995) apply *in toto* to the eight octant scales and circumplex of IASR-B5.

The final version of IASR-B5 therefore consists of 124 adjectives that are rated for self-descriptiveness on an eight-place Likert scale ranging from "1 = extremely inaccurate" to "8 = extremely accurate". The first 64 adjectives comprise the Dominance and Nurturance factors underlying the interpersonal circumplex and are used to score the eight octants (i.e., eight items per octant) of the Interpersonal Adjective Scales (Wiggins, 1995). Weighted combinations of these octant scores may then be computed for those wishing to work with factor scores. High loading Dominance items include dominant, assertive, domineering, and forceful, and high loading Nurturance items include tenderhearted, kind, charitable, and sympathetic.

The remaining 60 items of the IASR-B5 comprise the Neuroticism, Openness, and Conscientious factors (i.e., 20 items per factor, half of which are reverse-scored). High loading Neuroticism items include worrying, tense, anxious, and nervous. High loading Openness items include philosophical, inquisitive, imaginative, and abstract-thinking. And high scoring Conscientiousness items include organized, tidy, orderly, and planful.

The IASR-B5 takes approximately 20 minutes to complete and a glossary is provided to each respondent to ensure knowledge of word meanings. Although the IASR-B5 has primarily been used as a self-report inventory, more recent research has suggested that it may also be used in peer-report format. The IASR-B5 is suitable for use in research, industry, and clinical settings, although it is best employed among more educated respondents because a 10th grade reading level is required.

Table 1. Principal components of five-factor domain scales.

Scale	I	II	III	IV	V
Extraversion (NEO)	.84				
Dominance (IAS)	.82				
Sociability (HPI)	.81				
Ambition (HPI)	.71		.38		
Neuroticism (NEO)		.92			
Neuroticism (IAS)		.89			
Adjustment (HPI)		-.84			
Openness (IAS)			.85		
Openness (NEO)			.80	.35	
Intellect (HPI)			.72		
Love (IAS)				.83	
Agreeableness (NEO)				.81	
Likability (HPI)	.45			.68	
Conscientiousness (IAS)					.84
Conscientiousness (NEO)					.83
Prudence (HPI)					.65

Note: Adapted from Wiggins and Pincus (1994, p. 84). N = 581; loadings < .33 omitted. NEO = NEO Personality Inventory; IAS = Extended Interpersonal Adjective Scales; HPI = Hogan Personality Inventory.

Psychometric characteristics

Convergent and discriminant validity

The convergent and discriminant validities of the IASR-B5 were established (Wiggins & Pincus, 1994) with reference to a sample of 581 undergraduates who had been administered the NEO-PI (Costa & McCrae, 1985), the Hogan Personality Inventory (HPI; Hogan, 1986), and the IASR-B5 (Trapnell & Wiggins, 1990). These findings appear in Table 1. Overall, it was concluded that IASR-B5 has an excellent structure on the item level, internally consistent scales, and promising convergent and discriminant properties when compared with the NEO Personality Inventory and the Hogan Personality Inventory (Trapnell & Wiggins, 1990).

Peer ratings

Costa and McCrae (1995) administered the Revised NEO Personality Inventory in peer rating format to 380 participants (aged 19 to 96) in the Baltimore Longitudinal

Table 2. Correlations of Wiggins' and Goldberg's measures with NEO-PI-R facets in peer ratings

NEO-PI-R Facet Scale	N		E		O		A		C	
	W	G	W	G	W	G	W	G	W	G
N1: Anxiety	.72	.47								
N2: Angry Hostility	.68	.66					-.54	-.61		
N3: Depression	.61	.43								
N4: Self-Consciousness	.48		-.43							
N5: Impulsiveness										
N6: Vulnerability	.62	.44	-.40							-.41
E1: Warmth				.42			.57	.52		
E2: Gregariousness			.54	.46						
E3: Assertiveness			.84	.52						
E4: Activity			.54	.42						
E5: Excitement Seeking										
E6: Positive Emotions				.45			.52			
O1: Fantasy										
O2: Aesthetics						.49				
O3: Feelings										
O4: Actions			.40							
O5: Ideas					.78	.50				
O6: Values										
A1: Trust	-.45	-.59					.66	.66		
A2: Straightforwardness		-.61	-.52				.57	.60		
A3: Altruism		-.44					.75	.68		
A4: Compliance		-.57	-.64				.48	.64		
A5: Modesty		-.50	-.47				.51	.64		
A6: Tender-Mindedness							.57	.57		
C1: Competence						.43			.61	.57
C2: Order									.74	.51
C3: Dutifulness									.56	.59
C4: Achievement Striving			.47						.46	.54
C5: Self-Discipline									.72	.64
C6: Deliberation									.45	.45

Note: Adapted from Costa & McCrae (1995, p. 35). NEO-PI-R = Revised NEO Personality Inventory, N = Neuroticism, E = Extraversion, O = Openness to Experience, A = Agreeableness, C = Conscientiousness, W = Wiggins' Revised Interpersonal Adjective Scales - Big Five Version (IASR-B5), G = Goldberg's Transparent Trait Rating Form (TTRF). N = 150 for IASR-B5, N = 128 for TTRF. Correlations above ± .40 are given; all are significant at $p < .001$.

Study of Aging. Peer ratings were also obtained from some of these participants on either the Goldberg (1992) Big Five transparent adjectival markers ($N = 150$) or the IASR-B5 ($N = 128$). Table 2 presents the correlations of Wiggins' and Goldberg's measures with NEO-PI-R facets in these peer ratings.

Table 3. Internal consistency of IAS scales (Cronbach's alpha).

	Sample	
	Adult*	College student
IAS Scale	(N = 1,083)	(N = 2,825)
Assured-Dominant (PA)	.790	.848
Arrogant-Calculating (BC)	.865	.841
Cold-hearted (DE)	.810	.841
Aloof-Introverted (FG)	.840	.860
Unassured-Submissive (HI)	.815	.852
Unassuming-Ingenuous (JK)	.755	.733
Warm-Agreeable (LM)	.850	.865
Gregarious-Extraverted (NO)	.835	.843

Note: Adapted from Wiggins (1995, p. 44); * Adult sample includes employment selection, BLSA, and volunteer samples.

With the exception of the Openness dimension, the facets of the NEO-PI-R are reasonably well represented in both the Goldberg (G) and the Wiggins (W) adjectival scales. With respect to the Openness to Experience dimension, the IASR-B5 shares the Goldberg approach of focusing primarily upon cognitive aspects (i.e., intellect or ideas) of openess, unlike the broader approach of the NEO-PI-R that assesses additional facets. Also, the Goldberg and Wiggins scales provide substantial markers of Neuroticism facets, although the Goldberg scales might also be considered a negative measure of NEO-PI-R Agreeableness. Similarly, the Wiggins' measure of Extraversion is negatively loaded on NEO-PI-R Agreeableness. In general, however, the IASR-B5 performs well under peer-rating instructions with respect to the NEO-PI-R.

Internal consistency of IASR-B5 self-report

The results of studies of the internal consistency of the eight interpersonal adjective scales of IAS-R apply to IASR-B5 for reasons already discussed. Table 3 presents Cronbach's alpha coefficients in an adult sample (N = 1,083) consisting of an employment selection group, a sample from the Baltimore Longitudinal Study of Aging, and a volunteer sample of adults. Alpha coefficients were also computed in a university sample (N = 2,825). With the possible exception of the Unassuming-Ingenuous scale (JK), the coefficients of internal consistency are substantial[2]. Internal consistency coefficients were also reported by Trapnell and Wiggins (1989), based on a sample of 941 undergraduates, for Neuroticism, Conscientiousness, and Openness to Experience. A later analysis is also available, however, based on a much larger sample (N = 2,825), in which alphas were: .90 for Neuroticism; .93 for Conscientiousness; and, .87 for Openness.

---

[2] The relative lack of internal consistency of the IAS-R JK scale would appear to reflect on the dimension itself rather than on the measuring instrument. A preliminary review of the literature strongly suggested that this dimension tends to be the least internally consistent for almost all circumplex measures, regardless of content.

Table 4. Internal and temporal reliability estimates for informant ratings using IAS.

	Time 1[a]			Time 2[a]					
	M	SD	∝	M	SD	∝	Retest r	ES	SEM
Dominance Coordinate (DOM)	0.59	1.17	--[b]	0.45	0.96	--[b]	.75	-.13	0.53
Nurturance Coordinate (LOV)	0.66	1.59	--[b]	0.86	1.40	--[b]	.73	.13	0.83
Octant Scales:									
Assured-Dominant (PA)	5.3	1.1	.85	5.3	1.0	.80	.67	.05	.064
Arrogant-Calculating (BC)	3.1	1.5	.91	3.0	1.5	.92	.71	-.06	.083
Cold-hearted (DE)	2.1	1.2	.88	2.2	1.1	.91	.67	.09	.068
Aloof-Introverted (FG)	2.1	1.1	.89	2.2	1.1	.88	.70	.12	.060
Unassured-Submissive (HI)	3.0	1.2	.85	2.9	1.2	.86	.64	-.05	.074
Unassuming-Ingenuous (JK)	4.7	1.4	.83	4.9	1.3	.84	.62	.14	.088
Warm-Agreeable (LM) *	6.3	1.2	.92	6.1	1.2	.91	.69	-.15	.067
Gregarious-Extraverted (NO)	6.6	1.0	.89	6.4	1.0	.87	.70	-.12	.057

Note: Adapted from Kurtz *et al.* (1999, p. 108). IAS = Interpersonal Adjective Scales; Time 1 = first administration; Time 2 = second administration 6 months after Time 1; ES = effect size for mean score change; SEM = standard error of measurement; [a] *N* = 109. [b] Coefficient alpha was not computed for DOM and LOV coordinates, since these are weighted composites of the octant scores; * *p* < .05 for mean score difference between Time 1 and Time 2.

Internal consistency and temporal stability of IAS-R informant ratings[3]

Because it is both brief and comprehensive, IAS-R is well suited for use in peer-rating and spouse-rating studies, particularly those calling for repeated measurements. In this respect, Kurtz, Lee, and Sherker (1999) have provided important data regarding both the internal consistency and temporal stability of informant ratings based on IAS-R. The findings of Kurtz *et al.* are reproduced in Table 4 in which alpha coefficients are provided for both Time 1 and Time 2 (separated by six months), as well as retest correlations.

The mean values for the Dominance (DOM) and Nurturance (LOV) coordinates reported in Table 4 were calculated employing geometric formulae of weighted octant z-scores where DOM = $.3[(zPA - zHI) + .707(zNO + zBC - zFG - zJK)]$ and LOV = $.3[(zLM - zDE) + .707(zNO - zBC - zFG + zJK)]$ (see Wiggins, 1995, p. 17). The alpha coefficients are substantial for both Time 1 and Time 2 and the retest coefficients are moderate (range .62 to .71). One of the more important values for personality appraisal with IAS-R is the *angular location* which provides a directional summary of an individual's self-report (or of an informant's report) and thereby indicates the typological octant in which these reports may be classified. To the extent that these angular locations vary over time, an important change has taken place in the individual's self-view (or in the informant's view of the individual). Kurtz *et al.* (1999) provide an excellent discussion of this issue as it relates to diagnostic classification with IAS-R.

---

[3] Such information is currently available only for the circumplex portion and not for the N, C, and O components of IASR-B5.

Circumplex measures of personality may be used to classify or diagnose an individual as being a certain "type", depending on the octant in which the individual's DOM and LOV scores fall, and as expressing that type with differing degrees of clarity or intensity (vector length). It is therefore expected that the temporal stability of both self- and other-reported types will be related to vector length. An extremely extraverted person with substantial vector length is likely to be classified as falling within the NO octant six months or even six years from now. An individual with a much smaller vector length will not have a clear pattern of scores and therefore will be more likely to be classified within a different octant on re-testing. Thus, in Kurtz *et al.*'s (1999) sample "Stability of Angular Location was found to vary inversely and significantly with Vector Length at Time 1 ($r = -.43$; $p < .001$) and Time 2 ($r = -.36$; $p < .001$)" (p. 109).

As a consequence of the above relations, less than half of these respondents remained classified in their original octants on re-testing six months later. This situation is not peculiar to circumplex analysis and it will be encountered whenever respondents fail to report, or are perceived not to have, a "distinctive personality". Kurtz *et al.* recommended that IAS-R not be used to classify respondents with vector length scores less than 60 and they emphasized that IAS-R classification is generally more appropriate for clinical groups, particularly personality disorders.

IASR-B5 and the personality disorders

". . . the recently discovered success of the FFM in clarifying psychiatric conceptions of personality disorders in DSM-III-R (Costa & Widiger, 1994) must be attributed in large part to the two circumplex dimensions of that model which stem from a clinical tradition which has already served a similar function for the personality disorders of DSM-I (e.g., Leary, 1957), DSM-II (e.g., Plutchik & Platman, 1977), and DSM-III (e.g., Wiggins, 1982)" (Wiggins & Trapnell, 1996, p. 89).

MMPI personality disorder scales

Morey, Waugh, and Blashfield (1985) developed MMPI scales for the eleven personality disorders described in DSM-III (American Psychiatric Association, 1980). Under a combined rational/empirical strategy, MMPI items were assembled into both overlapping and non-overlapping sets of eleven scales. The then current research on these MMPI personality disorder scales was reviewed in a symposium held at the 1987 meetings of the American Psychological Association (Greene, 1987). At that symposium, Wiggins (1987) presented the results of a study designed to evaluate the hypothesis that the MMPI personality disorder scales may be construed within the framework of a circumplex model of personality. Two prior studies suggested this hypothesis: (a) Schaefer (1961) had made a convincing case for the interpretation of the two-dimensional structure of the MMPI as a circumplex of clinical scales and (b) Plutchik and Platman (1977) had demonstrated that when psychiatrists rated seven personality disorder labels from DSM-II on twelve interpersonal trait terms, the first two components extracted from the intercorrelations among trait terms exhibited a clear circumplex structure. Wiggins (1987) found support for these earlier findings, but emphasized that "Although the MMPI personality disorder scales are likely to have interpersonal correlates, the dimensions of dominance and nurturance are unlikely to capture other non-interpersonal characteristics associated with these scales. A more appropriate frame of reference for examining the content of these scales is provided by the so-called "Big Five" dimensions of personality."

An extensive multitrait-multimethod investigation of this topic was later conducted by Wiggins and Pincus (1989). A sample of 581 university students were administered the MMPI personality disorder scales developed by Morey *et al.* (1985) as well as the personality disorder scales of the Personality Adjective Check List developed by Strack (1987). Participants also completed the NEO Personality Inventory (NEO-PI; Costa & McCrae, 1985) and the Interpersonal Adjective Scales—Big 5 version (IASR-B5; Trapnell & Wiggins, 1990). Clear and meaningful projections of the personality disorder scales of Morey *et al.* and of Strack onto the IASR-B5 circumplex were found for the histrionic, dependent, avoidant, schizoid, and narcissistic disorders. These encouraging findings were qualified by the statement: "Although the circumplex model illuminated conceptions of some of the disorders, the full 5-factor model was required to capture and clarify the entire range of personality disorders" (Wiggins & Pincus, 1989, p. 305).

Within five years time, this conclusion had become canonical (e.g., Costa & Widiger, 1994).

Profile analysis

The expanded profile analysis obtained from the combination of the five-factor and circumplex components of the IASR-B5 made possible a more comprehensive diagnostic device than was available with either component alone. Figure 3 displays the IASR-B5 profiles of high scoring respondents on each of three MMPI personality disorder scales: avoidant ($N = 44$), schizoid ($N = 50$), and antisocial ($N = 50$) from a study by Trapnell & Wiggins (1990). As a group, the antisocial respondents clearly fell within the cold-hearted octant, the schizoid respondents fell within the aloof-introverted octant, and the avoidant respondents fell within the unassured-submissive octant.

Although standard circumplex analysis would end at this point, the IASR-B5 profile provides additional structural information in the bar graphs for neuroticism, conscientiousness, and openness to experience. Here it is apparent that: neuroticism further distinguishes avoidant from schizoid respondents; avoidant respondents are somewhat less conscientious than schizoid respondents; and antisocial respondents are quite low on conscientiousness. A final distinguishing feature of avoidant respondents is that they are closed to experience in comparison with schizoid and antisocial groups.

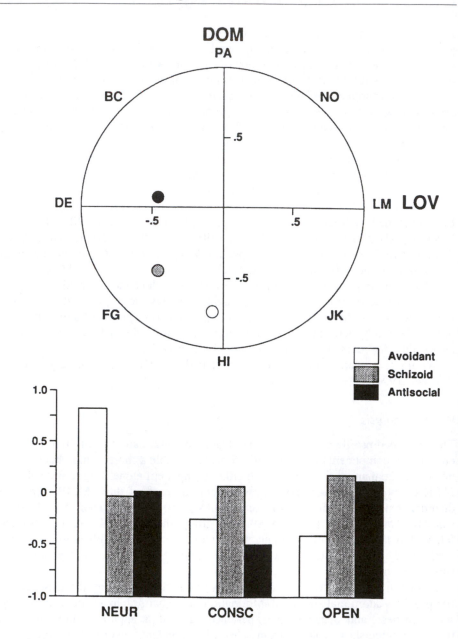

Figure 3. IASR-B5 profiles of respondents scoring high on MMPI personality disorder scales: Avoidant (*N* = 44), Schizoid (*N* = 50), and Antisocial (*N* = 62)(from Trapnell & Wiggins, 1990, page 789).

Other applications of IASR-B5

The circumplex portion of the IASR-B5 (i.e., IAS or IAS-R) has been used extensively in clinical, social, and personality research; the interested reader may consult the IAS manual (Wiggins, 1995) or Wiggins and Trobst (1997) for details. Here we will restrict our review to those published studies that have employed the full IASR-B5.

The brevity of IASR-B5 and the extent to which it provides markers of both the five-factor and circumplex structures make it a highly efficient tool for pilot and exploratory studies of new domains. The complete IAS-R remains intact within this instrument and thus provides a measure of eight interpersonal dimensions of central importance to personality and social psychology (Wiggins & Broughton, 1985), is ideally suited for repeated testing, mass screening, and exploratory investigations (Wiggins *et al.*, 1988), and may be confidently used for classification of persons into typological categories (Wiggins *et al.*, 1989). The IASR-B5 markers of the remaining three dimensions of the five-factor model are less comprehensive, but they are sufficiently related to more comprehensive measures of the Big Five to serve in an exploratory capacity in pilot studies of new domains.

The IASR-B5 has served as a criterion measure for evaluating the validity of other instruments such as the NEO-PI-R (Caldwell-Andrews, Baer, & Berry, 2000), as a marker in the development of other self-report measures such as psychopathy scales (Hill, 2000), and as an observer form in comparing university students and incarcerated offenders (Hart & Hare, 1994). IASR-B5 has also served as a frame of reference for evaluating the (limited) range of behaviors assessed by a variety of social support measures (Trobst, 2000). An Italian language version of IASR-B5 has been developed (Di Blas, 2000) and has been related to other Italian markers of the Big Five (Perugini, Gallucci, & Livi, 2000). Gallo and Smith (1999) used IASR-B5 to classify the distinctions among aggressive traits in Buss and Perry's (1992) Aggression Questionnaire.

Three studies of IASR-B5 stand out, in particular, for their non-obvious and/or surprising results. Sear and Stephenson (1997) assessed the interviewing performance and skill of 19 police officers attached to a London Metropolitan Police Department. They filled out police interview evaluation forms for four audiotaped interviews by each of 19 officers (76 interviews in total). All officers were also administered the IASR-B5. Results indicated that only Openness was significantly associated with interviewing skill but in the opposite direction to that predicted. The more skillful police interviewers were *closed* to experience.

The distributive justice dilemma is a classic paradigm for studying moral responses to a task that involves allocating money to self and three others and making judgments about such allocation behaviors. In an interesting study of this dilemma, Day (1998) randomly assigned 106 female and 95 male university students to one of three conditions: (1) a group that responded to a hypothetical dilemma, (2) a group that responded to a real situation with play money, or (3) a group that responded to a real situation with real money. Participants also completed the Moral Judgment Interview (MJI; Colby & Kohlberg, 1987) and the IASR-B5. In these situations, Openness scores on IASR-B5 were as predictive of allocation behavior as were responses to the Moral Judgment Interview!

Fehr and Broughton (2001) have demonstrated the utility of IASR-B5 in clarifying typologies of love, a topic that had previously been investigated almost exclusively within a social psychological framework. Earlier, Berscheid and Hatfield (1974) had made an influential distinction between *passionate* love (characterized by intense emotions, physiological arousal, and strong sexual attraction) and *companionate* love (deep affectional bonds based on trust, respect, caring, and honesty). In a university student sample, Fehr and Broughton administered IASR-B5 and the Views of Love Questionnaire (Fehr, 1994), in which respondents rate how similar their own view of love is to descriptions of 15 different types of love. The projections of these types of love onto the IASR circumplex were quite revealing; for example, romantic love fell near the center of the arrogant-calculating octant (BC), sexual love fell near the center of the cold-hearted octant (DE), maternal love fell near the center of the unassuming-ingenuous octant (JK), and parental love fell near the center of the gregarious-extraverted octant (NO). Correlations of types of love with the remaining three dimensions of the Big Five were equally interesting. For example, passionate kinds of love (e.g., sexual love, infatuation) were positively correlated with neuroticism, and companionate kinds of love (emphasizing emotional stability and calmness) were negatively related to neuroticism. Openness to experience was negatively related to committed love, especially for men.

The revised Interpersonal Adjective Scales (IAS-R) provide a well documented assessment of the two major dimensions of interpersonal behavior (e.g., Wiggins 1995). The remaining three scales of personality included in IASR-B5 provide well established markers of neuroticism, conscientiousness and openness to experience as documented here and elsewhere (e.g., Trapnell & Wiggins, 1990). Taken together in IASR-B5, these dimensions provide a highly useful preliminary survey of dimensions of personality that has proved helpful in a variety of different contexts.

Personality and interpersonal behavior

In a highly integrative and informative paper, McCrae and Costa (1989) characterized the relations between the interpersonal circumplex, as measured by the IAS (Wiggins, 1979) and the five-factor model of personality, as measured by the NEO Personality Inventory (Costa & McCrae, (1985).

The circumplex is intended to include only dispositions related to interpersonal interactions (Wiggins, 1979); the five-factor model aims at comprehensiveness and so includes affective, experiential, and motivational traits as well as interpersonal traits (McCrae & Costa, 1989, p. 586). McCrae and Costa (1989) also indicated that *love* and *status*, the conceptual underpinnings of the interpersonal circumplex ". . . are essentially interactional concepts that describe the relationships between two individuals; they are useful in the analysis of enduring social roles or dynamic social encounters. . . *Love and status are not, however, necessarily the best concepts for understanding enduring dispositions in individuals"* (p. 591, emphasis added).

The five-factor model of personality has been interpreted from several rather different theoretical perspectives (Wiggins, 1996) and one of these views, the "dyadic interactional perspective" (Wiggins & Trapnell, 1996), is clearly at variance with the position of McCrae and Costa just described. Earlier, Wiggins (1991) had argued that the broad philosophical concepts of *agency* and *communion* (Bakan, 1966) should serve as conceptual coordinates for the understanding and measurement of interpersonal behavior. More recently, Wiggins and Trapnell (1996) argued that agency and communion may be clearly identified in the two higher-order factors of the five-factor model (FFM). Our argument was based, in part, on Digman's (1997) extensive series of higher-order factor analyses of the FFM in which he indicated the fruitfulness of such an interpretation. This work may be summarized as demonstrating that love (communion) and status (agency) are indeed fruitful concepts for understanding enduring dispositions in individuals.

Conclusions

As will surely be apparent to any reader of this book, there are multiple approaches to the measurement and interpretation of the five-factor model of personality. What differentiates the IASR-B5 from other FFM inventories is its emphasis upon the interpersonal domain and the psychometric precision provided by circumplex assessment. To the rich literature of correlates of the FFM, the interpersonal circumplex approach adds a similarly rich literature of correlates of the interpersonal circumplex (see Kiesler, 1996). The structure of the circumplex allows for simultaneous examination of dominant and nurturant tendencies and in so doing provides not only dimensional, but also categorical information and an assessment of the rigidity of interpersonal expression (Wiggins, 1995). With this as its strong suit, the IASR-B5 might be preferentially employed when one is interested in the nature and character of interpersonal interaction in functional or dysfunctional form.

References

Allport, G.W., & Odbert, H.S. (1936). Trait-names: A psycho-lexical study. *Psychological Monographs, 47* (1, Whole No. 211).

American Psychiatric Association (1980). *Diagnostic and statistical manual of mental disorders* (3rd ed.). Washington, DC: Author.

Bakan, D. (1966). *The duality of human existence: Isolation and communion in Western man*. Boston: Beacon.

Buss, A.H., & Perry, M. (1992). The Aggression Questionnaire. *Journal of Personality and Social Psychology, 63*, 452-459.

Caldwell-Andrews, A., Baer, R.A., & Berry, D.T. (2000). Effects of response sets on NEO-PI-R scores and their relations with external criteria. *Journal of Personality Assessment, 74*, 472-488.

Carson, R.C. (1969). *Interaction concepts of personality*. Chicago: Aldine.

Colby, A., & Kohlberg, L. (1987). *The measurement of moral judgment: Vol 1. Theoretical foundations and research validation*. New York: Cambridge University Press.

Costa, P.T., Jr., & McCrae, R.R. (1985). *The NEO Personality Inventory manual*. Odessa, FL: Psychological Assessment Resources.

Costa, P. T., Jr., & McCrae, R. R. (1995). Domains and facets: Hierarchical personality assessment using the revised NEO Personality Inventory. *Journal of Personality Assessment, 64*, 21-50.

Costa, P.T., Jr., & Widiger, T. (1994). (Eds.), *Personality disorders and the five-factor model of personality*. Washington, DC: American Psychological Association.

Day, R.W.C. (1998). Relations between moral reasoning, personality traits, and justice decisions on hypothetical and real-life moral dilemmas (Doctoral Dissertation, Simon-Fraser University, Canada). *Dissertation Abstracts International, 58*, 6795.

Di Blas, L. (2000). A validation study of the interpersonal circumplex scales in the Italian language. *European Journal of Psychological Assessment, 16*, 177-189.

Digman, J.M. (1997). Higher-order factors of the Big Five. *Journal of Personality and Social Psychology, 73*, 1246-1256.

Berscheid, E. & Hatfield, E. (1974). A little bit about love. In T.L. Huston (Ed.), *Foundations of interpersonal attraction* (pp.355-381). New York: Academic Press.

Fehr, B. (1994). Prototype-based assessment of laypeople's view of love. *Personal Relationships, 1*, 309-331.

Fehr, B., & Broughton, R. (2001). Gender and personality differences in conceptions of love: An interpersonal theory analysis. *Personal Relationships, 8*, 115-136.

Gallo, L.C., & Smith, T.W. (1999). Construct validation of health-related personality traits: Interpersonal circumplex and five-factor analyses of the Aggression Questionnaire. *International Journal of Behavioral Medicine, 5*, 129-147.

Goldberg, L.R. (1977, August). *Language and personality: Developing a taxonomy of trait-descriptive terms*. Paper presented to the Division of Evaluation and Measurement at the annual meeting of the American Psychological Association, San Francisco.

Goldberg, L.R. (1992). The development of markers for the Big-Five factor structure. *Psychological Assessment, 4*, 26-42.

Greene, R.L. (Chair). (1987, September). *Current research on MMPI personality disorder scales*. Symposium conducted at the meeting of the American Psychological Association, New York.

Guttman, L. (1954). A new approach to factor analysis: The radex. In P.R. Lazarsfeld (Ed.), *Mathematical thinking in the social sciences* (pp. 258-348). Glencoe, IL: Free Press.

Guttman, L. (1966). Order analysis of correlation matrices. In R.B. Cattell (Ed.), *Handbook of multivariate experimental psychology* (pp. 438-458). Chicago: Rand McNally.

Hart, S.D., & Hare, R.D. (1994). Psychopathy and the Big 5: Correlations between observers' ratings of normal and pathological personality. *Journal of Personality Disorders, 8*, 32-40.

Hill, J.K. (2000). Development of a psychopathy self-report measure (Social Personality Inventory) (Doctoral Dissertation, University of Saskatchewan, Canada, 2000). *Dissertation Abstracts International, 60*, Z5055.

Hogan, R. (1986). *Hogan Personality Inventory*. Minneapolis, MN: National Computer Systems.

John, O.P., Angleitner, A., & Ostenforf, F. (1988). The lexical approach to personaltiy: A historical review of trait taxonomic research. *European Journal of Personality, 2,* 17-203.

Kiesler, D.J. (1983). The 1982 Interpersonal Circle: : A taxonomy for complementarity in human transactions. *Psychological Review, 90,* 185-214.

Kiesler, D.J. (1996). *Contemporary interpersonal theory and research: Personality, psychopathology, and psychotherapy.* New York: Wiley.

Kurtz, J.E., Lee, P.A., & Sherker, J.L. (1999). Internal and temporal reliability estimants for informant ratings of personality using NEO PI-R and IAS. *Assessment, 6,* 103-113.

Leary, T. (1957). *Interpersonal diagnosis of personality.* New York: Ronald Press.

McCrae, R.R., & Costa, P.T., Jr. (1989). The structure of interpersonal traits: Wiggins' circumplex and the five-factor model. *Journal of Personality and Social Psychology, 56,* 586-595.

Morey, L.C., Waugh, M.H., & Blashfield, R.K. (1985). MMPI scales for DSM-III personality disorders: Their derivation and correlates. *Journal of Personality Assessment, 49,* 245-251.

Norman, W.T. (1967). *2800 personality trait descriptors: Normative operating characteristics in a university population.* Department of Psychology, University of Michigan, Ann Arbor.

Peabody, D., & Goldberg, L.R. (1989). Some determinants of factor structures from personality trait-descriptors. *Journal of Personality and Social Psychology, 57,* 552-567.

Perugini, M., Gallucci, M., & Livi, S. (2000). Looking for a simple five factorial structure in the domain of adjectives. *European Journal of Psychological Assessment, 16,* 87-97.

Plutchik, R., & Platman, S.R. (1977). Personality connotations of psychiatric diagnosis: Implications for a similarity model. *Journal of Nervous and Mental Disease, 165,* 418-422.

Schaefer, E.S. (1961). Converging conceptual models for maternal behavior and for child behavior. *Parental attitudes and child behavior* (pp. 124-146). Springfield, IL: Charles C Thomas.

Sear. L., & Stephenson, G.M. (1997). Interviewing skills and individual characteristics of police investigators. *Issues in Criminological and Legal Psychology,* No. 29, 27-34.

Strack, S. (1987). Development and validation of an adjective checklist to assess the Millon personality types in a normal population. *Journal of Personality Assessment, 51,* 572-587.

Trapnell, P.D., & Wiggins, J.S. (1990). Extension of the Interpersonal Adjective Scales to include the Big Five dimensions of personality. *Journal of Personality and Social Psychology, 59,* 781-790.

Trobst, K.K. (2000). An interpersonal conceptualization and quantification of social support transactions. *Personality and Social Psychology Bulletin, 26,* 971-986.

Wiggins, J.S. (1979). A psychological taxonomy of trait-descriptive terms: The interpersonal domain. *Journal of Personality and Social Psychology, 37,* 395-412.

Wiggins, J.S. (1982). Circumplex models of interpersonal behavior in clinical psychology. In P.C. Kendall & J.N. Butcher (Eds.), *Handbook of research methods in clinical psychology* (pp. 183-221). New York: Wiley.

Wiggins, J.S. (1987, September). How interpersonal are the MMPI personality disorder scales? In R.L. Greene (Chair), *Current research on MMPI personality disorder scales.* Symposium conducted at the meeting of the American Psychological Association, New York.

Wiggins, J.S. (1991). Agency and communion as conceptual coordinates for the understanding and measurement of interpersonal behavior. In W. Grove & D. Cicchetti (Eds.),
Thinking clearly about psychology: Essays in honor of Paul E. Meehl (Vol. 2, pp. 89-
1130.

Wiggins, J.S. (1995). *Interpersonal Adjective Scales: Professional manual*. Odessa, FL:
Psychological Assessment Resources, Inc.

Wiggins, J.S. (Ed.)(1996). *The five-factor model of personality: Theoretical perspectives*.
New York: Guilford Press.

Wiggins, J.S., & Broughton, R. (1985). The interpersonal circle: A structural model for the
integration of personality research. In R. Hogan & W. H. Jones (Eds.), *Perspectives in
personality* (Vol. 1, pp. 1-47). Greenwich, CT: JAI Press.

Wiggins, J.S., Phillips, N., & Trapnell, P. (1989) Circular reasoning about interpersonal
behavior: Evidence concerning some untested assumptions underlying diagnostic classification. *Journal of Personality and Social Psychology, 56*, 296-305.

Wiggins, J.S., & Pincus, A.L. (1989). Conceptions of personality disorders and dimensions
of personality. *Psychological Assessment, 1*, 305-316.

Wiggins, J.S., & Pincus, A.L. (1992). Personality: Structure and assessment. In M. R. Rosenzweig & L.W. Porter (Eds.), *Annual review of psychology* (Vol. 43, pp. 473-504).
Palo Alto, CA: Annual Reviews, Inc.

Wiggins, J.S., & Pincus, A.L. (1994). Personality structure and the structure of personality
disorders. In P.T. Costa, Jr., & T. A. Widiger (Eds.), *Personality disorders and the five-
factor model of personality* (pp. 73-93). Washington, DC: American Psychological Association.

Wiggins, J.S., Steiger, J.H., & Gaelick, L. (1981). Evaluating circumplexity in personality
data. *Multivariate Behavioral Research, 16*, 263-289.

Wiggins, J.S., & Trapnell, P.T. (1996). A dyadic-interactional perspective on the five-factor
model. In J. S. Wiggins (Ed.), *The five-factor model of personality: Theoretical perspectives* (pp. 88-162). New York : Guilford Press.

Wiggins, J.S., & Trapnell, P.T. (1997). Personality structure: The return of the Big Five. In
R. Hogan, J. Johnson, & S. Briggs (Eds.), *Handbook of personality psychology* (pp. 737-
765). San Diego: Academic Press.

Wiggins, J.S., Trapnell, P., & Phillips, N. (1988). Psychometric and geometric characteristics of the revised Interpersonal Adjective Scales (IAS-R). *Multivariate Behavioral Research, 23*, 517-530.

Wiggins, J.S., & Trobst, K.K. (1997). Prospects for the assessment of normal and abnormal
interpersonal behavior. In J. A. Schinka & R. L. Greene (Eds.), *Emerging issues and
methods in personality assessment* (pp. 113-129). Mahwah, NJ: Erlbaum.

Chapter 12

The Big Five Marker Scales (BFMS) and the Italian AB5C taxonomy: Analyses from an etic-emic perspective

Marco Perugini
Lisa Di Blas

Introduction

In recent years several psycholexical studies to uncover the main personality factors have been undertaken in different languages and countries such as the USA, Germany, The Netherlands, Hungary, Turkey, Japan, and Korea (for recent reviews, see De Raad, 2000; Saucier, Goldberg, & Hampson, 2000). While these studies shared many commonalities, some procedural differences were also present. Italy represented a unique situation: two independent psycholexical projects were conducted in the same language by using different approaches. These two studies have already been compared in some detail elsewhere (De Raad, Di Blas, & Perugini, 1998; Di Blas & Perugini, 2001). In this chapter, after a brief description of the two independent projects and a comparison of their results, we merge the data. The final result is given in the form of a new adjective list offering a brief measure of the Big Five. This list, named the Big Five Marker Scales (BFMS), has two specific main features: a) it represents an optimal Big Five structure, with optimality meaning a factorially simple structure, and b) it can be used to map all other personality descriptive terms, henceforth providing a comprehensive taxonomy of personality descriptors in the Italian language.

Big Five Assessment, edited by B. De Raad & M. Perugini. © 2002, Hogrefe & Huber Publishers.

The two Italian projects

The first psycholexical study was conducted in Rome, the capital of Italy located in the center of the country, by Perugini and Caprara. Starting with an abridged dictionary, they finally selected a pool of 492 personality relevant–adjectives (Perugini, 1993; Caprara & Perugini, 1994). The pool was chosen on the basis of lay judges' implicit conceptions of personality, a criterion already applied in the Dutch lexical project (Brokken, 1978). The 492 adjectives were then administered for a self-rating task to 274 participants. Factor analyses were performed on the data set, and results indicated five dimensions only approximately comparable to the American Big Five. In a second study, the set of adjectives was reduced to 285 by discarding adjectives with low communalities in the five-factor solution of the first study and adding a few adjectives. The 285 adjectives were administered to 961 participants, who provided self- and peer-ratings. A five-factor solution again emerged, with factors called Extraversion/Energy, Conscientiousness, Quietness, Selfishness, and Conventionality. The first two closely resembled the Big Five factors Extraversion (I) and Conscientiousness (III); of the other three, Quietness and Selfishness were shown to be rotational variants of the Big Five factors Agreeableness (II) and Neuroticism (IV). Finally, Conventionality resembled more the fifth of the Dutch lexical dimensions rather then the fifth of the more common psycholexical Big Five (Intellect).

The other psycholexical research was conducted in Trieste, which is located in the North-East of Italy, very close to Slovenia and Croatia. Differently from the Roman project, Di Blas and Forzi (1998) firstly reduced a large set of person adjectives on the basis of lay judges' implicit conceptions, and secondly they further selected the adjectives by applying the categorization system of the German lexical project (Angleitner, Ostendorf, & John, 1990). Di Blas and Forzi collected 427 self-ratings and 277 other ratings on the final set of 314 adjectives, and performed factor analyses on the pooled data sets. Results showed a stable three-factor solution, resembling the Big Three of Peabody and Goldberg (1989). A five-factor solution yielded Conscientiousness, Assertiveness, Sociability, Quietness/Placidity, and Tendermindedness. These findings were replicated in subsequent taxonomic studies. In particular, Di Blas and Forzi (1999) used a broader set of personality adjectives, and performed factor analyses on 369 self-ratings: The five-factor solution again did not replicate exactly the Big Five, whereas the three-factor solution reproduced the Big Three. This solution was further developed in an Abridged Big Three Circumplex (AB3C) configuration (see also Di Blas, Forzi, & Peabody, 2000).

The two Italian taxonomic projects yielded seemingly inconsistent results. Caprara and Perugini (1994) argued for a cross-cultural replicability of the Big Five (after target rotation), whereas Di Blas and Forzi (1998, 1999) did not. How can these findings be reconciled? Can they be ascribed to procedural differences? De

Table 1. A representation of the five-factor structure from the pooled data sets of the Italian taxonomic projects

Exuberant, extroverted, social, vivacious, cheerful, unconstrained	Silent, introverted, shy, taciturn, reserved, solitary
Peaceful, patient, calm, tranquil, tolerant, meek	Irritable, aggressive, quarrelsome, domineering, choleric
Precise, orderly,consistent disciplined, industrious, responsible	Unruly, disorderly, absent-minded, inaccurate, uncautious
Assured, resolute, strong, enterprising, decisive, bold	Suggestible, timid, anxious, vulnerable, emotional, fragile
Sensitive, altruistic, generous, sentimental, loyal, human	Insensitive, insincere, disloyal, ruthless, greedy, perfidious

Raad, Di Blas, and Perugini (1998) compared the two taxonomies. They used the Triestian 314-item set (Di Blas & Forzi, 1998, Study 1), and the Roman 260-item set (Caprara & Perugini, 1994, Study 2). First, they factor analyzed a pooled data set of 1,664 ratings on 158 personality adjectives in common to the two projects, and found a stable five-factor structure which at best replicated the first four of the Big Five: Sociability (I), Placidity (II/IV), Conscientiousness (III), Self–Assurance (IV/II). The fifth factor was a blend of Nurturance and Integrity (Table 1). Analyses performed on the adjective sets specific to the two studies revealed that they covered comparable underlying broad dimensions, roughly dealing with factor I and a blend of factors III and V of the Big Five. These findings suggested that differences in selection procedures among the Italian studies are matters of emphasis in contents more than of structural discrepancies (see also De Raad, Perugini, Hřebíčková, & Szarota, 1998). In particular, it appeared that dissimilar selection criteria had an impact on the content of the fifth factor, which emerged as Conventionality in the Roman data and as Culture and Abilities in the Triestian data.

More recently, Di Blas and Perugini (2001) compared larger sets of Roman and Triestian adjectives. In particular, they analyzed the Roman set of 492 terms (Caprara & Perugini, 1994, Study 1), and the Triestian set of 369 adjectives (Di Blas & Forzi, 1999, Study 1). The two sets had 250 adjectives in common, 119 were specific to the Triestian study, and 242 to the Roman study. Extensive factor analyses spanning different factorial solutions were performed on the adjectives in common (765 self-ratings), and coefficients of congruence indicated three to five stable dimensions across subsamples of participants. Again, the five-factor solution did not reproduce the common Big Five; rather, the five dimensions were comparable to those found by De Raad *et al.* (1998). As regards the specific sets, the five-factor solutions appeared comparable in terms of content (basically, they could be interpreted as facets of Extraversion, Agreeableness, and Conscientiousness), with one main exception again concerning the fifth factor: in the Roman data it was defined as Conventionality and in the Triestian data as Culture.

In sum, these findings indicate the peculiar composition of the five-factor solution in the Italian language with respect to the common Big Five. Together with some other studies (e.g., Almagor, Tellegen, & Waller, 1995), they counterbalanced the enthusiastic claims that the Big Five are the universal dimensions of personality (McCrae & John, 1992).

The Big Five in the Italian language

A "standard" Big Five taxonomy failed to emerge in the Italian language from an emic perspective, that is, from studies of personality lexicon conducted from within the cultural system (Berry, 1969). It might be argued that the Big Five failed to emerge because they were not well represented in the Italian studies. However, this is not the case. In fact, Di Blas and Perugini (2001) could develop a brief adjectival Big Five measure from a set of 250 adjectives in common to the two Italian projects through applying an etic–emic strategy. First, they followed an etic approach, and selected 82 adjectives already classified as Big Five markers in previous lexical studies (De Raad, Hendriks, & Hofstee, 1994; Goldberg, 1992; Hofstee, De Raad, & Goldberg, 1992; Perugini & Leone, 1996; Trapnell & Wiggins, 1990). Then, they followed an iterative procedure, ideally resulting in a Big Five factor solution with orthogonal dimensions, each loaded by 10 markers. These socalled Big Five Marker Scales (BFMS) are presented in Table 2. Note that the fifth dimension encompasses adjectives mainly referring to divergent (Creativity) rather than convergent thinking (Intellect). Briefly, the Big Five do not represent particularly well the emic five–factor structure in Italian, but they can be recovered fairly well using *ad hoc* procedures.

This is the case for other languages as well: The Big Five are not neatly reproduced in emic studies, but Big Five markers can be rather easily selected (e.g., Boies, Lee, Ashton, Pascal, & Nicol, 2001; Hahn, Lee, & Ashton, 1999). Do these findings support the cross–cultural generality of the Big Five? Have taxonomers found the basic coordinates of a cross–cultural map of personality lexicon? Probably the answer to these questions might be *No* if we adopt the view that the coordinates should correspond to these lexical dimensions emerging consistently from independent emic studies conducted in many different languages (John, Goldberg, & Angleitner, 1984). In fact, it has been already shown that the Big Five do not fully satisfy rigorous psychometric tests of cross–cultural stability (De Raad *et al.*, 1998; Hofstee, Kiers, De Raad, Goldberg, & Ostendorf, 1997; for a different view, see Saucier *et al.*, 2000). The answer, however, may be *Yes* if we decide on *a priori* or conventional coordinates of such an international taxonomy. Many studies have shown that the Big Five can be recovered adopting a more etic-oriented perspective. Therefore, a convenient strategy might be to find an optimal Big Five structure that can be used as a grid on which other aspects of personality can be located and understood, whereby for optimal is especially meant a factorially simple structure (cf. Perugini, 1999; Perugini, Gallucci, & Livi, 2000).

In this chapter we look at our data from this latter perspective, and present a con-

Table 2. Big Five Marker Scales (BFMS) in the Italian language

I Extraversion	
Extroverted (Estroverso)	Reserved (Riservato)
Warm-hearted (Espansivo)	Shy (Timido)
Open (Aperto)	Silent (Silenzioso)
Exuberant (Esuberante)	Introverted (Introverso)
Vivacious (Vivace)	Reserved (Chiuso)
II Agreeableness	
Altruistic (Altruista)	Egoistic (Egoista)
Agreeable (Disponibile)	Revengeful (Vendicativo)
Generous (Generoso)	Cynical (Cinico)
Sympathetic (Comprensivo)	Egocentric (Egocentrico)
Hospitable (Ospitale)	Suspicious (Sospettoso)
III Conscientiousness	
Precise (Preciso)	Untidy (Disordinato)
Orderly (Ordinato)	Inconstant (Incostante)
Diligent (Diligente)	Careless (Impreciso)
Methodical (Metodico)	Careless (Sbadato)
Conscientious (Coscienzioso)	Rash (Incosciente)
IV Emotional Stability	
Self-assured (Sicuro)	Nervous (Nervoso)
Serene (Sereno)	Anxious (Ansioso)
Calm (Calmo)	Emotional (Emotivo)
Impassive (Impassibile)	Susceptible (Suscettibile)
Jealous (Geloso)	Touchy (Permaloso)
V Creativity	
Creative (Creativo)	Superficial (Superficiale)
Imaginative (Fantasioso)	Obtuse (Ottuso)
Original (Originale)	
Ingenious (Ingegnioso)	
Poetic (Poetico)	
Intuitive (Intuitivo)	
Intelligent (Intelligente)	
Rebellious (Ribelle)	

tribution in the development of such a conventional Big Five structure of personality adjectives.

The Big Five Marker Scales

The main aim of this chapter is to present the Big Five Markers Scale (BFMS), an adjective list composed of 50 adjectives that have been specifically selected in order to optimize the simplicity of the five-factor solution based on the combined data of the two Italian psycholexical studies (Di Blas & Perugini, 2001). In the original study, the markers were shown to have satisfying structural properties: the average value of the Kaiser's index of factorial simplicity was .86 (Kaiser, 1974); the average inter-scale correlation was .14 (absolute values); Everett's (1983) generalizability coefficient showed values ranging from .96 to .99 across the Roman and Triestian data sets. In this chapter we will present some additional data and review the psychometric properties of the BFMS. Furthermore, we will present a comprehensive Italian adjective trait taxonomy, which can be useful for comparisons with taxonomies developed in other languages as well as for measuring specific aspects of personality within the Italian context. We arranged the whole set of personality-adjectives selected in the Italian studies (611 terms) according to an Abridged Big Five Circumplex structure (AB5C; cf. Hofstee *et al.*, 1992). The coordinates of this AB5C space were based on the factorial space created by the BFMS.

Sample

The psychometric properties of the BFMS were assessed on a data set of 1,029 selfratings provided by 668 females (average age = 23.3, *SD* = 7.7), and 331 males (average age = 26.6, *SD* = 10.4). Thirty participants had missing information. Participants were instructed to rate on a 7-point scale (from 1 = not at all, to 7 = very much) the extent to which an adjective can be applied to him/herself. Note that the data set comprehends 765 self–ratings already used by Di Blas and Perugini (2001) to develop the BFMS, as well as 264 new self–ratings collected alongside other Big Five measures. In particular, 92 participants completed the NEO-PI-R (24 males and 68 females; average age = 23.8, *SD* = 8.0), 94 completed the Big Five Questionnaire–BFQ (14 males and 80 females; average age = 20.9, *SD* = 3.0), and 78 completed both the Five Factor Personality Inventory–FFPI and the International Personality Item Pool–IPIP (31 males and 45 females; average age = 26.3, *SD* = 11.2).

Structural validity

Table 3 presents the varimax rotated five-factor solution of the Big Five markers resulting from 1,029 self-ratings. Data were ipsatized before factoring in order to remove idiosyncratic components in the use of rating scales. The first ten eigenvalues were 6.34, 5.57, 3.48, 3.08, 2.24 (41.4 per cent of the total variance explained), 1.52, 1.34, 1.18, 1.06, and 1.05. A major jump between the fifth and sixth component suggested that a five-factor solution was adequate. An inspection of the factor loadings (Table 3) indicated that the factors were defined by the expected markers with medium to high loadings. Most adjectives presented a marker index higher than .40 (Perugini *et al.*, 2000), and high Kaiser's factorial simplicity values, indicating that the markers were factorially simple and that the resulting factor structure approximated a simple structure very well. The only exception was for a few adjectives measuring the fifth dimension, Creativity.

When Oblimin rotation was applied to the five-factor solution, factor correlations ranged between -.11 to .17. Therefore, the BFMS approximated well orthogonality,

Table 3. Five-factor solutions of the BF markers (after varimax rotation)

	I	II	III	IV	V	h^2	MI	FSI
Extroverted (Estroverso)	**.79**	-.05	.15	.07	.05	.66	.74	.95
Warm-hearted (Espansivo)	**.73**	-.05	.31	.04	.09	.64	.59	.83
Open (Aperto)	**.69**	.03	.28	.08	.00	.56	.58	.85
Exuberant (Esuberante)	**.60**	-.10	.03	.04	.24	.43	.53	.84
Vivacious (Vivace)	**.59**	-.05	.18	.19	.16	.45	.55	.77
Reserved (Riservato)	**-.59**	.20	.09	.19	.00	.43	.54	.81
Shy (Timido)	**-.69**	-.03	.20	-.13	-.09	.55	.63	.87
Silent (Silenzioso)	**-.72**	.06	.08	.13	-.01	.54	.69	.96
Introverted (Introverso)	**-.79**	-.01	-.04	.01	.00	.63	.79	.99
Reserved (Chiuso)	**-.80**	-.01	-.08	-.04	-.03	.65	.78	.98
Altruistic (Altruista)	.09	-.02	**.72**	.02	.02	.52	.71	.99
Agreeable (Disponibile)	.16	.00	**.69**	.06	.00	.50	.65	.95
Generous (Generoso)	.08	-.09	**.66**	.04	.04	.45	.65	.97
Sympathetic (Comprensivo)	.02	.06	**.59**	.07	.04	.36	.58	.97
Hospitable (Ospitale)	.17	-.04	**.53**	.10	.04	.33	.50	.85
Suspicious (Sospettoso)	-.04	.00	**-.41**	-.23	-.12	.23	.37	.73
Egocentric (Egocentrico)	.15	-.12	**-.42**	.06	.15	.24	.40	.74
Cynical (Cinico)	-.08	-.10	**-.43**	.09	.06	.21	.42	.88
Revengeful (Vendicativo)	.12	-.08	**-.48**	-.11	-.04	.26	.47	.89
Egoistic (Egoista)	-.06	-.08	**-.58**	.01	-.04	.35	.57	.96
Precise (Preciso)	-.07	**.74**	.00	.14	.10	.59	.70	.93
Orderly (Ordinato)	-.06	**.73**	.06	.11	-.03	.55	.71	.97
Diligent (Diligente)	-.07	**.67**	.21	.04	-.07	.50	.61	.90
Methodical (Metodico)	-.15	**.64**	-.01	.08	-.11	.46	.61	.89
Conscientious (Coscienzioso)	-.10	**.60**	.27	.03	-.06	.46	.52	.78
Rash (Incosciente)	.08	**-.47**	-.09	.07	.10	.25	.46	.94
Careless (Sbadato)	-.09	**-.60**	.11	-.10	-.02	.39	.59	.92
Careless (Impreciso)	-.06	**-.63**	.11	-.04	-.18	.44	.59	.90
Inconstant (Incostante)	.01	**-.64**	-.09	-.16	-.05	.45	.61	.91
Untidy (Disordinato)	.01	**-.71**	.06	.00	.00	.50	.70	1.0
Self-assured (Sicuro)	.29	.20	-.04	**.61**	.15	.52	.51	.72
Serene (Sereno)	.20	.18	.30	**.59**	-.14	.53	.49	.66
Calm (Calmo)	-.26	.17	.25	**.58**	-.11	.51	.51	.66
Impassive (Impassibile)	-.17	.01	-.22	**.44**	-.07	.28	.40	.69
Jealous (Geloso)	.07	-.04	-.11	**-.33**	-.14	.15	.32	.73
Touchy (Permaloso)	.02	-.06	-.21	**-.46**	-.21	.30	.42	.70
Susceptible (Suscettibile)	.04	-.11	-.13	**-.53**	-.18	.34	.50	.83
Emotional (Emotivo)	-.15	-.02	.26	**-.58**	-.04	.43	.51	.78
Anxious (Ansioso)	-.14	.08	.04	**-.65**	-.09	.45	.62	.94
Nervous (Nervoso)	-.06	-.02	-.17	**-.66**	-.03	.47	.62	.93
Creative (Creativo)	.11	.05	.07	.05	**.74**	.57	.72	.96
Imaginative (Fantasioso)	.17	.14	.11	-.04	**.68**	.52	.64	.89
Original (Originale)	.21	.08	.00	.14	**.61**	.44	.56	.85
Ingenious (Ingenioso)	.01	-.06	-.08	.23	**.59**	.41	.58	.85
Poetic (Poetico)	-.03	.07	.12	-.15	**.46**	.25	.44	.85
Intuitive (Intuitivo)	.03	-.04	.03	.14	**.41**	.19	.39	.88
Intelligent (Intelligente)	.04	-.07	-.09	.28	**.38**	.23	.32	.63
Rebellious (Ribelle)	.20	.28	-.23	-.11	**.27**	.26	.22	.28
Superficial (Superficiale)	-.03	**.34**	-.04	.15	-.27	.21	.19	.35
Obtuse (Ottuso)	.00	.08	.03	-.04	-.24	.07	.24	.82

Note: MI = marker index; FSI = factorial simplicity index

which constituted the main psychometric rationale we used to develop the AB5C taxonomy. The simplicity was formally assessed by calculating correlations between scale scores and factor scores (cf. Ten Berge & Knol, 1985). The observed values were .99, .95, .99, .98, and .96 for I to V of the Big Five, respectively, and off-diagonal values ranged from -.025 to .041. These results demonstrate the overall simplicity of the factor structure. The stability of the structure was ascertained by calculating Everett's generalizability coefficient on two random subsamples: the values were .99, .99, .99, .98, and .97 for factor I to factor V, respectively.

Descriptive statistics and reliability

Descriptive statistics and reliability values are reported in Table 4. Separate statistics were calculated for gender and age (below and above 25 years old). Table 4 shows that there were no significant differences for the Extraversion and the Creativity scales. Significant differences were found for the Conscientiousness scale with older people describing themselves as more conscientious than younger participants, and for the Emotional Stability scale with females having higher average score than males. For the Agreeableness scale differences were significant both for gender and age with females being more agreeable than males, and older participants more agreeable than younger. Internal consistency values varied from .73 for Creativity to .89 for Extraversion. From an applied point of view, we suggest to use orthogonalized factor scores instead of raw scores to measure the five dimensions. These can be obtained by multiplying the z-scores on each factor, which can be calculated by using the values given in Table 4, with the factor weights reported in Appendix 1.

Convergent validity

To assess convergent validity, factor scores on the BFMS were correlated with scores on four well-known Big Five questionnaires that are extensively described elsewhere in this book and therefore presented very briefly in this context.

NEO-Personality Inventory-Revised

The NEO-PI-R is a widely used measure of the Big Five dimensions of personality, developed by Costa and McCrae (1985, 1992), and containing 240 items, 48 for each of the five main scales: Neuroticism, Extraversion, Openness to Experience, Conscientiousness, and Agreeableness. Each scale has six facets. For the present sample, reliability values (Cronbach's alphas), were .93, .89, .88, .88, and .92 for Neuroticism to Agreeableness, respectively; they ranged from .64 to .86 for twenty-six subscales, and were .38 for O6-Values, .47 for O2-Aesthetics, .50 for A6-Tendermindedness, and .55 for E5-Excitement Seeking. The five dimensions were not completely orthogonal: Neuroticism correlated -.48 with Extraversion, and -.42 with Conscientiousness; Extraversion correlated .39 with Openness to Experience.

Table 4. Descriptive statistics and reliability values for the Big Five Marker Scales

		Scales				
		Extraversion	Agreeableness	Conscientiousness	Emotional Stability	Creativity
Males						
Young (*N* = 220)	Mean	43.18	49.08	42.49	39.42	50.12
	SD	9.98	8.68	10.65	9.13	7.11
Adult (*N* = 107)	Mean	44.78	50.92	49.30	39.83	48.72
	SD	10.44	7.66	9.21	8.98	7.56
Females						
Young (*N* = 554)	Mean	45.17	52.63	44.48	33.19	49.33
	SD	12.31	7.53	10.91	8.76	7.65
Adult (*N* = 106)	Mean	44.73	54.41	50.18	36.29	47.99
	SD	10.87	7.65	9.65	9.68	8.56
ANOVA						
Age			F = 9.75*	F = 50.36**		
Gender			F = 30.67**		F = 44.36**	
Alphas		.89	.76	.86	.77	.73

*Note: *p < .01, ** p < .001*

Big Five Questionnaire

The BFQ is a Big Five measure developed in the Italian language (Caprara, Barbaranelli, Borgogni, & Perugini, 1993). It is composed of 132 items, 20 for each of the five main scales: Energy, Friendliness, Conscientiousness, Emotional Stability, and Openness. Twelve items form the Lie scale. Each Big Five scale has two facets. For the present sample, Alpha values were .81, .72, .82, .87, and .76 for Energy to Openness, respectively, and they ranged from .57 (Openness to Experience) to .83 (Impulse Control) for the ten facets. For the Lie scale, the internal consistency was .62. The inter-correlation matrix revealed the relative orthogonality of the five main scales; only the fifth dimension presented significant correlations (at $p = .01$) of .33 with Conscientiousness, and .30 with Friendliness.

Five Factor Personality Inventory

The FFPI is a Big Five questionnaire containing 100 brief statements (Hendriks, 1997; Hendriks, Hofstee, & De Raad, 1999). It was developed on the basis of previous lexical studies in Dutch culminating in the Abridged Big-Five Dimensional Circumplex (AB5C) model (De Raad, Hendriks, & Hofstee, 1992, 1994; Hofstee *et al.*, 1992). The statements were selected across the AB5C space in order to represent the five dimensions also in their nuances. Differently from the NEO-PI-R and BFQ, the fifth factor is defined as Autonomy. For the present sample, alpha reliabilities were .91, .82, .86, .93, and .85 for Extraversion (I) to Autonomy (V), respectively. Only one of the correlations between the factors (using orthogonalized factor scores as recommended by Hendriks, 1997) was significant (-.29 between Conscientiousness and Autonomy).

International Personality Item Pool

The IPIP is a Big Five inventory described by Goldberg (1999), and it includes 100 items. In the present study, we used the shorter 50-item version. For the present sample, alpha reliabilities were .85, .85, .83, .87, and .75 for the first to the fifth of the Big Five, respectively. The inter-correlation matrix did not present any significant value, with correlations ranging from -.11 to .23.

Correlations between the BFMS scales and the other Big Five measures are reported in Table 5. Consider first the NEO-PI-R. Evidence of convergent validity was found for all five Big Five Marker scales, with each factor correlating mainly with the corresponding BFMS factor. A secondary correlation of -.39 between BFMS-III and NEO-PI-R Openness to Experience emphasizes the content of the Italian Conscientiousness scale, which refers to order and dutifulness without indulging in fantasies.

As regards the correlations of the BFMS with the NEO-PI-R facets, results provide evidence of convergent validity for twenty-two of the thirty facets, having their highest correlation with the expected BFMS scale. A clear convergent validity was observed for BFMS-III, with values ranging from .46 to .80; Order (C2), Self-Discipline (C5), and Dutifulness (C3) were shown to characterize the Italian Conscientiousness scale. Although more modest in magnitude (.44 to .59), convergent correlations were found for BFMS-II; among the NEO-PI-R Agreeableness facets, Modesty (A5) and Compliance (A4) appeared to be peripheral to BFMS Agreeableness, being also correlated to BFSM-I and -IV, respectively. Correlations higher than .44 were observed between BFMS-I and NEO-PI-R Extraversion facets; Warmth (E1) was located between BFMS-I and -II; and Excitement Seeking (E5) was unrelated to the BFMS-I, whereas it did correlate significantly with BFMS-III (-.36). If the value of -.28 found between BFMS-III and Impulsiveness (N5) is also considered, then it can be concluded that impulse control variables are related to the third of the Big Five in the Italian context. As regards BFMS-IV, convergent validity was partially supported, with low levels of Anxiety (N1) and Angry-Hostility (N2) being primarily related to the Italian Emotional Stability scale. For the fifth of the Big Five, convergent values ranged from .30 to .41. They suggest that creativity is relatively marginal to the definition of NEO-PI-R Openness, which is conceived in terms of readiness to appreciate rather than produce art, new ideas and values.

Concerning the relations with the BFQ measure, convergent validity was supported for the first, third and fourth of the Big Five, both for the general factors and the specific facets. A correlation of .51 was observed between BFMS-II and BFQ-Friendliness, with Politeness (F2) being also related to BFMS-IV and -V. As regards the fifth dimension, a correlation of .24 (p = .03) was observed between the two measures: the relation can be mainly ascribed to the facet Openness to Culture (.30). However, the values clearly indicate that BFMS and BFQ represent different aspects of the debated fifth of the Big Five. Correlations observed between BFMS and IPIP and FFPI questionnaires are also reported in Table 5. Results provide clear evidence of convergent validity for all factors. However, the FFPI-Autonomy scale was found to have a sizable secondary correlation with BFMS-I (.32)

In general, results support convergent validity of the BFMS. The composition of the fifth factor of the BFMS is peculiar, and it seems to be more linked to the productive aspects of creativity and intelligence rather than to openness to new experiences or culture.

An AB5C taxonomy of Italian personality trait adjectives

The BFMS provided the conventional Big Five map on which all other adjectives could be located. In particular, the BFMS were related with the 200 adjectives in common to the two Italian lexical projects (765 self-ratings), the 242 adjectives unique to the Roman study (275 self-ratings), and the 119 adjectives specific to the Triestian study (491 self-ratings), for a total of 561 adjectives. Following the AB5C model of Hofstee *et al.* (1992), the five-factor space was ordered into ten circum-

Table 5. Significant correlations observed between BFMS (factor scores) and NEO-PI-R (raw scores), BFQ (T-scores), IPIP (raw scores), FFPI (orthogonalized factor scores).

	Big Five Marker Scales				
	I	II	III	IV	V
NEO-PI-R					
Extraversion (E)	.74				
Agreeableness (A)		.76			
Conscientiousness ©			.83		
Neuroticism (N)	-.36			-.57	
Openness (O)			-.39		.48
Warmth (E1)	.47	.48			
Gregariousness (E2)	.45				
Assertiveness (E3)	.65	-.31			
Activity (E4)	.52		.33		
Excitement Seeking (E5)			-.36		
Positive Emotions (E6)	.48				
Trust (A1)		.47		.28	
Straightforwardness (A2)		.53			
Altruism (A3)		.59			
Compliance (A4)	-.31	.56		.43	
Modesty (A5)	-.41	.44			
Tendermindedness (A6)*		.45			
Competence (C1)			.52		

(Continued)

Table 5. continued	I	II	III	IV	V
Order (C2)			.80		
Dutifulness (C3)			.66		
Achievement Striving (C4)			.60		
Self-Discipline (C5)			.75		
Deliberation (C6)			.46		
Anxiety (N1)				-.61	
Angry Hostility (N2)		-.40		-.54	
Depression (N3)	-.36			-.47	
Self-Consciousness (N4)	-.37			-.34	
Impulsiveness (N5)			-.28		
Vulnerability (N6)	-.28			-.52	
Fantasy (O1)			-.35		.39
Aesthetics (O2)*		.32	-.31		.30
Feelings (O3)					.41
Actions (O4)			-.36		.31
Ideas (O5)					
Values (O6)*			-.30		
BFQ					
Energy (E)	.72				
Friendliness (F)		.51			
Conscientiousness (C)			.67		
Emotional Stability (ES)				.68	
Openness (O)					(.24)
Lie (L)					
Dynamism (E1)	.71				
Dominance (E2)	.48				
Cooperativeness (F1)		.46			
Politeness (F2)		.39		.34	-.30
Scrupulousness (C1)	-.36		.68		
Perseverance (C2)			.46		
Emotion control (ES1)				.71	
Impulse Control (ES2)				.48	
Op. to Culture (O1)					
Op. to Experiences (O2)					.30
IPIP					
Extraversion	.77				
Agreeableness		.66		-.32	
Conscientiousness			.80		
Emotional Stability				.69	
Intellect					.53
FFPI					
Extraversion	.73				
Agreeableness		.60			
Conscientiousness			.83		
Emotional Stability				.67	
Autonomy	.32				.39

Note: Correlations are significant at p < .01. The highest values are given in bold. * Alpha reliability values ^{2} .50.

plexes, each formed by pitting each of the Big Five factors against one another. The two highest observed correlations between a given term and the BF marker factors served first to assign the term to one of the ten circumplexes and second to calculate the angular location (AL) and the vector length (VL) of a given adjective within the pertaining circumplex. For each adjective, AL and VL were calculated as follows:

$$AL = ARCTAN\left(\frac{bf_y}{bf_x}\right)$$

$$VL = \sqrt{\left(bf_y^2 + bf_x^2\right)}$$

with bf_y and bf_x being the correlations of a given item with the the the two Big Five co-ordinates (y axis and x axis) of the assigned circumplex. After each adjective is assigned to one of the ten bi-dimensional spaces, and its VL and AL are calculated, the next issue is how to divide each bi-factorial space. Two main alternatives are available (cf. Perugini, 1999): eight sectors of 45 degree each, lending to a total of 25 bipolar spaces and twelve sectors of 30 degrees each, for a total of 45 bipolar spaces.

As shown in Table 6a, however, in this latter case, which is the option adopted by the Dutch-English AB5C model (cf. Hofstee *et al.*, 1992), a relevant number of bipolar spaces was poorly represented. Indeed, twenty four spaces (that is, 27 per cent) contained between 0 and 2 adjectives, often with a VL lower than .30 (in total, 160 of the 561 adjectives had a VL <.30). Therefore, we opted for the first alternative of using larger sectors of 45 degrees, giving a total of 25 bipolar spaces. Table 6b reports frequencies of adjectives classified in each octant.

Figure 1 presents illustrative adjectives (selected among those with the highest vector lengths) of the ten two-factor spaces, and plots of all the adjectives assigned to each circumplex.

This AB5C taxonomy of Italian personality adjectives provides interesting information. First, of the ten bi-dimensional spaces, those for BF II x III, III x IV, II x IV, and I x IV included the largest numbers of adjectives, and the space formed by BF IV x V included the smallest number of terms. These findings are comparable to those reported for both Dutch and American-English taxonomies (De Raad *et al.*, 1994; Hofstee *et al.*, 1992). Second, the cells are filled by adjectives consistent in terms of content, although some of them were selected from the independent Triestian and Roman data sets. Third, of the possible 25 bipolar facets, 18 are well-defined: theoretically opposite octants (e.g. I+II+ vs. I-II-) contain adjectives opposite in terms of content, and include at least three items with VL > .30. For example, of the nine possible facets for factor I, seven are well-defined: Talkative-Silent, Sociable-Aloof, Mild-Domineering, Prudent-Rash, Unconstrained-Insecure, Quiet-Frenetic, Brilliant-Boring. The bipolar sectors I+V- versus I-V+, III-IV+ versus III+IV-, and IV-V+ versus IV+V- are insufficiently represented. Of the remaining cells, only one pole is well-defined (e.g. I-III- but not I+III+). It should also be noted that IV+ and V- octants are poorly represented as well. This result is consistent with

Table 6. AB5C ordering of personality adjectives in Italian.

A. Number of adjectives assigned to the 30° sectors of the ten circumplexes.

	I+	II+	III+	IV+	V+	I-	II-	III-	IV-	V-
I+	7	9	0	11	5	/	14	7	5	0
II+	9	13	9	5	1	1	/	2	5	1
III+	0	17	11	16	1	1	9	/	1	2
IV+	13	9	40	5	9	2	10	3	/	1
V+	16	2	5	4	9	2	4	3	0	/
I-	/	6	12	4	0	7	8	7	11	9
II-	7	/	9	3	1	5	9	16	15	1
III-	7	2	/	0	10	4	12	11	20	2
IV-	3	3	0	/	0	5	10	21	6	3
V-	0	7	7	3	/	14	10	9	10	3

Note: The adjectives had a primary correlation on the column Big Five dimension, and a secondary correlation with the row Big Five dimension

B. Number of adjectives assigned to the 45° sectors of the ten circumplexes.

	I+	II+	III+	IV+	V+	I-	II-	III-	IV-	V-
I+	8									
II+	17	24								
III+	0	21	25							
IV+	22	12	47	10						
V+	21	3	6	12	11					
I-	/	5	11	6	2	9				
II-	15	/	13	10	5	11	22			
III-	12	3	/	3	11	10	28	21		
IV-	7	6	1	/	0	14	25	33	16	
V-	0	7	8	3	/	23	9	10	10	3

previously developed AB5C taxonomies in Dutch and American-English. Finally, the findings illustrated in Figure 1 allow emphasizing further consistencies between AB5C structures developed in different languages. There appear to be striking similarities between the continua observed by Hofstee *et al.* (1992), De Raad *et al.* (1994) and those presented here for the spaces formed by BF I x II, I x IV, I x V, II x IV, II x V, III x V. Interestingly, similarities can be found not only for the well-filled circumplexes (e.g., I x II), but also for those that are less filled, such as BF III x V (industrious and refined are located between III+ and V+ both in American-English and Italian taxonomies). More in detail, it can easily be noted, for example, that the Dutch, American-English, and the present AB5C structure locate optimism- and forcefulness-related adjectives in the I+IV+ sector; peacefulness-related terms in the II+IV+ section; stability and persistence-referring adjectives in the III+IV+ sector; simplicity in the II+V- cell; dependence in the IV-V- octant, and so forth. Some differences emerged as well. For example, the fifth positive pole is largely represented by adjectives suggesting divergent thinking, whereas this cell was not represented in

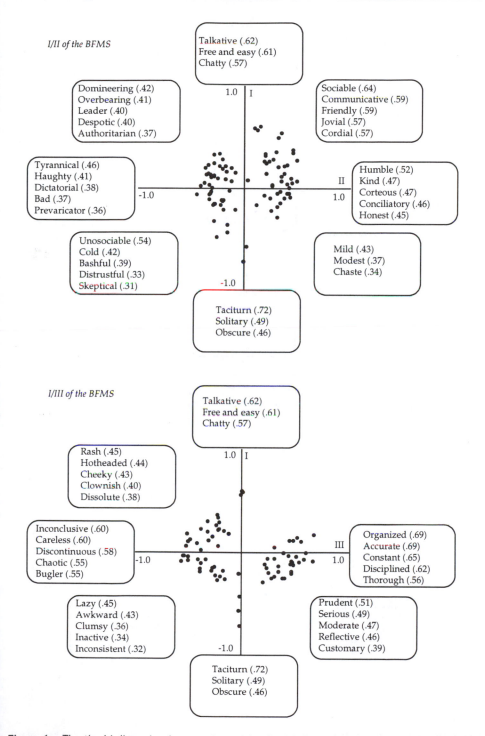

Figure 1a. The the bi-dimensional spaces formed by the BFMS factors: Illustrative items with the highest vector length are reported.

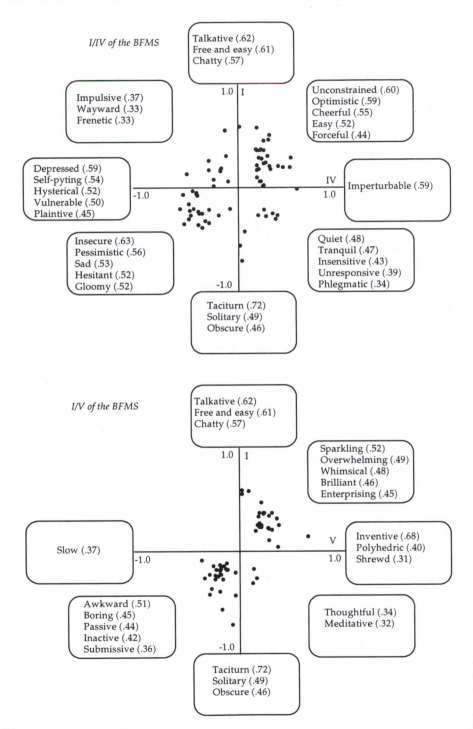

Figure 1b. Bi-dimensional spaces.

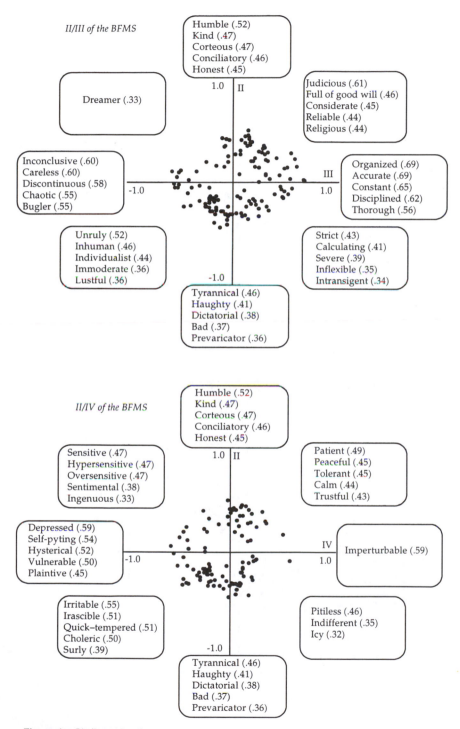

Figure 1c. Bi-dimensional spaces.

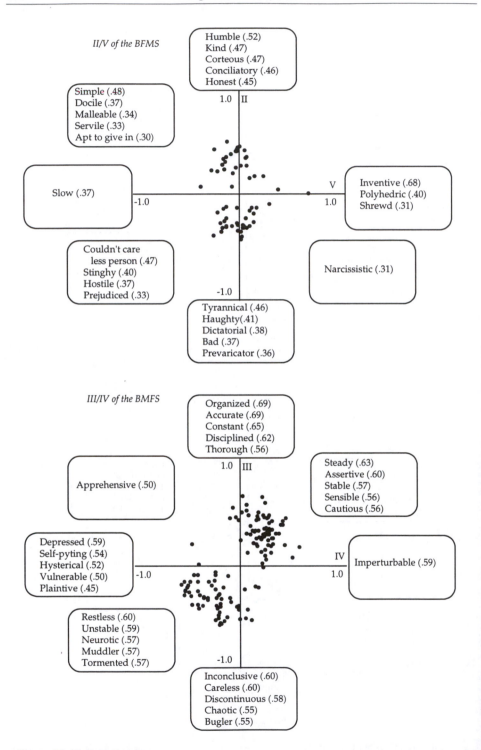

Figure 1d. Bi-dimensional spaces.

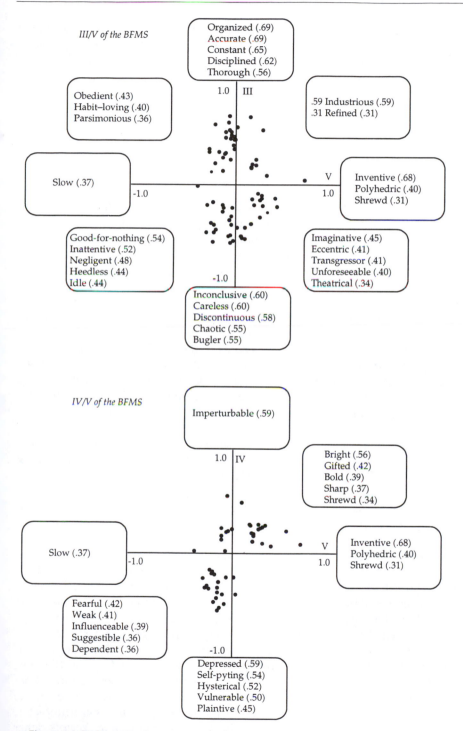

III/V of the BFMS

Organized (.69)
Accurate (.69)
Constant (.65)
Disciplined (.62)
Thorough (.56)

Obedient (.43)
Habit–loving (.40)
Parsimonious (.36)

1.0   III

.59 Industrious (.59)
.31 Refined (.31)

Slow (.37)

-1.0

V   1.0

Inventive (.68)
Polyhedric (.40)
Shrewd (.31)

Good-for-nothing (.54)
Inattentive (.52)
Negligent (.48)
Heedless (.44)
Idle (.44)

-1.0

Imaginative (.45)
Eccentric (.41)
Transgressor (.41)
Unforeseeable (.40)
Theatrical (.34)

Inconclusive (.60)
Careless (.60)
Discontinuous (.58)
Chaotic (.55)
Bugler (.55)

IV/V of the BFMS

Imperturbable (.59)

1.0   IV

Bright (.56)
Gifted (.42)
Bold (.39)
Sharp (.37)
Shrewd (.34)

Slow (.37)

-1.0

V   1.0

Inventive (.68)
Polyhedric (.40)
Shrewd (.31)

Fearful (.42)
Weak (.41)
Influenceable (.39)
Suggestible (.36)
Dependent (.36)

-1.0

Depressed (.59)
Self-pyting (.54)
Hysterical (.52)
Vulnerable (.50)
Plaintive (.45)

Figure 1e. Bi-dimensional spaces.

Dutch; conversely, the negative pole of the fifth factor was well filled in Dutch but not in Italian. Aggressiveness is a relevant component of the first of the Big Five in American but not in Dutch or Italian. Depression and anxiety represent Emotional Instability in Italian, whereas sensitiveness-related terms define the pure IV- sector in Dutch, and moody and possessive characterize the same cell in American-English.

Big Five for ever?

When the structure of personality-referring adjectives is analyzed in the Italian language from an emic perspective, findings consistently show that the Big Five are only partially replicated. Here, we analyzed a larger pool of adjectives ($N = 611$) than those used in previous studies (Caprara & Perugini, 1994; Di Blas & Forzi, 1998, 1999) since we merged the data of the two Italian lexical projects and analyzed them from an emic-etic perspective. We focus this final paragraph on two points.

First, whereas our approach follows an emic-etic perspective, it is not meant to be a full-fledged application of the emic-etic methodology. We developed a five-factor taxonomy whose coordinates were determined a priori as the Big Five. In particular, we first assessed some psychometric properties of the BFMS, then we used the resulting Big Five dimensions as coordinates of an AB5C taxonomy, and located 561 personality adjectives within this space. The AB5C taxonomy developed using the BFMS factors as coordinates revealed clear cross-cultural consistencies with other taxonomies. It is in this sense therefore that our study follows an emic-etic perspective. This approach to study personality-related adjectives in Italian has shown that the Big Five can be replicated in this language, whereas emic studies have demonstrated that the Big Five structure does not emerge in its common form (Caprara & Perugini, 1994; De Raad *et al.*, 1998; Di Blas & Forzi, 1999).

How, then, can we reconcile these findings? We think that the preceding findings may perhaps appear as paradoxical at first glance, but they actually are quite consistent and perhaps reveal something more general about the Big Five. We argue that the emic lexical structures simply reflect the largest areas of the AB5C space. For example, the first component in the Italian emic studies was Conscientiousness: the AB5C ordering of the Italian adjectives shows that the bipolar facets III+IV+/III-IV-, III+II+/II-III-, and III+/III- include the largest number of terms. Similarly, the component Placidity versus Irritability, emerging as the fourth factor in both the Roman and the Triestian study, is defined by adjectives assigned to the very large II+IV+/II-IV- cell. Therefore, when data are analyzed from an emic perspective, the main axes appear to be positioned in correspondence of the most filled areas of adjectives. Interestingly, plots of the bi-dimensional spaces formed by the Big Five factors in different languages show that the so-called mixed sectors are often more represented and better defined than the so-called pure sectors. This is true for the first and second factor, and it is particularly striking for the fourth and fifth factor. These latter factors appear to be systematically more defined by mixed sectors rather than pure ones. If "the degree of representation of an attribute has some correspondence with the general importance of the attribute" (Saucier & Goldberg, 1996, p. 26), then quantitative similarities are worth to be emphasized across taxonomies of different languages, because they suggest what the most important perceived individual differences across cultures are. In other words, the numbers of personality adjectives assigned to the AB5C sectors indicate that personality attributes different from the Big Five (or some of them) may be basically important according to everyday personality theories. For example, this is the case for sections located between BF I and IV (I+IV+ vs. I-IV-, that is, Assurance vs. Insecurity), BF I and II (I+II+ vs. I-II-, that is, Friendliness against Interpersonal coldness), BF II and III (II+III+ vs. II-III- or Reliability vs. Unreliability) or still between BF II and IV (II+IV+ vs. II-IV-, that is Placidity vs. Irritability). Of course, this is not the only possible interpretation of the results and our speculation need independent empirical support in future studies.

Second, our results do not solve the question about the universality of the Big Five. By definition, any study in a single country cannot be sufficient to establish universality. However, they allow us to elaborate on this issue. Here, we showed that a Big Five factor structure and an AB5C taxonomy can be developed from the joint Italian data set. The Big Five factors can be reliably assessed in the Italian context using the BFMS, and the AB5C taxonomy can be very valuable in understanding other dimensions which can be located in this space. The Big Five, however, emerged mainly when forcing the variables to conform to a Big Five structure. Therefore, these findings provide evidence that the Big Five are among the most important categories for ordering personality attributes. However, they are not necessarily the universal coordinates of personality unless we so decide. Moreover, the distribution of the adjectives in the AB5C cells — consistently with AB5C ordering of personality adjectives in Dutch and in English — indicates that other categories, mainly consisting of mixed factors when adopting a Big Five conventional map, may be equally if not even more important for lay people. Some of these "mixed" factors may well show to be of more practical importance than their pure counterparts, and this might lead to a revision on what kind of conventional map is more convenient in a given language or across languages. The Big Five represents a very significant achievement of personality psychology and a point of no-return in personality research. But, ultimately, time will tell whether they will maintain this status in the new century or rather will represent a starting point from which other more convenient taxonomies will be developed.

References

Almagor, M., Tellegen, A., & Waller, N.G. (1995). The Big Seven model: A cross-cultural replication and further exploration of the basic dimensions of natural language trait descriptors. *Journal of Personality and Social Psychology, 69*, 300-307.

Angleitner, A., Ostendorf, F., & John, O.P. (1990). Towards a taxonomy of personality descriptors in German: A psycho-lexical study. *European Journal of Personality, 4*, 89-118.

Berry, J.W. (1969). On cross-cultural comparability. *International Journal of Psychology, 4*, 119-128.

Boies, K., Lee, K., Ashton, M.C., Pascal, S., & Nicol, A.M. (2001). The structure of the French personality lexicon. *European Journal of Personality, 15*, 277–295.

Brokken, F.B. (1978). *The Language of Personality*. Krips, Meppel.

Caprara, G.V., Barbaranelli, C., Borgogni, L., & Perugini, M. (1993). The "Big Five Questionnaire": A new questionnaire to assess the Five Factor Model. *Personality and Individual Differences, 15*, 281-288.

Caprara, G.V., & Perugini, M. (1994). Personality described by adjectives: Generalizability of the Big Five to the Italian lexical context. *European Journal of Personality, 8*, 357-369.

Costa, P.T., Jr., & McCrae, R.R. (1985). *The NEO-PI Manual*. Odessa, FL: Psychological Assessment Resources.

Costa, P.T., Jr., & McCrae, R.R. (1992). *Revised NEO Personality Inventory (NEO-PI-R) and NEO Five-Factor Inventory (NEO-FFI) professional manual*. Odessa, FL: Psychological Assessment Resources.

De Raad, B. (2000). *The Big Five personality factors: The psycholexical approach to personality*. Gottingen, Germany: Hogrefe & Huber Publishers.

De Raad, B., Di Blas, L., & Perugini, M. (1998). Two independently constructed Italian trait taxonomies: Comparisons among Italian and between Italian and Germanic languages. *European Journal of Personality, 12*, 19-41.

De Raad, B., Hendriks, A.A.J., & Hofstee, W.K.B.(1992). Towards A refined structure of personality traits. *European Journal of Personality, 6*, 301-319.

De Raad, B., Hendriks, A.A.J., & Hofstee, W.K.B.(1994). The Big Five: A tip of the iceberg of individual differences. In C.F. Halverson, G.A. Kohnstamm, and R.P.Martin (Eds.), *The developing structure of temperament and personality from infancy to adulthood* (pp. 69-90). Hillsdale, NJ: Lawrence Erlbaum Associates.

De Raad, B., Perugini, M., Hřebičková, M., & Szarota, P. (1998). Lingua franca of personality: Taxonomies and structures. *Journal of Cross-Cultural Psychology, 29*, 212-232.

Di Blas, L., & Forzi, M. (1998). An alternative taxonomic study of personality descriptors in the Italian language. *European Journal of Personality, 12*, 75-101.

Di Blas, L., & Forzi, M. (1999). Refining a descriptive structure of personality attributes in the Italian language: The abridged Big Three circumplex structure. *Journal of Personality and Social Psychology, 76*, 451-481.

Di Blas, L., Forzi, M., & Peabody, D. (2000). Evaluative and descriptive dimensions from Italian personality factors. *European Journal of Personality, 14*, 279-290.

Di Blas, L., & Perugini, M. (2001). L'approccio lessicale nella lingua italiana: due studi tassonomici a confronto [The psycholexical approach in the Italian language: Comparisons among Italian taxonomic studies]. *Giornale Italiano di Psicologia, 28*, 177-203.

Everett, J.E. (1983). Factor comparability as a means of determining the number of factors and their rotation. *Multivariate Behavioral Research, 18*, 197-218.

Goldberg, L.R. (1992). The development of markers for the Big Five factor structure. *Psychological Assessment, 4*, 26-42.

Goldberg, L.R. (1999). A broad-bandwidth, public-domain, personality inventory measuring the lower-level facets of several five-factor models. In I. Mervielde, I. Deary, F. De

Fruyt, & F. Ostendorf (eds), *Personality psychology in Europe*, vol. 7 (pp. 7–28). Tilburg University Press: Tilburg, The Netherlands.

Hahn, D.W., Lee, K., & Ashton, M.C. (1999). A factor analysis of the most frequently used Korean personality trait adjectives. *European Journal of Personality, 13*, 261–282.

Hendriks, A.A.J. (1997). *The construction of the Five-Factor Personality Inventory (FFPI)*. Doctoral Dissertation, University of Groningen, The Netherlands.

Hendriks, A.A.J., Hofstee, W.K.B., & De Raad, B. (1999). The five-factor personality inventory (FFPI). *Personality and Individual Differences, 27*, 307–325.

Hofstee, W.K.B., De Raad, B., & Goldberg, L.R. (1992). Integration of the Big Five and circumplex approaches to trait structures. *Journal of Personality and Social Psychology, 63*, 146-163.

Hofstee, W.K.B., Kiers, H.A.L., De Raad, B., Goldberg, L.R., & Ostendorf. F. (1997). Comparison of the Big-Five structures of personality traits in Dutch, English, and German. *European Journal of Personality, 11*, 15-31.

John, O.P., Goldberg, L.R., & Angleitner, A. (1984). Better than the alphabet: Taxonomies of personality descriptive terms in English, Dutch and German. In H. Bonarius, G. Van Heck, & N. Smid (Eds), *Personality Psychology in Europe*, vol. 1 (pp. 83-100). The Netherlands: Tilburg University Press.

Kaiser, H.K. (1974). An index of factorial simplicity. *Psychometrika, 39*, 31-35.

McCrae, R.R., & John, O.P. (1992). An introduction to the five-factor model and its applications. *Journal of Personality, 60*, 175-215.

Peabody, D., & Goldberg, L.R. (1989). Some determinants of factor structures from personality trait-descriptors. *Journal of Personality and Social Psychology, 57*, 552-567.

Perugini, M. (1993). Un approccio circomplesso gerarchico alle tassonomie delle caratteristiche di personalità [*A circumplex hierarchical approach to taxonomies of personality characteristics*]. Doctoral Dissertation, University of Rome: Italy.

Perugini, M. (1999). A proposal for integrating hierarchical and circumplex modelling in personality. In I. Deary, F. De Fruyt, I. Mervielde, & F. Ostendorf (Eds.), *Personality Psychology in Europe*, vol. 7 (pp. 85-99). The Netherlands: Tilburg University Press.

Perugini, M., Gallucci, M., & Livi, S. (2000). Looking for a simple Big Five factorial structure in the domain of adjectives. *European Journal of Psychological Assessment, 16*, 87-97.

Perugini, M., & Leone, L. (1996). Construction and validation of a Short Adjective Checklist to measure Big Five (SACBIF). *European Journal of Psychological Assessment, 12*, 33-42.

Saucier, G., & Goldberg, L.R. (1996). The language of personality: Lexical perspectives on the five-factor model. In J.S. Wiggins (ed.), *The five-factor model of personality* (pp. 21-50). New Jork: The Guilford Press.

Saucier, G., Hampson, S.E., & Goldberg, L.R. (2000). Cross- language studies of lexical personality factors. In I. Mervielde & S.E. Hampson (Eds.), *Advances in Personality Psychology* (Vol. 1). London: Routledge.

Ten Berge, J.M.F., & Knol, D.L. (1985). Scale construction on the basis of components analysis: A comparison of three strategies. *Multivariate Behavioral Research, 20*, 45-55.

Trapnell, P.D., & Wiggins J.S. (1990). Extension of the interpersonal adjective scales to include the Big Five dimensions of personality. *Journal of Personality and Social Psychology, 59*, 781-790.

Appendix 1. BFMS orthogonalized factor scores (OFS) from raw data after standardization (SRS) (see Table 4).

OFS I BF	=	1.051*SRS I	−	.077*SRS II	+	.069*SRS III	−	.057*SRS IV	−	.149*SRS V.
OFS II BF	=	− .075*SRS I	+	1.022*SRS II	−	.042*SRS III	−	.067*SRS IV	−	.024*SRS V.
OFS III BF	=	.071*SRS I	−	.043*SRS II	+	1.062*SRS III	−	.196*SRS IV	+	.012*SRS V.
OFS IV BF	=	− .059*SRS I	−	.070*SRS II	−	.197*SRS III	+	1.066*SRS IV	+	.015*SRS V.
OFS V BF	=	.147*SRS I	−	.024*SRS II	+	.011*SRS III	+	.015*SRS IV	+	1.034*SRS V.

Chapter 13

Japanese Adjective List for the Big Five

Shigeo Kashiwagi

Introduction

In Japan, Aoki (1974) was the first to adopt the psycholexical approach to study personality traits. He published his *Dictionary for personality traits* containing about 2,400 Japanese adjectives describing traits, which were classified by Aoki into seven bipolar categories, namely politeness versus selfishness, gentleness versus stubbornness, sociability versus shyness, kindness versus cool-heartedness, activity versus impatience, steadiness versus carelessness, and brightness versus stupidity. Under the influence of psychological studies both in the United States and in Europe (e.g., John, 1990; Hofstee, De Raad, & Goldberg, 1992), several Big Five related investigations were performed based on Aoki's "dictionary". These were Kashiwagi, Wada, and Aoki (1993), Kashiwagi and Yamada (1995), Wada (1996), Kashiwagi and Wada (1996), and Kashiwagi (1999). All were published in Japanese, with only brief English summaries. These adjective based studies were performed in order to see whether the hypothetical Big Five model would hold in Japanese.

Kashiwagi *et al.* (1993), for example, *confirmed* the relevance of the Big Five by applying different methods of rotation. Kashiwagi *et al.* (1993) had a group of 583 university students (348 men and 235 women) who were requested to respond to a list of 200 adjectives, using a seven-point scale. Those 200 adjectives had been selected by Wada (1991) as being suitable for describing the Big Five concepts from the 2,400 adjectives in Aoki's dictionary. Kashiwagi *et al.* (1993) first applied the incomplete orthogonal procrustes factor rotation method of Browne (1972) to the 200 adjectives.

With this method it is possible to rotate the factorial structure towards a target structure that specifies the assumed theoretical model (i.e., Big Five), under the constraints of factor orthogonality. Browne's method has been shown to perform well under these conditions (see Kashiwagi *et al.*, 1993; Kashiwagi & Yamada, 1995; Kashiwagi & Wada, 1995; Kashiwagi, 1995). Moreover, if used iteratively, it allows

Big Five Assessment, edited by B. De Raad & M. Perugini. © 2002, Hogrefe & Huber Publishers.

to select items that best approximate the target simple structure.

Upon applying this rotation method, 131 adjectives turned out to provide the best tentative approximation of the Big Five; 69 adjectives were deleted. Next, the same factor rotation was applied to this reduced set of 131 adjectives, and subsequently to the smaller sets of 110 and 91 adjectives, until the Big Five assumption could be confirmed more satisfactorily. Finally, the 91 adjectives were accepted as the optimal set. More details concerning the computational aspects of this method of Browne can be found in the paragraphs "Structure of trait adjectives" and "Concurrent validity: the Big Five versus the psychoanalytic concepts" of this chapter.

Then, in order to polish up the orthogonal solution in the sense of a Big Five simple structure, and to get to know the correlations among the primary axes, the incomplete oblique factor rotation of Jöreskog (see Mulaik, 1972) was applied. The method of Jöreskog may be considered as an oblique case of the incomplete orthogonal procrustes factor rotation method of Browne (1972), therefore relaxing the orthogonality constraints and allowing for correlated factors. Some computational aspects of the method of Jöreskog are described in the paragraph "Big Five and interdependence" of this chapter paper.

The incomplete oblique procrustes factor rotation method of Jöreskog yielded possibly the first Big Five Adjective structure in Japan. The numbers of adjectives for Factor I (Extraversion) through Factor V (Openness to Experience) were 24, 21, 17, 10, and 19, respectively. The α-coefficients for the five factors were .92, .88, .87, .84 and .88, respectively. The correlations among the primary axes indicated that the pairs Factor I (Extraversion) and Factor V (Openness to Experience), Factor V (Openness to Experience) and Factor II (Agreeableness), and Factor II (Agreeableness) and Factor III (Conscientiousness) were each mutually correlated, which suggested that Factor IV (Neuroticism) might be relatively independent of the other four factors.

Following the work of Piedmont, McCrae, and Costa (1991), Wada (1996) and Kashiwagi and Wada (1996) also investigated the Big Five structure concurrently through joint factor analyses on data from both the Chiba University Personality Inventory (CUPI; Yanai, Kashiwagi, & Kokushou, 1987) and the previously mentioned list of 91 Japanese adjectives. The CUPI has twelve factors or scales each consisting of ten items. The factors or scales are named Neuroticism, Depression, Inferiority Complex, Extraversion, Activity, Stand Out, Enterprising, Aggressiveness, Agreeableness, Empathetic, Conscientiousness, and Endurance, respectively. The CUPI contains 120 Japanese items of the sentence type, such as "Others often tell me that I look always alive and vivid" for the factor Extraversion, "I like to help even an unknown person when in trouble" for the factor Agreeableness, "I always make plans before I perform anything" for the factor Conscientiousness, "I worry whenever I fail even in trivial matters" for the factor Neuroticism, "I like to come up with new ideas that no one has proposed before" for the factor Enterprising, and the like. In particular, Wada (1996) applied the Promax method, which is an oblique procrustes factor rotation method through a reference structure to a primary pattern based on the Varimax solution as an initial factor position (see Mulaik, 1972), to the factors and scales of both the CUPI and the Big Five based 91 adjectives. They confirmed that the scales Neuroticism, Depression, and Inferiority Complex of the CUPI correspond to the trait Neuroticism in the 91 adjectives list. Furthermore, they confirmed that Extraversion, Activity, and Stand Out of the CUPI correspond to Extraversion in the 91 list, Enterprising of the CUPI to Openness to Experience in the 91 list, Aggressiveness, Agreeableness, and Empathetic of the CUPI to Agreeableness in the 91 list, and Conscientiousness and Endurance of the CUPI to Conscientiousness in the 91 list, respectively.

Moreover, Kashiwagi (1999) demonstrated that the factor structure of the Tokyo University Egogram (TEG; Suematsu, Wada, Nomura, & Tamura, 1995), which was constructed on the basis of psychoanalytic concepts, could be circumplexically organized in terms of the Big Five. He did this through the incomplete orthogonal procrustes factor rotation method of Browne (1972). Some parts of this study are discussed in the paragraph "Concurrent validity; the Big Five versus psychoanalytic concepts" of this chapter.

Following this brief history of the findings, the possibility of arriving at a more refined Japanese Adjective List will be investigated. To that end, the development of trait-facet systems and the issue of using single adjectives versus sentences will be discussed.

The construction of a trait-facet system

The construction of a hierarchical Big Five structure containing both traits and facets can be approached in different ways. The most common approach is the one used in the NEO-PI-R (Costa & McCrae, 1991) which may be considered as one of the few broadly used and standardized personality inventories of the sentence type. It has Extraversion (E), Agreeableness (A), Conscientiousness (C), Neuroticism (N), and Openness to Experience (0) as the Five Factor labels. Each factor scale consists of six facets and each facet is described by eight items. Thus, the total number of items in the inventory amounts to 240. On data obtained for the 240 *items*, a Varimax rotation was applied and then the Big Five structure was identified in the sense of simple structure. A similar Big Five structure was also found after Varimax rotation of the thirty *facets*. However, as the number of trait factors was the same in both solutions, it may be said to be rather intuitive to discriminate between a trait factor and its six related facets. In other words, as both solutions may be said *not* to be *different* in the sense of hierarchical levels, the discrimination between a trait factor and the related six facets may not be easy. For example, the trait factor Extraversion may not be discriminated from its facet Activity only through both Big Five solutions unless the hierarchical relations concerning trait factors to facets were not assumed before starting the analysis.

Hofstee *et al.* (1992) adopted the so-called Abridged Big Five Dimensional Circumplex (AB5C) approach to seek the hierarchical relations between trait factors and facets in 636 adjectives. They estimated the factor loading matrix on the basis of 100 adjective markers of the Big Five. In other words, they obtained the rotated factor loading matrix *approximately* by making use of the principle $A = k\, Z'F$, where A, k, Z', and F respectively are the factor loading matrix to be estimated approximately, a scalar, the transposed standardized score matrix, and the factor score matrix based on the marker items. The adjectives in the approximately obtained orthogonal factor loading matrix were each grouped into the facets to be psychologically interpretable through plotting them graphically onto their circumplex planes.

Although the AB5C approach may be considered an improvement in comparison to the approach followed by Costa and McCrae, in the sense that it can discriminate a trait factor from its related facets more objectively, the grouping of factor loadings into a two dimensional or circumplex space may make it to be efficient to select adjectives with the help of inspection. In other words, the speed in the work for selection may be accelerated with the help of the assumption before starting the analysis concerning hierarchical relations of trait factors to facets.

A possible new type of approach to discriminate a trait factor from its related facets is discussed here for the construction of personality inventories. The Varimax and the Orthomax criteria, instead of the Varimax alone, are applied to a specific principal factor matrix in order to attain both the trait factors and the facets in an *objective* way. In other words, the Varimax is applied to attain the Big Five trait factors, and next *one* of the Orthomax criteria, which contain Quartimax, Varimax, Equamax, Parsimax, Factor-parsimony and others (see Mulaik, 1972), is applied to attain the related facets in each trait factor. Users can easily choose one of the Orthomax criteria in common standard statistical packages such as SAS. The main reason for applying the Orthomax in stead of the Varimax to define facets is that the Varimax *may* provide sometimes biased results when the number of items or the number of factors or both are so large (see Kashiwagi, 1965; Hofstee *et al.*, 1992; Goldberg, Sweeney, Merenda, & Hughes, 1996).

Take, for instance, the CUPI, described briefly above. Yanai *et al.* (1987) failed at an initial stage to attain the Varimax solution for 120 variables in twelve factors in the sense of simple structure. In other words, the Varimax did not work well and did not provide an interpretable answer from a psychological point of view. However, in order to get around this kind of trouble, a more psychologically interpretable and satisfactory answer in the sense of simple structure could be attained by applying the Equamax as one of the Orthomax criteria. Although the uses of the Orthomax criteria, instead of Varimax, may not be so popular at present, the application of the Varimax is *not always appropriate* for the reason given above. Moreover, even if the assumption for the Big Five based on the vast number of variables is confirmed, the facets in a number of factors larger than five may not always be interpretable when the Varimax is applied. In general, unless Varimax solutions can meet satisfactorily the user's pre-assigned assumption, the applications of the Orthomax criteria instead of Varimax should be considered. It may very well be possible to attain more satisfactory solutions from a theoretical point of view.

Adjectives versus sentences

We distinguish two types of personality inventories, one consisting of adjectives and the other consisting of sentences, henceforth respectively called the adjective type and the sentence type inventories. On the basis of common sense, the sentence type inventory may be preferred over the adjective type because adjectives are more abstract and inexact than sentences both in evaluating and in describing personality traits (see Widiger & Trull, 1997). In fact, almost all the widely used personality inventories, such as the NEO-PI-R, belong to the sentence type inventory. Goldberg (1999) asserted that the personality inventories of the sentence type are preferable, and consequently he presented the International Personality Item Pool (IPIP) consisting of short behavior-descriptive sentences. He used an item format that is more contextualized and thus longer than trait adjectives, yet more compact and thus shorter than the items in most personality inventories. The Groningen personality team of Hofstee, De Raad, and Hendriks has been the major proponent of this item format, and they have used it to develop an initial pool of Dutch items which might cover many of the facets of the Big Five structure (Hendriks, 1997). Based on their approach, Goldberg (1999) has worked further with their itempool and has proposed the IPIP in English.

Although adjectives may be more inexact and less contextualized than sentences in describing and evaluating personality traits, the advantage of personality inventories of the adjective type is that they are less time-consuming and more easily understood by foreigners. Moreover, studies by Piedmont *et al.* (1991) and Kashiwagi (1999) show that, also from a test theoretic point of view, personality inventories of the adjective type need not always be inferior to those of the sentence type. For example, the α-coefficient brought about when using adjectives may be larger than the one brought about when using sentences, with the same number of variables for facets or traits. From a factor analytic point of view, however, there are, to my knowledge, very few examples satisfying the trait-facet system in the personality inventories of the adjective type. Therefore, it is of great interest to develop further a personality inventory of the adjective type, which can be evaluated for both traits and facets simultaneously. This is one of the main aims of this paper.

Method

Two kinds of factor analytic studies were conducted. The first analysis (Study-1) involves the proposal of a Japanese Big Five Adjective List consisting of 120 adjectives, not to be confused with the CUPI (Chiba University Personality Inventory) which is also composed of 120 items.

The second analysis (Study-2) involves a hierarchical evaluation form based on traits and facets, using 105 items which were selected from the Adjective List achieved in Study-1. The data that were used for both analyses were obtained from 218 subjects, all university students among whom 33 foreign students. Especially considering the foreign students, who may not be so familiar with the Japanese words, an easy format was used.

Study-1

Material and procedure

The 200 adjectives selected by Wada (1991) from Aoki's "dictionary" were used. The subject were asked to provide self-ratings using a 3-point scale, with the answering possibilities "Yes", "Questionable", and "No", scored as 1, 0, and -1, respectively.

Results

Structure of trait adjectives

The self-ratings were factored following the principal axes method. Five factors were extracted, which were rotated according to Varimax. As some items turned out to be rather complex in terms of a Big Five simple structure, the number of items was decreased in the four steps described below, down to 120 through applying successively the factor analyses based on the numbers of the items 200, 180, 160, and 120.

At the *first* step, Varimax was applied to the 200 adjectives, and 20 items that were complex in the sense of Big Five simple structure were deleted. At the *second* step, analyses were done on the remaining 180 adjectives. A target matrix was constructed in such a way that the Varimax factor loadings less than and larger than .35 were set to be *zero* and *unknown,* respectively, and the incomplete orthogonal procrustes factor rotation method of Browne (1972) was applied. In this way the squared sum of the factor loadings corresponding to the zero elements in the target matrix was minimized in the sense of least squares with the orthogonal constraints of the factors rotated. Then each rotated value was converted into zero or unknown, yielding a new target matrix. At the *third* step, through the comparison between the initial targets and the newly obtained ones in terms of their mutually corresponding converted elements, the incomplete orthogonal procrustes factor rotation method was applied to the 160 adjectives, after deleting the twenty items that did not match to each other in terms of their mutually corresponding elements in both targets. At the *fourth* and final step, after deleting forty items on the basis of the comparison of both targets, the incomplete orthogonal procrustes'factor rotation method of Browne (1972) was applied to the 120 adjectives. At this stage, the initial and obtained targets agreed perfectly to each other in terms of their mutually corresponding converted elements, and also they were very satisfactory in the sense of the Big Five simple structure. Therefore, the 120 adjectives were finally retained.

The Varimax rotation was then applied to the 120 adjectives attained through the preceding four steps, the solution of which is presented in Table 1. The Japanese adjectives are presented in their alphabetic or *Rooma-Ji* form, and the translations in English are presented as well. The author translated the adjectives into English through consulting the works of Bond, Nakasato and Shiraishi (1975), Isaka (1990), Hofstee *et al.* (1992), and Goldberg *et al.* (1996). The study by Hofstee *et al.* (1992) was translated into Japanese by Murakami and Murakami (1999) and the study by Goldberg *et al.* (1996) was translated into Japanese by the present author.

In Table 1, the symbols between parentheses are labels for facets (e.g., E2, E1 for Sociable), to be explained in Study-2. For each trait-factor, the trait-adjectives are grouped into those with a positive loading and those with a negative loading, arranged from largest to lowest with regard to their absolute values. The values over | .35| are shown in boldface, and, if more factor loadings over | .35| are found for a trait-adjective, they are shown together with the trait factor symbol in parentheses. "Humorous", for example, loads on both the trait factors E and O with the values .38 and .36, respectively. The numbers of positively loading trait adjectives and negatively loading ones are, respectively, 19 and 10 for Extraversion, 16 and 4 for Agreeableness, 9 and 12 for Conscientiousness, 1 and 25 for Neuroticism, and 24 and 0 for Openness to Experience. The corresponding α-coefficients are .93, .88, .86, .91, and .90, respectively.

Big Five and interdependencies

In order to investigate the degree of interdependencies among the Big Five trait factors, the incomplete oblique procrustes factor rotation method of Jöreskog (Mulaik, 1972, pp. 314-318) was applied. According to this method, the squared sum of the elements in the obtained factor rotation matrix corresponding to the zero elements in the target matrix is minimized so as to attain *indirectly* the primary pattern through the reference structure. And, although this method may provide rather oblique solutions, they are *not affected at their initial factor positions*. Each row vector in the target matrix corresponding to the adjectives belonging to the trait factor Extraversion in Table 1 is given by [? 0 0 0 0]. Those for the trait factor Agreeableness are given by [0 ? 0 0 0], those for Conscientiousness are [0 0 ? 0 0], for Neuroticism [0 0 0 ? 0], and for Openness to Experience [0 0 0 0 ?]. The question mark "?" and the number "0" respectively represent the *unknown* and *zero* elements in the target matrix.

Table 1. Varimax solution for the Big Five in the 120 Japanese Adjectives List.

Adjectives		Facets	Loadings
Factor I (Extraversion: E)			
Shakoutekina	Sociable	(E2, E1)	.75
Akarui	Cheerful	(E4, E2, E1)	.74
Katsudoutekina	Active	(E3, E2)	.72
Gaikoutekina	Extraverted	(E3)	.68
Kaikatsuna	Merry	(E3, E2, E4)	.67
Youkina	Effervescent	(E2)	.67
Tomodachinoooi	Good-mixer	(E3, E1)	.65
Sekkyokutekina	Aggressive	(E3)	.61
Hitonattsukkoi	Affable	(E2)	.58
Hanashizukina	Talkative	(E4)	.55
Aisonoyoi	Amiable	(E1)	.54
Genki	Energetic	(E3)	.52
Koudou-han-inohiroi	Social	(E2)	.49
Riidaashippunoaru	Vibrant	(E4)	.48
Kigaruna	not-Reluctant	(E4)	.47
Hyoukinna	Jocular	(E2)	.47
Iyokutekina	Enthusiastic	(E3)	.46
Hitotoisshogasuki	Gregarious	(E4, N1)	.44
Yuumoanoaru	Humorous	(E2, O1)	.38 (.36; O)
Mukuchina	Quiet	(E1, E2, E4)	-.67
Uchikina	Shy	(E1, N1)	-.63
Hitogirai	Unsociable	(E1)	-.56
Uchitokenai	not-Affable	(E1)	-.55
Jimina	Sober	(E1)	-.54
Buaisona	not-Amiable	(E1	-.48
Ishihyoujishinai	Aloof	(E1)	-.47
Naiseiteki	Introspective	(E4)	-.46
Fusagigachi	Depressed	(E1)	-.45 (-.35; N)
Kodokuna	Alone		-.36
Factor II (Agreeableness: A)			
Onkouna	Cordial	(A3)	.69
Odayakana	Mild	(A3	.65
Hankoutekidenai	not-Antagonistic	(A2)	.63
Ryoushintekina	Honest	(A1, A3)	.63
Onwa	Gentle	(A3, A1)	.62
Shinsetsuna	Generous	(A1)	.58
Yasashii	Affectionate	(A1)	.51
Kyouryokutekina	Helpful	(A1)	.49 (.35; E)
Hitonoyoi	Good-natured	(A1)	.48
Reigitadashii	Polite	(A1, C2)	.47
Kinonagai	Patient	(A3, A2)	.45
Hitoatarinoyoi	Agreeable		.45 (.42; E)
Kandaina	Charitable	(A3)	.43
Omoiyarinoaru	Sympathetic	(A1)	.43
Nasakebukai	Compassionate	(A1)	.38
Jikochuushintekidenai	not-Self-centered	(A2)	.36

Hankouteki	Antagonistic	(A2, A3)	-.61
Togenoaru	Harsh	(A2)	-.52
Wagamamana	Selfish	(A2)	-.41
Zukezukemonowoiu	Abusive	(A2, O3)	-.38

Factor III (Conscientiousness: C)

Kichoumenna	Neat	(C2)	.49
Sekininkannotsuyoi	Responsible		.48
Rouwooshimanai	Diligent	(C1, N3)	.46
Ganbaru	Hardworking		.41
Keikakuseinoaru	Systematic	(C2)	.41
Teineina	Respectful	(C2)	.40
Kinbenna	Industrious	(C2)	.38
Shinchouna	Cautious	(C2)	.37
Faitonoaru	Spirited		.36

Iikagenna	Disorganized	(C1)	-.67
Keisotsuna	Rash	(C1)	-.62
Musekininna	Irresponsible	(C1)	-.61
Akkippoi	Weary	(C1)	-.55
Keihakuna	Frivolous	(C1, A2)	-.51
Ruuzuna	Unpunctual	(C2)	-.50
Bukkirabou	Blunt		-.50
Kimagure	Illogical	(C1)	-.48
Utsurigina	Fickle	(C1)	-.48
Taidana	Negligent		-.46
Rakkantekina	Optimistic	(C1)	-.41
Ishinoyowai	Weak-will		-.39

Factor IV (Neuroticism: N)

Kuyokuyoshinai	Unworried		.46

Bikubikusuru	Fearful	(N2, N1)	-.68
Kinochiisai	Timid	(N1, N2)	-.68
Urotaeru	Upset	(N2)	-.68
Odoodosuru	Fidgety	(N2)	-.62
Douyoushiyasui	Restless	(N2)	-.61
Okubyouna	Cowardly	(N1, N2)	-.60
Fuanninariyasui	Insecure	(N2)	-.59
Dokyouganai	not-Daring	(N1)	-.58
Shinkeishitsuna	Nervous	(N3)	-.58
Yuuutsuna	Gloomy	(N3)	-.57
Taninwokinisuru	Apprehensive	(N2)	-.53
Awateyasui	Unstable	(N2)	-.53 (-.35; C)
Hikantekina	Pessimistic	(N1, N3)	-.53
Mijimena	Miserable	(N3)	-.48
Sabishigariya	Lonely		-.47
Shinpaishou	Anxious		-.46
Rettoukannotsuyoi	Defensive	(N1, N3)	-.46
Hazukashigariya	Bashful	(N1)	-.45
Nayamigachi	High-strung	(N3)	-.44
Kinchousuru	Tense	(N1)	-.44
Zaiakukannotsuyoi	Self-critical	(N3)	-.43

Hitonoiinari	Dependent		-.43
Kizutsukiyasui	Vulnerable	(N3)	-.42
Kigurounoooi	Worried	(N3)	-.39
Hunbetsunoaru	Sensible		-.32

Factor V (Openness to experience: O)

Atamanokaitennohayai	Smart	(O2, O1)	.70
Omoitsukinoyoi	Insightful	(O1, O2)	.65
Nouritsunoyoi	Proficient	(O2)	.62
Kitennokiku	Flexible	(O2, O3)	.62
Yuunouna	Able	(O2)	.62
Atamanoyoi	Intellectual	(O2)	.60
Aideanoyoi	Intuitive	(O1, O2)	.57
Tasaina	Versatile	(O2)	.55
Handannohayai	Clever	(O3, O2)	.54
Souzouryokunitonda	Imaginative	(O1)	.53
Bitekikankakunosurudoi	Aesthetic	(O1)	.53
Nomikominohayai	Wise	(O2)	.52
Dousatsuryokunoaru	Perceptive	(O1)	.52
Dokusoutekina	Creative	(O1)	.49
Chakusougaii	Witty	(O1)	.48
Kannoii	Brilliant	(O2)	.45
Kibinna	Prompt	(O2)	.43
Tayorigainoaru	Dependable	(O2)	.40
Dokuritsushita	Independent	(O3, E1)	.39
Rinkiouhenna	Accommodating	(O3)	.39
Kanjounoyutakana	Artistic	(O1, N2)	.39
Kidatenoyoi	Soft-hearted		.37 (.36; A)
Yuuzuunokiku	Bright	(O3)	.35
Tegatai	Trustworthy		.32

Note: The adjectives are in Japanese Rooma-Ji and English

For space-saving purposes, the whole body of the primary pattern matrix is not presented, as the simple structure configuration of the Big Five is almost the same as the orthogonal one presented in Table 1. The matrix with correlations among the primary axes is presented in Table 2. Table 2 shows substantial correlations among the primary axes Factor I (Extraversion) and Factor V (Openness to Experience), Factor V (Openness to Experience) and Factor III (Conscientiousness), and Factor III (Conscientiousness) and Factor II (Agreeableness). Factor IV (Neuroticism) seems to be relatively independent of the other four trait factors. The relations for I-V, II-III, and the relative independence of IV were also found for the earlier described 91-list.

Table 2. Correlation among Primary Axes for the Big Five in 120 Japanese Adjectives

	A	C	N	O
E	.24	.14	.29	**.42**
A		**.37**	.05	.07
C			-.30	**.46**
N				.25

Note: The values over |.35| are shown in boldface

Study-2

In this second study we applied an Orthomax criterion, instead of Varimax, in order to define facets in an objective way. More specifically, the Parsimax, being one of the Orthomax criteria, was applied to the Japanese Adjective List with 120 items, obtained through the Varimax in Study-1. However, when applying this method, some items obtained in Study-1 may be excluded so that the final Big Five structure for the facets in Study-2 are satisfactory in the sense of the simple structure. An item belonging to a factor through Varimax in Study-1 may be regarded as belonging to a facet of another factor through the Parsimax in Study-2. "Spirited" for example, which loads .36 on Factor III (Conscientiousness) through Varimax (see Table 2), turns out to load on a facet of Factor I (Extraversion) through Parsimax (See Table 3 ahead).

Parsimax solution

The Parsimax for the orthogonal factor rotation (see Mulaik, 1972, pp. 263-265) was applied to the same data as used in Study-1. Before starting the analysis, the number of the facets was assumed to be *fifteen,* in the hope that every facet might have eight items on average and that all the α-coefficients for the facets might be larger than .75. The computation was continued until each of the rotated factor loadings stabilized within the tolerance limit of |.001|. The number of the cycles for the iterations was 112. The solution is presented in Table 3, where, for space-saving purposes, only the factor loadings belonging to the facets for each trait-factor are presented. For example, for the trait factor E, only the factor loadings corresponding to the four facets E1 to E4 are presented; others are not. In each trait-factor, the adjectives evaluated positively are different from those evaluated negatively, and they are grouped into two parts. In each part, they are arranged from the largest to the smallest in terms of the absolute values with regard to factor loadings.

Excluded adjectives

The Big Five assumption, brought about through Varimax, may not always be reproduced perfectly in the fifteen facets brought about through Parsimax when the factor loadings over |.35| are considered. When comparing Tables 1 and 3, the following *fifteen adjectives* may not always belong to the appropriate facets assumed previously following the Varimax procedure: *Alone* (Kodokuna) in E, *Agreeable* (Hitoatorinoyoi) in A, *Spirited* (Faitonoaru) in C, *Responsible* (Sekininkannotsuyoi) in C, *Hard-working* (Ganbaru) in C, *Blunt* (Bukkirabou) in C, *Negligent* (Taidana)

Table 3. Parsimax solution for the fifteen Facets in the 120 Japanese Adjective List

Factors	Facets			
I Extraversion	E1	E2	E3	E4
Amiable	.54	.27	-.02	.33
Jocular	.05	.65	.14	.03
Humorous	-.10	.61	.12	.08
Affable	.23	.53	.01	.34
Effervescent	.29	.52	.21	.30
Sociable	.39	.47	.21	.33
Social	.06	.39	.23	.24
Enthusiastic	.04	.05	.72	.17
Active	.20	.42	.49	.23
Aggressive	.20	.26	.48	.23
Energetic	.26	.18	.45	.29
Good-mixer	.36	.33	.43	.20
Merry	.14	.39	.41	.37
Extraverted	.25	.34	.37	.32
not-Reluctant	.11	.22	-.04	.59
Cheerful	.35	.36	.32	.46
Gregarious	.10	.17	.18	.42 (-.43; N1)
Talkative	.27	.31	.09	.38
Vibrant	.11	.15	.24	.35
not-Amiable	-.78	-.14	-.03	-.06
Depressed	-.57	-.01	-.21	-.10
Aloof	-.52	-.16	-.14	-.01
Quiet	-.43	-.41	-.17	-.35
not-Affable	-.41	-.25	-.06	-.31
Shy	-.39	-.25	-.25	-.27
Unsociable	-.37	-.25	-.23	-.20
Sober	-.35	-.21	-.24	-.29
Introspective	-.13	-.17	-.19	-.35
Alone(*)	-.28	-.20	-.10	-.27
II Agreeableness	A1	A2	A3	
Sympathetic	.68	.15	.06	
Affectionate	.67	.10	.23	
Generous	.62	.14	.32	
Good-natured	.59	.04	.19	
Honest	.53	.11	.44	
Compassionate	.46	.08	.11	
Helpful	.39	.23	.17	
Polite	.36	.13	.27 (.37; C2)	
not-Antagonistic	.12	.65	.31	
not-Self-centered	.17	.57	.00	
Mild	.24	.16	.68	
Cordial	.30	.15	.66	
Patient	-.15	.36	.56	

Charitable	.15	.14	.49
Gentle	**.38**	.20	**.44**
Agreeable(*)	.27	.13	.30 (**.36**; E1; **.35**; E4)
Selfish	.06	**-.62**	-.22
Antagonistic	-.16	**-.59**	-.35
Harsh	-.20	**-.50**	-.22
Abusive	-.21	**-.36**	-.11 (**.42**; O3)

III Consientiousness	C1	C2	
Diligent	**.35**	.10 (**-.36**; N3)	
Neat	.10	**.62**	
Cautious	.08	**.62**	
Respectful	.12	**.54**	
Systematic	.16	**.51**	
Industrious	.17	**.51**	
Spirited (*)	.10	.25 (**.61**; E3)	
Responsible (*)	**.33**	.18	
Hardworking (*)	.20	.11 (**.64**; E3)	
Rash	**-.66**	-.20	
Illogical	**-.62**	-.02	
Weary	**-.54**	-.17	
Fickle	**-.54**	-.17	
Irresponsible	**-.52**	-.21	
Disorganized	**-.51**	-.30	
Optimistic	**-.50**	.07	
Frivolous	**-.47**	-.16	
Unpunctual	-.34	**-.50**	
Blunt (*)	-.30	-.34 (**-.41**; E1)	
Negligent (*)	-.19	-.30	
Weak-will (*)	**-.33**	-.09	

IV Neuroticism	N1	N2	N3
Unworried (*)	**.32**	.29	.23
Timid	**-.60**	**-.41**	-.17
Not-Daring	**-.55**	-.32	-.13
Tense	**-.49**	-.13	-.18
Pessimistic	**-.49**	-.14	**-.40**
Bashful	**-.46**	-.16	-.06
Cowardly	**-.43**	**-.43**	-.18
Defensive	**-.38**	-.13	**-.38**
Restless	-.27	**-.63**	-.13
Unstable	-.11	**-.55**	-.29
Upset	-.29	**-.51**	-.26
Fearful	**-.43**	**-.47**	-.29
Fidgety	-.34	**-.45**	-.27
Insecure	-.30	**-.44**	-.34
Apprehensive	-.26	**-.41**	-.20
Miserable	-.11	-.19	**-.57**

Vulnerable	-.15	.03	-.54
Nervous	-.06	-.31	-.51
Self-critical	-.05	-.02	-.51
Worried	-.05	-.14	-.46
Gloomy	-.28	-.20	-.44
High-strung	-.09	-.28	-.41
Dependent (*)	-.31	-.23	-.26
Lonely (*)	.19	-.33	-.28
Anxious (*)	-.20	-.28	-.34
Sensible (*)	-.11	-.16	-.10

V Openness	O1	O2	O3
Aesthetic	.69	.10	.06
Imaginative	.64	.15	.00
Creative	.62	.02	.19
Intuitive	.53	.38	-.03
Perceptive	.49	.33	.16
Insightful	.42	.42	.26
Artistic	.41	.08	.23
Witty	.41	.23	.09 (.42; E4)
Wise	.12	.67	.03
Intellectual	.22	.62	.09
Smart	.39	.61	.23
Proficient	.15	.58	.30
Able	.34	.54	.12
Versatile	.27	.50	.20
Prompt	-.04	.47	.31
Brilliant	.23	.45	.13
Flexible	.29	.43	.41
Dependable	.07	.38	.31
Accommodating	.15	.14	.61
Clever	.07	.43	.56
Independent	.01	.05	.56
Bright	.15	.08	.54
Soft-hearted (*)	.14	.25	.14 (.41; A3)
Trustworthy (*)	.05	.24	.00 (.40; C2)

Note: (*) indicates excluded adjectives in the Fifteen Facets. Loadings over |.35| are in boldface.

in C, *Weak-will* (Ishinoyowai) in C, *Unworried* (Kuyokuyoshinai) in N, *Dependent* (Hitonoiinari) in N, *Lonely* (Sabishigariya) in N, *Anxious* (Shinpaishou) in N, *Sensible* (Hunbetsunoaru) in N, *Soft-hearted* (Kidatenoyoi) in O, and *Trustworthy* (Tegatai) in O. These were excluded from the list of 120 Japanese adjectives; the remaining 105 Japanese adjectives were adopted for the *fifteen facets*. The excluded adjectives are indicated by (*) in Table 3.

In Study-1, the largest absolute value with regard to the factor loadings was the most important guide to classify an adjective into a specific trait or facet. With such a criterion adopted here, five more adjectives (*Gregarious* in E, *Polite* in A, *Abuse* in A, *Diligent* in C, and *Witty* in O) should be excluded further (see Table 3); but this rather strict criterion was not followed.

The final list of 105 Japanese Adjectives

For space-saving purposes, the results of the Varimax solution of the 105 Japanese adjectives are not presented. The results, however, strongly resemble the simple structure configuration of the Big Five. Some statistics for the Big Five scales are presented in Table 4. The α-coefficients are very satisfactory with the exception may be of the value .83 for C. The scores for the scales are each nearly normally distributed as indicated by their standard deviations, skewnesses, and kurtosises. Therefore, these Big Five scales may be considered as very suitable for measuring the Big Five traits.

Fifteen facets and the Big Five

For the set of 105 adjectives that were attained, the following facets for each trait factor were defined as the result of the Parsimax solution presented in Table 3. The trait factor E has four facets, called Friendliness (E1), Sociability (E2), Activity (E3), and Gregariousness (E4). The trait factor A has three facets, called Understanding (A1), Generosity (A2), and Gentleness (A3). The trait factor C has two facets, called Reliability (C1) and Orderliness (C2). The trait factor N has three facets, called Toughness (N1), Stability (N2), and Happiness (N3). Finally, the trait factor O has three facets, called Imagination (O1), Competence (O2), and Quickness (O3). The names for the facets are based on the studies of Goldberg (1999) and of Saucier and Ostendorf (1999). The three facets for Neuroticism are given names that are the reverse of the trait factor. Table 5 contains the facet-names together with their factor loadings.

Except for the adjectives of the trait factor Neuroticism, Varimax was applied to the data based on the *fifteen facets* after reflecting the signs of the scores for the adjectives evaluated *negatively* in Table 3. The number of factors was of course five.

Table 4. Statistics for 105 Japanese Big Five Adjectives

Traits	E	A	C	N	O
number of items	28	19	15	21	22
α-coefficient	.93	.87	.83	.90	.90
mean	5.37	6.54	-1.03	-6.50	1.03
standard deviation	11.68	6.04	5.22	8.97	8.26
skewness	-.26	-.74	.09	.39	.08
kurtosis	-.54	.68	-.91	-.69	-.28

Table 5. Big Five Varimax solution in the fifteen facets of the 105 Japanese Adjective List (left part); Primary Pattern by the Incomplete Oblique Procrustes rotation method of Jöreskog (right part)

	E	A	C	N	O	E	A	C	N	O
I (Extraversion)										
E1 (Friendliness)	**.83**	.04	.13	-.27	-.07	**.94**	-.01	.20	-.16	.33
E2 (Sociability)	**.84**	.07	-.10	.00	.22	**.86**	.05	-.08	.10	.06
E3 (Activity)	**.82**	.01	.03	-.09	.25	**.84**	-.03	.06	.02	.06
E4 (Gregariousness)	**.84**	.00	-.16	-.09	.15	**.87**	-.02	-.13	.00	-.01
II (Agreeableness)										
A1 (Understanding)	.32	**.75**	.19	.10	.19	.28	**.75**	.07	.18	.08
A2 (Generosity)	-.16	**.67**	.31	-.16	-.24	-.13	**.68**	.21	-.15	-.31
A3 (Gentleness)	.00	**.85**	-.01	-.04	.18	-.13	**.90**	-.22	-.04	.19
III (Conscientiousness)										
C1 (Reliability)	-.08	.18	**.82**	-.22	-.02	.00	.08	**.85**	-.12	-.18
C2 (Orderliness)	-.01	.15	**.73**	.14	.33	-.01	.04	**.74**	.26	.23
IV (Neuroticism)										
N1 (Toughness)	.25	.00	.15	-**.81**	.21	.16	-.05	.08	-**.78**	.12
N2 (Stability)	.06	-.06	.24	-**.85**	.21	-.04	-.13	.17	-**.84**	.15
N3 (Happiness)	.09	.14	-.27	-**.80**	.02	-.02	.17	-**.39**	-**.86**	-.02
V (Openness to Experience)										
O1 (Imagination)	.21	.03	.04	-.01	**.75**	.02	-.01	-.04	.04	**.79**
O2 (Competence)	.16	.05	.30	-.18	**.79**	-.03	-.04	.21	-.10	**.79**
O3 (Quickness)	.10	.10	-.02	-.20	**.77**	-.14	.07	-.16	-.17	**.85**

Note: The values over |.35| are shown in boldface.

The result is presented in the left half of Table 5. They are neatly organized in terms of Big Five simple structure. In order to see the degree of the interdependencies among the Big Five and to be able to compare them to the results of Table 2, the incomplete oblique procrustes factor rotation method of Jöreskog was applied to the same data. The row vectors [?,0,0,0,0], [0,?,0,0,0], [0,0,?,0,0], [0,0,0,?,0], and [0,0,0,0,?] in the target matrix are given for the facets of the traits Extraversion, Agreeableness, Conscientiousness, Neuroticism, and Openness to Experiences, respectively, where the question mark "?" and the zero "0" represent the unknown and zero elements. The result is presented in the right half of Table 5. Although some complexity appeared in facet N3 (Happiness) in the primary pattern, the results are not really different from those in the left part of this table. However, when the correlations among the primary axes, as presented in Table 6, are compared to those in Table 2, only the linear relation of the trait factor E to the trait factor O turned out to be substantial.

Table 6. Correlations among Primary Axes for the Big Five in 105 Japanese Adjectives

	A	C	N	O
E	.11	-.03	-.22	**.46**
A		.34	-.10	.17
C			-.24	.28
N				-.17

Note: The values over |.35| are shown in boldface

Discussion

Hierarchical relations between traits and facets

The Parsimax solution of Table 3 indicates that some adjectives are complex in terms of simple structure. For example, for the trait factor Extraversion, *Merry* (Kaikatsuna) loads simultaneously on the three facets E3 (Activity), E2 (Sociability), and E4 (Gregariousness). In comparison, the trait variable *Extraverted* (Gaikoutekina) loads only on the facet of E3 (Sociability). The trait adjective *Extraverted* may therefore be considered *subordinate* to *Merry*, in terms of a hierarchical relation, as both of them load on the facet E3 (Activity). The importance of hierarchical relations between trait factors and facets from a factor analytic point of view, and the possibility to search for such relations, are emphasized for future studies of personality.

Statistics for Study-2

In Table 7 the statistics for the Big Five facets of the 105 Japanese Adjective List corresponding to the Parsimax solution are presented. Although the values of α-coefficients fluctuate from .86 to .62, it should be noted that their average is .78 as expected before starting this study. The lowest value .62 for the facet O3 (Quickness) is thought to be obtained because of its smallest number (four) of adjectives. The scores for the fourteen facets are nearly normally distributed though those for facet A1 are relatively sharper in terms of kurtosis. And, although the number (four) of the items for the facet O3 and the number (five) for facet A3 should possibly be increased, the fifteen facets obtained here are very suitable for the evaluations through their profiles together with the Big Five traits.

Table 7. Statistics for the Big Five facets on 105 Japanese adjectives (Parsimax)

Facet	number of items	α's	mean	sd	skewness	kurtosis
E1	9	.83	1.48	4.46	-.10	-.86
E2	6	.78	1.14	3.01	-.32	-.60
E3	7	.85	1.58	3.53	-.27	-.58
E4	6	.71	1.17	2.62	-.40	-.26
A1	8	.82	4.19	3.19	-.98	1.17
A2	6	.77	.23	2.22	-.10	-.84
A3	5	.70	2.12	2.24	-.77	.17
C1	9	.80	-1.55	3.31	.31	-.72
C2	6	.74	.52	2.89	-.10	-.75
N1	7	.81	-1.86	3.57	.29	-.99
N2	7	.84	-2.08	3.77	.34	-.95
N3	7	.72	-2.56	3.12	.59	-.34
O1	8	.79	1.67	3.23	-.14	-.37
O2	10	.86	-1.22	4.61	.19	-.43
O3	4	.62	.58	1.98	-.22	-.45

Concurrent validity: the Big Five versus psychoanalytic concepts

As was mentioned in the introductory section, Kashiwagi (1999) discussed the concurrent validity study, based on both an adjective type list (Adjective List or AL) and the sentence type list of the TEG (Tokyo University Egogram). The analysis was based on the *items* of both inventories. In the present chapter, this discussion is confined to the *scales* of both inventories. First, however, it is necessary to give some more details about the TEG and the AL.

The TEG is a psychodiagnostic type of personality inventory widely used in Japan, requiring self-ratings based on five kinds of psychoanalytic concepts. The five TEG scales each consist of ten items of the sentence type. The scale concepts are Nurturing Parent (NP), Critical Parent (CP), Adult (AD), Adapted Child (AC), and Free Child (FC). Each concept is represented by ten items such as "You love others as you do yourself" for NP, "Others say frequently that you are very strict to them as well as to yourself " for CP, "Others say that you are very logical" for AD, "I am very nervous of the critics to myself" for AC, and " Others say that you are cheerful" for FC. The subjects are requested to respond in terms of "Yes", "Questionable", and "No". These concepts of TEG were confirmed through Varimax, and the standardization for TEG was performed (For details about basic statistics, see Kashiwagi, 1999).

The AL scales are composed of fifty Japanese adjectives for the Big Five, which are selected from the results of Table 1 in a nearly random way, as the adjectives are very satisfactory in the sense of the Big Five. The items of the AL for the five scales are presented in Table 8. Also the AL has three answering options "Yes", "Questionable", and "No".

Self-Ratings were collected from 250 subjects (165 men and 85 women), on both the TEG items and the AL items, and these data were used to investigate the interrelationships between the Big Five concepts and the psychoanalytic concepts. For

Table 8. Japanese Adjective List translated into English used for concurrent validation

---

Extraversion (E)
+　　active, aggressive, effervescent, extraverted, talkative
-　　aloof, sober, shy, unsociable, quiet
Agreeableness (A)
+　　affectionate, charitable, gentle, generous, sympathetic, good-natured, honest not-self-centered
-　　antagonistic, harsh
Conscientiousness (C)
+　　industrious
-　　rash, illogical, fickle, weary, irresponsible, disorganized, negligent, optimistic, unpunctual
Neuroticism (N)
+　　insecure, anxious, high-strung, restless, fearful, tense, nervous, unstable, vulnerable, up-set
Openness to Experience(0)
+　　aesthetic, versatile, wise, proficient, perceptive, creative, independent, smart, flexible, accommodating

---

this purpose, two joint factor analyses were carried out on the scales from both inventories followed by an application of the incomplete orthogonal procrustes factor rotation of Browne (1972).

The first analysis involved the application of Browne's method, but restricted to the AL scales among the scales from both questionnaires. The second analysis involved the application of the same method, but restricted to the TEG scales. Preceding the factor rotations, the signs of all the scores for the adjectives that were evaluated negatively in the AL were reversed.

The target matrix for the first analysis is presented in the left upper part of Table 9. The squared sum of the rotated factor loadings corresponding to the zero elements in the target matrix was minimized in the sense of least squares with the orthogonal constraints of the factors rotated in both analyses. The rotated result for the first analysis is presented in the upper right part of Table 9. This may suggest that the TEG scales for the psychoanalytic concepts can be understandably described circumplexically in terms of the *Big Five,* as the AL scales for the Big Five are, factor analytically, mutually independent. In other words, the concept NP in the TEG can be described in everyday wordts by such terms as *active* and *affectionate*, the concept CP can be described by words such as *harsh* and *high-strung,* the concept AD can be described by such words as *wise* and *proficient* , the concept AC can be described by *shy, fickle* and *nervous*, and the concept FC can be described by *active* and *effervescent.* As expected, the mean of the α-coefficients for the AL scales of the adjective type (.81) is larger than the one for the TEG scales of sentence type (.75).

The AL scales were evaluated from the perspective of the TEG scales in the second analysis. The target matrix for the second analysis is presented in the left side of the middle part of Table 9. The rotated result for the second analysis is presented in the right side of that table. This may suggest that the AL scales can be described circumplexically in terms of the *four* dimensions of the psychoanalytic TEG scales except for NP or for FC. In other words, it may be said that the psychoanalytic concepts of both NP and FC are rather closely related to each other.

Table 9. Incomplete Orthogonal Procrustes Factor Solutions for AL and TEG scales

Scales	Target	E	A	C	N	O	α
			(Constrained by AL Scales)				
E	? 0 0 0 0	.87	.00	.04	.16	.25	.86
A	0 ? 0 0 0	.00	.88	.24	.07	.07	.72
C	0 0 ? 0 0	.04	.23	.93	.17	.11	.82
N	0 0 0 ? 0	.16	.07	.18	.87	.14	.82
O	0 0 0 0 ?	.25	.07	.12	.14	.87	.82
							mean of α =.81
NP	? ? ? ? ?	.53	.61	.12	-.21	.24	.78
CP	? ? ? ? ?	.04	-.75	-.07	-.56	.07	.67
AD	? ? ? ? ?	.08	.14	.34	.15	.83	.73
AC	? ? ? ? ?	-.45	.20	-.35	-.62	-.26	.80
FC	? ? ? ? ?	.80	.22	-.29	.19	.31	.79
							mean of α =.75

Scales	Target	NP	CP	AD	AC	FC
		(Constrained by TEG Scales)				
E	? ? ? ? ?	.37	.11	.08	-.49	.68
A	? ? ? ? ?	.56	-.68	.21	-.14	-.05
C	? ? ? ? ?	.48	-.22	.34	-.56	-.49
N	? ? ? ? ?	-.23	-.53	.19	-.66	.20
O	? ? ? ? ?	.12	.04	.81	-.20	.37
NP	? 0 0 0 0	.75	-.19	.20	.04	.36
CP	0 ? 0 0 0	-.15	.92	-.06	.09	-.07
AD	0 0 ? 0 0	.17	-.06	.87	-.24	.11
AC	0 0 0 ? 0	.04	.10	-.25	.83	-.26
FC	0 0 0 0 ?	.33	-.07	.12	-.26	.82

The orthogonal rotation matrices through the initial principal axes solution to the rotated orthogonal ones for both analyses were obtained. In addition, the orthogonal rotational interrelations between the personality traits for the Big Five in the AL scales and the five psychoanalytic TEG scales were obtained. The orthogonal rotation matrix obtained for the second analysis was transposed, and it was postmultiplied by the orthogonal rotation matrix for the first analysis. The result is presented in the correlation matrix of Table 10.

The result explained above based on the scales for both the AL and the TEG is *essentially similar* to the one analyzed on the basis of the items for both the AL and the TEG (Kashiwagi, 1999), which was suggested in the first part of this section. Although the previous result based on the items is not shown here, the present analysis based on their scales indicate that the psychoanalytic concept AD in the TEG correspond *almost perfectly* to the trait O in the AL. And the other four psychoanalytic concepts may be described *circumplexically* in terms of the remaining four Big Five personality factors.

Table 10. Correlations between AL scales and TEG scales

Concepts	AL scales				
	E	A	C	N	O
NP	.50	.55	.45	-.49	.03
CP	.21	-.75	.03	-.62	.15
AD	-.20	.09	.23	.05	.95
AC	-.44	-.35	-.58	-.59	-.04
FC	.69	.07	-.64	-.18	-.28

Final conclusion

It is concluded that the Big Five dimensions of personality traits were confirmed in Japanese. Although the results presented in Table 2 suggested some oblique relations among the Big Five factors through the incomplete oblique procrustes factor rotation, their almost perfect mutual orthogonalities were confirmed in the results based on at least eighty-eight percent (105 to 120) of the items. This was the case through the application of both the Varimax for the Big Five factors and the Parsimax for the related fifteen facets (see Table 5 and Table 6).

It is emphasized that the sentence type for personality inventories is to be preferred over the adjective type. The preferred format should be the short behavior-descriptive sentence so that subjects are able to respond more exactly and more easily. Still, at the same time, profiles or results obtained may very often be read and interpreted in related Big Five adjective terms. When using the short behavior-descriptive sentence type for personality inventories, for their interpretation in terms of the Big Five, it may be of help to use Big Five adjectives as well. Therefore, it is important to continue using adjective lists like the one in this study in personality research.

References

Aoki, T. (1974). *Dictionary for Personality Traits*. Diamond Press (in Japanese).

Bond, M.H., Nakasato, H., & Shiraishi, D. (1975). Universality and distinctiveness in dimensions in Japanese person perception. *Journal of Cross Cultural Psychology*, 6, 346-357.

Browne, M.W. (1972). Orthogonal rotation to a partially specified target. *British Journal of Mathematical and Statistical Psychology*, 25, 115-120.

Costa, P.T. Jr. & McCrae, R.R. (1991). *NEO-PI-R Professional Manual Revised NEO Personality (NEO-PI-R) and NEO Five-Factor Inventory (NEO-FFI)*. Psychological Assessment resource, Inc: Florida.

Goldberg, L.R. (1999). A broad-bandwidth, public-domain, personality inventory measuring the lower-level facets of several Five-Factor models. In I. Mervielde, I.J. Deary, F. De Fruyt, & F. Ostendorf (Eds). *Personality Psychology in Europe*, Volume 7, (pp. 7-28). Tilburg, Tilburg University Press.

Goldberg, L.R., Sweeney, D., Merenda, P.F., & Hughes, J.E. Jr, (1996). The Big-Five factor structure as an integrative framework: An analysis of Clarke's AVA model. *Journal of Personality Assessment, 66*, 441-471.

Hendriks, A.A.J. (1997). *The Construction of the Five-Factor Personality Inventory (FFPI)*. Groningen, The Netherlands: Rijksuniversiteit Groningen.

Hofstee, W.K.B., De Raad, B., & Goldberg, L.R. (1992). Integration of the Big Five and circumplex approaches to trait structure. *Journal of Personality and Social Psychology, 63*, 146-163.

Isaka, H. (1990). Factor analysis of trait terms in everyday Japanese languages. *Personality and Individual Differences, 11*, 115-124.

John, O.P. (1990). The "Big Five" Factor Taxonomy: Dimensions of Personality in the Natural Language and in Questionnaires. In L.A. Pervin. (Ed.), *Handbook of Personality: Theory and Research* (pp. 66-100). New York: The Guilford press.

Kashiwagi, S. (1965). Geometric vector orthogonal rotation method in multiple factor analysis. *Psychometrika, 30*, 515-530.

Kashiwagi, S. (1999). The trait theoretic evaluation of the TEG from the view of the Five-Factor Model. *The Japanese Journal of Psychology, 69*, 468-477 (in Japanese).

Kashiwagi, S., & Wada, S. (1996). A study on the concurrent validity of personality inventory from the view of the Five-Factor Model concerning personality traits. *The Japanese Journal of Psychology, 67*, 300-307 (in Japanese).

Kashiwagi, S., Wada, S, & Aoki, T. (1993). The Big Five and the oblique primary pattern for the items of the ACL Japan version. *The Japanese Journal of Psychology, 64*, 153-159 (in Japanese).

Kashiwagi, S., & Yamada, K. (1995). Evaluation of the Uchida-Kraepelin test based on The Five-Factor Model of personality traits. *The Japanese Journal of Psychology, 66*, 24-32 (in Japanese).

Mulaik, S.A. (1972). *The foundation of factor analysis*. McGraw Hill.

Murakami, Y., & Murakami, C. (1999). *The recent development of the Big Five theory in personality research*. Baifuukan (in Japanese).

Piedmont, R.L., McCrae, R.R., & Costa, P.T. Jr., (1991). Adjective Check List scales and the Five-factor model. *Journal of Personality and Social Psychology, 60*, 630-637

Saucier, G., & Ostendorf, F. (1999). Hierarchical subcomponents of the Big Five personality factors : A cross-language replication. *Journal of Personality and Social Psychology, 76*, 615-627.

Suematsu, H., Wada, M., Nomura, S., & Tawara, R. (1995). *EgoGram Pattern*. Kaneko Shoboh (in Japanese).

Wada, S. (1991). *A factor analytic study of the Big Five - (1) The structure of Japanese ACL* - (Unpublished paper in Japanese for the degree of master in the Chiba University of Japan).

Wada, S. (1996). Construction of the Big Five Scales of personality trait items and concurrent validity with NPI. *The Japanese Journal of Psychology, 67*, 61-67 (in Japanese).

Widiger, T.A. & Trull, T.J. (1997). Assessment of the Five-Factor Model of Personality, *Journal of Personality Assessment, 68*, 228-250

Yanai, H., Kashiwagi, S., & Kokushoh, R. (1987). Construction of a new personality inventory by means of factor analysis on Promax rotation. *The Japanese Journal of Psychology, 58*, 158-165 (in Japanese).

BIG FIVE ASSOCIATED INSTRUMENTS

Chapter 14

The Hogan Personality Inventory

Robert Hogan
Joyce Hogan

Introduction

We began developing the Hogan Personality Inventory (HPI) in 1976 for two reasons. First, from 1964 to 1976, we worked with the California Psychological Inventory (CPI: Gough, 1975), and by 1976 we had a substantial set of archival data on hand. We had read Norman's (1963) research but regarded it as lacking practical significance. To test this view, we constructed CPI content scales based on Norman's taxonomy, and reanalyzed our archival data. We found that the CPI content scales substantially outperformed the standard scales, and this persuaded us that future inventories of normal personality should be based on the Five-Factor Model (FFM; Wiggins, 1996). Second, although we had no desire to develop a personality inventory (it is too much work), the major inventories at the time were perhaps 30 years old, and none of them were likely to be reconfigured in terms of the FFM. We began working on the HPI as a teaching exercise in a graduate course in psychometrics and one thing led to another. We arrived at the current (1995) version of the inventory through a constant process of evaluation and revision over a period of 20 years.

We began work on the HPI while we were at Johns Hopkins University and we originally called it the Hopkins Personality Inventory (HPI). We moved to the University of Tulsa in 1982; we had published papers using the term HPI, so we retained it, with one small modification. The HPI differs from the other inventories described in this book in seven ways, and each of these differences is important.

1. The HPI has a well-defined conceptual foundation — it is based on Socioanalytic theory (Hogan, 1983; 1991; 1996). Socioanalytic theory combines elements of traditional interpersonal theory (Carson, 1969; Leary, 1957; Sullivan, 1953; Wiggins, 1979) with evolutionary theory, and is intended to explain individual differences in interpersonal competence and effectiveness. The theory is based on five

Big Five Assessment, edited by B. De Raad & M. Perugini. © 2002, Hogrefe & Huber Publishers.

key assumptions: (1) personality must be understood in the context of evolutionary theory; (2) people evolved as group living and culture using animals; (3) the most important human motives facilitate group living and enhance individual survival; (4) people are compelled to interact, and interaction involves negotiating for acceptance and status; and (5) some people are more effective at these negotiations than others (Hogan, 1996; Hogan, Jones, & Cheek, 1985).

The theory starts with two generalizations about social life: (1) people always live (work) in groups, and (2) groups are always structured in status hierarchies. This leads to two conclusions about human motivation. First, people need acceptance and approval from others, (and want to avoid rejection); this need is manifested in terms of behavior designed to allow one to "get along" with other members of the group. Second, people need status and the control of resources (and want to avoid losing them); this need translates into behavior designed to allow one to "get ahead" or achieve status within the group(s) where one lives. These generalizations make sense in Darwinian terms: historically, people who could not get along with others and who lacked status and power had reduced opportunities for reproductive success.

Anthropologists (cf. Redfield, 1960, p. 345) tell us that all societies require their members to work on "getting a living and living together." "Getting a living" concerns completing crucial life tasks, and "living together" concerns maintaining group solidarity. Social psychologists (cf. McGrath, Arrow, & Berdahl, 2000) tell us that group living allows people: "(a) to complete group projects and (b) to fulfill member needs. A group's success in fulfilling these two functions affects the viability and integrity of the group as a system" (p. 98). Small group research (cf. Forsyth, 1990; Mann, 1959) tells us that people provide their groups with task inputs and socio-emotional inputs. Task inputs promote the achievement of group goals, whereas socio-emotional inputs promote group solidarity. Personality is the heart of these processes — because the core of personality binds people to the groups where they live and work. People differ in their strategies for getting along (living together) and getting ahead (getting a living). These strategies, and the deep needs to get along and get ahead which they serve, are the core of personality.

Socioanalytic theory distinguishes between personality from the perspective of the actor and personality from the perspective of the observer. Personality from the actor's view is a person's identity, and it reflects his/her hopes, dreams, fears, aspirations, and career intentions. Identity is a person's self-view; self-views are unique and idiosyncratic, and they are difficult to study empirically. On the other hand, personality from the observers' view is a person's reputation. Reputation is defined in terms of trait evaluations — friendly, helpful, talkative, competitive, calm, etc. Reputation reflects, from an observer's perspective, an actor's characteristic ways of behaving in public. The Five-Factor Model (FFM) represents the structure of observers' ratings based on 75 years of factor analytic research (cf. Goldberg, 1993; Thurstone, 1934) — i.e., the FFM is a taxonomy of reputation (cf. Digman, 1990; Saucier & Goldberg, 1996). The observer's view of an actor's personality is easy to study and can be assessed reliably using ratings.

Identity is the person you believe you are; reputation is the person we believe you are. Your identity guides your behavior during social interaction; your reputation is the result of how we evaluate your performance after social interaction. Although identity is hard to measure, reputation is easy to measure and it is inherently valid — because the best predictor of future behavior is past behavior (Hough & Oswald, 2000), and reputation is based on past behavior.

2. The HPI is based on a theory of item responses that is very different from the standard self-report view of item responses (cf. Hogan & Hogan, 1998). From our perspective, the psychological processes involved in responding to questionnaire items are formally identical to those that guide social interaction more generally. People use their item responses to tell others how they want to be regarded — e.g., as calm, ambitious, hardworking, flexible, or enthusiastic. That is, people respond to items in terms of their identity, their theory of what they stand for. As such, item responses are self-presentations, not self-reports. When a test is scored, item responses are in essence interpreted by an anonymous observer behind the questionnaire — i.e., the scoring key (Hogan & Hogan, 1998, p. 39). Reputations are the result of a person's self-presentations being evaluated by others, and profiles on well-developed personality inventories predict reputation.

In summary, people do not respond to questionnaire items in terms of putatively veridical self-reports. Rather, they respond to questionnaire items in the same way that they respond to interview questions. They use their identities to guide their responses, and their responses (self-presentations) are intended to tell the "interviewer" how they want to be seen. Our model of item responses follows directly from Socioanalytic theory; thus, we can explicitly account for our own data base.

3. The HPI shares the measurement goals of the California Psychological Inventory (CPI; Gough, 1975). From the original publication of the CPI to the present, Gough has maintained that it is designed to predict two classes of phenomena: (a) indices of competence and effectiveness; and (b) how people will be described by persons who know them well. We adopted these measurement goals because they are pragmatic, they lead to real world pay-offs, and they explicitly focus on validity.

We believe that most test authors do not take validity seriously, although they would obviously disagree with our characterization. Test authors in the factor analytic tradition define validity as the degree to which the factor structure of their inventories will replicate across samples. Others, relying on the rather ill-defined concept of "construct validity", evaluate the validity of their inventories in terms of correlations with other tests and scales. Still others rather preposterously define validity in terms of the degree to which clients agree with their assessment results (cf. Hogan & Hogan, 1998).

Following Gough (1965), we define validity in terms of the number of empirically justified inferences we can make about a person on the basis of his or her score on a scale or measure. The more valid inferences we can make, the more valid the measure. In our view, assessment has a job to do — the job is to predict real world outcomes. Peoples' success in life, and how others describe them, are crucial outcomes, and validity is *the* critical index of how well an assessment device is doing its job.

4. The HPI further specifies *what* important real world outcomes it tries to predict. As stated in the first section, we believe that there are two broad classes of out-

comes that are crucial in human affairs. The first concerns the degree to which a person is liked, admired, respected, and accepted in his/her local community. Alternatively, it is sometimes useful to be able to identify persons who are loathed, feared, or shunned — and perhaps understand why they are seen in that way. The second outcome concerns the degree of status, power, and/or control of resources a person has been able to attain, or is likely to attain, in his/her local community. This includes identifying life's potential winners and losers. This information can be used for a variety of strategic purposes including hiring, promoting, and developing people.

We can summarize the foregoing by saying that the HPI is designed to assess individual differences in people's potential for getting along and getting ahead in the groups where they live and work.

5. The HPI was developed almost exclusively using data from working adults. Working adults provided the data for the original, and for the subsequent, developmental psychometrics. Working adults provided the normative data for the HPI. Current norms are based on over 300,000 working adults, and the norms are broken out separately for most relevant occupational categories: gender; race/ethnicity; age; status; applicants vs. incumbents; etc. Finally, the HPI was validated exclusively using data from working adults. To date we have conducted over 300 local validity studies in which HPI scale scores for job applicants or incumbents were compared with a wide variety of performance data, including supervisors' ratings, absenteeism, commendations, dismissals, subordinate appraisals, training performance, promotions, etc.

We have validity data for most of the common jobs in the U.S. economy, and we have studied jobs ranging from janitor to Chief Executive Officer, and from nanny to bomb disposal technician. In every study, the relevant HPI scales and/or subscales — those scales pertinent to the criteria in question — significantly predicted performance. The more reliable the performance criteria, the more strongly did the HPI forecast performance.

6. Reflecting our view that assessment has a job to do, the HPI is designed to predict significant outcomes — including how a person is described by others. At stake here is an important issue in the philosophy of science. Consider what has happened in psychological measurement since its beginning. Binet developed his test to forecast educational or training outcomes and he never mentioned the world "intelligence." Under the influence of Spearman and subsequent writers, the field of cognitive assessment changed from forecasting significant outcomes to measuring intelligence, a concept that has yet to be rigorously defined. And in the process of measuring intelligence, researchers tend to ignore validity. Similarly, the MMPI and the CPI were developed to predict significant outcomes. Under the influence of factor analysts, the field of personality assessment went from predicting outcomes to measuring traits, hypothetical entities that have yet to be discovered. The field moved from predicting something useful to measuring something that may not exist, and along the way it redefined the concept of validity so that predicting outcomes was no longer important for evaluating validity.

Trait theory assumes that traits are real, neuropsychic entities that literally exist, although they have yet to be discovered. Moreover, the strength of these traits controls item endorsements, so that a person's score on a personality measure reflects, in a point for point manner, the strength or intensity of the underlying trait. In this model, a person's aggressive behavior is explained in terms of a trait for aggressiveness. This is, of course, completely circular, but more importantly, it shuts down any subsequent debate about the causes of aggression. For example, we would argue that aggressive behavior is a form of self-presentation, it is an effort to tell others that one is not to be trifled with, that one is, somehow, a dangerous person. In our view, aggressiveness is a function of a person's identity and social learning experience rather than (necessarily) a function of a person's traits.

To say that behavior is explained by traits is to make a particular explanatory claim, and one that can be challenged by alternative explanatory accounts. In our view, purposive social behavior is best explained in terms of a person's intentions, not mythical neuropsychic entities. The intentions can then be further analyzed and broken down. No one believes more than we do in the importance of biology for providing ultimate explanations of human behavior. But at the every day level, intentions are more satisfying than traits as explanatory constructs.

7. Socioanalytic theory characterizes social behavior in terms of the two broad themes of "getting along" and "getting ahead". It follows that a personality inventory based on socioanalytic theory should have two dimensions. In our view, the dimension of the FFM are all aspects of getting along and getting ahead (cf. Wiggins & Trapnell, 1996). However, the task of predicting occupational outcomes requires more narrow band predictors than two or even five dimensions, and the HPI is about predicting practical outcomes. The HPI started as a classroom exercise designed to evaluate the FFM. Taking each dimension of the FFM one at a time, we asked what kinds of things would a person say or do so as to make others describe him/her as (for example, in the case of Adjustment) well or poorly adjusted. Among other things, we concluded this would involve seeming anxious, depressed, stressed, insecure, poorly attached, and having a lot of physical complaints. We wrote items for each of these components, called the components a dimension, and then moved on to the next dimension.

After writing items for the components of each dimension, we had over 420 items. The items were grouped into Homogenous Item Composites (HIC; Zonderman, 1980). Each composite was a coherent set of 3 to 5 items reflecting a single theme — e.g., anxiety, depression, stress, insecurity, etc. Our intent from the outset was to conduct validity research at the HIC level; we realized, however, that most test users are accustomed to interpreting profiles based on scales, so we set about composing scales. We began in a rational way, but once we had enough data, we carefully evaluated the factor structure of the HICs. We finally decided upon a seven-factor solution as optimal, and at no point was a five-factor solution ever contemplated—none of them fit the data. We believe that people think about themselves in a more complicated manner than they think about others. Consequently, although a five factor solution may be appropriate for rating other people, the factor structure of self-descriptions is necessarily more complex.

Thus, although we started with the FFM, we found a five factor solution did not fit our data. We think the FFM is the indispensable starting point for inventory construction, but it is not a structure than naturally inheres in nature.

Technical Features of the Hogan Personality Inventory

Guided by socioanalytic theory, the HPI is designed to predict individual differences in getting along and getting ahead in occupational settings. Although the inventory has broader uses (Axford, 1996), our research has been almost exclusively with job seekers and employed adults. Applications of the HPI include personnel selection, individualized assessment, placement, promotion, training, coaching and development, employee orientation, and career planning.

Our goals for the HPI also included certain desired operational features. We wanted an item pool that could be completed quickly. We wrote items to be easily understood by a wide range of people, trying to balance reading level with item complexity. We considered how test takers would react to the items, and tried to avoid items that were potentially invasive or intrusive. We wanted to assess the "bright side" of personality, i.e., to focus on characteristics that facilitate or inhibit a person's ability to get along with others and achieve his/her occupational goals, and we wanted to avoid the domain of psychopathology. We were committed to developing a measure that, when used for selection purposes, would have no adverse impact. Most importantly, we wanted to identify HICs that predicted significant occupational outcomes, including job performance. Finally, we wanted to develop an instrument that, when used appropriately, would yield financial payoffs for the user — reduced turnover, increased productivity, reduced shrinkage, increased retention, etc.

Description of the 1995 HPI

The Hogan Personality Inventory (Hogan & Hogan, 1995) is a 206-item true-false measure of normal personality designed to predict performance in real world settings. The inventory contains seven primary scales constructed from 41 HICs, which are groups of items that form sub-themes of the broader scale. The number of HICs per scale ranges from four (School Success) to eight (Adjustment). There is no item overlap among the primary scales. The inventory also contains six occupational scales and a validity scale to detect careless responding. The Flesch-Kincaid reading level analysis indicates that the items are written at the fourth grade level. This discussion is limited to the HPI primary scales; discussion of the occupational scales is presented in the HPI manual (Hogan & Hogan, 1995) and other publications (Hogan & Hogan, 1989; Hogan, Hogan, & Busch, 1984).

Table 1 presents the seven HPI primary scales and their definitions. Three of

Table 1. Hogan Personality Inventory Primary Scales and Definitions

	Definition
Adjustment	The degree to which a person appears calm and self-accepting.
Ambition	The degree to which a person seems socially self-confident, leader-like, competitive, and energetic.
Sociability	The degree to which a person seems to need and/or enjoy interacting with others.
Likeability	The degree to which a person is seen as perceptive, tactful, and socially sensitive.
Prudence	The degree to which a person seems conscientious, conforming, and dependable.
Intellectance	The degree to which a person is perceived as bright, creative, and interested in intellectual matters.
School Success	The degree to which a person seems to enjoy academic activities and to value educational achievement for its own sake.

these scales are directly aligned with FFM dimensions: Emotional Stability, Agreeableness, and Conscientiousness are represented by HPI Adjustment, Likeability, and Prudence. However, the HPI Ambition and Sociability scales cover the domain represented by the FFM Surgency dimension, and the HPI Intellectance and School Success scales cover the domain represented by FFM Intellect/Openness to Experience. The decision to include seven scales reflects the factor structure of the HICs. We intercorrelated scores on the HICs using a sample of 2500 employed adults. We decided on seven factors based on eigenvalues, a scree test, and the comprehensibility of alternative solutions. We refined the components using orthogonal varimax rotation. The factor matrix for the HPI HICs, as they load on the seven factors, appears in the test manual (Hogan & Hogan, 1995, p. 11).

We evaluated the internal consistency of the primary scales using Cronbach's alpha and a sample of 960 adults. We evaluated test-retest reliability with a sample of 150 respondents over an interval greater than four weeks. The internal consistency reliability and the test-retest reliability, respectively, for each scale is: Adjustment (.89/.86); Ambition (.86/.83); Sociability (.83/.79); Likeability (.71/.80); Prudence (.78/.74); Intellectance (.78/.83); and School Success (.75/.86). In Buros Mental Measurement Yearbook reviews, Axford (1996) and LoBello (1996) deemed the magnitude of these reliability coefficients adequate for research and application.

Table 2 presents the intercorrelations among the HPI primary scales based on a sample of 30,016 employed adults. As seen, Adjustment is correlated with all the other scales except Sociability. Ambition is moderately correlated with all the other scales. Sociability is positively related to Intellectance and negatively related to Prudence. In addition, Likeability is associated with Prudence and Intellectance is associated with School Success. Adjustment, Ambition, Prudence, and Likeability form one cluster of scales. Sociability is a second, and Intellectance and School Success form a weak third cluster. Other than these correlations the scales are reasonably independent.

Table 2. Hogan Personality Inventory primary scale intercorrelation matrix

	Adjustment	Ambition	Sociability	Likeability	Prudence	Intellectance
Adjustment	—					
Ambition	.50**	—				
Sociability	-.10**	.31**	—			
Likeability	.46**	.34**	.17**	—		
Prudence	.57**	.24**	-.31**	.38**	—	
Intellectance	.14**	.37**	.45**	.16**	-.05**	—
School Success	.26**	.35**	.14**	.16**	.21**	.38**

Note: N = 30,016; ** $p \leq .01$, two-tailed.

Figure 1 shows raw score means for each of the HPI primary scales by gender and by race/ethnicity. Scale means and standard deviations as well as norms appear in the technical manual by gender, age, and race (Hogan & Hogan, 1995). The striking feature of Figure 1, which is corroborated by the descriptive statistics, is that there are no practical differences in scale scores' means and standard deviations by race/ethnicity. However, for gender, females score lower than males on Adjustment, Ambition, and Intellectance.

Validity of the HPI

Understanding the meaning of a psychological measure is an ongoing task. Meaning is defined through a cumulative process of test validation. There are a number of ways to clarify meaning, although validity has historically been defined in terms of correlations between test scores and criterion variables. Considerable attention is typically paid to the correlations, but little consideration is typically given to criterion adequacy. In our view, the concept of validity applies to both predictor and criterion measures — we need to validate our scales and our criteria. The process of trying to validate both sets of measures can lead to an infinite regress; nonetheless, we can't evaluate the validity of a personality scale based on the correlation between scale scores and any single criterion measure. We understand the meaning of a test score by: (1) placing the construct in a theoretical context; (2) understanding the latent structure underlying both test scores and criterion measures (Campbell, 1990; Hogan & Nicholson, 1988); (3) examining what the scale predicts (convergent validity) and doesn't predict (divergent validity); and (4) gathering subsequent data to test further predictions. Theory provides an explanation for the covariations obtained.

Over the last 20 years, we have used four types of evidence to explore the construct validity of the HPI scales: (1) correlations with scales of other well-validated

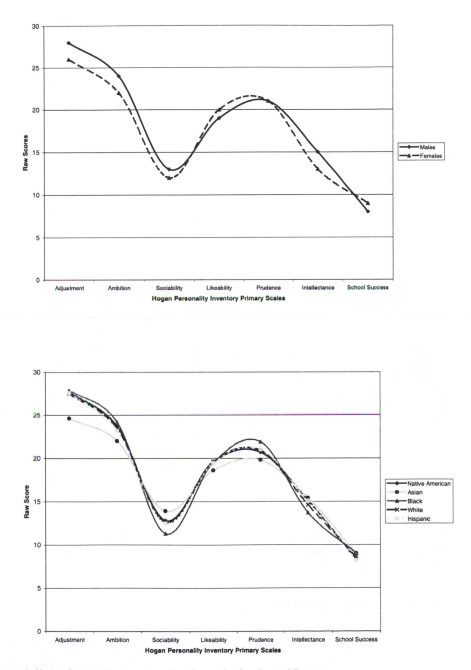

Figure 1. Hogan Personality Inventory Raw Scores by Gender and Race

Table 3. Links between the Hogan Personality Inventory and other Big Five measures

Source/ Big-Five Measure	Hogan Personality Inventory Scales						
	Adj	Amb	Soc	Lik	Pru	Int	Sch
Goldberg (1992)/							
Big-Five Factor Markers (N = 168)							
Surgency	.04	.55**	.44**	.31**	-.24**	.29**	-.03
Agreeableness	.13	-.11	.02	.56**	.23**	-.12	-.17
Conscientiousness	.10	.24**	-.26**	-.07	.36	-.17	-.08
Emotional Stability	.70**	.39**	-.04	.27**	.01	.28**	.11
Intellect	.05	.22**	-.04	-.01	.03	.33**	.35**
Salgado and Moscoso (1999)/							
Inventario de Personalidad de Cinco Factores (N = 200)							
IP-Neuroticism	.66**	.50**	.16	.31**	.32**	.26**	--
IP-Extraversion	.24**	.60**	.62**	.35**	.04	.41**	--
IP-Openness	.11	.44**	.51**	.25**	-.15	.69**	--
IP-Agreeableness	.22**	-.12	-.10	.37**	.25**	-.10	--
IP-Conscientiousness	.22**	.35**	.08	.30**	.49**	.19	--
Goldberg (2000)/							
NEO PI-R as part of IPIP project (N = 679)							
Neuroticism	.72**	.53**	.08	.27**	.22**	.14**	.16**
Extraversion	.16**	.54**	.63**	.44**	-.06	.21**	.08
Openness	.01	.20**	.38**	.19**	-.31**	.52**	.24**
Agreeableness	.30**	-.12**	-.24**	.47**	.46**	-.20**	-.08
Conscientiousness	.24**	.37**	-.05	.07	.42**	.05	.16**
Mount and Barrick (1995)/							
Personal Characteristics Inventory (N = 154)							
Extraversion	.39**	.64**	.26**	-.09	.04	.18	--
Agreeableness	.25**	.09	.61**	.21**	.50**	-.03	--
Conscientiousness	.39**	-.06	.17	.59**	.24**	.08	--
Stability	.59**	-.02	.46**	.25**	.69**	.06	--
Openness	.36**	.15	.17	-.05	.12	.57**	--

Note: ** $p \leq .01$, one-tailed

tests; (2) correlations with respondent's ratings; (3) correlations with organizational criteria; and (4) meta-analyses of scale correlates with job performance criteria. We describe these next.

Correlations with other tests

We obtained HPI matched data sets for four categories of measures to determine the convergent and divergent validity of the HPI scales. Correlations should be highest between those measures purporting to assess the same construct and lowest between those measures assessing different constructs. Categories of tests included normal personality, dysfunctional personality, motives and interests, and cognitive ability.

Table 4. Hogan Personality Inventory correlates with the Minnesota Multiphasic Personality Inventory-2

MMPI-2	Adjustment	Ambition	Sociability	Likeability	Prudence	Intellectance	School Success
L	.61**		-.20*	.32**	.45**	.12	.09
F	-.21*	-.13	.13	-.12	-.12	.02	-.23*
K	.59**	.45**	-.07	.41**	.55**	-.01	.14
Hs	-.66**	-.31**	.04	-.18	-.19	-.14	-.13
D	-.48**	-.56**	-.33**	-.22*	.07	-.47**	-.05
Hy	-.30**	.00	-.04	.03	.13	-.07	.07
Pd	-.64**	-.33**	.03	-.40**	-.43**	-.11	-.36**
Mf	-.31**	-.27*	-.05	.05	.13	-.29**	.21**
Pa	-.47**	-.28**	-.06	-.19	-.14	-.09	.05
Pt	-.76**	-.63**	-.02	-.46**	-.50**	-.24*	-.26*
Sc	-.72**	-.51**	-.05	-.50**	-.51**	-.19	-.26*
Ma	-.41**	.05	.45**	-.15	-.50**	.30**	-.17
Si	-.42**	-.77**	-.49**	-.48**	-.21*	-.55**	-.06

Note: $N = 71$; * $p \leq .05$; ** $p \leq .01$, one-tailed.

Table 3 presents correlations between the HPI scales and other well-constructed measures of FFM-based personality inventories. Median correlation coefficients summarize HPI relations with the NEO PI-R (Costa & McCrae, 1992; Goldberg, 2000), Goldberg's (1992) Big-Five Markers (R. Hogan & Hogan, 1995), Personal Characteristics Inventory (Mount & Barrick, 1995b), and the Inventario de Personalidad de Cinco Factores (Salgado, 1998; Salgado & Moscoso, 1999). Descriptions of procedures, methods, and samples are contained in the technical documents referenced above. The medians and ranges of correlations are as follows: Adjustment/Emotional Stability/Neuroticism (median $r = .73$; range $= .66$ to .81); Ambition/Extraversion/Surgency (median $r = .56$; range $= .39$ to .60); Sociability/ Extraversion/Surgency (median $r = 62$; range $= .44$ to .64); Likeability/Agreeableness (median $r = .50$; range $= .22$ to .61); Prudence/Conscientiousness (median $r = .51$; range $= .36$ to .59); Intellectance/Openness/Intellect (median $r = .57$; range $= .33$ to .69); and School Success/Openness/Intellect (median $r = .30$; range $= .05$ to .35). Although the off-quadrant correlations are not presented in the table, these are lower than correlations between scales sharing the same underlying construct. These data suggest that findings based on the HPI will generalize to other well-constructed measures of the FFM.

Tables 4 and 5 present correlations between the HPI scales and scales of the Minnesota Multiphasic Personality Inventory-2 (MMPI-2; Hathaway & McKinley, 1943; Butcher Dahlstrom, Graham, Tellegen, & Kaemmer, 1989) and the Hogan

Table 5. Hogan Personality Inventory and Hogan Development Survey primary scale correlates

HDS	Adjustment	Ambition	Sociability	Likeability	Prudence	Intellectance	School Success
Excitable	-.69**	-.47**	-.10**	-.39**	-.31**	-.10**	-.15**
Skeptical	-.38**	-.20**	.02	-.28**	-.28**	-.02	-.13**
Cautious	-.50**	-.66**	-.30**	-.32**	-.08**	-.21**	-.20**
Reserved	-.28**	-.31**	-.35**	-.57**	-.17**	-.15**	-.08**
Leisurely	-.28**	-.28**	-.06*	-.21**	-.14**	.03	-.06*
Bold	-.01	.25**	.33**	.02	-.09**	.18**	.12**
Mischievous	.03	.23**	.45**	.04	-.36**	.33**	.08**
Colorful	.08**	.40**	.60**	.18**	-.19**	.23**	.18**
Imaginative	-.18**	.06*	.38**	-.02	-.35**	.29**	.09**
Diligent	-.13**	-.05*	-.14**	.00	.33**	-.01	-.07*
Dutiful	-.06*	-.22**	-.12**	.16**	.20**	-.08**	-.17**

Note: N = 2,692; * $p \leq$ .05; ** $p \leq$ .01, one-tailed.

Development Survey (HDS; Hogan & Hogan, 1997), respectively. The MMPI was developed as an aid to psychiatric diagnosis and the original and revised versions are the most widely used tests of psychopathology in the world today. The HPI correlations in Table 4 are presented for the MMPI-2 basic validity keys and 10 clinical scales based on a sample of male and female police officer applicants (N = 71). As expected, there are substantial negative correlations between HPI Adjustment and all of the standard scales of the MMPI-2. The MMPI-2 scales most saturated with neuroticism — Hypochondriasis (Hs) and Psychasthenia (Pt) — yield the largest correlations with HPI Adjustment. Although HPI Adjustment is the scale most highly saturated with pathology, other correlations are also consistent with FFM predictions. Notable are negative correlations between HPI Ambition/Sociability and MMPI Social Introversion, HPI Likeability and MMPI Schizophrenia, and HPI Prudence and MMPI Psychopathic Deviate.

The HPI-HDS correlations in Table 5 were obtained from male and female job incumbents (N = 2,692) who completed the inventories during job coaching. The HDS is designed to assess eleven common dysfunctional dispositions derived, in part, from the DSM-IV, Axis 2 personality disorders taxonomy (American Psychiatric Association, 1994). Principal components analysis of the HDS yields three themes components that correspond to Horney's (1950) concepts of "moving away from people," "moving against people," and "moving toward people" (Hogan & Hogan, 1997, p. 10-12). The distinguishing feature of Table 5 is the negative manifold of relations for the first HDS component — Excitable, Skeptical, Cautious, Reserved, and Leisurely — with all HPI scales. This suggests that low HPI Adjustment scores reflect a syndrome that includes unstable relationships, suspiciousness, social anhedonia, and sensitivity to criticism. This should lead to poor interpersonal beha-

Table 6. Hogan Personality Inventory and Motives, Values, Preferences Inventory primary scale correlates

MVPI	Adjustment	Ambition	Sociability	Likeability	Prudence	Intellectance	School Success
Aesthetic	-.20**	-.05**	.23**	-.01	.18**	.39**	.17**
Affiliation	.28**	.36**	.41**	.38**	.15**	.15**	.08**
Altruistic	.10**	.08**	.03	.26**	.23**	.12**	.04*
Commercial	.11**	.25**	.21**	.13**	.18**	.19**	.16**
Hedonistic	-.34**	-.16**	.33**	-.02	-.39**	.07**	-.08**
Power	.05**	.37**	.36**	.06**	.01	.26**	.20**
Recognition	-.18**	.11**	.51**	.01	-.19**	.23**	.06**
Scientific	-.09**	-.04**	.05**	-.02	-.04*	.27**	.11**
Security	.02	-.09**	-.28**	.03	.34**	-.20**	-.11**
Tradition	.20**	.18**	-.10**	.11**	.34**	.04*	.08**

Note: N = 2,692; * $p \leq$ .05; ** $p \leq$ .01, one-tailed.

vior that inhibits social relations and a person's ability to get along with others and achieve occupational goals. In addition, note the correlations between HPI Ambition and Sociability with HDS Bold (Narcissistic) and Colorful (Histronic) scales as well as the relations between HPI Prudence and Diligent (Obsessive Compulsive) and Dutiful (Dependent). These relations suggest shortcomings associated with high scores on these scales.

Considering the relation between the HPI and assessments of interests, motives, and values, the correlations for Holland's (1985) Self-Directed Search appear in Hogan and Hogan (1995, p. 23). These results are sensible; the most interesting patterns occurred for Adjustment with no significant relations with any interests and for Investigative with significant correlations for all interests except SDS Conventional. Table 6 presents correlations between the HPI scales and scales of the Motives, Values, and Preferences Inventory (MVPI; Hogan & Hogan, 1996). The MVPI is a direct assessment of a person's motives and the assumption underlying the assessment is that values and interests are motivational concepts. The ten MVPI scales represent those dimensions that have historic presence in the literature on motivation. As such, the MVPI is based on a comprehensive taxonomy of motivational constructs. The HPI-MVPI correlations are based on a sample (N = 2,692) of male and female job applicants and incumbents. We hypothesized that there would be significant relations with every HPI scale, although some scales would be related to multiple motives and some relations would be negative.

As seen in Table 6, HPI Adjustment is positively related to Affiliation motives and negatively related to Aesthetic motives. This pattern is consistent with the creativity literature. HPI Ambition is most highly correlated with Power motives, while

HPI Sociability is most highly correlated with Recognition motives. HPI Likeability is correlated with both Affiliation and Altrustic motives. HPI Prudence is negatively related to Hedonistic motives and positively related to Security motives. Finally, HPI Intellectance has its strongest relation with Aesthetic motives and HPI School Success has its strongest relation with Power motives. These data provide useful interpretive information for HPI scale scores in the area of predicting what is likely to motivate an individual and what occupational environment is likely to be a good fit.

Tests of cognitive ability tend to be unrelated to the HPI scales with the exception of the Intellectance and School Success scales. We expect a modest positive correlation with Intellectance, because it contains a component of intellectual curiosity, and with School Success because it concerns interest in education and training. Hogan and Hogan (1995, p. 22) show that the only meaningful correlations between the HPI (r's ~ .20) and the Armed Services Vocational Aptitude Battery (ASVAB; U.S. Department of Defense, 1984) are with Intellectance and School Success. These results are corroborated by correlations between the HPI and several PSI Basic Skills Tests, the Industrial Reading Test, and the Watson-Glaser Critical Thinking Appraisal.

HPI correlations with others' descriptions

Correlations between others' descriptions and HPI scale scores allow us to evaluate the validity of the HPI and the adequacy of socioanalytic theory—on which the HPI rests. In a practical sense, the links between scale scores and reputational descriptions provide the information for individual feedback and coaching. For example, these correlations allow us to say, with some degree of accuracy, that people with high scores for Ambition are likely to be described by others as outgoing, assertive, polished, and forceful.

For this analysis we asked undergraduate and graduate student volunteers ($N = 128$) to complete the HPI and to distribute rating forms to two people who had known them for at least two years. The rating form contained 112 adjectives from Gough and Heilbrun's (1983) Adjective Check List (ACL); these adjectives were identified by John (1990) as prototypical markers of the FFM dimensions. Respondents rated the target person using a 5-point Likert scale, where "1" indicated "strongly disagree" and "5" indicated "strongly agree."

Correlations between the ACL items and the HPI scales appear in Table 7. The table lists the ten adjectives most highly correlated with each scale. As seen, these adjectives correspond closely to the scale definitions listed in Table 1 as well as the FFM dimension definitions that appear in John (1990). Close correspondence between descriptors and definitions suggest that the HPI scales are assessing the reputational features they were intended to assess. The negative correlations in the table are particularly interesting because they help interpret low scores and expand the understanding of the scale ranges.

Table 7. Hogan Personality Inventory and adjectival correlates

Adjustment	r	Ambition	R	Sociability	r
Tense	-.53**	Outgoing	.32**	Quiet	-.45**
Worrying	-.49**	Shy	-.31**	Talkative	.48**
Moody	-.46**	Retiring	-.30**	Shy	-.42**
Unstable	-.43**	Assertive	.28**	Outgoing	.37**
Self Pitying	-.39**	Spunky	.28**	Silent	-.37**
Temperamental	-.39**	Polished	.28**	Reserved	-.35**
Nervous	-.37**	Silent	-.27**	Show-off	.33**
Fearful	-.37**	Active	.26**	Spunky	.32**
Self Punishing	-.36**	Sociable	.26**	Outspoken	.32**
High Strung	-.35**	Forceful	.24**	Withdrawn	-.32**

Likeability	r	Prudence	R	Intellectance	r
Sympathetic	.44**	Noisy	-.43**	Narrow Interests	-.42**
Praising	.44**	Through	.38**	Ingenious	.34**
Outgoing	.43**	Wise	.37**	Artistic	.31**
Soft-hearted	.37**	Precise	.37**	Imaginative	.30**
Enthusiastic	.37**	Irresponsible	-.36**	Inventive	.30**
Sociable	.37**	Stable	.30**	Sharp-witted	.30**
Friendly	.36**	Show-off	-.34**	Active	.29**
Polished	.33**	Cautious	.30**	Energetic	.26**
Sensitive	.33**	Efficient	.31**	Witty	.26**
Pleasant	.31**	Practical	.31**	Original	.25**

School Success	r
Narrow Interests	-.26**
Insightful	.24**
Ingenious	.23**
Foresighted	.22**
Clever	.21*
Good Natured	-.22**
Thorough	.19*
Precise	.18*
Touchy	-.17*
Painstaking	.16*

Note: $N = 168$; * $p \leq .05$; ** $p \leq .01$, one-tailed.

HPI correlations with organizational criteria

The HPI is designed to forecast performance in real world settings; this has been a major focus of HPI validation research to date. The HPI has been used in hundreds of personnel selection studies to predict job performance. Using local validation research, we analyze the target job, develop hypotheses about the HPI components that should predict job performance, and develop criterion measures based on the job requirements. Next, we test applicants/incumbents and collect criterion data. Typically, these data are supervisors' ratings of the incumbents' job performance and objective performance measures. We compute various statistics, including correlations, to determine which HPI components are related to the criteria. Finally, we make recommendations for test implementation and follow-up.

Building a data base one study at a time, we now understand the organizational criteria best predicted by the HPI scales. Table 8 shows an example of the empirical links between the HPI scales and important organizational performance outcomes. Note that there is no listing for criterion variables of overall or summary job performance. Our strategy for validation research is to align predictors with criteria using the underlying construct. Historically, researchers pay considerable attention to measurement properties of predictors and virtually no attention to the adequacy of criterion data, often gathering that which is convenient rather than that which is valid. Campbell (1990) emphasized that the latent structure of constructs should extend across both predictor and criterion space and we organize our measures in this way. Therefore, the example criterion measures listed in Table 8 are criteria appropriate for their respective FFM dimensions. Matching test and criterion measures on the basis of a common construct is the key to maximizing the prediction of job performance.

The striking feature of Table 8 is that, across a range of jobs, organizations, and criteria, the HPI is consistently related to job performance. Although some writers believe conscientiousness as the only important FFM dimension (Ones, Viswesvaran, & Schmidt, 1993; Schmidt & Hunter, 1998), it is clear that when criteria are saturated with other personality-related content, the remaining FFM dimensions will also predict performance. When these results are compared to the mean validities reported by Barrick and Mount (1991), the virtues of aligning predictors with specific criteria become clear.

Meta-analyses of HPI Scales

We conducted a series of meta-analyses to answer the question of how well individual FFM dimensions predict criteria when they are aligned with the underlying construct (Hogan & Holland, 2001). We identified 43 independent samples (total N = 5,242) that met the following criteria: (1) the study used job analysis to estimate personality-based job requirements; (2) the study used a concurrent or predictive validation strategy with working adults; (3) the criteria were content explicit, not overall job performance; (4) the predictor variables were scales of the HPI; and (5) the sample was larger than N = 25. We excluded studies of the following type: (1) studies using clinical patients and therapists; (2) studies using undergraduate or graduate students; (3) studies using self-reported performance criteria; (3) studies using performance criteria other than ratings and objective productivity/personnel measures; (4) studies in which the only criterion was overall performance criteria; (5) laboratory or assessment center studies; (6) studies unrelated to work contexts; and (7) dissertation research.

Subject matter experts (SMEs; N = 13) reviewed the criterion variables in each study and identified the personality construct most closely associated with each performance criterion. The seven HPI scale constructs were defined and SMEs were asked to nominate only one scale for each criterion listed. Definitions of each performance criterion came from the original validation studies. The result was a nominal construct rating for each criterion, which allowed us to align the criteria with the predictors based on their common meaning (Campbell, 1990). We calculated Kappa to evaluate interrater agreement on nominal rating scales. For the seven personality

Table 8. Hogan Personality Inventory sample validation results

HPI Scale Source	Sample		Criteria	r
Adjustment				
Hogan, Rybicki, Heidelberg, & Shelton (1997)	27	Anchor handlers	Remains Even Tempered	.32
Rybicki & Hogan (1996)	27	Customer service reps	Shows Resiliency	.25
Holland, Shin, & Hogan (2000)	96	Managers	Manages People, Crisis, & Stress	.25
Ambition				
Holland, Shin, & Hogan (2000)	96	Managers	Exhibits Leadership	.34
Hogan & Gerhold (1995)	27	Financial consultants	Generates New Monthly Accounts	.33
Sinangil, Ones, & Cemalcilar (1997)	220	Expatriate managers	Takes Initiative	.24
Likeability				
Brinkmeyer & Hogan (1997)	328	Field representatives	Shows Interpersonal Skill	.26
Connolly (1996)	89	Managers	Shares Credit	.19
Hogan Assessment Systems (1999)	252	Customer service reps	Exhibits Capacity to Compromise	.13
Prudence				
Brinkmeyer & Hogan (1997)	101	Manufacturing workers		.31
Rybicki & Hogan (1997)	63	Deputy sheriffs		.26
Hogan & Rybicki (1997)	70	Correctional officers		.16
Intellectance				
Hogan & Rybicki (1997)	70	Correctional officers	Achieves Quality with Information	.24
Holland & Hogan (1999)	43	Clerical workers	Analyzes Finances/Operations	.21
Connolly (1996)	89	Managers	Seems Market Savvy	.18
School Success				
Rybicki, Brinkmeyer, & Hogan (1997)	112	Customer service reps	Exhibits Technical Skill	.31
Hogan, Hogan, & Klippel (2000)	148	Locomotive engineer trainees	Makes Progress in Training	.24
Shelton, Holland, & Hogan (2000)	49	Managers	Capitalizes on Training	.14

Note: Sociability is not represented in the table because there were not enough studies with Sociability-based criteria for inclusion.

constructs, the Kappa value was .48, which is within the .40 to .60 range considered as moderate to good interrater agreement.

We used the meta-analytic procedures specified by Hunter and Schmidt (1990) to cumulate results across studies and to assess effect sizes. All studies used zero-order product-moment correlations; this eliminated the need to convert alternative statistics to values of *r*. Corrections were made for sampling error and unreliability in the measures. Reliability of the personality measures was estimated using within-study coefficient alpha, rather than using the values reported in the HPI manual. No corrections were made for range restriction in the predictors or the criteria. We used artifact distributions to correct for unreliability in the criterion measures because we did not have sufficient information to correct each study individually. Following Barrick and Mount (1991) and Tett, Jackson, and Rothstein (1991), we used the .508 reliability coefficient proposed by Rothstein (1990) as the estimate of the reliability of supervisory ratings of job performance. For objective criterion data, we (conservatively) assumed perfect reliability, following Salgado (1997). The frequency-weighted mean of the job performance reliability distribution was .59, which is comparable to the value of .56 reported by Barrick and Mount (1991), and the mean square root reliability of .76 corresponds to the value of .778 reported by Tett *et al.* (1991). We did not correct correlation coefficients to estimate validity at the construct level.

Hunter and Schmidt (1990) point out that meta-analytic results can be biased unless each sample contributes about the same number of correlations to the total. To eliminate this problem, correlations within studies were averaged so that each sample contributed only one point estimate per predictor scale. This procedure takes into account both negative and positive correlations and avoids assumptions about using mean absolute values for averaging correlations. This is the major computational difference between these analyses and those presented by Tett *et al.* (1991), who used mean absolute value correlations for within-study averaging.

Table 9 presents validity results for HPI scales aligned by construct-classified criteria. Forty-two meta-analyses were computed to evaluate convergent and divergent validity of construct-aligned measures. There were too few studies with criteria categorized as sociability-related to compute meta-analyses for the HPI Sociability scale. However, there were sufficient studies to compute meaningful analyses for all other scales. The estimated true validities range from .25 (HPI School Success) to .43 (HPI Adjustment). The lower bound confidence intervals are all greater than .10, which suggests that scale validity generalizes across samples when criteria are classified by construct. In every case, the confidence intervals support the reliability of the validity coefficients.

Although not included in this table, we examined the convergent and discriminate validity of the FFM measures. For each dimension, correlations are highest between personality scales and the aligned, construct-specific criterion variables and this indicates convergence. The validity coefficient for HPI Adjustment (.43) is the largest in the table. Similarly, validity coefficients are smallest for the personality scales

Table 9. Hogan Personality Inventory Meta-Analysis Results for Criteria Aligned by Construct

	1	2	3	4	5	6	7	8	9
	K	total N	avg N	r obs	SD obs	rho	Sd rho	%VE	90% CV
Adjustment	24	2,573	107	.25	.114	.43	.117	62	.28
Ambition	28	3,698	132	.20	.077	.35	.000	119	.35
Sociability	na	na	na	na	na	na	na	na	na
Likeability	17	2,500	147	.18	.094	.34	.100	68	.21
Prudence	26	3,379	130	.22	.113	.36	.125	55	.20
Intellectance	7	1,190	170	.20	.037	.34	.000	357	.34
School Success	9	1,366	152	.15	.132	.25	.184	34	.01

Note: K = number of studies; total *N* = number of participants across k studies; average *N* = average number of participants within each study; *r* obs = mean observed validity; SD obs = SD of observed correlations; rho = true validity at scale level; SD rho = SD of true validity; %VE = percentage of variance explained; 90% CV = credibility value.

that are not aligned with the specific construct. For example, HPI Intellectance is unrelated to adjustment, likeability, and prudence criteria; HPI Sociability predicts none of the construct-based criteria. This pattern of lower correlations for the off diagonal scales supports discriminate validity. Another index of discriminate validity comes from the overlap of the credibility values among scales. Except for HPI School Success, no lower bound credibility values for construct-aligned measures overlap any other scale, which suggests independence. This pattern of findings provides further support for the discriminant validity of the predictor scales.

These analyses provide strong support for the contention that the HPI is a valid predictor of job performance. With the exception of Sociability, each HPI scale is useful in predicting organizational criteria saturated with the same construct. The scales predict less well or not at all organizational criteria saturated with different constructs.

Summary

We close our discussion by making (or remaking) four points regarding how the HPI differs from other personality inventories based on the FFM. First, the HPI is theory-based because it comes out of a theory of personality, not because it originated with an evaluation of the FFM. Personality theories begin with some assumptions about human nature. The FFM makes no such assumptions; consequently, it is a taxonomy of variables, not a theory of personality. We believe it is misleading to claim that a personality inventory is theory-based because it starts with the FFM.

Second, the HPI is based on a fully articulated model of personality — Socioanalytic theory. Socioanalytic theory argues that people are primarily motivated to get along and get ahead in life, that there are individual differences in peoples' ability to achieve these goals, and that these individual differences are captured in peoples' reputations. The HPI is designed to predict individual differences in reputation, which reflect individual differences in a person's success in life.

Third, the HPI is designed to predict individual differences in peoples' ability to get along and get ahead, and to predict how people will be described by others. The way a person is described by others is equivalent to that person's reputation. Therefore, the HPI is designed to predict a person's reputation.

Finally, the HPI (along with the CPI) has a single-minded focus on validity. And we define validity in terms of the degree to which a measure predicts significant and important non-self-report performance outcomes. Thus, the HPI takes seriously the notion that assessment has a job to do. However, we are not advocating old-fashioned dustbowl empiricism. The HPI combines a utilitarian focus with the ambitious theoretical agenda embodied in Socioanalytic theory.

References

American Psychiatric Association. (1994). *Diagnostic and statistical manual of mental disorders* (4th ed.). Washington, DC: Author.

Axford, S.N. (1996). Review of the Hogan Personality Inventory (Revised). In J.C. Impara & J.C. Coloney (Eds.), *The Supplement to the Twelfth Mental MeasurementYearbook.* Lincoln, NB: The University of Nebraska Press.

Barrick, M.R., & Mount, M.K. (1991). The Big-five personality dimensions and job performance: A meta-analysis. *Personnel Psychology, 44,* 1-26.

Brinkmeyer, K., & Hogan, R. (1997). *Preemployment screening preliminary report for manufacturing workers* (Tech. Rep. No. 136). Tulsa, OK: Hogan Assessment Systems.

Brinkmeyer, K., & Hogan, R. (1997). *Validity of the Hogan Personality Inventory for selecting field representatives* (Tech. Rep. No. 107). Tulsa, OK: Hogan Assessment Systems.

Butcher, J.N., Dahlstrom, W.G., Graham, J.R., Tellegen, A., & Kaemmer. B. (1989). *Manual for the restandardized Minnesota Multiphasic Personality Inventory: MMPI-2. An administrative and interpretive guide.* Minneapolis, MN: University of Minnesota Press.

Campbell, J. P. (1990). Modeling the performance prediction problem in industrial and organizational psychology. In M.D. Dunnette & L.M. Hough (Eds.), *Handbook of industrial and organizational psychology* (Vol. 1, 2nd ed., pp. 39-74). Palo Alto, CA: Consulting Psychologists Press.

Carson, R.C. (1969). *Interaction concepts of personality.* Chicago: Aldine.

Connolly, P.M. (1996). *Relations between Overseas Assignment Inventory ratings and Hogan Personality Inventory scores* (Tech. Rep. No. 193). Old Saybrook, CT: Performance Programs.

Costa, P.T., Jr., & McCrae, R.R. (1992). *Revised NEO Personality Inventory (NEO-PI-R) and NEO Five Factor Inventory (NEO-FFI) professional manual.* Odessa, FL: Psychological Assessment Resources.

Digman, J.M. (1990). Personality structure: Emergence of the Five Factor model. *Annual Review of Psychology, 41,* 417-440.

Forsyth, D.R. (1990). *Group dynamics* (2nd ed.). Pacific Grove, CA: Brooks/Cole.

Goldberg, L.R. (1992). The development of markers of the Big-Five factor structure. *Psychological Assessment, 4,* 26-42.

Goldberg, L.R. (1993). The structure of phenotypic personality traits. *American Psychologist, 48,* 26-34.

Goldberg, L.R. (2000). [Hogan Personality Inventory and NEO PI-R correlation coefficients]. Unpublished raw data based on International Personality Item Pool Project.

Gough, H.G. (1965). Conceptual analysis of psychological test scores and other diagnostic variables. *Journal of Abnormal Psychology, 70,* 294-302.

Gough, H.G. (1975). *Manual for the California Psychological Inventory.* Palo Alto, CA: Consulting Psychologists Press.

Gough, H.G., & Heilbrun, A.B., Jr. (1983). *The Adjective Checklist Manual: 1983 edition.* Palo Alto, CA: Consulting Psycholigists Press.

Hathaway, S.R., & McKinley, J.C. (1943). *Manual for the Minnesota Multiphasic Personality Inventory.* New York: Psychological Corporation.

Hogan Assessment Systems. (1999). *Validity of the Hogan Personality Inventory for selecting customer service representatives* (Tech. Rep. No. 171). Tulsa, OK: Hogan Assessment Systems.

Hogan, J., & Hogan, R. (1989). How to measure employee reliability. *Journal of Applied Psychology, 74,* 273-279.

Hogan, J., & Hogan, R. (1996). *Motives, Values, Preferences Inventory manual.* Tulsa, OK: Hogan Assessment Systems.

Hogan, J., & Hogan, R. (1998). Theoretical frameworks for assessment. In P. R. Jeanneret & R. Silzer (Eds.), *Individual psychological asessment* (pp. 27-53). San Francisco: Jossey-Bass.

Hogan, J., Hogan, R., & Klippel, D. (2000). *Validity of the Hogan Personality Inventory for selecting locomotive engineer trainees in the transportation industry* (Tech. Rep. No. 185). Tulsa, OK: Hogan Assessment Systems.

Hogan, J., & Holland, B. (2001). *Using theory to evaluate personality and job performance relations: A socioanalytic perspective.* Unpublished manuscript. Tulsa, OK: Hogan Assessment Systems.

Hogan, J., & Rybicki, S. (1997). *Validity of correctional officer selection procedures* (Tech. Rep. No. 119). Tulsa, OK: Hogan Assessment Systems.

Hogan, J., Rybicki, S., Heidelberg, H., & Shelton, D. (1997). *Validity of the Hogan Personality Inventory for selecting offshore anchor handlers* (Tech. Rep. No. 126). Tulsa, OK: Hogan Assessment Systems.

Hogan, R. (1983). A socioanalytic theory of personality. In M.M. Page (Ed.), *1982 Nebraska symposium on motivation* (pp. 55-89). Lincoln: University of Nebraska Press.

Hogan, R. (1991). Personality and personality measurement. In M.D. Dunnette & L.M. Hough (Eds.), *Handbook of industrial and organizational psychology* (Vol. 2, 2nd ed., pp. 327-396). Palo Alto, CA: Consulting Psychologists Press.

Hogan, R. (1996). A socioanalytic perspective on the five-factor model. In J. S. Wiggins (Ed.), *The five-factor model of personality* (pp.163-179). New York: Guilford.

Hogan, R., & Gerhold, C. (1995). *Validity of the Hogan Personality Inventory for selecting financial consultants* (Tech. Rep. No. 66). Tulsa, OK: Hogan Assessment Systems.

Hogan, R., & Hogan, J. (1995). *The Hogan Personality Inventory manual* (2nd ed.). Tulsa, OK: Hogan Assessment Systems.

Hogan, R., & Hogan, J. (1997). *The Hogan Development Survey manual.* Tulsa, OK: Hogan Assessment Systems.

Hogan, R., Hogan, J., & Busch, C. (1984). How to measure service orientation. *Journal of Applied Psychology, 69,* 157-163.

Hogan, R., Jones, W., & Cheek, J.M. (1985). Socioanalytic theory: An alternative to armidillo psychology. In B.R. Schlenker (Ed.), *The self and social life* (pp.175-198). New York: McGraw-Hill.

Hogan, R., & Nicholson, R. (1988). The meaning of personality test scores. *American Psychologist, 43,* 621-626.

Holland, B., & Hogan, J. (1999). *Validity of the Hogan Personality Inventory for selecting clerical support aides II and III* (Tech. Rep. No. 167). Tulsa, OK: Hogan Assessment Systems.

Holland, B., Shin, H., & Hogan, J. (2000). *Selecting project managers, superintendents, and estimators using the Hogan Personality Inventory, Hogan Development Survey, and Motives, Values, Preferences Inventory* (Tech. Rep. No. 182). Tulsa, OK: Hogan Assessment Systems.

Holland, J.L. (1985). *Making vocational choices: A theory of careers.* Englewood Cliffs, NJ: Prentice-Hall.

Horney, K. (1950). *Neurosis and human growth.* New York: Norton.

Hough, L.M., & Oswald, F. L. (2000). Personnel selection: Looking toward the future— Remembering the past. *Annual Review of Psychology, 51,* 631-664.

Hunter, J.E., & Schmidt, F.L. (1990). *Methods of meta-analysis.* Newbury Park, CA: Sage.

John, O. P. (1990). The "Big-Five" factor taxonomy: Dimensions of personality in the natural language and in questionnaires. In L.A. Pervin (Ed.), *Handbook of personality and research* (pp. 66-100). New York: Guilford.

Leary, T. (1957). *Interpersonal diagnosis of personality.* New York: Ronald Press.

LoBello, S.G. (1996). Review of the Hogan Personality Inventory (Revised). In J.C. Impara & J.C. Coloney (Eds.), *The Supplement to the Twelfth Mental Measurements Yearbook.* Lincoln, NB: The University of Nebraska Press.

Lord, F.M., & Novick, M.R. (1968). *Statistical theories of mental test scores.* Reading, MA: Addison-Wesley.

Mann, R.D. (1959). A review of the relationships between personality and performance in small groups. *Psychological Bulletin, 56,* 241-270.

McGrath, J.E., Arrow, H., & Berdahl, J.L. (2000). The study of groups: Past, present, and future. *Personality and Social Psychology Review, 4,* 95-105.

Mount, M.K., & Barrick, M.R. (1995). *The Personal Characteristics Inventory manual.* Unpublished manuscript. Iowa City, IA.

Norman, W.T. (1963). Toward an adequate taxonomy of personality attributes: Replicated factor structure in peer nomination personality ratings. *Journal of Abnormal and Social Psychology, 66,* 574-583.

Ones, D.S., Viswesvaran, C., & Schmidt, F.L. (1993). Comprehensive meta-analysis of integrity test validation: Findings and implications for personnel selection and theories of job performance. *Journal of Applied Psychology, 78,* 679-703.

Redfield, R. (1960). How society operates. In H.L. Shapiro (Ed.), *Man, culture, and society* (pp. 345-368). New York: Oxford University Press.

Rothstein, H.R. (1990). Inter-rater reliability of job performance ratings: Growth to asymptote level with increasing opportunity to observe. *Journal of Applied Psychology, 75,* 322-327.

Rybicki, S., Brinkmeyer, K., & Hogan, R. (1997). *Validity of the Hogan Personality Inventory for selecting customer service representatives, drivers, and delivery and installation/service* (Tech. Rep. No. 102). Tulsa, OK: Hogan Assessment Systems.

Rybicki, S., & Hogan, J. (1997). *Validity of the Hogan Personality Inventory Form-S for selecting correctional deputy sheriffs* (Tech. Rep. No. 120). Tulsa, OK: Hogan Assessment Systems.

Salgado, J.F. (1998). *Manual tecnico del Inventario de Personalidad de Cinco Factores (IP/5F)* [Technical Manual for the Personality Inventory of Five Factors (IP/5F)]. Santiago de Compostela, Spain: Torculo.

Salgado, J.F., & Moscoso, S. (1999, May). *Construct validity of two personality inventories based upon the five-factor model (FFM)*. Paper presented at the Fourteenth Annual Meeting of the Society for Industrial-Organizational Psychology, Inc., Atlanta, GA.

Saucier, G., & Goldberg, L.R. (1996). The language of personality: Lexical perspectives on the Five-Factor model. In J.S. Wiggins (Ed.), *The Five-Factor model of personality* (pp. 21-50). New York: Guilford.

Schmidt, F.L., & Hunter, J.E. (1998). The validity and utility of selection methods in personnel psychology: Practical and theoretical implications of 85 years of research findings. *Psychological Bulletin, 124*, 262-274.

Shelton, D., Holland, B., & Hogan, J. (2000). Validity of the Hogan Personality Inventory for selecting managers (Tech. Rep. No. 192). Tulsa, OK: Hogan Assessment Systems.

Sinangil, H.K., Ones, D.S., & Cemalcilar, Z. (1997). *Personality characteristics of expatriate managers working in Turkey* (Tech. Rep. No. 122). Minneapolis, MN: University of Minnesota.

Sullivan, H.S. (1953). *The interpersonal theory of psychiatry*. New York: Norton.

Tett, R.P., Guterman, H.A., Bleier, A., & Murphy, P.J. (2000). Development and content validation of a "hyperdimensional" taxonomy of managerial competence. *Human Performance, 13*, 205-251.

Tett, R.P., Jackson, D.N., & Rothstein, M. (1991). Personality measures as predictors of job performance: A meta-analytic review. *Personnel Psychology, 44*, 703-742.

Thurstone, L.L. (1934). The vectors of the mind. *Psychological Review, 41*, 1-32.

U. S. Department of Defense. (1984). *Manual for the Armed Services Vocational Aptitude Battery*. North Chicago, IL: U. S. Military Entrance Processing Command.

Wiggins, J.S. (1996) (Ed.). *The Five-Factor model of personality*. New York: Guilford.

Wiggins, J.S. (1979). A psychological taxonomy of trait-descriptive terms: The interpersonal domain. *Journal of Personality and Social Psychology, 37*, 395-412.

Zonderman, A.B. (1980). *Inventory construction by method of homogenous item composites*. Unpublished manuscript. Baltimore, MD: Johns Hopkins University.

Chapter 15

The Six Factor Personality Questionnaire

Douglas N. Jackson
Paul F. Tremblay

Introduction

The Six Factor Personality Questionnaire (SFPQ; Jackson, Paunonen, & Tremblay, 2000) extends and in certain ways redefines the popular Big Five factors. The immediate impetus for developing the SFPQ arose as a result of a series of confirmatory factor-analytic studies using the scales of the Personality Research Form (PRF; Jackson, 1984), a published personality questionnaire that measures 20 variables of personality drawn largely from the work of Murray (1938). These factor-analytic studies, which are briefly described in this paper, revealed that a six factor solution consistently provided a better fit than did a five factor solution (Jackson, Paunonen, Fraboni, & Goffin, 1996). The factors are *Extraversion, Agreeableness, Independence, Openness to Experience, Methodicalness,* and *Industriousness.* The fifth and sixth factors represent a division of the Big Five Conscientiousness factor into two: one factor reflecting Methodicalness and the other, Industriousness. These two factors are correlated but distinguishable. In the SFPQ we provide the option of combining them into a general Conscientiousness factor. The SFPQ profile provides both a score for the Conscientiousness factor and a set of scores for Methodicalness and Industriousness. Users who prefer to distinguish the latter two factors may thus do so; those who prefer the broader Conscientiousness factor have that information. Those who are interested in information on how Methodicalness and Industriousness combine to yield a certain Conscientiousness score can also be satisfied.

Another departure of the SFPQ from the Big Five conceptualizations is our identification of an Independence factor that has been shown to define the opposite pole of the Neuroticism factor (Jackson, Ashton, & Tomes, 1996). We deliberately avoided any attempt to label any of the SFPQ scales as "Neuroticism" for several reasons. First, neuroticism as a construct is poorly defined and is not represented in

Big Five Assessment, edited by B. De Raad & M. Perugini. © 2002, Hogrefe & Huber Publishers.

standard psychiatric nomenclature such as the DSM-IV (1994). Second, professionals have demonstrated an inability to agree on its manifestations (Gough, 1957), in contrast to other terms like depression. Third, the blueprint for the development of the SFPQ was to encompass normal dimensions of personality, just as its predecessor, the PRF, did. Fourth, popular Neuroticism scales have been shown to be confounded with an independent desirability factor (Jackson, Ashton, & Tomes, 1996). Finally, a strong Independence factor has consistently emerged from factor analyses of the PRF, and we believe it should have a prominent place among the factors of normal personality.

A number of researchers have investigated the factor structure of the PRF since its introduction in the late 1960's. In some studies, the Big Five factors of personality have been identified and claimed to account for the common variance in the PRF trait scales (Costa & McCrae, 1988; Paunonen, Jackson, Trzebinski, & Forsterling, 1992; Paunonen, Keinonen, Trzebinski, Forsterling *et al.*, 1996; Skinner, Jackson, & Rampton, 1976; Stumpf, 1993). In other studies, however, factor structures have included more than five factors. For example, Nesselroade and Baltes (1975) found eight oblique factors in a large sample of PRF respondents. In another study with the PRF, Stricker (1974) found six factors.

Studies that have found more than five factors tended to split one of the Big Five Factors, Conscientiousness, into two factors. In the study by Nesselroade and Baltes (1975), for example, one factor was defined by Cognitive Structure, Order, and low Impulsivity. An equally clear factor was defined by Achievement and Endurance. The two factors correlated .43 when they were rotated using an oblique rotation. In our factor analyses we have chosen to label these factors as Methodicalness and Industriousness, respectively.

The SFPQ was developed to realize a number of aims: (a) to measure the major factors of normal personality functioning in a brief, compact format; (b) to develop factor scales that meet modern standards for convergent and discriminant validity by emphasizing at the earliest stages of scale development, the suppression of response biases and the optimization of relevant content, while minimizing irrelevant content and correlations between scales; (c) to employ personality questionnaire items that are short, that have a clear, straight-forward vocabulary, that represent characteristic behavior that most normal adults have experienced or observed, and that have been subjected to rigorous multivariate item analyses. Because the original item pool was well over 3,000 items, the ratio of original to retained items was more than 30 to 1.

Development

The foundation for the SFPQ was the Personality Research Form. Chapter 2 of the *PRF Manual* (Jackson, 1984) provides a detailed outline of the steps in its development. These steps are outlined briefly here: (a) develop careful definitions of each pole of the 20 variables of personality based on the work of Murray (1938) and his colleagues; (b) prepare large item pools for each personality dimension, which in the aggregate consisted of well over 3,000 items; (c) edit and select items for empirical evaluation; (d) conduct item analyses based on a total item pool of more than 2,700 items using a procedure designed to maximize each item's content saturation while suppressing desirability variance and eliminating items correlating too highly with irrelevant scales; (d) developing parallel forms based on an algorithm minimizing statistical differences between forms; (e) constructing Form E based on a new item analysis using an algorithm developed for the purpose of maximizing the correlation of an item with its own scale, while minimizing correlations between scales. For-mulas and flow charts describing these procedures are contained in the *PRF Manual*. The starting point for the SFPQ was the set of items contained in the PRF Form E. These items had already been selected from the original pool with a selection ratio of approximately 10 to 1.

We followed three distinct stages in constructing the SFPQ, which are described in an article by Jackson *et al.* (1996). The first stage was to compare five-factor and six-factor models of personality structure using confirmatory factor analysis of PRF scale scores. In the second stage, we assembled a questionnaire specifically designed to measure the proposed six-factor model of personality, and we evaluated some of its psychometric properties. That questionnaire, the SFPQ, was then used in the third stage to assess the predictability of the separate Industriousness and Methodicalness factors in relation to some criteria of social importance. The first two stages are summarized below. The third stage is described in the Validity section.

Comparison of the Five-Factor and Six-Factor models

Jackson *et al.* (1996) tested five-factor and six-factor models of personality structure based on two samples of PRF respondents. The first sample consisted of 306 first-year university undergraduates (143 men and 163 women). The second sample con-sisted of 2,141 men between the ages of 17 to 24 who completed the PRF as part of a selection procedure for a training program in the Canadian armed forces.

The first model was based on the five-factor structure reported by Costa and McCrae (1988). In their study, Costa and McCrae factored the 20 PRF content scales along with marker scales from their NEO Personality Inventory. The six-factor model was based on the earlier research studies about the relations among the 20 PRF traits, and it divides Conscientiousness into two separate factors we have labeled Industriousness and Methodicalness. The Industriousness factor was defined by the PRF traits of high Achievement, high Endurance, and low Play. The Meth-odicalness factor was defined by high Cognitive Structure and Order, and low Im-pulsivity. Jackson had proposed this division of the Conscientiousness factor as early as 1967 in the original PRF Manual (1967/1984) based on rational and theo-retical considerations. Empirical support for this division is also found in the studies by Nesselroade and Baltes (1975), and Siess and Jackson (1970). Other minor dif-ferences between Costa and McCrae's (1988) five factor model and the six-factor model are described in Jackson *et al.* (1996). Results of the confirmatory factor analyses consistently revealed that the oblique six-factor model provided a statistically significantly better fit than did the oblique modified five-factor model for both samples.

Evaluation of a Six-Factor personality measure

The second stage of the development of the SFPQ was based on the previous confirmatory factor analyses. The previous sample of 306 respondents and a second sample of 113 undergraduates completed both the PRF and the Jackson Personality Inventory-Revised (1994) in a true/false format. Based on knowledge of scale content and on previous exploratory factor analytic work, three PRF scales were chosen to define each of the six factors identified by Jackson *et al.* (1996). Three facet scales were chosen because three variables is the minimum number required to define a factor in common factor analysis (Thurstone, 1947), and we wished to keep the SFPQ brief. Seventeen of the 18 facet scales were derived from the PRF. One JPI-R scale, Breadth of Interest, was introduced to help define the Openness to Experience factor because we found this scale to have a higher loading than did the PRF Sentience scale that it replaced. The PRF scales Harmavoidance and Nurturance were omitted due to their tendency to split into several factors.

An item analysis was conducted on the 18 trait facets for the purpose of selecting the best six items (three positive and three negative exemplars) from the item pool. The item analysis was based on the sample of 306 respondents. Item means, variances, item-scale correlations, and the Item Efficiency Index (Neill & Jackson, 1970) were investigated. The item analysis revealed that Sentience did not contribute as strongly as was expected to the Openness factor. It was, therefore, replaced by the JPI Breadth of Interest scale. Selection of the items from the Breadth of Interest scale was based on an inspection of the PRF and JPI responses of the sample of 113 undergraduates, and on extensive previous item analyses. Two confirmatory factor analysis models, a five-factor and a six-factor model were tested by Jackson *et al.* (1996) using the sample of 113 undergraduates. A χ^2 nested model comparison was conducted between the two models. The χ^2 results indicated that the six-factor solution provided a significantly better fit to the data than did the five-factor model (χ^2 change = 24.77, df = 5, $p < .001$).

Description of the SFPQ

The SFPQ is comprised of six factor scales and 18 facet scales. Three facet scales are subsumed under each factor scale, and each facet scale is measured by six items, resulting in a total of 108 items. The SFPQ requires approximately 20 minutes to administer. The instructions direct respondents to answer on a five-point scale whether they strongly disagree, disagree, are neutral, agree or strongly agree with the statements. Facet scale scores are obtained by summing the five-point items, taking into account the direction of keying. Factor scale scores are calculated by summing scores for each of the three relevant facet scales. In addition to a paper-and-pencil format, the SFPQ is also available for administration and scoring via personal computer.

The SFPQ scales were developed to be bipolar. Thus the direction of scoring for any given scale was arbitrarily chosen. For example, a scale called Even-tempered could just as well have been scored in the direction of Aggression. This arbitrariness is particularly true because, for each facet scale, three items were selected to represent the positive pole of the dimension and three to represent the negative pole.

Based on previous research with the Personality Research Form (Reddon & Jackson, 1989), we judge the vocabulary used in the SFPQ items to be below the fifth grade level. The fifth-grade level is the reading level of the Personality Research Form, from which most of the items were drawn. However, in the selection process for the SFPQ, preference was given to short, simple items. Furthermore, we introduced minor editorial changes to simplify items drawn from the PRF. The major reason for choosing short, simple items is that they have been shown, in general, to be more valid (Holden, Fekken, & Jackson, 1985). In Table 1, factor scales, facet scales, and scale definitions for high scorers are provided.

Norms

Adult SFPQ norms were based on the responses of 1,067 participants (483 men and 584 women) from the United States and Canada. The method for obtaining names of potential SFPQ respondents was to review U.S. census data and to identify from a data base containing approximately 72 million telephone numbers and addresses, the names and addresses of persons representing a geographically diverse area. Respon-

Table 1. Factor scales (in bold/italics); Facet scales (italics); Scale definitions for high scorers.

Extraversion	Enjoys the company of others; confident and comfortable in social situations; tries to control environment and influence or direct people; likes to have an audience and to be the center of attention.
Affiliation	Enjoys being with friends and people in general; accepts people readily; makes efforts to win friendships and maintain associations with people.
Dominance	Attempts to control environment and to influence or direct other people; expresses opinions forcefully; enjoys the role of leader and may assume it spontaneously.
Exhibition	Wants to be the center of attention; enjoys having an audience; engages in behavior that wins the notice of others; may enjoy being dramatic or witty.
Agreeableness	Is considerate, likable and cooperative; accepts criticism and blame; avoids confrontations and conflicts; is not easily offended.
Abasement	Shows humility; accepts blame and criticism even when not deserved; willing to accept an inferior position; tends to be self-effacing; readily fulfills others' requests; is helpful.
Even-tempered	Imperturbable when faced with instigation to anger; avoids confron-

	tations and conflicts; does not express hostility, either verbally or physically; is not concerned with "getting even;" is forgiving of others' mistakes.
Good-natured	Is willing to concede mistakes; willingly changes own opinions to ensure positive relationships; is not angered or upset by criticism; does not respond to attack or question; is not easily offended; has "nothing to hide."
Independence	Is self-determined and shows a high level of autonomy; enjoys being free and unrestrained in various situations; is little concerned about reputation or others' praise or disapproval.
Autonomy	Tries to break away from restraints, confinement, or restrictions of any kind; enjoys being unattached, free, not tied to people, places, or obligations; may be rebellious when faced with restraints.
Individualism	Unconcerned about reputation or social standing; insensitive to others' praise or disapproval; does not necessarily conform to socially-approved norms in behavior and appearance.
Self Reliance	Does not look to others for guidance or support; is able to maintain oneself without aid; has confidence in and exercises own judgment; confronts problems alone; does not seek help, advice, or sympathy.
Openness to Experience	Likes change and new experiences; is curious about many areas of knowledge; has a wide variety of interests.
Change	Likes new and different experiences; dislikes routine and avoids it; may readily change opinions or values in different circumstances; adapts readily to changes in environment; enjoys travel.
Understanding	Wants to understand many areas of knowledge; values a synthesis of ideas, verifiable generalizations, logical thought, particularly when directed at satisfying intellectual curiosity.
Breadth of Interest	Is attentive and involved; motivated to participate in a wide variety of activities; interested in learning about a diversity of things.
Methodicalness	Does not like ambiguity; thinks before acting; is organized and neat.
Cognitive Structure	Does not like ambiguity or uncertainty in information; wants all questions answered completely; desires to make decisions based upon definite knowledge rather than upon guesses or probabilities.
Deliberateness	Acts with deliberation; is on an even keel; ponders issues and decisions carefully; thinks before acting; avoids spontaneity.
Order	Concerned with keeping personal effects and surroundings neat and organized; dislikes clutter, confusion and lack of organization; interested in developing methods for keeping materials methodically organized.
Industriousness	Maintains high standards of work and aspires to reach challenging goals; persistent and unrelenting in work habits; is drawn more towards work than play; takes a serious approach to life.
Achievement	Aspires to accomplish difficult tasks; maintains high standards and is willing to work towards distant goals; responds positively to competition; willing to put forth effort to attain excellence.
Endurance	Willing to work long hours; doesn't give up quickly on a problem; persevering, even in the face of great difficulty; patient and unrelenting in work habits.
Seriousness	Is subdued in thought, appearance, and manner; takes a serious approach to life and to work; does not seek fun or amusement; avoids frivolity and idle pursuits.

Table 2. Characteristics of the Normative Sample

	Percentage		
Variable	Male	Female	Total
Age			
< 20	4.9	8.3	6.8
20-29	7.8	8.0	7.9
30-39	17.6	19.8	18.8
40-49	23.4	20.5	21.8
50-59	14.8	13.9	14.3
60-69	18.0	15.6	16.7
70+	13.5	13.9	13.7
Total	100.0	100.0	100.0
Education			
Grade 8 or less	2.9	1.4	2.1
Some high school	4.1	3.7	3.9
High school graduate	23.1	34.3	29.2
1-3 yrs college or university	31.9	35.0	33.6
College or university graduate	22.2	12.8	17.0
Post graduate education	15.8	12.8	14.2
Total	100.0	100.0	100.0
Marital status			
Never married	18.1	20.3	19.3
Married	71.2	56.6	63.2
Separated or Divorced	7.2	10.2	8.8
Widowed	3.5	12.9	8.7
Total	100.0	100.0	100.0
Location			
Northwest	16.6	18.4	17.6
Southwest	13.3	14.8	14.1
South Central	15.6	15.0	15.2
North Central	28.9	29.2	29.1
Pacific / Mountain	18.1	12.4	15.0
Canada	7.5	10.2	9.0
Total	100.0	100.0	100.0

dents were selected randomly and a letter, together with a small monetary incentive, was sent to 1,500 potential respondents. Table 2 provides a breakdown of the normative sample by age, sex, education, marital status and geographic location.

Normative information provided in the SFPQ manual include descriptive statistics (means, standard deviations, skewness, and kurtosis) and percentile tables for males, females, and for the combined sample.

Appropriate populations

Because SFPQ norms span virtually all segments of the adult population, the SFPQ is applicable in a wide variety of assessment contexts. The relatively modest reading level of the SFPQ makes it appropriate for use with a large proportion of the general population, and in addition, to specialized populations not necessarily possessing high-level reading skills. Some of these specialized populations might include adolescents, psychiatric patients, prison inmates, linguistic minorities, and immigrant samples. The SFPQ provides a broad assessment that can be useful in counseling, selection, and research. As with most instruments of assessment, the SFPQ should be used in conjunction with other reliable information in making decisions about respondents.

Reliability

Cronbach alpha values for the six factor scales and the individual facet scales of the SFPQ are presented in Table 3. These reliabilities are from two sources, the North American normative sample ($N = 1,067$) and an Oregon community sample gathered by Lewis R. Goldberg ($N = 671$, personal communication). It can be seen that these values range from .76 to .86 (median = .81) for the factor scales and from .55 to .84 (median = .65) for the facet scales in the normative sample. These internal consistency reliabilities should be interpreted in light of the breadth of the factor scales and the relative shortness of the facet scales (6 items each).

Validity

Convergent and discriminant validity

The purpose of this stage of the SFPQ development was to examine the convergent and discriminant validity of the six-factor model within the framework of the multitrait-multimethod matrix (Campbell & Fiske, 1959). A sample of 94 paid volunteer undergraduates (34 men and 60 women) were asked to participate in a roommate rating study. Participants were same-sex roommate pairs from a university residence who had lived together for at least seven months. They were first asked to provide a self-report of their behavior by completing the SFPQ. They were then asked to rate their roommates' behavior using the SFPQ.

The multitrait-multimethod matrix framework requires the assessment of two or more traits by two or more methods. The validity coefficients (correlations between measures of the same trait by two different methods) should be higher than the correlations between different traits measured by different methods (heterotrait-heteromethod correlations), and also higher than the correlations for different traits measured by the same method (heterotrait-monomethod). The correlation matrix of

Table 3. Internal Consistency Reliability

	Cronbach's alpha	
Scale	Normative Sample	Oregon Sample
Extraversion	.86	.88
Affiliation	.73	.78
Dominance	.83	.86
Exhibition	.77	.80
Agreeableness	.80	.78
Abasement	.60	.54
Even-Tempered	.66	.65
Good-Natured	.60	.58
Independence	.76	.78
Autonomy	.54	.59
Individualism	.72	.74
Self-Reliance	.57	.57
Openness to Experience	.81	.82
Change	.61	.63
Understanding	.73	.74
Breadth of Interest	.65	.69
Methodicalness	.84	.83
Cognitive Structure	.55	.56
Deliberateness	.66	.68
Order	.84	.78
Industriousness	.77	.69
Achievement	.58	.47
Endurance	.61	.59
Seriousness	.65	.61

SFPQ traits' self-ratings and peer ratings appears in Table 4. It can be seen that the validity coefficients are relatively high (mean $r = .56$) and significant (all $p < .01$). These coefficients were generally higher than the heterotrait-heteromethod correlations (mean absolute $r = .09$) and higher than the heterotrait-monomethod correlations (not shown). The mean absolute heterotrait-monomethod correlation was .13 for self-ratings and .20 for peer ratings. Table 4 also reveals a modest average correlation ($r = .41$) obtained between Methodicalness and Industriousness. This correlation was expected based on the conceptual relatedness of these two constructs.

Composite direct product analysis

A composite direct product analysis (Browne, 1984) was used by Jackson *et al.* (1996) as a substitute for the more common confirmatory factor analytic procedure for multitrait-multimethod (MTMM) matrices because the interpretation of multitrait-multimethod results with only two methods of measurement is generally not possible due to the under-determination of factors (see Goffin, 1988; Goffin & Jackson, 1992; Kenny & Kashy, 1992; Widaman, 1985). The MUTMUM computer program (Browne, 1990) was used to conduct this analysis. The overall fit of a six-

Table 4. SFPQ convergent and discriminant correlation coefficients based on self and peer ratings

	Self Ratings					
Peer Ratings	**AG**	**EX**	**IP**	**OP**	**IT**	**ME**
Agreeableness (AG)	*.45***	-.14	-.02	-.13	.00	.04
Extraversion (EX)	-.02	*.58***	.04	.16	.04	-.16
Independence (IP)	-.04	-.21	*.56***	.01	-.05	-.16
Openness to Experience (OP)	-.07	-.01	.11	*.53***	.10	-.21
Industriousness (IT)	-.13	-.14	-.03	.10	*.55***	.33*
Methodicalness (ME)	.00	-.16	-.02	-.11	.49**	*.69***

Note: *p < .01, **p < .001. N = 94.; Convergent validity coefficients in italics; Correlations above the diagonal are based on self-ratings and those below the diagonals are based on peer ratings.

factor model and a five-factor model were compared in the context of the present MTMM data. Method factors were specified in addition to trait factors. The models incorporate method factors to account for method variance, and this allows one to evaluate the possibility that one or more of the trait factors are composed mainly of method variance. The five-factor model tested was identical to the six-factor model, with the exception that the correlation between the Methodicalness and Industriousness factors was constrained to unity in the former case.

The five-factor oblique model applied to the MTMM data resulted in a $\chi^2 = 77.8$, $df = 44$. The three fit indices, Expected Cross-Validation Index (ECVI; Browne & Cudeck, 1989), Root Mean Square Error of Approximation (RMSEA; Steiger, 1989), and Relative Noncentrality Index (RNI; MacDonald & Marsh, 1990), for this model were 1.57, 0.09, and 0.90 respectively. The six-factor oblique model resulted in a $\chi^2 = 51.1$, $df = 43$. The ECVI, RMSEA, and RNI for this model were 1.30, 0.05, and 0.98 respectively. These results indicated that the six-factor model had a consistently better fit than did the five-factor model on all indices. The χ^2 difference test of nested models revealed a significant increment in model fit by specifying six factors (χ^2 change = 26.68, $df = 1$, $p < .001$) rather than five. These results are consistent with those of Stages 1 and 2, indicating that a six-factor model provides a better fit than does a five-factor model for the personality domain encompassed by the variables of the PRF.

Criterion predictability

Jackson *et al.* (1996) addressed the differential predictability of the Industriousness and Methodicalness factor scales. If the two domains of behavior really pertain to one and the same personality factor (i.e., Conscientiousness), then they should both predict the same criterion variables approximately equally well (or equally poorly). Rather, if they are distinct (albeit correlated) factors, then they will each add incrementally to the other in the prediction of certain criteria. To evaluate the situation with the SFPQ, the Industriousness and Methodicalness factor scales were correlated with various criterion variables measured in a sample of 94 dormitory roommates.

Industriousness predicted grade point average ($r = .24$, $p < .05$) to a moderate degree, whereas Methodicalness did not ($r = -.01$, *ns*). Methodicalness was negatively correlated with smoking behavior ($r = -.25$, $p < .05$), but the correlation between Industriousness and smoking behavior was not significant ($r = -.16$, *ns*). Finally, Methodicalness was negatively correlated with selection of a liberal arts program of study ($r = -.22$, $p < .05$), but Industriousness was not significantly correlated with this criterion ($r = -.07$, *ns*). This differential pattern of predictive validities between Industriousness and Methodicalness supports the utility for our conceptualization of two correlated facets of Conscientiousness within a six-factor model of personality structure. However, these findings need to be verified in a more definitive manner such as the development of a more extensive array of criterion variables for which a panel of knowledgeable judges would make differential predictions for industriousness and methodicalness and the comparison of these predictions with empirical results.

Confirmatory factor analysis of the normative sample

Correlations among the SFPQ factor scales and the facet scales are presented in Table 5. The correlations in the bottom triangle are based on the normative sample; the correlations in the top triangle are based on a community sample collected by L. R. Goldberg (1999). The correlation between Methodicalness and Industriousness is .41 in the normative sample and .34 in the Oregon sample. There is also a modest correlation between Extraversion and Openness to Experience ($r = .36$ in the normative sample and $r = .28$ in the Oregon sample). The other correlations between factor scales are small, suggesting that there is minimal overlap among the scales.

A confirmatory factor analysis of the SFPQ was performed on the normative sample. The standardized solution is presented in Tables 6 and 7, with Table 7 containing the correlations among the SFPQ factors. All loadings shown are statistically significant. The solution revealed a $\chi^2 = 1221.85$ ($df = 122$, $p < .01$), an ECVI = 1.22 and a RMSEA = .09. These results are similar to those found by Jackson *et al.* (1996), confirming the presence of six factors.

Relations between the SFPQ and Five other personality inventories

Evidence of convergent validity of the SFPQ has been found by inspecting its statistical relations with five other personality inventories. The data were from a large collaborative research project on the structure of personality conducted by L. R. Goldberg at the Oregon Research Institute. Goldberg (1999) collected personality

Table 5. Correlations among Factor Scales and Facet Scales

Variable	(1)	(2)	(3)	(4)	(5)	(6)	(7)	(8)	(9)	(10)	(11)	(12)	(13)	(14)	(15)	(16)	(17)	(18)	(19)	(20)	(21)	(22)	(23)	(24)
(1) Extraversion		-.06	-.22	.28	.02	.11	.78	.77	.88	.05	-.12	-.05	-.13	-.24	-.11	.16	.21	.29	-.05	-.04	.10	.28	.16	-.17
(2) Agreeableness	.09		.11	.04	-.06	.03	.09	-.14	-.07	.77	.80	.83	.03	.22	-.02	.00	.02	.07	-.11	.04	-.07	.07	.07	-.03
(3) Independence	-.17	.03		.17	-.12	.03	-.29	-.11	-.15	.08	.10	.08	.82	.73	.78	.23	.12	.05	-.19	-.04	-.07	-.02	.16	-.06
(4) Openness to Experience	.36	.05	.10		.20	.07	.22	.21	.25	.09	-.04	-.06	.24	.03	.12	.70	.83	.84	-.25	-.14	-.11	.26	.14	-.19
(5) Methodicalness	.00	.06	-.03	.03		.34	-.01	.10	-.06	-.15	.03	-.05	-.12	-.11	-.04	-.23	-.12	-.12	.78	.80	.83	.22	.24	.26
(6) Industriousness	-.02	.06	.09	.13	.41		-.02	.26	.00	.03	.02	.09	.08	-.13	.13	-.02	.11	.07	.22	.34	.08	.72	.77	.69
(7) Affiliation	.76	.06	-.28	.27	.01	-.06		.32	.63	.11	.03	-.17	.03	-.13	-.25	.10	.14	.27	-.05	-.07	.08	.20	.02	-.23
(8) Dominance	.75	-.18	.00	.28	.08	.16	.26		.50	-.03	-.17	-.13	.03	-.27	.02	.15	.18	.19	.03	.08	.12	.31	.28	-.01
(9) Exhibition	.87	-.09	-.14	.30	-.10	-.17	.60	.48		.04	-.14	-.07	-.08	-.18	-.06	.10	.15	.24	-.10	-.12	.05	.16	.06	-.20
(10) Abasement	-.05	.80	.08	.09	-.15	.03	.11	-.03	.04		.37	.51	.04	.18	.01	.01	-.09	-.02	.13	.03	-.10	.02	.05	-.05
(11) Even-tempered	-.12	.79	.10	-.04	.03	.02	.03	-.17	-.14	.37		.48	.01	.18	.01	-.09	-.02	.01	-.03	.13	-.01	.01	.00	.01
(12) Good-natured	-.04	.83	.08	-.06	-.05	.09	-.29	-.13	-.07	.51	.48		.00	.22	-.07	.01	.05	.07	-.06	.03	-.08	.08	.19	-.03
(13) Autonomy	-.12	.03	.82	.24	-.12	.08	.03	.03	-.08	.04	.01	.00		.34	.28	.14	.01	.00	-.14	.01	.00	.06	.22	.01
(14) Individualism	-.24	.22	.73	.03	-.11	-.13	-.13	-.27	-.18	.18	.18	.22	.34		.31	.02	.18	.09	-.12	.18	-.06	.10	.03	-.10
(15) Self Reliance	-.02	-.02	.78	.12	-.04	.13	-.25	.02	-.06	.01	.01	-.07	.28	.31		.16	.09	.04	-.01	.10	.00	.06	.20	.21
(16) Change	.31	.00	.23	.70	-.23	-.02	.10	.15	.10	.01	-.09	.01	.14	.02	.16		.33	.39	.03	.03	-.09	.32	.04	-.20
(17) Understanding	.20	.04	.12	.83	-.12	.11	.14	.18	.15	-.09	-.02	.05	.01	.18	.09	.33		.66	-.03	.13	-.01	.26	.12	-.17
(18) Breadth of Interest	.35	.11	.05	.84	-.12	.07	.27	.19	.24	-.02	.01	.07	.00	.09	.04	.40	.61		.18	-.09	-.05	.24	.11	.24
(19) Cognitive Structure	-.07	-.03	-.19	-.25	.77	.22	-.05	.03	-.10	.13	-.03	.08	-.17	-.12	-.01	-.18	-.03	-.17		.54	.46	.24	.22	.34
(20) Deliberateness	-.02	-.15	-.04	-.14	.80	.34	-.07	.08	-.12	.03	.13	.03	.01	.18	.10	.13	.13	-.09	.54		.53	.18	.26	.30
(21) Order	.05	.02	-.07	-.11	.83	.08	.08	.12	.05	-.10	-.01	-.08	.00	-.06	.00	-.10	-.01	-.05	.46	.53		.21	.26	.18
(22) Achievement	.15	.05	-.02	.26	.22	.72	.20	.31	.16	.02	.01	.08	.06	.10	.06	.26	.24	.28	.24	.26	.21		.52	.44
(23) Endurance	.09	.05	.16	.14	.24	.77	.02	.28	.06	.05	.00	.19	.22	.03	.20	.10	.12	.18	.22	.29	.26	.52		.33
(24) Seriousness	-.27	.04	.01	-.19	.26	.69	-.23	-.01	-.20	-.05	.01	-.03	.01	-.10	.21	-.09	-.17	.24	.34	.30	.18	.44	.33	

Table 6. Confirmatory Factor Analysis of the Normative Sample

Facet Scales	Factors					
	EX	AG	IP	OP	ME	IT
Affiliation	.66					
Dominance	.51					
Exhibition	.91					
Abasement		.66				
Even-tempered		.57				
Good-natured		.85				
Autonomy			.69			
Individualism			.43			
Self reliance			.70			
Change				.42		
Understanding				.71		
Breadth of Interest				.92		
Cognitive Structure					.70	
Deliberateness					.77	
Order					.62	
Achievement						.71
Endurance						.73
Seriousness						.45

Note: EX = Extraversion, AG = Agreeableness, IP = Independece, OP = Openness to Experience, ME = Methodicalness, IT = Industriousness; Blank scales refer to parameters fixed at zero.

data on an Oregon community sample of over 800 participants using several well known personality inventories. In Table 8 we present the correlations between the factor scales of the SFPQ and the NEO Personality Inventory-Revised (NEO-PI-R; Costa & McCrae, 1992).

This section also presents a summary of the results regarding relations between the SFPQ factor scales and those of the 16 Personality Factor Questionnaire (16 PF; Cattell, Cattell, & Cattell, 1993), the NEO Personality Inventory-Revised (NEO-PI-R; Costa & McCrae, 1992), the California Psychological Inventory (CPI; Gough,

Table 7. Correlations among factors

Factor Scales	Factors					
	EX	AG	IP	OP	ME	IT
Extraversion (EX)						
Agreeableness (AG)	-.09					
Independence (IP)	-.20					
Openness to Experience (OP)	.39	.13				
Methodicalness (ME)	-.09	.12		.11		
Industriousness (IT)		.12	.22	.30	.54	

Note: EX = Extraversion, AG = Agreeableness, IP = Independece, OP = Openness to Experience, ME = Methodicalness, IT = Industriousness; Blank scales refer to parameters fixed at zero.

Table 8. Correlations between the SFPQ factor scales and NEO-PI-R factor scales

SFPQ Factor Scales	NEO-PI-R Scales				
	Ex	Ag	N	Op	Co
Extraversion	.71	-.16	-.26	.25	.19
Agreeableness	.00	.43	-.34	-.04	.00
Independence	-.25	-.13	-.22	.14	-.01
Openness to Experience	.23	-.03	-.10	.67	-.04
Methodicalness	-.03	.08	-.19	-.27	.66
Industriousness	.00	.02	-.10	-.03	.44

Note: Ex = Extraversion, Ag = Agreeableness, N = Neuroticism, Op = Openness to Experience, Co = Conscientiousness.

1996), the Hogan Personality Inventory (HPI; Hogan & Hogan, 1995), and the Jackson Personality Inventory-Revised (JPI-R; Jackson, 1994). The relations between the SFPQ and the other personality inventories are presented in the SFPQ manual. Some important results are summarized in Table 9. Specifically, we list each SFPQ factor scale and its 9 highest correlations with the other five inventories. These correlations generally support the convergent validity of the SFPQ factor scales with respect to conceptually related published personality scales.

Relations between the SFPQ and the NEO-PI-R

A study by Jackson, Ashton, and Tomes (1996) provided evidence in support of the hypothesis that the present six-factor model of personality structure can be represented by NEO-PI-R scales, as well as those of the SFPQ. A sample of 144 undergraduate university students (80 men and 64 women) completed the SFPQ and NEO Personality Inventory-Revised (NEO-PI-R; Costa & McCrae, 1992). The NEO-PI-R is a 240-item questionnaire measuring the Big Five factors with 30 facet scales. To investigate the extent to which social desirability variance is present in the NEO-PI-R and the SFPQ, two desirability scales from the AA and BB forms of the PRF were converted to a five-point response format and included in the study. In contrast to the approach taken in the construction of the PRF and the SFPQ, where response styles, including social desirability, were minimized at several stages of test development, the selection of NEO-PI-R items did not include explicit minimization of social desirability variance (Costa & McCrae, 1988, p. 259). The authors of the NEO PI-R argued that it would be difficult to measure inherently desirable traits if socially desirable items were removed. However, a serious problem can emerge when response style variance is confounded with content variance. The presence of response style variance can contribute to correlations between scales and therefore limit the convergent and discriminant validity of the test.

A principal components analysis was conducted on the combined SFPQ and NEO-PI-R data, followed by an orthogonal rotation to a targeted criterion (Schönemann, 1966). A procedure proposed by Paunonen (1997) to evaluate whether or not results from the targeted rotation can be attributed to capitalization on chance was also used.

Table 9. Correlations between the SFPQ factor scales and facet scales from other personality inventories

SFPQ Extraversion	SFPQ Agreeableness
.79 Social Confidence (JPI-R)	.56 Compliance (NEO PI-R)
.72 Sales Potential (HPI)	-.54 Angry Hostility (NEO PI-R)
.71 Social Boldness (16PF)	.51 Service Orientation (HPI)
.71 Sociability (CPI)	.50 Empathy (HPI)
.70 Dominance (CPI)	-.48 Tension (16 PF)
.65 Ambition (HPI)	.48 No hostility (HPI)
.65 Self Acceptance (CPI)	.46 Adjustment (HPI)
.64 Sociability (HPI)	.44 Even-tempered (HPI)
.64 Assertiveness (NEO PI-R)	.40 Good Impression (CPI)

SFPQ Independence	SFPQ Openness to Experience
-.62 Cooperativeness (JPI-R)	.78 Breadth of Interest (JPI-R)
-.51 Sociability (JPI-R)	.59 Openness to Change (16 PF)
-.43 Not autonomous (HPI)	.59 Ideas (NEO PI-R)
-.41 Gregariousness (NEO PI-R)	.59 Complexity (JPI-R)
.39 Self Reliance (16 PF)	.56 Aesthetics (NEO PI-R)
-.39 Empathy (JPI-R)	.56 Innovation (JPI-R)
-.34 Warmth (16 PF)	.53 Actions (NEO PI-R)
-.33 Anxiety (JPI-R)	.52 Culture (HPI)
-.32 Appearance (HPI)	.51 Intellectance (HPI)

SFPQ Methodicalness	SFPQ Industriousness
.71 Organization (JPI-R)	.46 Achievement Striving (NEO PI-R)
.66 Order (NEO PI-R)	.39 Self-Discipline (NEO PI-R)
.64 Perfectionism (16 PF)	.34 Dutifulness (NEO PI-R)
.53 Deliberation (NEO PI-R)	.31 Mastery (HPI)
-.50 Flexibility (CPI)	.31 Energy Level (JPI-R)
.50 Self Discipline (NEO PI-R)	.30 Organization (JPI-R)
.48 Dutifulness (NEO PI-R)	.29 Perfectionism (16 PF)
-.47 Abstractedness (16 PF)	.29 Activity (NEO PI-R)
.40 Prudence (HPI)	.27 Competitive (HPI)

Note: All correlations are significant, $p < .01$. JPI-R = Jackson Personality Inventory-Revised (Jackson, 1994), HPI = Hogan Personality Inventory (Hogan & Hogan, 1995), NEO PI-R = Revised NEO Personality Inventory (Costa & McCrae, 1992), 16 PF = 16 Personality Factor Questionnaire (Cattell, Cattell, & Cattell, 1993), CPI = California Psychological Inventory (Gough, 1996).

Six factors corresponding to those in the SFPQ were hypothesized, plus one for the Desirability scales. For the Extraversion, Agreeableness, and Openness to Experience factors, all SFPQ and NEO-PI-R facet scales originally designed to assess these factor scales were targeted on their appropriate factor. Scales targeted for the Independence (low Neuroticism) factor included the three Independence facet scales from the SFPQ and the Neuroticism facet scales (assigned negative target loadings) from the NEO-PI-R. The targeted variables for the Methodicalness and Industriousness factors included the respective facet dimensions from the SFPQ. Furthermore, all the Conscientiousness facet scales from the NEO-PI-R were targeted on both Methodicalness and Industriousness factors. The seventh factor was targeted using the two desirability scales and one facet scale from each of the SFPQ and NEO-PI-R factor scales which correlated most strongly (in the present analysis) with the desirability scales. The reason for targeting one facet scale from each of the NEO-PI-R and SFPQ factors was to ensure that the desirability factor so derived would be determined by a heterogeneous set of content scales rather than only those content scales most highly related to desirability.

Although the rotated matrix of factor loadings is not presented here, it can be found in the article by Jackson, Ashton, and Tomes (1996). However, Table 10 displays the mean factor loadings for targeted NEO-PI-R and SFPQ scales on the six factors. It can be seen that the average loading is 0.63 for the SFPQ and .54 for the NEO-PI-R, indicating that both measures define the six factors, with a somewhat higher average loading for the SFPQ.

One potential issue regarding the comparison of the NEO-PI-R and the SFPQ is that the NEO-PI-R Concientiousness scales were targeted on both the Methodicalness and Industriousness factors. This might lead to a reduced average loading when the two factors are considered together. One alternative is to calculate the average loading for the NEO-PI-R on the Methodicalnness and Industriousness factors by using only the three highest Conscientiousness scale loadings. This results in an average mean loading of .59 for the Methodicalness factor, .57 for the Industriousness factor, and .58 for the overall average. It is particularly noteworthy that the SFPQ achieves at least a comparable level of factor separation and loading magnitude to the NEO PI-R with less than half the items (108 vs 240).

Also found in Table 10 are the desirability saturation values for each SFPQ and NEO-PI-R factor. These values were obtained by averaging the corresponding loadings for each SFPQ facet scale and each NEO-PI-R facet scale on the Desirability factor. It can be seen that the saturation values are noticeably higher for all of the five NEO-PI-R factors than they are for the corresponding SFPQ factors. On average, the desirability saturation value is higher in the NEO-PI-R than it is in the SFPQ (mean = .30 vs .17).

SFPQ modal profiles

The SFPQ provides a set of scale scores that can be interpreted individually or as a series of standardized scale scores in a profile. To interpret an individual's profile, one could, for example, identify the scores that are at or below the 16th percentile, and at or above the 84th percentile. This exercise would provide a clear description of an individual's salient attributes. In addition to this descriptive information, one might be interested in evaluating the similarity of an individual's pattern of personality attributes to 'typical' or 'modal' profiles for some group. A modal profile refers to the pattern of personality attributes that is characteristic of a subset or cluster of persons in a particular population who share certain high and low personality characteristics.

In some cases, typical profiles have been extensively researched and documented. Consider the example of Type A behavior, in which modal profile analysis casts additional light on what was believed to be a unitary syndrome. It was commonly

Table 10. Mean factor loadings and desirability saturation for targeted NEO-PI-R and SFPQ scales

Factors	Factor Loadings		Desirability Saturation	
	SFPQ	NEO PI-R	SFPQ	NEO PI-R
Extraversion	0.69	0.54	0.16	0.31
Agreeableness	0.62	0.56	0.17	0.41
Openness to Experience	0.68	0.62	0.14	0.23
Independence	0.57	0.61	0.17	0.27
Industriousness	0.60	0.46	0.24	
Methodicalness	0.60	0.47	0.11	
Conscientiousness				.26
Average	0.63	0.54	0.17	0.30

believed that the Type A behavior pattern was characterized by a sense of time urgency, proneness to anger and hostility, high competitiveness, impatience, and achievement strivings. However, Gray, Jackson, and Howard (1990) demonstrated that there was not a strong unitary Type A pattern. Rather, three distinct profiles of Type A behavior were identified, each with its unique patterning of high and low points.

Consider another application of profile analysis. That method was used extensively by Jackson and Williams (1975) in the development of interpretive information for the Jackson Vocational Interest Survey (Jackson, 2000). Profiles of professional and academic interests were developed for different occupational groups. For example, a cluster of several engineering specialists (e.g., mechanical, electronic, civil) emerged defined by high interests in mathematics, physical science, engineering, and skilled trades, and low interests in social service, elementary education, and author-journalism, among others.

In other cases, such as that described below for the SFPQ, profile analysis has been used as an exploratory procedure to discover patterns and similarities among people and attributes. This particular application is useful in the early stages of a research program. In the case of the SFPQ, no specific patterns of attributes were hypothesized and, therefore, modal profile analysis was used as an exploratory procedure. The validity of a particular profile can be established and could be considered as a new conception to describe particular types of individuals. One initial step in establishing the stability of such a particular profile or set of profiles is its replication in diverse samples drawn from different populations of individuals.

The first author and his colleagues have maintained an active interest in the classification of personality and the development of procedures to derive modal profiles. This work has evolved into a statistical procedure labeled *modal profile analysis* (Jackson & Williams, 1975; Skinner, Jackson, & Hoffmann, 1974; Skinner, Reed, & Jackson 1976). This technique is a multivariate classification strategy. Unlike clustering techniques, which place entities displaying specific attributes into discrete categories, modal profile analysis locates clusters of entities in a multidimensional space. This is done by performing a singular value decomposition (related to principal components analysis) using a data matrix in which the columns are people and the rows are personality attributes. Whereas principal components analysis (or factor analysis) is usually used to find patterns among a subset of variables, the objective of modal profile analysis is to find patterns among people. The principal component scores represent the projections of each attribute in a multivariate space defined by the entities (in the present case, people).

One important advantage of modal profile analysis over other numerical clustering procedures is that it does not require that an individual be placed in a discrete category. Instead, one can evaluate the extent to which an individual fits a modal profile on a continuous similarity scale. For example, one could correlate an individual's profile with various modal profiles and compare the fit by examining the magnitude of the correlations of the individual's profile with each modal profile. In general, there will not usually be a perfect fit between an individual and a given profile; however, the individual's profile will usually resemble one modal profile more closely than it will resemble other profiles.

Description of the SFPQ modal profiles

The SFPQ male and female modal profiles were derived from the normative sample. Five profiles were derived for each sex, based on an inspection of the eigenvalues. Each profile represents a bipolar dimension and can therefore be reversed to produce the 'negative' pole by subtracting the value of each attribute in the profile by the maximum scale score and taking the absolute value of the difference. The five profiles are arbitrarily labeled as representing the positive pole of the typal dimensions. Table 11 presents the percentile scores for the positive and negative exemplars of the five male and five female SFPQ modal profiles. It was necessary to define distinct male and female modal profiles because measured personality does differ markedly between males and females as reflected both in mean scores and in the organization of types. We deemed it more appropriate to center each sex's set of modal profiles on sex-based norms, rather than using combined norms because the latter strategy would spuriously confound typal differences with mean differences.

Comparison of classification efficiencies

Using the criterion that an individual's profile must correlate at least .50 with a given modal profile to be considered classifiable, the classification rate was 72.6 per cent for males and 66.5 per cent for females in the SFPQ normative sample. Persons not classified with respect to a profile type can be considered as representing mixed or infrequently occurring types.

Individuals representing modal profiles

Provided in Figure 1 are the SFPQ profiles of two individuals in the normative sample. The first profile depicts a male who is Independent, somewhat Open to Experience somewhat Industrious, not Agreeable, and not Methodical. His scores on the

Table 11. SFPQ modal profile percentiles

Modal Profile	Affiliation	Dominance	Exhibition	Abasement	Even-tempered	Good-natured	Autonomy	Individualism	Self Reliance	Change	Understanding	Breadth of Interest	Cognitive Structure	Deliberateness	Order	Achievement	Endurance	Seriousness
						MALES												
1+	16	2	14	84	92	82	18	42	31	92	66	92	79	76	73	16	21	34
2+	31	16	10	54	73	73	86	92	69	14	2	10	50	86	84	66	66	84
3+	79	58	66	98	93	96	54	46	54	62	31	14	12	4	12	42	34	58
4+	5	50	4	46	34	50	73	66	54	84	86	79	16	18	8	84	90	96
5+	38	88	31	84	31	82	2	14	4	34	24	46	84	58	73	92	92	66
1-	84	98	86	16	8	18	82	58	69	8	34	8	21	24	27	84	79	66
2-	69	84	90	46	27	27	14	8	31	86	98	90	50	14	16	34	34	16
3-	21	42	34	2	7	4	46	54	46	38	69	86	88	96	88	58	66	42
4-	95	50	96	54	66	50	27	34	46	16	14	21	84	82	92	16	10	4
5-	62	12	69	16	69	18	98	86	96	66	76	54	16	42	27	8	8	34
						FEMALES												
1+	2	21	7	69	42	42	18	21	21	84	93	98	62	58	42	46	62	76
2+	24	31	10	92	62	76	58	50	31	5	12	16	27	79	82	93	92	88
3+	50	14	31	82	93	92	82	79	79	86	50	34	10	5	4	27	42	76
4+	24	73	31	8	8	8	93	86	93	24	76	62	31	31	21	76	86	90
5+	76	90	84	82	42	58	7	12	34	12	69	66	50	3	5	79	86	62
1-	98	79	93	31	58	58	82	79	79	16	7	2	38	42	58	54	38	24
2-	76	69	90	8	38	24	42	50	69	95	88	84	73	21	18	7	8	12
3-	50	86	69	18	7	8	18	21	21	14	50	66	90	95	96	73	58	24
4-	76	27	69	92	92	92	7	14	7	76	24	38	69	69	79	24	14	10
5-	24	10	16	18	58	42	93	88	66	88	31	34	50	97	95	21	14	38

three Extraversion facet scales differ substantially showing an average level of Dominance and Exhibition but a very low level of Affiliation. It is noteworthy that he displays a relatively high level of Industriousness but a low level of Methodicalness. This is an example of a case where information would be lost if Industriousness and Methodicalness scales were aggregated into a Conscientiousness scale. Instead, the SFPQ Methodicalness-Industriousness configuration reveals someone who works hard but is not well organized. This male profile correlates .64 with the male modal profile 4+ presented in Table 11.

Female Profile

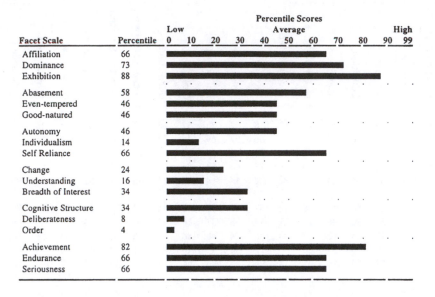

Male Profile

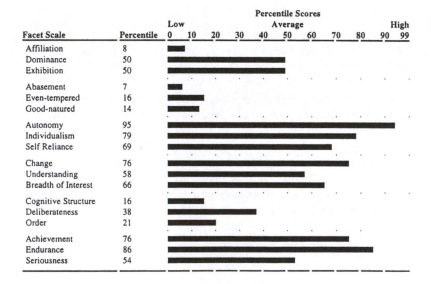

Figure 1. SFPQ profiles of a male and a female in the normative sample

The second profile depicts a female who is somewhat Extraverted, somewhat Industrious, not Open to Experience, and not Methodical. She also has a moderate level of Agreeableness and Independence (although a low score on Individualism). This female profile correlates .75 with the female modal profile 5+ (see Table 11).

Research using modal profiles

The evaluation of SFPQ modal profiles can be viewed as an alternative to the more typical evaluation of relationships of single personality variables to external criterion variables. Using modal profiles, one is interested in the external characteristics or behaviors associated with typical individuals who define a given modal profile. For example, are certain profile types more likely to be more satisfied or more effective workers? Or, as has been done with the Personality Research Form (Jackson, Peacock, & Smith, 1980; Rothstein & Jackson, 1980), one could evaluate the judged suitability or probable success of job applicants showing different modal profiles. The relation of personality profile membership and vocational preferences and interests (Siess & Jackson, 1970) is another possibility.

Conclusions

The structure of the SFPQ has been supported by a number of confirmatory factor analyses. Evidence of convergent and discriminant validity also is presented. Noteworthy is the average uncorrected validity of .56 when the SFPQ factor scales are correlated with peer ratings. The separation of the Conscientiousness factor into Methodicalness and Industriousness was substantiated by several confirmatory factor analyses and also by the predictive validity indices. These promising results were obtained even though the SFPQ was developed in such a way as to suppress the desirability confound. Indeed, SFPQ scales show low desirability factor loadings and correlations with desirability scales. Given the need for brief yet comprehensive assessment measures, the SFPQ appears well suited to measure personality on a broad range of personality traits.

References

American Psychiatric Association. (1994). *Diagnostic and statistical manual of mental disorder (4ᵗʰ ed.)*. Washington, DC: Author.

Browne, M.W. (1984). The decomposition of multitrait-multimethod matrices. *British Journal of Mathematical and Statistical Psychology, 37*, 1-21.

Browne, M.W. (1990). *MUTMUM PC User's Guide*. Unpublished manuscript. Department of Statistics, University of South Africa, Pretoria.

Browne, M.W., & Cudeck, R. (1989). Single sample cross-validation indices for covariance structure. *Multivariate Behavioral Research, 24,* 445-455.

Campbell, D.T., & Fiske, D.W. (1959). Convergent and discriminant validation by the multitrait-multimethod matrix. *Psychological Bulletin, 56,* 81-105.

Cattell, R.B., Cattell, A.K., & Cattell, H.E. (1993). *Sixteen Personality Factor Questionnaire, Fifth Edition.* Champaign, IL: Institute for Personality and Ability Testing.

Costa, P.J., Jr., & McCrae, R.R. (1985). *The NEO Personality Inventory manual.* Odessa, FL: Psychological Assessment Resources Inc.

Costa, P.J., Jr., & McCrae, R.R. (1988). From catalog to classification: Murray's needs and the five factor model. *Journal of Personality and Social Psychology, 55,* 258-265.

Costa, P.J., Jr., & McCrae, R.R. (1992). *Revised NEO Personality Inventory professional manual.* Odessa, FL: Psychological Assessment Resources, Inc.

Goffin, R.D. (1988). *The analysis of multitrait-multimethod matrices: An empirical and Monte Carlo comparison of two procedures.* Unpublished doctoral dissertation. The University of Western Ontario, London, Ontario, Canada.

Goffin, R.D., & Jackson, D. N. (1992). Analysis of multitrait-multirater performance appraisal data: Composite direct product method versus confirmatory factor analysis. *Multivariate Behavioural Research, 27,* 363-386.

Goldberg, L. R. (1999). *The Eugene-Springfield community sample: Information available from the research participants.* Technical Report, Vol 39. Oregon Research Institute.

Gough, H.G. (1957). *California Psychological Inventory: Manual.* Palo Alto, CA: Consulting Psychologists Press.

Gough, H.G. (1996). *CPI Manual: Third Edition.* Palo Alto, CA: Consulting Psychologists Press.

Gray, A., Jackson, D.N., & Howard, J.H. (1990). Identification of a coronary-prone profile of business managers: Comparison of three approaches to Type A assessment. *Behavioral Medecine, 16,* 67-75.

Hogan, R., & Hogan, J. (1995). *Hogan Personality Inventory Manual: Second Edition.* Tulsa OK: Hogan Assessment Systems.

Holden, R.R., Fekken, G.C., & Jackson, D.N. (1985). Structured personality test item characteristics and validity. *Journal of Research in Personality, 19,* 386-394.

Jackson, D.N. (1967, 1984). *Personality Research Form manual.* Port Huron, MI: Sigma Assessments Systems.

Jackson, D.N. (1994). *Jackson Personality Inventory manual—Revised.* Port Huron MI: Sigma Assessments Systems.

Jackson, D.N. (2000). *Jackson Vocational Interest Survey manual—Second Edition.* Port Huron, MI: Sigma Assessment Systems.

Jackson, D.N., Ashton, M.C., & Tomes, J.L. (1996). The six-factor model of personality: Facets from the big five. *Personality and Individual Differences, 21,* 391-402.

Jackson, D.N., Paunonen, S.V., Fraboni, M., & Goffin, R.D. (1996). A five-factor versus six-factor model of personality structure. *Personality and Individual Differences, 20,* 33-45.

Jackson D.N., Paunonen, S.V., & Tremblay, P.F. (2000). *Six Factor Personality Questionnaire Manual.* Port Huron, MI: Sigma Assessment Systems.

Jackson, D.N., Peacock, A.C., & Smith, J.P. (1980). Impressions of personality in the employment interview. *Journal of Personality and Social Psychology, 39,* 294-307.

Jackson, D.N., & Williams, D.R. (1975). Occupational classification in in terms of interest patterns. *Journal of Vocational Behavior, 6,* 269-280.

Kenny, D.A., & Kashy, D.A. (1992). Analysis of multitrait-multimethod matrix by confirmatory factor analysis. *Psychological Bulletin, 112,* 165-172.

McDonald, R.P., & Marsh, H.W. (1990). Choosing a multivariate model: Noncentrality and goodness-of-fit. *Psychological Bulletin, 107,* 247-255.

Murray, H.A. (1938). *Explorations in personality.* New York: Oxford University Press.

Neill, J.A., & Jackson, D.N. (1970). An evaluation of item selection strategies in personality scale construction. *Educational and Psychological Measurement, 30,* 647-661.

Nesselroade, J.R., & Baltes, P.B. (1975). Higher order factor convergence and divergence of two distinct personality systems: Cattell's HSPQ and Jackson's PRF. *Multivariate Behavioural Research, 10,* 387-407.

Paunonen, S.V. (1997). On chance and factor congruence following orthogonal procrustes rotation. *Educational and Psychological Measurement, 57,* 33-59.

Paunonen, S.V., Jackson, D.N., Trzebinski, J., & Forsterling, F. (1992). Personality structure across cultures: A multimethod evaluation. *Journal of Personality and Social Psychology, 62,* 447-456.

Paunonen, S.V., Keinonen, M., Trzebinski, J., Forsterling, F., Grishenko-Rose, N., Kouznetsova, L., & Chan, D.W. (1996). The structure of personality in six cultures. *Journal of Cross-Cultural Psychology, 27,* 339-353.

Reddon, J. R., & Jackson, D. N. (1989). Readability of three adult personality tests: Basic Personality Inventory, Jackson Personality Inventory, and Personality Research Form-E. *Journal of Personality Assessment, 53,* 180-183.

Rothstein, M., & Jackson, D.N. (1980). Decision making in the employment interview: An experimental approach. *Journal of Applied Psychology, 65,* 271-283.

Schönemann, P.H. (1966). A generalized solution of the orthogonal Procrustes problem. *Psychometrika, 31,* 1-16.

Siess, T.F., & Jackson, D.N. (1970). Vocational interests and personality: An empirical integration. *Journal of Counseling Psychology, 17,* 27-35.

Skinner, H.A., Jackson, D.N., & Hoffmann, H. (1974). Alcoholic personality types: Identification and correlates. *Journal of Abnormal Psychology, 83,* 658-666.

Skinner, H.A., Jackson, D.N., & Rampton, G.M. (1976). The Personality Research Form in a Canadian context: Does language make a difference? *Canadian Journal of Behavioural Science, 8,* 156-168.

Skinner, H.A., Reed, P.L., & Jackson, D.N. (1976). Toward the objective diagnosis of psychopathology: Generalizability of modal personality profiles. *Journal of Consulting and Clinical Psychology, 44,* 111-117.

Steiger, J.H. (1989). EZPATH: *A supplementary module for SYSTAT and SYSGRAPH.* Evanston, IL: SYSTAT, Inc.

Stricker, L.J. (1974). Personality Research Form: Factor structure and response style involvement. *Journal of Consulting and Clinical Psychology, 42,* 529-537.

Stumpf, H. (1993). The factor structure of the Personality Research Form: A cross-national evaluation. *Journal of Personality, 61,* 27-48.

Thurstone, L.L. (1947). *Multiple factor analysis.* Chicago: University of Chicago Press.

Widaman, K.F. (1985). Hierarchically nested covariance structure models for multitrait-multimethod data. *Applied Psychological Measurement, 9,* 1-26.

Chapter 16

Zuckerman-Kuhlman Personality Questionnaire (ZKPQ): An alternative five-factorial model

Marvin Zuckerman

Introduction

The ZKPQ was developed as the result of an attempt to define the basic factors of personality or temperament. The question arose in preparation for writing my book "Psychobiology of Personality" (Zuckerman, 1991). The book needed some framework for a top-down approach from personality traits through levels of intermediate biological levels to the genetic bases of personality traits (Zuckerman, 1993a). But what is a basic factor and which factors are basic? (Eysenck, 1992; Zuckerman, 1992). Factor analysis has been the classical method used to answer these questions. However, as we all know, what you get out of a factor analysis is limited by what you put into it. Our guiding assumption was that basic personality traits are those with a strong biological-evolutionary basis. Therefore we started with scales which had been used in psychobiological research and embodied concepts amenable to translation into comparative behavior among other species. For example, aggression rather than agreeableness, and impulsive sensation seeking rather than conscientiousness. Sensation seeking has been shown to have many biological correlates (Zuckerman, Buchsbaum, & Murphy, 1980) and to be a useful comparative model (Zuckerman, 1984). However, when it has been included in other systems it is usually in the form of a single scale ignoring the facets or subtypes of the trait which have differential associations with some biological traits.

The "Big Five" originated in lexical analyses of words (generally adjectives) with connotations for personality. We started with scales which had been used as measures of temperament or involved in psychobiological studies of personality. Eysenck's (1967) "Big Three" (extraversion, neuroticism, psychoticism) were an obvious starting point. Ostensible measures of temperament such as the Buss-Plomin (1975) scales for emotionality, activity, sociability, and impulsivity, and scales from Strelau's (1983) Temperament Inventory, based on Pavlovian theory,

Big Five Assessment, edited by B. De Raad &t M. Perugini. © 2002, Hogrefe &t Huber Publishers.

were included. Sensation seeking is a trait that has shown a high heritability and many psychophysiological and biochemical correlates suggesting a biological basis for the trait (Zuckerman, 1979; 1984; 1994a). However, the most widely used form of this scale contains four subfactors and some studies had suggested that the biological bases were sometimes specific to one or the other of the factors, therefore all four were included in our analyses. Similarly, impulsivity has been measured in a number of different ways and we felt it was necessary to include several markers for this trait. Emotional traits like anxiety and aggression-hostility are considered basic to most theories of temperament and such measures were also included. Measures of socialization and responsibility were also included. Measures of social desirability were also included to be sure that none of the basic factors were primarily defined by this response set.

In total we included at least three scale markers for each of nine hypothesized factors: sociability, general emotionality (neuroticism), anxiety, hostility, socialization, sensation seeking, impulsivity, activity, and social desirability. No measures of cultural interests or intellectual styles were included because of our conception of basic personality traits as comparative to traits in other species (Zuckerman, 1984). This is why we could not find a trait like "Openness to Experience," one of the Big Five.

Procedure of development

Based on the rationale described above, a total of 46 scales were selected from eight different questionnaires to represent the hypothesized factors with anywhere from three to nine potential markers for each factor (Zuckerman, Kuhlman, & Camac, 1988). The subjects were 271 students (73 men and 178 women) from an undergraduate class in personality psychology. Both oblique and orthogonal rotations were used with nearly identical results from both. A scree test suggested that four or five factors would be sufficient, but in order to clarify the possible hierarchal nature of the structure we analyzed the results at the seven-, five-, and three-factor levels. In this way we could see how primary factors merged to form the superordinate factors going from the seven- to three-factor levels. Figure 1 shows the correlations between factors across the three levels.

At the three-factor level Eysenck's Big Three were clearly identified. His E and N scales had the highest loadings on the first two factors and his P scales had the second highest loading on the third factor. The E factor contained scales measuring sociability and activity. The N factor was comprised of scales for neuroticism, anxiety, anger, hostility, general emotionality, lack of emotional control, and work efficiency. Other than P itself, the P factor consisted of a scale for autonomy or independence, nearly all of the sensation seeking and impulsivity subscales, and at the opposite pole, scales for socialization, planning, responsibility, restraint, and social desirability. This factor was labeled *Impulsive Unsocialized Sensation Seeking* (ImpUSS). These three factors were compared across genders and were nearly identical in structure in men and women.

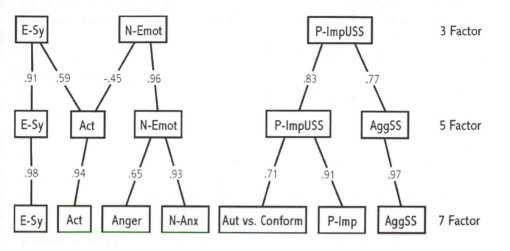

Figure 1. Factors at each level (three-, five-, and seven-factor analyses) and factor score correlations across levels. (E = Extraversion, Sy = Sociability, N = Neuroticism, Emot = Emotionality, P = Psychoticism, ImpUSS = Impulsive, Unsocialized Sensation Seeking, Act = Activity, AggSS = Aggressive Sensation Seeking, Anx = Anxiety, Aut vs Conform = Autonomy vs. Conformity, Imp = Impulsivity. From 'What lies beyond E and N? Factor analyses of scales believed to measure basic dimensions of personality' by M. Zuckerman, D. M. Kuhlman, & C. Camac, 1988, *Journal of Personal and Social Psychology, 54,* figure 2, p. 103. Copyright 1988 by American Psychological Association.

In the five-factor analysis the extraversion factor split into its sociability and activity components and the P-ImpUSS factor was split into impulsive and aggressive sensation seeking factors. In the seven-factor solution the neuroticism factor split into separate anger and anxiety factors.

A second study was done in order to sharpen the hierarchal model with a larger sample of subjects ($N = 525$) and a reduced number of scales (33) with several markers for each of the narrower factors revealed in the first study (Zuckerman, Kuhlman, Thornquist, & Kiers, 1991). This time factor rotations were done for three, four, five, six, and seven factors. Figure 2 shows the correlations between factor scores of subjects across the three- to six-factor levels. The seven-factor solution had a factor consisting of only one scale and therefore was ignored in further analyses. Separate sociability and activity factors emerged at the six-factor level. The sociability factor remained unchanged through the five-, four-, and three-factor levels. The activity factor was largely absorbed into the N-Anxiety factor in the four-factor analysis, but shifted to the sociability factor in the — supraordinate — three-factor analysis. N-Anxiety and Aggression-Hostility formed two separate fact-

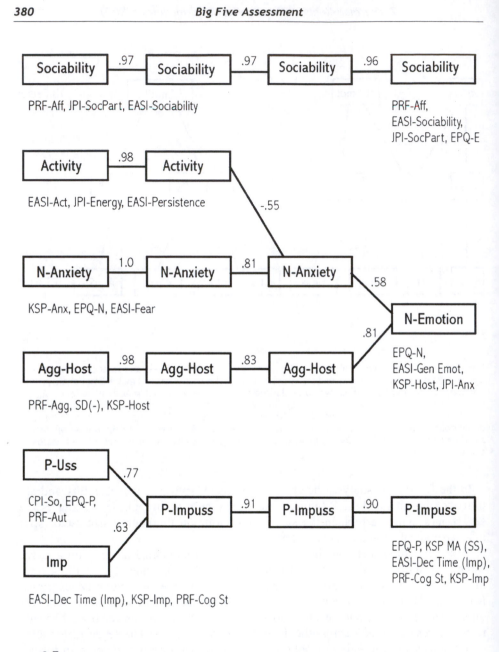

Figure 2. Factors at each level (three-, four-, five-, and six-factor analyses) and factor score correlations across levels for the total group. (N = Neuroticism, Agg-Host = Aggression-Hostility, Emotion = Emotionality, PUss = Psychopathy (Psychoticism) - Impulsive Unsocialized Sensation Seeking, Imp = Impulsivity. The strongest loading scales defining each factor at six- and three-factor levels are indicated. From "Personality from top (traits) to bottom (genetics) with stops at each level between" by M. Zuckernan in *Foundations of Personality* (Figure 3, p. 77) edited by J. Hettema & I.J. Deary, 1993, Dordrecht, Netherlands: Kluwer Academic Publishers. Copyright 1993 by Kluwer Academic publishers. Reproduced with permission of Kluwer.

ors from the six- to the four-factor levels but at the three-factor level the hostility scales shifted to the N-Anxiety and the aggression scales to the P-ImpUSS factor. At the six-factor level sensation seeking and impulsivity scales formed separate factors with the P scale itself more strongly attached to the sensation seeking factor. But from the five-factor through the three-factor solutions the sensation seeking and impulsivity scales were merged into a common P-ImpUSS factor.

All of the above results were based on the combined gender group. Factor reliabilities were the primary determinants of the analyses to use in the development of a questionnaire. Certainly, one would want factors that were the same for men and women. We therefore calculated congruency coefficients comparing male and female participants. Both three- and five-factor solutions were equally robust with average coefficients from .95 to .96 for corresponding factors and low coefficients for divergent factors averaging close to zero. However, the four-factor solution was not as reliable and in the six-factor solution the impulsivity factor could not even be identified in women. In view of these results we decided to proceed with the five-factor results because they offered the maximum specificity with no reduction of factor reliability. This is what led to the combination of impulsivity and sensation seeking in a single scale. Apart from the high coherence of these traits from the five-factor analysis up to the three-factor one, the theory and past research suggested that this was "a marriage of traits made in biology" (Zuckerman, 1993b).

Development of the ZKPQ full scale

The items from all of the scales used in the 1991 study, except for those in the Eysenck Personality Questionnaire (EPQ), were correlated with the five-factor scores, calculated for each subject ($N = 522$). The five factors were: Impulsive Sensation Seeking (ImpSS), Sociability (Sy), Neuroticism-Anxiety (N-Anx), Aggression-Hostility (Agg-Host), and Activity (Act). Twenty items were selected to represent each factor on the basis of their demonstrating high correlations with that factor and lower correlations with other factors and a social desirability scale. At this point some of the items were rewritten. This first form of the ZKPQ containing 100 items was given to a new group of 589 subjects and the items were factor analyzed. Scree tests unambiguously indicated the appropriateness of a five-factor solution. Of the 100 items selected on the basis of item-total score correlations, 89 loaded significantly and primarily on the factors to which they had been previously assigned. However, some of the items in the Sy scale had to be rewritten because of an extreme skewness in the distribution of scale scores. Ten new items were added for a validity scale to eliminate individual records influenced by an extreme social desirability set. The final form of the ZKPQ therefore consists of 99 true-false items and is usually completed in 15 to 20 minutes testing time.

Facet scores for the ZKPQ

Factor analyses were done on the items within each of the five major scales described above in order to see if facet or subfactor scales within the major scales could be derived. For two of the scales, N-Anx and Agg-Host, the scree plots indicated the sufficiency of a one-factor solution. For the remaining three scales, ImpSS, Sy, and Act, two-factor solutions were indicated. The Sy scale contained factors for (1) liking lively parties and friends, and (2) intolerance of social isolation. The ImpSS scale factors were (1) sensation seeking, and (2) impulsivity (particularly of the nonplanning type). The two factors in the Act scale were (1) need for general activity, and (2) need for work activity.

Scale descriptions

Impulsive Sensation Seeking (ImpSS)

This scale has 19 items. The impulsivity items describe a lack of planning and a tendency to act quickly on impulse without thinking. The sensation seeking items describe a general need for thrills and excitement, a preference for unpredictable situations and friends, and the need for change and novelty. Unlike earlier forms of the sensation seeking scale (forms II, IV, and V) this scale contains no items mentioning specific activities like drinking, drugs, sex, or risky sports. Such items were eliminated to avoid confounding in studies of persons who actually engage in one or another of these activities.

Neuroticism-Anxiety (N-Anx)

The 19 items in this scale describe emotional upset, tension (i.e., "I sometimes feel edgy and tense"), worry, fearfulness, obsessive indecision (i.e., "I often have trouble trying to make choices"), lack of self-confidence, and sensitivity to criticism (i.e., "I tend to be sensitive and easily hurt by thoughtless remarks and actions of others").

Aggression-Hostility (Agg-Host)

About half of the 17 items of this scale reflect a readiness to express verbal aggression (i.e., "It is natural for me to curse when I am mad"). Other items include rude, thoughtless or antisocial behavior (i.e., "If people annoy me I do not hesitate to tell them so"), vengefulness, spitefulness, a quick temper and impatience with others (i.e., "When people disagree with me I cannot help getting into an argument with them").

Sociability (Sy)

This scale has 17 items. One group of items describes a liking of big parties, interacting with many people (i.e., "I tend to start conversations at parties") and having many friends. The second group indicates an intolerance for social isolation in highly sociable subjects and a liking or tolerance for isolation in unsociable subjects (i.e., "I would not mind being socially isolated in some place for some period of time").

Activity (Act)

The activity scale has 17 items. The first factor describes the need for general activity and impatience and restlessness when there is nothing to do (i.e., "I like to keep busy all the time"). The second factor indicates a preference for challenging and hard work (i.e., "I like a challenging task more than a routine one") and lot of energy for work and other tasks (i.e., "When I do things I do them with lots of energy").

Infrequency

Infrequency (10 items). This is not a scale but it is used to eliminate subjects with possibly invalid records. The items are most true scored and if endorsed indicate exaggerated socially desirable content, unlikely to be true(i.e., "I never met a person I didn't like", "I have always told the truth"). Scores higher than 3 are considered to indicate questionable validity for that record.

Norms

T scores and percentile norms are available in an unpublished form from the authors based on 1,144 male and 1,825 female college students. Means, standard deviations, and frequency distributions are also provided. A copy of the ZKPQ is available from the authors.

Short form (ZKPQ-S)

A short form, consisting of 35 items (7 items for each of the 5 major factors) has been developed by Zuckerman and Kuhlman. We began by analyzing the items with the highest correlations with the total scores on each of the five factors and the greater response variance using the normative sample referred to above. On the basis of these data the seven highest correlating items for each factor were selected for the short form. Some items were eliminated because of redundancy of content and the next highest correlating items were substituted.

The short 35 item form was given to new samples of students, 208 males and 820 females, from the same college population. A factor analysis of the 35 items among the females confirmed the assignments of every item to its particular scales based on the previous analyses. There were some differences in results among the males, perhaps due to the smaller N. A copy of this form with the college norms for it are available from the authors.

Reliabilities

Internal reliability (Alpha)

Table 1 shows the internal reliabilities (Cronbach's alphas) for the total and sub-scales in the American sample and a Spanish translation (Zotes, 1999), and for translations of the total scales in Japanese (Shiomi, Kuhlman, David, Zuckerman, & Joireman, 1996), German (Ostendorf & Angleitner, 1994), Chinese, (Wu, Wang, Du, Li, Jiang, & Wang, 2000), and Catalan (Goma-Friexenet, 2000). The last sample was from the area of Spain around Barcelona where Catalan is the common language rather than Spanish. The reliabilities for the short-form described above are also shown in Table 1.

All of the alphas for males and females in the American sample are good with most ranging between .70 and .80. The only questionable one is for the subscale of General Activity in the female group (.56). The results were similar for the Spanish sample except for low reliabilities for the subscale of Work Effort. N-Anx has the highest reliabilities in all samples, above .79 for both males and females. The Japanese, German, and Catalan samples had good reliabilities for the total scales, but the Chinese sample had lower reliabilities; those for four of the scales were in .60's. Only the reliability for N-Anx was high (.81).

The reliabilities of the short form of the ZKPQ were all satisfactory ranging from .62 to .78 for males and .67 to .73 for females. As expected from reduction in the length of scales, the reliabilities were somewhat less for the short than for the long form for four of the five scales. On Sy they are about the same.

Retest reliabilities

American students ($N = 153$) were tested twice on the ZKPQ with an interval of three to four weeks between tests. Retest reliabilities were: ImpSS, .80; N-Anx, .84; Agg-Host, .78; Act, .76, and Sy, .83. Retest reliabilities for males and females were quite similar.

Table 1. ZKPQ reliabilities (Cronbach's Alphas)

Scales	USA Long Form		USA Short Form		Spanish		German	Catalan	Chinese	Japanese	
N's	1,144	1,825	208	820	186	581	730	933	333	206	230
	Male	Female	Male	Female	Male	Female	Both	Both	Both	Male	Female
Impulsive Sensation Seeking	.77	.81	.62	.71	.76	.81	.83	.79	.68	.77	.79
Sensation Seeking	.74	.77			.73	.80					
Impulsivity	.64	.68			.70	.71					
Neuroticism-Anxiety	.82	.84	.70	.72	.79	.85	.86	.84	.81	.82	.85
Aggression-Hostility	.76	.76	.66	.67	.75	.75	.71	.67	.62	.74	.74
Activity	.74	.77	.67	.72	.75	.73	.75	.74	.61	.69	.73
Need for General Activity	.74	.56			.74	.71					
Need for Work Activity	.75	.72			.47	.50					
Sociability	.77	.79	.78	.79	.79	.76	.75	.76	.63	.81	.73
Parties and Friends	.73	.77			.75	.72					
Isolation Intolerance	.69	.72			.66	.65					

Table 2. Four-factor analysis of NEO, ZKPQ, and EPQ personality scales

Scale	Factor Loadings			
	Factor 1	Factor 2	Factor 3	Factor 4
NEO Extraversion	**.88**	-.14	-.05	.17
EPQ Extraversion	**.79**	-.32	.17	-.08
ZKPQ Sociability	**.76**	-.16	.10	-.07
ZKPQ Activity	**.60**	.01	-.18	.02
ZKPQ N-Anxiety	-.13	**.92**	-.01	.08
NEO Neuroticism	-.15	**.90**	.10	-.11
EPQ Neuroticism	-.16	**.91**	-.04	-.08
NEO Conscientious	.15	-.07	**-.86**	-.02
EPQ Psychoticism	-.09	-.08	**.80**	-.28
ZKPQ ImpSS	.48	.08	**.74**	-.02
NEO Agreeabieness	-.04	-.07	-.31	**.81**
ZKPQ Agg-Host	.35	.34	.24	**-.72**
NEO Openness	.27	.14	.18	**.67**

Note: From "A comparison of three structural models for personality: The Big Three, the Big Five, and the Alternative Five," by M. Zuckerman, D. M. Kuhlman, J. Joireman, P.Teta, and M. Kraft, 1993, *Journal of Personality and Social Psychology, 65*, p. 762. Copyright 1993 by the American Psychological Association Reprinted with permission.

Gender differences

Significant gender differences were found in the normative American samples of college students. Men scored higher on ImpSS, Agg-Host, and Act; women were higher on N-Anx and Sy. On the short form men scored higher on ImpSS and women were higher on N-Anx.

Validity

Convergent and discriminant validity

The ZKPQ, Costa and McCrae's (1992) NEO-PI-R, and the Eysenck Personality Questionnaire (EPQ-R; Eysenck, Eysenck, & Barrett, 1985) scales were intercorrelated and subjected to a factor analysis in order to see the extent of overlap between the two five-factor models and Eysenck's three-factor one. The subjects were 157 undergraduate students. Four factors accounted for 74 per cent of the variance and additional factors added little to the solution. Table 2 shows the results of the varimax rotated four-factor analysis.

The results show a high degree of convergence between the factors as represented by scales in each of the three tests. Measures of neuroticism were virtually similar in all three tests with loadings of .90 and above on factor 2. Convergence was also high on the other factors: .76 - .88 for extraversion and sociability scales (factor 1); -.86, .74, and .80 for conscientiousness, impulsive sensation seeking, and psychoticism scales (factor 3); and .81 and -.72 respectively for the agreeableness and aggression-hostility scales (factor 4). The fifth factor in the NEO, openness to experience, loaded on factor 4 and the fifth factor in the ZKPQ, activity, loaded on the extraversion factor 1. A five-factor solution showed no convergence of openness and activity in the fifth factor. Discriminant validity was also good: most loadings on irrelevant factors were very low; one exception was the secondary loading of ImpSS on the extraversion factor 1.

Bivariate correlations of the ZKPQ scales with the NEO, EPQ, EASI (Buss & Plomin, 1984), the SSS form V (Zuckerman, Eysenck, & Eysenck, 1978), and Ego-Control and Ego-Resilience scales (Block & Block, 1980) are shown in Table 3. The N for the correlations of the ZKPQ with the NEO and EPQ was 157. The N's for the correlations with the other scales varied from 135 to 177, depending on the numbers of subjects who took particular tests. ZKPQ Sy correlated very highly with EPQ and NEO E scales, and with EASI Sociability. N-Anx correlated very highly with EPQ and NEO N scales, and with EASI Emotionality. ImpSS correlated highly with EPQ P, NEO Conscientiousness, with EASI Impulsivity, Block's Undercontrol, and the SSSV Total score. Correlations between ImpSS and the SSS subscales, with the exception of Boredom Susceptibility (BS), were all moderate and close in magnitude. Agg-Host correlated highly and inversely with the NEO Agreeableness scale, and moderately with EASI Emotionality and Impulsivity, and lower with several other scales including NEO N and EPQ N and P. ZKPQ Act correlated highly with EASI Act and low with EPQ E and NEO E and Conscientiousness. NEO Openness did not correlate with any of the ZKPQ scales. ZKPQ Sy, N-Anx, ImpSS, and Act all show good convergent and discriminant validity. Agg-Host had good convergent validity with NEO Agreeableness.

Cloninger's personality model resembles the alternative five model in many respects. Zuckerman and Cloninger (1996) correlated the scales of the ZKPQ with those of the Temperament and Character Inventory (TCI; Cloninger, Przybeck, Svrakie, & Wetzel, 1994). Four of the five ZKPQ scales showed good convergent validity with four of the TCI scales. ImpSS correlated .68 with TCI Novelty Seeking; N-Anx correlated .66 with Harm Avoidance; Agg-Host correlated -.60 with Cooperativeness; Act correlated .46 with Persistence. All of these were markedly higher than correlations with other scales of the ZKPQ and TCI (discriminant validity). A curious thing about the Cloninger model is that it has no scale for extraversion or sociability. The ZKPQ Sy scale correlated .37 with Novelty Seeking and -.38 with Harm Avoidance. The EPQ Extraversion scale, also used in this study, showed the same pattern of correlations with the two TCI scales.

Table 3. Correlations of ZKPQ Scales with EASI, SSS and Block Ego Undercontrol and Ego Resilience Scales.

		ZKPQ Scales				
		Impulsive Sensation Seeking	Sociability	Neuroticism-Anxiety	Aggression-Hostility	Activity
EPQ	Psychoticism	**.55****	-.05	-.05	.32**	-.05
EPQ	Extraversion	.28**	**.70****	-.24**	.13	.36**
EPQ	Neuroticism	.01	-.21*	**.79****	.35**	-.13
NEO	Conscientiousness	**-.51**	-.04	-.09	-.13	.31**
NEO	Extraversion	.28**	**.70****	-.24**	.13	.36**
NEO	Neuroticism	.01	-.21	**.79****	.35**	-.13
NEO	Agreeableness	-.23**	-.05	.04	**-.63****	.09
NEO	Openness	.00	.06	.00	-.14	.11
EASI	Emotionality	-.11	-.13	**.68****	.46**	-.14
EASI	Sociability	-.25**	**.67****	-.28**	.24**	.27**
EASI	Impulsivity	**.70****	.23**	-.06	.42**	-.03
EASI	Activity	.08	.19*	-.18	.11	**.59****
SSS	Total Score	**.66****	.20*	-.10	.31**	.01
SSS	Thrill & Adventure	.49**	.21**	-.24**	.11	.17*
SSS	Experience Seeking	.46**	-.05	.00	.07	-.12
SSS	Disinhibition	.48**	.23**	.05	.36**	-.09
SSS	Boredom Susceptibility	.37**	.15	-.08	.30**	.11
Block	Ego Undercontrol	**.63****	.24**	-.15	.30**	.11
Block	Ego Resiliency	.14	.17*	-.30**	-.24**	.23**

Note: Correlations in bold-face are those showing good convergent validity with similar scales; $p < .05$, two-tailed test; ** $p < .01$, two-tailed test

Motivational and emotional traits

In a number of personality models it is suggested that personality traits represent expressions of more basic motivational, cognitive, or emotional traits. Gray (1982), for instance, has proposed two basic dimensions: anxiety and impulsivity. The former is based on sensitivitiy to signals of punishment and the latter to sensitivity to signals of reward. A third system, fight-flight, is expressed in aggression or anger and based on sensitivity to signals of punishment or non-reward. Tellegen (1985) identifies two major dimensions associated with emotions: positive emotionality associated with extraversion and negative emotionality associated with neuroticism. His third dimension is constraint, associated with behavioral inhibition versus impulsivity. Costa and McCrae (1992) also identify extraversion with positive emotions and warmth, and neuroticism with anxiety, depression, and hostility, although they include other kinds of traits as facets of these two primary factors. Among Zuckerman's (1991) five basic factors are: sociability, identified with behavioral approach tendencies, generalized reward expectancy, and positive affect; and neuroticism, associated with a behavioral inhibition mechanism, generalized reward expectancy, and emotions of anxiety and depression. Impulsive sensation seeking was hypothesized to be associated with behavioral disinhibition and the emotion of anger and the attitude of hostility.

These models, together with Eysenck's basic three factors, were related to measures of motivational and emotional traits in a study by Zuckerman, Joireman, Kraft, and Kuhlman (1999). Motivational traits of sensitivities to reward and punishment were measured by scales developed by Torrubia *et al.* (1995) based on Gray's model. Generalized reward and punishment expectancy scales were those developed by Ball and Zuckerman (1990). Trait affect scales for anxiety, depression, hostility, positive affect, and sensation seeking (surgent) affect were assessed using the revised Multiple Affect Adjective Check List (MAACL-R; Zuckerman & Lubin, 1985; Lubin & Zuckerman, 1999).

The associations between personality, motivational, cognitive, and emotion traits were investigated using factor analysis with replication using Procrustes rotations to target. An extraversion factor (EPQ E, ZKPQ Sy) was associated with generalized reward expectancy, sensitivity to signals of reward, and both surgent and positive affect. The neuroticism factor (EPQ N, ZKPQ N-Anx) was strongly related to generalized punishment expectancy, sensitivity to signals of punishment, and trait anxiety. The third factor, a combination of the EPQ P scale and the ZKPQ ImpSS and Agg-Host scales, was weakly related to sensitivity to reward and strongly related to trait hostility. Trait depression was equally related to the neuroticism and P-ImpSS-Agg-Host factors. Although there were some secondary loadings of the motivational, cognitive, and emotion scales on the factors other than the primary ones described above, the general pattern supports the discriminant as well as the convergent validity of the measures.

Construct, concurrent, and predictive validity

Psychopathy

Thornquist and Zuckerman (1995) rated prison inmates enrolled in a drug program for psychopathy using the Hare (1991) Psychopathy Check List. The participants were also evaluated on a passive-avoidance learning task developed by Newman and Kosson (1986). All subjects were given the ZKPQ. Psychopathy ratings correlated with ImpSS in White but not in African-American or Hispanic groups. ImpSS correlated with passive avoidance errors (learning not to respond to signals of punishment) across all subjects. None of the other scales in the ZKPQ were related to either the psychopathy rating, based on case history and interview, or the deficit in passive-avoidance learning in the experimental setting.

Drug Abuse

Ball (1995) gave the ZKPQ to 450 cocaine abusers seeking treatment in an outpatient facility. Unlike the relative independence of the ZKPQ subscales in the college population, ImpSS, N-Anx, and Agg-Host subscales were substantially correlated in the substance abuser sample. The high intercorrelation of these scales may have something to do with their immediate circumstance of seeking treatment. Early use of cocaine was related to ImpSS, Agg-Host, and Act. Number of past treatment episodes was related to N-Anx. Severity of drug abuse and addiction was related to ImpSS, N-Anx, and Agg-Host. Other psychiatric problems were also related to these three subscales. Only Agg-Host was related to a history of violence.

Treatment outcome (predictive validity) was predicted by the ImpSS, Agg-Host, and N-Anx scales. Cocaine abusers who continued using cocaine during treatment had scored higher on ImpSS and Agg-Host on admission. There was also a marginal effect for Agg-Host. Early drop-outs scored higher on Agg-Host than those patients completing treatment. ImpSS was the only scale correlated with number of treatment appointments kept. Cocaine abusers who scored higher on ImpSS were less successful at remaining at least one month in treatment and were also judged in need of inpatient treatment. Cocaine abusers referred for treatment also scored higher on N-Anx and Agg-Host.

Cluster analyses of the ZKPQ scales yielded two subtypes, one characterized by patients scoring higher on ImpSS, Agg-Host, and N-Anx and lower on Sy. This latter subtype scored higher than the other subtype on drug-abuse, family, and psychiatric severity. The other subtype was primarily men stipulated by the criminal justice system, not abused as children, and free of psychiatric symptoms, or in other words "normal" criminals. We would hypothesize that the subtype with elevated ZKPQ scores were personality disorders, primarily of the antisocial personality type.

Black (1993) used the ZKPQ to study drug abusers entering an outpatient drug treatment facility. Based on their drug histories the clients were divided into primary users of alcohol, cocaine, or marijuana. Primary alcohol users were higher on Sy than cocaine users, whereas the primary cocaine users were significantly higher on N-Anx and Agg-Host. There were no significant differences between primary marijuana users and the other two groups on any of the scales. Those who successfully completed the program were higher on Sy and those who were violators of the prohibition on drug use during the program were higher on N-Anx and Agg-Host. The results of this study were similar to those of Ball except for the absence of ImpSS as a correlate of cocaine use or a predictor of therapy outcome.

Prostitution

Studies of drug abusers in treatment programs confound long term personality characteristics with the stress of the program and the implicit demand to admit psychopathology. These situational features have their greatest effects on scales of neuroticism which are elevated in the early parts of the programs but markedly reduced in those who remain in the program (Zuckerman, Sola, Masterson, & Angelone, 1975).

We had the opportunity to test a group of prostitutes who were actively practicing their profession on a highway leading out of a city, soliciting motorists and truck drivers at bars and restaurants (Sullivan, Zuckerman, & Kraft, 1996). This was an unusually risk-taking group because a year before the study a serial killer had been murdering prostititutes along the same highway and some of the women knew the victims. More than half of the group were cocaine users. The prostitutes were interviewed and tested in a diner and paid $10 for their participation. Their ZKPQ scores were compared with those of a control group composed of food service workers at a university. Despite an attempt to match for race, marital status, age, and education the controls were still significantly older and educated.

The prostitutes scored significantly higher than the controls on ImpSS, N-Anx, and Agg-Host, but after controlling for age and education differences only the difference on ImpSS ($p < .001$) remained significant, although the difference on Agg-Host approached significance ($p = .08$). Cocaine users among the prostitutes scored significantly higher than non-drug or other drug users on ImpSS. ImpSS was also higher in polydrug than in no drug or one drug users. This relationship between sensation seeking and number of drugs used has been found in many other studies using the SSS (Zuckerman, 1994).

General and specific risk-taking

Zuckerman and Kuhlman (2000) studied the relationships between personality, using the ZKPQ, and risk-taking among college students in six areas: smoking, drinking, drugs, risky sex, reckless driving, and gambling. Most of these types of risk-taking, particularly the first four, were significantly intercorrelated. A composite risk-taking score was constructed for each subject. High general risk-takers were higher than medium and low risk-takers on ImpSS, Agg-Host, and Sy. These three scales independently predicted general risk-taking. Gender differences on risk-taking were mediated by ImpSS only. Analyzing the types of risk-taking separately, we found that whereas all three of the above described traits were related to drinking, only ImpSS was independently related to smoking and drug use, only ImpSS and Agg-Host were related to risky sex, only Agg-Host and low N-Anx were related to reckless driving, and only Sy was related to gambling. It is interesting that in this general population N-Anx did not appear as a predictor of substance use. This supports our belief that anxiety appears as a predictor of substance use only in groups asking for or actually in treatment. ImpSS is the main predictor of drug abuse and antisocial forms of behavior sometimes accompanied by elevated Agg-Host.

The lack of association between ImpSS and reckless driving was not expected because of a large literature relating the SSS to driving violations, reported speed of driving, and even behavioral observations of reckless driving (Zuckerman, 1994). Although ImpSS correlated equally with Thrill and Adventure Seeking (TAS), Experience Seeking, and Disinhibition subscales of the SSS (see Table 2) some as yet anecdotal evidence has suggested that the ImpSS scale is not picking up the TAS component measured in the SSS. Some persons, above college age, who report engaging in many kinds of risky or extreme sports do not score high on ImpSS, and some who are actually aversive to any kind of physical risk-taking manage to get high scores on ImpSS. Studies of ImpSS scores in persons engaging in extreme sports have not been done. Perhaps the impulsive part of ImpSS is not characteristic of persons who take these kinds of physical risks, but may be limited to those who take other kinds of physical risk like smoking, drug use, or criminal activity.

Gambling

Sensation seeking, as defined by the SSS, has been related to gambling activity in the general population, although not to pathological gambling as represented by those who participate in Gamblers Anonymous or enter therapy for the compulsion. A recent community-wide study used only the ImpSS scale from the ZKPQ (McDaniel & Zuckerman, unpublished). Both gender and age were strong determinants of ImpSS scores; ImpSS was higher in men than in women and decreased with age in both sexes. ImpSS was significantly related to gambling interest and variety of gambling activities in both men and women. There were some differential relationships between ImpSS and specific types of gambling in men and women. ImpSS correlated with sports betting and video poker playing in both sexes, but it correlated with slot machine playing and off-track betting only in women and with lottery playing only in men.

Breen and Zuckerman (1999) used the ImpSS in a study of gambling behavior in a controlled laboratory paradigm. The outcomes of the betting of participants was fixed in a decreasing rate of winning over trials so that all participants started by winning at a high rate but the pay-off gradually decreased with each successive block of trials. Subjects could quit at any time. Those who persisted until they lost all of their initial stake were called "chasers" and those who quit before losing all of their starting money were termed "non-chasers." The Imp component of the ImpSS differentiated chasers from nonchasers — the chasers were higher — but the SS component did not. The study illustrates why it may be important to look at the facet scores separately as well as at the total score.

Team sport participants

Sensation seeking, as measured by the SSS, has not been found to be high in participants in ordinary sports or physical activities even if these are moderately risky, but it is high in participants of extreme sports like sky diving, scuba-diving, hanggliding, mountain climbing, etc. We used the ZKPQ to investigate the personality profiles in male and female participants in team sports. Male members of baseball and football teams, and female members of field hockey and lacrosse and equestrian teams were given the ZKPQ. They were compared with general college norms from the school they attended (O' Sullivan, Zuckerman, & Kraft, 1998)

Members of all of the teams were characterized by a distinctive profile on the ZKPQ. All four teams were significantly higher on Activity and lower on the Neuroticism-Anxiety scales than the general college population. The fact that athletes of all types are high on Act supports the construct validity of this scale. The low scores on N-Anx may represent the lack of fear since physical harm is a risk in most of these sports. Members of the male teams actually scored lower than the general college population on ImpSS. Although conventional sports participation has not been related to sensation seeking, the lower scores of male participants on ImpSS was not expected. The results, however, confirm our feeling that ImpSS is not relevant to the kind of physical risk-taking in ordinary sports.

Final Comments

The development of the ZKPQ began in the 1980's (Zuckerman *et al.*, 1988) before Costa and McCrae (1992) had expanded their NEO from three to five factors to fit the popular big-five theory evolved from the lexical analyses of Goldberg (1990) and others (Norman, 1963). The definitions of the major five factors in the two models differ, and the content inclusion is somewhat narrower in the alternative-five model, but there is strong convergence of three of the five factors and moderate conversion on a fourth (ImpSS vs. Conscientiousness). The fifth factors are entirely different, Openness in the big-five and Activity in the alternative-five. The differences among the first four factors are in the placement of facet traits in the NEO and the ZKPQ and in what is a facet, or minor trait, and what is a major trait. My investigation of the realm of traits began as an attempt to see where sensation seeking fits in the broader family of traits and therefore we included several types of sensation seeking as well as impulsivity scales in our initial factor analyses. The reasons for sampling more widely among sensation seeking and impulsivity scales was that these constructs had proven to be quite important in psychobiological research and we were striving to establish a framework for a psychobiological model of personality (Zuckerman, 1991). Similarly, traits like aggression and activity were selected because of their importance in the biological and comparative literature.

Reliability findings for the scales are fairly robust even though we can identify subfactors in three of the five major scales. Convergence and discriminant validities are also strong. Research shows good concurrent and predictive validity in the areas of psychopathy, drug abuse, and risk-taking in general. Translated scales in German, Spanish, Catalan, Japanese, and Chinese have shown good factor reliabilities and internal scale reliabilites suggesting cross-cultural generality of the personality contructs. We hope that the easy availability of the ZKPQ gratis to all interested researchers will continue to stimulate research with the instrument, particularly in the areas of genetics, psychopharmacology, psychophysiology, and psychopathology. This particular five-factor model is based on an evolving psychobiological model but much more research is needed to develop the model to its fullest potential.

References

Ball, S.A., & Zuckerman, M. (1990). Sensation seeking, Eysenck's personality dimensions and reinforcement sensitivity in concept formation. *Personality and Individual Differences, 11,* 343-353.

Black, J.J. (1993). *Predictors of outcome at an outpatient substance abuse center.* Unpublished doctoral dissertation, University of Delaware, Newark, DE.

Block, J.H., & Block, J. (1980). The role of ego-control and ego-resilience in the organization of behavior. In W.A. Collins (Ed.) *The Minnesota symposium on child psychology, Vol. 13: Development of cognition, affect and social relations* (pp. 39-101). Hillsdale, NJ: Erlbaum.

Breen, R.B., & Zuckerman, M. (1999). "Chasing" in gambling behavior: Personality and cognitive determinants. *Personality and Individual Differences, 27,* 1097-1111.

Buss, A.H., & Plomin, R. (1975). *A temperament theory of personality development.* New York: Wiley.

Cloninger, C.R., Przybeck, T.R., Svrakic, D.M., & Wetzel, R.D. (1994). *The temperament and character inventory (TCI): A guide to its development and use.* St. Louis, MO: Center for Psychobiology of Personality.

Costa, P.T., Jr., & McCrae, R.R. (1992). *NEO-PI-R: Revised NEO Personality Inventory (NEO-PI-R).* Odessa, FL: Psychological Assessment Resources.

Eysenck, H.J. (1967). *The biological basis of personality.* Springfield, IL: Charles C. Thomas.

Eysenck, H.J. (1992). Four ways five factors are not basic. *Personality and Individual Differences, 13,* 667-673.

Eysenck, S.B.G., Eysenck, H.J., & Barrett, P. (1985). A revised version of the psychoticism scale. *Personality and Individual Differences, 6,* 21-29.

Gray, J.A. (1982). *The neuropsychology of anxiety: An enquiry into the function of the septohippocampal system.* New York: Oxford University Press.

Hare, R.D. (1991). *The Hare Psychopathy Checklist-Revised.* Toronto: Multihealth Systems.

Lubin, B., & Zuckerman, M. (1999). *MAACL-R: Manual for the Multiple Affect Adjective Check-List.* San Diego, CA: Educational and Industrial Testing Service.

McDaniel, S., & Zuckerman, M. (2000). *Impulsive sensation seeking and interest and participation in gambling activities.* Manuscript submitted for publication.

Newman, J.P., & Kosson, D.S. (1986). Passive avoidance learning in psychopathic and non-psychopathic offenders. *Journal of Abnormal Psychology, 95,* 252-256.

Ostendorf, F., & Angleitner, A. (1994). A comparison of different instruments proposed to measure the big-five. *European Review of Applied Psychology, 44,* 45-53.

O'Sullivan, D.M., Zuckerman, M., & Kraft, M. (1996). The personality of prostitutes. *Personality and Individual Differences, 21,* 445-448.

O'Sullivan, D.M., Zuckerman, M., & Kraft, M. (1998). Personality characteristics of male and female participants in team sports. *Personality and Individual Differences, 25,* 119-128.

Shiomi, K., Kuhlman, D.M., Zuckerman, M., Joireman, J.A., Sato, M., & Yata, S. (1996). Examining the validity of a Japanese version of the Zuckerman-Kuhlman Personality Questionnaire (ZKPQ). *Hyago University of Teacher Education Journal, 2,* 1-13.

Strelau, J. (1983) *Temperament, personality, activity.* London: Academic Press.

Tellegen, A. (1985). Structure of mood and personality and their relevance to assessing anxiety, with an emphasis on self-report. In A.H. Tuma, & J.D. Maser (Eds.), *Anxiety and the anxiety disorders* (pp. 681-706).

Thornquist, M.H., & Zuckerman, M. (1995). Psychopathy, passive-avoidance learning and basic dimensions of personality. *Personality and Individual Differences, 19,* 525-534.

Torrubia, R., Avila, C., Moltó, J., & Grande, I. (1995). Testing for stress and happiness: The role of the behavioral inhibition system. In C.D. Spielberger, I.G. Sarason, M.T. Brebner, E. Greenglass, P. Laungani, & A.M. O'Roark (Eds.), *Stress and emotion: Anxiety, anger, and curiosity, Vol. 15* (pp. 191-211). Washington, DC: Taylor & Francis.

Wu, Y-X., Wang, W., Du, W-Y., Li, J., Jiang, X-F., & Wang, Y-H (2000). Development of a Chinese version of the Zuckerman-Kuhlman Personality Questionnaire: Reliabilities and gender/age effects. *Social Behavior and Personality, 28,* 241-250.

Zotes, J.A.G. (1999). *Spanish Version for the Zuckerman-Kuhlman Personality Questionnaire.* Unpublished manuscript.

Zuckerman, M. (1979). *Sensation seeking: Beyond the optimal level of arousal.* Hillsdale, NJ: Erlbaum.

Zuckerman, M. (1984). Sensation seeking: A comparative approach to a human trait. *Behavioral and Brain Sciences, 7,* 413-471.

Zuckerman, M. (1991). *Psychobiology of personality.* Cambridge, UK: Cambridge University Press.

Zuckerman, M. (1992). What is a basic factor and which factors are basic? Turtles all the way down. *Personality and Individual Differences, 13,* 675-681.

Zuckerman, M. (1993a). Personality from top (traits) to bottom (genetics) with stops at each level between. In J. Hettema & I.J. Deary (Eds.), *Foundations of Personality* (pp. 73-100). Dordrecht, Netherlands: Kluwer Academic Publishers.

Zuckerman, M. (1993b). Sensation seeking and impulsivity: A marriage of traits made in biology? In W.G. McCown, J.L. Johnson, & M.B. Shure (Eds.), *The impulsive client: Theory, research, and treatment* (pp. 71-91). Washington, DC: American Psychological Association.

Zuckerman, M. (1994). *Behavioral expressions and biosocial bases of sensation seeking.* New York: Cambridge University Press.

Zuckerman, M., Buchsbaum, M.S., & Murphy, D.L. (1980). Sensation seeking and its biological correlates. *Psychological Bulletin, 88,* 187-214.

Zuckerman, M., & Cloninger, C.R. (1996). Relationships between Cloninger's, Zuckerman's, and Eysenck's dimensions of personality. *Personality and Individual Differences, 21,* 283-285.

Zuckerman, M., Eysenck, S.B.G., & Eysenck, H.J. (1978). Sensation seeking in England and America: Cross cultural, age, and sex comparisons. *Journal of Consulting and Clinical Psychology, 46,* 139-149.

Zuckerman, M., Joireman, J., Kraft, M., & Kuhlman, D.M. (1999). Where do motivational and emotional traits fit within three factor models of personality. *Personality and Individual Differences, 26,* 487-504.

Zuckerman, M., & Kuhlman, D.M. (2000). Personality and risk-taking: Common biosocial factors. *Journal of Personality, 68,* 999-1029.

Zuckerman, M., Kuhlman, D.M., & Camac, C. (1988). What lies beyond E and N? Factor analyses of scales believed to measure basic dimensions of personality. *Journal of Personality and Social Psychology, 54,* 96-107.

Zuckerman, M., Kuhlman, D., Thornquist, M., & Kiers, H. (1991). Five (or three) robust questionnaire scale factors of personality without culture. *Personality and Individual Differences, 12,* 929-941.

Zuckerman, M., & Lubin, B. (1985). *Manual for the Multiple Affect Adjective Check List-Revised (MAACL-R).* San Diego, CA: Educational and Industrial Testing Service.

Zuckerman, M., Sola, S., Masterson, J., & Angelone, J.V. (1975). MMPI patterns in drug abusers before and after treatment in therapeutic communities. *Journal of Consulting and Clinical Psychology, 43,* 286-296.

Chapter 17

Second-order factor structure of the Cattell Sixteen Personality Factor Questionnaire

Scott M. Hofer
Herbert W. Eber

Introduction

The Cattell Sixteen Personality Factor (16PF) Questionnaire[©] has been one of the most studied instruments in the history of personality research. A conservative estimate of research using the 16PF Questionnaire would include upwards of 2100 publications since 1974 (see IPAT, 1991 for 1974-1991 references). The 16PF Questionnaire (Cattell, 1949) has undergone four revisions, in 1956, 1962, 1967-1969 (Cattell, Eber, & Tatsuoka, 1970), and in 1988-1993 resulting in the current, Fifth Edition of the Sixteen Personality Factor Questionnaire (Cattell, Cattell, & Cattell, 1993; Conn & Rieke, 1994; Russell & Karol, 1994).

Theoretical and historical rationale

In the early 1940's, Cattell (1943, 1945) began a vigorous program of research into the structure of personality, one that was based on factor analysis of what he termed the "personality sphere"— a complete range of trait-variables that have been defined in language. Given the limits of performing factor analysis at that time, it was necessary to reduce the number of variables to a smaller number of clusters on which to base an empirical analysis of personality (for a historical review, see H.E.P. Cattell, 1996; John, Angleitner, & Ostendorf, 1988). Subsequent factor and cluster analysis led to continued refinement of the primary scales over his career, work that continues at the Institute for Personality and Ability Testing (Cattell et al., 1993; Conn &

Big Five Assessment, edited by B. De Raad & M. Perugini. © 2002, Hogrefe & Huber Publishers.

Rieke, 1994).

Development of the 16PF Questionnaire, from the beginning, has included information from peer or observer ratings, self-reports, and objective behavioral data.
Cattell's approach was multivariate in all forms — consistent personality attributes
should be observable by others, reported in questionnaire format, and manifest in an
individual's behavior. Replication across these three modes was considered to lead
to source traits defining significant components of personality. Consistent structures
across methods were an integral aspect within Cattell's development scheme.

Cattell conceptualized personality in terms of a hierarchical factor structure. He
emphasized the likelihood that real influences would, in general, be correlated and
thus he eschewed orthogonal factor solutions. Simple structure was to be the ultimate guide, based on the obvious logic that, within any system of multiple causes,
any one behavior was most likely influenced by far fewer than the total set of potential causes. That, in turn, demanded zeroes (or near-zeroes) in the factor pattern matrix. Cattell developed ingenious methods, not always totally objective, for rotating
to this simple structure.

Given that primary factors were permitted to be correlated, the hierarchical notion
of second (or higher) order factors becomes obvious. Although the emphasis was at
the primary level of personality structure, Cattell and colleagues reported second-
order global factors of personality based on these primary factors. Indeed, researches
that have led to an emphasis on the five broad factors of personality were initially
based on Cattell's 35 variable set which formed the basis for the 16PF (Norman,
1963; Tupes & Christal, 1961; see also H.E.P. Cattell, 1996). Extensive reviews of
the historical achievements in personality research, including Cattell's contributions,
may be found elsewhere (H.E.P. Cattell, 1996; John *et al.,* 1988).

Primary factor structure of the 16PF questionnaire

The 16PF Questionnaire consists of fifteen personality scales and a brief reasoning
scale. The primary structure has been satisfactorily replicated in studies based on
samples differing in language, culture, and education that ensured sufficient variability (see Mershon & Gorsuch, 1988 for a review; e.g., Cattell, 1946; 1947; 1956b;
1973; Cattell *et al.,* 1970; Cattell & Krug, 1986; Howarth & Browne, 1972). The
16PF primary scales are shown in Table 1.

Second-order factor structure of the 16PF Questionnaire

At the second-strata, at least five broad personality factors have been identified with
considerable confidence across diverse samples of subjects (e.g., Bolton, 1977;

Table 1. The 16PF primary scales

Factor name and label		Descriptors of high range	Descriptors of low range
Warmth	A	Warm, Outgoing, Attentive to Others	Reserved, Impersonal, Distant
Reasoning	B	Abstract	Concrete
Emotional Stability	C	Emotionally Stable, Adaptive, Mature	Reactive, Emotionally Changeable
Dominance	E	Dominant, Forceful, Assertive	Deferential, Cooperative, Avoids Conflict
Liveliness	F	Lively, Animated, Spontaneous	Serious, Restrained, Careful
Rule-Consciousness	G	Rule-Conscious, Dutiful	Expedient, Nonconforming
Social Boldness	H	Socially Bold, Venturesome, Thick-Skinned	Shy, Threat-Sensitive, Timid
Sensitivity	I	Sensitive, Aesthetic, Sentimental	Utilitarian, Objective, Unsentimental
Vigilance	L	Vigilant, Suspicious, Skeptical, Wary	Trusting, Unsuspecting, Accepting
Abstactedness	M	Abstracted, Imaginative, Idea-Oriented	Grounded, Practical, Solution-Oriented
Privateness	N	Private, Discreet, Non-Disclosing	Forthright, Genuine, Artless
Apprehension	O	Apprehensive, Self-Doubting, Worried	Self-Assured, Unworried, Complacent
Openness to Change	Q1	Open to Change, Experimenting	Traditional, Attached to Familiar
Self-Reliance	Q2	Self-Reliant, Solitary, Individualistic	Group-Oriented, Affiliative
Perfectionism	Q3	Perfectionistic, Organized, Self-Disciplined	Tolerates Disorder, Unexacting, Flexible
Tension	Q4	Tense, High Energy, Impatient, Driven	Relaxed, Placid, Patient

Note: Adapted from the 16PF Fifth Edition Technical Manual (Conn & Rieke, 1994; Table 1.5) with permission from the publisher.

Cattell, 1956a; 1956b; Cattell & Cattell, 1995; Cattell *et al.*, 1970; Gerbing & Tuley, 1991; Gorsuch & Cattell, 1967; Hofer, Horn, & Eber, 1997; Horn, 1963; Karson, 1961; Karson & Pool, 1958; Krug & Johns, 1986; Matthews, 1989). These second-order factors account for much of the reliable covariance among the primary factors. For example, in the 16PF Fifth Edition Questionnaire, a six-factor solution (including an intelligence factor indicated by the B primary scale) accounts for 70 per cent of the total variance of the 16PF primary scales (Conn & Rieke, 1994). The brief reasoning scale (B primary) indicates a separate and sixth factor. The results of many studies have shown that intellectual ability factors of this kind are separate from, although some are correlated with, self-report dimensions of personality. The five major second-order personality factors and the significant primary scales that indi-

cate them are shown in Table 2. However, historically, the diversity of factor analytic techniques and use of different mathematical rotations (e.g., orthogonal versus
oblique) to evaluate the factor structure across diverse samples has made the evidence for this second-order structure somewhat mixed (see Cattell, H.E.P., 1995; Cattell
& Cattell, 1995; Chernyshenko, Stark, & Chan, 2001; Hofer *et al.*, 1997; Horn,
1963). In a large-scale reanalysis of the national standardization sample of the
Fourth Edition of the 16PF Questionnaire and Clinical Analysis Questionnaire
(CAQ), Krug and Johns (1986) found that seven major personality dimensions account for most of the variance of the 16PF primary personality scales. The five major factors that closely resemble the Big-Five factors are Extraversion, Anxiety,
Tough-Mindedness, Independence, and Self-Control.

The results of Krug and Johns (1986) differed only slightly from an earlier analysis of second-order factors reported by Cattell *et al.* (1970). Additionally, the five
major second-order factors were sufficiently replicated in a study by Noller, Law,
and Comrey (1987) and reanalyzed by Boyle (1989) where the 16PF Questionnaire
was analyzed with the Eysenck Personality Questionnaire and the Comrey Personality Scale. However, several studies of the second-order structure of the Fourth and
earlier versions of the 16PF Questionnaire report divergent findings on the number
of factors. Gorsuch and Cattell (1967) and Cattell (1994) extracted eight factors.

Table 2. Global factor dimensions of the Sixteen Personality Factor Questionnaire

Factor Name	Label	Extraversion	Anxiety	Tough-Mindedness	Independence	Self-Control
Warmth	A	.74		-.35		
Reasoning	B					
Emotion. Stabil.	C		-.70			
Dominance	E				.87	
Liveliness	F	.70				-.39
Rule-Conscious	G					.78
Social Boldness	H	.44			.43	
Sensitivity	I			-.75		
Vigilance	L		57		.31	
Abstactedness	M			-.39		-.58
Privateness	N	-.67				
Apprehension	O		76			
Open. to Change	Q1				-.68	.49
Self-Reliance	Q2	-.81				
Perfectionism	Q3					.82
Tension	Q4		.86			

Note: Rotated factor loadings (decimals and loadings < .30 omitted) based on the national
standardization sample (*N*=3,498). Adapted from the 16PF Fifth Edition Technical Manual (Conn &
Rieke, 1994; Table 1.3) with permission from the publisher.

Argentero (1989) extracted eight factors with orthogonal rotation on an Italian version of the 16PF with the finding that five factors were found to be robust across men and women: Extraversion, Anxiety, Control, Tough-Mindedness, and Intelligence while the Independence factor was not identified. A similar second-order factor structure of the 16PF Questionnaire across men and women were reported by Karson and O'Dell (1974).

Hofer *et al.* (1997) reported results from an analysis of factorial invariance of the second-order structure of two forms of the 16PF Questionnaire across large samples of police applicants and convicted felons. Evidence for a five-factor second-order structure, based on the primary scales and excluding the ability factor, was obtained across diverse samples and forms. The factor structure was largely congruent with the findings of Boyle (1989; see also Noller *et al.*, 1987), Krug and Johns (1986), and Cattell *et al.* (1970). The tests of factorial invariance showed that constraints of strict factorial invariance (equivalent factor loadings, variable means, and variable uniquenesses) as well as substantive model constraints of invariant factor intercorrelations and variances provided a reasonable fit across samples within the major groups of police applicants and felons. Chernyshenko *et al.* (2001) report clear findings for sixteen primary factors and five second-order factors based on hierarchical factor analysis (i.e., Schmid-Leiman procedure) of multiple-item composites from a large sample of respondents ($N = 11,846$). These studies provide strong evidence in support of a five personality factor structure of the 16PF Questionnaire that closely approximates the Big Five factor pattern.

Several recent studies have examined the factor-level correlations among the 16PF global factors and broad factors from questionnaires used to indicate the Big Five (e.g., Barbaranelli & Caprara, 1996; Boyle, 1989; H.E.P. Cattell, 1995; 1996; Noller *et al.*, 1987). The Fifth Edition 16PF Technical Manual contains comparisons of the 16PF primary and global factors with other scales, including the NEO-PI-R, shown in Table 3. The global factors for the two tests are highly congruent, with many of the NEO PI-R facet scales having their highest association with the corresponding 16PF Global scale. H.E.P. Cattell (1996) reported comparisons across the 16PF Fifth Edition and the NEO-PI-R and found a high degree of concordance across the five broad factors but also important differences in the conceptualization of these factors. We would expect no less; strict concordance despite different methods is not yet always a realistic expectation in our science.

Extraversion and Anxiety (Neuroticism or, conversely, Adjustment) have been well-identified across different questionnaires. It almost could not be otherwise. These two broad factors are so pervasive that any personality data in which they do not appear should be suspect as to data errors. Self-Control (Conscientiousness) shows a high degree of concordance across questionnaires. The Independence (Agreeableness) and Tough-Mindedness (Openness to Experience) factors exhibit the least correspondence across questionnaires (e.g., H.E.P. Cattell, 1993; 1996). While there are clearly nuances in how each of these factors are defined across different broad-factor systems, it is clear that each represents a high degree of similarity conceptually.

Table 3. Correlations between global factor dimensions of the Sixteen Personality Factor Questionnaire and the NEO PI-R Scales.

	16PF Global Factor Dimension				
	Extraversion	Anxiety	Tough-Mindedness	Independence	Self-control
NEO PI-R Factor Scales					
Extraversion	.65	-.21		.36	-.29
Neuroticism	-.31	.75		-.27	
Openness			.56		-.25
Agreeableness			.28	-.42	
Conscientiousness	-.21		.29		.66
NEO-PI-R Facet Scales					
E1: Warmth	.61	-.24		.20	
E2: Gregariousness	.70	-.23		.32	-.23
E3: Assertiveness	.45	-.26		.60	
E4: Activity	.21			.40	
E5: Excitement Seeking	.39			.25	-.25
E6: Positive Emotion	.47	-.29		.22	-.22
N1: Anxiety	-.21	.63		-.23	
N2: Angry Hostility		.59			
N3: Depression	-.28	.66		-.22	
N4: Self-Consciousness	-.31	.55		-.44	
N5: Impulsiveness		.30			-.32
N6: Vulnerability	-.22	.51		-.28	
O1: Fantasy	.26		-.41		-.35
O2: Aesthetics	.24		-.53		
O3: Feelings	.24		-.37		
O4: Actions		-.21	-.31		-.32
O5: Ideas				.24	
O6: Values			-.33	.20	-.24
A1: Trust	.38	-.47			
A2: Straightforwardness				-.31	.20
A3: Altruism	.32		-.22		
A4: Compliance		-.23		-.44	
A5: Modesty				-.34	
A6: Tender-Mindedness	.24		-.26		
C1: Competence				.22	.39
C2: Order			.28		.57
C3: Dutifulness					.42
C4: Achiev. Striving			.23		.44
C5: Self-Discipline			.21		.44
C6: Deliberation	-.22		.23		.57

Note: Correlations below .20 and decimals omitted. (N=257). Adapted from the 16PF Fifth Edition Technical Manual (Conn & Rieke, 1994; Table 6.1 and Appendix 6D) with permission from the publisher.

Description of the Sixteen Personality Factor Questionnaire

The Fifth Edition of the Sixteen Personality Factor Questionnaire (Cattell *et al.*, 1993; Conn & Rieke, 1994; Russell & Karol, 1994) is comprised of 185 items and provides scores on 16 primary factor scales, five second-order factors, and an impression management scale. One of the primary scales is a brief reasoning scale (16PF Scale B) involving verbal analogies (both common and esoteric). Each primary factor scale contains 10-15 items, with each item scored on a three-choice response format. The b response choice for all personality items (except for the Reasoning [B] scale) appears as a question mark.

The 16PF Questionnaire is designed to be administered to individuals aged 16 years of age and older and has been evaluated on diverse samples of individuals, nationally and internationally, in clinical, occupational, and other settings. Alternate forms of the 16PF have been developed for particular populations or situations. These include part of the *Clinical Analysis Questionnaire* (Krug, 1980), a *Form E* (Eber & Cattell, 1976) useable with adults down to 3rd grade reading level, and even some tape recorded presentations to permit testing of virtual illiterates. Forms for younger ages, not always covering all the factors because they sometimes were not clearly identifiable, included the *Jr.-Sr. High School Personality Questionnaire* (Cattell, Beloff, & Coan, 1958; Cattell, Cattell, & Johns, 1990), *the Child Personality Questionnaire* (Porter & Cattell, 1963), and even an *Early School Personality Questionnaire* and a *Pre-School Personality Questionnaire* (Cattell & Coan, 1973). A new *Adolescent Personality Questionnaire* (Schuerger, 2001) is in press.

The 16PF Questionnaire can be self-administered individually or in group format using either computer-based or paper-and-pencil formats (permitting either hand or computer scoring). Test-completion time ranges from 35-50 and 25-35 minutes for the paper-and-pencil and computer administration, respectively. The questionnaire is designed for administration to individuals with at least a fifth-grade reading proficiency level.

Normative data for the 16PF Fifth Edition is based on a population stratified sample of 2,500 individuals that closely corresponds to gender, race, age, and education percentages of the 1990 U.S. census. These data were provided from experienced 16PF administrators in a variety of settings and who were provided testing materials free in exchange for the normative data. Sten ("standardized ten") scores — having a mean of 5.5, standard deviation of 2.0 and ranging from 1-10 — were computed for each scale to provide a basis for comparison across primary scales with norms based on both combined-sex and sex-specific samples.

Reliability

Internal consistency coefficients for the 16PF Fifth Edition primary scales averaged .75 (.66 - .86) across two general population samples and one university student sample (Conn & Rieke, 1994). It was not possible to compute internal consistency coefficients for the Global Scales since they were derived from weighted composites of the primary scales. In two independent university samples, the median test-retest reliability coefficients for the second-order scales were .87 (.84 - .91) and .80 (.70 - .82), for two-week and two-month retest intervals, respectively (Conn & Rieke, 1994).

Validity

Construct Validity

Various versions of the 16PF have been compared to questionnaires designed to measure the Big Five factor structure. These studies provide evidence for a high degree of correspondence between the 16PF and other questionnaires designed to measure personality at the broad factor level (H.E.P. Cattell, 1996; Conn & Rieke, 1994; Gerbing & Tuley, 1991). For example, comparison of the 16PF Fifth Edition with NEO-PI-R (H.E.P. Cattell, 1996) resulted in moderate to high correlations between corresponding broad factors. Further inspection of the primary scale loadings on these factors across the two questionnaires, however, finds different emphases at the broad factor level and should be an important issue for further development of both primary and secondary factors within personality taxonomies (H.E.P. Cattell, 1996).

Criterion Validity

A substantial body of validity data has been obtained for concepts at the level of the 16 factors of the Cattellian system (e.g., Cattell *et al.*, 1970; Cattell & Krug, 1986). Mershon and Gorsuch (1988) investigated the criterion validity of the 16PF in terms of whether the 16 primary factors or the fewer second-order factors account equally for the variance in a criterion variable measuring "aggregated behavior" (job tenure or supervisors ratings) with shrunken r's computed to reduce bias associated different numbers of predictors. The 16 primary scales accounted for twice the amount of variance in the criterion variables than did the second-order factors. These findings further support the idea that fine-grained personality distinctions may have greater utility for many purposes than broad factors (e.g., Goldberg, 1972). In a recent study, Goldberg (in press) compared several personality inventories and their International Personality Item Pool equivalents (IPIP; see Goldberg, 1999) in a predictive validity study of six clusters of behavioral acts varying in social desirability. Although all questionnaires showed a high degree of predictive validity, the 16PF Questionnaire, particularly the IPIP version of the 16PF, was found to have the highest validity coefficients.

Cross-Cultural Generalizability

The 16PF Questionnaire has been translated into over 40 languages and validated in numerous countries worldwide. The primary structure of the 16PF Questionnaire has been evaluated across cultures and has resulted in confirmation of all or most of the 16 factors (e.g., Adcock & Adcock, 1977; Cattell & Nesselroade, 1965; Cattell, Pichot, & Rennes, 1961; Krug, 1971; Meschieri & Cattell, 1960; Motegi, 1982; Schneewind, 1977; Tsujioka & Cattell, 1965). Generalization across boundaries of language, of custom, of ethnicity and of geography involve whole new classes of problems which fall outside the present scope. In general, difficulties and inconsistencies multiply with increased specificity. Broad concepts typically transport well, both in research and in application. Narrower focus translates less well.

Summary

Analyses based initially on items comprising the 16PF Questionnaire (or adjective scales which Cattell developed and on which the 16PF Questionnaire was based) as well as on subsequently developed items have led to a five factor theory of personality known popularly as the *big five* (see Block, 1995, for a review; also Fiske, 1949; Goldberg, 1990; McCrae & Costa, 1985). The view that five factors — extracted at the primary factor level — accounts for a significant proportion of individual differences in self-report data of questionnaires is supported by numerous studies and reviews (e.g., De Raad, 1998; Digman, 1990; Goldberg, 1981; Norman, 1963; Saucier & Goldberg, 1996; Tupes & Christal, 1961).

It is the case that the global factors extracted at the second-order level of the 16PF Questionnaire are highly similar to factors known as the Big Five. Science has been advanced by the fact that there is much agreement at the broad factor level among the NEO-PI-R (Costa & McCrae, 1992), the Goldberg Big Five (Goldberg, 1990; 1992), and other personality instruments. Disagreements in the definition of these broad factor concepts may be a matter of emphasis or may define the next generation of problems for personality psychologists. Is there a reason that we should not have six factors, or seven, or more that describe major features of personality? Cattell regarded the primary factors of personality to be representative of real causes — solutions that mixed primary and secondary levels of such factors were regarded as incorrect. However, from other viewpoints, mixing levels of analysis may not be so negative. Nonetheless, the critical issue is that the developing stabilities of personality assessment in terms of broad factor structures are well-represented by the 16PF as well as by other questionnaires.

References

Adcock, N.V., & Adcock, C.J. (1977). The validity of the 16 PF personality structure: A large New Zealand sample item analysis. *Journal of Behavioral Science, 2*, 227-237.

Argentero, P. (1989). Second-order factor structure of Cattell's 16 Personality Factor Questionnaire. *Perceptual and Motor Skills, 68*, 1043-1047.

Barbaranelli, C., & Caprara, G.V. (1996). How many dimensions to describe personality? A comparison of Cattell, Comrey, and the Big Five taxonomies of personality traits. *European Review of Applied Psychology, 46*, 15-24.

Block, J. (1995). A contrarian view of the five-factor approach to personality description. *Psychological Bulletin, 117*, 187-215.

Bolton, B. (1977). Evidence for the 16PF primary and secondary factors. *Multivariate Experimental Clinical Research, 3*, 1-15.

Boyle, G.J. (1989). Re-examination of the major personality type factors in the Cattell, Comrey and Eysenck scales: Were the factor solutions by Noller *et al.* optimal? *Personality and Individual Differences, 10*, 1289-1299.

Cattell, H.E.P. (1995). Some comments on a factor analysis of the 16PF and the NEO Personality Inventory-Revised. *Psychological Reports, 77*, 1307-1311.

Cattell, H.E.P. (1996). The original big five: A historical perspective. *European Review of Applied Psychology, 46*, 5-14.

Cattell, H.E.P. (2001). The Sixteen Personality Factor Questionnaire. In W.I. Dorfman & M. Hersen (Eds.), *Understanding Psychological Assessment*. New York: Plenum Publishers.

Cattell, H.E.P., Mead, A.D., & Cattell, R.B. (In press). The 16PF. In S.R. Briggs, J.M. Cheek, & E.M. Donahue (Eds.), *Handbook of Adult Personality Inventories*. New York: Plenum Publishers.

Cattell, R.B. (1943). The description of personality: I. The foundations of trait measurement. *Psychological Review, 50*, 559-594.

Cattell, R.B. (1945). The description of personality: Principles and findings in a factor analysis. *American Journal of Psychology, 58*, 69-90.

Cattell, R.B. (1946). *The description and measurement of personality*. New York: World Book.

Cattell, R.B. (1947). Confirmation and clarification of primary personality factors. *Psychometrika, 12*, 197-220.

Cattell, R.B. (1949). *Sixteen Personality Factor Questionnaire*. Champaign, IL: Institute for Personality and Ability Testing, Inc.

Cattell, R.B. (1956a). Second-order personality factors in the questionnaire realm. *Journal of Consulting Psychology, 20*, 411-413.

Cattell, R.B. (1956b). Validation and intensification of the sixteen personality factor questionnaire. *Journal of Clinical Psychology, 12*, 205-214.

Cattell, R.B. (1973). *Personality and mood by questionnaire*. San Francisco: Jossey-Bass.

Cattell, R.B. (1994). Constancy of global, second-order personality factors over a twenty-year-plus period. *Psychological Reports, 75*, 3-9.

Cattell, R.B., Beloff, H. & Coan, R.W. (1958) *Handbook for the IPAT High School Personality Questionnaire*. Champaign, IL: Institute for Personality and Ability Testing, Inc.

Cattell, R.B., Cattell, A.K., & Cattell, H.E. (1993). *Sixteen Personality Factor Questionnaire*, Fifth Edition. Champaign, IL: Institute for Personality and Ability Testing, Inc.

Cattell, R.B., & Cattell, H.E.P. (1995). Personality structure and the New Fifth Edition of the 16PF. *Educational and Psychological Measurement, 55*, 926-937.

Cattell, R.B., Cattell, M.D., & Johns, E. (1990). *High School Personality Questionnaire*. Champaign, IL: Institute for Personality and Ability Testing, Inc.

Cattell, R.B., & Coan, R.W. (1973). *Early School Personality Questionnaire (ESPQ)*. Champaign, IL: Institute for Personality and Ability Testing, Inc.

Cattell, R.B., & Delhees, K.H. (1980). *Clinical Analysis Questionnaire*. Champaign, IL: Institute for Personality and Ability Testing, Inc.

Cattell, R.B., Eber, H.W., & Tatsuoka, M.M. (1970). *Handbook for the Sixteen Personality Factor Questionnaire (16 PF)*. Champaign, IL: Institute for Personality and Ability Testing, Inc.

Cattell, R.B., & Krug, S.E. (1986). The number of factors in the 16PF: A review of the evidence with special emphasis on the methodological problems. *Educational and Psychological Measurement, 46*, 509-522.

Cattell, R.B., & Nesselroade, J.R. (1965). Untersuchung der interkulturellen konstanz der Personlichkeitsfaktoren in the 16PF test. *Psychologische Beiträge, 8*, 502-515.

Cattell, R.B., Pichot, P., & Rennes, P. (1961). Constance interculturelle des facteurs de personalite measures par le test 16 PF: Comparison franco-americaine. *Revue de Psychologie Appliqueé, 11*, 165-196.

Chernyshenko, O.S., Stark, S., & Chan, K.Y. (2001). Investigating the hierarchical factor structure of the Fifth Edition of the 16PF: An application of the Schmid-Leiman orthogonalization procedure. *Educational and Psychological Measurement, 61*, 290-302.

Conn, S.R., & Rieke, M.L. (1994). *The 16PF Fifth Edition Technical Manual*. Champaign, IL: Institute for Personality and Ability Testing, Inc.

Costa, P.T., Jr., & McCrae, R.R. (1976). Age differences in personality structure: A cluster analytic approach. *Journal of Gerontology, 31*, 564-570.

Costa, P.T., & McCrae, R.R. (1992). *Revised NEO Personality Inventory (NEO-PI-R) and NEO Five-Factor Inventory (NEO-FFI) Professional Manual*. Odessa, FL: Psychological Assessment Resources.

De Raad, B. (1998). Five big, big five issues: Rationale, content, structure, status and crosscultural assessment. *European Psychologist, 3*, 113-124.

Digman, J.M. (1990). Personality structure: Emergence of the five-factor model. In M.R. Rosenzweig & L.W. Porter (Eds.), *Annual Review of Psychology* (Vol. 41, pp. 417-440). Palo Alto, CA: Annual Reviews.

Eber, H.W. & Cattell, R.B. (1976). *Manual for Form E of the 16PF*. Champaign, IL: Institute for Personality and Ability Testing, Inc.

Fiske, D.W. (1949). Consistency of factorial structures of personality ratings from different sources. *Journal of Abnormal and Social Psychology, 44*, 329-344.

Gerbing, D.W., & Tuley, M.R. (1991). The 16PF related to the five-factor model of personality: Multiple-indicator measurement versus the a priori scales. *Multivariate Behavioral Research, 26*, 271-289.

Goldberg, L.R. (1972). Parameters of personality inventory construction and utilization: A comparison of predictive strategies and tactics. *Multivariate Behavioral Research Monographs, 72-2*, 1-59.

Goldberg, L.R. (1981). Language and individual differences: The search for universals in personality lexicons. In L. Wheeler (Ed.), *Review of personality and social psychology*: Vol. 2 (pp. 141-165). Beverly Hills, CA: Sage.

Goldberg, L.R. (1990). An alternative "description of personality": The big-five factor structure. *Journal of Personality and Social Psychology, 59*, 1216-1229.

Goldberg, L.R. (1992). The development of markers of the big five factor structure. *Psychological Assessment, 4*, 26-42.

Goldberg, L.R. (1999). A broad-bandwith, public-domain, personality inventory measuring the lower-level facets of several five-factor models. In I. Mervielde, I. Deary, F. De Fruyt, & F. Ostendorf (Eds.), *Personality Psychology in Europe: Vol. 7* (pp. 7-28). Tilburg, The Netherlands: Tilburg University Press.

Goldberg, L.R. (in press). The comparative validity of adult personality inventories: Applications of a consumer-testing framework. In S.R. Briggs, J.M. Cheek, & E.M. Donahue (Eds.), *Handbook of Adult Personality Inventories*. New York: Plenum.

Gorsuch, R.L., & Cattell, R.B. (1967). Second stratum personality factors defined in the questionnaire realm by the 16 P.F. *Multivariate Behavioral Research, 2*, 211-223.

Hofer, S.M., Horn, J.L., Eber, H.W. (1997). A robust five-factor structure of the 16PF: Evidence from independent rotation and confirmatory factorial invariance procedures. *Personality and Individual Differences, 23*, 247-269.

Horn, J.L. (1963). Second-order factors in questionnaire data. *Educational and Psychological Measurement, 23*, 117-134.

Howarth, E., & Browne, J.A. (1971). An item factor analysis of the 16 PF. *Personality, 2*, 117-139.

Institute for Personality and Ability Testing. (1991). *Administrator's Manual for the Sixteen Personality Factor Questionnaire*. Champaign, IL: IPAT.

John, O.P., Angleitner, A., & Ostendorf, F. (1988). The lexical approach to personality: A historical review of trait taxonomic research. *European Journal of Personality, 2*, 171-203.

Karson, S. (1961). Second-order factors in positive mental health. *Journal of Clinical Psychology, 17*, 14-19.

Karson, S.E., & O'Dell, J.W. (1976). *Clinical use of the 16PF*. Champaign, IL: Institute for Personality and Ability Testing, Inc.

Karson, S., & Pool, K.B. (1958). Second-order factors in personality measurement. *Journal of Consulting Psychology, 22*, 299-303.

Krug, S.E. (1971). *The 16PF in Latin America*. Champaign, IL: Institute for Personality and Ability Testing, Inc.

Krug, S.E., & Cattell, R.B. (1980). *Clinical Analysis Questionnaire manual*. Champaign, IL: Institute for Personality and Ability Testing, Inc.

Krug, S.E., & Johns, E.F. (1986). A large scale cross-validation of second-order personality structure defined by the 16PF. *Psychological Reports, 59*, 683-693.

Krug, S.E., & Laughlin, J.E. (1978). Second-order factors among normal and pathological primary personality traits. *Journal of Consulting and Clinical Psychology, 45*, 575-582.

Matthews, G. (1989). The factor structure of the 16PF twelve primary and three secondary factors. *Personality and Individual Differences, 10*, 931-940.

McCrae, R.R., & Costa, P.T., Jr. (1985). Updating Norman's "adequate taxonomy": Intelligence and personality dimensions in natural language and in questionnaires. *Journal of Personality and Social Psychology, 49*, 710-721.

Mershon, B., & Gorsuch, R.L. (1988). Number of factors in the personality sphere: Does increase in factors increase predictability of real-life criteria? *Journal of Personality and Social Psychology, 55*, 675-680.

Meschieri, L., & Cattell, R.B. (1960). *The international cross cultural constancy of personality factors examined in the 16 PF: Italian American relations.* Unpublished report. Champaign, IL: Laboratory of Personality and Group Analysis. University of Illinois.

Motegi, M. (1982). *Japanese translation and adaptation of the 16PF.* Tokyo: Nihon Bunka Kagakusha.

Noller, P., Law, H., & Comrey, A.L. (1987). Cattell, Comrey, and Eysenck personality factors compared: More evidence for the five robust factors? *Journal of Personality and Social Psychology, 53,* 775-782.

Norman, W.T. (1963). Toward an adequate taxonomy of personality attributes: Replicated factor structure in peer nomination personality ratings. *Journal of Abnormal and Social Psychology, 66,* 574-583.

Porter, R.B., & Cattell, R.B. (1963) *Child Personality Questionnaire.* Champaign, IL: Institute for Personality and Ability Testing, Inc.

Russell, M.T., & Karol, D.L. (1994). *The 16PF Fifth Edition Administrator's Manual.* Champaign, IL: Institute for Personality and Ability Testing, Inc.

Saucier, G., & Goldberg, L.R. (1996). The language of personality: Lexical perspectives on the five-factor model. In J. S. Wiggins (Ed.), *The five-factor model of personality: Theoretical perspectives* (pp. 21-50). New York: Guilford.

Schneewind, K.A. (1977). Development of a German version of the 16 Personality Factor Questionnaire. *Diagnostica, 23,* 188-191.

Tsujioka, B., & Cattell, R.B. (1965). Constancy and difference in personality structure and mean profile, in the questionnaire medium, from applying the 16PF test in America and Japan. *British Journal of Social and Clinical Psychology, 4,* 287-297.

Tupes, E.C., & Christal, R.E. (1961). *Recurrent personality factors based on trait ratings* (Tech. Rep. Nos. 61-67). Lackland, TX: U. S. Air Force Aeronautical Systems Division.

Chapter 18

A "Big Five" scoring system for the Adjective Check List

Deborah FormyDuval Hill
John E. Williams
Jonathan F. Bassett

Introduction

In this chapter, we describe the development of a Five Factor scoring system for the 300-item Adjective Check List. Designed primarily for use in research studies rather than for individual personality assessment, the system permits the scoring of any selected set of adjective descriptors in terms of the Big Five. We employed ratings made by American university students to determine the degree to which each of the 300 person-descriptive adjectives of Gough and Heilbrun's (1980) Adjective Check List was associated with each of the five factors described by the Five Factor Model: Extraversion, Agreeableness, Conscientiousness, Emotional Stability, and Openness to Experience. These ratings were found to be highly reliable (.97 to .98) and to have a high degree of convergent validity with the results of earlier ACL studies by John (1989) and McCrae and Costa (1992).

The scoring system provides a mean score for each of the five factors for any given sub-set of the 300 adjectives, i.e., those chosen as descriptive of a given target. Illustrative applications include the cross-cultural examination of gender stereotypes in 27 countries (Williams, Satterwhite, & Best, 1999; Williams, Satterwhite, Best, & Inman, 2001) and a 20-country study of cross-cultural similarities and differences in the relative importance of various psychological traits (Williams, Satterwhite, & Saiz, 1998). There are many potential research applications involving the use of the system to obtain Big Five profiles for individuals or groups, real or hypothetical, or any other "target" that can be meaningfully personified and administration typically takes 15 minutes or less. Information is provided concerning computer scoring systems and the availability of translations of the ACL item pool to languages other than English.

Big Five Assessment, edited by B. De Raad & M. Perugini. © 2002, Hogrefe & Huber Publishers.

Development of the ACL item pool

The Adjective Check list (ACL) is a set of 300 person-descriptive adjectives developed by Harrison Gough and his associates at the University of California, Berkeley (Gough & Heilbrun, 1980). The ACL is used to record the psychological characteristics associated with individual persons or groups and has been employed in a wide variety of assessment and research contexts. This chapter reports on the development of a system for scoring ACL item sets in terms of the Five Factor Model (FFM) of personality. The primary purpose of this system was to enable the study of the characteristics associated with groups in terms of the FFM (e.g., gender stereotypes) rather than for individual personality assessment, for which excellent instruments already existed. Before proceeding to a description of the new five-factor system — designated ACL-FF — we will review the history of the ACL and briefly describe three other theory-based scoring systems that have been used with ACL item sets.

The origin and development of the Adjective Check List item pool has been described in detail by Gough and Heilbrun (1980). It was initially proposed as a method of obtaining observers' descriptions of other individuals (i.e., staff members' observations of individuals studied in assessment programs). However, it was quickly observed that the item set could be used in self-descriptions and has been so employed quite extensively. The ACL item pool has also been used to characterize one's ideal self, a fictitious individual or persona, geographical regions, and other "targets" that can be quite easily personified. Inasmuch as language, particularly adjectives, is used to describe and specify, the Adjective Check List is then rooted in language itself and must therefore be universally applicable for descriptive purposes.

The first attempts at categorizing such descriptive terms was undertaken by Allport and Odbert in their 1938 monograph in which they enumerated 17, 953 English words. This list was condensed by R. B. Cattell (1943, 1946) who developed a trait list of 171 variables, obtained ratings of the items from subject samples, and factor analyzed the results, reducing the surface clusters to twelve "primary source traits of personality." Initial attempts to develop the Adjective Check List, made in 1949, drew 125 adjectives from Cattell's 171 variables and other items were added following review of the theoretical viewpoints of Freud, Jung, Mead, and Murray. For instance, *stingy* was added to reflect Freud's concept of the anal character, *rational* was added to reflect the Jungian rational functions (thinking and feeling), *adaptable* reflects Mead's concept of skill in role-taking, and *understanding* was taken from Murray's concept of needs. Following review of the instrument in 1950, by the Institute of Personality Assessment and Research in Berkeley, it was determined that some important terms had not been included and thus several changes were made to alleviate lack of items descriptive of physical characteristics (i.e., *attractive, good-looking,* and *handsome*) and words representing reactions of males to females (i.e., *charming, fickle, flirtatious*, and *sexy*) among other things. The ACL existed in its current 300-item form by the end of 1952.

The 300 ACL items provide for a relatively comprehensive description of the target being considered. The large size of the item pool permits the inclusion of many nearly synonymous adjectives with subtle differences in meanings: e.g., *steady, stable, unemotional, unexcitable*. Despite the large number of items, persons using the ACL usually take no more than 20 minutes to complete the description of a given target. The 300 English language ACL items are presented in the Appendix at the end of this chapter.

Translations of the ACL items

The 300 English language items have been translated into more than 20 of the world's major languages. Williams and Best and their associates employed translations from English to 16 other languages, namely: Bahasa-Malaysia, Chinese, Dutch, Finnish, French, German, Hebrew, Italian, Japanese, Korean, Norwegian, Polish, Portuguese, Spanish, Turkish, and Urdu. Their studies have resulted in the 300 items being scaled for (1) relative association with women and men (gender stereotypes) in 27 countries (Williams & Best, 1990a), (2) relative association with young adults and old adults (age stereotypes) in 19 countries (Williams, 1993), (3) psychological importance (i.e., central vs. peripheral traits) in 20 countries (Williams *et al.*, 1998), and (4) favorability (positive vs. negative characteristics) in 10 countries (Williams *et al.*, 1998).

The use of translated materials in psychological research is always somewhat problematic. Richard Brislin (1980), an authority on this topic, notes that the translation of individual words is more difficult than the translation of sentences or paragraphs that suggests that our translators faced a most challenging task. On the other hand, Brislin notes the value of redundancy in translated materials and this was a positive feature in making our translations. While each of the 300 English adjectives has at least a slightly different meaning, there are many near synonyms in the item pool. For example, it seems clear that the adjectives *stable, steady, unemotional*, and *unexcitable* share a substantial common meaning factor. If, for some reason, one item is not well translated, one can hope that the others will be and in this way the common meaning factor will be represented in the translated item pool. Thus, while one must be very cautious in making cross-translation comparisons of responses to individual items, one seems on safer ground in making such comparisons between broad factor scores that are based on responses to many items.

We have no formal basis for judging the adequacy of the translation of the item pool from English to the other languages. We know that the translations were done with care by our cooperating researchers who employed recommended methods such as back translation and committee approaches.

We do have one set of findings that bears indirectly on the question of the fidelity of the ACL translations. Denotative meaning aside, a critical aspect of translation fidelity concerns affective meaning, particularly the evaluative connotations of words that Osgood, May, and Miron (1975) found to be the principal affective meaning component in each of the diverse sample of world languages they studied.

Our study (Williams *et al.*, 1998) employed samples of university students who rated the favorability of each ACL item, or its translated equivalent, on a five-point scale. The students were from the United States, Nigeria, Singapore, Chile, China, Korea, Norway, Pakistan, Portugal, and Turkey. Subjects in the first three countries rated the favorability of the items in the standard English language form, while subjects in the other seven countries rated the items as translated into their respective national languages. After computing mean favorability ratings for each of the items in each sample, a correlation coefficient was computed between the mean ratings in each pair of countries, across the 300 items. The results were then grouped by language of administration with the following results: among the three English language samples, the median is .82; among the seven other languages, the median is .82.

These findings indicated a high degree of agreement in the favorability ratings across the eight languages employed, despite the likelihood of at least some bonafide cultural differences in the favorability associated with particular psychological traits. The results support the idea of reasonable translation fidelity with regard to the important affective meaning dimension of favorability.

In sum, we feel that our language translations, everything considered, are reasonably adequate for the uses to which they have been, and may be, employed.

Earlier scoring systems

The use of the ACL often results in the selection of 80 - 100 items as descriptive of a given target person or group. While analyses may be conducted at the level of individual items (e.g., Williams & Best, 1990a, chapter 3; Williams *et al.*, 1998, chapter 5), it is often more useful to employ scoring systems that abstract or summarize the factors underlying the responses to the individual items. Prior to the development of the Five Factor system described below, there were three major theoretically based scoring systems available dealing, respectively, with psychological needs, affective meanings, and ego states.

Psychological needs

The original ACL scoring system (Gough & Heilbrun, 1980) yields scores indicating relative loading on 15 psychological needs (e.g., Dominance, Deference, Nurturance, Achievement, etc.) for selected ACL item sets. This system was developed by providing psychology graduate students with definitions taken from Edwards (1959) and having them select adjectives considered indicative or counter-indicative of each of the 15 needs. Consensus among the raters was used to code each of the 300 adjectives for each of the psychological needs.

Affective meanings

Based on the three-factor theory of affective meaning developed by Charles Osgood and his associates (Osgood *et al.*, 1957, 1975), this system enables one to obtain scores reflecting the relative Favorability, Strength, and Activity for selected ACL item sets (Best, Williams, & Briggs, 1980; Williams & Best, 1977). In developing the system, American university students rated each of the 300 ACL adjectives for it's favorability, strength, or activity with a separate group of judges employed for each factor. The mean values obtained in this manner provide a score on each of the three factors for each of the 300 items.

Transactional Analysis Ego States

Based on the Transactional Analysis Ego States theoretical system of Eric Berne (1961, 1966), this system provides scores for each ACL adjective that reflect its "loading" on each of the five functional ego states of Transactional Analysis (TA) theory: Critical Parent, Nurturing Parent, Adult, Free Child, and Adapted Child (Williams & Williams, 1980). The ego state scores were based on the mean ratings of the 300 items by 15 expert judges who were highly trained in TA theory. The system enables one to compute mean scores reflecting the relative loading on the five ego states for any given set of ACL items.

The theory-based scoring systems just described have been found useful in a variety of studies in the personality-social area including: gender stereotypes (Williams & Best, 1990a), age stereotypes (Williams, 1993), self and ideal self (Williams & Best, 1990b), and the importance of psychological traits (Williams *et al.*, 1998). The Five Factor scoring system for the ACL was constructed to enable such research findings to be expressed in terms of this important, more recently developed, conceptual system.

Development of the ACL-FF system

Here we provide a general description of the development of the ACL-FF scoring system. Additional details may be found in FormyDuval (1993) and in FormyDuval, Williams, Patterson, and Fogle (1995). In these earlier reports, the general adjustment factor was labeled "Neuroticism" with high scores indicative of poor adjustment. In more recent writings, including the present chapter, we have reversed this factor and called it "Emotional Stability" with high scores indicative of good adjustment.

The subjects for this scaling study were 244 male and 251 female introductory psychology students at Wake Forest University, primarily freshmen and sophomores, who participated in order to meet a course requirement. Separate groups of students rated each of the five factors: 47 men and 49 women rated the Extraversion factor, 51 men and 50 women rated the Agreeableness factor, 48 men and 48 women rated the Conscientiousness factor, 48 men and 52 women rated the Emotional Stability factor, and 50 men and 51 women rated the Openness to Experience factor.

Inasmuch as the five factors appear to be meaningful folk psychology concepts and not simply esoteric abstractions of personality psychologists (see McCrae, Costa, & Piedmont, 1993), one would reasonably assume that laypersons should be able to understand and make judgments about the five factors. Thus, it was considered reasonable to employ undergraduate students for the present study.

Subjects were provided a booklet containing both an extensive set of instructions and all 300 ACL items. They were initially given a brief description of all five factors (referred to as "characteristics") and told "personality psychologists believe that a description of an individual containing information regarding all five [factors or 'characteristics'] is a reasonably complete one." Subjects were then given a more complete set of instructions regarding the particular characteristic they were asked to rate. Costa and McCrae (1992) describe the factors in terms of their *facets* and these *facet* descriptions were used in the present study to illustrate the factors to the subjects. Illustrative examples were provided with three ACL items obtained from John's (1989) list that "may be representative [indicative] of this characteristic" and three items that "may suggest the opposite [counterindicative] of this characteristic." Finally, the subjects were instructed to rate all 300 ACL items in terms of the extent to which they seemed indicative or counterindicative of their single assigned factor on a 5-point scale from -2 (highly counterindicative) to 2 (highly indicative) with a rating of 0 to indicate in-between or not related. Specific instructions were given as follows:

Characteristic I (Extraversion): "You will be asked to consider individual adjectives and to give your impression of the extent that each adjective is representative of Characteristic I or the opposite of Characteristic I. Characteristic I consists of several different facets. These include gregariousness, assertiveness, activity, excitement-seeking, positive emotions, and warmth.... You are asked to think about each adjective in terms of the degree to which it is representative of one or more of the facets of Characteristic I....For each adjective, circle the number which you feel best reflects the degree of Characteristic I...." Illustrative items were outgoing, active, and warm; and reserved, retiring, and withdrawn.

Characteristic II (Agreeableness): "Characteristic II consists of several different facets. These include trust, straightforwardness, altruism, compliance, modesty, and tender-mindedness. An adjective which suggests one or more of these facets is considered indicative of the characteristic...however, an adjective which suggests the opposite of one or more of these facets is considered counterindicative of the characteristic...." Illustrative items were trusting, modest, and sympathetic; and fault-finding, quarrelsome, and stingy.

Characteristic III (Conscientiousness): "Characteristic III consists of several different facets. These include competence, order, dutifulness, achievement-striving, self-discipline, and deliberation...." Illustrative items were reliable, conscientious, and deliberate; and careless, disorderly, and frivolous.

Characteristic IV (Emotional Stability): "Characteristic IV consists of several different facets. These include anxiety, angry hostility, depression, self-consciousness, impulsiveness, and vulnerability...." Illustrative items were contented, unemotional, and stable; and anxious, touchy, and impulsive.

Characteristic V (Openness to Experience): "Characteristic V reflects openness to new or unfamiliar experiences. This openness may be reflected in an appreciation of knowledge, various art forms, and nontraditional values as opposed to an appreciation of tradition and the status quo. This characteristic may be revealed in several different facets of an individual's behavior, including values, ideas, actions, feelings, fantasy, and appreciation of aesthetics...." Illustrative items were imaginative, artistic, and original; and shallow, narrow-interests, and commonplace.

To control for possible order/fatigue effects, the order of the items was counterbalanced by dividing the ACL into thirds such that set A consisted of items 1-100, set B consisted of items 101-200, and set C consisted of items 201-300. Booklets were then distributed with the ACL items presented in the following orders: ABC, ACB, BAC, BCA, CAB, CBA. Each of the six orderings was distributed equally among the subjects.

The study was carried out over two semesters with approximately one-half of the ratings obtained during the fall semester and one-half completed during the spring semester. Ratings for all five factors were obtained in both semesters to prevent the confounding of factor ratings with semester. The same female examiner presented the procedure to groups of approximately 30 individuals with most subjects finishing in 20 to 30 minutes.

The original rating scale presented to subjects ranged from -2 to +2. This scale was converted to a 1 to 5 scale where 1 is highly counterindicative, 3 reflects an intermediate (or unrelated) position, and 5 is highly indicative or highly characteristic of the factor. Following this transformation, means were computed separately by gender across all 300 items for each factor with the results shown in Table 1. Note that all means are close to the mid-point of the scale (3.00) suggesting relatively equal numbers of items considered indicative and counterindicative of each factor. Standard deviations were sizable, indicating diversity among the adjectives in the extent to which they were thought indicative or counterindicative of the five factors.

Table 1. Factor means, standard deviations, and correlations between gender groups for 300 ACL items

Factor	Male subjects	SD	Female subjects	SD	r
Extraversion	3.07	0.86	3.02	0.99	.98*
Agreeableness	2.96	0.89	2.95	0.99	.98*
Conscientiousness	3.15	0.84	3.16	0.82	.98*
Stability	2.92	0.68	3.00	0.80	.97*
Openness to Experience	3.05	0.72	3.05	0.80	.97*

*p<.001.

Data were initially analyzed by gender to determine the degree of agreement in the ratings by women and men subjects. Pearson product-moment correlation coefficients were computed between men's and women's ratings across the 300 ACL items for each factor. As can be seen in Table 1, the results revealed high degree of agreement between men and women raters. Such high correlations suggest high reliability in the ratings, given that any true gender effects would serve to reduce the correlations. Thus, these correlation coefficients can be viewed as an indication of the lower limit of the reliability of the ratings. Given such high agreement between men and women, it was deemed appropriate to pool the male and female ratings in further analyses. Factor scores for each item were calculated by summing all of the subjects' ratings of that item (approximately 100 subjects for each of the five factors), after which the average was calculated for that item. The mean five-factor ratings for each of the 300 ACL items are listed in the Appendix at the end of this chapter.

To examine the relations among the five factors, product-moment correlations between the 300 ratings for each pair of factors were computed, the results of which are shown as the left-hand values in Table 2. Given that the Five-Factor Model has historically been derived from orthogonal factor rotations, the five factors were expected to be relatively independent. However, as seen in Table 2, inter-factor correlations were rather high. Indeed, the mean common variance between pairs of scales was 48 per cent. Since previous research had shown each of the factors to have a substantial favorability component (see below), it was hypothesized that the common variance among the factors might be attributable to this shared favorability. To examine this hypothesis, the authors employed data from a previous study (Williams & Best, 1977) in which the 300 ACL items had been rated for favorability by university student judges. These mean item favorability ratings were correlated with mean item factor ratings for each of the five factors resulting in high correlations between each factor and favorability: .84 for Extraversion; .94 for Agreeableness; .80 for Conscientiousness; .80 for Emotional Stability; .72 for Openness. In this analysis, favorability accounted for anywhere between 52 per cent and 88 per cent of the variability in factor ratings. (To ensure that the high agreement between men and women raters could not be attributed solely to favorability, partial correlations between males' and females' ratings for each factor were examined, controlling for the favorability variable. The resulting correlations were: .93 for Extraversion; .88 for Agreeableness; .95 for Conscientiousness; .92 for Neuroticism; .95 for Openness.

Table 2. Interfactor correlation matrix.

Factor	Agr	Con	Sta	Opn
Ext	.79(03)	.70 (.11)	.64 (-.08)	.89 (.76)
Agr		.71 (-.19)	.79 (.19)	.64 (-.13)
Con			.63 (-.01)	.56 (-.03)
Ems				.51 (-.16)

Note: Extraversion (Ext), Agreeableness (Agr), Conscientiousness (Con), Emotional Stability (Ems), and Openness to Experience (Opn). In parentheses are correlations after favorability was partialled out.

Thus, it appeared that the agreement between the sexes was indeed independent of favorability.)

To remove the influence of favorability from the principal analyses, partial correlation coefficients were computed for each pair of the five factors while controlling for favorability. The partial correlations are presented in parentheses in Table 2. Examination of this table reveals that removal of the variance attributable to favorability resulted in a dramatic reduction of the inter-factor correlations such that the factors appear to be generally independent of one another, with the exception of the relation between Openness to Experience and Extraversion. These two factors remained relatively highly correlated with a common variance of 58 per cent. According to university student judges, therefore, there appears to be an empirical, positive relationship between these two factors.

One possible explanation for the aforementioned relationship between the factors Openness to Experience and Extraversion is the relative poverty of certain types of trait adjectives in the ACL item pool that might be considered indicative of an individual who is indeed open to experience. In John's (1989) previous study, graduate student raters placed a large number of adjectives associated with stimulus-seeking individuals in the Openness to Experience dimension (e.g., imaginative, inventive, interests wide), adjectives that may also be descriptive of extraverted individuals. Indeed, the student judges in this study rated those three items rather high on the extraverted dimension with scores of 4.14, 4.00, and 4.47, respectively. Therefore, the ACL item pool may not include a sufficient number of items that distinctively represent the Openness to Experience factor. Since "misery loves company," note that, among five factor researchers, this same factor has often been found to be the most difficult to define and conceptualize, as reflected in the variety of different names that have been offered (Digman, 1990; see also De Raad & Van Heck's, 1994 special issue of the European Journal of Personality).

Convergence with findings from other ACL studies

Earlier work by John (1989) linking the ACL and Big Five resulted in groupings of ACL items rated by graduate student judges as being either indicative (I) or counterindicative (CI) of each of the five factors. For each factor, data from the present study were used to compute the mean rating of John's groups of I and CI adjectives. Mean ACL-FF scores for John's I and CI items, respectively, were: Extraversion, 4.23 and 1.53; Agreeableness, 4.47 and 1.58; Conscientiousness, 4.47 and 1.58;[1] Emotional Stability, 4.27 and 1.66; and Openness to Experience, 3.86 and 1.97. These values show high differentiation in the expected direction for each set of John's items, thus providing substantial evidence of convergent validity between John's system and the ACL-FF system. As noted earlier, the undergraduate student raters in the present study were given only brief descriptions of each factor. Howe-

---

[1] The identical reported values for Agreeableness and Conscientiousness are correct.

ver, their ratings were highly congruent with those of trained graduate students, thus supporting the idea that the five factors are easily understood "folk psychology" concepts.

In another earlier study, McCrae and Costa (1992) identified ACL items found to be significantly correlated with one or more facets of each of the five factors, positively or negatively, as measured by the NEO-PI-R. Within each factor, we computed the mean ACL-FF score for the sets of ACL items collapsed across facets with the following results for positively and negatively correlated items, respectively: Extraversion, 4.31 and 1.65; Agreeableness, 4.49 and 2.48; Conscientiousness, 4.55 and 2.11; Emotional Stability, 3.82 and 1.84; and Openness to Experience, 3.93 and 2.24. These findings indicate substantial convergent validity between the new ACL-FF system and the widely used NEO-PI-R.

The favorability of the five factors

It was shown above that, for each of the five factors, the scoring weights were found to have substantial correlations with the independently rated favorability of the 300 ACL items. Thus, an ACL description that is relatively high on the five factors will be a generally favorable one and, conversely, a generally favorable description will tend to be relatively high on the five factors.

Further evidence of the evaluative nature of the factors is found in two studies reported by Goodman and Williams (1996) and summarized by Williams *et al.,* (1998). These studies employed Costa and McCrae's (1992) NEO-Five Factor Inventory (NEO-FFI) for the assessment of the five factors, with the Neuroticism factor reversed as Emotional Stability. In the first study, it was demonstrated that, for each factor, items phrased in an "indicative" manner (e.g., extraverted, agreeable, etc.) were rated more favorably than items phrased in a "counter-indicative" manner (e.g., introverted, disagreeable, etc.). In a second study, one group of participants was instructed to "fake good" on their NEO-FFI self-descriptions while a second group was instructed to "fake bad." The result was that, for each factor, the mean "fake good" scores were much higher than the "fake bad" scores. Both studies were considered to support the idea that, for each factor, higher scores are more favorable than lower scores. We suspect that similar results would be found with most other Big Five assessment procedures, such as those described elsewhere in this book.

How should one view the linkage between favorability and the dimensions of the Big Five? Should it be viewed as a "problem" for which one attempts to make corrections (á la social desirability)? Or are the five factors intrinsically evaluative and should be accepted as such? We favor the latter view, based on the following considerations.

Osgood and his associates (Osgood *et al.,* 1975) explored the dimensions of affective (connotative) meaning in a large group of the world's languages. They studied English-speaking Americans and 22 other language/culture groups and found that, in each sample, the primary dimension was Evaluation, or favorability. Denotative meanings aside, the connotative meanings of words reflected, primarily, their relative "goodness/badness" in their respective languages. Since the Five Factor Model was based on a lexical approach, identifying personality descriptive terms in the English language, it should not be surprising that the five factors carry evaluative connotations. If, as many believe, the five factors reflect the basic concerns, which people have when behavior is being assessed, we should not be surprised that an important element of this assessment is separating the "good guys" from the "bad guys." Persons who are extraverted, agreeable, conscientious, emotionally stable, and open-minded are viewed more favorably than persons who are introverted, disagreeable, irresponsible, neurotic, and close-minded. This appears to be the view that emerges from the language itself.

There is, of course, the possibility of "too much of a good thing:" Excessive extraversion might border on the manic; excessive conscientiousness on the compulsive, etc. With such possible exceptions, we conclude that, through the greater part of their score ranges, all five factors have an intrinsic positive association with favorability. While researchers sometimes may choose to study the five factors with favorability controlled (e.g., see Table 2 above), they must bear in mind that they are examining artificially contrived concepts rather than the naturally occurring factors with their intrinsic favorability components.

Two illustrative research applications

Gender Stereotypes

Here we describe two recent studies in which the ACL-FF scoring system has been used. The first study involved the re-analysis of the gender stereotype data from the Williams and Best (1990a) project in which the data originally had been analyzed in terms of the three earlier scoring systems described above. In each of 27 countries from the Americas, Europe, Africa, Asia, and Oceania, university students had judged each ACL item (or its translated equivalent) as to whether, in their respective cultures, the adjective was more frequently associated with men or with women, or not differentially associated by gender.

In each sample, a stereotype index score — called the M% score — was computed for each of the 300 items by employing the responses of all subjects and dividing the frequency of association with men by the sum of the frequencies associated with men and with women (the frequency of equal association responses was not used). Computed in this way, high M% scores indicated items highly associated with men and low M% scores indicated items highly associated with women.

In the first report from this study (Williams *et al.*, 1999), pancultural gender stereotypes were examined by computing the mean M% score for each item across all groups of student raters. The 79 items with mean M% scores of 67 and above —

items associated with men at least twice as often as with women — constituted the pancultural male stereotype; the 56 items with mean M% scores of 33 and below — items associated with women at least twice as often as with men — constituted the pancultural female stereotype. The ACL-FF scoring system was then applied to these two item sets to obtain the following mean Five Factor scores for the male and female pancultural stereotypes, respectively: Extraversion, 3.23 and 2.95 ($p < .10$); Agreeableness, 2.79 and 3.15 ($p < .05$); Conscientiousness, 3.43 and 2.89 ($p < .001$); Emotional Stability 3.11 and 2.79 ($p < .01$); and Openness to Experience 3.27 and 2.95 ($p < .05$). Thus, the pancultural female stereotype was higher on Agreeableness and the male stereotype was higher on the other four factors.

In a second report from this study (Williams *et al.*, 2001), the data from each country were analyzed separately using the local M% scores to identify the items composing the focused male stereotype (M% of 67 and above) and the items composing the focused female stereotype (M% of 33 and below). The two item sets in each sample were scored using the ACL-FF system to yield mean Big Five scores for each of the two gender stereotypes in that country. Relative to the female stereotype, the male stereotype was higher in Conscientiousness (all 27 countries), Openness to Experience (26 of 27 countries), Extraversion (24 of 27), and Emotional Stability (24 of 27). On the other hand, the female stereotype was high in Agreeableness in 22 of the 27 countries. As would be expected, the grand means of the individual country means for each of the two stereotypes revealed the same pancultural patterns found in the earlier analyses, with the female stereotypes higher on Agreeableness and the male stereotypes higher on the other four factors.

An additional analysis involved computing an index of the degree to which the two stereotypes in each country were differentiated in terms of the Big Five factors. This differentiation index was found to be largest in Nigeria, Japan, and South Africa, and smallest in Venezuela and France. Further analyses revealed that the differentiation scores were correlated with a number of cultural comparison variables; for example, the stereotypes tended to be more differentiated in countries where the prevailing sex-role ideology was more traditional (i.e., male dominant), in countries where fewer women entered higher education, and in countries where Schwartz (1994) found strong Hierarchy and Conservatism values. It was also found that stereotype differentiation was relatively low in countries where the female stereotypes were more favorable than the male stereotypes, and relatively high in countries where the male stereotype was more favorable.

This re-analysis of the stereotypes in terms of the five factors should prove useful to scholars interested in relating the study of gender stereotypes to the growing literature on applications of the Five Factor model in other areas of personality and social psychology.

The importance of psychological traits

A second illustration of a research application of the ACL-FF scoring system is found in a study of the relative importance of various psychological characteristics in different cultures (Williams *et al.*, 1998). University students in 20 countries rated the importance of each of the 300 ACL adjectives — or their translated equivalents — on a 1 to 5 scale ranging from "little or no importance" to "critical or outstanding importance." Importance was defined as the degree to which an adjective describes a more basic or central personality characteristic as opposed to a more superficial or peripheral characteristic; more important adjectives are very informative (or diagnostic) as to "what a person is really like;" less important adjectives are less informative. It was found that the psychological importance ratings were highly reliable in different cultures (Williams *et al.*, 1998). University students in 20 countries rated the importance of each of the 300 ACL adjectives — or their translated equivalents — on a 1 to 5 scale ranging from "little or no importance" to "critical or outstanding importance." Importance was defined as the degree to which an adjective describes a more basic or central personality characteristic as opposed to a more superficial or peripheral characteristic; more important adjectives are very informative (or diagnostic) as to "what a person is really like;" less important adjectives are less informative. It was found that the psychological importance ratings were highly reliable in each country. Inter-country correlations were positive but only moderate in magnitude suggesting substantial cultural variation in the importance assigned to various traits.

The ACL-FF system was employed to determine the characteristics associated with psychological importance in each of the 20 countries. In each country, the mean ratings of psychological importance were correlated with each of the five factor scales across the 300 ACL items. These analyses revealed substantial between-country variations in the relative importance of the five factors.

In some countries, psychological importance was found to be equally associated with all of the five factors. In other countries, certain factors were more important than others. The 10 countries with the most highly differentiated patterns of association between five-factor scores and psychological importance scores are shown in Table 3. For example, in Hong Kong, Agreeableness (A) was much more important

Table 3. Relative strength of the relationship of psychological importance scores to each of the five factor scores in 10 countries[a].

Country	Pattern[b]
Australia	E A >> S C O
Hong Kong	A >>> C E S >>> O
India	A C E >>> S O
Japan	C >>> A S E O
Korea	C A >> E S >> O
Nepal	A > C E >> S > O
Nigeria	A C >> E > S > O
Pakistan	A > C > E S >>> O
Singapore	S >>> E C > A O
Venezuela	E >>> A O > C >>> S

[a] Difference in common variance between adjoining factors: > + 5-9%; >> = 10-14%; >>> = 15% and up.

[b] E = Extraversion; A = Agreeableness; C = Conscientiousness; S = Emotional Stability; O = Openness to Experience.

than Conscientiousness (C), Extraversion (E), and Emotional Stability (S), which, in turn, were much more important than Openness to Experience (O).

In sum, this application of the ACL-FF system enabled us to better understand the cross-cultural variations in the importance attached to various psychological characteristics.

Other potential applications

The ACL adjectives constitute a general set of person descriptors, which can be used in many different ways to describe real or imaginary individuals or groups. The wide variety of research questions that can be addressed via the ACL item pool, previously summarized by Williams and Best (1983), includes descriptions of individual persons (e.g., politicians, spouses, children, etc.), descriptions of groups of persons (e.g., traits that collectively characterize groups of persons such as successful employees or successful students, individuals with clinical diagnosis A versus clinical diagnosis B, etc.), social stereotypes (i.e., subjects might be asked to describe their beliefs about the psychological characteristics of individuals within broad social or ethnic groups such as men versus women), historical figures (e.g., impressions of Stalin, Roosevelt, Churchill, Hitler), or even personified concepts. In the latter example, for instance, Gough and Heilbrun (1980, p. 40) report on studies comparing Fiat and Volkswagen automobiles and comparing the cities of Rome and Paris.

Bassett and Williams (2000) recently employed the ACL scoring system in a study of personified concepts. Here, university students used the ACL item pool to describe the characteristics associated with God, Satan, and self in order to study the inter-relationships among these three concepts. With the availability of the ACL-FF scoring system, the results of studies of the aforementioned types can now be examined in terms of the Five Factor model of personality.

Information on computer scoring and translations

Inquiries concerning computer scoring for the ACL-Five Factor system may be sent to: Jonathan F. Bassett, Dept. of Psychology, Georgia State University, Atlanta, GA 30303-3083 (*gs07jfb@panther.gsu.edu*); or to John E. Williams, 4750 Bell Circle, S.E., Conyers, GA 30094 (*jnwms@mediaone.net*); or to Deborah F. Hill, Wake Forest University School of Medicine, Medical Center Blvd., Winston-Salem, NC 27157 (*dfhill@wfubmc.edu*).

Inquiries concerning translations of the ACL items to other languages may be sent to Deborah L. Best, Department of Psychology, Wake Forest University, Box 7778, Winston-Salem, NC 27109 (*best@wfu.edu*).

References

Allport, G.W., & Odbert, H.S. (1936). Trait names: A psycho-lexical study. *Psychological Monographs, 47* (1, Whole No. 211).

Baron, F. (1953). Complexity-simplicity as a personality dimension. *Journal of Abnormal and Social Psychology, 48*, 163-172.

Bassett, J.F., & Williams, J.E. (2000). *Self, God, and Satan as seen in Adjective Check List descriptions*. Unpublished paper, Georgia State University.

Berne, E. (1961). *Transactional analysis in psychotherapy*. New York: Grove Press.

Berne, E. (1966). *Principles of group treatment*. New York: Oxford University Press.

Best, D.L., Williams, J.E., & Briggs, S.R. (1980). A further analysis of the affective meanings associated with male and female sex-trait stereotypes. *Sex Roles, 6*, 735-746.

Brislin, R.W. (1980). Translation and content analysis of oral and written materials. In H. C. Triandis and J.W. Berry (Eds.), *Handbook of Cross-Cultural Psychology* (Vol. 2). Boston: Allyn & Bacon.

Cattell, R.B. (1943). The description of personality: 2. Basic traits resolved into clusters. *Journal of Abnormal and Social Psychology, 23*, 476-507.

Cattell, R.B. (1946). *Description and measurement of personality*. Yonkers-on-Hudson, NY: World Book Company.

Costa, P.T., Jr., & McCrae, R.R. (1992). *The Revised NEO Personality Inventory manual*. Odessa, FL: Psychological Assessment Resources.

De Raad, B., & Van Heck, G.L. (1994). The fifth of The Big Five. *European Journal of Personality, 4*, special issue.

Digman, J. M. (1990). Personality structure: Emergence of the five-factor model. *Annual Review of Psychology, 41*, 417-440.

Edwards, A.L. (1959). *Edwards Personal Preference Schedule manual*. New York: The Psychological Corporation.

FormyDuval, D.L. (1993). *Scaling the Adjective Check List for the five-factor model of personality*. Master's thesis, Wake Forest University, Winston-Salem, NC.

FormyDuval, D.L., Williams, J.E., Patterson, D.J., and Fogle, E.E. (1995). A "Big Five" scoring system for the item pool of the Adjective Check List. *Journal of Personality Assessment, 65*, 59-76.

Goodman, R.C., & Williams, J.E. (1996). *Social Desirability: Favorability Gradients in the Five Factor Model of Personality*. Paper presented at the meeting of the Southeastern Psychological Association, Norfolk, VA.

Gough, H.G., & Heilbrun, A.B., Jr. (1980). *The Adjective Check List manual*. Palo Alto, CA: Consulting Psychologists Press.

John, O.P. (1989). Towards a taxonomy of personality descriptors. In D. M. Buss & N. Cantor (Eds.), *Personality psychology: Recent trends and emerging directions* (pp. 261-271). NY: Springer:Verlag.

McCrae, R.R., & Costa, P.T., Jr. (1992). Discriminant validity of NEO-PI-R facet scales. *Educational and Psychological Measurement, 52*, 229-237.

McCrae, R.R., & Costa, P.T., Jr., & Piedmont, R.L. (1993). Folk concepts, natural language, and psychological constructs: The California Psychological Inventory and the five-factor model. *Journal of Personality, 61*, 1-26.

Murray, H.A. (1938). *Explorations in personality*. New York: Oxford University Press.

Osgood, C.E., May, W.H., & Miron, M.S. (1975). *Cross-cultural universals of affective meaning.* Urbana: University of Illinois Press.

Osgood, C.E., Suci, G.J., & Tannenbaum, P.H. (1957). *The measurement of meaning.* Urbana: University of Illinois.

Schwartz, S.H. (1994). Beyond individualism/collectivism: New cultural dimensions of values. In U. Kim, H.C. Triandis, C. Kagitcibasi, S. Choi, & G. Yoon (Eds.), *Individualism and collectivism: Theory, method, and applications.* Thousand Oaks, CA: Sage.

Williams, J.E. (1993). Young adults' view of aging: A 19 nation study. In M.I. Winkler (Ed.), *Documentos: Conferencias del XXIV Congreso Interamericano de Psicologia* (pp. 101-123). Santiago, Chile: Sociedad Interamericana de Psicologia.

Williams, J.E., & Best, D.L. (1977). Sex stereotypes and trait favorability on the Adjective Check List. *Educational and Psychological Measurement, 37,* 101-110.

Williams, J.E., & Best, D.L. (1983). The Gough-Heilbrun Adjective Check List as a cross-cultural research tool. In J.B. Deregowski, S. Dziurawiec, & R.C. Annis (Eds.), *Expectations in Cross-Cultural Psychology.* Lisse, Netherlands: Swets & Zeitlinger.

Williams, J.E., & Best, D.L. (1990a). *Measuring sex stereotypes: A multination study* (revised ed.). Beverly Hills, CA: Sage Publications.

Williams, J.E., & Best, D.L. (1990b). *Sex and psyche: Gender and self-concepts viewed cross-culturally.* Newbury Park, CA: Sage Publications.

Williams, J.E., Satterwhite, R.C., & Best, D.L. (1999). Pancultural gender stereotypes revisited: The Five Factor Model. *Sex Roles, 40,* 513-525.

Williams, J.E., Satterwhite, R.C., Best, D.L., & Inman, G.L. (2001). *Gender stereotypes in 27 countries examined via the Five Factor Model.* Unpublished paper, Georgia State University.

Williams, J.E., Satterwhite, R.C., & Saiz, J.L. (1998). *The importance of psychological traits: A cross-cultural study.* New York: Plenum.

Williams, K.B., & Williams, J.E. (1980). The assessment of Transactional Analysis ego states via the Adjective Check List. *Journal of Personality Assessment, 40,* 120-129.

Appendix

Five Factor scores for the 300 items of the Adjective Check List. Ext = Extraversion; Agr = Agreeableness; Con = Conscientiousness; Ems = Emotional Stability; Opn = Openness

Adjective	Five Factor scores				
	EXT	AGR	CON	EMS	OPN
1. absent-minded	2.32	2.27	1.37	2.56	2.72
2. active	4.77	3.65	4.19	3.12	4.29
3. adaptable	4.19	4.14	4.08	4.17	4.43
4. adventurous	4.76	3.49	3.49	3.40	4.78
5. affected	3.04	3.37	3.14	2.18	3.06
6. affectionate	4.24	4.48	3.19	3.74	3.36
7. aggressive	3.91	2.50	3.90	2.17	3.86
8. alert	4.10	3.61	4.32	3.07	3.93
9. aloof	2.19	2.21	2.40	2.65	2.50
10. ambitious	4.35	3.39	4.79	3.35	4.11
11. anxious	2.98	2.62	3.38	1.37	3.14
12. apathetic	1.93	2.19	2.21	3.04	2.15
13. appreciative	3.85	4.38	3.56	3.62	3.76
14. argumentative	2.75	1.80	3.22	1.84	2.87
15. arrogant	2.47	1.50	2.76	2.68	2.44
16. artistic	3.43	3.19	3.26	3.14	4.26
17. assertive	4.53	3.26	4.44	3.21	3.78
18. attractive	3.57	3.21	3.07	3.17	3.23
19. autocratic	3.04	2.69	3.49	2.86	2.97
20. awkward	2.00	2.45	2.36	2.25	2.50
21. bitter	1.42	1.47	2.33	1.61	2.09
22. blustery	2.60	2.38	2.58	2.45	2.76
23. boastful	2.73	1.59	2.78	3.04	2.79
24. bossy	2.87	1.65	3.09	2.58	2.51
25. calm	3.02	4.00	3.65	4.27	3.10
26. capable	3.93	4.01	4.64	3.39	3.89
27. careless	2.39	1.88	1.40	2.47	2.77
28. cautious	2.57	3.43	3.99	3.24	2.33
29. changeable	3.55	3.49	3.10	3.07	4.19
30. charming	4.11	3.98	3.21	3.68	3.39
31. cheerful	4.67	4.21	3.32	4.33	3.64
32. civilized	3.76	3.88	3.96	3.42	3.18
33. clear-thinking	3.72	4.11	4.68	4.13	3.66
34. clever	3.93	3.60	4.28	3.28	3.93
35. coarse	2.09	2.03	2.69	2.24	2.56
36. cold	1.35	1.40	2.55	2.22	2.17
37. commonplace	2.25	2.83	2.73	3.06	1.82
38. complaining	1.71	1.71	2.35	1.82	2.04
39. complicated	2.59	2.59	3.15	2.14	3.06
40. conceited	2.36	1.41	2.61	2.89	2.40
41. confident	4.47	3.82	4.44	4.17	4.26
42. confused	2.17	2.39	1.94	1.99	2.37

43. conscientious	3.61	4.00	4.37	2.99	3.21
44. conservative	2.50	3.31	3.51	3.20	1.68
45. considerate	4.04	4.72	3.56	3.72	3.41
46. contented	3.55	3.81	3.31	4.27	2.72
47. conventional	2.72	3.19	3.41	3.51	1.90
48. cool	3.41	3.14	3.26	3.53	3.22
49. cooperative	3.87	4.43	4.14	3.79	3.75
50. courageous	4.18	3.59	3.88	3.63	4.43
51. cowardly	1.67	2.33	2.13	2.40	1.49
52. cruel	1.52	1.20	2.37	2.40	2.34
53. curious	4.17	3.61	3.88	3.02	4.72
54. cynical	1.86	1.90	2.68	1.82	2.17
55. daring	4.24	3.15	3.41	3.20	4.61
56. deceitful	1.87	1.32	2.18	2.47	2.56
57. defensive	2.26	2.20	2.94	1.63	2.27
58. deliberate	3.21	3.03	4.09	2.96	2.93
59. demanding	2.99	2.18	3.78	2.29	3.05
60. dependable	3.89	4.59	4.70	3.81	3.15
61. dependent	2.48	2.53	2.31	2.14	2.31
62. despondent	2.17	2.39	2.50	2.28	2.55
63. determined	4.35	3.71	4.70	3.35	4.02
64. dignified	3.65	3.57	3.82	3.67	3.25
65. discreet	2.67	3.42	3.15	3.58	2.63
66. disorderly	2.41	2.30	1.23	2.27	2.92
67. dissatisfied	2.21	2.16	2.45	1.71	3.21
68. distractible	2.60	2.34	1.95	2.13	3.05
69. distrustful	1.91	1.34	2.03	2.18	2.30
70. dominant	3.84	2.26	3.73	3.08	3.04
71. dreamy	3.36	3.12	2.65	2.78	4.00
72. dull	1.57	2.44	2.59	3.00	1.74
73. easy-going	4.01	4.09	3.06	4.16	3.86
74. effeminate	2.75	3.14	2.90	3.11	2.90
75. efficient	3.73	3.75	4.73	3.63	3.20
76. egotistical	2.66	1.65	2.93	2.84	2.70
77. emotional	3.67	3.70	2.88	1.66	3.45
78. energetic	4.77	3.87	4.09	3.28	4.40
79. enterprising	4.24	3.60	4.39	3.55	4.38
80. enthusiastic	4.77	4.13	4.14	3.80	4.42
81. evasive	2.22	2.13	2.55	2.73	2.44
82. excitable	4.41	3.53	3.51	2.54	4.11
83. fair-minded	3.56	4.02	3.68	3.75	3.56
84. fault-finding	2.19	1.62	2.97	1.91	2.09
85. fearful	1.93	2.36	2.48	1.91	1.78
86. feminine	2.81	3.25	2.81	3.07	2.92
87. fickle	2.48	2.28	2.48	2.29	2.58
88. flirtatious	3.73	2.97	2.78	3.23	3.44
89. foolish	2.57	2.21	1.97	2.61	2.95
90. forceful	3.16	2.15	3.51	2.95	3.15
91. foresighted	3.30	3.43	4.14	3.58	3.28

92.	forgetful	2.42	2.17	1.47	2.61	2.65
93.	forgiving	3.83	4.50	3.42	3.83	3.50
94.	formal	2.87	2.97	3.51	3.32	2.50
95.	frank	3.62	3.88	3.72	2.83	3.43
96.	friendly	4.72	4.58	3.62	3.81	3.77
97.	frivolous	3.08	2.45	2.15	2.89	3.36
98.	fussy	2.13	1.96	2.86	1.99	2.25
99.	generous	4.06	4.38	3.45	3.68	3.65
100.	gentle	3.69	4.46	3.19	3.83	3.35
101.	gloomy	1.30	1.95	2.32	1.65	1.98
102.	good-looking	3.31	3.11	3.03	3.29	3.15
103.	good-natured	4.33	4.34	3.67	3.92	3.88
104.	greedy	2.02	1.59	2.73	2.61	2.49
105.	handsome	3.30	3.08	3.03	3.29	3.17
106.	hard-headed	2.55	1.97	3.11	2.30	2.07
107.	hard-hearted	1.85	1.50	2.89	2.27	2.36
108.	hasty	2.81	2.28	2.18	2.21	3.03
109.	headstrong	3.65	2.64	3.90	2.83	3.04
110.	healthy	3.85	3.44	3.60	2.67	3.57
111.	helpful	4.25	4.59	4.03	2.78	3.60
112.	high-strung	3.33	2.38	3.16	1.90	3.22
113.	honest	3.82	4.79	3.96	3.43	3.49
114.	hostile	1.85	1.43	2.46	1.54	2.35
115.	humorous	4.21	3.68	3.21	3.75	3.68
116.	hurried	2.94	2.47	2.65	2.18	2.71
117.	idealistic	3.60	3.41	3.65	3.23	3.46
118.	imaginative	4.14	3.61	3.69	3.11	4.62
119.	immature	2.52	2.08	1.89	2.26	2.66
120.	impatient	2.71	1.58	2.42	1.74	2.63
121.	impulsive	3.88	2.60	2.32	1.62	4.23
122.	independent	4.03	3.23	4.30	3.66	4.39
123.	indifferent	2.20	1.86	2.34	3.13	2.44
124.	individualistic	3.81	3.08	3.90	3.19	4.22
125.	industrious	3.92	3.50	4.68	3.52	3.86
126.	infantile	2.34	2.27	2.04	2.27	2.48
127.	informal	3.25	3.05	2.63	3.01	3.43
128.	ingenious	3.52	3.36	3.87	2.43	3.83
129.	inhibited	1.82	2.37	2.64	2.45	1.76
130.	initiative	4.40	3.79	4.59	3.62	4.29
131.	insightful	3.87	3.94	4.29	3.51	4.03
132.	intelligent	3.71	3.74	4.44	3.10	3.87
133.	interests narrow	1.66	2.09	2.52	2.41	1.32
134.	interests wide	4.47	3.96	3.69	3.59	4.79
135.	intolerant	1.99	1.44	2.65	1.94	1.72
136.	inventive	4.00	3.53	4.02	3.39	4.25
137.	irresponsible	2.21	1.79	1.30	2.30	2.78
138.	irritable	1.86	1.57	2.43	1.46	2.38
139.	jolly	4.36	4.06	3.27	4.26	3.62
140.	kind	4.39	4.65	3.35	3.79	3.45

141.	lazy	1.76	2.27	1.38	2.62	2.01
142.	leisurely	3.00	3.17	2.16	3.40	3.05
143.	logical	3.34	3.60	4.38	3.70	3.15
144.	loud	3.64	2.54	2.94	2.60	3.19
145.	loyal	3.87	4.64	3.79	3.46	2.95
146.	mannerly	3.49	3.78	3.89	3.67	2.89
147.	masculine	3.07	2.93	3.12	3.05	3.07
148.	mature	3.49	4.01	4.27	3.88	3.47
149.	meek	1.91	2.98	2.62	2.92	2.30
150.	methodical	2.88	3.18	4.37	3.27	2.46
151.	mild	2.42	3.36	2.97	3.70	2.72
152.	mischievous	3.35	2.25	2.34	2.54	3.63
153.	moderate	2.74	3.35	3.24	3.52	2.84
154.	modest	2.76	4.21	3.27	3.36	2.61
155.	moody	2.21	2.06	2.61	1.35	2.73
156.	nagging	1.92	1.74	2.64	1.96	2.40
157.	natural	3.81	3.74	3.27	3.50	3.72
158.	nervous	2.11	2.44	2.70	1.72	2.22
159.	noisy	3.41	2.40	2.71	2.52	3.09
160.	obliging	3.37	3.88	3.40	3.33	3.20
161.	obnoxious	2.63	1.68	2.32	2.17	2.71
162.	opinionated	3.51	2.44	3.48	2.12	2.96
163.	opportunistic	4.04	3.09	4.22	3.09	4.12
164.	optimistic	4.53	4.22	4.14	4.32	4.19
165.	organized	3.61	3.75	4.87	3.64	3.14
166.	original	4.07	3.62	3.92	3.38	4.35
167.	outgoing	4.87	4.19	3.89	3.93	4.37
168.	outspoken	4.32	3.03	3.67	3.09	3.68
169.	painstaking	2.77	2.93	3.53	2.85	2.76
170.	patient	3.18	4.42	3.82	4.25	3.44
171.	peaceable	3.55	4.39	3.63	4.13	3.47
172.	peculiar	2.89	2.81	2.97	2.25	3.60
173.	persevering	3.76	3.65	4.49	3.37	3.61
174.	persistent	4.11	3.42	4.70	3.12	3.64
175.	pessimistic	1.60	1.67	2.03	1.58	1.80
176.	planful	3.44	3.57	4.59	3.62	2.85
177.	pleasant	4.17	4.33	3.45	4.10	3.55
178.	pleasure-seeking	4.73	3.56	3.05	3.24	4.30
179.	poised	3.65	3.52	3.85	3.70	3.22
180.	polished	3.54	3.38	3.89	3.89	3.07
181.	practical	3.25	3.72	4.40	3.71	2.74
182.	praising	3.85	4.22	3.36	3.95	3.38
183.	precise	3.25	3.37	4.46	3.49	2.88
184.	prejudiced	2.04	1.64	2.42	2.45	1.71
185.	preoccupied	2.56	2.16	2.67	2.01	2.19
186.	progressive	3.78	3.34	3.73	3.36	4.22
187.	prudish	2.05	2.48	2.88	2.81	1.93
188.	quarrelsome	1.95	1.34	2.46	1.75	2.37
189.	queer	2.15	2.27	2.58	2.59	2.99

190.	quick	3.78	3.19	3.59	3.01	3.50
191.	quiet	1.69	3.06	2.90	3.36	2.47
192.	quitting	1.54	1.83	1.24	2.34	1.90
193.	rational	3.44	3.71	4.34	4.11	3.02
194.	rattlebrained	2.39	2.17	1.65	2.09	2.66
195.	realistic	3.22	3.66	4.21	3.87	2.90
196.	reasonable	3.70	4.05	4.26	4.08	3.34
197.	rebellious	3.26	2.06	2.19	2.11	3.79
198.	reckless	3.05	1.91	1.68	2.11	3.60
199.	reflective	3.13	3.70	3.74	3.34	3.32
200.	relaxed	3.36	3.84	3.18	4.40	3.58
201.	reliable	3.78	4.52	4.77	3.96	3.16
202.	resentful	1.66	1.55	2.24	1.81	2.24
203.	reserved	1.67	2.96	3.00	3.18	1.80
204.	resourceful	4.14	3.58	4.58	3.59	4.02
205.	responsible	3.83	4.30	4.89	3.71	3.32
206.	restless	3.55	2.45	2.68	1.88	3.77
207.	retiring	1.65	2.64	2.34	3.24	2.19
208.	rigid	1.87	1.90	3.13	2.57	1.61
209.	robust	3.45	2.96	3.06	3.16	3.42
210.	rude	1.82	1.25	2.38	2.11	2.60
211.	sarcastic	2.28	1.64	2.60	1.90	2.62
212.	self-centered	2.36	1.35	2.69	2.20	2.42
213.	self-confident	4.42	3.78	4.32	4.03	4.22
214.	self-controlled	3.63	3.88	4.46	3.98	3.47
215.	self-denying	2.52	2.93	2.77	2.74	2.16
216.	self-pitying	1.75	1.89	2.09	1.83	2.02
217.	self-punishing	1.83	2.18	2.79	2.05	2.24
218.	self-seeking	3.12	2.59	3.41	2.75	3.91
219.	selfish	2.17	1.37	2.37	2.26	2.57
220.	sensitive	3.87	4.63	3.38	2.87	3.50
221.	sentimental	3.56	4.07	3.05	3.12	3.10
222.	serious	2.72	3.49	4.33	2.54	2.76
223.	severe	2.03	2.19	3.03	2.17	2.47
224.	sexy	3.44	3.06	2.94	3.32	3.38
225.	shallow	2.31	1.75	2.42	2.65	1.85
226.	sharp-witted	3.82	3.43	3.90	3.17	3.80
227.	shiftless	2.59	2.34	2.63	2.75	2.61
228.	show-off	3.44	1.81	2.70	3.13	3.33
229.	shrewd	2.65	2.74	3.55	2.81	3.03
230.	shy	1.40	2.69	2.51	2.53	1.84
231.	silent	1.42	2.48	2.47	2.84	2.15
232.	simple	2.48	3.18	2.85	3.39	2.42
233.	sincere	3.84	4.60	3.75	3.48	3.43
234.	slipshod	2.53	2.40	2.34	2.74	2.80
235.	slow	2.01	2.72	2.03	3.03	2.37
236.	sly	2.97	2.17	2.93	2.70	3.25
237.	smug	2.33	1.93	2.70	2.71	2.55
238.	snobbish	2.13	1.42	2.55	2.78	2.06

239.	sociable	4.85	4.20	3.54	3.99	4.23
240.	soft-hearted	3.88	4.52	3.12	3.58	3.40
241.	sophisticated	3.41	3.36	3.70	3.49	3.47
242.	spendthrift	2.91	2.75	2.93	2.92	3.00
243.	spineless	1.90	1.94	2.09	2.53	1.84
244.	spontaneous	4.50	3.38	2.89	2.68	4.63
245.	spunky	4.49	3.45	3.15	3.40	4.27
246.	stable	3.47	3.94	4.28	4.61	2.86
247.	steady	3.40	3.95	4.30	4.47	2.74
248.	stern	2.41	2.56	3.48	2.82	2.41
249.	stingy	1.91	1.80	2.74	2.70	2.17
250.	stolid	2.46	2.70	3.03	3.15	2.62
251.	strong	3.84	3.67	3.95	3.62	3.59
252.	stubborn	2.70	2.21	3.43	2.37	2.08
253.	submissive	1.90	2.81	2.18	2.86	2.55
254.	suggestible	3.37	3.35	3.21	2.87	3.51
255.	sulky	1.84	2.07	2.52	1.81	2.33
256.	superstitious	2.73	2.58	2.63	2.40	2.55
257.	suspicious	2.34	2.07	2.87	1.93	2.37
258.	sympathetic	3.83	4.59	3.20	3.52	3.42
259.	tactful	3.71	4.07	4.09	3.58	3.38
260.	tactless	2.13	1.75	1.91	2.46	2.61
261.	talkative	4.58	3.57	3.32	3.12	3.70
262.	temperamental	2.84	2.34	2.65	1.69	2.83
263.	tense	2.11	2.30	3.11	1.69	2.24
264.	thankless	2.07	1.72	2.30	2.52	2.42
265.	thorough	3.50	3.62	4.74	3.33	3.34
266.	thoughtful	4.14	4.66	3.93	3.65	3.65
267.	thrifty	3.04	2.97	3.66	3.07	3.05
268.	timid	1.47	2.65	2.38	2.69	1.85
269.	tolerant	3.70	4.28	3.50	3.95	3.85
270.	touchy	2.39	2.33	2.65	1.71	2.37
271.	tough	3.28	2.90	3.74	3.19	3.35
272.	trusting	3.97	4.52	3.73	3.81	3.77
273.	unaffected	2.63	2.55	2.98	3.96	3.00
274.	unambitious	1.61	2.35	1.31	2.80	1.75
275.	unassuming	2.61	2.99	2.55	3.50	2.85
276.	unconventional	3.16	2.79	2.60	2.82	3.97
277.	undependable	2.01	1.48	1.17	2.32	2.69
278.	understanding	4.13	4.71	3.80	3.67	3.74
279.	unemotional	1.72	1.94	2.91	4.20	2.42
280.	unexcitable	1.49	2.19	2.64	3.94	1.76
281.	unfriendly	1.27	1.38	2.45	3.57	2.18
282.	uninhibited	3.55	3.04	2.76	3.27	4.04
283.	unintelligent	2.13	2.34	1.54	3.12	2.45
284.	unkind	1.61	1.30	2.41	2.57	2.38
285.	unrealistic	2.56	2.45	1.87	2.37	3.18
286.	unscrupulous	2.39	2.20	2.40	2.85	2.87
287.	unselfish	3.65	4.31	3.27	3.65	3.55

288.	unstable	2.21	2.15	1.69	1.48	2.99
289.	vindictive	1.90	1.51	2.48	2.08	2.62
290.	versatile	4.13	3.83	4.04	3.52	4.54
291.	warm	4.56	4.51	3.38	3.83	3.57
292.	wary	2.25	2.44	3.03	2.19	2.25
293.	weak	1.75	2.47	1.99	2.43	2.17
294.	whiny	1.73	1.73	2.13	1.88	2.01
295.	wholesome	3.60	3.90	3.55	3.53	3.07
296.	wise	3.45	3.89	4.40	3.47	3.73
297.	withdrawn	1.36	2.19	2.46	2.07	1.84
298.	witty	4.06	3.58	3.61	3.36	3.61
299.	worrying	2.03	2.49	2.94	1.61	1.96
300.	zany	4.20	3.18	2.87	3.24	4.00

The MMPI-2 Personality Psychopathology—Five (PSY-5) scales and the Five Factor Model

John L. McNulty
Allan R. Harkness

Introduction

Recent sources detailing personality assessment options (e.g., Butcher & Rouse, 1996; Butcher & Williams, 2000; Friedman, Lewak, Nichols, & Webb, 2001; Greene, 2000; Millon & Davis, 2000; Widiger & Trull, 1997) have described the Personality Psychopathology - Five scales (PSY-5; Harkness, McNulty, & Ben-Porath, 1995) that can be scored from the item responses to the Minnesota Multiphasic Personality Inventory-2 (MMPI-2; Butcher *et al.*, 2001). Although mention of the MMPI-2 causes many psychologists to reflexively think of empirical scale construction, the MMPI-2 PSY-5 scales were constructed in a process that is the polar opposite of contrasted-groups empirical construction. In the development of the PSY-5, psychological theory, hence trait constructs were developed first, followed by the construction of MMPI-2 scales designed to optimize quantified communication (Harkness & Hogan, 1995; Harkness, in press) between the test-taker and test-interpreter. In this chapter, we describe the PSY-5 and compare them with the Five Factor Model (FFM). Next, we detail the development of the PSY-5 theoretical constructs (Harkness & McNulty, 1994) from markers of normal personality (Tellegen, 1982) and fundamental topics in the personality disorders (Harkness, 1992). We then describe the procedures used to build MMPI-2 PSY-5 scales optimized for quantified communication (Harkness, McNulty, & Ben-Porath, 1995). Psychometric properties and summary of recent validity studies are presented next, followed by general administration and scoring recommendations. Finally, we present guidelines for clinical interpretation of the MMPI-2 PSY-5 scales. This chapter complements a University of Minnesota Press Test Report on the PSY-5 (Harkness, McNulty, Ben-Porath, & Graham, in press).

Big Five Assessment, edited by B. De Raad & M. Perugini. © 2002, Hogrefe & Huber Publishers.

The PSY-5 theoretical constructs: Similarities to and distinctions from the FFM

Because many readers are familiar with the FFM, particularly as implemented by Costa and McCrae (1992) in the NEO-PI-R, the most pressing need is to begin this chapter with a description of the PSY-5 theoretical constructs, and a discussion of how the PSY-5 constructs are similar to and distinct from the FFM constructs.

PSY-5 Aggressiveness

Aggression can take on many forms. PSY-5 Aggressiveness focuses on aggression that is used to accomplish goals or intimidate others. PSY-5 Aggressiveness does not emphasize the aggression seen when one is cornered or reacting to the aggression of others. Interpersonally, high PSY-5 Aggressiveness is linked with dominance and hate.

PSY-5 Psychoticism

Some patients with personality disorders show some degree of disconnection from reality. This is seen, for example, in schizotypal (but not schizoid), and paranoid personality disorders. Some patients with borderline personality disorder have micro-psychotic episodes in which they appear to take leave of reality for a circumscribed period of time. The grandiose self-evaluations of some narcissistic personality disorder patients are clearly at odds with reality. Although "degree of connection to reality" has not been classically considered a part of personality, it clearly colors the effects of all other personality variables.

The PSY-5 dimension of Psychoticism assesses this degree of disconnection from reality. Unshared beliefs, as well as unusual sensory and perceptual experiences are examples of disconnection. Alienated and unrealistic expectations of harm from others are also assessed. PSY-5 Psychoticism is phenotypic: it is not linked to any specific etiology.

PSY-5 Disconstraint

Tellegen's (1982) Constraint concept led to identifying PSY-5 Disconstraint (the current PSY-5 name is now reversed from the original name Constraint) in aggregated normal personality and personality psychopathology markers (Harkness & McNulty, 1994). This construct has been further described by Watson & Clark (1993). The high disconstraint person is more open to physical risk taking, more spontaneous and less controlled, and less rule bound than the more constrained person.

PSY-5 Negative Emotionality/Neuroticism

The personality disposition to experience negative (valence) affects and emotions was articulated by Tellegen (1982) and further described in Watson and Clark's (1984) review. To focus on problematic features of incoming information, to worry, to be self-critical, to feel guilty, and to concoct worst-case scenarios are common features of elevated Negative Emotionality/Neuroticism.

PSY-5 Introversion/Low Positive Emotionality

Although linked with the corresponding social dimension of Introversion versus Extroversion, Tellegen (1982; 1985) and Watson and Clark (1997) argued persuasively that the core of this individual differences dimension is affective. People differ in the readiness to experience the positive emotions. We retain both labels to emphasize the link between the two. The current label of PSY-5 Introversion/Low Positive Emotionality is reversed from the original label of Extraversion/Positive Emotionality. This change of label was done for the assignment of MMPI-2 Uniform T scores (Tellegen & Ben-Porath, 1992) for which any skew must be aligned as positive.

Comparing the PSY-5 and the Five Factor Models[1]

Harkness and McNulty (1994) suggested that these PSY-5 constructs are linked to, yet distinct from, other personality trait models such as the FFM. They noted that both PSY-5 and FFM shared the Negative Emotionality/Neuroticism and Introversion/Low Positive Emotionality (i.e., reversed Extraversion) constructs. The authors asserted that although PSY-5 Aggressiveness shares some features of FFM reflected Agreeableness, the PSY-5 construct emphasizes more extreme aggression, cruelty, and violence. Finally, Harkness and McNulty argued that PSY-5 Disconstraint is not comparable to FFM Conscientiousness, and that PSY-5 Psychoticism is not tapped by the FFM.

Widiger and Trull (1997) subsequently compared the FFM and the PSY-5. They acknowledged the similarity of FFM Neuroticism and Extraversion to PSY-5 Nega-

---

[1] Many of the studies summarized in this chapter were conducted using the original scoring direction and names for the Constraint en Extraversion/Positive Emotionality scales. For clarity and consistency of presentation, results of those studies are reported here using the current scoring direction and Disconstraint and Introversion/Low Positive Emotionality scale names, respectively. The direction of relations with extratest data involving these two scales has been reversed from that reported in the original source, where appropriate.

tive Emotionality/Neuroticism and Introversion/Low Positive Emotionality, respectively, and focused most of their discussion on PSY-5 Aggressiveness, Disconstraint, and Psychoticism. They concluded that high PSY-5 Aggressiveness may be similar to low FFM Agreeableness, but that opposite ends of the constructs may be dissimilar. Widiger and Trull suggested that the difference between FFM Conscientiousness and PSY-5 Disconstraint may result from a different organization of FFM facets. For example, Trull, Useda, Costa, and McCrae (1995) noted the relation between NEO PI-R Excitement Seeking ($r = .41$, sign of correlation is reversed to reflect PSY-5 renaming), a facet of Extraversion, and PSY-5 Disconstraint. Furthermore, they argued that the MMPI-2 item pool is limited in having a small number of items tapping FFM Conscientiousness (e.g., Costa, Zonderman, McCrae, & Williams, 1985). Finally, Widiger and Trull acknowledged the clear difference between PSY-5 Psychoticism and FFM Openness to Experience. In general, Widiger and Trull's comparison of FFM and PSY-5 reached conclusions similar to those in Harkness and McNulty (1994).

History of the development of the PSY-5 constructs

The development of the PSY-5 began in 1989 with Allan Harkness's (1989 / 1990) University of Minnesota doctoral dissertation. From a pool of symptoms and characteristics of both normal personality functioning and personality disorder, 60 major topics in human personality were identified. Thirty-nine of these were derived from symptoms of the DSM-III-R personality disorders (PD) and Cleckley's (1982) descriptors of psychopathy and 26 were derived from characteristics of normal personality included in Tellegen's (1982) Multidimensional Personality Questionnaire (five of the PD markers duplicated normal personality markers and were fused into single items). Harkness (1992) published the development of the 39 PD "fundamental topics," and 26 normal personality markers, documenting their similarity to inclusive marker sets generated by Clark (1990) and Livesley, Jackson, and Schroeder (1989). These topics comprised an inclusive set of topics for "facet" level construction of personality disorder assessment.

Harkness and McNulty (1994) used the 60 fundamental topics of PDs and normal personality to develop the PSY-5 constructs. They reported eigen-vector analyses of a psychological distance matrix generated from the judgments of 201 lay persons. The summed similarity matrix collected short and long psychological distances as well as metrifying opposite relationships among the 60 markers of normal and disordered personality (slightly over a million independent judgments of lay people). Following these analyses, the authors described the five highest-order marker aggregates, labeled them the PSY-5, and linked them to relevant literature. The PSY-5, as described above, provided five broad individual differences vectors for distinguishing personalities.

The PSY-5 scale development

With the PSY-5 constructs in hand, Harkness, McNulty, and Ben-Porath (cf., 1995) set about building scales to measure them from items of the MMPI-2 (Butcher, Graham, Dahlstrom, Tellegen, & Kaemmer, 1989) item pool. The MMPI-2 offered several potential advantages. First, the MMPI-2 had been used in a wide variety of clinical, forensic, and correctional contexts as a measure of personality functioning and psychopathology. Therefore, extensive data were already available. Second, the 567 items of the MMPI-2 cover a wide range of personality characteristics and symptoms of psychopathology. Third, the MMPI-2 had been standardized in 1989, providing a large normative sample representative of the population of the United States. Fourth, the MMPI-2 contains validity scales that allow assessment of the respondent's test-taking approach. Persons evidencing content nonresponsiveness, or content responsive distortions (Berry, 1995; Nichols, Greene, & Schmolck, 1989) could be identified.

Harkness, McNulty and Ben-Porath (1994) developed Replicated Rational Selection (RRS) for identifying potential PSY-5 items. In RRS, many persons were taught the psychological features contained in each of the PSY-5 constructs. These trained item selectors then examined the entire MMPI-2 item pool for candidate items for each construct. Items for which a majority of selectors replicated each other's judgments were then further examined. The candidate items were reviewed to ensure they could be clearly keyed, were not projective in nature, and were relevant to only one construct. Items that failed this review were eliminated. The resultant scales were psychometrically analyzed in four samples, and items that evidenced poor internal consistency or were more strongly correlated with another scale were deleted.

The final version of the PSY-5 scale's item composition and scoring direction are shown in Table 1, and item examples for each of the scales are shown in Table 2.

Psychometric properties

Harkness, McNulty, and Ben-Porath (1995) reported the psychometric properties of the PSY-5 scales using the MMPI-2 normative sample (Butcher *et al.*, 1989), a college sample, and three clinical samples. Across the five samples, coefficient alphas ranged from .65 to .88, with higher alphas found in samples having greater baserates of psychopathology. In the MMPI-2 normative sample (for men, $N = 1,121$; for women, $N = 1,446$) coefficient alphas ranged from .65 (Disconstraint) to .84 (Negative Emotionality/Neuroticism) for men, and from .65 (Aggressiveness and Disconstraint) to .84 (Negative Emotionality/Neuroticism) for women. Normative sample intercorrelations evidenced a lower level than found among many sets of MMPI scales (Watson & Clark, 1984). The strongest intercorrelation is between Psychoti-

Table 1: Scoring Keys For The PSY-5 scales

AGGR - Aggressiveness (18 items)

True	27 50 85 134 239 323 324 346 350 358 414 423 452 521 548
False	70 446 503

PSYC - Psychoticism (25 items)

True	24 42 48 72 96 99 138 144 198 241 259 315 319 336 355 361 374 448 466 490 508 549 551
False	184 427

DISC - Disconstraint (29 items)

True	35 84 88 103 105 123 209 222 250 284 344 362 385 412 417 418 431 477
False	34 100 121 126 154 263 266 309 351 402 497

NEGE - Negative Emotionality/Neuroticism (33 items)

True	37 52 82 93 116 166 196 213 290 301 305 329 375 389 390 395 397 407 409 415 435 442 444 451 513 542 556
False	63 223 372 405 496 564

INTR - Introversion/Low Positive emotionality (34 items)

True	38 56 233 515 517
False	9 49 61 75 78 86 95 109 131 174 188 189 207 226 231 244 267 318 330 340 342 343 353 356 359 370 460 531 534

Note: From MMPI-2 (Minnesota Multiphasic Personality Inventory - 2): Manual for Administration, Scoring and Interpretation (2nd ed.), by J. Butcher, J. Graham, Y. Ben-Porath, A. Tellegen, W. Dahlstrom, and B. Kaemmer, 2001. Copyright 2001 by the Regents of the University of Minnesota. Adapted and reprinted by permission.

cism and Negative Emotionality/Neuroticism, at $r = .52$. The level of intercorrelation is directly comparable to the strongest intercorrelation reported between domain scores on the NEO PI-R, $r = -.53$ between Neuroticism and Conscientiousness (Costa & McCrae, 1992). The mean absolute correlation between the PSY-5 scales was $r = .25$ (range = -.05 to .52) in the MMPI-2 normative sample, and is comparable to the domain level intercorrelation found in the NEO PI-R (mean absolute $r = .21$). Trull *et al.* (1995) reported six month test-retest stabilities ranging from .62 (Aggressiveness) to .86 (Disconstraint) in a sample of 44 clinic outpatients. Harkness, Spiro, Butcher, and Ben-Porath (1995) reported five year test-retest stabilities for the PSY-5 scales that ranged from .69 (Psychoticism) to .82 (Negative Emotionality/Neuroticism) in the Boston VA Normative Aging Study samples.

PSY-5 scale raw score means and standard deviations from the MMPI-2 normative sample, by gender, are reported in Harkness *et al.* (in press), along with tables for converting raw scale scores to uniform T scores. Measures of each scale's internal consistency (Cronbach's Coefficient Alpha), standard errors of measurement, scale intercorrelations and one week test-retest correlations calculated from the MMPI-2 normative sample (by gender) are provided in Harkness *et al.* (in press).

Table 2: Example items from the MMPI-2 based PSY-5 scales (Scoring direction in parentheses)

AGGR: Aggressiveness

27	(T)	When people do me a wrong, I feel I should pay them back if I can, just for the principle of the thing.
70	(F)	I am easily downed in an argument.
239	(T)	I am entirely self-confident.
324	(T)	I can easily make other people afraid of me, and sometimes do for the fun of it.
521	(T)	I like making decisions and assigning jobs to others.
548	(T)	I've been so angry at times that I've hurt someone in a physical fight.

PSYC: Psychoticism

48	(T)	Most anytime I would rather sit and daydream than do anything else.
96	(T)	I see things or animals or people around me that others do not see.
198	(T)	I often hear voices without knowing where they come from.
241	(T)	It is safer to trust nobody.
336	(T)	Someone has control over my mind.
508	(T)	I often feel I can read other people's minds.

DISC: Disconstraint

100	(F)	I have never done anything dangerous for the thrill of it.
105	(T)	In school I was sometimes sent to the principal for bad behavior.
126	(F)	I believe in law enforcement.
266	(F)	I have never been in trouble with the law.
309	(F)	I usually have to stop and think before I act even in small matters.
497	(F)	It bothers me greatly to think of making changes in my life.

NEGE: Negative Emotionality/Neuroticism

223	(F)	I believe I am no more nervous than most others.
301	(T)	I feel anxiety about something or someone almost all the time.
372	(F)	I am not easily angered.
405	(F)	I am usually calm and not easily upset.
442	(T)	I must admit that I have at times been worried beyond reason over something that really did not matter.
513	(T)	Sometimes I get so angry and upset I don't know what comes over me.

INTR: Introversion

49	(F)	I am a very sociable person.
61	(F)	I am an important person.
75	(F)	I usually feel that life is worthwhile.
318	(F)	I usually expect to succeed in things I do.
353	(F)	I enjoy social gatherings just to be with people.
515	(T)	I am never happier than when I am by myself.

Note: From *MMPI-2 (Minnesota Multiphasic Personality Inventory - 2): Manual for Administration, Scoring and Interpretation* (2nd ed.), by J. Butcher, J. Graham, Y. Ben-Porath, A. Tellegen, W. Dahlstrom, and B. Kaemmer, 2001. Copyright 2001 by the Regents of the University of Minnesota. Adapted and reprinted by permission.

Validity research on the PSY-5 scales

Discrimination studies

Several validity studies have focused on the issue of discriminability. For example, in a sample of 171 participants from an inpatient/outpatient psychiatric hospital, McNulty, Harkness, and Wright (1994) compared the mean PSY-5 scale scores of two clinical subgroups to those of the balance of the sample. Mean PSY-5 scale scores of participants whose diagnoses indicated the presence of psychotic features were significantly different from the scales' scores in the remainder of the sample only for the Psychoticism scale. In comparison to participants diagnosed with a primarily depression-related disorder, PSY-5 scale scores for the remainder of the participants were significantly lower on the Negative Emotionality/Neuroticism and Introversion/Low Emotionality scales. These results were consistent with each of the PSY-5 constructs, as the lack of significant differences between non-diagnosis-related scales, along with the mentioned differences in each comparison, were construct relevant.

Harkness, Sprio *et al.* (1995) examined the links between PSY-5 measured individual differences and alcohol consumption and self-defined alcohol problems in three groups identified from the Boston VA Normative Aging Study sample. In this study, high volume drinkers were considerably more likely to evidence higher levels of both Disconstraint and Introversion/Low Positive Emotionality than low volume drinkers. Furthermore, high volume drinkers who had experienced drinking related problems during the course of their lives were considerably more likely to evidence higher levels of Negative Emotionality/Neuroticism than those high volume drinkers who had not experienced such problems. Given these results, Harkness, Spiro *et al.* speculated on the role alcohol consumption may play as a mechanism for enhancing or adapting to one's trait related personality characteristics, and how knowledge of a client's standing on these traits can play a role in understanding and intervening with various drinking patterns.

In a European sample comprised of both psychiatric inpatients and outpatients, Egger, Derksen, and DeMey (1997) explored how well the PSY-5 scales discriminated between three common profile types, identified via cluster analysis of the MMPI-2 clinical scales. Their analyses clearly showed that the pattern of PSY-5 scale elevations differentiated between the three groups in construct relevant ways. For example, the first cluster was characterized primarily by elevations on scales 8 and 9. The PSY-5 profile for this cluster evidenced an elevation only on the Psychoticism scale. The cluster dominated by elevations on scales 2 and 7 evidenced an elevation on the PSY-5 Introversion/Low Positive Emotionality scale only. The third cluster, characterized by elevations on scales 8, 7, 6, 4, and 2, showed PSY-5 elevations on the Psychoticism, Negative Emotionality/Neuroticism, and Introversion/Low Positive Emotionality scales.

Rouse, Butcher, and Miller (1999) showed how the PSY-5 Disconstraint scale was able to distinguish between substance abusers who had been classified as non-abusers (false negatives), and non-substance abusers who had been correctly classified (true negatives), based on optimum cutoffs on the MAC-R, AAS, and APS scales. Their results indicated that substance abusers miss-classified as non-abusers obtained higher PSY-5 Disconstraint scale scores than correctly classified non-abusers.

In a study by Bagby, Buis, Nicholson, Parikh, and Bacciochi (1999), the ability of the MMPI-2 clinical, content, and PSY-5 scales to differentiate patients with major depression, schizophrenia, and bipolar disorder, depressed was evaluated. A comparison of PSY-5 scale mean scores across the three patient groups showed that the Disconstraint scale differentiated between the major depression and bipolar depressed groups, and the Introversion/Low Positive Emotionality scale differentiated between the major depressed and schizophrenia groups. Subsequent stepwise regressions showed that the PSY-5 Disconstraint scale was the most effective at distinguishing patients with bipolar depression from patients with major depression. Bagby *et al.* concluded that both the content and PSY-5 scales provided important information in differential diagnosis.

As indicated earlier, the strongest PSY-5 scale intercorrelation occurs between the Psychoticism and Negative Emotionality/Neuroticism scales. Harkness, McNulty, Finger, Arbisi, and Ben-Porath (1999) introduced the idea of item pleiometricity as an explanation for the magnitude of this relation. Pleiometricity refers to items that measure more than one construct. The authors hypothesized that psychoticism items are intrinsically pleiometric: They intrinsically involve detecting a problem in oneself. Thus they measure negative emotionality as well as psychoticism. To test this idea, the authors examined how the base-rate of psychotic patients in a sample influenced the factor structure of the items jointly comprising the PSY-5 Psychoticism and Negative Emotionality/Neuroticism scales. Confirmatory factor analysis using the MMPI-2 normative sample, a sample with a low base rate of psychotic problems, suggested that the items from the two scales were consistent with a single latent factor. In a normal sample, psychoticism items tended to function as high-psychometric difficulty indicators of negative emotionality. In a clinical sample that evidenced a higher base rate of psychotic patients, two factors were required for a plausible solution. Psychoticism items could be pleiometric in this sample, tapping both psychoticism, and the negative emotionality tendency to see problems in oneself. These results offer an explanation for the lack of a separate psychoticism factor in models based on normal personality functioning, such as the five factor model. In a test of the discriminability of the Psychoticism and Negative Emotionality/Neuroticism scales, Harkness, McNulty, Finger *et al.* multiply regressed both scales with the count of psychotic symptoms in the clinical sample. While the two scales have a positive intercorrelation, the Psychoticism scale had a significant positive beta weight with the number of psychotic symptoms, while the Negative Emotionality/Neuroticism scale had a significant negative beta weight with the number of psychotic symptoms. The Negative Emotionality/Neuroticism scale acted, in effect, as a suppressor variable on the Psychoticism scale; knowledge of a person's standing on Negative Emotionality or Neuroticism allows the clinician to suppress nuisance variance in the subject's self-report of psychotic phenomena.

Relations with other individual differences models

A series of studies had as their focus the relations between the PSY-5 scales and those of other models. Harkness, McNulty, and Ben-Porath (1995) presented an analysis of the relations between the PSY-5 scales and Tellegen's Multidimensional Personality Questionnaire (MPQ: manuscript in preparation) superfactor scales in a sample of 838 college students. PSY-5 Negative Emotionality/Neuroticism, Disconstraint, and Introversion/Low Positive Emotionality correlated as expected with MPQ superfactors of the same name: Negative Emotionality, Constraint, and Positive Emotionality, respectively.

Participants in the Boston VA Normative Aging Study were again the source for a study presented by Harkness, Spiro *et al.* (1995). The authors correlated the PSY-5 scales with a modified version of the Big Five factors based on Goldberg's 1992 adjective markers. The modified Big Five component scores showed the strongest convergent relations with PSY-5 Negative Emotionality/Neuroticism and Introversion/Low Positive Emotionality, consistent with Harkness and McNulty's (1994) speculations. While PSY-5 Aggressiveness, Disconstraint and Psychoticism, respectively, had no strong correlations with the Big Five Agreeableness, Conscientiousness, and Openness components, of interest was the correlation between PSY-5 Aggressiveness and Big Five Extraversion ($r = .39$). Upon investigation, Harkness, Spiro *et al.* found strong relations between the PSY-5 Aggressiveness scale and the bold, assertive, demanding, and timid (-) Goldberg extraversion markers, each consistent with the Aggressiveness construct. In a final set of analyses, Harkness, Spiro *et al.* correlated the PSY-5 scale scores with those of the Sixteen Personality Factor Questionnaire (16PF; Cattell, Eber, & Tatsuoka, 1970) administered approximately 25 years earlier. There was strong support for convergent and divergent construct validity, and the length of time between the administration of the instruments provided additional support for the stability of the PSY-5 constructs.

Trull *et al.* (1995) examined the relations between PSY-5, NEO-PI, and NEO-PI-R scores in community and clinical samples. Of particular interest are the results from the clinical sample ($N = 56$). As Harkness and McNulty (1994) predicted, the strongest relations between the PSY-5 and NEO-PI based FFM domain scores occurred between PSY-5 Negative Emotionality/Neuroticism and NEO-PI Neuroticism, and between PSY-5 Introversion/Low Positive Emotionality and NEO-PI Extraversion. PSY-5 Aggressiveness evidenced a moderate correlation with NEO-PI Agreeableness, also consistent with Harkness and McNulty's expectation. Finally, PSY-5 Disconstraint showed a moderate correlation with NEO-PI Conscientiousness, and PSY-5 Psychoticism was moderately correlated with NEO-PI Openness to Experience.

McNulty, Harkness, and Ben-Porath (1998) explored the relations between four individual differences models of personality in a college sample of 291 introductory psychology students: the PSY-5, Costa and McCrae's (1992) NEO Personality Inventory-Revised (NEO-PI-R), Tellegen's Multidimensional Personality Questionnaire (MPQ; manuscript in preparation), and the Alternative Five model (ZKPQ-III; Zuckerman, Kuhlman, Joireman, Teta, & Kraft, 1993). Scales at the five-factor level from each model were submitted to a multiple battery factor analysis, a factor analytic technique that minimizes the impact of battery specific variance on the resultant factor solution (cf., Browne, 1980; Millsap, 1995). Extraction and oblique rotation of a five factor solution provided the best representation of the variance common across the four models. These factors were labeled Neuroticism, Communal Positive Emotionality, Aggressiveness, Disconstraint, and Agentic Positive Emotionality.

Regarding the PSY-5 model, the Negative Emotionality/Neuroticism and Aggressiveness scales were strongly and uniquely related to the Neuroticism and Aggressiveness common factors, respectively. PSY-5 Introversion loaded primarily on the Communal Positive Emotionality factor, but had a secondary loading on the Agentic Positive Emotionality factor as well. This pattern suggested that the PSY-5 Introversion scale taps both aspects of the broad Positive Emotionality domain. PSY-5 Disconstraint showed a primary loading on the Disconstraint factor and a secondary loading on the Aggressiveness factor, suggesting that this scale reflects an aggressive impulsivity, a construct similar to that hypothesized by Siever and Davis (1991) as particularly relevant to the domain of personality disorders. Finally, PSY-5 Psychoticism loaded moderately on the Neuroticism factor.

Voelker and Nichols (1999) explored the relations between several MMPI-2 based scales, including the PSY-5, and the Factor 1, Factor 2, and Total scores of the Hare Psychopathy Checklist-Revised (PCL-R; Hare, 1991). The item content of PCL-R Factor 1 includes superficial charm, grandiose sense of self-worth, manipulative, and lack of empathy, each related to the PSY-5 Aggressiveness construct. For PCL-R Factor 2, the item content includes boredom proneness, poor behavior control, impulsivity, juvenile delinquency, and behavior problems, each related to the PSY-5 Disconstraint construct. In a sample of 100 correctional inmates, PSY-5 Aggressiveness was the strongest correlate of PCL-R Factor 1 ($r = .30$), while PSY-5 Disconstraint was the strongest correlate of PCL-R Factor 2 ($r = .34$). Furthermore, PSY-5 Aggressiveness was essentially uncorrelated with PCL-R Factor 2 ($r = .16$), PSY-5 Disconstraint was uncorrelated with PCL-R Factor 1 ($r = .10$), with only the PSY-5 Introversion/Low Positive Emotionality scale obtaining an additional moderate correlation with Factor 1 ($r = -.24$). Voelker and Nichols' results confirmed the convergent and discriminant aspects of both the Aggressiveness and Disconstraint PSY-5 constructs.

Relations between the PSY-5 scales and extratest criteria

Prediction of relevant extratest characteristics (e.g., diagnostic symptoms, personality characteristics) is the focus of a third set of validity studies. Trull *et al.* (1995) examined the relations between PSY-5, NEO-PI, and NEO-PI-R scores in community and clinical samples. In a final analysis, the validity of the PSY-5 scale scores was assessed in predicting symptom counts for the DSM-III-R personality disorders. Two instruments, the Structured Interview for DSM-III-R Personality — Revised (SIDP-R; Pfohl, Blum, Zimmerman, & Stangl, 1989) and the Personality Diagnostic Questionnaire — Revised (PDQ-R; Hyler & Reider, 1987), were administered to the clinical sample participants (N = 56). The PSY-5 scales were significant predictors of the symptom counts for all 13 of the structured interview (SIDP-R) PDs (mean R^2 = .29, range = .21 to .51), and 12 of the 13 self-report (PDQ-R) PDs (mean R^2 = .31, range = .19 to .64).

McNulty, Ben-Porath and Watt (1997) analyzed the incremental validity of the PSY-5 and Five Factor models in predicting SCID-II personality disorder symptomatology in a sample of substance abusers participating in a VA hospital addiction recovery program. In their summary of a series of regression analyses where the PSY-5 and NEO-PI-R domain scales were alternately entered first, the mean increase in R^2 for the PSY-5 scales was .085 (range, .033 to .206), compared with .024 (range = .000 to .047) for the NEO-PI-R scales. An important finding was the contribution of the PSY-5 Psychoticism scale to the prediction of SCID-II schizotypal personality disorder symptomatology. Consistent with Harkness and McNulty's (1994) speculations, the Psychoticism scale was the key to distinguishing between the schizoid and schizotypal personality disorder symptom scores.

Rouse (1997) studied the validity of the PSY-5 scales using data from the Minnesota Psychotherapy Assessment Project. Rouse first reported that the correlations between the PSY-5 scales and the MMPI-2 clinical, content, and supplementary scales were meaningful and relevant to the PSY-5 constructs. In a second set of analyses, Rouse utilized regression analyses to predict individual PSY-5 scale scores from symptom indices created from a priori judgements of construct relevant symptoms. From rater-identified symptoms relevant to each PSY-5 construct, an index was created for each PSY-5 scale. Each PSY-5 scale was then regressed on its associated symptom index. Multiple Rs ranged from .22 for the Psychoticism scale to .41 for the Disconstraint and Introversion/Low Positive Emotionality scales. As the multiple Rs reflected the relations between informant and self-report data, Rouse argued that these multiple Rs provided a "stress test", or lower bound, of the PSY-5 scales' construct validity. Rouse concluded that the significant correlations between the non-test measures (symptom indices) and the PSY-5 scales, and the pattern of correlations between the PSY-5 scales and the MMPI-2 clinical, content, and supplementary scales, supported the construct validity of the PSY-5 scales, and demonstrated the utility of the PSY-5 scales in understanding inpatient and outpatient psychopathology.

Perspectives on PSY-5 interpretation

Harkness (in press), Harkness and Lilienfeld (1997), Harkness and McNulty (in press), and Siever and Frucht (1997) have emphasized the relevance and importance of an individual differences perspective to understanding psychopathology, and have offered suggestions for incorporating individual differences models in assessment and treatment. With respect to the PSY-5, Harkness, Royer, and Gill (1996) presented an approach for organizing MMPI-2 assessment feedback using the PSY-5 scales. This individual differences approach, modeled on that developed by Stephen Finn (1996), was considered extremely or mostly accurate and helpful by over 95 per cent of the participants from an outpatient university counseling center sample.

PSY-5 scale interpretation issues have been addressed in two studies. In the first, Rouse, Finger, and Butcher (1999) applied an item response theory (IRT) approach to examining the psychometric properties of the PSY-5 scales. Full-information factor analyses confirmed that each of the PSY-5 scales is adequately unidimensional for IRT analysis. Test information functions for the PSY-5 scales indicated two different patterns. For the PSY-5 Aggressiveness, Psychoticism, and Negative Emotionality/Neuroticism scales, the greatest discrimination between test respondents occurred at the high end of the trait dimension. For the Aggressiveness and Negative Emotionality/Neuroticism scales, while respondents with low to normal range scores can be modestly discriminated from each other, scale scores of 60 or higher evidence much greater differential trait levels with each succeeding increase in score. The Psychoticism scale evidences little discriminability for persons scoring lower than 65. However, each change in T score above 65 offers a great deal of discriminant information. The second test information function pattern pertains to the PSY-5 Disconstraint and Introversion scales. For both of these scales, test discrimination is distributed bilaterally and broadly across trait levels.

Harkness *et al.* (in press) reviewed the correlations between extratest variables and each of the PSY-5 scales from a large outpatient community mental health sample (detailed information on the study site, sample characteristics, instruments, and procedures are found in Graham, Ben-Porath, & McNulty, 1999). Available extratest data included variables from a standardized intake interview and mental status exam, scale scores from the self-report SCL-90-R, responses to a 188-item patient description form (PDF) completed by the client's therapist following the third therapy session, and scores for 25 empirically derived scales that tap the important content domains reflected by the PDF items. The analyses were conducted by gender, and only with participants obtaining a valid MMPI-2 ($N = 410$ men, $N = 610$ women).

The pattern of Aggressiveness scale correlates reflected aggressive, physically abusive, and antisocial behavior in both men and women. Passive behavior in interpersonal relations was associated with low scores in both genders. For women, there were several additional construct relevant correlates, such as being perceived as narcissistic, assertive, egocentric, grandiose, selfish, overbearing in relationships, and over-evaluating their own worth.

In this study site, clients with severe psychopathology were referred elsewhere. Consequently, there was a noticeable lack of such pathology in the study sample. However, self-report paranoid ideation and psychoticism scale correlations from the SCL-90-R were the strongest for the PSY-5 Psychoticism scale. Otherwise, the pattern of correlations suggested generally low functioning, isolation, depression, and poor coping abilities, in both interpersonal and work-related situations. Only for women did evidence of hallucinations at intake correlate with Psychoticism.

The correlates of the PSY-5 Disconstraint scale suggested a general tendency to act out and behave impulsively. Substance abuse was a prominent feature of higher scores, as well as being in trouble with the law. Many of the aggression related correlates of the PSY-5 Aggressiveness scale were shared with the Disconstraint scale. Several Disconstraint relevant correlates were evidenced only by women, including procrastination, deception, evasiveness, failure to complete projects, insensitivity, manipulation, tending to intellectualize or rationalize, and feigning remorse when their behavior lands them in trouble.

There was a substantial degree of overlap in the correlates of the Negative Emotionality/Neuroticism and Introversion scales, primarily related to depression and related symptoms, and to anxiety. This is not unexpected, given the high degree of comorbidity between these two symptom patterns in clinical populations, as well as the magnitude of the correlation between these two constructs that is typically found. Anxiety did, however, show a generally stronger relation with the Negative Emotionality/Neuroticism scale, while depression was somewhat more strongly related to the Introversion scale. Correlates unique to Negative Emotionality/Neuroticism included histrionic behavior, low frustration tolerance, and being over-reactive. Correlates indicative of a lack of achievement orientation were relatively unique to the Introversion scale, as were being perceived by one's therapist as introverted, shy, socially awkward, and not sexually adjusted. These correlates of the Introversion scale indicated that it is measuring both of the agentic and communal domains included in the broader Positive Emotionality construct.

General administration and scoring recommendations

Consistent with the general administration guidelines provided in Butcher *et al.* (2001), we recommend administration of the entire MMPI-2 questionnaire. This will provide the test user with information concerning the respondent's test-taking approach as well as scores on the currently available clinical, content, and supplementary scales in addition to the PSY-5 scales. A review of the respondent's test-taking approach, as indicated earlier, was one of the primary reasons for developing the MMPI-2-based PSY-5 scales. Furthermore, information available from the other MMPI-2 scales can provide useful insights into an individual differences interpretation approach available through the PSY-5 scales. While an abbreviated administration of the first 370 MMPI-2 items provides sufficient information for computing the original validity and clinical scale scores, the items comprising the PSY-5 scales are spread throughout the MMPI-2 item pool. Consequently, such an abbreviated administration would not provide all of the responses required for calculation of PSY-5 raw scale scores.

With the availability of gender-based mean and standard deviation data for the PSY-5 scales (Butcher *et al.*, 2001), linear T scores can be manually calculated from PSY-5 scale raw scores. Recently, the MMPI-2-based PSY-5 scales were included in the computerized scoring and interpretation services provided by National Computer Systems (NCS; P.O. Box 1416, Minneapolis, MN 55440).

Clinical interpretation of the PSY-5 scales

The PSY-5 scales provide an overview of major personality trait features for the MMPI-2 test respondent. Interpretive approaches such as those suggested by Butcher and Williams (2000), Finn (1996), and Graham (2000) consider such a formulation to be a central ingredient in the overall interpretation. General interpretive statements for the PSY-5 scales are provided in Harkness *et al.* (in press) and in Butcher *et al.* (2001). We provide a summary in this chapter. The interpretation of high and low scale scores is guided by test information functions computed from the MMPI-2 normative sample (Rouse, Finger, & Butcher, 1999).

Elevated Aggressiveness scale scores (T scores greater than 65) suggest the tendency toward offensive aggression, toward using aggression in the pursuit of one's goals. A high scorer enjoys dominating others and derives satisfaction from the sense of power associated with aggressive displays. In the outpatient sample, high Aggressiveness scale scores were associated with a history of being physically abusive and therapist ratings as having aggressive and antisocial features. Men were more likely to have histories of committing domestic violence while women were more likely to have been arrested. Finally, women with high Aggressiveness scale scores were rated by their therapists as extroverted. The test information function for the Aggressiveness scale indicates that low scores should not be interpreted.

Elevated Psychoticism scale scores (T scores above 65) suggest difficulty in maintaining contact with consensually validated reality. Eccentric thought and behavior patterns, perceptual distortions, and difficulty in making appropriate cause and effect attributions (particularly in interpersonal situations) are the primary characteristics of high scorers. In an inpatient sample (Harkness *et al.*, 1999), persons with high scores were more likely to have admission notations of psychosis, paranoid suspiciousness, ideas of reference, loosening of associations, hallucinations, or flight of ideas. In an outpatient sample, with lower base-rates of psychotic phenomena, elevations were associated with lower functioning at admission and having few or no friends. Both outpatient men and women were characterized as depressed on mental status examination, and were rated by their therapists as not being achievement oriented. A sad mood at admission and therapist-rated anxiousness and depression were characteristics of outpatient men with high Psychoticism scale scores. Women with high Psychoticism scale scores were more likely to report hallucinations at admission. Low Psychoticism scores should not be interpreted.

High Disconstraint scale scores (T scores greater than 65) suggest that the respondent is not bound by traditional moral values and dictates, engages in risky behavior, and evidences a general lack of control in responding to internal or external situational contexts. Elevated scores in the outpatient sample were associated with a history of being arrested, and histories of alcohol, cocaine, and marijuana abuse in the outpatient sample. In addition, high Disconstraint scorers were rated by their therapists as aggressive and antisocial. Men had histories of committing domestic violence, while women were characterized as somewhat achievement oriented by their therapists. Low scores on Disconstraint (T scores less than 40) suggest a reduced tendency for risk taking, greater self-control, and reduced impulsivity. Low scorers evidence greater boredom tolerance, a tendency to be a rule follower, and a slight tendency to prefer romantic partners with similarly constrained personality patterns.

Elevated Negative Emotionality/Neuroticism scale scores (T scores greater than 65) suggest a tendency to attend to danger signals. High scorers view events and recollections through a filter with a bias toward catching signals of danger and problems. They tend to view the world as more threatening and dangerous than others do. The affect of high scorers tends to be dominated by worry, tension, and a propensity to experience guilt about one's actions. In the outpatient sample, elevated scores were associated with diagnoses of depression or dysthymia, low functioning, and the tendency to have few or no friends. Therapist ratings and results of mental status exams indicated anxiety, depression, and a sad mood state characterized high scorers as well. High scoring men were more likely to have committed domestic violence, characteristic with maintaining a focus on the flaws, problems, and irritations in one's spouse, life, and future prospects. Consistent with links reviewed by Watson and Pennebacker (1989), complaints of somatic symptoms were more common among high Negative Emotionality/Neuroticism scale scorers. Evidence of histories of alcohol abuse and therapist ratings as pessimistic and lacking achievement orientation characterized high scoring women. Low Negative Emotionality/Neuroticism scale scores should not be interpreted.

Men and women with high scale scores (T scores greater than 65) on Introversion/Low Positive Emotionality have a reduced capacity to experience positive emotions, and are much more comfortable engaging in solitary activities or interpersonal activities with only one or a few friends. High scores on the Introversion/Low Positive Emotionality scale also suggest a lower achievement orientation. Increased rates of dysthymia and depression, and feelings of depression and sadness during completion of a mental status exam were evident in the outpatient sample for elevated scores. Therapists rated high scorers as having a low achievement orientation, and as anxious, depressed, introverted, pessimistic, and complaining of somatic symptoms. Antidepressant medications were more likely to be prescribed to high scoring women, who were also seen as having few or no friends. Persons with low scale scores (T scores less than 40) exhibited an Extroverted/High Positive Emotionality pattern.

Such scores suggest a greater capacity to experience pleasure and joy, and more social interests and energy.

A Case example

Figure 1 shows the PSY-5 profile for a 26 year-old, single, Caucasian woman seen at an outpatient clinic. The validity scales were all within acceptable limits, suggesting that the client completed the MMPI-2 in a straightforward manner. Elevations on both of the PSY-5 Disconstraint and Psychoticism scales, the low Introversion/Low Positive Emotionality scale score, and the absence of clinically relevant scores for the Aggressiveness and Negative Emotionality/Neuroticism scales provide the organizing framework for understanding the client's prominent personality characteristics.

The client presented with interpersonal problems, primarily in her family, and alcohol and drug abuse. During the intake interview she acknowledged having previously received individual and group psychotherapy, an arrest record, a lifetime history of alcohol and marijuana abuse, and having been physically and sexually abused. She did not complete high school but had obtained her GED. During the intake interview, the client was cooperative and displayed a full range of affect, including happiness, anxiety, and sadness. Following the client's third therapy session, her therapist (who was blind to the MMPI-2 results) rated her on a number of personality characteristics. She was rated as ignoring or intellectualizing problems and having difficulty trusting others, tending to keep them at a distance. The therapist concluded that interpersonal relationships tend to be stormy, particularly within her family. She resents family members and feels that her family lacks love. The thera-

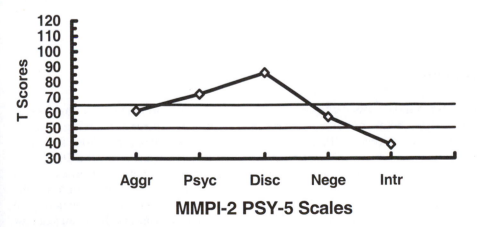

Figure 1. PSY-5 scale scores for a 26year-old female outpatient

pist further concluded that although she sees her interpersonal relationships as unfulfilling, she has a very strong need to be with others. The client was rated as moderately aggressive, angry, critical, and argumentative at times during therapy. However, her therapist indicated an absence of deep emotions.

From a PSY-5 individual differences perspective, one key issue concerns the basis of the client's interpersonal difficulties and the aggressive displays evidenced in therapy. Both PSY-5 Aggressiveness and Negative Emotionality/Neuroticism are within normal limits, suggesting that she does not attempt to dominate others nor is it likely that trait-like anxiety is the typical genesis for such behavior. Her therapist indicated that she has a strong need to be with other people, and her PSY-5 Introversion/Low Positive Emotionality score suggests that she enjoys the company of others and has the capacity to experience positive emotions. However, her ability to accurately interpret her social, interpersonal world may be compromised.

Thus the Psychoticism scale that may provide an essential clue. This client may have difficulty understanding the actions of others and may feel alienated as a result. Furthermore, she may interpret others' behavior as threatening and react with aggressive displays. This pattern may then be amplified by her inability to inhibit her responses, suggested by the elevated Disconstraint scale score. This conceptualization of the case suggests a different formulation and therapeutic approach compared to one focused solely on the client's aggression.

A second key issue concerns the client's substance abuse problem. Her elevated PSY-5 Disconstraint score points to difficulties inhibiting impulsive behavior, and is often found in persons with substance abuse problems. Her low Introversion/Low Positive Emotionality score, indicative of the Extroverted pattern, may also provide clues to the dynamics of her substance abuse. The client enjoys the company of others and likely seeks out interpersonal relationships. However, consistent with her high Psychoticism score, she may also have difficulty interpreting others' social cues; she feel alienated from others and view others' behavior as threatening. It is possible that alcohol and marijuana use dampen the sense of alienation and threat, helping the client to enjoy her interpersonal relations more fully. For both of these key therapeutic issues, PSY-5 Psychoticism provides information not readily available from other models.

Conclusion

The PSY-5 model was derived from indicators of both normal and abnormal personality. Using both types of markers resulted in PSY-5 constructs that resemble parts of the FFM. However, PSY-5 constructs differ in important ways from the FFM. Scales to measure the PSY-5 constructs were developed using the MMPI-2 item pool. The MMPI-2 PSY-5 scales evidence adequate psychometric properties as well as convergent and discriminant relations with clinically relevant extra-test data. Comparisons of the MMPI-2 based PSY-5 scales with other models, including the FFM, indicates common Negative Emotionality/Neuroticism and Introversion/Low

Positive Emotionality measures. PSY-5 Aggressiveness is also similar to FFM Agreeableness. There is less similarity between PSY-5 Disconstraint and FFM Conscientiousness. PSY-5 Psychoticism is quite different from any of the FFM constructs and provides a unique contribution to understanding personality functioning.

From a clinical perspective, a broad overview of major personality trait features is an important component of adequate case conceptualization and treatment planning (e.g., Harkness & Lilienfeld, 1997). The similarity and differences between the PSY-5 and FFM outlined in this chapter can help the clinician determine the appropriateness of either or both models in addressing important clinical issues.

References

Bagby, R.M., Buis, T., Nicholson, R.A., Parikh, S., & Bacchiochi, J.R. (1999, April). *Distinguishing bipolar depression, major depression, and schizophrenia using the MMPI-2 clinical, content, and PSY-5 scales*. Paper presented at the 34th Annual Symposium on Recent Developments in the Use of the MMPI-2 and MMPI-A. Huntington Beach, CA.

Berry, D.T.R. (1995). Detecting distortion in forensic evaluations with the MMPI-2. In Y.S. Ben-Porath, J.R. Graham, G.C.N. Hall, R.D. Hirschman, & M.S. Zaragoza (Eds.), *Forensic Application of the MMPI-2* (pp. 82-102). Thousand Oaks, CA: Sage.

Browne, M.W. (1980). Factor analysis of multiple batteries by maximum likelihood. *British Journal of Mathematical and Statistical Psychology, 33*, 184-199.

Butcher, J.N., Dahlstrom, W.G., Graham, J.R., Tellegen, A., & Kaemmer, B. (1989). *MMPI-2 (Minnesota Multiphasic Personality Inventory - 2): Manual for Administration, Scoring and Interpretation*. Minneapolis: University of Minnesota Press.

Butcher, J.N., Graham, J.R., Ben-Porath, Y.S., Tellegen, A., Dahlstrom, W.G., & Kaemmer, B. (2001). *MMPI-2 (Minnesota Multiphasic Personality Inventory - 2): Manual for Administration, Scoring and Interpretation* (2nd ed.). Minneapolis: University of Minnesota Press.

Butcher, J.N., & Rouse, S.V. (1996). Personality: Individual differences and clinical assessment. *Annual Review of Psychology, 47*, 87-111.

Butcher, J.N., & Williams, C.L. (2000). *Essentials of MMPI-2 and MMPI-A interpretation* (2nd ed.). Minneapolis: University of Minnesota Press.

Cattell, R.B., Eber, H.W., & Tatsuoka, M.M. (1970). *Handbook for the Sixteen Personality Factor Questionnaire*. Champaign, IL: Institute for Personality and Ability Testing

Clark, L.A. (1990). Toward a consensual set of symptom clusters for assessment of personality disorder. In J.N. Butcher, C.D. Spielberger *et al.* (Eds.), *Advances in Personality Assessment* (Vol. 8, pp. 243-266). Hillsdale, NJ: Lawrence Erlbaum Associates.

Cleckley, H. (1982). *The mask of sanity: An attempt to clarify some issues about the so-called psychopathic personality*. St. Louis: Mosby.

Costa, P.T., Jr., & McCrae, R.R. (1992). *NEO PI-R professional manual*. Odessa, FL: Psychological Assessment Resources.

Costa, P.T., Zonderman, A.B., McCrae, R.R., & Williams, R.B. (1985). Content and comprehensiveness in the MMPI: An item factor analysis in a normal adult sample. *Journal of Personality and Social Psychology, 48*, 925-933.

Egger, J.I.M., Derksen, J.L., & DeMey, H.M.R. (1997, June). *Validation of MMPI-2 scales and profiles in outpatient and inpatient settings*. Paper presented at the 32nd Annual

Symposium on Recent Developments in the Use of the MMPI-2 and MMPI-A. Minneapolis, MN.

Finn, S.E. (1996). *Manual for using the MMPI-2 as a therapeutic intervention.* Minneapolis: University of Minnesota Press.

Friedman, A.F., Lewak, R., Nichols, D.S., & Webb, J.T. (2001). *Psychological assessment with the MMPI-2.* Mahwah, NJ: Lawrence Erlbaum Associates.

Graham, J.R. (2000). *MMPI-2: Assessing personality and psychopathology* (3rd ed.). New York, NY: Oxford University Press.

Graham, J.R., Ben-Porath, Y.S., & McNulty, J.L. (1999). *MMPI-2 Correlates for outpatient community mental health settings.* Minneapolis: University of Minnesota Press.

Greene, R.L. (2000). *The MMPI-2: An interpretive manual.* Boston, MA: Allyn and Bacon.

Hare, R.D. (1991). *The Hare Psychopathy Checklist - Revised.* Toronto: Multi-Health Systems.

Harkness, A.R. (1989/1990). Phenotypic dimensions of the personality disorders (doctoral dissertation, University of Minnesota, 1989). *Dissertation Abstracts International, 50*(12B), 5880B.

Harkness, A.R. (1992). Fundamental topics in the personality disorders: Candidate trait dimensions from lower regions of the hierarchy. *Psychological Assessment, 4*, 251-259.

Harkness, A.R. (in press). Theory and measurement of personality traits. In J.N. Butcher (Ed.), *Clinical Personality Assessment: Practical Approaches* (2nd. ed.). New York: Oxford.

Harkness, A.R., & Hogan, R. (1995). Theory and measurement of traits: Two views. In J.N. Butcher (Ed.), *Clinical Personality Assessment: Practical Approaches* (pp. 28-41). New York: Oxford.

Harkness, A.R. & Lilienfeld, S.O. (1997). Individual differences science for treatment planning: Personality traits. *Psychological Assessment, 9*, 349-360.

Harkness, A.R., & McNulty, J.L. (1994). The personality psychopathology five (PSY-5): Issue from the pages of a diagnostic manual instead of a dictionary. In S. Strack & M. Lorr (Eds.), *Differentiating Normal and Abnormal Personality* (pp. 291-315). New York: Springer.

Harkness, A.R., & McNulty, J.L. (in press). Implications of personality individual differences science for clinical work on personality disorders. In P.T. Costa, Jr., & T.A. Widiger (Eds.), *Personality Disorders and the Five-Factor Model of Personality* (2nd Ed.). Washington, DC: American Psychological Association.

Harkness, A.R., McNulty, J.L., & Ben-Porath, Y.S. (1994, May). *A different answer to Meehl's (1945) Lt. Max Hutt assertion: Building MMPI-2 scales with replicated rational selection.* Paper presented at the 29th Annual MMPI-2 & MMPI-A Symposium, Minneapolis, MN.

Harkness, A.R., McNulty, J.L., & Ben-Porath, Y.S. (1995). The personality psychopathology five (PSY-5): Constructs and MMPI-2 scales. *Psychological Assessment, 7*, 104-114.

Harkness, A.R., McNulty, J.L., Ben-Porath, Y.S., & Graham, J.R. (in press). *Test report: The Personality Psychopathology Five (PSY-5) Scales.* Minneapolis: University of Minnesota Press.

Harkness, A.R., McNulty, J.L., Finger, M.S., Arbisi, P.A., & Ben-Porath, Y.S. (1999, April). *The pleiometric nature of psychoticism items, or why the Big-5 does not measure psychoticism.* Paper presented at the 34th annual MMPI-2 and MMPI-A Symposium, Huntington Beach, CA.

Harkness, A.R., Royer, M.J., & Gill, T.P. (1996, June). *Organizing MMPI-2 Feedback with Psychological Constructs: PSY-5 Scales and Self-Adaptation*. Paper presented at the 31st Annual MMPI-2 Symposium, Minneapolis, MN.

Harkness, A.R., Spiro, A. III, Butcher, J.N., & Ben-Porath, Y.S. (1995, August). *Personality Psychopathology Five (PSY-5) in the Boston VA Normative Aging Study*. Paper presented at the 103rd Annual Convention of the American Psychological Association, New York, NY.

Hyler, S.E., & Rieder, R.O. (1987). *PDQ-R personality questionnaire*. New York: New York State Psychiatric Institute.

Livesley, W.J., Jackson, D.N., & Schroeder, M.L. (1989). A study of the factorial structure of personality pathology. *Journal of Personality Disorders, 3*, 292-306.

McNulty, J.L., Ben-Porath, Y.S., & Watt, M. (1997, June). *Predicting SCID-II personality disorder symptomatology: A comparison of the PSY-5 and Big Five models*. Paper presented at the 31st Annual MMPI-2 & MMPI-A Symposium, Minneapolis, Minnesota.

McNulty, J.L., Harkness, A.R., & Ben-Porath, Y.S. (1998, March). *Theoretical assertions and empirical evidence: How MMPI-2 PSY-5 scales are linked with the MPQ, ZKPQ-III, and NEO PI-R*. Paper presented at the 32nd Annual MMPI-2 & MMPI-A Symposium, Tampa, Florida.

McNulty, J.L., Harkness, A.R., & Wright, C.L. (1994, April). *Chart diagnoses and the validity of MMPI-2 based PSY-5 scales*. Paper presented at the 40th Annual Convention of the Southwestern Psychological Association, Tulsa, Oklahoma.

Millon, T., & Davis, R. (2000). *Personality Disorders in Modern Life*. New York: Wiley.

Millsap, R.E. (1995). The statistical analysis of method effects in multitrait-multimethod data: A review. In P.E. Shrout & D.W. Fiske (Eds.) *Personality Research, Methods, and Theory* (pp. 93-109). Hillsdale, NJ: Lawrence Erlbaum Associates

Nichols, D.S., Greene, R.L., & Schmolck, P. (1989). Criteria for assessing inconsistent patterns of item endorsement on the MMPI: Rationale, development, and empirical trials. *Journal of Clinical Psychology, 45*, 239-250.

Pfohl, B., Blum, N., Zimmerman, M., & Stangl, D. (1989). *Structured interview for DSM-III-R personality: SIDP-R*. Iowa City, IA: Author.

Rouse, S. V. (1997). *The construct validity of the MMPI-2 PSY-5 scales in a clinical sample* (doctoral dissertation, University of Minnesota, 1997).

Rouse, S.V., Butcher, J.N., & Miller, K.B. (1999). Assessment of substance abuse in psychotherapy clients: The effectiveness of the MMPI-2 substance abuse scales. *Psychological Assessment, 11*, 101-107.

Rouse, S.V., Finger, M.S., & Butcher, J.N. (1999). Advances in clinical personality measurement: An item response theory analysis of the MMPI-2 PSY-5 Scales. *Journal of Personality Assessment, 72*, 282-307.

Siever, L.J., & Davis, K.L. (1991). A psychobiological perspective on the personality disorders. *American Journal of Psychiatry, 148*, 1647-1658.

Siever, L.J., & Frucht, W. (1997). *The new view of self: How genes and neurotransmitters shape your mind, your personality, and your mental health*. New York: Macmillan.

Tellegen, A. (1982). *Brief manual for the Differential Personality Questionnaire*. Unpublished manuscript, University of Minnesota, Minneapolis. [Since renamed Multidimensional Personality Questionnaire]

Tellegen, A. (1985). Structures of mood and personality and their relevance to assessing anxiety, with an emphasis on self-report. In A.H. Tuma & J.D. Maser (Eds.), *Anxiety and the Anxiety Disorders* (pp. 681-706). Hillsdale, NJ: Lawrence Erlbaum Associates.

Tellegen, A. *MPQ (Multidimensional Personality Questionnaire): Manual for administration, scoring, and interpretation.* Manuscript in preparation.

Tellegen, A., & Ben-Porath, Y.S. (1992). *The new uniform T scores for the MMPI-2: Rationale, derivation, and appraisal.* Psychological Assessment, 4, 145-155.

Trull, T.J., Useda, J.D., Costa, P.T., Jr., & McCrae, R.R. (1995). Comparison of the MMPI-2 Personality Psychopathology Five (PSY-5), the NEO-PI, and NEO PI-R. *Psychological Assessment, 7,* 508-516.

Voelker, T.L., & Nichols, D.S. (1999, April). *MMPI-2 correlates of the Psychopathy Check List-Revised (PCL-R).* Paper presented at the 34th Annual Symposium on Recent Developments in the Use of the MMPI-2 and MMPI-A. Huntington Beach, CA.

Watson, D., & Clark, L.A. (1984). Negative affectivity: The disposition to experience aversive emotional states. *Psychological Bulletin, 96,* 465-490.

Watson, D., & Clark, L.A. (1993). Behavioral disinhibition versus constraint: A dispositional perspective. In D.M. Wegner & J.W. Pennebaker (Eds.), *Handbook of Mental Control* (pp. 506-527). New York: Prentice Hall.

Watson, D., & Clark, L.A. (1997). Extraversion and its positive emotional core. In R. Hogan, J. Johnson, & S. Briggs (Eds.), *Handbook of personality psychology* (pp. 767-793). San Diego, CA: Academic Press.

Watson, D., & Pennebaker, J.W. (1989). Health complaints, stress, and distress: Exploring the central role of negative affectivity. *Psychological Review, 96,* 234-254.

Widiger, T.A. & Trull, T.J. (1997). Assessment of the five-factor model of personality. *Journal of Personality Assessment, 68,* 228-250.

Zuckerman, M., Kuhlman, D.M., Joireman, J., Teta, P., & Kraft, M. (1993). A comparison of three structural models of personality: The big three, the Big Five, and the Alternative Five. *Journal of Personality and Social Psychology, 65(4),* 757-768.

Chapter 20

The Professional Personality Questionnaire

Paul Barrett

Introduction

The Professional Personality Questionnaire (PPQ) was created by the late Paul Kline and his research student Sharon Lapham, in the late 1980s, with the first publication of its factor pattern and scale correlations in 1991. It is a brief questionnaire measuring five broad scales that are designed to assess the Big Five factors of McCrae and Costa (1987) in the work environment. The PPQ scales are named Insecurity versus Confidence (Big Five Anxiety), Conscientiousness versus Carelessness, Introversion-Extraversion, Tough versus Tender-Minded (Big Five Agreeableness), and Conventional versus Unconventional (Big Five Openness to Experience). A sixth Invalidity V scale is scored as a measure of inaccuracy/inconsistency of responding. The PPQ was constructed to provide a brief but reliable measure of these factors, suitable for use in Industrial/Organizational (I/O) personnel selection and staff development screening in the UK. An initial item pool of 100 items was generated in which all references to clinical and psychiatric terminology and symptoms were removed. The items were all configured to be "work-relevant" and face-valid. Guiding the item generation process was the consistent aim to acquire measures of the Big Five factors, but with items that were highly face-valid within the work context. Many more than the final 100 "pilot" items were generated by both test authors, to be followed by informal semantic analysis to remove obvious duplicates or ambiguous items. The initial set of 100 pilot items was then administered to 1472 university students. Each item uses a binary "yes/no" response format, and is scored 1/0 in the targeted direction. From the initial factor and item analyses, a subset of 68 items was selected; these items possessed desirable psychometric indices of reliability and validity. Although four papers were published by Kline and Lapham (1991a, 1991b, 1992a, 1992b), and one by Kline and Barrett (1994), the test itself was never published, marketed, or sold. It was originally sponsored for development by Personality Systems Ltd., a UK test publishing company; but the company became insolvent in early 1990 and subsequently ceased trading. The test thus remained a research in-

Big Five Assessment, edited by B. De Raad & M. Perugini. © 2002, Hogrefe & Huber Publishers.

strument that is only now being made available to the wider test community (with the agreement of Paul Kline's widow).

The questionnaire and score key

Appendices A and B provide a complete listing of the final 68 test items, including the test instructions, along with the score key for the test. As can be seen from the item listing, nearly all the items focus on the work-environment or aspects of work. About half the items are keyed "Yes", and acquiescence was checked in the item analyses and factor analyses by showing that there were no differences in factor loadings between positive and negative items. The average completion time for the test is about 10 minutes.

The psychometrics of the PPQ

Factor analysis

Kline and Lapham (1991a) administered the 100 item pilot test to 1,472 UK students, 906 females and 566 males in four universities. A principal components analysis was undertaken on the joint gender dataset, as according to Kline and Lapham (1991a) there were no sex differences in separate sample factors. Five factors were extracted using the scree test, and subsequently rotated using direct oblimin rotation with delta = 0.0. The complete table of factor loadings is given in this paper, albeit referenced to the 100-item questionnaire. The significant feature is that the 68 items chosen to form the PPQ do load their respective factors > |.30|, although there is some limited item complexity (but the targeted loading is always higher than any other loading on a different factor).

Table 1. Scale alpha reliability coefficients for the 68 item PPQ, based upon a sample of 1,472 mixed-gender UK university students and 253 mixed-gender UK adult volunteers

Scale	Number of Items	Student Alphas	Adult Alphas
Insecurity (Anxiety)	15	.76	.79
Conscientiousness	13	.78	.79
Introversion	13	.76	.80
Tender Minded (Agreeableness)	12	.70	.72
Unconventional (Openness to Experience)	15	.73	.77

Alpha Reliabilities

Within Kline and Lapham (1991a), the scale alphas computed using a total sample size of 1,472, are reported. They are shown here in the "Student Alphas" column of Table 1.

As can be seen, all alphas are greater than or equal to .70, with the Tough-Minded scale having the lowest alpha coefficient of .70. A second sample of data also provided further evidence of alpha reliabilities of greater than .70 for all scales. This evidence was drawn from 253 adult volunteers (186 females and 67 males) who also took part in a series of psychophysiological and chronometric tasks at the Biosignal laboratory in the Institute of Psychiatry. The total sample originally provided data for a joint-questionnaire multidimensional scaling analysis that was reported in Kline and Barrett (1994). Although this latter paper did not report the scale alphas, it is worthwhile reporting them in Table 1 for comparative purposes. As can be seen, these alphas are slightly higher than the student sample – although not appreciably different. To date, there is no reported evidence of test-retest reliability of the five scales.

With regard to the sampling characteristics of the Biosignal laboratory sample, the mean and standard deviation age of the female sample was 35 and 11.6 years, respectively, with a range of 16 to 59 years. For the 67 males, the mean was 34 years with a standard deviation of 11.5 years, with the same age range as the females. The adult volunteers were enlisted into the Biosignal Laboratory participant pool using advertising in local newspapers, local employment offices, and within surrounding adult-education colleges in the South London geographical area. Testing within the laboratory always took place during working hours, hence most of the female sample were housewives, part-time employees, and unemployed individuals. The male sample was primarily composed of part-time and unemployed individuals. Although educational histories and biographical information was not acquired from the individuals comprising the laboratory sample, IQ scores are available. These were acquired using the Jackson Multidimensional Aptitude Battery (1984), a group-administered version of the Wechsler Adult Intelligence Scales - Revised (1981). Table 2 below provides the descriptive statistics of the three summary IQ variables for this sample.

Table 2. Summary Multidimensional Aptitude Battery IQ variable statistics computed over the sample of 253 mixed-gender UK adult volunteers.

	Verbal IQ	Performance IQ	Full-Scale IQ
Mean	110.4	108.2	109.5
Median	111	110	111
Standard Deviation	12.34	13.72	12.11
Minimum Value	72	63	67
Maximum Value	137	137	136

Table 3. Scale score intercorrelations of the PPQ, based upon a sample of 1,472 mixed gender UK university students. The figures in brackets are the scale correlations computed using the sample of 253 volunteer adults from the Biosignal Laboratory panel.

Scale	Conscientious	Introversion	Tender Minded	Unconventional
Insecurity	.05 (.10)	.38 (.46)	.15 (.26)	-.29 (-.23)
Conscientious		.01 (.16)	-.25 (-.11)	-.42 (-.26)
Introversion			.35 (.39)	-.23 (-.28)
Tender-Minded				.13 (.00)
Unconventional				

It is clear that the IQ scores of this sample are above average (given a normative mean of 100 and standard deviation of 15), with 17 per cent of individuals with Full-Scale IQs less than 100.

Scale Inter-Correlations

The scale-score correlations between the five personality scales, which are also reported in Kline and Lapham (1991a), are provided in Table 3.

Within this table, both the student and Biosignal Laboratory sample inter-correlations are reported. These correlations indicate that certain scales are definitely not independent from one another. If we correct the highest student sample scale intercorrelations for unreliability of measurement using the alphas from the $N = 1,472$ student sample, it turns out that the observed correlation in the student sample data between Conscientiousness and Unconventionality of .42 then becomes .55. The observed correlation of .29 between Insecurity and Unconventionality then becomes .38. That between Introversion and Tender Mindedness (.35) then becomes .48, and the correlation of .38 between Insecurity and Introversion becomes .50. Whilst the corrected correlations are not observable, they do indicate that taking into account measurement error as defined within classical test theory, there is reasonably substantive correlation between certain scales of the test.

Table 4. Scale means and standard deviations for the PPQ personality and Invalidity V scale, computed using the $N = 1,472$ UK mixed gender university student sample. The figures in brackets are the values computed using the sample of 253 volunteer adults from the Biosignal Laboratory panel (the Invalidity scores were not computed for this sample).

Scale	Mean	Standard Deviation
Insecurity	3.5 (4.70)	3.0 (3.42)
Conscientious	4.8 (5.12)	3.2 (3.34)
Introversion	6.3 (7.06)	3.2 (3.43)
Tender-Minded	6.6 (6.68)	2.8 (2.88)
Unconventional	5.0 (5.53)	3.1 (3.44)
Invalidity V scale	3.1	2.4

Scale means and standard deviations

Kline and Lapham (1991b and 1992a) report the global means and standard deviations for each of the five PPQ personality scales, as well as for the Invalidity V scale. Table 4 lists these. Also in this table are the personality scale means and standard deviations computed using the Biosignal Laboratory sample of 253 volunteer adults. Kline and Lapham (1991b), using the $N = 1,472$ student sample, also provide a comprehensive set of tables of personality scale means and standard deviations as a function of the frequency distribution of the Invalidity Scores. These tables are useful for determining a threshold for "inconsistent responding" on each of the scales.

Furthermore, within Kline and Lapham (1992a) is a breakdown of the global student sample into constituent samples of Arts, Sciences, Social Sciences, Engineers, and Mixed groups. In Kline and Lapham (1992b), a new sample of data from 208 employees across 10 occupational groups in various organisations was obtained. The means and standard deviations of the five PPQ scales are reported in that paper, along with indications from analyses of variance and post-hoc Scheffe contrast tests that certain occupational groups can be meaningfully differentiated using particular scale scores.

Construct/concurrent validity

The final set of data presented in Kline and Lapham (1991a) establish some limited construct validity for the PPQ scales. The test authors concurrently administered the Eysenck Personality Questionnaire (EPQ: Eysenck & Eysenck, 1975) to 100 mixed gender UK university students (56 male, 44 female). The four EPQ scales of Psychoticism, Extraversion, Neuroticism and Social Desirability were subsequently correlated with the five PPQ scales. The results are presented in Table 5 below.

These correlations indicate that the PPQ scales only marginally overlap with their nearest EPQ counterparts. For example, EPQ-Psychoticism correlates at just -.06 with Tender-Minded (Tough-Minded being the opposite pole on the PPQ). As Kline

Table 5. Correlations between the Eysenck Personality Questionnaire (EPQ) and PPQ personality scales, using the scores from 100 UK mixed gender university students

Scale	EPQ			
	Psychoticism	Extraversion	Neuroticism	Social Desirability
PPQ-Insecurity	-.14	-.45	.37	.22
PPQ-Conscientious	-.17	-.02	.08	.22
PPQ-Introversion	-.19	-.41	.19	.28
PPQ-Tender-Minded	-.06	-.15	.13	-.02
PPQ-Unconventional	.23	.30	-.20	-.18

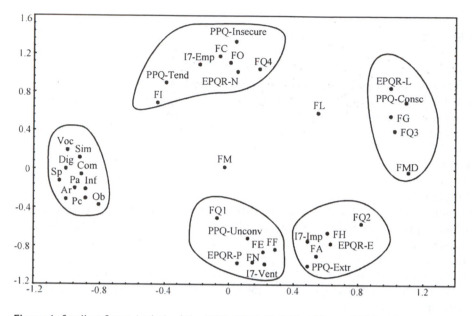

Figure 1. Smallest Space Analysis of the 15FQ, EPQR, I7, MAB ability, and PPQ scales

and Lapham indicate though, the PPQ Tough-Minded scale items contain no reference to cruel, bizarre, or aggressive behaviours, so this lack of correlation is to be expected. The strongest correlation is that between EPQ Extraversion and PPQ Introversion (-.41, corrected for unreliability = -.52, using the alpha of 0.85 from the N = 4,140 mixed gender UK reference EPQ sample). This is a moderate correlation that indicates that a significant amount of variance, over and above that in common with the EPQ, is being assessed by the PPQ.

Another set of data, partially presented in the Kline and Barrett (1994) paper, provides some additional concurrent validity for the PPQ. The questionnaire was administered to 253 Biosignal Laboratory panel volunteers (as detailed above). These respondents had also completed the Eysenck Personality Questionnaire – Revised (EPQR: Eysenck, Eysenck, & Barrett, 1985), the Fifteen Factor Personality Questionnaire (15FQ: Paltiel & Budd, 1992), the Jackson Multidimensional Ability Battery (MAB: Jackson, 1984), and the IVE-I7 (Eysenck, Pearson, Easting, & Allsopp, 1985) questionnaire. The 15FQ is a normative, three-option response format, personality test that has been developed for use in research, industrial, and organisational settings. The test consists of 191 items, assessing 15 bipolar personality dimensions similar to those measured using Cattell's 16PF Form A. In addition, a 16th scale provides a measure of motivational distortion that is similar to the concept of social desirability as measured via the Eysenck Personality Questionnaire-Revised version (EPQR, Eysenck, Eysenck, & Barrett, 1985). The Eysenck *et al.* IVE-I7 questionnaire assesses Impulsivity, Venturesome, and Empathy/Sensitivity. The MAB assesses ten of the subscales of the WAIS-R ability test in a group-administered and/or

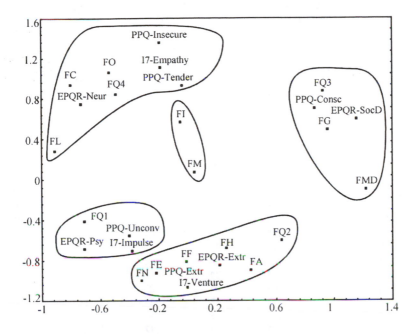

Figure 2. Smallest Space Analysis of the 15FQ, EPQR, I7, and PPQ scales

Table 6. Key to abbreviations used in Figures 1 and 2.

Fifteen Factor Personality Questionnaire (15FQ)	

Fifteen Factor Personality Questionnaire (15FQ)		Eysenck IVE-17	
FA	= Outgoing		
FC	= Stable (scored as *Instability*)	**Eysenck IVE-17**	
FE	= Assertiveness	I7-Imp	= Impulsivity
FF	= Enthusiastic	I7-Vent	= Venturesomeness
FG	= Detail-Conscious	I7-Emp	= Empathy/Sensitivity
FH	= Socially Bold	**Professional Personality Questionnaire (PPQ)**	
FI	= Aesthetic Sensitivity	PPQ-Insec	= Insecurity/Anxiety
FL	= Suspicious	PPQ-Extr	= Extraversion
FM	= Conceptual	PPQ-Unconv	= Unconventionality
FN	= Restrained (scored as *Unrestrained*)	PPQ-Consc	= Conscientiousness
FO	= Self-Doubting	PPQ-Tend	= Tender-Minded
FQ1	= Radical	**MAB: Multidimensional Aptitude Battery**	
FQ2	= Self-Sufficient (scored as *Group-Oriented*)	Voc	= Vocabulary
FQ3	= Disciplined	Sim	= Similarities
FQ4	= Tense-Driven	Dig	= Digit Symbol
FMD	= Motivational Distortion	Com	= Comprehension
Eysenck Personality Questionnaire-Revised (EPQR)		Sp	= Spatial
		Pa	= Picture Arrangement
Psy	= Psychoticism	Inf	= Information
Extr	= Extraversion	Ar	= Arithmetic
Neur	= Neuroticism	Pc	= Picture Completion
SocD	= Social Desirability/Conformity	Ob	= Object Assembly

Table 7. Pearson correlations between the PPQ scales, the Psytech 15FQ Personality scales, the Eysenck I7 and EPQ-R Personality scales, and Jackson's Multidimensional Aptitude Battery (MAB) ability scales

N = 193 mixed gender cases	Insecurity	Tender-minded	Extraversion	Conscientious
		PPQ		
15FQ_Outgoing	-.37	.02	.26	-.08	.13
15FQ_Stability	-.32	-.18	.13	.03	.06
15FQ_Assertiveness	-.39	-.31	.35	-.09	.26
15FQ_Enthusiastic	-.41	-.10	.41	-.12	.31
15FQ_Detail Conscious	.04	-.16	-.08	.42	-.08
15FQ_Socially Bold	-.38	-.06	.28	.07	.21
15FQ_Aesthetic Sensitivity	.02	.43	.12	.14	.11
15FQ_Suspicious	.10	-.17	.06	.16	.04
15FQ_Conceptual	-.11	.17	-.05	-.15	.28
15FQ_Restrained	.31	-.19	-.29	.26	-.29
15FQ_Self-Doubting	.24	-.17	-.19	.17	-.10
15FQ_Radical	-.15	-.02	.03	-.28	.41
15FQ_Group-Oriented	.22	.16	-.15	.06	.05
15FQ_Disciplined	.01	-.14	.02	.38	-.29
15FQ_Tense-Driven	.17	-.21	-.10	.14	.00
15FQ_Motivational Distortion	-.09	.01	-.07	.11	.05
EPQR_Psychoticism	-.12	-.15	.31	-.31	.46
EPQR_Extraversion	-.47	.08	.44	.03	.29
EPQR_Neuroticism	.21	.17	-.12	.03	-.01
EPQR_Social Desirability	.10	.04	-.24	.24	-.08
I7_Venturesomeness	-.20	-.12	.46	-.06	.25
I7_Impulsivity	-.37	-.26	.38	-.17	.32
I7_Empathy-Sensitivity	.22	.42	-.22	.06	-.05
MAB_Information	-.07	.05	-.14	-.27	.09
MAB_Comprehension	-.07	.15	-.09	-.22	.03
MAB_Arithmetic	-.20	-.11	.02	-.30	-.02
MAB_Similarities	-.04	.19	-.16	-.33	.01
MAB_Vocabulary	-.03	.09	-.21	-.21	-.15
MAB_Digit Symbol	-.19	.05	-.04	-.24	-.07
MAB_Picture Completion	-.13	-.10	-.06	-.15	-.11
MAB_Spatial	-.06	.05	-.08	-.22	.02
MAB_Picture Arrangement	-.17	.06	.00	-.23	.02
MAB_Object Assembly	-.22	-.02	.08	-.25	.09
MAB_Verbal IQ	-.11	.09	-.14	-.33	-.01
MAB_Performance IQ	-.19	.00	-.02	-.27	.00
MAB_Full-Scale IQ	-.16	.05	-.09	-.33	.00

*Note: correlations |.25| and above are highlighted

individual computer-administered format, excluding the Digit Span subtest. As with the WAIS-R, it provides estimates of Verbal, Performance, and Full-Scale IQ. The total sample size for this concurrent study is 193 mixed-gender respondents (48 males, 145 females). Rather than provide the entire correlation matrix for the 28 scales, a useful way of demonstrating concurrent validity is to compute a multidimensional scaling solution for the scale score data matrix. Figures 1 and 2 provide the scaling maps, with and without the MAB ability variables. The key to each figure provides the full name of each scale abbreviation, and the regional area names represented by the enclosed groups of scales.

As can be seen from Figure 1, the PPQ and other personality variables show no substantive relationship to the ability variables. The correlations reported in Table 7 between these variables and the 10 ability subset variables confirms this (although Conscientiousness is negatively related with an average correlation of -.26). In figure 2, it can be seen that the PPQ scales (as in figure 1) are closely associated with the key personality regions of the map. What is also noticeable is that in these data, PPQ Insecurity and PPQ Tender-Minded are placed fairly close together in the Euclidean personality space; their Pearson intercorrelation in these data is .28. Further, instead of five regions being associated with the Big Five "factors", only four have been identified using these questionnaires.

As an additional aid to understanding the relationships between the PPQ factors and the variables, all the correlations between the personality, ability, and PPQ scale scores are presented in Table 7.

The correlations do not exceed .50 between any of the PPQ scales and other related personality scales. Further, there is no substantive correlation between any of the ability scales and PPQ scales except for the Conscientious scale. These latter correlations were all negative, with the highest observed value of -.33 between Full-Scale and Verbal IQ, and the Similarities subtest. The complete scale score dataset is available from the author in SPSS and STATISTICA format.

In conclusion, the PPQ possesses the minimal psychometric properties required by a questionnaire for use as a measure of variants of the Big Five factors of McCrae and Costa (1987). It possesses adequate factorial validity, and internally consistent scales. It is relatively short, face-valid for the I/O work environment, and quick to complete. There is a limited amount of construct/concurrent validity with some other multi-scale personality tests and a multidimensional ability test. However, given the lack of substantive normative non-student data, it is probably best considered a "research-only" questionnaire until more norms, further factor analysis, and test-retest reliability indices are obtained.

References

Eysenck, H.J., & Eysenck, S.B.G. (1975). *Manual of the Eysenck Personality Questionnaire*. London: Hodder and Stoughton

Eysenck, S.B.G., Eysenck, H.J., & Barrett, P.T. (1985). A revised version of the Psychoticism scale. *Personality and Individual Differences, 6,* 1, 21-29.

Eysenck, S.B.G., Pearson, P.R., Easting, G., & Allsopp, J. (1985). Age norms for impulsiveness, venturesomeness, and empathy in adults. *Personality and Individual Differences, 6,* 613-620.

Jackson, D.N. (1984). *Manual for the Multidimensional Aptitude Battery*. Ontario: Sigma Assessment Systems Inc.

Kline, P., & Barrett, P. (1994). Studies with the PPQ and the five factor model of personality. *European Review of Applied Psychology, 44,* 35-42

Kline, P., & Lapham, S.L. (1991a). The validity of the PPQ: A study of its factor structure and its relationship to the EPQ. *Personality and Individual Differences, 12,* 631-635

Kline, P., & Lapham, S.L. (1991b). The Validity of the V scale of the PPQ. *Personality and Individual Differences,* 12, 6, 637-641

Kline, P., & Lapham, S.L. (1992a). Personality and faculty in British Universities. *Personality and Individual Differences, 13,* 855-857

Kline, P., & Lapham, S.L. (1992b). The PPQ: a study of its ability to discriminate occupational groups and the validity of its scales. *Personality and Individual Differences, 13,* 225-228

McCrae, R.R., & Costa, P.T., Jr. (1987). Validation of the five-factor model of personality across instruments and observers. *Journal of Personality and Social Psychology, 52,* 81-90

Paltiel, L., & Budd, R. (1992). *Manual for the 15FQ Personality Questionnaire.* Bedfordshire, UK: Psytech International Ltd.

Wechsler, D. (1981). *Manual for the Wechsler Adult Intelligence Scale – Revised.* New York: Psychological Corporation.

Appendix A: The 68 item PPQ including administration instructions

Instructions

In this test there are a number of statements which complete the unfinished sentence "Ideally, I would like to work in a job setting where ..." You should respond to each statement by circulating Yes, if you agreed with the statement or No, if you disagree.

For example: Ideally I would like to work in a job setting where ... The workday is 10am – 6pm as opposed to 9am – 5pm.

If your ideal job-setting is one in which the work day is 10am – 6pm then circle Yes. If you prefer 9am – 5pm then circle No. Remember this is not necessarily the way it is where you are working now or where you have worked before. It is the way things would be if everything was exactly the way you wanted it: your IDEAL job setting.

The following points should be remembered when completing the questionnaire.

There are no right or wrong answers – be as honest as you can and do not give an answer because it seems the right thing do say.

If you want to change an answer delete it completely and then circle your new response.

There is no time limit – however you should work as quickly as you can without pondering over any one question at length.

Do not worry about being consistent – answer each question individually.

There are 68 questions in this questionnaire – please ensure that you complete ALL the questions.

Turn over and begin the test when you are told.

Ideally I would like to work in a job setting where ...

1. It is easier to get ahead by plodding on deliberately than by taking chances.   Yes   No
2. More liberal methods are favoured over traditional ones.   Yes   No
3. People with the necessary abilities are taken on even if they are not punctual.   Yes   No
4. People believe they should be effective first, supportive second.   Yes   No
5. The atmosphere is calm and steady as opposed to fast and pressured.   Yes   No
6. It's important to everyone that shelves are dusted and floors vacuumed and/or dusted every week.   Yes   No
7. It's generally accepted that to get ahead you have to break a few rules.   Yes   No
8. I am often the centre of attention.   Yes   No
9. Attending to minute detail is not considered the only way to do an acceptable job.   Yes   No
10. The job involves more high profile activity than activity taking place behind the scenes.   Yes   No
11. The work requires me to be more empathic than logical.   Yes   No
12. Moderation, discipline and self-control are three of the emphasised values at work.   Yes   No
13. It if had to be one of the other I would be considered well-liked as opposed to the best in my field.   Yes   No
14. Employees are expected to maintain a particularly high standard of order and tidiness in their own personal workspace.   Yes   No
15. Unexpected situations, both good and bad, often occur.   Yes   No
16. Colleagues would describe me as more tough than sensitive.   Yes   No
17. Most of the work involves long term projects requiring a steady pace as opposed to short term projects requiring rapid action.   Yes   No
18. The impression that I make on people is not that important to my success.   Yes   No
19. I am rarely called upon to inspire confidence in others.   Yes   No
20. I am often making decisions that are crucial to the company.   Yes   No
21. Deadlines are rarely set – they are seen as limiting.   Yes   No
22. Quick decision making is favoured over taking time to contemplate issues.   Yes   No
23. Employees avoid pushing ideas that require stepping on a few toes.   Yes   No
24. Competitive people get ahead most quickly.   Yes   No
25. The methods I am dealing with could be described as more novel than established.   Yes   No
26. I often am expected to take and/or offer advice.   Yes   No
27. The work requires me to be more imaginative than pragmatic.   Yes   No
28. Employees are more concerned with expression individuality than identifying with one another.   Yes   No
29. The atmosphere is fast and pressured as opposed to calm and steady.   Yes   No
30. Waste not want not is one of the main rules emphasised at work.   Yes   No

31. I am directly answerable to someone who offers advice and keeps track of my progress as opposed to being a free agent.   Yes   No
32. It's the employee's prerogative whether to keep his/her personal workspace tidy or untidy.   Yes   No
33. Employees could be described as more creative than practical .   Yes   No
34. I am frequently in the position where I am asked for my opinion.   Yes   No
35. It's mandatory that employees check general files and/or supplies every week to make sure that they're arranged categorically.   Yes   No
36. If a choice had to be made, I would be putting ideas into action rather than being the one who comes up with them.   Yes   No
37. Colleagues would describe me as more firm than compliant.   Yes   No
38. I am hardly ever in the position where I have to advance my own views and challenge other people's.   Yes   No
39. If a choice had to be made, I'd associate more frequently with powerful people as opposed to people I'm close to who have little influence.   Yes   No
40. Colleagues would describe me as more sensitive than tough.   Yes   No
41. The hierarchy is strictly defined – I'm expected to treat superiors with greater respect than I would colleagues and people in lower status positions are expected to do the same for me.   Yes   No
42. I rarely am making decisions that are crucial to the success of the company.   Yes   No
43. If a choice had to be made, I'd have high job security with a mediocre income rather than low job security with a higher income.   Yes   No
44. It's not of much concern if shelves don't get dusted or floor don't get vacuumed and/or mopped every week.   Yes   No
45. The work requires me to be more subjective than objective.   Yes   No
46. I am required to present my ideas face-to-face more often than in writing.   Yes   No
47. If a choice had to be made, I'd be developing new ways of doing things as opposed to improving standard methods.   Yes   No
48. Unexpected situations, good or bad, rarely occur.   Yes   No
49. The general approach to work could be described as more conventional than progressive.   Yes   No
50. Taking time to contemplate issues is favoured over quick decision making.   Yes   No
51. I rarely am expected to take advice and /or offer it.   Yes   No
52. Most of my work involved independent as opposed to group projects.   Yes   No
53. At times the atmosphere is hectic and rushed.   Yes   No
54. The work requires me to be more demanding than consenting.   Yes   No
55. Most of the work involves short-term projects requiring rapid action as opposed to long-term projects requiring a steady pace.   Yes   No
56. The methods I am dealing with could be described as more established than novel.   Yes   No
57. I am often called upon to inspire confidence in others.   Yes   No
58. A place for everything and everything in its place is a rule that everyone must follow.   Yes   No
59. There is a standard of dress that people are expected to follow.   Yes   No
60. I am a free agent as opposed to directly answerable to someone who   Yes   No

offers advice and keeps track of my progress.

61. The work requires me to spend most of my time travelling around each day rather than remaining on site.   Yes   No

62. I can maintain a daily routine that is rarely broken.   Yes   No

63. Lateness is intolerable.   Yes   No

64. People believe they should be supportive first, effective second.   Yes   No

65. The work requires me to be more logical than empathic.   Yes   No

66. I rarely go into work knowing exactly what I'll be doing every hour; I just have a general idea and take things as they come.   Yes   No

67. I am in a lower status position where mistakes have little impact as opposed to a higher status position where mistakes can have serious consequences.   Yes   No

68. The work requires me to be more pragmatic than imaginative.   Yes   No

Appendix B: The PPQ ScoreKey

Insecurity vs Confidence (Anxiety) – 15 items
Score 1 if response is **Yes**: 18, 19, 23, 38, 42, 48, 51, 62, 67
Score 1 if response is **No** : 15, 20, 26, 34, 46, 57
A high score on the scale indicates Insecurity

Conscientiousness vs Careless – 13 items
Score 1 if response is **Yes**: 6, 12, 14, 30, 35, 41, 58, 59, 63
Score 1 if response is **No** : 3, 9, 32, 44
A high score on the scale indicates Conscientiousness

Introversion-Extraversion – 13 items
Score 1 if response is **Yes**: 1, 5, 17, 43, 50
Score 1 if response is **No** : 7, 8, 10, 22, 24, 29, 53, 55
A high score on the scale indicates Introversion

Tough vs Tender-Minded (Agreeableness) – 12 items
Score 1 if response is **Yes**: 11, 13, 40, 45, 64
Score 1 if response is **No** : 4, 16, 37, 39, 52, 54, 65
A high score on the scale indicates Tender-Minded

Conventional vs Unconventional (Openness to Experience) – 15 items
Score 1 if response is **Yes**: 31, 36, 49, 56, 68
Score 1 if response is **No** : 2, 21, 25, 27, 28, 33, 47, 60, 61, 66
A high score on the scale indicates Conventionality

Invalidity V scale – 15 item pairs
If both items in each pair are checked the same (a "Yes" or "No" on each item), then the respondent achieves a score of 1 on the Invalidity scale, or 0 otherwise. For example, if a respondent responds "Yes" on question 4, and "Yes" on question 64, then they would achieve a 1 on the Invalidity scale as the items are directly reversed in meaning.
A high score on the scale indicates invalid/inconsistent responding

Score 1 if both responses are the same for these item pairs:

4, 64	19, 57
5, 29	20, 42
6, 44	22, 50
11, 65	22, 56
14, 32	26, 51
15, 48	27, 68
16, 40	31, 60
17, 55	

Appendix C: PPQ SCORE DESCRIPTIONS

Raw Score 0 - 3   **Low Extraversion**   **Std. Score 0 - 2**

Your score on extraversion was lower than average. This means that you are the sort of person who is somewhat quiet and retiring and prefers to have a few real friends rather than a large number of superficial acquaintances. This score suggests that you would be happy in jobs where you had to be on your own quite a bit of the time and did not meet new people all the time. Quiet jobs rather than bustling environments are what you prefer.

Raw Score 4 - 8   **Average Extraversion**   **Std. Score 3 - 7**

Your score on extraversion was around the average for your group. This means that you can get on with people but are not particularly sociable or gregarious. On the other hand, you are not withdrawn or shy, or one who likes being on his or her own particularly. This score means that a wide variety of job settings would be quite suitable for you, although ones where you were much of the time on your own or ones where you had to meet new people every day would not be ideal.

9 +   **High Extraversion**   **Std. Score 8 +**

Your score on extraversion was higher than average. This means that you are an outgoing, sociable person who enjoys meeting and gets on well with other people. You are at your best in working situations where it is necessary to get along with a variety of people and where you do not have a lot of repetitive and careful work, or where you have to be on your own for long periods of time.

0 - 1   **Low Confidence**   **Std. Score 0 - 2**

Your score was below average for confidence. This has no clinical implications because our test was specifically designed for normal people who are not likely to require psychiatric care. Your score means that generally you do not feel particularly confident in difficult or strange situations, or situations where you are highly responsible for other people. This means that you feel happier in jobs where there is a good routine and where people know what is expected of them, even when this may be very difficult. Many professional positions are of this kind.

2 - 5   **Average Confidence**   **Std. Score 3 - 6**

Your score was around the average for confidence for your group.
This means that you are well capable of dealing with all the normal stresses and strains of life. It means that jobs which require you to act quickly and take responsibility will not be too irksome for you and are unlikely to cause you sleepless nights.

6 +   **High Confidence**   **Std. Score 7 +**

It is better not to have this category. The meaning of such a score is not clear and feedback of this kind could be dangerous. It is better to combine the category with the one above.

| **0 - 4** | **Low Tough-mindedness** | **Std. Score 0 - 3** |

Your score on tough-mindedness was below average. This means that you are a somewhat sympathetic person who does not like to make decisions that bear adversely upon the lives and feelings of others. This sensitivity to feelings means that you would be suited to jobs where this quality is regarded as necessary. The helping professions and personnel management are obvious possibilities.

| **5 - 8** | **Average Tough-mindedness** | **Std. Score 4 - 6** |

Your score on tough-mindedness was about average for your group. This means that you can take decisions which affect people adversely and hurt their feelings but you do not enjoy it and would rather not have to. This means that you would be suited to jobs where decisions about the fates and careers of people had to be made every once in a while but was not a major part of the work.

| **9 +** | **High Tough-mindedness** | **Std. Score 7 +** |

Your score was above average for tough-mindedness. This means that you do not object to taking decisions even where you may have to ruffle peoples' feelings or pride. You are able to face unpopularity if it is necessary and some people might regard you as ruthless. This means that you would be happy in jobs where it was necessary to be tough, as in some aspects of management and industry. You would be unlikely to be happy in jobs where it was important to be sympathetic to people or to help those who can't help themselves.

| **0 - 2** | **Low Openness to Experience** | **Std. Score 0 - 3** |

Your score on the measure of openness to experience was below average. This means that you are happiest working with tried and tested methods, where you can use approaches to problems that you know will work. You are suspicious of new things until they have been demonstrated to be effective. This means that you are best in jobs where you can use good, sound methods. Many of the professions are of this kind.

| **3 - 6** | **Average Openness to Experience** | **Std. Score 4 - 6** |

Your are around the average on our measure of openness to experience. This implies that you are capable of adapting to and using new methods but are also quite happy to use old ones, provided that they are efficient. This means that you are quite adaptable for most jobs but generally prefer those where there is an emphasis neither on completely new approaches nor on the rigid application of traditional methods.

| **7 +** | **High Openness to Experience** | **Std. Score 7 +** |

You are above average on the measure of openness to experience. This means that you enjoy novel methods and new approaches to thinking about things. You prefer trying new things out even when there are accepted ways of doing them. You would happy in jobs that exploited these characteristics, where you were allowed to do things your way and be generally creative.

0 - 2   **Low Conscientiousness**   **Std. Score 0 - 2**

You scored below average on the conscientiousness scale This means that you are not too concerned with the trivial details of how things are done but are more interested in the end result. Rules and regulations are only important where there is no other way and you see the pettiness of rule bound officials as just an excuse for not thinking. You would be happiest in jobs where you could do things in your own way and in your own time. You would hate regimented positions such as the armed forces, or jobs where you always had to wear a suit

3 - 7   **Average Conscientiousness**   **Std. Score 3 - 6**

You obtained an average score for conscientiousness. This means that you are conscientious and pay due regard to rules and regulations. You do things properly but are not heavy-handed about it and are not completely upset if you or a colleague are a tiny bit late or forget something. This means that you would fit well into most jobs except those where there was excessive emphasis on rules and regulations and the opposite of this where there was complete laxity.

8 +   **High Conscientiousness**   **Std. Score 7 +**

You are above average on conscientiousness. This means that you are a person with very high standards who likes everything to be done properly. You believe that old-fashioned virtues like punctuality, neatness and regard for rules and regulations are important. You prefer jobs where these qualities can come into play and are rewarded. Some accounting, legal and administrative positions are of this kind, as are jobs in the armed forces and police.

Author index

Subject index